U0633994

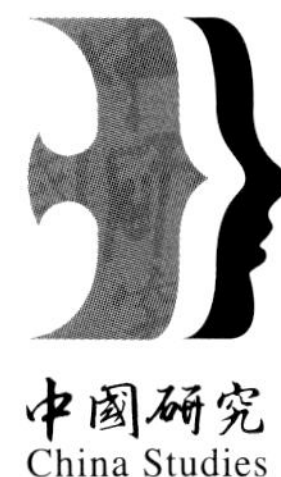

“汉学与当代中国”座谈会文集 2017

THE COLLECTED WORKS AT THE SYMPOSIUM ON CHINA STUDIES 2017

文化和旅游部对外文化联络局
中 外 文 化 交 流 中 心 编

中国社会科学出版社

图书在版编目（CIP）数据

2017"汉学与当代中国"座谈会文集. 汉英对照 / 文化和旅游部对外文化联络局，中外文化交流中心编. — 北京：中国社会科学出版社，2018.7

ISBN 978 - 7 - 5203 - 2836 - 4

Ⅰ. ①2… Ⅱ. ①文… ②中… Ⅲ. ①汉学—文集
Ⅳ. ①K207.8-53

中国版本图书馆 CIP 数据核字（2018）第 150904 号

出 版 人 赵剑英
责任编辑 夏 侠
责任校对 郭 莹
责任印制 王 超

出 版 中国社会科学出版社
社 址 北京鼓楼西大街甲 158 号
邮 编 100720
网 址 http://www.csspw.cn
发 行 部 010 - 84083685
门 市 部 010 - 84029450
经 销 新华书店及其他书店

印刷装订 环球东方（北京）印务有限公司
版 次 2018 年 7 月第 1 版
印 次 2018 年 7 月第 1 次印刷

开 本 710×1000 1/16
印 张 42.25
字 数 734 千字
定 价 298.00 元

凡购买中国社会科学出版社图书，如有质量问题请与本社联系调换
电话：010 - 84083683

2017 年 7 月 25 日，“汉学与当代中国”座谈会闭幕式后合影

Group photo at the closing ceremony of the “Symposium on China Studies” on July 25, 2017

2017“汉学与当代中国”座谈会开幕式前并行圆桌会议

The parallel round table sessions held before the opening ceremony of the “Symposium on China Studies”

2017“汉学与当代中国”座谈会现场

At the “Symposium on China Studies”

2017“汉学与当代中国”座谈会现场

At the “Symposium on China Studies”

2017“汉学与当代中国”座谈会现场

At the “Symposium on China Studies”

座谈会期间学者们相互交流

Sinologists communicating during the Symposium

座谈会期间学者们相互交流

Sinologists communicating during the Symposium

2017 年 7 月 26 日至 28 日，参加“汉学与当代中国”座谈会的中外学者一行 30 余人赴青海省进行“一带一路”调研考察，所到之处受到当地民众的热烈欢迎

Scholars on a visit to Qinghai Province for investigation on the theme of the “Belt and Road” from July 26 to 28, 2017

2017 年 7 月 28 日，赴青海考察的汉学家一行参观十世班禅大师故居

Sinologists on a visit to former residence of the 10th Panchen Lama on July 28, 2017

主办：中华人民共和国文化和旅游部　中国社会科学院
承办：中外文化交流中心

Hosts：Ministry of Culture and Tourism of the People's Republic of China
Chinese Academy of Social Sciences
Organizer: Network of International Culturalink Entities

目录

传统文化与当代中国

中国方案与全球治理

共同发展与共同价值

CONTENTS

Traditional Culture and Contemporary China

Chinese Solution and Global Governance

Mutual Development and Common Value

传统文化与当代中国

Traditional Culture and Contemporary China

宋代文明：世界历史中的首次文艺复兴

马麟 【美国】
美国堪萨斯城纳尔逊—阿特金斯艺术博物馆东亚部主任

文艺复兴向来被誉为人类历史的转折点以及沟通中世纪与现代的桥梁，而这种赞誉的确是实至名归的。文艺复兴运动源于 14 世纪晚期的意大利，到 1600 年至欧洲各地。它被定义为人类思想史上的革命期，不仅促进了方言文学的兴起，也重新唤起了人们对古典艺术与建筑的兴趣，令古典准则成为进一步探索艺术形式与建筑形式的基础。此外，文艺复兴推动了科学方法与科学技术的革新，中国的活字印刷术便是在这一时期内引入欧洲的。毫无疑问，古典兴味的复兴促进了科学思想的发展，近期以来，文艺复兴时期阿拉伯数学家的贡献正逐步得到当代学界的认可。虽然对于文艺复兴的概念尚存在诸多置疑，但这一时期无疑代表着人类史、特别是艺术史上的一段革命性的时期。

从世界艺术史的标准教材——玛丽琳·斯托克斯塔德的《艺术史》中便能看出文艺复兴在艺术及建筑领域内的重要性。该书用长达 140 页的篇幅讲述了 1430—1600 年间文艺复兴时期的艺术史。相比之下，关于有 300 多年历史的宋代（960—1279）的介绍则仅仅只有 7 页。

即使在中国，宋代也不如之前的唐朝和之后的明朝那样瞩目。与唐朝相比，宋朝军事力量孱弱，地理版图较小。相比之下，唐朝在历史上向来以“黄金时代”、“丝绸之路的世界主义时代”而著称，“大明王朝”则因紫禁城所折射出的巍巍皇权而传颂于世。

事实上，在很多方面，宋朝的重要性并不亚于唐朝和明朝。尽管历史性的跨文化比较常常有失精准，但宋朝与欧洲的文艺复兴之间的确存在着许多共性与平行（同时也存在诸多差异）。如果将文艺复兴视作中世纪与现代世界的桥梁，那么考虑宋朝时期的中国在何种程度上体现出现代性则并没有不当之处。首先我必须承认，我并不是研究中国历史或中国文学的专家，只是一位典藏研究员和艺术史学者。对于汉学家群体而言，我的讲述或有班门弄斧之嫌，因为宋史专家早已谙熟这个朝代的诸般成就。因此，我的目的在于向国际学者而非汉学家推广宋朝的文明成就。若问此举目的何在，我只能说，作为西方国家博物馆的一名典藏研究员，我也负责管理中国艺术品，但每天接触的历史或艺术史中都凸显着欧洲中心主义倾向。在我看来，宋代的现代性丝毫不弱于文艺复兴时期，甚至比同时代的（10—13 世纪）欧洲国家更为进步。

在审视物质文化之前，有必要对宋代文明的成就——知识复兴及科技创新——做一总括式回顾。在这一时期内，儒学得到复兴，科举制得到推广；在官吏选拔方面，选贤任能的观念深入人心；在科技方面，印刷术得到迅速推广，丰富了书籍品类；农业技术的进步成倍地提高了生产率，海洋技术取得了重大进步，包括指南针、船舵、防水壁的发明；此外，人们对古文物、器物的学术兴趣与日俱增，编纂了关于青铜器及书画作品的目录。

在对中欧文化进行对比之前，有必要指出两者在物质文化层面上的鲜明差异：中国古建筑多为木质，且明朝之前的宫殿建筑大多已损毁，外观气势上略逊于哥特大教堂，比如，沙特尔圣母大教堂（建于 1153—1260 年左右）的高度达到 136.57 米。相比之下，建于 1056 年的应县佛宫寺释迦塔只有 67.31 米，与比萨斜塔高度相仿。比萨斜塔始建于 1173 年，于 1360 年左右竣工，高 56.67 米。中国建筑并不追求高度，而是讲求空间搭配。由于找不到现存的宋代宫殿，紫禁城可算是目前现存的规模最大、最完整的古代宫殿建筑群。

在欧洲，许多收藏家和艺术家重新发掘了古希腊和古罗马雕塑艺术，而宋代的文物收集者也展现出对中国古代青铜器物的兴趣，然而这种兴趣并没有像文艺复兴一样，直接引发古代工艺的复兴。许多古文物被收入目录且进行了仿制，但采用的工艺却是“失蜡法”而非古代的“分铸法”，因而缺乏古代模具所特有的美学优点。在雕塑艺术上也可以进行类似的比较。中国的雕刻家并没有获得文艺复兴时期艺术家米开朗基罗那样声望，也没有像他一样执着于人物形体的塑造。尽管唐代已经流行石雕艺术，但宋代艺术家更青睐木材或黏土等材质。在中国的艺术品中，人物的身份往往通过服饰进行定义，裸体向来不受欢迎。但半裸的菩萨像却从未招致反对，这主要是受到印度佛教遗产的影响。需要指出的一点是，宋金时期的雕塑不论是在美感、规模、逼真程度还是绚烂程度上，都远远超过“前文艺复兴时代”欧洲各国的雕塑作品。纳尔逊艾特金斯艺术博物馆陈列的南海观音像虽然出自一位匿名匠人之手，但足可与米开朗基罗的《大卫》相媲美。大卫像虽然高达 17 英尺，且体积远远大于观音像，但与 71 米高的乐山大佛（建于唐代 713—803 年间）或独乐寺的黏土观音像（高 16 米，建于辽代）相比，委实要渺小许多。

下面，我将举两例说明宋代的艺术媒介具有无可否认的现代性以及远远超出同时代欧洲艺术的先进性。第一，瓷器。至少从唐代起，中国瓷器便因其先进的工艺和杰出的美感获得亚洲以及其他地区的青睐，但直到宋代，釉瓷才得到宫廷的追捧，如定窑白瓷、汝窑青瓷、龙泉青瓷等。这些瓷器的出众之处在于将釉质和外形放在首位，而将图案纹饰放在次要地位。几乎在所有“前现代”文化中，价值都是通过图案与纹饰来传达，图案纹饰越多，艺术品的价值便越高。然而在釉瓷器中，图案纹饰的数量往往被降至最低，甚至完全缺失。与唐三彩釉陶器不同，宋代的高火釉体现出明显的庄重与内敛。许多学者指出，宋代的釉色白中显青绿，应该是加入了银或玉等其他物质，只有从极富现代性的审美视角才能欣赏如此细腻的美感，这与 20 世纪上半叶兴起于欧洲的“鲍豪斯运动”具有诸多共同点。

然而在绘画领域，宋代取得的成就是最为显著且意义深远的。唐代的绘画注重人物表现，而宋代则将焦点转移至风景。正如历史学家西蒙·沙玛所说，“这是人类历史上首次以山水画来定义人类文明的壮举”。以现实主义笔法呈现风景，远比人物画更具挑战性。如何描绘远景？如何在版式相对受限的中国画中呈现出自然的渺远？此类问题在 10 世纪的中国已然得到了解答。这一时期最具代表性的山水画家要数李成（919—967），其作“峰峦重叠，间露祠墅，此为最佳。至于林木稠薄泉流深浅，如就真景”“近观李成笔锋，如在千里之外。”郭若虚则用“夫气象萧疏，烟林清旷，毫锋颖脱，墨法精微者，营丘之制也”来评价。

不论是当时的画作还是画论，都明显地表现出对“再现”这一命题的极大兴趣。例如，卓越而博学的沈括（1031—1095）曾对李成山水画及建筑画中的透视技法进行过批判与探讨。

“又李成（919—967）画山上亭馆及楼塔之类，皆仰画飞檐，其说以谓自下望上，如人平地望塔檐间，见其榱桷。此论非也。大都山水之法，盖以大观小，如人观假山耳。若同真山之法，以下望上，只合见一重山，岂可重重悉见，兼不应见其溪谷间事。又如屋舍，亦不应见中庭及后巷中事。若人在东立，则山西便合是远境；人在西立，则山东却合是远境。似此如何成画？李君盖不知以大观小之法，其间折高远，自有妙理，岂在掀屋角也。”

此番评论值得关注之处在于，沈括明确地指出了单点透视（消失点）的不恰当之处——在15世纪的欧洲绘画中，这种视角的使用极为频繁。从本质上讲，沈括的评论凸显出这样一种问题意识：使用单点透视无法呈现山峦的“纵深感”。或许，试图捕捉山峦影像的摄影师大多都会赞同这一观点。

李成的绘画技法在现存的几幅真迹中得到了完美的诠释。以《晴峦萧寺图》为例：前景中描绘的似乎是两家饭馆，一家档次较高，一家较为简陋，大概类似于麦当劳或饺子店。然而对两栋建筑的描绘手法却显得十分高明，巧妙地展现了沈括所谓“中庭中事”，以水墨营造雾气、通过精确缩小比例、远山的重叠等技法，惟妙惟肖地营造出距离感与纵深效果。

空间透视法在南宋夏圭的《山水十二景图》中得到了完美诠释。在这幅画作中，绢面大片留白，只有山水风景在雾气中若隐若现。王诜《烟江叠嶂图》（现存于上海博物馆）则更显极端，近半绢面大幅留白。

若观者徐徐展开画卷，所见者只有一片空白，并且会将这片空白解读为氤氲的雾气。这种迫使观者解读空白、参与想象的技法，从本质上讲，具有极强的现代性，类似的抽象作品直到20世纪早期才在卡西米尔·马列维奇（1878—1935）等极简主义画家的作品中出现。夏圭、王诜等人的作品与欧洲同时代画家的作品形成了有趣的对比。成书于1150年左右的《温彻斯特手抄本圣经》中绘有大量极富艺术价值的插图，然而不论是这部圣经还是同期的画作，都没有表现丝毫的空间意识和距离意识，直至15世纪早期，菲利波·布鲁内列斯基（1377—1466）才发明出单消失点的几何透视法。从15世纪的一副匿名画作中能够看出欧洲画家在单点透视法上取得的突破，与《烟江叠嶂图》相比，这幅画作的技法或许“科学性”更强，但在营造“烟雾弥漫、浩渺空旷”的意境方面，则要逊色许多。

中国画凸显出的幻觉现实主义风格似乎在11世纪遭到批判，或许是因为士大夫阶层将技艺精湛的画家视作威胁（在当时的画作批评中，画家的社会身份以及道德人格往往与艺术技巧同等重要），这场批判风潮大体可以用“写意”二字来概括。最先倡导这一理念且影响最为深远的人要数苏轼——宋代杰出诗人、政治家、书画家。苏轼有关画作最著名的论断莫过于“论画以形似，见与儿童邻”。

这番论断有时会被误解为“逼真”并不重要，但实际上，苏轼想要表达的是，仅凭“逼真”来衡量美学价值是不够全面的。苏轼的作品大多已经失传，但从仅存的少量作品来看，苏轼笔法可谓灵动与神韵兼备。笔法是中国书法艺术中最基本的元素，而中国书法与绘画间又存在着紧密联系，这种联系已经持续了几个世纪之久。苏轼的画作大多构图简单，不过在北宋（960—1127）的画作中，他所倡导的风格渐渐体现出更为复杂的表现形式，最佳的例证便是乔仲常的《后赤壁赋图》。当然，乔氏并非纤毫毕现地展示《后赤壁赋》这首诗的图景，而是通过笔锋来捕捉该诗的神韵。可以说，《后赤壁赋图》是世界上第一幅印象主义画作，在苏轼“登树”俯视滔滔江水的场景中，这种印象主义风格体现得尤为明显。此外，以诗提画更能体现苏轼“书画本一体”的理念。

然而在北宋后期，在社会及文化的其他领域，特别是在科技领域，革新的态势并没有持续下去。在绘画领域，宋代为后世绘画技法的创新奠定了基础，例如，笔墨技法的表现潜力在元代的绘画大师倪瓒（1301—1374）、黄公望（1269—1354）等人的作品中得到了充分的发挥，并被明末清初的画家所传承。董其昌（1555—1636）的山水画构图复杂且形式抽象，空间表现体现出刻意的模糊性，有时令人联想到毕加索的立体主义表现手法。龚贤（1618—1689）山水画的“点墨”技法远远早于乔治·修拉等点画派艺术作家的创作技法。当然，必须承认的是，在形式与内容的突破上，龚贤的作品比修拉的画作更为大胆。若是没有宋代这些革命性的突破，中国画坛则不会掀起一波又一波的新风潮。总之，无可否认的是，宋代是视觉艺术的革命期，在某些方面甚至超越了欧洲的文艺复兴，远比之前的罗马艺术及哥特艺术更为进步。

Song Civilization: the World's First Renaissance

Colin Christopher Mackenzie / United States of America

Senior Curator of East Asian Art, the Nelson-Atkins Museum of Art, Kansas City

The Renaissance is rightly celebrated as a crucial turning point in world history and as a bridge between the Middle Ages and the Modern Era. Beginning in the late 14th century in Italy, but eventually spreading to the rest of Europe by 1600, it is defined as a period of revolutions in intellectual pursuits, including a flowering of vernacular literature, a revival of interest in classical art and architecture and their use as a basis for further development forms, new developments in scientific method and new technological innovations such as the invention of the movable type.Although the revival of interest in the classical past was undoubtedly a spur to scientific thinking, more recently, the contribution of Arab mathematicians has been increasingly recognized. Although the concept of the renaissance has been questioned, it undoubtedly represents a revolutionary era in the history of mankind, particularly in art.

The artistic and architectural importance ascribed to the Renaissance is reflected in the number of pages devoted to it in the standard text book on the history of world art, Marilyn Stokstad's *Art History*. 140 pages, covering the years 1430-1600.

The Song Dynasty (960-1279), a period of some 300 years, by contrast, occupies only seven pages.

Even within China, the Song is less well known than the Tang which preceded it or the Ming which eventually followed it after the intervening Yuan. Compared with the Tang, it was militarily weaker and geographically smaller. Its demise at the hands of non-Han peoples has also contributed to its relatively lackluster reputation. Histories of the Tang dynasty, for instance, often describe it as Golden Age and cosmopolitan age of the Silk Road, while the Ming Dynasty is lauded for its imperial power that is still reflected in the Forbidden City.

Yet, in many respects, it was at least as significant as these two eras. And although historical cross cultural comparisons are always inaccurate and imprecise, there are many commonalities and parallels with the European Renaissance (although many differences also). But if we see the Renaissance as a bridge between the medieval and modern worlds, I think it is appropriate to consider in what ways Song dynasty China was modern. In the following brief discussion, I have to make some admissions. I am not a scholar of Chinese history or literature, but rather a curator and an art historian. Moreover I know that I am really preaching to the converted as far as the sinologist community is concerned—experts on Song history are well aware of its many achievements. My agenda is really one of boosting the reputation of the Song dynasty, not so much among sinologists, but in the international scholarly community. You might ask why this is important, but as a curator of Chinese art in a Western museum, I encounter a Eurocentric view of history and art history on a daily basis. My argument is that in many ways Song is as modern as the Renaissance and certainly far in advance of the contemporaneous European world of the 10th to 13th centuries.

Before focusing on material culture, it is worth outlining an overview of Song achievements, both in terms of the revival of knowledge and innovation: these include a revival of interest and scholarship in the Confucian classics; the expansion of the imperial examination system and the entrenchment of the idea of officials chosen on the basis of merit and the consequent development of a professional bureaucratic administration for the empire; in technology, the dramatic expansion of printing for a wide range of books; advances in agriculture which increased productivity by orders of magnitude; crucial advances in maritime technology including the invention of the compass, the rudder and bulkheads;a scholarly interest in the artifacts of antiquity and the compilation of catalogues of painting and bronzes.

In comparing the cultures of Europe of China, it is important to point out some very striking differences between the material culture of Europe and China: Chinese architecture was wood, and no intact palace structures have survived from before the Ming dynasty. Temple architecture does survive, but it is less impressive than the great Gothic cathedrals—Notre Dame at Chartres (ca 1153-1260) rises to a height of69 metres (226 ft), while dome of the Basilica of Saint Peters reaches a height of 136.57 metres (448.1 ft) By contrast, the wooden pagoda of Yingxian Fogong pagoda, completed in 1056, reaches a total height of 67.31 m (220.83 ft) tall, about the same height as the Leaning Tower of Pisa, begun in 1173 and completed around 1360, is (56.67 metres (185.93 feet tall).Height was, in any case, not the ultimate aim of Chinese architecture; it was encompassing space. In this respect although we don't have an Song palaces extant, the Forbidden City exceeds all other architectural complexes.

Just as collectors and artists rediscovered Classical, Hellenistic and Roman sculpture, so Chinese antiquarians became interested in ancient Chinese bronzes. Unlike Renaissance, however, this did not inspire a direct revival of the ancient craft. Ancient bronzes were illustrated in catalogues and reproductions were made using the lost-wax method rather than the section mold technique, and consequently lacked the aesthetic merit of their ancient models. In terms of sculpture, however, there is a closer comparison. Chinese sculptors never achieved the fame of Renaissance artists such as Michelangelo nor did they explore the human figure with the same passion. Although stone had been in fashion during Tang, by Song wood and clay were the preferred materials. In Chinese art, the human figure was defined by drapery and nudity generally disliked. However, certain semi-nude such as bodhisattvas were accepted, the legacy of Indian Buddhist influence. The point is that these Song-Jin sculptures surpassed in beauty and realism and magnificence anything that was being produced in pre-Renaissance Europe, both in terms of scale and realism. The Guanyin of the Southern Sea in the Nelson-Atkins Museum of Art, although an anonymous work, stands comparison with Michelangelo's David. And although the latter at 17 ft, is much larger, it is dwarfed by some of the great Chinese Buddhist sculptures such as the71-metre (233 ft) tall stone statue of Buddha at Leshan, built between 713 and 803 (during the Tang Dynasty), or the clay sculpture of Guanyin at Dulesi some sixteen meters in height, created during the Liao Dynasty (907-1125).

I am going to explore briefly two examples of artistic media that, in my opinion, are undeniably modern and indisputably more advanced than their equivalents in Europe at the time. First, ceramics: Chinese ceramics have been prized throughout Asia and beyond for their technical and aesthetic excellence since at least the Tang dynasty. But it was during the Song dynasty that glazed stonewares and porcelains became sought after by the imperial court, first the white Ding ware porcelains, then the blue-green celadons of Ru, Guan, and Longquan. What is so remarkable about these stonewares and porcelains is the subservience of decoration to form and glaze. In virtually all pre-modern cultures, decoration conferred value—the more decoration, the more valuable the work of art. But in the glazed stonewares, decoration is on the whole minimal or often totally absent.And unlike the bright three color glazes of Tang, the highfired glazes of Song are distinguished by their demure understated tones. It has been pointed out by a number of scholars that the colors of the glazes, white, green, and bluish, evoked other materials, such as silver and jade. It took a very modern sensibility to appreciate this subtle aesthetic, which has much in common with the European Bauhaus movement of the first half of the twentieth century.

It is in the field of painting, however, that the Song made the most dramatic and significant advances. Painting of the Tang dynasty focused on the figure, but by the Song Dynasty, it had shifted to landscape. As the historian Simon Schama has pointed out, "for the first time in history, civilization was defined by landscape painting."[1]Realistic depiction of landscape was a much more challenging venture than figure painting. How was one to depict objects further away? And how to encompass the huge distances and vast scale of nature within the relatively confined format of Chinese painting?During the course of the 10th century this challenge was overcome. The primary exponent was Li Cheng (919-967), whose style was described as "within the piled-up peaks and mountains of his paintings, temples and villas appear; this is the best thing of his art. The dense or sparse trees and the deep and shallow streams are depicted as the real scenery."[2]"Li Cheng's brushwork, when seen from nearby, seems a thousand miles away."[3]Another critic, Guo Ruoxu 郭若虚 , emphasized Li's ability to create atmospheric effects: "In the productions of [Li of] Yingqiu, the atmospheric effects have a sublime openness, the misty woods a pure spaciousness; his brush-point is distinguished, and his use of ink exquisitely subtle."[4]

What is very clear both from paintings of the time, but also the critics, is that the question of representation was one of great interest. The great polymath Shen Kuo 沈括(1031—1095), for instance, discusses the perspective involved in Li Cheng's buildings and landscape paintings in a somewhat critical tone.

"Further, when Li Cheng (919-967) painted such buildings as pavilions or towers

1 Simon Schama, referring to China, uses this phrase in the introduction to a series on world civilizations.

2 Wai-kam Ho, Sherman E. Lee, Laurence Sickman, and Marc F. Wilson, *Eight Dynasties of Chinese Painting*, p. 14. The text is from Liu Daochun.

3 Susan Bush, *Early Chinese Texts on Painting*, p. 117.

4 See Alexander Soper(translator).*Kuo Jo-Hsu's Experiences in Painting*< 圖畫見聞誌 > p. 19. Chinese text at the end unpaginated.

on a mountain, he always did the flying eaves as if one were looking up at them. The explanation is given that one is viewing what is above from below, just like a man on level ground looking up at house eaves sees their supporting rafters. This theory is wrong. Generally, the method of landscape painting is taking the larger view of the small, just as a man looks at an artificial mountain. If it were the same as the method of [viewing] actual scenery, then looking up from below, one would only see a single layer of the mountain. How could one see its whole, layer upon layer? Similarly, one would not see its valleys and other details. Again, in such things as buildings one would not see inner courtyards or events happening in the rear lanes..."[1]

What is so interesting about Shen Kuo's commentary is that he explains very clearly why a single vanishing point perspective such as emerged in Europe in the 15th century would not have been appropriate. Essentially, he realized that if one took a single-point perspective one would be unable to represent the depth of mountain ranges, a point with which any photographer who has tried to photograph mountain ranges would probably agree. Li Cheng's approach is best exemplified by one of the few surviving paintings that may actually have been painted by his hand, *Solitary Temple Amid Clearing Peaks*. In the foreground is depicted what seem to be two restaurants, a higher class version and a humbler one, perhaps the equivalent of McDonalds or a Jiaozidian (饺子店). The way the buildings are drawn cleverly opens up the interior space, just as Shen Kuo described the technique. Likewise the use of wash to create mists, the careful diminution of scale, and the overlapping of distant mountains are all cleverly marshalled to create an effect of depth and distance.

A fine example of the use of atmospheric perspective is the painting *Twelve Views of Landscape* by the Southern Song painter Xia Gui. In this painting much of the silk is left blank, with only elements of the landscape emerging from the mist. Even more extreme is the famous Serried Hills Over a Misty River by Wang

1 Susan Bush, *Early Chinese Texts on Painting*, p. 112.

Shen in the Shanghai Museum, which for over half the length of the scroll is blank. A viewer unrolling the scroll would see only blank silk that he would interpret as mist filled void. The sophistication of an artist who challenges the viewer to engage with essentially blankness is strikingly modern and can be anticipates the abstract works of early twentieth century European minimalist artists such as Kazimir Malevich(1878-May 15, 1935). It is interesting compare the Xia Gui and Wang Shen paintings with art of the same period in Europe. The manuscript leaf from the Winchester bible, created about 1150 is wondrous work of art, but there is no hint in this or other works of the time of any understanding of how to represent space or distance. It is only during the early 15thcentury that Filippo Brunelleschi (1377-1446) developed geometrical perspective with a single vanishing point. An anonymous 15th century painting shows the breakthrough in single-view point perspective. Compared with Solitary Temple, it may be more scientific, but in terms of conveying the illusion of monumental scene, it is no more successful.

During the 11th century, there seems to be a reaction against the illusionistic realism that had been achieved in Chinese painting. It originated among the literati (士大夫 shidafu) class, who perhaps felt threatened by the virtuoso technique of professional painters (in contemporaneouscritiques of painters, their social status and moral character is often as important as their artistry). This movement is encapsulated in the idea of xieyi (写意) “writing the idea”. One of the first and most influential proponents of this idea was the celebrated poet, politician, calligrapher and painter Su Shi苏轼. His most famous statement concerning painting is: “anyone judging painting on the criterion of likeness is the next thing to a child.” (论画以形似，见与儿童邻)[1]This has sometimes been misinterpreted to mean that likeness was not important, but in reality Su was arguing that likeness was not a sufficient criterion for judging aesthetic value. Very few of Su Shi’s paintings survive and those that do suggest that vitality of brushwork was crucial. Brushwork, of course, was the fundamental quality of calligraphy, and the close relationship between

1 The complete poem comes from《书郡陵王主薄所画折枝二首》.

calligraphy and Chinese painting had already existed for centuries. Su Shi's paintings are relatively simple compositions, but other paintings from the end of Northern Song (960-1127) show a much more sophisticated expression of the new literati style. Foremost among these is the *Illustration to the Second Prose Poem on the Red Cliff* 后赤壁赋图 by Qiao Zhongchang 侨中常 . In this handscroll, the artist does not merely illustrate the poem, he captures its poetic essence through brushwork. The *Red Cliff* has been claimed with some justification as the world's first expressionist painting. This is particularly true of the scene in which Su Shi climbs up the tree to look down on the boiling waters. Moreover, the integration of the poem itself into the painting exemplifies Su Shi's comment that poetry and painting are two sides of the same coin.

Whereas in other areas of society and culture, especially science and technology the innovations of Song did not see continued development in the later periods, in painting, the Song period set the groundwork for further innovations. It was in the following dynasties that the expressive potential of brush and ink was fully realized in the works of Yuan dynasty masters such as Ni Zan (倪瓒 , 1301-1374)and Huang Gongwang (黄 公 望 , 1269–1354). Their successors of the late Ming and Qing dynasties carried this brush and ink play further. Dong Qichang's (董其昌 , 1555-1636) landscapes are complex semi-abstract constructions of forms with deliberate spatial ambiguities that sometimes anticipate the cubist forms of Picasso's paintings. Gong Xian's (龚 贤 , 1618-1689) landscapes constructed of dots anticipate the pointillism of artists such as George Seurat. Indeed, it could be argued that Gong Xian's painting is much more daring in terms of its manipulation of form and texture than Seurat's. None of these later movements in Chinese painting could have occurred without the revolutionary breakthrough of Song. In conclusion, there can be no doubt that in the visual arts, the Song was as revolutionary and in some respects more so than the European Renaissance, as well as being far in advance of art of the preceding Romanesque and Gothic periods.

“六经”的价值论理和中国文化精神

刘梦溪 【中国】
中国艺术研究院终身研究员 / 中国文化研究所所长 / 中央文史研究馆馆员

一　中华文化的精神旨趣

20年前，我在《中国现代学术要略》中曾经提出：“学术思想是人类理性认知的系统化，是民族精神的理性之光。”以我多年研习中国文化的心得，于今思之，中华文化能够贡献给世界的，我认为是人之为人的、群之为群的、家之为家的、国之为国的一整套精神价值理念。这些价值理念的精神旨归，是使人成为健全的人，使群体成为和谐的群体，使家成为有亲有爱有敬的和睦的家，使国家成为讲信修睦、怀柔远人的礼义文明之邦。

二　六艺和六经

中国文化的最主要的价值理念都在“六经”。“六经”指《易》《诗》《书》《礼》《乐》《春秋》六种文本经典。《乐》这一经没有文本传下来，是为“五经”。但也有一种说法，认为《乐》本来就没有文本，它是跟《礼》结合在一起的，所以“礼乐”并称。尽管后来看到的是“五经”，可是学者们习惯上仍然称为“六经”，直到清代还是如此。所以清初的大学者王船山的一句有名的话是“六经责我开生面”。“经”是晚些时候的说法，开始的名称叫“六艺”。孔子教学生，就是以“六艺”作为教材。但当时有两种“六艺”，《易》《诗》《书》《礼》《乐》《春秋》是文本经典的“六艺”，另一种是“礼、乐、射、御、书、数”，我称之为实践课。这里的“书”，是指跟文字有关的“六书”，是识字课。“数”是计算，射是射箭，“御”是驾车。

文本经典的“六艺”即“六经”，孔子之前就有了。像《周易》，相传是伏羲画卦，文王演易，孔子作传。所以《论语》里记载孔子的话，说“五十以学《易》，可以无大过矣”。《诗经》是周代的诗歌，最早有三千多篇，经过孔子的删订，存留 305 篇，所以《诗经》也称“诗三百”。《书》是《尚书》，是包括虞、夏、商、周在内的上古文告、文献汇编。《礼》有三礼，包括《周礼》《仪礼》和《礼记》。作为“六经”的《礼》，一般指《礼记》。《春秋》是鲁国的一个大事纪，应该是孔子所作。如果不是孔子的原创，也是孔子在原有的一个大事纪基础上加工润色而成。因为记事简，措辞晦，寓意深，由此形成史家称道的所谓“春秋笔法”。

“六经”都经过孔子删订，是中国现存的最原初的文本经典，是古人智慧的结晶，也是现代人做人和立国的基本精神依据。20 世纪的大儒马一浮，称“六经”为中国文化的最高的特殊的形态，大哲学家熊十力则说，“六经”是现代人做人和立国的基本精神依据。这些大判断，时至今日也没有过时，反而愈见其精彩绝到。

三　六经的价值论理

我近年从“六经”里面，也包括后来成为“十三经”的《论语》《孟子》《孝经》里面，抽绎出几组价值理念，包括**诚信、爱敬、忠恕、廉耻、和同（“和而不同”）**五组概念。我觉得这些概念范畴，是中国文化中的具有永恒性、普世性的价值理念，既适用于古代，也适用于今天，不仅适用于中国人，也适用于全世界所有的人。

1. 诚信

首先是诚信，这是中国文化里面非常重要的价值理念。孔子讲，“民无信不立”、“人而无信，不知其可也”。孟子说，“朋友有信”。老子也讲，“信言不美，美言不信”。中华文化的原初经典把“信”放在非常高的位置。

信和诚是连载一起的，内里面有诚，外面才有信。无诚，便不可能有信。讲“诚”讲得最多的是《中庸》，其中说，“诚”是“天之道”，是“物之终始，不诚无物”。而想要“立诚”，是“人之道”。《中庸》把“诚”视作“天道”和“人道”的核心问题。

明代思想家王阳明的一个学生，他跟王阳明向学的时间很长了，最后需要离开老师，回到自己的家乡去。辞行的时候他对王阳明说：“下次见面不知何时，老师可有什么嘱托，让我一生受用。”王阳明说：“立诚。”这是个年龄比较大的弟子，他说天下的万事万物太多了，需要解决的问题无穷无尽，难道光一个“诚”就可以？还有没有其他的东西？王阳明回答说：“立诚。”

后来这个弟子终于体验到了“立诚”的确是应该终生以之的立德之本。

“立诚”的理念，早在《易经》里面，就明确提出来了。《易经》乾卦的倒数第三爻的爻辞写道：“忠信，所以进德也；修辞立其诚，所以居业也。”这里的“修辞立其诚”，就是明确提出的“立诚”。

人活在世界上，究竟何欲何求？仔细想来，《易经》乾卦这两句话全包括了。人生在世，一个无非是想把自己变得更好一些，使自己成为一个有修养的人，成为受人尊敬的人。而要做到这一点，首要的是要讲诚信。这就是九三爻辞说的“忠信所以进德也”。“进德”的核心价值理念是“忠信”。“忠”字的直接涵义是把自己的心放正，成为一个诚实的人，讲信义的人。这是人生的第一层要义。人生的第二层要义，就是事业有成，在哪一方面的专业上有自己的建树，能够安居乐业。而“居业”的前提是“立诚”，所以是“修辞立其诚，所以居业也”。

“立诚”是“居业”的前提。兹可见诚信的重要。“诚信”两字，是人的一生成败得失的关键，可以视为中国文化的核心价值理念。

2. 爱敬

中国文化的另一个核心价值理念是“爱敬”。“爱敬”是《孝经》里面的话，引用孔子的话说：“爱亲者，不敢恶于人；敬亲者，不敢慢于人。爱敬尽于事亲，而德教加于百姓。”

“爱敬”是从家庭秩序中衍生出来的。父子、夫妇、弟兄之间的关系，都有爱和敬存在。如果一个人对自己的尊长亲人能做到有爱有敬，对家庭以外的其他人也不至于太不好，至少不会轻慢别人。因此《孝经》还说：“生事爱敬，死事哀戚，生民之本尽矣，死生之义备矣。”把爱敬看做了人生之本和生死的大义。人的哀愁和悲痛的情感，最初也是从家庭亲人的困厄、不幸中因感同身受而产生的。夫妇之间，一般以为有爱就行了，其实光有爱是不能持久的，还须有敬，既亲密无间，又相敬如宾，才是典范的夫妇关系。

对“爱敬”这个价值理念，魏晋时期刘劭的《人物志》解释得最为恰切。《人物志》是一部很特别的书，既是相人之书，又是伦理之书，又是哲学之书。或者说是一部特殊的《人论》。只有魏晋时期的人，能写出如此奇书。刘劭在《人物志》里写道：“盖人道之极，莫过爱敬。是故《孝经》以爱为至德，以敬为要道。”把“爱敬”看成是人道之极，可见“爱敬”这个价值理念在中华文化中的位置。

“敬”当然可以包括尊敬师长、尊敬前贤、尊敬长辈。但“敬”的价值的哲理义涵，是指人作为生命个体的“自性的庄严”。“敬”是人的内在性格、性体、本性的精神安顿之所，传统文化中很多道德规范都跟“敬”有关系。

譬如“孝”,《论语》的一个例子说，一次子游问老师，到底什么是“孝”。孔子回答说，现在的人们以为“能养”就是孝，如果“能养”就是“孝”，那么犬马也“能养”，没有“敬”，何以别乎？所以人跟犬马的一个区别在于，在“孝”这个问题上，人有“敬”，犬马不会有敬。

由此可以看出，“孝”的精神内核是“敬”。所以人们通常把对老人的“孝”，称作“孝敬”，甚至泛称为“敬老”。中国传统社会对官员的察选，如果不孝敬父母，就没有做官的资格。忠敬、诚信的人，一定孝敬父母，能孝敬父母才能成为忠于职守、仁爱天下的贤者。

举凡一切礼仪，都必须有“敬”的精神。所以《孝经》里面讲：“礼者，敬而已矣。”孔子一段有名的话说：“为礼不敬，临丧不哀，吾何以观之哉？”礼是需要有人看的，因此有“观礼”之说。但礼仪如果没有“敬”，就不值得看了。孔子还有一句话，认为“祭神如神在”。他的意思是说，在祭祀的时候，要相信神是在场的，只有这样，才能使祭祀者保持诚敬之心。

祭祀在古代是头等重要的事情。《左传》里的一句话说：“国之大事，在祀与戎。”祀就是祭祀，戎则是军事行动。但无论祭祀还是军事行动，都不能没有“敬”。军事行动也要懂礼仪。《左传》有很多记载，很多战争的发生，都是由于“不敬”或“大不敬”，引起强者一方的军事行动。现代社会，处理国家与国家的关系，涉及外交事务，讲礼仪、懂敬，同样非常重要。

礼仪、敬，是文明的指标；文明与不文明的重要分野，在于文明讲礼仪。

3. 忠恕：“己所不欲，勿施于人”

“忠恕”是孔子的重要思想。一次孔子说：“吾道一以贯之。”曾子（曾参）说，是的。后来孔子离开了，其他弟子问曾参：“这话怎讲？”曾子说：“夫子之道，忠恕而已矣！”这说明，“忠恕”在孔子那里是通贯全体、贯彻始终的思想。忠和诚可以互训，诚者必忠，“主忠信”是孔子的至高的道德律令。弟子樊迟问什么是“仁”，孔子回答说：“居处恭，执事敬，与人忠。”可知“敬”和“忠”都是仁的构件。

“忠”和“信”更为密切。取信的要道是“忠”。曾子“吾日三省吾身”的一、二两项内容，第一是：“为人谋而不忠乎？”第二是：“与朋友交而不信乎？”忠和信是与人交往的随时需要反省的问题。

孔子还说：“言忠信，行笃敬，虽蛮貊之邦行矣。言不忠信，行不笃敬，虽州里行乎哉？”如果做到了“忠信”，而在行为上又能体现出庄重和礼敬，即使走到不那么文明的异邦，也能立得住脚跟。相反，如果言不由衷，对人不能以诚相待，得不到交往对象的信任，行为上又轻慢无礼，即使在自己的家乡也照样吃不开。

至于忠恕的“恕”，其重要性更显而易见。按孔子的解释，恕就是“己所不欲，勿施于人”。“恕”这一价值理念所蕴含和所要求的涵义，通俗地说，就是设身处地，将心比心，换位思考，自己不喜欢不希望的东西不要强加于人。我认为“恕”这个价值理念，彰显了中华文化的异量之美。这是中国文化贡献给人类的一个伟大的思想。世界人文学界非常重视孔子的这一思想，把它奉为人类共同遵行的道德金律。

4. 廉耻：“行己有耻”

《礼记·中庸》有一段讲修身，引用孔子的话写道：“好学近乎知，力行近乎仁，知耻近乎勇。知斯三者，则知所以修身。”这等于把好学、力行、知耻，当作了修身的三要素。一个人的修为，自然离不开吸取知识，这也就是《礼记·大学》所说的“格物致知”。因此“学”是修身的第一要素。

学了以后何为？如果成为装知识的器皿，或者从知识到知识，那是学了等于不学。学的要义，在于用，在于践行。此即古人常讲的“知行合一”。所以修身的第二要素是“力行”。学习了，也践行了，离“仁”就不远了，至少是走向通往“仁”的道路上。

但无法保证所做的每一件事都正确无误，难免会发生错误。出了错误怎么办？要能够反省，善于反思，找出原因，知错改错，力戒重犯错误。当认识到错误的时候，人的良知会让自己感到羞愧，感到后悔，感到不好意思。能做到这一层，就是“知耻”的表现。“知耻”是改过的前提。所以修身的第三要素是“知耻”。

智、仁、勇在古代被称作“达德”。具有了智、仁、勇的德品，就可以做到大的判断不致发生错误，遇到困难不会感到忧虑，面对威胁无所畏惧。就是孔子说的：“知者不惑，仁者不忧，勇者不惧。”（《论语·子罕》）子贡认为，他的老师孔子是兼有不惑、不忧、不惧特点的人。

修身的三要素中，第三要素“知耻”，尤不可轻视。我给学生讲课，多次讲：修身应该从知耻开始。耻感是人成为人的一个文明指标，人的文明的表现之一是有羞耻心，孟子称之为“羞恶之心”。孟子说，恻隐之心、羞恶之心、辞让之心、是非之心，是人的“四端”。“端”是开始的意思，意即“四端”是做人的开始，或者说是最起码的人之为人的标志。若果没有羞恶之心，孟子说就不是人。同样，没有恻隐之心、没有辞让之心、没有是非之心，也不是人。恻隐之心是不忍，也就是同情心，也就是“恕”，己所不欲，勿施于人；辞让之心指文明礼貌，是非之心指社会的公平正义，而羞恶之心则是“知耻”，修身的第三要素，亦即孔子所强调的：“行己有耻。”

“耻”跟“廉”构成一个组合概念，曰“廉耻”。管子的一个著名论述，是提出：“礼义廉耻，国之四维。”“礼”是文明秩序，“义”是社会正义，“廉”是节俭廉洁，“耻”是道德的约束和自律。礼义廉耻没有了，国家的处境就危险了。

明清之际的大学者顾炎武曾经说过：“廉耻，立身之大节。”他说，如果不廉，将无所不取；而不耻，将无所不为。他还说过：“士大夫之无耻，是为国耻。”

5. 和同（“和而不同”）

跟诚信、爱敬、忠恕、廉耻一样，“和同”也是中华文化最基本也是最重要的价值理念。中国文化倾向于不把人与人之间的关系搞得那么不可调和，“和而不同”是中国人面对这个世界的总原则。

“和同”的思想来源于《易经》。《易》的“同人”一卦，所演绎的就是关于“与人和同”的理念。《易》的系辞概括为：“天下同归而殊途，一致而百虑。”这是说，人们的不同，常常表现为途径和方法的不同，终极目标是相同的，所以最终会走到一起。人类社会的存在形态，人们的生活方式和风俗习惯，彼此之间是不同的，但生活的价值追求，人的心理指向，往往有相同的一面。孟子对此说得很明白：

> 口之于味也，有同耆焉；耳之于声也，有同听焉；目之于色也，有同美焉。至于心，独无所同然乎？心之所同然者何也？谓理也，义也。（《孟子·告子上》）

孟子这段话是说，好吃的食物、好听的音乐，多彩的颜色，人们都会喜欢，在这点上人和人是相同的。既然在这方面有同样的感受，那么人的“心”是不是也有相同的东西呢？回答是肯定的。人心所相同者，是“理”和“义”。

孟子讲的“心”，也可以做“心理”解。恰好大学者钱锺书先生说过：“东海西海，心理攸同。”所以，人与人之间的不同，远没有想象的那么多，夸大人类的不同，是文化的陷阱。而且在人类的不同之中，也有“同”的一面。正因为如此，人和人之间、文化和文化之间，才可以沟通，不同也能够共存于一个统一体中。

不同文化之间可以共存、沟通、融合，是中国文化的一个固有的理念。这个理念基于中国文化的“和”的观念。“和”是由诸多的“不同”构成的，没有不同，便无所谓和。所以孔子的著名论断是：“君子和而不同。”宋代的思想家张载，他的有名的四句教是：“为天地立心，为生民立命，为往圣继绝学，为万世开太平。”张载字横渠，所以这四句话又称“横渠四句教”。但他还有另外的“四句教”，是这样的四句话：

有象斯有对，
对必反其为，
有反斯有仇，
仇必和而解。

我把张载的这四句话称为“哲学四句教”。因为他是对整个宇宙世界发言的。大意是说，这个世界是由一个一个的生命个体组成，有人类的、动物的、植物的，这些生命个体都是不同的。古人有一句话：“佳人不同体，美人不同面。”西方也有一个说法：“世界上没有完全相同的两个个体。”这些不同的个体都是一个个的“象”。这些“象”是流动的，不是静止的。但“象”的流动方向是不同的，有的甚至相反。这就是张载哲学四句教第一、第二两句讲的“有象斯有对，对必反其为”。由于“有对”，甚至“反其为”，就会发生彼此之间的纠结，从而形成“有反斯有仇”的局面。

这个“仇”字，古代写作“雠”，左边一个隹，右边一个隹，中间是言论的言字。“隹”是一种尾巴很短的鸟。试想，这个“雠”字，其象征意涵，不就是两只短尾巴鸟在那里叽叽喳喳的说话吗？我们还可以推测，尾巴短的鸟往往叫的声音很高，那么它们就不是一般的说话，而是在讨论、争论、辩论，甚至是在斗嘴、吵架。讨论的问题我们无法得知，但结果，它们经过计较、辩驳、讨论、争论的结果，并不是这个鸟把那个鸟吃掉，而是或达成共识，或求同存异，总之是和解了。

所以是“仇必和而解”。

四 “冤仇宜解不宜结”

张载“哲学四句教”给我们的启示是深远的。反观现实，我们可以得出一个总括性的看法，就是：这个世界有差异，但差异不必然发展为冲突，冲突不必然变成你死我活，而是可以“和而解”的。有了这个观念，很多事情会得到更恰当的处理。

大文豪鲁迅有一首诗，这首诗是关于战后中国和日本的关系的，其中有两句：“渡尽劫波兄弟在，相逢一笑泯恩仇。”人与人之间、群体与群体之间、族群与族群之间、国与国之间，都不应该培养仇恨。“仇”是可以化解的，应该走向“和而解”。所以中国有另外一句俗语，云：“冤仇宜解不宜结。”

The Reasoning Regarding Values of the Six Classics and the Ethos of the Chinese Culture

Liu Mengxi / China

Tenured Fellow and Director of the Institute of Chinese Culture at the Chinese National Academy of Arts, Member of the Central Research Institute of Culture and History

I. Spiritual Purport of the Chinese Culture

Two decades ago, I put forward in the *Chinese Modern Academic Synopsis*: "the Academic thought represents the systematization of the human rational cognition and the light of rationality of the national spirit." Having studied Chinese culture for years and based on the experience deriving from thereof, I have thought about it again and have drawn a conclusion. On the basis of my way of thinking, what Chinese culture can contribute to the world lies in the completely whole set of value reasoning, meaning that the human being, group, family and nation being themselves. The spiritual orientation of these values is to cultivate and foster sound people, a harmonious group, a loving and cozy family, a courteous and civilized nation which embraces faith, promotes good will and cherishes talents from afar.

II. Six Arts and Six Classics

The most important and essential values of Chinese culture rest with "Six Classics", which refer to six classical texts consisting of the *Book of Changes*, the *Book of Songs*, the *Book of Documents*, *Ceremonial Etiquette*, the *Classic of Music*, the *Spring and Autumn Annuals*. Among them, the *Classic of Music* has been passed down without a written text, thus it should be called "Five Classics". However, another saying also prevails that the *Classic of Music* was not originally written as a text, and it was in combination with *Ceremonial Etiquette* and then acquired the jointed name of "Li-Yue" (this stems from the direct pronunciation of their corresponding Chinese characters). Although "Five Classics" had always been read and popular in later times, scholars still preferred to call them "Six Classics" instead, until the Qing dynasty. Therefore, there is a famous quote from the great scholar Wang Chuanshan of the early Qing dynasty, reading "Six Classics compel me to interpret the world from different perspectives." "Jing" (the direct pronunciation of its corresponding Chinese character) is an appellation in later times while it was originally dubbed as "Six Arts". Confucius taught students with "Six Arts" as the teaching material. What differs from modern times is that there were two kinds of "Six Arts" during that time, one of which is made up of the *Book of Changes*, the *Book of Songs*, the *Book of History*, *Ceremonial Etiquette*, the *Classic of Music*, the *Spring and Autumn Annuals,* all of which converge to become the classical "Six Arts" in the form of a written text; while that of the other consists of "Ritual, Music, Archery, Chariot-riding, Calligraphy and Mathematics", all of which are named as practical courses. "Calligraphy" hereof refers to the "Six categories of the traditional structural theory of Chinese characters" relating to words, which belongs to the scope of a literacy course. "Mathematics" is related to calculations while "Archery" is shooting and "Chariot-riding" is driving.

The classical "Six Arts" in the form of a written text are the so-called "Six Classics", which came into existence before Confucius. It is legendarily said that Fuxi painted the eight diagrams for the *Book of Changes*, King Wen deduced the remaining part of it, and then Confucius added the biography for it eventually. Therefore, Confucius's sentence was recorded in the *Analects of Confucius* because of the complex history of compiling, saying that "I will understand the *Book of Changes* without great misconceptions when I study it at the age of fifty". The *Book of Songs* refers to poems in the Zhou dynasty, which occupied a number of over three thousand and maintained three hundred and five after the revision that Confucius made of it. Thereafter, the *Book of Songs* is also called "Poem Three Hundred". *Shu* (the direct pronunciation of its corresponding Chinese character) means the *Book of Documents*, which contains the proclamations and literary compilation of ancient times, involving Yu, Xia, Shang and Zhou. *Li* (the direct pronunciation of its corresponding Chinese character) can be divided into three sections: *Rites of Zhou*, *Ceremonial Etiquette* and the *Book of Rites*. As a part of the "Six Classics", *Li* generally refers to *Ceremonial Etiquette*. The *Spring and Autumn Annuals,* which should be the work of Confucius, concentrates on a historic event of great significance in the Lu state. If not being the original creation of Confucius, it is probably a product based on the initial historic event, which was processed and polished by Confucius at a later time. Simple and easy understanding events recorded, obscure wordings employed and profound messages conveyed, jointly form the later "Techniques of Chun Qiu Writing" commended by historians.

The "Six Classics", which are believed to have been deleted and arranged by Confucius, are the most original classical texts existing in contemporary China. This book represents the crystallization of the wisdom of the ancients, and acts as the fundamental spiritual basis for the Homo sapiens to conduct themselves and found a state. The learned and famous scholar of the 20th century, Ma Yifu asserted that the "Six Classics" is the highest special form of Chinese culture; while the great philosopher Xiong Shili considered the "Six Classics" to be the fundamental spiritual basis for the Homo sapiens to conduct themselves and found a state. These great judgments and comments still prevail in modern times and are not obsolete and outdated, and they continue to demonstrate their further and deeper excellence and wonder with the passage of time.

III. The Reasoning Regarding the Values of the Six Classics

In recent years, I have deduced and summarized several sets of values, comprising the five sets of concepts naming sincerity and trust, love and reverence, loyalty and forbearance, honor and shame, harmony and diversity (meaning harmony in diversity) from the "Six Classics", the *Analects of Confucius*, the *Works of Mencius*, and the *Classic of Filial Piety*, the latter three of which are included in the "Thirteen Classics". These conceptual categories, from my standpoint of view, are the values which possess eternity and universality in Chinese culture. They apply to both ancient times and modern times, both Chinese people and those from all over the world.

1. Sincerity and trust

Honesty and integrity, which is a very important value concept in Chinese culture, comes first. Confucius once said: "Trust is the coin of the realm", and "It remains unknown what one could achieve if he is not trustworthy". And Mencius said: "Trust exists amongst friends". And Lao Tzu also said: "Trustworthy words may not be fine-sounding; fine-sounding words may not be trustworthy". "Trust" occupies a very important position in the original classic of Chinese culture.

Internal sincerity and external trust are interconnected, and they cannot exist without each other. "Sincerity" appears most frequently in *The Doctrine of the Mean*, in which there are words saying: "Sincerity" is "the way of heaven", and "Sincerity is the start and the end of everything; without sincerity, there would be nothing". However, to "establish sincerity" is "the way of people". In *The Doctrine of the Mean*, "sincerity" is regarded as the core issue of "the way of heaven" and "the way of people".

A student of Wang Yangming, an ideologist of the Ming dynasty, learned from him for a long time and he had to leave for his hometown. While saying goodbye before setting out, he said to Wang Yangming: “I don’t know when we will meet again, do you have any suggestions that can benefit me for my whole life?” Wang Yangming replied: “Be sincere”. The student was an old disciple. Myriad of things occur in this world and quantities of questions need to be solved in the world, so he doubted that whether the single “sincerity” could be the answer to everything and questioned if there were any other supporting factors. Wang Yangming replied again: “Be sincere”.

This disciple did realize that “sincerity” was indeed the life-long foundation of morality in his later life.

The ideology of “sincerity” was explicitly mentioned and discussed as early as in the *Book of Changes*. In this book, the statements in the third to the last line of the Qian diagram read like this: “A gentleman should be loyal and trustworthy, thus his moral character will be enhanced. And he should cultivate good words to establish sincerity, and then live and conduct his career in peace and contentment.” Thus, “sincerity” is explicitly proposed hereof.

What on earth do people pursue in this world? The two sentences of the Qian diagram in the *Book of Changes* indeed have summarized the essence when you think about it carefully. What one wants to achieve in his lifetime is indeed to become a better, cultivated and respected person. Sincerity and trust are the first value to achieve if one wants to succeed in doing so. This is what the statement, “A gentleman should be loyal and trustworthy, thus his moral character will be enhanced” means. The core value concept of “morality enhancement” is “loyalty and trust”. The direct and literal meaning of the word “loyalty” is to put oneself in the right place to become an honest and trustworthy person, which tops at the first level of life essentials. The second level of life essentials goes to a successful career, meaning that one should have his own construction and achievement in whatever fields he is professional in, and should be capable of living and conducting his career in peace and contentment. And “sincerity” is the premise of “living and conducting a career in peace and confidence", thus comes the "One should cultivate good words to establish sincerity, and then live and conduct his career in peace and contentment."

"Sincerity" is the premise of "living and conducting a career in peace and confidence". Sincerity and trust show their significance and importance hereby. "Sincerity and trust" is an essential element in determining the success or failure of the individual life, and can be regarded as the core value concept of Chinese culture.

2. Love and reverence

Another core value concept of Chinese culture lies in "love and reverence", which is quoted from the words of Confucius, reading "Those who love their own parents will not hate other parents, and who respect their own parents will not neglect other parents. People shall serve their own parents with Xin and soul, and conduct moral education to people around." in the *Classic of Filial Piety*.

"Love and reverence" come from family discipline and order. Love and reverence actually exist between father and son, husband and wife, and siblings. If one shows respect and reverence towards his own elders and beloved ones, he will not be unfriendly and impolite towards people outside his family, and at least will not treat them without proper respect. In addition, the *Classic of Filial Piety* also deems, "Serve parents when they are alive with love and reverence, and arrange the funeral with mourning when they pass away, by doing so, a filial son could fulfill his duty and responsibility in the world." Regard love and reverence as the principle and meaning of life and death. A man's emotions of sorrow and grief usually derive from the sympathetic feelings about the distress and misfortune of his family members. It is generally believed that love is sufficient to support the relationship between wife and husband; in fact, love is not long-lasting. Reverence is also a basic necessity as well. Being intimate and respectful is the key for a couple to become a paragon.

The *Records of Personages*, a book written by Liu Shao from the Wei and Jin dynasties, provides the most precise and appropriate explanation about the value concept of "love and reverence". The *Records of Personages* is quite special since it is a book of people, a book of ethics and a book of philosophy, or the special *An Essay on Man*. Only people in the Wei and Jin dynasties could write such a wonderful book. Liu Shao wrote in this book:

> Nothing is more appropriate than love and reverence for ultimate humanity. Therefore, the *Classic of Filial Piety* deems love as the majestic moral character, and reverence as the thoroughfare.

The value concept of "love and reverence" does have its significant position in Chinese culture since it is regarded as the ultimate value of humanity.

"Reverence" can certainly include respect for teachers, for virtuous people of the older generations and for elders. However, the philosophical meaning of the value of "reverence" refers to the "dignity of self-nature" of the human being as individual life. "Reverence" is the spiritual settlement of one's inner character, sexual body and natural instinct. In traditional culture, many moral norms are related to "reverence".

Take "filial piety" as an example. An instance in the *Analects of Confucius* goes like the following. Once Zi You asked Confucius what "filial piety" was and Confucius replied that people nowadays think that "being able to raise" is filial piety; if this is true, dogs can also "raise", however, dogs are without "reverence" when doing so, thus, how can the difference be distinguished? One difference between a man and a dog is that in the matter of filial piety, people can show "reverence" while dogs cannot.

It can be seen that "reverence" is the spiritual core of filial piety. Therefore, people usually refer to the attitude and actions towards the elderly as "filial piety", which is also known as "respect for the elderly". In the traditional Chinese society, officials have been chosen seriously. If they do not honor their parents with filial piety, they are not qualified to be officials. Loyal and sincere people must honor their parents with filial piety, and only by doing so can they become virtuous sages who devote themselves to duties and love the world.

All etiquettes in the universe should be equipped with the spirit of "reverence". Therefore, the *Classic of Filial Piety* says: "The ultimate meaning of Li (the direct pronunciation of its corresponding Chinese character) is reverence". One of the famous sayings of Confucius is, "How can I be able to stand the people who are in power, not to be lenient, not to be serious when they salute, and not to be sad when they attend funerals?" Etiquette is something that needs to be watched by others; thus comes the saying of "attend a celebration or ceremony". However, etiquette is not worth seeing if it is without "reverence". Another famous saying of Confucius is: "Offer sacrifice to the god as if it were there", meaning that one should believe that god is present when offering a sacrifice and only in this way can the worshippers be kept sincere.

Sacrifice was of paramount importance and significance in ancient times. A sentence in the *Zuo Commentary* goes like this: "The important matters of a nation are sacrifices and wars". The former means offering sacrifice to the god and the latter refers to military actions. However, neither sacrifice nor military action can be without "reverence". Military action should also be about etiquette. Lots of documents and records in the *Zuo Commentary* show that many wars occur because of "irreverence" or "great irreverence", which leads to the military actions of the powerful party. In modern society, it is also important to deal with the interrelationship among states, involving foreign affairs, etiquette and reverence.

Etiquette and reverence are the index of civilization. The important distinction between civilization and uncivilization lies in the fact that the former embraces etiquette.

3. Loyalty and forbearance: "Do not do to others what you would not have them do to you."

"Loyalty and forbearance" is an important thought of Confucius. Once Confucius said: "What I mean by morality is being loyal and consistent." Zeng Zi (Zeng

Shen) said: Yes. And then, Confucius left and other disciples asked Zeng Shen: "What does it mean?" Zeng Shen replied: "The morality of Confucius is loyalty and forbearance", which suggests that "loyalty and forbearance" is a consistent and thorough thought. Loyalty and sincerity can interact with each other. Those who are sincere must be loyal. "Loyalty and sincerity" is the supreme moral law of Confucius. Disciple Fan Chi asked what "Benevolence" was. Confucius replied: "Behave properly while staying at home, be serious while dealing with daily chores and be loyal while treating friendship." It can be known that both "reverence" and "loyalty" are the components of benevolence.

"Loyalty" and "trust" are even more closely intimate. The main way to get trust is to be "loyal". Zeng Zi once said: "I meditate on myself three times a day", amongst which there are two elements included, one is: "Do I try my best when I handle affairs for others?" and the other one is: "Am I trustworthy when I make friends with others?" Loyalty and trust are problems that need to be reflected upon in relationships with others.

Confucius also said: "It works even in the undeveloped and uncivilized areas if one is loyal and trustworthy, and behaves himself in a respectful way. However, if one does the opposite, it will not work even in his own country." If one can keep being "loyal and trustworthy" and behave solemnly and respectfully, he will be able to stand on his feet even in the less civilized state. On the contrary, if one is not sincere and not honest with others, and cannot win the trust of his partners and he behaves rudely, he will not be able to win respect in his own hometown.

"Forbearance" demonstrates its significance and importance more apparently. According to the explanation of Confucius, forbearance means: "Do not do to others what you would not have them do to you." The meaning contained in and required by "forbearance" as a value concept generally means to be considerate, feel for others, show mutual understanding and empathy and do not impose what is undesirable for oneself on others. I think the value concept of "forbearance" demonstrates the beauty of Chinese culture. This is a great idea that Chinese culture contributes to mankind. The literary world attaches great importance to the idea of Confucius and regards it as the moral golden rule of human beings.

4. Honor and shame: "One shall not do what he thinks is shameful."

In the *Book of Rites: the Doctrine of the Mean*, there is a paragraph about cultivating moral character, quoting from Confucius, "One is approaching wisdom if he is full of curiosity, getting close to benevolence if he practices diligently, and gets access to bravery if he is familiar with the sense of shame. Knowing these elements, one will know how to cultivate character."Therefore, being curious, practicing diligently and knowing the sense of shame are treated as the three basic elements of cultivating character. Cultivation cannot be separated from knowledge absorption; this is what the sentence "Study the nature of things and gain knowledge" in the *Book of Rites: Great Learning* means. Therefore, "learning" ranks first place in the cultivation of character.

What does it mean to learn? If the ultimate purpose is to become a vessel for knowledge, and nothing is transformed at all, then it is useless to learn. The key to learning is to use it in practice, this is what the ancients meant by "unity of knowledge and action". Thus, the second element goes to "practice diligently". If one has studied and practiced, then he is not far from "benevolence", at least he is on the way to it.

However, there is no guarantee that everything you do is right since mistakes always occur. So what if something goes wrong? One shall be able to carry out self-reflection and be good at it, thus to find out the reason, to correct mistakes and to avoid making mistakes repeatedly. When one realizes his own mistake, he will feel ashamed, regretful and embarrassed about what he did. If one succeeds in doing so, then he "knows the sense of shame", which is the prerequisite for correcting mistakes. Therefore, "knows the sense of shame" is the third element.

Wisdom, benevolence and courage were called an "unchanging morality" in ancient times. With wisdom, benevolence and courage, one can make great judgments without mistakes, and will not be worried when encountering difficulties, and will not be afraid of threats, which are of the same meaning with “One should constantly seek knowledge to reduce the confusion about the world, should be honest with others, and no longer worry about personal gain or loss and should practice bravely and not be afraid of any difficulties” by Confucius. (*Analects of Confucius: Zi Han*) Zi Gong believed that his teacher, Confucius, was a person who had no worries, doubts or fears.

Amongst the three elements of the cultivation of character, the third one is “knowing the sense of shame”, which can especially not be despised. I have told students so many times: The cultivation of character should begin with a sense of shame. Shame is a civilized indicator of human beings, and one of the manifestations of human civilization, which Mencius called the “sense of shame”. Mencius said that the sense of compassion, the sense of shame, the sense of modesty and yielding, and the sense of right and wrong are the “four starts” of human beings. The word “Duan” (the direct pronunciation of its corresponding Chinese character) means “start”, meaning that the “four starts” is the beginning of a human being, or at least the symbol of a human being. According to Mencius, a man without a sense of shame is not a human being. Similarly, a man without a sense of compassion, a sense of modesty and yielding, and a sense of right and wrong is not a human being either. The sense of compassion is intolerance, which is sympathy, meaning “forbearance”. Do not do to others what you would not have them do to you. A sense of modesty and yielding means to be civilized and polite, a sense of right and wrong refers to fairness and justice of society, while a sense of shame, which is the third element of the cultivation of character, means “know the sense of shame”. Also, it is what Confucius means by “One shall not do what he thinks is shameful”.

“Chi” and “Lian” (the direct pronunciation of their corresponding Chinese characters) constitute a combined concept, naming “Lian Chi” (“honor and shame” in English). One of the famous arguments of Guan Zi goes like this: “Etiquette, righteousness, honor and shame constitute the four dimensions of a state." "Etiquette" is the civilized order, "righteousness" is social justice, "honesty" is being thrifty and "shame" is moral restraint and self-discipline. A state will be in danger without these four elements.

Gu Yanwu, the great scholar of the Ming and Qing dynasties, once said: "Honor and shame is the vital element of getting on in the world and behaving oneself." According to him, without thriftiness, one will take everything; and without shame, one will do everything. Still, there is another sentence from him: "The shamelessness of scholar-officials is the national humiliation."

5. Harmony and diversity (harmony in diversity)

Like sincerity and trust, love and reverence, loyalty and forbearance and honor and shame, harmony and diversity is the most basic and important value concept of Chinese culture. Chinese culture tends not to make the relationship among people so irreconcilable. Harmony in diversity is the general principle for the Chinese to interact with the world.

The idea of "harmony and diversity" derives from the *Book of Changes*. The diagram "Tong Ren" (the direct pronunciation of their corresponding Chinese characters) in this book interprets the concept of "Harmony and diversity with human beings." The precepts of the *Book of Changes* are summarized as follows: "Different paths lead to the same destination, and different intentions and thoughts have the same purpose in this world." This is to say that differences in people are often expressed in diverse ways and methods with the same ultimate goal. Therefore, by doing so, people finally gather together. The form of existence of human society, people's lifestyle as well as customs and habits are different among each other, however, the value of their life pursuit and their psychological orientation are often of the same. Mencius made this point clear:

> People have the same taste for food, deriving from the mouth; people have the same taste for sound, deriving from the ear; people have the same taste

> for color, deriving from the eye; thus, when it comes to the Xin (the direct pronunciation of its corresponding Chinese character), is there no such thing as the same? What do people have in common about Xin? It lies in principle and righteousness. (*Mencius · Gao Zi Shang*)

What Mencius means by this paragraph is that people all like delicious food, wonderful music and diverse colors, the respect for which is the same with human beings. Since there is a similar feeling in this respect, what about “Xin”? The answer is without any doubt. The same point of Xin lies in principle and righteousness.

“Xin”, which is from Mencius, can be understood as “psychology”. Qian Zhongshu, the great scholar, once said: “The psychological states of the east sea and the west sea are the same.” Therefore, the differences among people are far fewer than imagined. It is a cultural trap to exaggerate the human differences. And there is a “same” point within human differences. Because of this, there is inter-communication among people and among cultures, and therefore, difference can coexist in a unity.

The coexistence, communication and integration of different cultures are an inherent concept, which is based on the concept of “harmony” in Chinese culture. “Harmony” is composed of a myriad of “diversities”. It will not come into existence without diversities. Then, here comes the famous claim: “Gentlemen seek harmony but not uniformity.” Chang Tsai, a famous ideologist of the Song dynasty, is famous for his four teachings: “Ordaining conscience for the public; securing safety and fortune for common people; preserving cultural property from elder generations and carrying it forward; establishing peace for all future generations.” Since Chang Tsai is famous with the pseudonym of Heng-chu, thus the famous four sentences are called the “Heng-chu Four-Sentences Teaching”. Another “four teachings” are also well-known, which go like this,

> All phenomena in this world consist of opposite sides, which will lead to opposite moving directions, which will further lead to revenge and battle,

however, leading to an ultimate result of harmony.

I refer to these four sentences as the "four philosophical teachings", which specifically aim at the entire universe. These teachings generally mean that the universe is made up of single individuals, including human beings, animals and plants, and all of these individuals are different. The ancients had a saying that reads "Beauties do not share the same body and the same face." There is also a famous saying in the west, which reads: "There are no two identical individuals in the world." These different individuals are single "phenomena", which are fluid instead of static. However, these individual phenomena flow in different directions, some even move towards the opposite direction, and all of these consist of the first and second sentences of Chang's philosophy. Since "opposite" exists, there will be a conflict between each other, thus forming a situation of "revenge and battle".

The word "revenge" was written as " 讎 " in ancient times, with a letter 隹 (zhui) on the left, a letter 隹 (zhui) on the right, and a letter 言 (yan) in the middle. " 隹 " is a bird with a short tail. It can be imagined that the word " 讎 " symbolizes that two short tail birds are flapping there, just as if they were talking to each other. It can also be speculated that birds with short tails tend to cry very loudly, so they are not just talking, but arguing, debating, or even bickering and quarreling with each other. We have no idea about what they are communicating, but the result of their deliberation, rebuttal, discussion, and argument will not be that the birds have eaten each other, but that they have reached a consensus, or a common ground or harmony in diversity. Therefore, there follows the phrase "an ultimate result of harmony".

IV. "Better to Make Friends than to Make Enemies"

The implications of the "philosophical four teachings" from Chang Tsai are far-reached and profound. In reality, we can get a sweeping view: The world is different, but the difference does not necessarily develop into a conflict. Conflict does not necessarily become a zero-sum game, but can be "solved in harmony". By bearing this idea in mind, a lot of things will be dealt with more appropriately.

A poem, coming from the great literary expert Lu Xun, is about the relationship between China and Japan in the postwar period. Two sentences of this poem are: “Disasters are never powerful enough to separate real friends. A smile is all they need to eliminate the gratitude and resentment.” There should be no enmity among people, among communities, among ethnic groups and among nations. “Revenge” can be resolved with a result of “harmony”. Therefore, there is another saying in China, which reads, “Better to make friends than to make enemies.”

人文精神和中国文化

吉耶斯 【法国】
法国国立集美亚洲艺术博物馆（巴黎）前馆长 / 法国文化部前文化事务总监

人文精神包含了博大精深的中华思想，又汲取了西方哲学的精华，翻译成中文有两个汉字组成，即“人文”（*ren wen*）。人指人性，文则代表文化。在这一固有的语言表达形式背后，体现的是一个具有学术意义的术语，指中国的文化史中最重要的是文化的伦理价值。

对于一个西方人来说，原始术语的这种关联性即使是极度相关的，也并不一定就能意识到。这就需要对这一术语所涉及的概念进行解释，尤其是“文化”与“人文主义”之间的哲学关系。因为这些概念是中华文化的基础，展示了她几千年的历史。这就是我希望讨论的文化的核心。

一

我想谈谈中西方之间文化的差异。“人文主义”一词的现代翻译恰好再现了西方思维中所涉及的文化伦理差异。西方的“人文主义”一词有两层含义：一是指在哲学领域，这是一个将对人类问题的思考放在首位的思想体系；二是指在历史研究领域，其源于意大利文艺复兴时期的文化运动——古希腊和古罗马思想的复兴。

但是，可以说，文化和哲学这两个含义存在于中国人对“仁慈”一词的思考中，这是对古典文化“古人之道”的一种类似的回归，这在人文主义的道德价值上是明晰的。

我突然发现，这里的"人文主义"与西方的Humanism的对等性让人震惊，或者说把Humanism翻译成"人文主义"再恰当不过了。对比古代文化研究，所谓"古道"，显然是包括人文精神的道德价值的。或者在这种情况下，它只是一种现代的表达方式，以专门区别于众所周知的含义。

尽管如此，为了明确主题，这里最好把这种从西方借用的人文主义的现代翻译放在括号里，因为这是中西方两种文化的转换，非常明显的是中国和欧洲各自的发展最终以不同的语言表达了这些重要的人类真理。 在这方面回顾中国古典语言所表达的意义就会发现，这些字符所表达的含义都是完全独立的，与目前现代翻译中的情况相反，很少出现能与西方话语完全匹配的表达。

这就是孔子（公元前6世纪）强调文化（指斯文）和仁慈以及人性的美德，这种至高无上的理想之间联系的重要性。不仅把美德放在第一位，而且它也是文化的同义词。《论语》里有话为证，当然，这也需要进一步评论。

孔子在匡地被包围，他说，"文王既没，文不在兹乎。天之将丧斯文也，后死者不得与于斯文也；天之未丧斯文也，匡人其如予何！"（《论语》）

在本文中，我们将重点讨论"天之未丧斯文也，匡人其如予何！"

二

本文将论证为了尊重别人的"自我剥夺"（*dispossession of Self*）是以诚信为本的：这包括孔子所谓的人性美德、仁德。孔子在《论语》中很清楚地说明了中华古典思想的基本概念：

> "夫仁者，己欲立而立人，己欲达而达人。能近取譬，可谓仁之方也已。"

因此，这种对以自我为中心的"自我剥夺"就是走向崇高理想和道德完整的道路：人性（仁）的美德。为了达到这样的要求，孔子曾毫不犹豫地说：

> "志士仁人，无求生以害仁，有杀身以成仁。"（《论语》）

为了避免给人以中国的传统思想只有孔子和他的弟子传授的思想学派的印象，在本文中我们也将介绍孔子同一时代的另一代表思想学派——道家学派。这一学派始于老子和庄子（以及他们的作品），在中国传统文化中同样具有权威性。

与孔子的儒家学派截然相反，人们通常认为人性的原则（仁德）尽管从来没有在这里表达过——或者是故意避开了——因为它与文化不可分割地联系在一起，隐含在庄子的思想里。这就是我们想在此说明的。

因此按照真实性和返朴归真的想法，也就是我们最初是什么的观点，我们首先需要讨论庄子所言的“真”——本性、本原——哲学的直觉。

在庄子看来，自然真实性（真）决定了智者（圣人）或真正之人（真人）的形象。圣人或真人是指能够理解事物的本质并与它和谐相处的人。

当一个人能完美和谐地与“他者”相处（与“以自我为中心的我”不同），这个“他者”，从内部的核心义来看，就是世界，或者说是“道”（*dao*）。

重要的是，除了强调自然与文化的对立——这一对立就能分别定义孔子的儒家思想和庄子的道家思想体系——他们有本质上的相通性：真。

很显然，这两种思想体系都基于“真实”或“真诚”，因此，在二者分别按照自己的学说向不同方向发展之前，“求真”是他们的重要共通之处。

三

因此本研究中“仁”和“真”的概念（人文精神与真实性）的基石原来是以“自我的剥夺”，即“己欲立而立人”（自己的脚要先站稳，才能够扶起摔倒的人）。作为通向这一最高理想的路径则是道德的完整性和自我的真实性。

在孔子看来，诚实守信是仁德的保证；在庄子看来，与“道”的完美和谐相处的方式是本真。

对“自我剥夺”的劝告在庄子的学说中达到极致，有他的观点作为佐证：

> “形固可使如槁木，而心固可使如死灰乎？今之隐机者，非昔之隐机者也？”（《庄子·齐物论》）

按照我们的理解，自我通过对客观世界的感知到对客观现实的认识，就像木头和灰烬一样。这个自我客体就可据此称客体，即外部现实，“形固可使如槁木，而心固可使如死灰乎”。

如《庄子》所言，这一“自我客体”的减小暗示了完全的“自我剥夺”。这就是庄子客观描述的“自我剥夺”——似乎按照佛教“无我”的概念，这没有什么价值。的确如此么？

但我们不会只停留在对这种“自我剥夺”的印象（可借鉴让-保罗·萨特的《辩证理性批判》中的表达）。因为在中国的思想体系中，确切地说，在佛教引入中国之前，并没有这种“缺失”，自我否定。因此我们用这个中位的术语，以自我为中心的“自我剥夺”，来准确地翻译庄子之言。

要证明这一点，只能引用《庄子》中对“真”（真理、真诚）这个词的定义。即“真者，精诚之至也。不精不诚，不能动人。”《庄子·杂篇·渔父》

这就是“人本思想”的证明。“激发他人的情感和激情”；奉行孔子的教义：诚实、真诚；庄子将这些统统合成一个词组：精诚。

当然，这是从众生中的圣人智者的角度看，在精神上处于孤立，在现实中与他们距离却并不遥远。圣人的任务是以自身来示范。

要想深入分析《庄子》，就需要掌握“真”（精诚）的含义：

> “真者，所以受于天也，自然不可易也。故圣人法天贵真，不拘于俗。”(《庄子杂篇·渔父》)

四

我们分别从以孔子和庄子为代表的中国两个传统思想体系中看到，人文思考最终走向了类似的人文关怀。庄子主张道法自然，即原始真实性，不受世俗的约束。“故圣人法天……不拘于俗。”

“客观化自我剥夺”（*objectifying dispossession of Self*）所刻画的“形容枯槁”就是精神练习，一种达到美妙本质的方法，即自然法则。在任何情况下（尽管从纯粹的修辞上与此相反，如庄子的格言）都不会忽略或撇开人文主义的反思。

关于这一点，我想提到《天道》(《庄子·外篇》)。这是关于尧舜间的对话中所强调的孔子和庄子的理想之间的深刻的理解：

“昔者舜问于尧曰：天王之用心何如？”尧曰：“吾不敖无告，不废穷民，苦死者，嘉孺子而哀妇人。此吾所以用心也。舜曰：美则美矣，而未大也。”

但应该注意的是，庄子的人文主义，与孔子传授的人文主义相比，更具有真理的主题形成了。虽然二者间的关系是紧密的，决定了总体上的相对性。因此，有人可能会想：没有庄子，哪儿来的孔子的示范价值？

事实上，这段对话里几乎每一个字都介绍了孔子关于人性美德的最高理想的实现：

子贡曰：“如有博施于民而能济众，何如？可谓仁乎？”子曰：“尧舜其犹病诸！”

并继续解释，“夫仁者，己欲立而立人。”

五

因为它显然出现在第一和主要概念的这个层次上，说明来源于上述两种思想之间的关系。

我可以看到中国传统思想的这种一致性以及超越哲学体系的多样性。更值得一提的是，一谈到人文价值观和文化，我就会谈及中国思维的独特性。正如我们刚刚看到的，这种思维支配着哲学体系的道德有效性，即使对那些声称完全摆脱哲学体系的人也是如此。因此，应该提到的是，那些总是被提到的、在文人圈子内传播的且人人都离不开的，是老子和庄子的教义。

人文与文化的契合，体现了中国传统文化的独特性。事实上，这一特点也延伸到与之密切相关的艺术创作领域。11 世纪伟大的诗人苏轼（1037—1101）的诗句就是很好的证明。在他的诗中，提到了他同时代的文同（1018—1079）的画作。对我们来说，诗中表现出被剥夺的自我的积极含义。

我们把这首描写文同的画的诗放在这儿，因为它说明了这些理想的文化持久性。

苏轼评论这首诗里“客观化自我剥夺”，佛教以及庄子的思想是北宋学者关于当下的概念形成的来源。以下是这首诗的部分内容，它说明了这些理想的文化持久性。

与可画竹时，见竹不见人。
岂独不见人，嗒然遗其身。
其身与竹化，无穷出清新。
庄周世无有，谁知此凝神。

（苏轼：《书晁补之所藏与可画竹三首》）

Humanism and Chinese Culture

Jacques Gies / France

Former President-Director of the Musée Guimet - National Museum of Asian Art, Paris and Former General Inspector of Cultural Affairs, French Ministry of Culture. (Retired)

Introduced as such in the universe of Chinese thought, the term "humanism", adopted following the meeting with Western philosophy, had to receive a modern translation by the pair of characters *renwen* 人文 : expression made from the prefixes of the two terms: *renxing* 人性 "humanity" and *wenhua* 文化 "Culture". Behind the ready-made linguistic expression, arises a very scholarly composition of the term referring to the cultural history of China; namely, first and foremost, to the ethical values of Culture.

For a Westerner the expression of this correlation of the original term is not immediate, even though it turns out to be deeply relevant. It requires the explanation of the concepts in question, and particularly the philosophical relationship made here between "Culture" and "humanism". For, these concepts are at the very foundations of the Chinese civilisation, determining its several-thousand-year history. It is this cultural singularity we wish to consider here.

I

I'm just talking about the cultural distance between the West and China. It so happens that the modern translation into Chinese of the term humanism accurately reproduces the cultural and ethical nuances involved in the Western thinking.

The thing is quite remarkable to be mentioned. Thus, the double meaning given in the Western to the term "humanism": on the one hand, in philosophy, a system of thought attaching prime importance to human matters; on the other hand, in historical studies, a Renaissance cultural movement in Italy (14th-16th centuries), which revived interest in ancient Greek and Roman thought and antique Art.

However, one could say that these two meanings, cultural and philosophical, exist in the Chinese thinking about the term "humanity" (*ren ci* 仁 慈), that is a comparable return to the antique Culture, "the Way of the Ancients", is plainly inclusive in the moral value of humanism.

Let it be said at once that the parallelisms are striking. Can we talk about a genius of the Chinese translation? Or, as is the case, it is but a modern expression, precisely unique in its use, to distinguish it from a well-known thing, in other respects.

Nonetheless, for the clarity of the subject, it is preferable here to put in brackets this modern translation of *humanism* (*renwen zhuyi* 人文主义) borrowed from the West; because the respective developments in these two cultural worlds, China and Europe, to finally express these cardinal human truths, are very distinct. It will be recalled, in this regard, that the Chinese classical language use of words (characters) in their full and independent meanings, rarely combined in pairs — contrary to what is the case in the present modern translation of the term.

That is all the merit of Confucius (6th century BC) to have emphasized the importance of the link between Culture (*wen* 文): "this culture of ours" (*si wen* 斯 文), which he declared himself the "depositary and guarantor", and the virtue of humanity (*ren* 仁), this supreme Ideal. Not only this ideal shed light on the first, but still it is a synonym. That is evidence in reading the Analects of Confucius. Of course, it deserves a commentary.

> “ Threatened with death in Kuang, the Master (Confucius) said: “After the death of King Wen, its culture (*wen* 文) should not live here in me? If heaven had wanted to bury this Culture (*si wen* 斯文), a mortal like me would not have been let known about it. However, if that is not the intention of heaven, what can the men of Kuang do to me? ” *(Analects*, IX-5).

In this paper, we will focus on the conclusion, “If that is not the intention of heaven, what have I to fear from *Kuang*?”

II

The line taken in this paper proposes to demonstrate that *dispossession of self for the sake of respect for others* is the path to the (proper) sincerity, honesty (*cheng* 诚) : that includes the Confucian notion of virtue of humanity, both of perfect virtue (*ren de* 仁德). Cardinal notion of the Classical Chinese thinking, very clearly expressed by Confucius in his *Analects:*

> “Practice the virtue of humanity (*ren* 仁) is to start with oneself: wanting to establish others as much as we want to establish ourselves, and wishing their success as much as we want our own. Draws in you the idea of what you can do for others — that is what put you on the path to perfect virtue (*ren* 仁)!” (*Analects* VI-30.)

Therefore, such dispossession of ego-centered Self is the path to the lofty ideals and moral integrity: the active virtue of humanity (*ren* 仁). This, in its integrity, is of such a requirement that Confucius does not hesitate to say that:

> “The follower committed to the Way, the man of true benevolence (*ren* 仁), far from caring for his live if it costs to the *ren*, will be brave enough to sacrifice his life to accomplish the quality of the *ren*.” (*Analects* XV-9.)

In order to avoid giving the impression that all the classical Chinese thoughts hold in the teaching of Confucius and his disciples, we will also consider in this paper, another thought, the Taoism: announced by Laozi and extended by Zhuangzi, whose authority is just as essential in traditional Chinese culture.

Far from professing a teaching diametrically opposed, as it is often presented, the principle of humanity (*ren de* 仁德), though never formulated as such here, or knowingly eluded, because it is indissolubly linked to Culture, is, in some ways, implicit in Zhuangzi. That is what we want to show.

Therefore, we must begin with this philosophical intuition that Zhuangzi refers to by the term *zhen* 真 (*Truth*); here in the sense of 'nature' (*ben xing* 本性), "natural state" (*ben yuan* 本原), according to the idea of original simplicity, original authenticity: what is "us" originally.

For Zhuangzi, the natural authenticity (*zhen* 真) determines the figure of the Wise (*sheng* 圣) or the "Real man" (*zhenren* 真 人).The saint or the "real man" is the one who understands the nature of things, who lives in harmony with it, spreading his wonderful and effective virtue within the universe. In other words, one that is in perfect harmony with what is "the Other"(different, for his limited self-centered ego), but that is "*His*", internally, in essence : namely here, the world or Nature : the Way (*dao* 道).

What matters here, beyond the opposition stressed between Nature and Culture — opposition that would define the respective systems of thoughts of Confucius and Zhuangzi — it is their first common requirement of Truth, Sincerity.

It is clear that these two systems of thought are based on the common basis of the imperative of the 'Truth' (*zhen* 真), the "Sincerity" (*cheng* 诚). Thus, the essential kinship, before that happens the well-known divergence of their respective developments in separate doctrines.

III

It would seem that the cornerstone of these remarks about the concept of "humanity-authenticity", turns out to be the principle of dispossession of Self in equality of respect for others, "If one wants to establish each other as much as he wants to establish himself", as a path to this supreme ideal that is moral integrity or original authenticity to oneself.

For Confucius, sincerity, moral integrity (cheng 诚) is the guarantee to accomplish the cultivation of the quality of humanity (ren 仁); for Zhuangzi, the truth (zhen 真) is the pledge of the fulfillment of the perfect harmony with the way (dao 道).

The injunction of the dispossession of Self is even taken to the extreme in Zhuangzi, as it is said in the famous sentence of the chapter. II, *Of the equality of things*:

> "Can your body really become thus like a withered tree and your heart like dead ashes, doesn't feel we do part of the wonderful Essence?" (*Zhuangzi*)

According to our interpretation, this body of mine perceived through my objectification of the world, transformed into an objective reality as wood and ashes: this "me-object" that happens to me, and on which a judgment may be reported to as a *simple objet*, referred to an external reality:" like a withered tree and your heart like dead ashes…"

This *me-object* on which a drastic reduction can take place, as Zhuangzi says, indicates a total dispossession of Self. Such is the Zhuangzi's *objectifying* dispossession of Self —anticipating, it seems, on the Buddhist concept of "absence, negation of Self", it is worth noting. But is it so?

Nonetheless, we will not stay on this impression of a total dispossession of Self ("of a bleeding without return", to borrow a term from Jean-Paul Sartre in *Critique of dialectical reason*.) In the Chinese thinking, precisely before the introduction of Buddhism, it has not been conceived such absence, negation of Self. Hence, the median expression of "dispossession of Self" we use to translate accurately the words of Zhuangzi.

To demonstrate this, it is but to refer to the definition that Zhuangzi gives to the term *zhen* 真 (*Truth, natural Authenticity*), or better said here, of (proper)Truth:

> "The natural disposition means the apex of absolute sincerity. Without absolute sincerity, you will never be able to elicit the emotions and passions of others."[1] (*Zhuangzi*)

As it is here, a real proof of a humanist thought. The Sincerity is therefore envisaged in the relationship to others: "to elicit the emotions and passions of others." Moreover, the demonstration use the terms specific to those of Confucius: honesty, sincerity (*cheng* 诚); Zhuangzi simply affixed a superlative: pure authenticity (*jing cheng* 精诚).

As well, the perspective proposed here is really that of the wise man present among men, and not distant from them in his spiritual solitude, whose mission is to teach them the *Way* by the example he gives of himself.

Further reading this chapter of the Zhuangzi is needed to grasp what this concept of pure authenticity (*jing cheng* 精诚) means.

> "the Truth is that which is received from the Heaven; natural, it is immutable. Therefore, the Sage takes his law from Heaven and prizes it highly as his (proper) Truth, without submitting to the restrictions of custom." (*Zhuangzi*)

IV

What we have seen through the two systems of Chinese traditional thinking, respectively from Confucius and from Zhuangzi, is eventually the convergence

1 *Zhuangzi*, Hunan Publishing House, Changsha, 1997, p. 660.

towards a comparable humanistic consideration.

Zhuangzi appeals to the law of Heaven, to the principle of Nature. This is defined the original authenticity, to which he opposed the Customs (*su* 俗), "Therefore, the Sage takes his law from Heaven… without submitting to the restrictions of custom."

The *objectifying dispossession of Self*, inscribed in the phrase "Can your body really become thus like a withered tree…" is nothing else than a spiritual exercise, a way to reach the wonderful essence, the law of Heaven who rules over everything. In no case (despite the contrary, purely rhetorical, formulas such as Zhuangzi's) is ignored or leave aside a humanistic reflection.

In this regard, we should mention this passage from the chapter "The Way of Heaven", of Zhuangzi (Outer *Chapiter*, chap. 30.). This imaginary dialogue between the Wise Kings of Mythology: Yao and Shun, emphasizes the linkage, in a profound understanding, between the ideal of Confucius and that which is proper to Zhuangzi:

> "Anciently, Shun asked Yao, saying, 'In what way does your Majesty by the Grace of Heaven exercise your mind?' The reply was, 'I simply show no arrogance towards the helpless; I do not neglect the poor people; I grieve for those who die; I love their infant children; and I compassionate their widows."

Shun rejoined, "Admirable, as far as it goes; but it is not what is great."

But it should be noted that the (more celestial) thesis of Zhuangzi — thesis developed in all its relevance — is formed in this way compared to the humanism taught by Confucius. The relationship is intimate; it determines the objection in all its terms. Thus, one may wonder: without the first, which would have been the demonstrative value of the second?

In fact, this dialogue resumes almost word for word that presents Confucius about the realization of the supreme ideal of the virtue of humanity (*Analects*, VI.

30.), as given here:

> "Zi Gong: Master, if there is a man who extensively conferring benefits on the people, and able to assist all, would he not deserve the name of *ren* (perfectly virtuous) ? The Master: (…) Even Yao and Shun were still solicitous about this."

Follows this comment (by which we started):

> "Practice the *ren* (the virtue of humanity) (...) it is wanting to establish the others as much as one wants to establish oneself..."

V

It follows from the foregoing evidence of a kinship between the two thoughts, as it obviously appears at this level of the first and prime concepts.

I can see this consistency of the traditional Chinese thought, beyond the diversity of philosophical systems. But, better still, I could talk, as soon as it comes to humanistic values —and Culture that subtends —of the uniqueness of the Chinese thinking. Because, as we have just seen, this thinking dominates the moral validity of philosophical systems, even those that claim precisely to break free from it. As such, it should be mentioned those that deliver, in a quest interior and undivided for everyone, the teachings of Laozi and Zhuangzi.

This correspondence between humanism and culture characterizes the uniqueness of the Chinese traditional culture. Indeed, it extends into the intimate domain of artistic creation. It is evidenced by the poem of the great scholar of the 11th century, Su Shi (1037-1101), about the art of his contemporary, Wen Tong (1018-1079); it becomes clear to us the positive meaning that must be given to the dispossession of Self.

We give this poem on Wen Tong's painting, in its entirety, because it illustrates the cultural permanence of these ideals.

Su Shi comments in it the *objectifying dispossession of Self*, legacy of Buddhism, but also of Zhuangzi's thinking, as a very present concept for the scholars of the Northern Song.

> When Yuke painted bamboo,
> He saw bamboo and nor himself.
> Not simply unconscious of himself,
> Trance-like, he left his body behind.
> His body was transferred into bamboo,
> Creating inexhaustible freshness.
> Zhuangzi is no longer in this world,
> So who can understand such concentration?[1]

1 A Poem of Wen Tong's Painting, Trad. Susan Bush, *The Chinese Literati on Painting*, Harvard University Press, Cambridge, Massachusetts, and London, 1971, p. 41.

天下主义与“一带一路”

王柯平 【中国】

中国社会科学院哲学研究所研究员 / 研究生院哲学系博士生导师 / 美学研究室主任

中国传统的“天下”（all under heaven）观，在语用意义上近乎于希腊传统的“世界”（*Oikoumenē*）说。史学家汤因比（Arnold J. Toynbee）与沃格林（Eric Voegelin）在纵论天下局势与人类现状时，将“天下”观发展成“天下主义”(ecumenism)，以此代表一种类乎世界主义的价值取向和思维方式，同时从历史实践角度将其上溯到汉高祖的治国策略，继而根据其积极效应将其奉为构建人类社会前景与世界秩序的重要参照系。譬如，在《人类与大地母亲》这部世界叙述史里，汤因比特意指出：当今全球境域里的各个主权国家，已经没有能力维护和平，没有能力拯救生物圈免遭人为的污染，更没有能力保护生物圈里不可替代的自然资源。在这个技术与经济层面依然整合的世界上，政治层面上的世界无政府状态再也无法持续下去了。中国传统的“天下”观，主要基于“泛爱众”的仁慈感，期待人人都将自己的爱心无私奉献给他人和同胞。这种仁慈或仁爱，既包含熟人故友所激发的爱心，也包含共同人类大众所激发的爱心。公元前 2 世纪期间，中国王朝的治理方式在世界上是出类拔萃，与其他地方的治理方式相比，它使很大一部分人类多年生活在和平有序的时代里。但是，后来有些中国的王公大臣，出于个人利益的诉求，背离了这种天下观，滥用了手中的权力，结果给中国带来灾难。如果中国汲取历史教训，采取积极有效措施，预防重复这类错误，不仅会给自己国家带来巨大益处，而且会给整个人类带来巨大益处，尤其当人类处在迷离道路上的这一关键阶段。[1]

不过，从中国历史的实情来看，汉兴之初所奉行的天下主义，本质上是一种失衡模式，其利弊同在、代价甚高，更有利于草原帝国匈奴的恣意扩张，致使他们在西域纵马横行，开疆拓土，先后摧毁或驱逐了久居当地的乌孙、月氏诸国。另外，根据汉朝与匈奴之间的和议条文，前者每年向后者供奉大量食物、丝绸和奢侈用品，等同于以朝贡方式赎买和平。然而，擅长骑射、好战成性的匈奴游牧，每到冬春季节，时常不顾彼此禁止犯界的和约条文，随意侵扰汉界边陲城镇（如代郡、上郡等），屠杀当地军民，致使汉代边防守将李广率部驱敌，往来奔驰，如同救火，由此赢得"飞将军"之称。但就总体而言，"汉兴至孝文二十余年，天下和洽"，确是事实。在司马迁所著的《史记·平准书》里，对此时期的政治和解、经济繁荣以及民生状况均有较为翔实的描述。

需要指出的是，汤因比是从大历史观出发，着重强调了汉匈的和解方式与政治效应，有意忽略了从未中断的汉匈冲突与杀伐，其思想倾向似乎有意将汉初实施天下主义的国策予以理想化和范式化了。实际上，到了汉武帝刘彻之时，汉朝经过多年忍辱负重和励精图治，终于从休养生息中强大起来，从政治软弱的阴影中走了出来，有能力有意志直面匈奴的骄横攻伐与长期纠缠。在数年准备之后，刘彻采取积极防卫和纵深打击的双重策略，终于将匈奴从汉朝边陲赶往遥远漠北，由此彻底解除了边境压力，赢得了真正和平。与此同时，刘彻在张骞等大臣的辅佐下，着力推行天下主义的平衡模式，促进了中原地区与西域诸国的联系合作，开辟了古代丝绸之路，打通了东西横跨欧亚大陆的商贸与文化交流通道。

根据英国历史学家弗兰科潘（Peter Frankopan）的最新研究结果：上述这些交流通道是整个世界的中枢神经系统，将各民族各地区联系在一起。当时，丝绸之路沿线所及，地域辽阔，文化多样，是世界主要宗教的发祥地，是各种语言群体相互竞争的熔炉，许多相关国家绝非处在全球事务的边缘，而是处在国际交往的正中心，并且自古以来就是如此。人类文明实则是从这里诞生。[2] 实际上，当时的中国汉代都城长安，所面对的是一个似乎正在变得越来越小的世界。人类历史上

---

1 Arnold Toynbee, *Mankind and Mother Earth: A Narrative History of the World* (Oxford: Oxford University Press, 1976), pp. 589-593.

2 ［英］弗兰科潘：《丝绸之路：一部全新的世界史》邵旭东、孙芳译，徐文琪审校，浙江大学出版社 2016 年版，第 3—4 页。

的全球化通常看作是当代社会独有的现象，但早在2000年前它就已经随着丝绸之路的开拓应运而生，它提供着机遇，带来了问题，也推动着技术的进步。[1]

就天下主义发展的内在逻辑而论，我认为诚心尚"和"（和合，和洽，和谐与和平）的和谐论（harmonism）才是其关键所在，才是决定其成其所能为的根本途径。中国传统思想中的"和"，原本是礼乐文化中所用的一个音乐概念，意在将不同乐器的音调和舞蹈的动作有机配合、融为一体，形成乐舞和谐、感化人心的效果，实现移风易俗、人文化成的目的。后来儒家推举"和为贵"之说，将其引入政治、社会与道德领域，从而使"和"成为一种融合、协调与汇通不同要素的思想运作方法和治国理政准则，通常显现出相辅相成、相反相成、求同存异、化解矛盾、和而不同等主要特征。春秋时期的政治家和思想家晏婴，曾以"和如羹"的喻说，对"和"的妙用进行了形象而生动的阐释；另外在《国语》里，也相继提出了"和实生物，同则不继"等著名论断。到了宋代理学勃兴之时，关中学派代表张载强调"反"、"仇"与"和"等几种力量之间的交互作用，标举一种解决矛盾或化解冲突的和解与合理方式。他概括说："有象斯有对，对必反其为；有反斯有仇，仇必和而解。"[2] 从辩证角度看，张载所言揭示了事物相互对立、相互依存而又相互协调的动态关系。具体说来，世间的万事万物（象）之间，客观地存在着对立关系（反）；这种对立关系必然反映在彼此不同的功能作用（为）上，并在一定条件下演变为某种冲突关系（仇）；当这种冲突关系达到一定程度时，就需要借助协调或和解方式（和）予以纾缓或消减，否则就会失去控制，酿成更大的困局或灾难，从而对双方造成不可弥补的损失。这种因"象"而生"反"，因"反"而成"仇"，因"仇"而趋"和"的过程，在逻辑上呈现出一种朴素的辩证统一链接，在效应上凸显出和则互利的实用思想。需要指出的是，这种辩证模式在自然界里表现得并不尽然，但在人世间却表现得异常突出。要知道，在人与人、家与家、村与村、部落与部落、公司与公司、民族与民族乃至国家与国家之间，由于追求各自不同的利益，经常引发出不同的矛盾与冲突，有时甚至导致不同形式或不同规模的斗争与战争。在此情况下，无论是用"强权即公理"的方式以大欺小，还是用非理性、非人道的极端方式以小搏大，都无法从根本上解决相互之间的问题，反而会进而加剧彼此之间的敌意。这就需要采用"仇必和而解"的和解原则，切

1 ［英］弗兰科潘：《丝绸之路：一部全新的世界史》，邵旭东、孙芳译，徐文琪审校，浙江大学出版社2016年版，第10页。

2 张载撰，王夫之注：《张子正蒙注》，中华书局1975年版，第25页。

合实际地缓解或消解矛盾冲突，最终取得彼此谅解与互惠双赢的可能结果。当然，以“和”化“仇”，以和平手段化解冲突，是有条件的，是需要双方协同努力的，也需要以相应实力作为后盾的。因为，任何一厢情愿、单方面绥靖退让的做法，非但不能化解冲突，反倒会自取其辱，甚至酿成更大的冲突。

自汉代以降的两千余年来，连接东方与西方的丝绸之路，不仅直接促进了中国、印度、波斯、阿拉伯、希腊、罗马等不同文化的交流，也在很大程度上始终影响或主宰人类经济活动与文明发展的历史进程。在丝绸之路漫长的沿线上与广袤的地区里，不同种族、不同宗教、不同背景和不同诉求的帝王、臣子、军队、僧侣、商人、奴隶，冒着不同风险往来在这条路上，历经自然、暴力、死亡的重重考验，创造并传递着财富、智慧、信仰、艺术、战争、疾病和灾难，等等。

如今，“一带一路”的倡议和构想，作为一种国际公共产品，所能惠及的地域、人口与规模之大，远远超出历史上人类参与过的任何经济与文化交流活动。不过，自然风险与疾病风险由于现代交通与医疗科技的发展已然淡化，但不同形式、不同程度的政治风险、经济风险、生态风险与暴力风险依然存在。譬如，丝绸之路沿线的恐怖主义威胁，就是今日人类挥之不去的梦魇。因此，风险管控是建设“一带一路”的关键所在。对于政治风险，需要开展全方位外交，充分考量每个国家不同政党和民众团体的不同诉求和利益关切；对于经济风险，需要在遵守市场规律和有效经营原则的前提下，具体情况具体分析，充分汲取发达国家风险投资的经验与教训；对于生态风险，需要因地制宜，坚持绿色发展理念，杜绝先污染后除污或先破坏后修复的错误做法；对于暴力风险，需要参照历史经验和组织国际力量，建立强大的反暴机动能力，真正发挥保驾护航的积极作用。总之，在此背景下，需要认真研究可行性、有效性与具体应对措施，联系和谐论的相关要素，重思天下主义的积极作用，探索其在现代条件下与时俱进的鼎新模式，以便有助于促进沿线国家与民族达成“三通”共识，有助于推动“一带一路”倡议的成功实施，有助于消减贫富之间的差距，有助于缓解因霸权、贫困与绝望所导致的不同文明和种族之间的紧张关系。

当然，“一带一路”的倡议，承载着开放、包容、发展和推进建设性全球化前行的思路。当世界上更多国家与地区参与其中时，就需要通过对话和共商等方式，创构一套不断追求完善的有效运作机制，这样既可增加合作共赢共享的概率，同时也可促使这些国家参与全球经济、安全、社会、生态等公共领域的治理。面对全球治理与国家治理的同步和落差这一现实境况，参与“一带一路”建设的国家或地区，需要在动态发展过程中贡献自己的智慧，补充合理的规则，设立对接的条件，减少相关的落差，提升治理的水平，在构建人类命运共同体的伟大实践中发挥更大的作用。

Rethinking Ecumenism for the "Belt and Road" Initiative

Wang Keping / China

Researcher and Director of the Section of Aesthetics under the Institute of Philosophy at the Chinese Academy of Social Sciences, Doctoral Advisor of the Graduate School of the Chinese Academy of Social Sciences

The Chinese notion of *tian-xia* (天下) as "all under heaven" can be traced back to the ancient times. Somewhat corresponding to the Hellenic idea of *Oikoumenē*, it bears the cardinal aspects of ecumenism coined by some historians and thinkers later. As discerned in Arnold J. Toynbee and Eric Voegelin who have dated it back to the regime of Liu Bang during the early Han Dynasty, ecumenism is perceived as a historically successful experimentation in the domain of international interaction, and therefore recommended as a working alternative to facilitating global peace and order for the common good of humankind. To my understanding, ecumenism as such is underlined significantly by the Confucian conception of *he* (和) qua harmony not merely as the fundamental rationale of its practical application, but also as the ultimate goal of its teleological pursuit from the past to the present.

Today the "Belt and Road" initiative is taken by and large as an international public product, for it is proposed to benefit a much larger size of area, population and scale in voluminous economic and cultural exchange than what has ever occurred in the human history. This being the case, it is of need to reconsider ecumenism under the current context in order to find a more effective mode with the passage of time. All this will help enhance a possible consensus of mutual understanding, inter-transportation system and trade interflow, push forward the active implementation of the Belt and Road proposal, narrow down the widening gap between the rich and the poor, and reduce the increasing tension between certain national states and ethnic groups, and make it possible to build up a better world order to benefit all peoples on this planet.

Ecumenism in View of All under Heaven

Currently, the Chinese idea of "tianxia" has turned up to be reexamined by some academics around the world. Sebastian Harnisch, for example, assumes that the idea as such "does not depict a geographical, but a cultural community, whose boundaries are determined by knowledge and practices of China's Confucian philosophical and moral traditions." [1] I partly agree with this explanation. Yet, when reviewed from a historical perspective, it is claimed to imply three things interrelated. Say, when used in a geographical sense, it means the entire territory of China in ancient time; when used in a political sense, it indicates the governance or regime of the whole region; then, when used in a cosmopolitan sense, it denotes international interactions and collaborations beyond borders. According to *The Historical Records* (*Shiji*), [2] "Jia Yi affirms that "tianxia" all enjoys peaceful collaboration in more than two decades during the regime of Han Wendi (Liu Heng)".[3] What "tianxia" suggests in this case is one of the typical proofs to justify the three implications of the term afore-mentioned. Historically, Han Gaozu (Liu Bang) made a duce agreement with

---

1 Sebastian Harnisch, "China's historical self and its international role," in S. Harnisch and J-C Gottwald (ed.s), *China's International Roles, Challenging or Supporting International Order?* (New York & London: Routledge, 2016), pp. 39-40.

2 *The Historical Records* (*Shiji* 史记) by Sima Qian (司马迁) is also rendered as *The Records of the Historian in the Han.*

3 Sima Qian, "Qu Yuan and Jia Yi" , in *The Historical Records* (《史记・屈原贾生列传》). Its original statement follows: "贾生以为汉兴至孝文二十余年，天下和洽" .

his rival Empire of Huns headed by Modun after an unsuccessful confrontation at Pingcheng (modern Datong of Shanxi province) in 200 BC, and ever since then, his successors to the throne continued to carry it on until about 127 BC. All this facilitated a long time of peace between the Han Dynasty and the Huns Empire, and led to such a positive outcome as Sima Qian depicts:

> The seven decades or so witnessed a peaceful period ever since the founding of the Han Dynasty. People across the country lived a self-sufficient life all these years except for some disturbances caused by draughts and floods. Fully saturated with grain or money were the official barns and treasuries at all levels. For example, the capital treasury was reported to store up billions of coins, and the capital barn to have an abundant amount of grain. Both of them were far beyond either the fiscal or consumption demands.[1]

Interestingly, Toynbee takes this special period as a poster example with particular reference to the Chinese ideal of "tianxia" when working in the tri-dimensional field with focus on the unity of the past, the present and the future. He deliberately argues that the "immutable past does not present the same appearance always and everywhere. It looks different at different times and places, and either an increase or a decrease in our information may also change the picture. Our view of the relations of past events to each other, of their relative importance, and of their significance, changes constantly in consequence of the constant change of the fugitive present."[2]

Evidently, Toynbee is highly aware of the relative importance of the constantly changing past as is reconsidered at different times and places. By virtue of a comparative study of the past against the present with regard to the human condition, he sharply observes "a disparity between Man's technological

1 Sima Qian, "Peace and Development Documents," in *The Historical Records* (《史记・平准书》).

2 Arnold Toynbee, *Mankind and Mother Earth: A Narrative History of the World*, Oxford: Oxford University Press, 1976, p. 589.

progression and his social performance", and "the 'morality gap' between Man's physical power for doing evil and his spiritual capacity for coping with this power". He thus arrives at the conclusion that during the last 5,000 years, the gap that "has yawned as wide open as the mystical jaws of Hell" "has caused mankind to inflict on itself grievous disasters. Man's spiritual inadequacy has set a limit to his social progress and therefore to his technological progress too."[1] This indicates the imbalance between human immaturity and technological achievement that will create more problems in the moral realm than benefits in the economic sector. As a consequence, "the present-day global set of local sovereign states is not capable of keeping the peace, and it is also not capable of saving the biosphere from man-made pollution or of conserving the biosphere's non-replaceable natural resources. This ecumenical anarchy on the political plane cannot continue for much longer in an *Oikoumenē* that has already become a unity on the technological and economic planes."[2]

Then, what could be done to help humankind move out of this plight? Toynbee looks into the past for a historical alternative. After an elaborate comparison, he focuses his attention on the Chinese worldview of "All under Heaven" (*tian-xia*).[3] The worldview is largely based on "a sense of compassion for any other human being", which expects a human being to love and serve all his fellow human beings with an impartial devotion. In other words, it leads to a mixture of "love inspired by personal acquaintance and love for all fellow human beings simply in virtue of a common humanity." Toynbee gives much credit for the Chinese view of "All under Heaven" as the Chinese paradigm of ecumenism. He finds it well embodied and operated in "the Chinese Imperial civil service in the second century B.C. Just as he emphasizes in the following statement,

> The Chinese Imperial civil service had been the best of any in the

---

1 Ibid., pp. 591-592.

2 Ibid., p. 593.

3 The Chinese notion of *tian-xia* is rendered in English as all under heaven, all below heaven, all-under-heaven, or all-under-sky, etc.

> Oikoumenē; it had held together a larger number of human beings in peace and order for a greater number of years than any other civil service anywhere. Yet, time after time, the Chinese civil servants had betrayed their trust and had brought China to grief by abusing their power for their own personal advantage. China's leaders have taken steps to prevent this from happening again. Whether they will be more successful than earlier Chinese reformers remains to be seen, but at least the vigour of their current action is a good augury. If the Chinese take to heart the lesson of past Chinese errors, and if they succeed in saving themselves from repeating these errors, they may do a great service, not only to their own country, but to the whole of mankind at a critical stage in mankind's enigmatic course.[1]

It goes without saying that Toynbee as a humanistic historian displays a strong sense of mission when he comes to reconsidering the prospect and destiny of humankind in the global society. His sense of mission reveals itself not merely in the above argument per se, but also through his dialogue with Japanese scholar Daisaku Ikeda as presented in the *Choose Life*. [2] The title of this book is in fact derived from a divine logos in the *Bible*, say, "I call Heaven and earth to witness against you today that I have set before you life and death, blessings and curses. Choose life so that you and your descendants may live."[3] Apparently, he expects humankind to choose life as a vital action to salvage human destiny by a revolution in thinking and morality. He perceives it as a critical necessity because of the hard fact that humans today are pursuing their present course towards self-defeat and self-destruction. Since the survival of human race is threatened by the imbalance between human immaturity and technological achievement, he attempts to look for a human-made cure to harness the dramatic increase of human-made evils here and there across the world. Being a humanistic historian and an international

---

1 Ibid., p. 595.

2 Arnold Toynbee & Daisaku Ikeda, *Choose Life: A Dialogue* (Oxford: Oxford University Press, 1977).

3 *Holy Bible* (Nanking: National TSPM & CCC, 2000), Deuteronomy 30:19.

sage, Toynbee advices a double check of what the Chinese civil service did in the Han Dynasty. He thereby recommends the Chinese conception of *tianxia* as ecumene or oikoumenē due to its compassionateness, peacefulness, inclusiveness and cooperativeness in the domains of politics, economy, and culture in particular. According to his comparative analysis, he placed more emphasis on the way of governance and the form of ecumenism exercised by Liu Bang, the first Emperor of the Han Dynasty. He regarded Liu as a historical example to unify all under heaven with particular reference to the global unification in order to resist global conflict. To his mind, Liu Bang learned the bitter lessons from the past events in Chinese history and abandoned the war-like spirit as well as punish-ridden governance. Instead he embraced the concept of "all under heaven" and conducted state affairs in accordance with the supreme principle of harmony (*hé*) as the fundamental basis of securing peace and order. Toynbee gave much credit for the civil service of the Han Dynasty mainly because of its ecumenic orientation and corresponding capacity. Such ecumenic orientation requires a humanistic stance to treat all humans as fellow beings in one sense, and in the other sense, an unconditional acceptance of a universal humanity under all circumstances. Such capacity lies in the virtues of peace-loving spirit, dynamic engagement, working diligence, persistent courage and practical wisdom, among others.

I assume that "the Chinese errors" may vary from time to time, but stay principally in the form of social disorder or chaos within China as a result of political corruption and misleading governance. For in many cases such disorder would work destructively to weaken the institutional adequacy and undercut the social structure, and worse still, to cause civil wars or foreign invasions that would turn the entire kingdom into horrible catastrophe or split states (*guo*).

In this respect, Eric Voegelin, a political philosopher, has made a meaningful distinction between the *tian-xia* as "all below Heaven" and the *guo* as states after his comparative analysis of the Chinese ecumenism and its Western counterpart. According to his observations, the Chinese *tianxia* is "neither the cosmos nor the earth as a territorial expanse under heaven, but the earth as the carrier of human society...It is the exact equivalent of the Greek *oikoumenē* in the cultural sense." He therefore renders it as "ecumene" whenever it occurs.[1] Moreover, Chinese ecumenism received its peculiar coloration from the unbroken consciousness of the identity of China with mankind.[2]

> The tianxia is organized as a manifold of guo, while the guo recognize themselves as part of the ecumene... there are guo that try to overthrow and replace the dynasty; but there are no guo that pretend to form a rival ecumene. The Chinese kinship over 'all below Heaven,' though it is definitely a position of power, acquired and held by force, is singularly devoid of associations with imperial conquest. The extant documents let tianxia and guo exist in a pre-established harmony...[3]

Conducted in recent years is a critical reflection on the Chinese notion of "tianxia" as "all under heaven". According to one of the active thinkers today, "tianxia" can be taken as a spiritual concept as it deals with the interaction between the human Dao and the heavenly Dao in principle. And meanwhile it can be perceived as a sentimental conception as it contains an important part of China's history, tradition, experience and spirituality as a whole.[4] An interpretation of his exposes the three-dimensional world in view of all below heaven. That is, *tianxia* can be treated as a conception of the world within a structure of trinity. For it is referred to the entire world in a geographical sense, to the common choice of all peoples over the world in a socio-psychological sense, and the world polity in a political sense.[5] Incidentally, the conception as such is reconceived as a new perspective that is directed to the general problem of the world order per se. It is therefore beyond

1 Eric Voegelin, *The Ecumenic Age* (ed. Michael Franz, Columbia: University of Missouri Press, 2000), p. 352.

2 Eric Voegelin, *The Ecumenic Age,* p. 354,

3 Ibid., pp. 361.

4 Zhao Tingyang, *Tian-xia de Dang Dai Xing* (A Possible World of All-under-heaven System, China Citic Press, 2016), pp. v-vi.

5 Ibid., pp. 60-63.

China proper but concerned with "a world of worldliness", "the wordlization of world", and a possible "order of co-existence".[1]

Personally, I share much sympathy with all these efforts to rediscover the practical merits of tianxia-based policy exercised during the early Han Dynasty with due consideration of the status quo of the human condition and the global reality. The idea of "tianxia" in this regard can be seen as the kernel of ecumenism based on the present-day preoccupations in respect to the possibility of a better world order for humankind in its entirety. Apart from being something spiritual and sentimental, the idea itself can be viewed as a transcultural concept as it goes beyond the borders of all cultures or civilizations in the world. Moreover, it can be employed as an international asset as calls for the collaboration among all nations living on the same planet. Accordingly, it can be deployed as a co-relational concept as it requires the harmonization of human relations among all human beings who tend to embrace the sense of compassion for all other fellow human beings.

However, I must point out the hidden tendency to idealize the political setting of the period concerned. In my observation drawn from the historical documents, the peaceful collaboration between the Han and the Huns was not always smooth but rather costly, because the Huns not merely asked for more compensation (living materials, luxuries and forced brides etc.) every year from the Han Dynasty, but also launched sporadic incursions into the North China (Daijun, Shangjun et al) with brutal slaughtering and plundering. Moreover, the long-term compromise on the part of the Han Dynasty conduced to the dominant power of the Huns who took the advantage to have conquered a number of kingdoms (Wusun Kingdom, for example) in the west region and driven Rouzhi Kingdom to Yili area then. All this led to the development of the hegemonic Empire of the Huns and its more frequent invasion of the North China then. Accordingly, it made the Han court to pay much more price to the aggressive Huns for the sake of conflict and war avoidance. Hence I am inclined to perceive the exercise of ecumenism at that stage as an

1 Ibid., p.2.

unbalanced mode that benefited more to the Huns rather than the Han in one sense, and in the other sense, plunged other small kingdoms adjacent to the Huns into their prey and victims. [1]

As the Chinese old saying shows, "Anything that goes to extremes will be bound to reverse." It was during the regime of Han Wudi (Liu Che) that a new policy was implemented to fight against the Huns. The initial confrontations were difficult and not successful, and the later campaigns turned out to be highly effective. After years of tough warfare, the Han army eventually succeeded in banishing the Huns from their headquarters close to China's borderline, and driving them down to the far north of Mongolia. It was under such circumstances that the Han Dynasty had released the heavy pressure of foreign invasion, secured the national safety along the Northern section of the Great Wall, and restored its entire sovereignty in the pure sense of this term. By so doing did Han Wudi develop a balanced mode of ecumenism that helped to open up the Silk Road for trade and cultural interactions with other countries. The Silk Road was extended as far as to the Middle East at the first stage, and then to the Rome at the subsequent stage.

"Belt and Road" Initiative for Ecumenic Renovation

It is over 2000 years so far ever since the opening up of the Silk Road in the early Han Dynasty. The linkage between the East and the West as the Silk Road initially brought forth have enhanced a large-scaled interactive exchange among Chinese, Indian, Persian, Arabic, Greek and Roman cultures, among others. Meanwhile, it has remained as a determinant impact upon the historical progression of both economic activities and civilizational developments of humankind in its entirety. Historically speaking, along the Road are the broad and remote areas where peoples of different backgrounds from different cultures, religions and ethnic groups would travel back and forth at the risk of their lives in pursuit of their different goals and interests. They would of course experience a diversity of natural hardships, violent confrontations, unexpected deaths and so on. And meanwhile, they would

1 Sima Qian, "The Huns" , in *The Historical Records* (《史记·匈奴列传》).

make fortune, create wealth, trans-communicate wisdom, ideas, faiths, arts, physical ills, and other good or bad things as well.[1]

Now the Belt and Road Initiative is proposed as an international public product. Its tentative scheme is stimulating and inviting to the world sustainable development as it is designed to act upon such principles as interactive mechanism, win-win cooperation and open-to-all inclusiveness, among many others. However, it needs to be more specified during the dynamic process of step-by-step development. This calls for detailed feasibility studies as it is schemed to accommodate more participants as shareholders. By now what can be definitely said about it is the fact that it is by nature a most complex and challenging project. For it is assumed to involve a huge number of multiple nations, geographical zones, economic structures, political institutions, cultural values, religious faiths, economic discrepancies, and differing expectations, among others. In a word, the size of area and population it is supposed to cover is so wide and large that it goes far beyond any kind of human practice involving economic and cultural exchange in history. Nevertheless, kinds of risk do exist here and there. Even though natural and disease risks can be well handled with the help of modern transportation and advanced medical science, what are bound to turn up are political, economic and violence risks in varied forms and degrees. For instance, that terrorist threat prevails along the belt and road leads to a haunting nightmare for years. This being true, risk control is the key to Belt and Road construction. Broadly speaking, as regards political risk, it requires all-round diplomacy by taking into due consideration of distinct expectations and concerns of all political entities and groups within each country involved. With respect to economic risk, it ought to comply by the market rules and adopt efficient management, and under such circumstances, case-by-case analysis ought to be conducted with particular reference to the experiences and lessons drawn from risk investments by developed countries. As for eco-environmental risk, it must insist on the principle of green development in accord with the geographical features,

1 Peter Frankopan, *The Silk Roads: A New History of the World*, pp. IV, 1-23.

and resolutely turn down such wrong policy as that pollution precedes depollution and destruction precedes restoration. When it comes to violence risk, it must take up historical experiences, organize international forces, strengthen anti-terrorist capacity, and secure the active role of effective protection against any threat.

Undoubtedly, the open scope of the Belt and Road Initiative is internationally and globally oriented for certain. As expressed in some observations today, this initiative displays China's new role that "indeed reintroduces the traditional 'tianxia' concept."[1] Accordingly, With respect to its long-term development, "some Central and Eastern European countries are even included in the important diplomatic scope of China's 'greater neighborhood.'[2] This being the fact, it is of critical necessity to reconsider the positive aspects of harmonism in the light of the global context in one sense, and in the other sense, to explore the possibility of renovating a new mode of ecumenism in terms of the global governance under new and changing circumstances. To my mind, the possibility of this kind lies in the implementation of the Belt and Road Initiative in the years to come. It will thus serve to elicit a constructive mode of ecumenism that depends principally upon a relevant modification and freedom of idiosyncratic mentality, ethno-centralistic mentality, cold-war mentality, and unilateral mentality altogether. If this mode of ecumenism is solidly established at the time when the Belt and Road experimentation turns out to be a success story, it will give rise to a better world order for the common good of all humans alike. All this sounds like a world dream to form a community of shared destiny for the future of humankind. Accordingly, it will help build up a general consensus of mutual understanding, inter-transportation system and trade interflow, push forward the active application of the Belt and Road Initiative, narrow down the widening gap between the rich and the poor, and reduce the increasing tension between certain civilizations, nation-states and ethnic groups caused mainly by

1 Bart Dessein, "The Belt and Road and China's 'Tianxia' Concept," in China Ministry of Culture Sino-Foreign Cultural Centre (ed.), *The Collected Works at the Symposium on China Studies*, China Social Sciences Press, 2016, p. 85.

2 Mu Chunshan, "How Does Europe Rank in China's Diplomacy," *The Diplomats*, 5 April 2014.

hegemony, poverty and despair.

Above all, what should be done first with this most complex and challenging project? According to the Daoist sage, "It is a rule in the world that the most difficult things begin with the easy, and the largest things arise from the minute. Hence tackle the difficult while it is still easy, and achieve the large while it still minute."[1] Compared with other domains related to the Belt and Road Initiative, the economic domain is considered to be the first priority or a relatively easy part of an agreeable plan for development owing to social and market demands. It is now to be bolstered by AIIB mainly in the aspect of infrastructure construction across the regions concerned. This will make it possible to set up inter-transportation and inter-communication networks as serve to assure trade exchange and logistic interflow amidst the countries involved. Yet, when it comes to enhancing the level of mutual understanding among the ethnic groups of different backgrounds, any kind of overriding emphasis on economic factor does not suffice to accomplish this goal. It therefore calls for transcultural studies and contacts in order to facilitate not merely a sense of tolerance and prudence, but also a sense of sympathy and empathy through reciprocal consciousness and trustworthy sincerity. Moreover, the potential threat to safety and the hidden cost should be taken into account when planning and distributing the investment. In this regard, it is rather crucial to introduce a multi-lateral consultation among the AIIB members, the World Bank advisors and all the participants engaged. On such occasion, it requires collective wisdom and joint efforts, and accordingly, it relies on the synthetic mode of harmony as it will shed light on human intelligence and win-win cooperation.

In the final analysis, the Belt and Road Initiative is multidimensional in essence. Based on such principles of openness, inclusiveness and peaceful development, it is intended to push forward a more healthy type of globalization. As it gets more and more countries and regions involved in it, it needs to create a set of shared rules and a kind of efficient operational organism by virtue of equal-footed dialogue and

1 Laozi, *The Dao De Jing*, Section 63.

consultation among the participants. By doing so, it can not merely increase the ratio and index of win-win cooperation, but enable the participants to take part in the global governance of economic, safety, social, and eco-environmental and other public spheres. Naturally, facing the synchronous connection as well as present-day gap between global governance and nation-state governance, all the countries and regions engaged in the Belt and Road program are expected to contribute their respective wisdom to remolding more reasonable and complementary regulations for a better collaboration worldwide. This will also work to procure more favorable conditions for the two kinds of governance to dock with one another, reduce the developmental gap, upgrade the governmental level, and play a more constructive role in the process of building a global community of shared destiny for the humankind.

文明从饮食开始

龚文庠 【中国】
北京大学新闻与传播学院教授、博士生导师 / 北京大学文化与传播研究所所长

我将用四个汉字开始今天的演讲，因为我想用汉字跟其他历史文献做个比对，从这几个汉字可以回溯中国几千年的文明史。

不管何种文化，人都要吃。中国人的吃有什么特别？中国独特的地方是，我们使用汉字来描述我们饮食的方式，通过汉字可以追溯到中国文明的发展史，所以，中国饮食史和文明史同步发展，汉字是见证。

第 1 个字——“炮”。原来的发音是二声。汉字是象形文字，每个字就像一幅画。炮字左边是“火”，右边是“包”，“包”就是包裹、包起来。最开始我们是怎么样做东西吃的？最简单的方式是在野地里烧烤，以火烧烤用泥裹起来的猎物。据考古发现，这种烧烤的方式持续了 100 多万年，直到公元前 6000 年发明了陶器。

第 2 个字——礼。刘梦溪教授也谈到“礼”这个字，礼是儒教文化的核心。我引用了《礼记》里面的一句话：“夫礼之初，始诸饮食。”礼是儒家文化的核心。让我们看一下原来样子的“禮”字，左边的偏旁是“示”，天垂象，见吉凶，所以示人也。从“二”。二是古文上字，就是天。三垂日月星也，观乎天文，以察时变，示神事也。右边为“豊”，行礼之器。左右合在一起的“禮”就是我们把最好的礼物和食物献给上天，也就是祭祀。鬼神用飨，国受其福，民众得到保佑。“禮”有很多意思，这里主要的意思是要以尊重敬重的态度对待我们的食物，这是我们

文明的开端。

吃和管理是联系在一起的，中国有一句话叫“民以食为天”。在《论语》里“政”字出现了41次，“食”字也出现了41次。当代中国的领导人经常说“温饱是最基本的人权”，首先要让人民吃饱穿暖。中国民众非常认可这句话，因为我们相信民以食为天。

第3个字——“饗”。这个字的古体是“卿”，两个人对面而坐，中间摆放着食物，标志着中国人吃饭的方式。世界上有两种主要的饮食方式，第一个是聚食制，第二个是分食制。中国是典型的聚食制。在中国去餐馆，大家请记住，如果你是跟一帮朋友一块儿出去吃饭，你就要为大家点菜，不是只为自己，因为每一个朋友都能够夹桌子上的每一盘菜，所以用转桌子上面的转盘方式，比较适合中国人聚餐。在一起吃饭时，是分享爱、分享尊敬和友谊的最好方式。

第4个字——尊。古体是，像两只手捧一个器物，器物里装着酒。以两手捧举表示尊敬和恭敬；尊是盛酒的器皿，同时也是尊敬的意思。《周礼》中“周公定制”，就是定下吃饭的规矩。《论语》中孔子和齐景公有一段非常有名的对话。齐景公问孔子怎样治理国家，孔子说：“君君，臣臣，父父，子子。”齐景公说：“说得好！假如君不君，臣不臣，父不父，子不子，即使收了粮食，我能吃到嘴吗？”

中国饮食文化的传统一直延续到今天。中国媒体报道，国家领导人与普通民众一道进餐，为他们夹菜，是表达感情最直接的方式。

中国的饮食哲学是古今相通的，天人合一是中国非常重要的理论和哲学，今天的中国人依然相信饮食的中庸之道，“不极五味之调”，走极端对身体有危害。饮食之道表现出中国人追求天、地、人的和谐精神。

Civilization Starts from the Diet

Gong Wenxiang / China

Professor and Doctoral advisor of the School of Journalism and Communication at Peking University, Director of the Institute of Culture and Communication at Peking University

I will start today's speech with four Chinese characters, because I want to compare the Chinese characters with other historical documents. Through these characters, we can trace the history of Chinese civilization over thousands of years.

No matter what kind of culture, people have to eat. What is the uniqueness of the Chinese people in eating? The unique feature of China is that we use Chinese characters to describe the way we eat. Through Chinese characters, we can trace back the history of the development of Chinese civilization; therefore, the history of Chinese food and the history of civilization have developed simultaneously, and Chinese characters are the witnesses of that development.

The first character is " 炮 ". The original intonation is the second tone. Chinese characters are pictographs; each character is like a picture. The left side of the 炮 is " 火 ", which means fire, the right side is " 包 ", which means wrapping up. At the very beginning, how did our ancestors cook? The easiest way was to barbecue the pray wrapped up with mud in the wild. According to archaeological discoveries, this way of barbecuing had lasted about 1,000,000 years until pottery was invented in 6000 BC.

The second character is 礼（禮）, which means rite. Professor Liu Mengxi also talked about the word " 礼 ", which is the core of the Confucian culture. I quoted a sentence in *The Book of Rites:* "The behavioral norm in dietary activities is the origination of ritual." The rite is the core of the Confucian culture. Let's take a look at the original appearance of the word " 禮 ". The left side is " 示 ". As the natural phenomenon tells us whether it is a blessing or a curse, therefore, it means indication. From " 二 ", we can see it means heaven. " 三 " means the sun, the moon and the stars. Through the above things, the god will tell people weal and woe. On the right is " 豊 ", the vessel used for the ceremony. When combined together, the " 禮 " means that we consecrate the best gifts and food to the god, which is also called the worship ceremony. Gods or the ghosts take these sacrifices and bless the people. There is a lot of meaning in " 禮 ". The main idea here is to treat our food with respect. This is the beginning of our civilization.

Eating and management are interlinked. As a Chinese saying goes, "food is the first necessity of people". In the book of *The Analects of Confucius*, the word " 政 " which means politics appeared 41 times, and the word " 食 " which means eating also appeared 41 times. Leaders of contemporary China often say that "food and clothing are the most basic human rights". The top priority is providing people with enough food and warm clothing. The Chinese people agree with this saying very much, because we believe that food is God for the people.

The third character is " 饗 ", the old style of which is " 鄉 ". Form this old style character [illegible], we can see that there are two people sitting face to face, in the middle of them is food, which marks the eating style of Chinese people. There are two main ways of eating in the world. The first is eating food together by sharing the same dishes, the second is individual serving. China adopts a typical dining together system. When you go to a restaurant in China, please remember that if you are out to dinner with a group of friends, you need to order for everyone, not only for yourself, because every friend can have each dish on the table, so the table that is round and can be rotated might be more suitable for the Chinese people. Sitting together is the best way to share love, respect and friendship.

The forth character is 尊 . The old style of it is 𡬠, which is like a container filled with wine and held by two hands. The two hands mean respect and modesty. " 尊 " is a vessel for wine, and at the same time it also means respect. In the book of *The Rites of Zhou*, the Duke Zhou regulation for drawing means making rules on eating. There is a very famous dialogue between Confucius and Monarch Jing of the State of Qi in the Spring and Autumn Period and the Warring States Period called in *The Analects of Confucius*. Monarch Jing asked Confucius: "How should the country be governed?" Confucius said: "The Monarch is obliged to do what the Monarch is obliged to do, before he can enjoy the proper treatment of the Monarch; the minister should be obliged to assist the Monarch in normal affairs; the father also needs to fully fulfill the duty of father, before he can enjoy the right that a father should enjoy; children should fulfill their obligation of filial piety." Monarch Jing quite agreed with it and said, "It should be so; otherwise, how can I eat the food even though there is a good harvest?" If there are no rules, we will become wild animals.

The tradition of Chinese food culture has continued to this day. Once, Premier Zhou Enlai entertained President Nixon; when he picked up food with chopsticks and put it on the Nixon's plate, Nixon seemed puzzled. Chinese media often reported that the leaders of the state had meals with ordinary people and picked up food with chopsticks for them, which was considered the most direct way to strengthen a relationship.

China's philosophy of diet is interlinked in ancient and modern times. Harmony between man and nature is a very important theory and philosophy in China. People believe that eating liver nourishes the liver, eating brain nourishes the brain, and eating turtles makes it possible to live long. Today, the Chinese people still take the middle road of the diet. They will not pursue the extremity of the five flavors, as going to extremes is harmful to one’s health. The way of their diet shows the Chinese people’s pursuit of harmony between heaven, earth and man.

沟通过去与未来的桥梁：布鲁克林博物馆的亚洲艺术新展廊

宁珊 【美国】
布鲁克林博物馆亚洲艺术馆助理馆长

布鲁克林博物馆是美国规模最大、历史最悠久的艺术博物馆之一，位于纽约市布鲁克林区，与布鲁克林植物园相邻。该馆成立于 1823 年，并于 1897 年面向公众开放。其成立之初，布鲁克林还是一座独立的城市，尚未划归纽约市，因此起初被命名为布鲁克林市博物馆。如今，布鲁克林区的人口几乎与芝加哥齐平，美国人口普查局预计十年之内，布鲁克林人口将超过芝加哥。

布鲁克林博物馆是一座百科全书式的博物馆，永久藏品超过 150 万件，几乎涵盖世界各类文化，历史跨度超过 5000 年。馆内分为埃及艺术部、近东及古典艺术部、美洲艺术部（美洲原住民及前哥伦比亚艺术）、非洲艺术部、美国艺术部、欧洲艺术部、当代艺术部、伊斯兰世界艺术部，当然还有亚洲艺术部。该馆收藏的埃及艺术品享誉世界，曾于今年年初在韩国首尔的国家博物馆进行过专题展出。

除永久藏品的范围较广之外，该馆的现当代艺术专题展也享有较高的声誉，从巴斯奎特到乔治·亚欧姬芙，展品种类繁多，不一而足。此外，该馆与纽约的艺术家保持着紧密联系，这些艺术家时常参与该馆举办的教育项目。

作为中国艺术部的典藏研究员，我关注的问题主要在于，如何让中国艺术引起广泛关注、如何向西方观众展示中国艺术。如果观众对亚洲一无所知，该采用何种方式来展示中国艺术？如何才能营造出古代艺术品与当代语境的关联，从而引起观众共鸣，鼓励观众频繁来访？

在展出亚洲及中东艺术方面，该馆正经历着一场转折：博物馆二楼的永久藏品展廊正在进行大幅整改，这恰好是进行自我改进、调整亚洲艺术品展览方式的绝佳机遇。当然，所谓的整改并非只是重新刷漆，而是将原有展廊彻底拆除，重新装修，从藏品以及捐赠品（这要感谢慷慨的捐赠者）中精心拣选，在陈列方式及陈列顺序上，要达到给访客以最大震撼的效果。因此可以利用这个机会重新规划，以通过增强展品的关注度来推介中国历史和中国文化。

由于地处纽约市内，该馆的访客可谓形形色色，且大多访客相对年轻——60% 的观展者年龄低于 45 岁。此外，许多学生群体会在教师的带领下，在本馆内进行现场学习。如果展览的手段足够有效，就可以促使这些访客在年轻时培养起对中国艺术和中国文化的浓厚兴趣。这种兴趣或许可以持续终身。此外，还可以促进他们与纽约市庞大的美籍华人群体进行交流和互动。

这便是整改亚洲艺术展廊的目的所在。以下，我将对过去的展示方法进行简要介绍，并以几个例子来说明，如何构建中国艺术与当代艺术的关联，从而引起更多的关注。

早在 20 世纪早期，布鲁克林博物馆便开始展出中国艺术品，亚洲艺术部的首位典藏研究员——斯图亚特・科林自 1903 年起开始在本部工作，一直到 1929 年去世。科林本人通晓汉语，这在 20 世纪早期的美国博物馆典藏研究员中实属罕见。1906 年、1909 年，以及 1913—1914 年，科林曾先后带领团队到中国考察，并在北京、上海及广东等地生活过一段时间。关于几次考察的详细报告、照片等资料，目前存放在该馆的资料室。此外，科林还去过日本、韩国、斯里兰卡、印度等亚洲国家和地区。

对新展廊竣工后采用的展示方式，我们计划不仅展品要以经典作品为主，同时还要突出能够引起各类访客共鸣的主题。例如，全球化与中国古代的国际贸易这一主题。该馆藏有一件宋元时期的镀漆钱柜，原产地在浙江温州，或许是丝绸之路沿线的商贾随身携带之物。这件藏品将在以亚洲贸易为主题的展廊内进行展示。一件产于景德镇官窑的凤首壶，是当时向印度尼西亚出口的商品，北京的国家博物馆中也有类似的藏品。唐三彩跪驼像中便有类似的凤首壶，陶瓷质地中显露出金属的色泽，应该是古丝绸之路上通行的贸易商品。伊斯坦布尔的托普卡比萨雷博物馆中藏有一副波斯画作，画中描绘的瓷器花瓶类似于明代洪武年间的釉底红彩壶。除贸易主题外，该馆将继续发掘跟中国古代文化相关的各类主题，以此构建当代艺术与传统艺术间的对话。

再来看几个例子。图 1 是一尊乾隆年间的景泰蓝佛龛，1909 年，这尊佛龛与 200 余件明清时期的景泰蓝艺术品一同被捐赠给布鲁克林博物馆，并于 1912 年进行过专题展览。这张照片是在该馆近期的专题展览中拍摄。在举办的“无垠的蓝色”主题展中，展出的各类永久藏品均突出了蓝色这一主题。照片中展示的亚洲陶瓷器可以追溯到唐代贸易，当时许多钴蓝釉瓷从中东运到中国，而中国的制瓷技术也在这一时期传至中东地区。馆方对亚洲传入西方的瓷器，以及采用亚洲技术和亚洲设计的西方瓷器进行了发掘。馆方还会把当代艺术家的作品与传统展品共同展出。其中一尊景泰蓝香炉便是与中国当代画家苏笑柏的漆画一同展出。

图 1：景泰蓝佛龛

此外，新画廊也会展出各类山水画，但展示方式却与传统方式不同。比如，我们会把一副关于灵璧石的水墨画与一尊用墨块雕成的灵璧石放在一起展出。这幅手卷展示的是数字时代的上海图景，而这位画家却将风景绘在了自己的身体上，显然是一种表演艺术。在以下的几个例子中，一个汉代陶瓷花瓶与一位当代艺术家创作的硅质花瓶放在一起展出。此外，还可以通过展品说明来吸引观众。例如，对一尊青瓷罐，作品说明中却采用了一个十分吉祥的标题：“八仙过海”。展览要事先为中小学生准备资料，让他们选择自己想成为哪一位仙人，想拥有哪种超能力。为此，工作人员专门参考了元代和明代的文学文本以及戏剧作品。

可以看出，布鲁克林博物馆 1930 年建成的亚洲艺术展廊和 1938 年成立的中国艺术展廊保持了很多年。

截至 2013 年，在整改业洲展廊之前，两间展廊一直都没有发生太大的变化。亚洲艺术展廊位于博物馆二楼，瑟缩在难以找到的角落，过道十分狭窄。为此，博物馆将原有的墙壁和天花板全部拆除，重新进行规划并设计了新展廊的平面图。另外，在博物馆大厅新建了精美的玻璃楼梯，访客可以沿着楼梯直接来到二楼的亚洲艺术展廊。上楼的过程中便能看到右侧的中国艺术展廊。由于墙壁都是由玻璃制成，因此上楼时便能看到陈列的艺术展品。中国展廊被设置在博物馆的最佳位置，在大厅里便能看到。这种设计规划能够引起访客兴趣、鼓励访客探索中国的宝贵遗产、学习中国艺术及文化。布鲁克林博物馆以及新建的中国展廊期待各位的光临！

Bridging Past and Future: the New Asian Art Galleries at the Brooklyn Museum

Susan L. Beningson / United States of America

Assistant Curator of Asian Art, Brooklyn Museum

The Brooklyn Museum is one of the oldest and largest art museums in the United States. It is located in downtown Brooklyn, New York City, next to the Brooklyn Botanical Gardens. The museum was founded in 1823 and the current building opened to the public in 1897. At the time the museum was built, Brooklyn was an independent city and not a borough of New York City as it is today, so it was created as the museum of the City of Brooklyn. Today Brooklyn has almost the same population as Chicago, and the U.S. Census projects that in 10 years Brooklyn will be larger than Chicago.

We are an encyclopedic museum and our permanent collection contains over 1.5 million objects representing nearly every culture worldwide and over 5000 years of history. Our departments include Egyptian Art, Near-Eastern and Classical Art, Arts of the Americans (Native American and Pre-Columbian Art), African Art, American Art, European Art, Contemporary Art, Arts of the Islamic World, and of course, Asian Art. Our Egyptian collection is world-renowned and was on view in a special exhibition at the National Museum of Korea in Seoul earlier this year.

In addition to the broad scope of our permanent collections, we are well known for our special exhibitions of modern and contemporary art ranging from Basquiat to our current Georgia O'Keefe exhibition. We have strong relationships with New York based artists who often participate in our educational programs.

As the curator of Chinese art, my main concern is how to highlight Chinese art and present it to a western audience. How do I present Chinese art to an audience that may know nothing about Asia? How do I create a contemporary relevance to engage our audience and encourage them to make repeat visits?

We are also at a turning point in presenting the Arts of Asia and the Middle East at the Brooklyn Museum. We are in the middle of a major reinstallation of the second floor of the museum which is devoted to these permanent galleries. We have the rare opportunity to reinvent ourselves and how we present Asian art. When I talk about reinstalling the Asian galleries, I am not just talking about a new coat of paint. We literally demolished the old galleries and started from scratch, selecting objects from our collection, acquiring new objects thanks to the generosity of donors, and placing and sequencing the objects for the maximum impact on our museum visitors. We can seize this moment and create new strategies to highlight our collection and promote Chinese history and culture.

We are located in New York City. Our audience is diverse and unlike many other museums in the city, we have a young demographic: 60% of our visitors are under the age of 45. In addition, we have many school groups that teach in the galleries of the museum. If we are effective, we can engage visitors when they are young and create an environment for them to focus on Chinese art and culture throughout their lives and also engage with the large Chinese-American community in New York.

So these are the goals of our new reinstallation of our permanent galleries of Asian Art. Let me now give you a brief introduction to our *past* history of presenting

Asian Art at the museum and give you a few examples of how we intend to make traditional Chinese art relevant to our very contemporary art focused audience in the *future*.

The Brooklyn Museum has a long history of presenting Chinese art since the early 20th century. Our first curator of Asian Art, Stewart Culin worked at the museum from 1903 until his death in 1929. He spoke some Chinese which was rare for American museum curators in the early 20th century. In 1906, 1909, and 1913-1914 he organized museum expeditions to China and spent time in Beijing, Shanghai and Guangdong. The museum has all of his detailed expedition reports and photographs in our extensive Archives. He also visited Japan, Hong Kong, Korea, Sri Lanka, India and many other countries in Asia and other parts of the world.

Our plan for the future is not only to focus on masterpieces in the collection but also to highlight themes that have resonance with our diverse audience in Brooklyn. For example, Globalization and International Trade in Ancient China: This lacquered traveling coffer from the Southern Song or Yuan dynasty, was made in the city of Wenzhou in Zhejiang province. However, it was most likely made for merchants or others who traveled across the trading routes on the Silk Route. It will be shown in our new gallery devoted to Asian Trade. This phoenix-headed ewer was made in the imperial kilns at Jingdezhen, but it was made for export to Indonesia. Similar examples are in the National Museum here in Beijing. Tang Dynasty sancai sculpture of a kneeling camel, that similar ewers were brought in both ceramic and metalwork forms, across the ancient trading routes. A ceramic vase similar to our Ming dynasty underglaze red ewer from the Hongwu period, is depicted in a Persian painting in the Topkapi Saray Museum in Istanbul, Turkey. Other themes to be explored in our gallery include the richness and diversity of ancient Chinese culture, as well exploring dialogues between contemporary artists and traditional art.

To give you a few more examples, the figure one cloisonne shrine dating to the Qianlong period was part of a large gift of over 200 cloisonne objects dating to the Ming and Qing dynasties, donated to the Brooklyn Museum in 1909. Here it is displayed in a special exhibition in 1912. Here it is in a special exhibition in the museum today. Our new exhibition "Infinite Blue" is a cross collection show highlighting blue throughout all our permanent collections. The stories told involve the trade in cobalt from the Middle East to China during the Tang dynasty, and the later transmission of porcelain technology from China back to the Middle East. We explore export ceramics from Asia to the west as well as the western adaptation of Asian designs and technologies. Here our cloisonne censer is juxtaposed with a contemporary lacquer painting by the Shanghai artist Su Xiaobai.

Figure 1: Cloisonne

In our new galleries we will also explore different forms of landscape but not always in a traditional way. For example an ink painting of a scholar's rock will be shown with a sculpture we commissioned of a scholar's rock made out of black ink! This handscroll shows a digitally manipulated landscape of modern-day Shanghai and here the artist paints the landscape on his body as a form of performance art. The last few examples show a Han dynasty ceramic vessel in dialogue with a silicon vase created by a contemporary artist responding to its form. Another way to engage our audience is through didactics such as this one for our celadon jar with the auspicious theme of the "8 Immortals Crossing the Sea". (*baxian guo hai*). We created a handout for school children where they can choose which Immortal they want to be and which superpowers they want! To do this we examined Yuan and Ming dynasty literary texts and plays.

In conclusion, the photos of the installation of the Asian galleries at the Brooklyn Museum in 1930 and of the Chinese gallery in 1938 show that it didn't look much different at the time we de-installed the galleries for construction in 2013! The Asian galleries on the 2nd floor of the museum were hard to find and had narrow corridors. We demolished the space and took down the floors, walls and ceiling and started from scratch. This is the plan for our new galleries. In addition, we have built a dramatic new glass staircase in the Great Hall of the Museum, just off the Lobby which will take you directly into the Asian Galleries on the second floor. As you come up the stairs you will see the new Chinese galleries on your right. The wall is open with the bottom glass so the art will be visible as you walk across the platform from the stairs. The Chinese galleries will be in the best location in the museum, and will be visible from the Great Hall inviting our visitors to come explore the treasures of China and to learn about Chinese art and culture. We welcome you to visit the Brooklyn Museum and the new Chinese galleries!

传统文化的“传”和“承”

葛剑雄 【中国】
复旦大学资深教授 / 中央文史研究馆馆员

一

传统文化并非一切过去的文化，而是在以往流传了相当长一段时间，为主流社会所接受或具有较大影响的文化。

早在两千多年前，司马迁在《史记》中就引用谚语：“百里不同风，千里不同俗。”风，就是流行、时尚，形成得快，变化或消失得也快，所以其影响范围往往只有百里，百里外就是另一种时尚了。俗，是习俗，即有的风经受了时间的考验保存下来，形成习惯，成为人们的生活方式、行为规范、意识形态、思想观念、价值观、婚丧礼俗、节庆仪式、法律制度，相当稳定，影响范围也扩大到千里之内。时间长了，俗就成为传统。

风之所以只能影响百里，固然是由于自身的不成熟、不稳定，更主要的是对地理环境的适应性。一种在一个特定空间范围形成不久的风尚，未必适应此范围以外的人文和自然地理条件，因而未必能为此范围以外的人们所接受。俗的适应性虽较风强得多，影响或起作用的空间范围也大得多，还是离不开地理环境的影响，特别是在人们的生产力有限的条件下。一旦形成传统，尤其是精神方面的传统，为了维护和延续这种传统，人们会极大地发挥其主观能动性，使之适应变化了的地理环境。但是，如果一种传统文化赖以存在和延续的物质基础已完全改变或不复存在，这种文化的消亡只是时间问题，除非它本身已经彻底改变，或者成功地完成了转变。

正因为如此，对传统文化的传承应该分为“传”与“承”两个部分，这是两个不同的概念，应当区别对待。“传”需要我们把前人留下来的精神的、物质的文化遗产，尽可能完整地、无条件地保存下来，无论是精华还是糟粕，它都是历史的一部分。“承”，是要使它能得到延续和继承，应该是有选择性的，有的需要摒弃，有的需要在正确理解的基础上进行科学转换，只有极少部分才能按照原样继承。

二

三、四千年以来，中国长期以来是以小农经济为基础的农业社会和以游牧为主的牧业社会，而就整体而言，当今中国早已进入工业社会，一些发达地区已进入后工业社会、信息社会甚至智慧社会。就社会制度而言，也已由封建、专制、集权、封闭转变为民主、自由、开放的初级阶段的社会主义、市场经济的社会主义。社会制度和经济基础发生了根本性的变化，与此相适应的文化和上层建筑当然必须随之转变。如果不是采取特殊的保护措施，传统文化中不适应新社会的那部分已经或将要消失。

无论是以马克思主义为指导的新文化，还是以西方文化为主的外来文化，都对传统文化产生了巨大的冲击和持续的影响，其中一些糟粕和弱势部分已被扫荡殆尽。

传统文化赖以存在的物质基础相对落后，即使没有人为的破坏，也难以持久。如古旧建筑大多是土木结构，民间技艺缺乏记录手段，一些必需的自然资源已接近枯竭。传统文化往往缺乏传播手段，或者相当落后，有些本来就处于自生自灭状态。

中国的传统文化是非宗教性的，连已经本土化的佛教也已在很大程度上世俗化、物质化，所以无法依附于宗教而得到保护和延续。

“传”具有极其紧迫性，所以不必争论先进还是落后，不应考虑有用还是无用，就是不能让它们在我们这一代手中断绝，就是要尽最大的努力延续它们的生命或存在。有的古建筑就在人们争论它该不该被保护、如何保护时倒塌了。有的非物质文化传承人，就在主管部门和专家学者讨论他是否能被确定为传承人的过程中去世了。

即使明显属于糟粕、落后、反动甚至罪恶，也应该适当保存。量不必大，但应尽可能有代表性，尽可能完整。因为它们同样是我们历史的一部分，不了解它们，就不能真正了解和理解历史。奥斯维辛集中营被联合国教科文组织列为世界文化遗产，正是为了使人类能永远记住历史上曾经出现的这场浩劫，具体了解法西斯骇人听闻的罪行，否则我们善良的后代或许不会相信、无法想象这些灭绝人性的罪行的残酷程度。

妇女缠足，无论如何总是一种陋习，属于中国传统文化的糟粕。但如果我们不将可以保存的实物和记载保存下来（包括那些欣赏、赞美“三寸金莲”的文学艺术作品），我们的后代又如何能了解从宋朝到清朝汉族妇女曾经有过怎样一段惨痛的历史，如何理解妇女的社会地位，如何研究这持续了上千年的畸形审美观念。

人类的精神、思想、智慧并非始终处于上升阶段，也不一定后者胜过前者。古人的智慧，今人未必都能理解，更未必能超越。所以应该先保存下来，而不必肯定它先进与否，或今后有什么用。如果将它毁灭了，或者任其自生自灭，等我们或后人意识到了，或许已经没有办法再深入了解和研究，更谈不上继承弘扬了。

比如辛亥革命以后，中国废除沿用了三千多年的农历（夏历），完全实行公历。几十年下来，绝大多数人不仅不知道农历，还将它看成是落后的，甚至将它与风水、皇历、迷信视为一体。但实际上农历并非单纯的阴历，而是阴阳合历，适合传统的农业社会。特别是其中的二十四节气，不仅完全符合科学原理，而且早就成为国人的生产、生活节律，是很高的生存智慧。中国以有限的耕地生产充足的粮食和生活资料，养活世界上最多的人口，建立在二十四节气基础上的生产和生活方式起了重要作用。有些少数民族的特殊生活、生产方式，今天或许被当成迷信、陋习，或许也是在古代特殊条件下更有利于生存和环保的方式，不妨先保存下来，等科学技术进步了再慢慢研究。

三

“承”就不同了，应该是有选择的，有条件的。我们需要继承、传播、发扬、发展的，只能是传统文化中的精华，那些今天还有积极意义和利用价值的部分，还要剔除其中不可避免的糟粕。我们不仅需要正确理解传统文化的精神实质，肯定它在历史上曾经起过的积极作用，还要考虑如何使它适应现实的需要，使之形成社会实践。一旦转换成功，就能在中国产生巨大的效益，解决其他文化无法解决的难题。

以对中国古代社会具有长久、深远影响的孝道为例。

孟子在评价舜结婚的事情时说：“不孝有三，无后为大。舜不告而娶，为无后也，君子以为犹告也。”（《孟子·离娄上》）这段话的意思很明白，所以君子认为他做得对，保证有后比事先告知父母更重要。舜结婚前虽然没有告知父母，是因为怕不结婚会无后，这样做等于告知了父母。可见孝道就是要保证家庭有后，而无后就是最大的不孝，这是当时君子们的共识。这是因为在先秦时代，由于生产力不发达，人口普遍营养不良，医疗保健水平很低，妇女婚龄晚，人口有偶率低，产妇和婴儿死亡率高，产妇哺乳期长，人口平均预期寿命短等各方面的不利因素，要保证每个家庭都有后很不容易，要使一个家族人口繁衍更加困难。

《易传》称：“有万物，然后有男女。有男女，然后有夫妇。有夫妇然后有父子，有父子，然后有君臣。有君臣，然后有上下。”也是将家庭及其生育繁衍作为君臣关系的前提和基础。而《说文解字》将“孝”字解释为：“善事父母者。从老省，从子，子承老也。”更多是从文字结构的角度出发，因而只是应用了孝道的普遍要求之一，属表层现象，而非精神实质。另一方面也应该看到，到了《说文解字》问世的东汉时代，随着物质条件的进步和人口总量的增加，无后的矛盾已不如春秋战国时那么尖锐，因而社会对孝道的要求更多注重于精神层面。

汉朝标榜“以孝治天下”，不仅皇帝的谥号都带“孝”字，更表现在采取了一系列政策奖励、保证百姓有后。如汉高祖七年（前 200 年）就下令：“民产子，复勿事二岁。”[1] 即免除家里生了孩子的户主二年徭役，作为对增加人口者的奖励。汉惠帝六年（前 189 年）又下令“女子年十五以上至三十不嫁，五算”[2]；对三十岁还不出嫁的妇女征收五倍的人头税作为惩罚。东汉章帝元和二年（85 年）下诏：“令云‘人有产子者复，勿算三岁。’今诸怀妊者，赐胎养谷人三斛，复其夫，勿算一岁，著以为令。”[3] 即在原有对生育家庭给予三年免人头税的基础上，再增加奖励孕妇三斛谷子，丈夫免除一年人头税，条件比西汉初更加优惠，奖励的力度更大。对生育的奖励措施一直为历代统治者所沿用，如唐贞观三年（629 年）曾下诏：“妇人正月以来产子者粟一斛。”[4]

---

1 《汉书》卷 1《高帝纪》。

2 《汉书》卷 2《惠帝纪》。

3 《后汉书》卷 3《章帝纪》。

4 《新唐书》卷 2《太宗纪》。

另一方面，为了使妇女能早婚早育，法定婚龄定得很低。北周建德三年（574年）、唐开元二十二年（734年）和北宋天圣年间都曾将法定婚龄降至男十五岁、女十三岁[1]，自南宋至清代的法定婚龄都是男十六岁、女十四岁。

在特殊情况下，统治者甚至会采取极端措施，而不顾某些伦理道德标准。如西晋武帝规定，女子年满十七岁父母还未使其婚嫁的，由官府配婚[2]。北齐后主竟下令将“杂户”中二十岁以下、十四岁以上的未嫁女子统统集中起来配婚，家长敢隐匿就处死[3]。唐太宗贞观元年（627年）曾颁布《令有司劝勉庶人婚聘及时诏》，规定：“宜命有司，所在劝勉，其庶人之男女无家室者，并仰州县官人，以礼聘娶，皆任同类相求，不得抑取。男年二十，女年十五以上，及妻丧达制之后，孀居服纪已除，并须申以媒媾，命其好合。”“刺史、县令以下官人，若能使婚姻及时，鳏寡数少，量准户口增多，以进考第。如其劝导乖方，失于配偶，准户减少，以附殿失。”[4]不仅要求对符合条件的男女强制婚配，还作为官员政绩考核的重要内容。

早在汉代，对一些地方普遍存在的杀婴现象，有的地方官已采取严厉措施，严禁杀婴，甚至规定与杀人同罪[5]。宋代也曾多次制定法令严禁民间“生子弃杀”，高宗时甚至还规定“杀子之家，父母、邻保与收生之人，皆徒刑编置”[6]。

由于孝道必须保证“有后”的观念深入人心，成为社会的共识，甚至可以打破种族与政治的界限。张骞首次出使西域时被匈奴扣留了十余年，他始终忠于国家，“持汉节不失”，但并不拒绝匈奴配给他的妻子，并且“有子”[7]。另一位汉使苏武出使匈奴，被扣押19年，历尽艰辛，坚贞不屈，多次以死抗争，但也娶了匈奴妻子。归汉后苏武的儿子因罪被杀，丧失了继承人。汉宣帝怜悯，问左右：“（苏）武在匈奴久，岂有子乎？”可见汉人滞留匈奴而娶妻在当时很正常。苏武报告：“前发匈奴时，胡妇适产一子通国，有声问来”，请求用金帛赎回，得到宣帝批准。以后苏通国随使者来归，被封为郎[8]，成为苏武的合法继承人和苏氏家族的传人。

1 《周书》卷3《武帝纪》，《新唐书》卷52《食货志》，《玉海》卷65。
2 《晋书》卷3《武帝纪》：泰始九年“冬十月辛巳，制女年十七父母不嫁者，使长吏配之”。
3 《北齐书》卷8《后主纪》武平七年二月。
4 宋敏求编《唐大诏令集》卷110，商务印书馆1959年版。
5 如《后汉书》卷77《酷吏传·王吉》：为沛相，“生子不养，即斩其父母”。又见卷67《党锢传·贾彪》。
6 《历代名臣奏议》卷8《论举子钱米疏》，《四库全书》本。
7 《汉书》卷61《张骞传》。
8 《汉书》卷54《苏武传》。

在天翻地覆、国破家亡之际，总是将家族的延续放在重要地位，当作尽孝的实际行动。我在研究中国人口史时发现，往往每当战乱一结束，就会迎来人口迅速增长，原因之一就是在战乱之中、颠沛流离之际，育龄妇女的生育并未停止，甚至为了保证有后而加紧生育，多生育。即使个人因忠于国家而无法尽孝，也会通过家族的努力或特殊手段争取忠孝两全。例如南宋的忠臣文天祥，自己舍生取义，杀身成仁，为宋朝尽忠，但允许其弟文璧出仕元朝，为家族尽孝，保证文氏家族的绵延。[1]

早在公元初，汉朝已经拥有 6000 万人口，以后多次遭遇天灾人祸，人口数量曾急剧下降，但每次都能得到恢复，并且不断增加，在 12 世纪初的北宋末突破 1 亿，17 世纪初的明代接近 2 亿，在 1853 年超过 4.3 亿。中国的人口数量始终在世界人口中占有很高的百分比，汉族一直是世界上人口最多的民族，虽然有多方面的原因，但孝道无疑起着独特而重要的作用。孝道的本质是维系家族的精神支柱，保证家族和社会的繁衍，所以才有“不孝有三，无后为大”的说法。孝道的继承和弘扬，使先民一代又一代，自觉或不自觉地尽可能生育，尽最大努力抚养后代，还积极与外族通婚，争取外族的同化和融合。

今天现代化国家和发达地区都面临着生育率降低、人口数量下降、老龄化加剧的难题，随着国民收入的提高，社会保障的稳定，信息交流的便捷，职业竞争的激化，家庭观念的淡薄，这种现象日益严重，找不到解决的办法。一些国家企图通过经济和法律手段加以缓解，但事实证明，经济手段作用有限，对衣食无忧的中产阶层更无计可施。而法律只能保护已有的生命，却无法强制人们生育。

今天中国也面临着这样的难题，在一些发达地区和城市，人口已多年处于负增长。晚婚晚育、不婚不育、丁克家庭已占相当比例，并有扩大的趋势。如果仅仅讲物质因素和现实需要，这类现象是很难改变的。例如，如果说生育是“养儿防老”，随着社会保障体系的建立，养老服务的社会化，人均寿命的延长，老人健康条件的改善，人际交流的便捷，文化生活的丰富，的确已经没有必要。如果计算生育和抚养一个孩子的直接和间接的成本，在绝大多数情况下，总是无法得到政府和社会的补偿。即使生育和抚养的成本全部由社会承担，甚至再给予额外补贴，对只考虑个人的自由、身材的健美、生活的舒适、职场的竞争、成功的追求的人们也无济于事。

1 何隽《文天祥首肯文璧降元及其原因》，《文献》1995 年第 1 期。

如果将传统的孝道转化为现代的价值观念，即保证家庭和社会的繁衍是每一个人的义务，更是青年不可推卸的职责。如果我们的后代从小就受到这样的教育和熏陶，将孝道融入逐渐确立的基本价值观念，以后就会将家庭和睦、生儿育女、尊老爱幼看作人生不可或缺的内容和应尽的职责，不会仅仅从个人的幸福考虑，或者从物质方面斤斤计较。那么这种孝道就能在中国发挥独特的巨大作用，有望解决现代化过程中至今无法解决的难题。

传统的孝道也有其历史性的局限，需要在转换过程中摒弃，并且在实践在继续消除其影响。

一是“无后”的“后”原来只指男性，而不包括女性。所以如果生了女婴，无论连生了几个，非但不能被当成“后”，而且会被视为不吉不祥，当成家族的不幸或遭受的惩罚。富贵人家往往因此而溺杀女婴以隐瞒真相。贫困家族则为了保证未来的男婴能得到供养而溺杀并不需要的女婴。无男性“后”也是休妻和纳妾的合法理由。由此造成中国人口长期存在的高性别比，实际上降低了人口的有偶率、生育率和净繁殖率，成为中国人口增长率始终不高的原因之一。

在实施计划生育政策阶段，这一陈旧的观念依然在起作用，特别是在农村和贫困地区，多数家族往往要生到有男孩子为止，成为一孩政策的最大阻力。如果这一观念不改变，连续生育两个女孩的家庭也会坚持生第三胎，对女孩和女性的歧视也难以消除。

一是将生育和抚养的责任全部推给女方。在传统社会，不能生育的责任一般都由女方承担，既有医学知识的局限，也有男尊女卑观念的影响。所以即使在当代，一些男性还不愿共同承担起生育的责任，在遇到障碍时不积极配合，轻易放弃生育的可能性。

传统社会对男性的要求只是负经济供养和教育之责，而将抚养子女的重担完全交给女性。女性基本留在家庭内的农业社会，这样的分工有一定的合理性。到了现代社会，特别是在女性与男性拥有同样的职业选择和社会地位时，这样的分工既不合理，也不人性，必须改变。

The “Passing down” and “Inheritance” of the Traditional Culture

Ge Jianxiong / China

Senior Professor of Fudan University, Member of the Central Research Institute of Culture and History

I

Traditional culture is not all the culture of the past. It should be a culture that has been spread for quite some time and widely accepted by the mainstream society, or that has tremendous influence.

As early as more than two thousand years ago, Sima Qian quoted the proverb in the *Records of the Historian*, “There are different fashions within a hundred miles; there are different customs within thousands of miles.” “Fashion” here refers to popularity, which develops quickly, changes or disappears quickly, so its range of influence is usually only hundreds of miles and a hundred miles away there is another fashion. “Custom” refers to convention & habits, which have stood the test of time and been preserved. It has become a people’s way of life, norms of behavior, a code of conduct, ideology, ideas, values, wedding and funeral customs, festival ceremonies, and a legal system. It is quite stable and the scope of influence also extends up to a thousand miles. As time goes by, "custom" becomes "tradition".

A fashion that could only influence an area of hundreds of miles is due to its self-immaturity and instability, and more importantly, its adaptability to the geographical environment. A newly-formed fashion in a particular space is not necessarily adapted to the human and natural geographical conditions outside this scope, and therefore may not be acceptable to people outside this scope. Although the adaptability of the custom is much stronger and the spatial scope of the influence or function is much larger than that of fashion, it is still subject to the influence of the geographical environment, especially in the conditions of a limited productivity. Once the tradition has been formed, especially a tradition on spiritual level, in order to maintain and continue this tradition, people will greatly exert its subjective initiative to make it adapt to the changing geographical environment. However, if the material basis for the existence and continuity of a traditional culture has completely changed or disappeared, the extinction of this culture is only a matter of time, unless it has changed completely or successfully transformed itself.

Just because of this, the passing down and inheritance of traditional culture should be divided into two parts: "passing down" and "inheritance", which are two different concepts and should be treated differently. "Passing down" requires us to preserve the spiritual and material cultural heritage left by our predecessors as completely and unconditionally as possible. It is a part of history, be it the essence or the dregs. "Inheritance" is to enable it to be extended and inherited. It should be selective, some inheritance needs to be abandoned, and some of it needs to be scientifically converted on the basis of correct understanding. Only a very small part can be inherited completely.

II

Over the past three thousand or four thousand years, China has long been an agricultural society based on a small agricultural economy and a nomadic pastoral society. On the whole, it has already entered the industrial society, and in some developed areas it has entered the post-industrial society, the information society and even the intellectual society. As far as the social system is concerned, it has also changed from a feudal, autocratic, centralized and closed society to the primary stage of socialism featuring democracy, freedom and opening-up and a kind of socialism with a market economy. Fundamental changes have taken place in the social system and the economic foundation, and the culture and superstructure corresponding to it must change accordingly. Without special protective measures, the part of traditional culture that has not adapted to the new society has disappeared or will disappear.

Whether it is a new culture guided by Marxism or a foreign culture dominated by Western culture, it has had a huge and lasting impact on the traditional culture, and some of the dross and weak parts have been swept away.

The material base that the traditional culture depends on is relatively backward. Even if there is no deliberate destruction, it is also difficult to be persistent. For example, most of the old buildings are made of earth and wood; folk skills lack the means of recording; and some essential natural resources have disappeared. Traditional culture is often lacking in means of communication, or rather backward, and some are originally in a state of self-destruction.

China's traditional culture is non-religious, and even the native Buddhism has been widely vulgarized and materialized, so it cannot be linked to religion in order to seek protection and continuity.

The "passing down" is extremely urgent, so it is not necessary to argue for advanced or backward, nor should it be considered useful or useless. What we need to do is to do our best to continue the life or existence of what is passed down rather than let it die out in our generation. Some ancient buildings collapsed when people were in dispute whether they should be protected or as to how to protect them. Some intangible cultural successors died when the competent authorities, experts and scholars were in the process of discussing whether they could be identified as successors.

Even if it is obviously dross, backward, reactionary or even evil, it should be properly preserved. The volume is not necessarily large, but it should be as representative and as complete as possible. Because these aspects are also a part of our history, and without knowing them, we cannot really know and understand our history. The Auschwitz Concentration Camp is listed as a world cultural heritage by UNESCO so that human beings will always remember this period of havoc in history and understand the horrific crimes carried out by fascists; otherwise, our kind descendants may not believe and cannot imagine the cruelty of these inhuman crimes.

Women's foot-binding is anyhow a bad corrupt custom, which is the dross of Chinese traditional culture. However, if we do not save the objects and records, including those literary and artistic works which appreciate and praise "three inches of Golden Lotus", how can our descendants understand the painful history of the women of the Han nationality from the Song Dynasty to the Qing Dynasty, how can they understand the social status of the women and how can they study the deformed aesthetic concept that lasted for thousands of years.

The human spirit, thought and wisdom are not always on the rise, and not necessarily the latter triumphs over the former. The wisdom of the ancients may not always be completely understood, nor may it be necessarily surpassed. Therefore, we should first save it without having to be sure whether it is advanced or not, or what role it will play in the future. If it was destroyed, or left on alone to run its own course, when we or later generations become aware of its value, perhaps there is no way to further understand and study it, let alone inherit it and carry it forward.

For example, after the Revolution of 1911, China abolished the lunar calendar (Xia Li), which had been used for more than three thousand years, and implemented the Gregorian calendar. For decades, most people not only did not know the lunar calendar, but also regarded it as backward, and even considered it the same as

Feng Shui (a geomantic omen), the Chinese almanac and superstition. However, actually, the lunar calendar is not purely a lunar calendar, but a combination of a lunar and a Gregorian calendar, which is suitable for the traditional agricultural society. The twenty-four solar terms in particular are not only fully in line with the principles of science, but also become the production and life rhythm of the Chinese people. It is high-level survival wisdom. Why could China produce enough grain and life materials with limited cultivated land, and raise the world's largest population? The production and lifestyle based on the twenty-four solar terms has played an important role in this. Some ethnic minorities' special manners of life and production may be regarded as superstitious, bad habits. However, they might also be more conducive to survival and environmental protection under the special conditions of ancient times. We might as well preserve them first and study them gradually when the science and technology progresses further.

III

"Inheritance" is different. It should be selective and conditional. We need not only inherit, spread, carry forward and develop the essence of traditional culture that still has positive significance and a value for use nowadays, but we should also eliminate the inevitable dross. We need not only correctly understand the spiritual essence of traditional culture and affirm the positive role it has played in history, but we should also figure out how to make it adapt to the needs of reality and make it become social practice. Once the conversion is successful, it will bring huge benefits to China and solve the problems that other cultures cannot solve.

As an example, take the doctrine of filial piety, which has a long-lasting and far-reaching influence on ancient Chinese society.

Mencius once commented on the marriage of Shun (the name of a legendary monarch in ancient China), saying: "There are three things that are not in accordance with the doctrine of filial piety; the most serious one is not fulfilling one's obligation to one's parents. The fact that Shun got married without having told his parents is the most serious case. However, from the point of view of a man of noble character, that is pretty much the same as telling his parents." (*Mencius·Lilou I*) The meaning of this passage is very clear, so the gentleman thought he was right. It is more important to ensure that he has gotten married and had babies than to tell his parents beforehand. Shun did not tell his parents before marriage, because he was afraid that if he did not marry, he would not fulfill his filial duty to his parents. Therefore, getting married first was equal to telling his parents. Apparently, filial piety is about a guarantee that there are descendants in the household. Remaining without descendants would have been the worst case in filial piety at that time, and this was the consensus of the gentleman at that time in history. This is because in the pre-Qin period, due to underdeveloped productivity, malnutrition, poor healthcare, late marriage age, low population rate, high maternal and infant mortality, long breastfeeding period, short life expectancy and so on, it was not an easy task to guarantee that each household had descendants and it was even harder to get the big family booming in family members.

Yi Zhuan claims, "All things on earth came first, men and women appear afterwards, and then there were couples, and then there were fathers and sons and then there were monarchs and ministers, and then there was a hierarchy." Family and their reproduction are the premise and foundation of the relationship between monarchs and ministers. In the book of *Shuowen Jiezi*, the word "filial piety" is interpreted as "Be filial to parents. The virtue of filial piety should be started from the old, inherited by you and passed down to generations after you." It is more from the perspective of word structure; it only applies one of the universal requirements of filial piety, which is a superficial phenomenon rather than a spiritual essence. On the other hand, in the Eastern Han Dynasty, when the *Shuowen Jiezi* came out, with the progress of the material conditions and the increase in the total population, the contradiction of the reproduction was not as sharp as that in the Spring and Autumn Period and the Warring States Period, when, with the respect of social demand for filial piety, people paid more attention to the spiritual level.

The Han Dynasty proclaimed "rule the country with the doctrine of filial piety". Not only did the emperor's posthumous title carry the word "filial piety", but also a series of policy incentives were adopted to ensure that the people had their own descendants. In the 7th year (200 BC), the Emperor Gaozu of the Han Dynasty ordered: "If the wife gives birth to a baby, her husband will be exempt from taxes and corvée for two years."[1] This was considered the reward for increasing the population. In the 6th year (189 BC), Emperor Hui of the Han Dynasty also ordered: "If women aged between fifteen and thirty do not marry, they will be fined 600 copper coins"[2]; those girls aged above 30 who haven't married would be levied five times the poll tax as a punishment. In the 2nd year of the Yuanhe period (85AD), Emperor Zhang of the Eastern Han Dynasty ordered: "If a woman gives birth to a baby, she will be excepted from the poll tax for three years. Those who are pregnant now will be granted three buckets of grain and their husbands will be exempt from the poll tax for one year."[3], which means that in addition to the exemption of the poll tax for three years, the household who once again has a baby will be given three buckets of grain for the pregnant woman and the husband will be exempt from the poll tax for one year. The policy was more favorable than that of the Western Han Dynasty, and the reward was more generous. The reward measures for reproduction had been used by rulers of all dynasties, for example, in the 3rd year of Zhenguan (629 AD) of the Tang Dynasty, an imperial edict was once issued: "Every woman who gives birth to a baby from the first month of the lunar year will be granted one bucket of rice."[4]

On the other hand, in order to enable women to get married and have children earlier, the legal age of marriage is very small. In the 3rd year of Jiande (574AD) of the Northern Zhou Dynasty, in the 22nd year of Kaiyuan (734AD) of the Tang Dynasty and during the Tiansheng period of the Northern Song Dynasty, the legal

---

1 *History of the Han Dynasty* (Volume 1): *The Biography of Emperor Gao*

2 *History of the Han Dynasty* (Volume 2): *The Biography of Emperor Hui*

3 *History of the Post-Han Dynasty* (Volume 3): *The Biography of Emperor Zhang*

4 *New History of the Tang Dynasty* (Volume 2): *The Biography of Emperor Taizong*

age for marriage was reduced to fifteen years for males and thirteen years for females, respectively[1]. The marriage age from the Southern Song Dynasty to the Qing Dynasty was sixteen years for males and fourteen years for females.

Under special circumstances, rulers even took extreme measures, regardless of certain ethical standards. For example, the emperor of the Western Jin Dynasty stipulated that if the woman was seventeen years old and her parents had not arranged marriage for her, the marriage would be arranged by the government.[2] The last emperor of the Northern Qi Dynasty ordered that all unmarried women aged between 14 and 20, whose households were socially inferior, would be gathered together and allocated marriage, and parents who intended to hide their daughters would be executed.[3] In the 1st year of the Zhenguan period (627AD), Emperor Taizong of the Tang Dynasty once promulgated a *Decree of Asking the Competent Authority to Persuade Those Socially Inferior People to Get Married In Time,* which stipulated that "the related competent authority should persuade the men and women who all came from socially inferior households to get married by means of the male's family sending betrothal presents to the female's family. Everyone had to conform to this decree and no one would be allowed to go against it. It should be arranged for the men who were 20 years old, women above 15 years of age as well as the widows who have finished the prescribed mourning period, to get married with the help to matchmakings." "If the prefectural governors, the county magistrates or lower level officials are able to arrange marriages for the people under their jurisdiction in a timely manner, so as to reduce the number of widowers and widows and increase the population, they could be promoted correspondingly,

1 *History of the Zhou* Dynasty (Volume 3): *The Biography of Emperor Wu*, *New History of the Tang Dynasty* (Volume 52): *Shi Huo Zhi*, *Yu Hai* (Volume 65)

2 *History of the Jin Dynasty* (Volume 3): *The Biography of Emperor Wu:* In the 9th year of Taishi period, "in October of the winter, all girls who have turned 17 but have not been arranged marriage by their parents, that will be arranged by the government officials" .

3 *History of the Northern Qi Dynasty* (Volume 8): *The Biography of the Last Emperor,* February, the 7th year of Wuping period (576AD).

otherwise, they would be punished accordingly."[1] It required not only compulsory marriage for eligible men and women, but it also considered it as an important part of official performance appraisal.

Early in the Han Dynasty, some local officials had taken strict measures against infanticide, which was prevalent in some places. Infanticide was strictly prohibited and the government even ordered that anyone who committed infanticide would be on a par with a murderer.[2] In the Song Dynasty, a number of decrees had been made to strictly prohibit the "abandoning and killing" of the infants. During the reign of Emperor Gaozong of the Song Dynasty, he even stipulated that "the family that kills the child, the parents, the neighbors and people that help with infanticide, shall all be put in prison."[3]

Because the doctrine of filial piety must ensure that the households do "have descendants" was deeply rooted in the minds of the people and had become the consensus of the society, it could even break the boundaries between race and politics. Zhang Qian had been detained by the Huns for more than ten years in the western regions on his first journey there. He was all along loyal to the country and never gave up to them, but did not refuse the wife that the Huns arranged for him and "had a son".[4] Another envoy of the Han Dynasty named Su Wu went to the Huns and was detained for 19 years there. He went through hardships and remained faithful and unyielding, but he also married a woman of the Huns. After he returned to the Han region, his son was killed due to committing a crime, thus he lost his successor. Emperor Xuan of the Han Dynasty took pity on him and asked his ministers if Su Wu had sons among the Huns since he had lived there for so long

1 Song Minqiu (ed.), *The Imperial Edict of the Tang Dynasty* (Volume 110), The Commercial Press, 1959 Edition.

2 Such as in the *History of the Post-Han Dynasty* (Volume 77): *The Biography of Cruel Official · Wang Ji:* He served as the Pei Minister and ordered that if the parents abandoned their children, they would be beheaded immediately. Please also refer to *History of the Post-Han Dynasty* (Volume 67): *The Biography of Danggu · Jia Biao.*

3 *Memorials Submitted to the Throne by Important Officials of Successive Dynasties* (Volume 8): *About Financial Relief*, The Si Ku Quan Shu Edition.

4 *History of the Han Dynasty* (Volume 61): *The Biography of Zhang Qian.*

time. Obviously, it was normal at that time that a man from the Han Dynasty would marry a woman of the Huns when being detained there. Su Wu reported: "When I was with the Huns, my wife of the Huns people, Hu, had given birth to a boy named Tongguo. There was news from the Huns requesting the redemption with gold and silk." And Emperor Xuan approved. Later, Su Tongguo returned with the envoy and was bestowed Assistant Minister.[1] Therefore, he became a legal heir to Su Wu and a successor to the Su family.

When undergoing fundamental changes and on the verge of country ruin, people always put the family continuity in an important position and considered it as a practical action of fulfillment of filial piety. In the study of the history of China's population, I found that when each war ended, the population had grown rapidly. One of the reasons is that in the war, the women of childbearing age did not stop getting pregnant and in order to ensure that there were more descendants they gave birth to more children. Even if one could not fulfill the filial piety due to loyalty to the state, he would strive for loyalty and filial piety through family efforts or special means. For example, Wen Tianxiang, a loyal minister of the Southern Song Dynasty, lost his own life for the Song Dynasty, but his brother Wen Bi was allowed to be an official of the Yuan Dynasty to fulfill the filial piety and guarantee the continuation of the family.[2]

In the early years of the Christian era, the Han Dynasty had a population of 60 million. Even though suffering from natural and man-made disasters many times and the number of people had fallen sharply, each time the population managed to recover, and increased in number continuously. At the beginning of the 12th century, in the late Northern Song Dynasty, it exceeded 100 million; in the early 17th century, during the Ming Dynasty, it was close to 200 million, and it surpassed 430 million in 1853. The population of China has always had a very high percentage of the world's population. The Han nationality has always been the most populous nation

1 *History of the Han Dynasty* (Volume 54): *The Biography of Su Wu.*

2 He Juan, Wen Tianxiong Approved of His Younger Brother Wen Bi's Surrendering to the Yuan Dynasty and the Reasons, *Literature*, 1995(1), pp.99-114.

in the world. Although there are many reasons, the doctrine of filial piety plays a unique and important role. The essence of the doctrine of filial piety is the spiritual support of a family and is to ensure the reproduction of the family and society. That is why there is a saying that "there are three situations that run contrary to the doctrine of filial piety, 'with no descendants' is the most serious one." The inheritance and promotion of the doctrine of filial piety makes the ancestors from generation to generation, consciously or unconsciously, give birth to as many as possible, try their best to raise their offspring, and actively marry people who are not of the same clan in a bid to strive for the assimilation and integration with the other nationalities.

Today, both modern countries and developed areas are facing difficulties of a low fertility rate, declining population and aging. With the improvement of national income, the stability of social security, the convenience of information exchange, the intensification of professional competition, and the weak concept of family, this phenomenon is becoming more and more serious and cannot be solved. Some countries are trying to mitigate it by economic and legal means, but the fact is that the role of economic means is limited. Especially, for the middle class who have nothing to worry about, the government has no good ways of changing their ideas. The law can only protect the existing life, but cannot force people to have babies.

Today, China is also facing such a problem. In some developed regions and cities, the population has been in a negative growth rate for many years. Late marriage, late childbirth, no marriage and no children and dink families have accounted for a considerable proportion, which is continuing to grow. Only from the perspective of material factors and practical needs, is it hard to change those phenomena. For example, in the past, we often said that raising children was to guarantee that the parents could be taken care of when they were old. However, with the establishment of the social security system, the socialization of the old-age service, the prolongation of the life expectancy, the improvement of the health conditions of the elderly, the convenient interpersonal communication and the rich cultural life, it is really not necessary to have children. In terms of the direct and indirect cost of raising children, in most cases, the government and society will not make up for it. Even if the costs of the birth and raising of children are all borne by the society, and even with additional subsidies, it is of no help for those who only pay attention to their individual freedom, body-building, comfortable life, competition in the workplace, the pursuit of success and so on.

If the traditional doctrine of filial piety is transformed into a modern concept of value, it is the obligation of every person to guarantee the reproduction of the family and the society, and it is also the inescapable responsibility of the youth. If our descendants are taught and nurtured from an early age to integrate the doctrine of filial piety into their gradually established basic value and take family harmony, the birth of a child, respecting the old and cherishing the young as the indispensable contents of their life and their duty, you will not only take the individual happiness into consideration and haggle over every ounce from the material aspects. This kind of doctrine of filial piety can play a unique role in China and is expected to solve the problems that cannot be solved in the process of modernization.

The traditional doctrine of filial piety also has its historical limitations, which need to be abandoned in the process of transformation and their influence needs to be eliminated in practice.

“Having no descendants” originally means without male descendants, and did not include females. If the descendants were females, no matter how many there were, they were not considered real descendants. And even worse, it was regarded as an ominous thing for the whole family as it was interpreted as a kind of misfortune or punishment to the family. Wealthy families often drowned their baby girls to hide the truth. The poor families drowned the girls to reduce the expenditure so as to ensure that they would be able to raise future boys. If the wife was not able to give birth to boys, it was justifiable for the man to divorce or marry other women. As a result, the high sex ratio of the Chinese population for a long time had actually reduced the marriage rate, the fertility rate and the net reproduction rate, which was one of the reasons for the low rate of growth of the population in China.

In the implementation of the family planning policy, this obsolete concept is still working, especially in rural and poor areas. Most families will not give up until they have a boy, which becomes the biggest obstacle to the one–child policy. If this concept is not changed, families with two girls will continue to have third births, and discrimination against girls and women will not be eliminated.

To be specific, the responsibility of giving birth to and raising children is undertaken by women. In traditional society, the responsibility of infertility is usually borne by the woman, due not only to the limitations of medical knowledge, but also to the view that males are superior to females. Therefore, even in the contemporary era, some men are unwilling to shoulder the responsibility of childbearing together, do not cooperate actively with their wives in the face of obstacles, and easily give up the possibility of reproduction.

The traditional society's demand for men was only the responsibility of economic support and education, while the burden of raising children was completely handed over to women. Such a division of labor was reasonable in an agricultural society where women basically stayed at home. By contrast, in modern society, especially when women and men have the same career choices and social status, this division of labor is neither reasonable nor human-based and must be changed.

书籍、作者与译者——新丝绸之路建设的一种可能性途径

克拉拉 【匈牙利】

匈中友好协会主席 / 匈牙利文学翻译家协会会员、文学翻译

> “不要认为在书籍（的世界）中寻求慰藉的人是在逃避生活；
>
> 相反，他或许在试着拓展生活的边界：他不满足于时代或命运分配给他的生活，而是渴望着更多的生活体验。”
>
> 米哈利·巴比茨[1]

我在开篇引用的，是匈牙利一位著名诗人的话。这位诗人同时也是一名作家和文学译者，生活在 19 世纪、20 世纪之交，是为匈牙利文学期刊《西方》（Nyugat）供稿的“第一代”作家。之所以用这句话作为开篇序语，是因为这位作家的观点与我不谋而合——书籍并不会将读者“驱逐”出现实世界，而是能够拓展读者的生活世界，为读者提供“更多的生活体验”。例如，书籍可以帮助读者了解各类人群、了解不同的地域和时代，让读者站在他人的立场思考，理解他人的思想，体会他人的感受。大多数人或许永远都没有机会去身处实地的考察遥远的异国文化，但读者却可以通过一本译著，对异域文化进行窥视。

一个国家“健康”发展的先决条件是，接受他国文化影响，但不会令本国的文化价值观沦为从属地位，或是在外界条件影响下逐渐“枯萎”。在当今全球化的语境下，各国间的互动日趋频繁，各国人民之间的联系甚至趋向日常化，因而

1　米哈利·巴比茨（1883—1941，布达佩斯），作家、诗人、文学史学者、文学译者。

文学翻译的重要性也在日益加深。翻译不仅能够促进我们对不同文化的理解，同时还能让我们意识到，我们是“大群体”中的一员。为了更好地了解这个“大群体”，仅凭经济指标或线上线下的媒体短评是远远不够的，我们必须对彼此的文化、思想、哲学、文学等领域进行深入而系统的了解，若没有文学翻译，这一目标是无法达成的。文学翻译不会引起文化的合并与杂糅，而是能够揭示各个文化间的异同之处。

之所以用“书籍、作者与译者——新丝绸之路建设的一种可能性途径”作为题目，是因为我一直深信，书籍以及纯文学翻译是构建新丝绸之路所需的基础材料，能够帮助中国与世界上的重要区域建立紧密的联系。语言是表达思想、传播理念、表述感受的重要手段，而书籍则是促进人们相互理解的重要“工具”。当然，除了此类“基础材料”外，作为“中间媒介”的作者和译者也能在“新丝路的建构”中发挥重要作用。

我来自中东欧地区的一个小国家，匈牙利。尽管我国的国土面积和人口数量与中国相差甚远——匈牙利的人口数量不足1000万人，甚至比不上中国一些大城市的人口数量——但中匈两国一直保持着密切的友好关系，特别是当前两国间的外交关系和经贸交往比以往任何时期都要密切。在很早之前，匈牙利便已认可中国的国际地位，并造就了一批饮誉国际的汉学家和中国研究学者。这一点是值得强调的，因为蓬勃发展的匈牙利汉学正是扎根于两国源远流长的友好历史，因而在中国文化走向全球的过程中，匈牙利才能扮演如此积极的角色。中国和匈牙利不仅仅是两个不同的国家，各自的文化渊源和语言文字之间也存在着根本性的差异。两国的语言几乎找不到任何共同点：中国人使用的汉字属于语素文字（又称表意文字），汉语是一种措辞简洁的孤立语（又称分析语），语义关联层次丰富，而匈牙利语采用的则是衍生版的拉丁字母（比原始拉丁字母表多出á, é, í, ó, ö, ő, ú, ü, ű几个字母），是一种措辞冗长的黏着语，表意更为具体。两国的文化语言差距过大，相互比较时只有少数几个“参照点”可以把握，所谓的类比和联想更是无从谈起。想要跨越地理界限、在两国文化或思想界之间构建一座“桥梁”或一条“道路”，委实不易。但这是一项崇高的任务，或者说，是一份崇高的事业或使命。总之，这便是文学翻译者肩负的重任。

匈牙利人民对东方国家，特别是对中国思想和中国文化持有相对开放的态度，近年来对“东方”的兴趣正在持续复兴，当然，其中原因十分复杂，在此我只想强调三点：（1）由于中东欧地区的国家生活着许多中国人，匈牙利民众与中国人的接触已变得日常化。匈牙利国内设有许多专门机构，如中匈双语小学、中学，佩奇市的中医孔子学院，以及匈牙利法门佛教学院等，此外还有多家中国跨国企业，比如米什科尔茨的华为和万华等，中国银行也在匈牙利设立了总部，在中东欧地区开设了第一家分行；同时，许多非政府组织——如匈中友好协会等，也为推动中匈文化交流发挥了积极的作用。（2）由于匈牙利民族与东方文化渊源颇深，几个世纪以来，东方学一直备受重视。（3）两国外交互动十分活跃，近年来两国高层领导人互访频繁，仅在几周前，中国国务院副总理刘延东刚刚结束对匈牙利的访问。在两国领导层进行会晤和磋商的过程中，文化因素往往扮演着重要的角色，从这个角度来讲，不论是中国的“一带一路”倡议还是匈牙利的“向东方开放”政策，都不是仅仅出于商业、政治或经济层面的考虑，同时也涉及文化、教育层面的互动和交流。两国文化合作的范例不胜枚举，在此仅列举几例：2013 年，匈牙利文化中心在北京成立；随后，中国各地大学纷纷设立匈牙利专业（如重庆的四川外国语大学）以及匈牙利研究中心；2017 年，匈牙利科学院设立中东欧研究院；2014 年，中东欧汉语教师培训中心在布达佩斯挂牌成立；2017 年，国际中国语言学学会第 25 届年会召开；2016 年，第 1 届中东欧文学论坛开幕；中匈两国的交换生与留学生数量日益增多；大型艺术展（如布达佩斯举办的《齐白石精品展》、上海举办的《茜茜公主与匈牙利》）、电影节、艺术节相继拉开帷幕，各类戏剧、歌剧、音乐艺术在两国的舞台上分别亮相，各类书籍纷纷出现在两国的图书市场上。值得一提是，匈牙利于 2016 年以主宾国的身份参与了北京国际图书博览会。

1949 年 10 月 4 日，中国与匈牙利正式建立外交关系，两国已建交近 70 年，交流史则更为久远。

据证实，早在公元 14 世纪时期，便有匈牙利的传教士到达中国，但在接下来的几十年里，由于奥斯曼帝国控制了所有通往远东的路线，两国间的联系在很长一段时间内出于中断状态，直到 17 世纪，又有数名匈牙利传教士来到了中国。18 至 19 世纪，一些探险家和科学家先后访问中国，其中名望最著者，要数乔玛·德克勒希（1784—1842）。在 19 世纪 20 年代，这位语言学家及图书学家长期生活在西藏地区的寺院里，尽管他并没有在那里寻找到匈牙利人之“根”，但却凭借一本藏–英字典、一本语法书以及几部科学著作，成为了举世闻名的“藏学之父”；1877—1881 年间，“匈牙利最伟大的政治家”伊什特万·塞切尼之子——探险家厄尔·贝拉·塞切尼（1837—1908）游历了中国多个地区，探险队的成员中也包括世界著名地质学家、地理学者拉吉奥斯·洛克奇（1902 年，在德国汉堡召开的东方学家大会上，洛克奇做了关于敦煌的报告，阐明了石窟中佛教壁画的重要性）。1898 年，厄尔·杰诺·兹奇取道陆路抵达北京；匈裔英籍考古学家、探险家奥莱尔·斯坦因于 1907 年前往敦煌，带走了千佛洞中的艺术品，这一行为至今仍遭到中国人民的谴责。

至于中国与奥匈帝国之间的种种关联、中匈两国在两次世界大战期间的关系，恐怕要另写一篇文章才能尽述。我的导师尤山度教授曾专门就这一课题发表了论著，因此我的发言只关注 20 世纪两国之间的“二度接合”，这次“接合”被认为是匈牙利汉学史上的里程碑。匈牙利是在新中国成立几天之后便与之建立外交关系的为数不多的国家之一。这不仅是两国政治合作和经济合作的开端，更开启了两国之间的文化、教育以及科技交流。

第一批匈牙利政府奖学金来华留学生于 1950 年抵达北京，1950—1966 年间，在华留学的匈牙利学生大约有 30 人，其中包括文学批评家高恩德（Endre Galla）——杰出的鲁迅研究者，鲁迅作品、匈牙利文学的译介者；文学批评家梅维佳（Vilma Mészáros），中国现当代史学者尤山度（Sándor Józsa），以及艺术批评家、文学翻译家米白（Pál Miklós）。米白出版了多部中国艺术及文化史专著，其中最主要的一部便是关于敦煌千佛洞的学术著作。此外还有匈牙利科学院的经济学家、政治学家戴伯纳（Barna Tálas），著名文学翻译家、政治学家鲍洛尼·彼得（Péter Polonyi）、著名文学翻译家、匈牙利著名出版社——欧罗巴出版社资深编辑姑兰·埃娃（Éva Kalmár），文学批评家、匈牙利前驻华大使叶桐（Ottó Juhász）；随后的几批留学生包括艺术、文化批评家范凌思（Mária Ferenczy）等。尽管匈牙利国内大学早已成立远东系，但匈牙利的汉学基本上是由杜克义（Ferenc Tőkei）、陈国（Barnabás Csongor）以及艾之迪（Ildikó Ecsedy）等语言学者、哲学研究者以及文学翻译者建立起来的。

这些学者功底深厚，文笔优美，翻译了大量中国（古典及现代）文学作品和哲学作品，取得了较高的成就，且在汉学各个领域均有建树。罗兰大学的汉语教师培训中心已经成为培养未来汉学家的摇篮以及中—匈文学翻译基地。培训中心传授了深刻的汉学知识和科学的研究方法，从专业启蒙到现在，中心一直给予我无私的帮助，对此，我深表感激。

在两次世界大战期间，匈牙利国内已经出现少数中国文学作品的译本，例如，1931 年著名诗人及文学翻译家戴兹索・科斯托兰伊翻译了一本中日诗歌集，尽管并非从汉语直接译介，而是从中介语翻译而来，但由于他对原作的解读十分透彻和贴切，这部诗歌集在匈牙利产生了重要影响；1937 年，拉吉奥斯・安格翻译了另一部古典诗歌作品——《中国诗歌 100 篇》。

在来华留学生以及罗兰大学几名教授的努力下，匈牙利于 20 世纪 50 年代开始了对中国文学的大规模译介。20 世纪 50 年代至 70 年代之间，一些汉学家与当时最著名的一批匈牙利诗人，如劳伦克・萨扎波、桑朵・威欧利、盖乌拉・伊利斯、伊斯万・瓦斯、拉斯洛・纳吉等人，合作翻译了屈原、杜甫、白居易、李白等人的诗作，以及《诗经》、《乐府诗》、蒲松龄的作品、《水浒传》、《孽海花》、《老残游记》、《儒林外史》以及《西游记》等作品；80 年代，鲁迅、矛盾、巴金、老舍以及溥仪等人的作品被翻译为匈牙利语并出版；至于中国最经典的作品，如《唐诗集》（李白、白居易、杜甫）、著名小说《红楼梦》（从德语本译介）、《水浒传》、《金瓶梅》（从德语译介）、《西游记》以及《道德经》、《论语》等，几乎在每个匈牙利知识分子的家里都能找到。在这一时期，中国的伟大经典作品曾多次再版重印。

由于篇幅和时间所限，此处无法对匈牙利著名汉学家及其译作进行详细阐述，仅仅列举一些最具影响力的中国作家及作品的译介情况：陈国翻译了《水浒传》、《西游记》、中国古典诗歌以及其他各类文学作品；范伦克・图凯翻译了三卷《中国古代哲学》，以及包括戏剧、诗歌等体裁在内的经典作品；高恩德翻译了鲁迅和老舍的作品；米白翻译了老舍、郭沫若及曹禺的作品；姑兰・埃娃翻译了《元曲》、莫言的《酒国》以及多部现当代中短篇小说；鲍洛尼・彼得翻译了《儒林外史》、《老残游记》以及余华和王蒙的作品；尤山度翻译了溥仪、艾芜等人的作品；艾之迪翻译了《三国演义》的前六回。以上翻译家对中国文学及哲学著作进行了绝佳的阐述，为中国文学及中国文化在匈牙利的普及做出了重要贡献。

20 世纪 80 年代尚且有一些中国古典文学作品及当代作家（王蒙、余华、谌容等人）的作品在匈牙利国内出版，但从 90 年代开始，“纯中国文学”、特别是现当代中国文学的译介渐趋衰微，主要原因在于，在各大出版社的编辑中，已经找不到像范伦克・图凯或姑兰・埃娃这样既能准确把握中国文学趋势，又有丰富翻译经验的汉学家。

2008年，中国作为“荣誉嘉宾”参加第十五届千禧年图书节，中国各大出版社纷纷推出“中国丛书”，这对中国文学作品的译介产生了一定的促进作用，许多中国文学作品、艺术作品以及教育类书籍得以出版，比如鲁迅的杂文、高行健的《灵山》、姜戎的《狼图腾》、吴帆的《二月花》等。我本人翻译了《狼图腾》和《二月花》两部作品，姑兰·埃娃则编写了一套20世纪中国短篇小说集。

莫言于2012年获诺贝尔文学奖后，中国当代文学在匈牙利得到了进一步的认可，各大媒体均对莫言的作品、生活以及中国当代文学及文学翻译产生了浓厚的兴趣，这一期间，我本人也参与了几次访谈节目。几个月后，文学月刊《世界》（Nagyvilág）刊载了莫言的几部短篇小说（2012年12月—2013年2月），科苏斯出版集团（匈牙利国内历史最悠久、规模最大的纯文学出版机构）旗下的诺兰—利布罗出版社买下了《酒国》（2013）及《蛙》（2014）两部作品的版权，分别由姑兰·埃娃和我本人担任译者。在此，我真诚希望能有机会继续出版莫言的全部作品。

目前，中国作家及作品占据了部分匈牙利图书市场，尽管数量有限，但都是著名出版社（欧罗巴、麦格维托、诺兰-利布罗、莱布理）推出的精品，比如刘慈欣和麦家的畅销作品等，最近几年还引进了青年作家颜歌的小说。我本人翻译了颜歌的《我们家》，除这部作品以外，几乎其他所有作品都是从中介语翻译而成。几个月前，吉狄马加的诗集出版上市，我的最近一部译著——刘震云的《我不是潘金莲》将在最近几天出版。目前，各大出版社正与中方出版社洽谈，准备继续推出一系列中国当代文学作品。尽管文学作品不像文化产品或艺术产品一样容易“消化”（既不似中国武术一般“壮观”，也不像音乐或视觉艺术那样易于理解），但中国文学的普及和推广却依然展现出良好的势头，对此，我是有切身体会的。不论是在近期还是在将来，匈牙利将继续引进丰富多彩的当代中国文学精品，对于这一点，我有绝对的信心。

目前，我担任匈—中友好协会会长一职。匈—中友好协会成立于1959年，是匈牙利国内最早的非营利性、非政府组织，致力于推动两国友好关系，1988年，在塔洛什·鲍尔瑙担任会长期间，协会进行了重组。塔洛什是匈牙利著名科学家，至今仍担任友好协会的名誉主席一职。协会的成员及支持者大多为专家学者、科学家、外交官、媒体人士、艺术家、中国侨民以及始终关注着中国的重要人士。

匈—中友好协会属于民间组织，并不隶属于任何政治党派或国家机构，运作资金来自于成员缴纳的会费和各界人士的捐赠，协会的宗旨为：促进匈中两国历史、文化、文明以及现代化成就的普及。为此，我们定期举办友好交流会，组织开展互访活动，承办或协办文化活动（艺术展、音乐会等），出版书籍、举办新书发布会，参与并协办学术交流会以及科学研讨会，推广与中国有关的各类文化活动。

作为匈—中友好协会的会长和一名文学翻译者，我有幸承担了多场文学活动的组织与安排工作，在此仅列举影响最大的几次活动：2016年5月，“第一届中国—中东欧文学论坛”在巴拉顿菲赖德和布达佩斯召开；《山东汉代石雕作品集》与吉狄马加诗集的图书发布会在塞切尼国家图书馆举行，发起这次活动的，是匈牙利人民的好朋友余泽民。余先生是著名作家、文学翻译家，目前生活在布达佩斯，曾获得匈牙利政府颁发的匈牙利文化贡献奖。此类文化活动得到了匈牙利民众的高度重视。

继2014年出版《中—匈友好65年》之后，本协会即将推出《美丽的拱桥：中国人眼中的匈牙利》，两部作品均得到中国驻匈牙利大使馆的赞助与支持。《中—匈友好65年》一书中收集了11位匈牙利作家——包括一些著名汉学家和外交官关于中国的回忆和撰写的散文。《美丽的拱桥》一书中收录了23篇文章，这些文章大多出自中国大使、外交官、学者、记者、艺术家之手，从中国人的视角描述匈牙利。这些作者均在匈牙利度过了或长或短的一段时间，为两国的文化交流做出了巨大贡献。两本书均以双语（匈牙利语和汉语）写成，其中收录了每位作者的传记。

每逢与中国作家、出版社或是文学代表见面时，不论是官方会见还是私下会面，我都感到无比欣慰。我曾在布达佩斯见过余华、马原、龙冬等，见过前来匈牙利参加“布达佩斯国际文化艺术节”的颜歌，见过中国作家协会的吴义勤（文学批评家）、熊育群、张楚、刘文艳、吴欣蔚，这些作家都是“第一届中国—中东欧文学论坛”的官方代表；此外还有著名文艺期刊《十月》的主编陈东捷、编辑室主任赵雪芹，以及多名中国出版社（中国出版集团、凤凰出版传媒、译林出版社、山东出版集团）的代表。令我欣慰的是，我本人也能为中国文学新作品的出版、普及以及为两国的进一步合作，做出一份或多或少的贡献。我坚信，匈牙利将会完成越来越多的中国文学项目，越来越多的中国文学精品会得到译介，越来越多的匈牙利人会通过文学翻译来了解中国。

Books, Writers, Translators – One Possible Way of Building the New Silk Road

Klára Zombory / Hungary

Literary Translator, President of the Hungarian-Chinese Friendship Association, Member of the Hungarian Literary Translators' Association

> "Do not believe that he who escapes into (the world of) books is a fugitive from life. Rather, he might try to stretch the boundaries of his life:he is hungry for more life than he has been allotted by the age and his destiny."
>
> Mihály Babits[1]

I start my presentation with a quotation with the thought of a famous Hungarian poet, writer and literary translator, who lived in the turn of the 19th and 20th century, and who was one of the most prominent members of the "first generation" of the so called *Nyugat (East)* literary periodical, which promoted literary translation that time. I choose this quotation as a motto of my presentation, since it demonstrates the writer's opinion – which does not differ from that of mine –, that books do not "expel", on the contrary, they "extend" the world, moreover they

1 Mihály Babits (1883, Szekszárd – 1941, Budapest) writer, poet, literary historian, literary translator.

provide opportunity to live “more life”, i.e. they help the reader to get acquainted with different people, lands and ages; to imagine himself/herself in someone else's shoes, to understand other peoples' thoughts and feel their feelings. A translated book often gives a glance into far-away cultures, which without the opportunity of personal and on-the-spot experience might be unrevealed and unreachable forever to the majority of the people.

The precondition of a nation's “healthy” development is letting other cultures' influence in without having its own cultural values to be subordinated, or moreover, to be “wilted” by the influences coming from outside. In today's globalized world there are more and more interactions with other nations, we have almost daily connection with distant people, so the importance and the role of literary translation is growing day by day. Translations do not only make us possible to understand different cultures, but they also make us understand that we are the members of a “greater community”. And to become familiar with this “greater community” the economic indicators and the short online or offline press releases are far not enough, the thorough knowledge of each other's culture, thoughts, philosophy and literature etc. is also indispensable, which of course would be unattainable without literary translations. Literary translations do not mix and merge different cultures into one another, but help to understand the similarities and the differences.

Books, writers, translators – One possible way of building the New Silk Road is the title of my presentation, since I firmly believe, that books, including belles-lettres' translations as well, are basic fundaments and “building blocks” of the so called New Silk Road which connects China with several important destinations around the world. Language is the most important way of expressing thoughts, ideas, feelings etc., so books are one of the most important “devices” to get acquainted with each other. And of course besides these “building blocks”, the writers, and the translators, who have the “intermediary function” also play a very important role in this “construction”.

I came from Hungary, a small CEE country, which in spite of the differences in size (population, area etc.) – the population of Hungary is that of a bigger Chinese city, not even 10 million people – traditionally foster very good relationship with China, and nowadays the diplomatic, economic and cultural ties are tighter than ever. Hungary started the recognition of China quite early, and contributed several internationally acknowledged sinologists and China-explorers to the world. I feel it important to mention and emphasize this fact, since the highly developed Hungarian Sinology is rooted in the long history of the connection between the two countries, and that is why Hungary can also take a very active part in the globalization of the Chinese culture. Though we are talking about two very different countries, the cultural roots and the languages are also fundamentally different. As for the language we hardly find any similarities: while Chinese is using characters, has a logographic writing system, and is an isolating and concise-wording language, with several associations' layer in meaning; Hungarian is using the extended version of the Latin alphabet (extra letters: á, é, í, ó, ö, ő, ú, ü, ű), is an agglutinating language and fairly "verbose"-wording, moreover rather concrete in meaning. Between two such distant cultures and languages there are only a few common "benchmarks", the "handholds" and the similar associations are almost totally missing. To build an intellectual or intercultural "bridge" or "road" between cultures separated by continents not easy at all, but a very noble task. Or rather a profession? Or vocation? Whatever it is called… this is exactly what a literary translator needs to do.

Hungarian people have relative openness to Eastern, especially Chinese thinking and culture, and the interest towards the "East" is living its renaissance in these days. Of course there are several reasons contribute to this fact, but I would like to emphasize only 3 of them: 1. Very huge, one of the biggest Chinese colonies of the CEE region is living in Hungary, so the average Hungarian has daily contact and connection with Chinese people. Hungary has quite a few special institutions (such as the Chinese-Hungarian Bilingual Primary & Secondary School, a special

Confucius Institute dedicated the Traditional Chinese Medicine (TCM) at the city of Pécs, the Dharma Gate Buddhist College etc.), a few big multinational Chinese companies (such as Huawei, Wanhua at the city of Miskolc etc.) also established headquarters in Hungary, the Bank of China also opened its first branch in the CEE region and so on; several NGOs – such as the Hungarian-Chinese Friendship Association – are promoting the Chinese-Hungarian cultural exchanges. 2. Due to the supposed Eastern roots of the Hungarian nation, orientalism has been a very important discipline for centuries. 3. The diplomatic relations between the two countries are very active – there were several high-level, even premier-level, mutual visits in the near past, e.g. Vice Premier Liu Yandong visited Hungary only a few weeks ago, and on the meetings and negotiations cultural issues often play very important role, thus the so called "Belt and Road" Initiative of China and the "Opening to the East" policy of my country hint not only commercial, political and economic, but also cultural and educational interactions and exchanges. I would mention only a few cultural co-operations without completeness to demonstrate this: the Hungarian Cultural Institute in Beijing was established /2013/; new Hungarian faculties (e.g. in Sichuan International Studies University in Chongqing etc.) and Hungarian Studies Research Centers were established throughout China; the China-CEE Institute at the Hungarian Academy of Sciences /2017/ and the Central and Eastern European Regional Center of Confucius Institutes /2014/ were opened in Budapest; conferences are organized (25th Annual Meeting of the International Association of Chinese Linguistics /2017/, 1st China-CEE Literary Forum /2016/ etc.); more and more Hungarian scholarship students study in China and vice versa; several huge art exhibitions (*Qi Baishi*, *Treasures of Ancient China*, *From the East*… in Budapest, and *Sissi & Hungary* in Shanghai etc.), movie and other art festivals were organized; theater, opera and music performances could be seen in both countries; different genres' of books are published in both countries, and Hungary among the other CEE countries was one of the guests of honor of the Beijing International Book Fair in 2016, etc.

I. Overview of the Hungarian-Chinese Relations

China and Hungary built up diplomatic relation in 4th October 1949, almost seventy years ago, but the first intercourse between the two countries had started much earlier.

It is proved that as early as in the 14th century a few Hungarian missionaries reached China, but in the following decades since the Turkish (Ottoman) Empire controlled all the routes to the Far East, the connection had broken for a long time, up till the 17th century, when again several Hungarian missionaries arrived to the Middle Kingdom. In the 18th-19th century quite a few adventurers and scientists visited China, just to mention the most acknowledged ones: Sándor Kőrösi Csoma or Sándor Csoma de Kőrös (1784-1842), linguist and librarian, who in the 1820's spent a long time in different Tibetan monasteries, and although he could not find the traces of the Hungarians' roots, with his Tibetan-English dictionary and grammar book, along with other scientific works he became the worldwide respected "founder" of Tibetology; Earl Béla Széchenyi (1837-1908), the son of the "greatest Hungarian", István Széchenyi, with his expedition between 1877-81 visited several parts of China; Lajos Lóczy (1849-1920), the world-renowned geologist and geographer, member of the Széchenyi expedition; Earl Jenő Zichy (1837-1906), who arrived to Beijing in 1898 through the continent; Aurél Stein (1862–1943), the British nationality archeologist and explorer with Hungarian origin, who went to Dunhuang in 1907, and whose activity in the Thousand Buddha Caves is rather condemned by the Chinese – only to mention the most famous ones.

To discuss in details the relation between China and the Austro-Hungarian Monarchy, and the relation of the two countries between and under the two World Wars would require a separate paper, it was explored and published by my professor Sándor Józsa (尤山度), so I would only speak about the "reconnection" of the two countries in the 20th century that is considered to be the milestone regarding to the establishment of Hungarian Sinology. Hungary was among the first countries that only after a few days of the declaration of the People's Republic of China already established diplomatic relation with the New China. It was not only the starting point of political and economic cooperation between the two countries, but it also contributed to cultural, educational and scientific exchanges.

II. The First Group of the Hungarian Scholarship Students to China: the Revival of the Hungarian Sinology

The first group of the Hungarian scholarship students arrived to Beijing in 1950, and between 1950 and 1966 almost thirty Hungarian students studied in China, such as Endre Galla (高恩德) literary historian, an excellent researcher and translator of Lu Xun, and he also explored the traces of the Hungarian literature in China; Vilma Mészáros (梅维佳) literary historian; Sándor Józsa (尤山度), the already mentioned historian, whose research field is the modern and contemporary history of China; Pál Miklós (米白) art historian, literary translator, who published several studies on Chinese art and cultural history, one of his major works is about the Dunhuang Thousand Buddha Caves; Barna Tálas (戴 伯 纳), economist and researcher of political science, member of the Hungarian Academy of Sciences; Péter Polonyi (鲍洛尼 · 彼得) renowned literary translator, also a researcher of political science; Éva Kalmár (姑兰 · 埃娃) renowned literary translator, editor of one of the most prestigious Hungarian publishing houses, Európa Publishing, for over 15 years; Ottó Juhász (叶桐) literary historian, former Ambassador of Hungary in China; and among the later generations: Mária Ferenczy (范凌思) art and cultural historian etc. Although the Far Eastern Department was established much earlier, but basically they were the ones, along with a few philologists, philosophers and literary translators (Ferenc Tőkei (杜 克 义), Barnabás Csongor (陈 国), Ildikó Ecsedy (艾之迪) who established Sinology in Hungary. They have translated several classical and modern Chinese literary and philosophical works into Hungarian with the greatest competence, wild range of knowledge and stylistic sense. They also published articles on different fields of Sinology. The Faculty of Chinese at the Eötvös Loránd University (ELTE) became the educational center of the following sinologist generations and the base of the Chinese-Hungarian literary translation.

I am more than grateful to them for the in-depth knowledge and approach towards Sinology they have transferred to us, and also for the great support and altruistic help at the beginning – and even in these days – of my professional career.

III. Overview of the Literary Translation from Chinese

1. A brief retrospection

In Hungary between the two World Wars there were already a few Chinese literary works translated into Hungarian for example in 1931 (it has several reprints) an anthology of Chinese and Japanese poems translated by Dezső Kosztolányi, poet and excellent literary translator – although he translated from intermediate languages, but since he did excellent interpretations of the original poems, these literary pieces had great influence in Hungary – and another collection of classical Chinese poetry in 1937, the *100 Chinese poems* translated from original Chinese by Lajos Ágner.

The beginning of the literary translation from original Chinese language in larger amount started in the 50's as a result of the work of the scholarship students mentioned before, and the students and professors of Eötvös Loránd University. Between the 50's–70's Qu Yuan, Du Fu, Bai Juyi, Li Bai poems, *The Book of Songs, The Music Palace* – translated by sinologists in cooperation with the best poets of the time, such as Lőrinc Szabó, Sándor Weöres, Gyula Illyés, István Vas, László Nagy, Pu Songling, *Water Margin, Flower in the See of Sin, The Travels of Lao Can, The Scholars, Journey to the West* etc.; and in the 80's Lu Xun, Guo Moruo, Mao Dun, Ba Jin, Lao She, Pu Yi etc., quite a great amount of Chinese works were published in Hungary. In those times the "great Chinese classics" such as the *Tang-poets' anthologies* (Li Bai, Bai Juyi, Du Fu), the famous romances (*Dream of the Red Chamber* /translated from German/, *Water Margin, Jin Ping Mei* /translated from German/, *Pilgrim to the West*) or the *Dao De Jing* and *Lun Yu* could be found in almost every Hungarian intellectual family's bookshelf. Several great Chinese classics were reprinted in those decades.

The length and time limits of this presentation and also the topic do not allow me to talk about the renowned Hungarian sinologists and their literary translations in detail, but I would like to mention them at least by name along with the most important writer(s) or literary work(s) they have translated into Hungarian: Barnabás Csongor (*Water Margin, Journey to the West*, classical Chinese poems and other genres), Ferenc Tőkei (Chinese philosophical texts in three volumes *Chinese Philosophy: Antiquity, Vol. 1-3.*, and several other genres – drama, poetry etc. – classical Chinese texts), Endre Galla (*Lu Xun, Lao She*), Pál Miklós (*Lao She, Guo Moruo, Cao Yu*), Éva Kalmár (Yuan-dramas, Mo Yan's *The Republic of Wine* and other modern and contemporary writer's short stories and novellas), Péter Polonyi (*The Scholars, The Travels of Lao Can,* Gu Hua, Wang Meng), Sándor Józsa (Pu Yi, Ai Wu) and Ildikó Ecsedy (*Romance of the Three Kingdoms,* 1-6. chapters) etc. They all have done excellent interpretations of the Chinese literary and philosophical works, and did a great contribution to the popularization of classical and modern Chinese literature and culture in Hungary.

2. Present

Even in the 80's, several classical and contemporary (Wang Meng, Gu Hua, Shen Rong etc.) literary works were published, but from the 90's less and less "pure Chinese literature", especially modern and contemporary writings emerged in Hungary, so the situation was worse than that of in the 50's-80's. Only one factor is that there is not a single sinologist among the editors of the renowned publishing houses, like earlier Ferenc Tőkei or Éva Kalmár, who were not only well-informed about the trends and works of Chinese literature, but also initiated several Chinese novels, dramas and other genres' publication.

The 15th Jubilee Book Festival in 2008 – where China was the "guest of honor" has effected a kind of "breakthrough" in comparison with the previous decade, since almost all the important publishers came out with their own "China-book", thus several Chinese literary, art educational and other China related books were published for the event, such as Lu Xun essays, *Soul Mountain*, *Wolf Totem*, *February Flowers* by Fan Wu – the latest two are my translation – and a 20th

century Chinese short story collection edited by Éva Kalmár, only to mention the most important ones.

The Nobel-prize of Mo Yan in 2012, of course, has given another impulse to the process of the recognition of Chinese contemporary literature in Hungary, the media was interested in his works, life, Chinese contemporary literature and literary translation in general, so I was invited to several interviews at that time. A few months later a few of his short stories were published in a literary periodical *Worldiwide* [Nagyvilág, 2012/12 and 2013/02] and a prestigious publisher, Noran Libro Publishing – part of one of the biggest and oldest publishing groups (Kossuth Publishing) specializing in best-sellers, has bought the copyright two of Mo Yan's novels, the *Republic of Wine* (2013) and *Frogs* (2014), the earlier is translated by Éva Kalmár, and the later one by myself. Hopefully there will be continuation in the publication of his oeuvre.

Chinese books and writers are present at the Hungarian book market, and although not in a great number, but they are published by very renowned Publishing Houses (Európa, Magvető, Noran Libro, Libri etc.), for example Liu Cixin's and Mai Jia's bestsellers, and Yan Ge's novel appeared in the past few years – although except Yan Ge's *My Family* which is my translation, all of them were translated from intermediate language. Jidi Majia's poetry collection was published a few months ago, my latest translation, Liu Zhenyun's *I am not Pan Jinlian* is about to be published in these days, and negotiations with different publishers about some contemporary Chinese writings are under process – so the promotion and popularization of Chinese literature, even if not as rapidly as other cultural and art "products" that are easier to "consume" (without doubt literature not as "spectacular" as martial arts, and not understandable without words as music or visual arts), shows very positive trends, what I also feel on my own "skin". I am absolutely confident about that this positive tendency – about the introduction of the multicolor, interesting and high-quality contemporary Chinese literature – will continue in the near and far future as well.

IV. Hungarian-Chinese Friendship Association

Currently I hold the post as the chair of the Hungarian-Chinese Friendship Association, which is the oldest non-profit and non-governmental organization in Hungary fostering friendly relationship between the two countries. It was founded in 1959, and reorganized in 1988 under the chairmanship of Barna Tálas – a renowned scientist also mentioned before –, he is the honorary chairman of the Association up to the present. The members and the supporters of the Association are experts, scientists, diplomats, journalists, artists and other personages interested in China, along with Chinese residents. Hungarian-Chinese Friendship Association is a civil initiative, it does not belong to any political parties or state organizations, it receives only membership fees and occasional voluntary contributions from the supporting members and donators. The main objectives of the Association: popularize the history, the culture, the civilization and modernization results of China to the Hungarian people, and vice versa. To attain our objectives we arrange friendly meetings, initiate and organize mutual visits; serve as main- or co-organizer of cultural activities (exhibitions, concerts etc.); publish books and arrange book launches; attend and co-organize professional meetings and scientific conferences; popularize different cultural activities in connection with China.

As the chairman of the Hungarian-Chinese Association, and also as a literary translator I am very proud to take part in the organization of several literary events from which the most important ones are: the 1st China-CEE Literary Forum held in Balatonfüred and Budapest in 2016 May; the book launches of the Hungarian publication of the *Collection of the Shandong Han Dynasty Stone Reliefs* and the poetry collection of Jidi Majia, both of them took place at the National Széchényi Library, initiated by my very good friend, Yu Zemin, who himself is a writer and one of the best, Pro Cultura Hungarica laureate, literary translators resided in Hungary, and on the invitation of the Hungarian-Chinese Association and others these events attracted a big audience.

Now we are compiling a book (*Beautiful arched bridges – Remembrance of*

Chinese Personalities to Hungary) which is the continuation of a former book of our Association (*Beijing Hungarian Rhapsody – Memories from the 65 years of the Hungarian-Chinese Relations*) published in 2014, both with the support of the Embassy of the People's Republic of China in Hungary. The former book collected stories, memories and essays about China from 11 Hungarian authors, including famous sinologists, diplomats etc., and this one, which is to be published this year – so now we are in the middle of the finalization process – will consist of 23 writings about Hungary from Chinese personalities (ambassadors, diplomats, professors, correspondences, artists etc.) who had spent longer or shorter period of time in Hungary, and who have contributed to a great extent to the cultural relationship between China & Hungary. Both books are bilingual (Hungarian & Chinese) and besides the essays they include biographical notes about the authors.

I take all opportunity to receive and meet with Chinese writers in Hungary, either officially or privately, since it always makes me very glad and enthusiastic when Chinese writers, publishers or other literary delegations come to visit my country. I could meet in Budapest with Yu Hua, Ma Yuan, Long Dong and Zhao Lanzhen (*October* literary periodical); with Yan Ge, who arrived to Hungary to the "Budapest Transfer International Festival"; Wu Yiqin (critic),Xiong Yuqun, Zhang Chu,Liu Wenyan and Wu Xinwei (CWA),who were the members of the official delegation to the "1st CEE Countries–China Literary Forum"; Chen Dongjie and Zhao Xueqin also from the famous *October* literary periodical, and several Chinese publishers' (China Publishing Group, Phoenix Publishing & Media Group, Yilin Press, Shandong Publishing Group etc.) delegations. It makes me happy if greater or smaller extent I can contribute to a new publication, to further cooperation or to the popularization of Chinese literature. I firmly believe that more and more Chinese literary projects will be fulfilled in Hungary, more and more excellent books will be translated, and more and more Hungarian people will be familiar with China through literary translations.

“一带一路”的文化启示：重新发现“蓝色”中国

方李莉 【中国】
中国艺术研究院艺术人类学研究所所长、博士生导师

“一带一路”倡议，让我们重新审视古代丝绸之路上的中国贸易，重新审视中国古代物质文化的世界流向。在这一研究的过程中，我们感觉到中国古代的文明就像是冰山，浮在水面上的部分是黄色部分，而蓝色部分即走向世界的商贸文明一直被遮蔽在水面之下的冰山中，我们虽视而不见，但其不仅存在，还非常巨大，因此，当我们重新关注和研究这一部分，就会看到一个以往被我们忽略掉了的，由物质文化构成的中国的另一方面。

以上提到的“黄色”是代表农耕文明，而“蓝色”则代表的是面向大海的商贸文明。在大家的常识中，常常以黄色代表中华文明，以蓝色代表欧洲文明，前者是以农耕取胜，后者是以海上商贸取胜。但实际上任何文明都不是绝对的，尤其是像中国这样一个巨大的文明体，她的构成是复杂多样的，绝不是单一的。在中国，黄色代表黄河、长城、农业优先、大陆至上、命令式经济体制、儒家文官制度。蓝色则意谓长江下游、市场经济、自给自足、文化互动、长距离贸易、迎向海洋。在中国的历史上这两种文明一直在博弈，前者是政府主导，自然常占上风；后者是以民间主导为主，当然常被遮蔽。

有关这一问题的讨论，让我们不仅看到了中国在陆上丝绸之路的贡献，还看到了中国在海上丝绸之路的贡献，同时，还看到了在人类早期全球化过程中，中华文明所起的作用和所作出的巨大贡献，对今天“一带一路”倡议的实施是有巨

大意义的。

从20个世纪80年代开始，“全球化”这个名词就越来越频繁地出现于各种媒体和学者们的文章中，大家似乎有一个共识，人类社会走向全球互动是从15世纪欧洲地理大发现开始的，但事实上，在欧洲地理大发现之前，人类社会就开始了全球化的进程。正如美国学者罗伯特·芬雷所认为的那样：“人类物质文化首度步向全球化，是在中国的主导下展开。”我们翻开历史就可以看到，人类社会最早的远距离贸易在中国汉代就开始了，那时中国的丝绸就通过陆路的丝绸之路运送到了古罗马。但真正的，具有更加广袤的世界性贸易网络，是内河的运输和海上远洋的运输发达以后才可能构成。因为水运比陆运更快速，量更大，也更安全。

人类远距离的大规模的海上物质交流很早就已经开始，但在6、7世纪这样的贸易的加速，这是因为在那个时期，欧亚非大陆诸文明之间的格局因两个重大事件的出现而改变。第一个大事件：中国的黄河、长江以及这两大河流的支系，通过人工建造的大运河得以沟通，开辟了一条贯通全国的，既便宜又安全的水上通道，这一系列从春秋至隋朝开凿的人工河流，至隋唐时期得以修建完成。正如亚当·斯密所言：“各行各业可及的市场，因水运而扩大，此为陆运所不及。所以唯有在滨海地区以及可航行内河的沿岸，各类工业才会开始进行分工与改良。”水运交通促进了中国商业的发达，同时也促进了中国手工生产的进步，使其逐步成为当时的“世界手工业工场”。

如果说，隋唐时期中国大运河的出现是当时世界上的一个大事件，那么，与此同时出现的一个广泛的伊斯兰教的世界则是第二个大事件。7世纪时期，阿拉伯人征服波斯，此时伊斯兰势力在阿拉伯世界建立根基。接下来阿拉伯穆斯林征服了伊拉克、美索不达米亚、埃及等国家，造成从西亚到北非全面统一在伊斯兰旗下。这样的统一体使这个地区变得日益强大，并以此为力量渗透到周边国家，从而形成了一个巨大的消费市场。两大文明的崛起形成了远距离财富交流的需求。

当时的中国由于大运河的开通，促使当时各地生产的手工艺品得以运销到沿海港口，然后从东海、南海进入印度洋，继而到达旧大陆各个国家，在当时主要是伊斯兰和佛教国家。如唐代出口白瓷、三彩制品和青花瓷的重要窑口——巩县窑，其位置正处于洛水与黄河交汇的洛汭地带，这里曾是沟通北方大半个中国的漕运枢纽。这里溯洛水进入黄河东去，可抵郑州、开封，转入大运河，向北直通华北大平原，由天津到朝鲜、日本；向南直达当时重要港埠、国内国际商贸城市扬州；再顺长江东去，可直航海外至东亚、南亚与中东地区。还有当时的长沙窑生产的釉下彩瓷器远销亚非不同的国家，其地理位置处于湘江附近，其产品从湘江到洞庭湖，然后达长江口转入海外。当时著名的瓷器产地越窑，属于明州地区，也是当时的重要港口，可以直通海外。正是这种便利的水运交通，让中国的瓷器通过国内的人工及河流运输到达沿海港口，经内海再穿过马六甲进入印度洋走向欧亚非大陆。

8 世纪起，西亚船舶开始来到广州，大批阿拉伯人和波斯人在此定居。有各种外国货轮，每年均驶来广州与中国进行贸易。船高数丈，置梯以便上落，堆积宝货如山。每有蕃舶到港时，郡邑为之喧阗。可见当时的贸易，一方面是中国的商人内陆航运广州，另一方面是西亚等地的商人再将这些货物运往世界各地，形成的一种循环的流动，在旧大陆的亚非欧之间形成了一个复杂的商业网络，而这一商业网络的形成是在中华文明和伊斯兰文明的主导下形成的。

到南宋女真建立的金国征服北中国，结束了宋王朝的第一阶段。接下来金国又击败契丹辽国，几乎切断了宋朝与中亚的所有接触，从 1126 年至 1279 年蒙古灭宋为止，宋朝君主只能从长江之南、位于浙江杭州的临时国都，治理他们残存的帝国疆域，统治面积仅为原有中土的三分之二。北方强权横亘阻绝，丝路不再可及，南宋毅然转身，迎向海洋。1087 年，继广州、杭州和明州以后，朝廷在泉州建立了第 4 个市舶司，从此泉州成为对外交流的中心。当时的中国承运商充分利用穆斯林商人的知识，开始加入海上贸易的队伍，最有代表性的有广东商人、浙江商人、福建商人。其中以福建商人的声誉最高，队伍最壮大。南宋时，皇家册封福建商人信仰的妈祖为天妃娘娘，让其成为所有海上运输商人们的保护神，一方面是代表了对福建商人业绩的肯定，另一方面也说明当时海上贸易的繁荣与商人队伍的壮大。

宋代经济繁荣，城市化得到加速，首都开封城市人口达到 100 余万，通过宋代画家张泽端画的“清明上河图”，让我们看到了当时开封的繁荣，同时画面中段主要描绘汴河上的虹桥码头区，那是属于名为“通济渠”的大运河，也说明大运河开通以后极大地促进了宋代中国的经济发展。“海洋与文明”的作者林肯·佩恩在文章中写道：“在宋代，估计有 600 万中国人居住在城市里，大约占当时全世界城市人口的一半。”城市的发展是商品经济发展的重要动力，一方面是繁荣的城市生活需要有更丰富的商品来满足日益增长的人口和日益富裕的生活。另一方面，城市的发展更利于手工业的生产，这些产品也需要有对应的城市来进行财富的交换。亚当·斯密曾认为宋代的中国由于手工业产量的增加，人口的增长，技术的孵化繁殖和各种发明创新的爆炸式涌现，使宋代的中国比以往任何时期——或者比同时代世界的任何地区——都更为繁荣富庶。正是因为这样的繁荣和富庶促进了当时的海外贸易，也推动中国的手工业生产开始向沿海一带转移。以陶瓷业为例，当时江西的景德镇窑、江苏的宜兴窑、福建的德化窑、广东的潮州窑等等开始兴盛。

到元代，不仅是水路交通，就是陆路交通也开始繁盛起来。但海路还是更安全快捷，所以元代大量的商业贸易还是沿着唐宋时期的海道在进行。近年有关元时期的沉船遗址不断被发现，北礁一号沉船遗物点、北礁三号沉船遗物点、大练一号沉船遗物点等，还有在朝鲜半岛发现的元新安沉船，都发现了大量当时运往海外的中国货物，包括瓷器、金属制品、石制品、木制品等。

我最近看到一本伊朗学者写的“丝绸之路”的著作，里面写道，在19世纪欧洲工业产品席卷全球之前，中国的物质产品一直是世界最优良的商品，当时在海上和陆上的丝绸之路中，商人们贩运的不仅是中国的丝绸、茶叶、瓷器，还有铁器、铜器、漆器等，其中包括铜镜、铁锅、火钳都从中国购买过来。当时中国的物质文化影响了整个的旧大陆。即使到15世纪以后，欧洲的商人也主要是以中国的物质产品的贩运为主，而且自那以后中国的物质产品才真正被全球化了，不仅深入到欧洲市场，更被欧洲人运送到美洲和大洋洲市场。因此，美国学者罗伯特·芬雷认为，从汉代一直到19世纪初，中国都是世界经济的引擎。

通过研究，我们越来越多地看到了中国在历史上的海上贸易网络中的重要价值，因此，中国不仅是一个黄色的中国，也是一个蓝色的中国。有人会说，海上丝绸之路的贸易，不是由中国商人所主导的，所以和中国的关系不大。但大家不能否认的有两点：第一，阿拉伯、波斯和欧洲商人们与中国人做生意，只是在沿海城市，而贸易的产品却遍及中国，是谁将这些产品运送到港口的，当然是中国商人。第二点，在海外贸易的过程中大量是外国商人，但也不能否定有中国商人的参与，近年在中国的海域发现的一些中国宋代沉船，还有在韩国、在印尼、在波斯湾等地发现的沉船，不少被证明是中国的船只。在明代以前，中国的政府是不禁止中国的商人出海的，即使在明代以后，政府命令禁止中国商人出海，但有不少的走私船仍然在冒险经商。现在我们看到的生活在东南亚一带的华人，其中许多人就是当年的中国商人被滞留在那些地方的后代子孙。

最近，我看到一份资料显示，即使到了19世纪中期，欧洲商人一霸天下，在机器轮船逐步取代中国木帆船的情况下，中国还有不少的帆船往来于中国和新加坡。

有一点可以肯定：长期以来中国都处于某种可称为“黄色中国”对“蓝色中国”的紧张关系之中，尤其是明代以后的精英阶级坚持大陆观点，使中国曾经有过的，经由海上贸易及物质文化对世界产生过巨大影响的辉煌被严严实实地遮蔽了。在“一带一路”倡议影响整个世界格局变化的今天，我们需要重新阅读这一历史，读懂这一历史有助于我们理解中国文化的实质，这一实质就是中华文明的内涵是极其丰富的，不能仅以农业文明一而概之，里面还包括了商贸文明、手工业文明等，其中还有很丰厚的物质文化领域的研究是我们以前关注得还不够的地方。尤其是中华文明在历史上是以何种方式与远距离的一些文明世界互动和互相影响，以形成了当今中国文化的种种特色等，这一方面的研究都是需要进一步挖掘的。所谓的文化自信首先要建立在对自己历史文化充分了解的基础上。

另外，“一带一路”倡议不仅要让我们关注今天中国的发展，还需要我们去关注今天中国的发展和中国历史的关系是什么。任何文化的发展都是有基础的，我们只有对我们的基础部分越了解，我们才能对我们今天的发展有更深刻的思考。

Cultural Revelation of the "Belt and Road" Initiative: Rediscovering "Blue" China

Fang Lili / China

Director and Doctoral Advisor of the Art Anthropology Research Center at the Chinese National Academy of Arts

The "Belt and Road" Initiative allows us to review China's trade along the ancient Silk Road, and the flow of the ancient Chinese material culture throughout the world. In the course of study, we feel that the ancient Chinese civilization is like an iceberg, with a yellow part floating on the surface of the water. However, the blue part, which represents the civilization of the business trade to the world, has always been hidden in the iceberg under the ocean. We often ignore it, but as a matter of fact, it not only exists but also is very large in size. Therefore, when we refocus and study this part, we will see another aspect of China that has been overlooked and is made up of material culture.

The foregoing "yellow" represents the farming culture, while the "blue" represents the sea-oriented trading culture. Common sense suggests that the Chinese civilization is often represented by yellow and the European civilization by blue. The former is based on farming and the latter is based on seaborne trade.

In fact, any civilization is not absolute, especially a giant civilization like the Chinese one. Undoubtedly, the Chinese civilization has complex and diversified components rather than a single component. In China, yellow represents the Yellow River, the Great Wall, the priority to agriculture, the supremacy of the mainland, the imperative economic system and the Confucian civil service system, with indifference to the world of the ocean. Blue means the lower reaches of the Yangtze River, a market economy, self-sufficiency, cultural interaction, long-distance trade, and an orientation towards the sea. In the history of China, the two civilizations have always battled with each other. The former is government-oriented, which prevails beyond all questions. By contrast, the latter is non-government-oriented, which is, of course, often cast into the shade.

Discussions on this issue enable us to see the contributions of China on the Land Silk Road, the contributions of China on the Maritime Silk Road, and the roles and great contributions of the Chinese civilization in the early globalization of mankind, which are of great significance to the implementation of the Belt and Road Initiative today.

Since the 1980s, the term "globalization" has appeared in the articles of various media and scholars more and more frequently. Seemingly, there is a consensus that human society started moving towards global interaction at the time of the Great Geographical Discovery of Europe in the 15th century. In fact, human society started the process of globalization before the Great Geographical Discovery of Europe. As Robert Finlay, an American scholar, believes, "The first globalization of human material culture proceeds under the leadership of China." From an overview of history, we can see that the earliest long-distance trade in human society began during the Han Dynasty in China, and at that time, Chinese silk was transported to ancient Rome along the Land Silk Road. However, it would possible to establish a more extensive real worldwide trading network only after the flourishing of inland water transportation and ocean-going transportation. This is because water transportation is faster, more extensive and safer than land transportation.

The long-distance large-scale oceanic material exchanges began very early, but such trade was accelerated during the 6th and 7th centuries. This was because, at that time, the pattern among the European, Asian and African civilizations had changed due to two major events. The first major event: China's Yellow River, the Yangtze River, and the branches of the two major rivers communicated with each other through the artificially constructed Grand Canal, opening up an inexpensive and safe waterway throughout the country. The series of artificial rivers built from the Spring and Autumn Period to the Sui Dynasty were completed during the Sui and Tang Dynasties. As Adam Smith put it: "Every market accessible to all walks of life is extended by water transportation, which has a much larger capacity than land transportation. Therefore, various industries begin the division of labor and improvement only in coastal areas and on the coast of navigable inland rivers." Water transportation has not only promoted the development of China's businesses, but it has also facilitated the progress of China's handcraft production, enabling China to gradually become the "world's handicraft workshop".

If the emergence of the Grand Canal in China during the period of the Sui and Tang Dynasties was a major event in the world at that time, the emergence of the broad Islamic world at the same time was the second major event. In the 7th century, the Arabs conquered and took over Persia, and then, the Islamic forces established a foundation in the Arab world. Afterwards, Arab Muslims conquered Iraq, Mesopotamia, Egypt, and other countries, resulting in the complete unification of Islam from West Asia to North Africa. Such unification made this area increasingly powerful and it further infiltrated the neighboring countries, eventually forming a huge consumer market. The rise of the two major civilizations generated the demand for long-distance exchanges of wealth.

At that time, the opening of the Grand Canal enabled China's handicraft works produced in various regions to be shipped to coastal ports, then from the East China

Sea and the South China Sea to the Indian Ocean, and then to the countries of the Old Mainland, mainly the Islamic and Buddhist countries. For instance, the Gong County Kiln, an important kiln for exporting white porcelains, three-color glazed pottery products and blue and white porcelain during the Tang Dynasty, was located precisely in the Luorui area where Luoshui and the Yellow River flow together. This was once a hub of water transportation across most of northern China. From here, along the Luoshui, it is possible to enter the Yellow River eastward and arrive in Zhengzhou and Kaifeng; in the event of transit through the Grand Canal, it is also possible to reach the Great Plains of Northern China by traveling northward, and eventually on north to North Korea and Japan from Tianjin; if one is traveling southward, it is possible to reach Yangzhou, an important port and commercial city both at home and abroad at that time, and if along the Yangtze River you head eastward, it allows you direct sailing overseas to reach East Asia, South Asia and the Middle East. At that time, the underglaze colour of the porcelain produced by the Changsha Kiln was exported to different countries in Asia and Africa. Located near the Xiangjiang River, the Changsha Kiln had its products shipped from the Xiangjiang River to Dongting Lake, and then along the Yangtze River in order to get access to the overseas markets. At that time, the Yue Kiln, a famous place for the production of porcelain, was located in Mingzhou. Mingzhou was an important port for direct access overseas. Hence, it is the convenient water transportation that allows Chinese porcelain to be shipped to coastal ports through domestic artificial and river transportation, reach the inner sea and then cross Malacca, enter the Indian Ocean and eventually reach Europe, Asia and Africa.

From the 8th century, West Asian ships began to arrive in Guangzhou, where a large number of Arabs and Persians settled. There were various types of foreign freighters that came to Guangzhou every year to trade with China. It was described in this way: "Because the ships are so tall, ladders are set up to make it easy to get on and off the ships. All kinds of treasures are accumulated together, like a mountain. Every time a foreign ship arrives in the port, the county and town are full of hustle and bustle." Therefore, the trade at that time, on the one hand, was the inland water transportation of Chinese merchants, and on the other hand, the transportation of goods by the merchants from West Asia and other places to all of the regions of the world, forming a cyclical flow and a complex business network in Asia, Africa and Europe on the old continent. The business network was established precisely under the leadership of the Chinese civilization and the Islamic civilization.

During the period of the Southern Song Dynasty, the Jin Dynasty established by the Jurchens people conquered Northern China and ended the first stage of the Song Dynasty. Subsequently, the Jin Dynasty defeated the Liao Dynasty established by the Qidan people again and almost cut off all contacts between the Song Empire and Central Asia. From 1126 to 1279, when the Song Dynasty was overthrown by Mongolia, the Chinese monarchs could only govern the remaining territory of the empire from the temporary capital of Hangzhou, located in Zhejiang Province to the south of the Yangtze River. The remaining territory only accounted for two-thirds of the original area of the central zone. The powerful northern dynasty blocked the Silk Road and made it no longer accessible, so that the Southern Song Dynasty resolutely turned to the sea. In 1087, the imperial court established the 4th Bureau for Foreign Shipping in Quanzhou, followed by those in Guangzhou, Hangzhou and Mingzhou. Since then, Quanzhou has become the hub of foreign exchanges. At that time, Chinese carriers took full advantage of the knowledge of Muslim merchants and began to join the ranks of maritime trade. The most representative were the Guangdong merchants, the Zhejiang merchants and the Fujian merchants, among whom the Fujian merchants owned the highest reputation and the largest team. In the Southern Song Dynasty, the royals granted Mazu, a Fujianese God revered by the Fujian merchants, as Celestial Queen to be the patron saint of all merchants involved in maritime transportation. On the one hand, this represented the affirmation of the achievements of Fujian merchants; on the other hand, it illustrated the prosperous maritime trade and the expanding merchants at that time.

Thanks to economic prosperity, urbanization was accelerated in the Song Dynasty. The population of the capital of Kaifeng City reached more than 1 million. The *Riverside Scene at Qingming Festival*, a work by Zhang Zerui (a painter in the Song Dynasty), allowed us to see the prosperity of Kaifeng at that time. At the same time, the middle part of the painting depicted the Hongqiao wharf area of the Bianhe River, which belonged to the Grand Canal named "Tongji Canal"; showing the opening of the Grand Canal greatly promoted the economic development of China during the period of the Song Dynasty. Lincoln Penn, author of *The Sea and Civilization*, wrote in an article, "In the Song Dynasty, an estimated 6 million Chinese people lived in cities, accounting for about half of the world's urban population at that time." The development of cities is an important driving force for the development of a commodity economy. On the one hand, a prosperous urban life requires more abundant goods to satisfy the needs of the growing population and the increasingly affluent life. On the other hand, the development of cities is more conducive to the production of the handicraft industry, and the handicraft products also need corresponding cities to exchange wealth. Adam Smith once believed that in the Song Dynasty of China, the increase in the production of handicrafts, the growth of the population, the incubation and popularization of technologies, and the explosive emergences of various inventions and innovations made China's Song Dynasty more prosperous and thriving than any other period or any other region of the contemporary world. It was precisely the prosperity and thriving that promoted overseas trade at that time and contributed to the shift of handicrafts production in China to the regions along the coast. Take the ceramics industry as an example; the Jingdezhen Kiln in Jiangxi, the Yixing Kiln in Jiangsu, the Dehua Kiln in Fujian, and the Chaozhou Kiln in Guangdong started to flourish.

In the Yuan Dynasty, both waterway traffic and land traffic began to flourish. However, the marine traffic and land traffic were safer and faster, so that a large quantity of commercial trade in the Yuan Dynasty was carried out along the sea lanes of the Tang and Song Dynasties. In recent years, the shipwreck sites of the Yuan Dynasty were discovered one after another, such as the North Reef No.1 shipwreck site, the North Reef No.3 shipwreck site, the Dalian No.1 shipwreck site, and the Yuanxin'an shipwreck found on the Korean Peninsula. A large number of Chinese goods shipped overseas at that time were discovered, including porcelain, metal products, stone products, and wood products.

I recently saw a book *The Silk Road* written by Iranian scholars, stating that before the European industrial products swept across the globe in the 19th century, China's material products had always been the world's finest commodities. On the Land Silk Road and the Maritime Silk Road, merchants sold Chinese silk, tea, and porcelain, ironware, bronze ware, and lacquer ware, including bronze mirrors, iron pots, and tongs. At that time, China's material culture affected the entire Old World. Even after the 15th century, European merchants also mainly transported Chinese material products for sale. Since then, China's material products have truly been globalized, which not only penetrated into the European market, but were also transported by Europeans to the markets in the Americas and Oceania. Therefore, Robert Finley, an American scholar, believed that China was the engine of the world's economy from the Han Dynasty to the early 19th century.

Through research, we are deeply impressed with the important value of China in the history of the network of maritime trade. Therefore, China is not only a yellow China but also a blue China. Some people may say that the trade on the Maritime Silk Road is not dominated by Chinese merchants, so there is little relationship with China. However, there are two undeniable aspects. First, Arabic, Persian and European merchants do business with the Chinese people only in coastal cities, but the products of trade are from all of the regions throughout China. Who transports these products to the port? The answer is, of course, Chinese merchants. Second, a large number of foreign merchants are involved in the process of overseas trade, but the participation of Chinese merchants cannot be denied. In recent years, some of the sunken ships from the period of China's Song Dynasty were found in Chinese waters, and in addition, some sunken ships found in South Korea, the Persian Gulf and other places in Indonesia were proved to be Chinese ships. Before the Ming Dynasty, the Chinese government did not ban Chinese merchants from going to the sea. Even after the Ming Dynasty, the government explicitly banned the Chinese merchants from going to the sea, many smuggling vessels still ventured into business. Now, we can see that a number of ethnic Chinese people live in Southeast Asian regions, many of whom are indeed the descendants of the Chinese merchants who were stranded in these places at that time.

Recently, I saw a document showing that quite a number of Chinese sailing ships were still sailing between China and Singapore, even by the middle of the 19th century when European merchants dominated the world and the mechanical ships were gradually replacing Chinese wooden sailing ships.

However, it is certain that China has long been in a state of tension between the "yellow China" and the "blue China". Especially, since the elites of the Ming dynasty insisted on the mainland viewpoint, the brilliance of maritime trade and material culture exerting tremendous impact on the world has been fully put into the shadows. Nowadays, as the Belt and Road Initiative affects the entire world, we need to review the history again, which will help us understand the essence of Chinese culture. In another word, Chincse civilization has abundant connotations. It not only covers agricultural civilization, but also includes trade civilization and handicraft civilization. There is also a lot of research in the field of material culture that we have not paid enough attention to before. In particular, how Chinese civilization has interacted with and affected distant civilized worlds throughout history to form the characteristics of today's Chinese culture requires further in-depth research and exploration. The so-called cultural confidence must first be based on the full understanding of its own cultural history.

In addition, the Belt and Road Initiative requires us not only to attach importance to the development of China today, but also to pay attention to the relationship between the development of China today and Chinese history. The development of any culture has a foundation. Only by a profound understanding of our foundation can we have more profound thoughts on our development today.

中国方案与全球治理

Chinese Solution and Global Governance

文化与世界秩序

博泰尔·赫林 【丹麦】
哥本哈根大学政治学院欧洲及国际安全问题让·莫内教席教授 / 军事研究中心中国安全研究主任 / 哥本哈根大学中国问题智库 ThinkChina.dk 联合创始人及协调人

一 引言

中国是独特而卓越的。中国代表着文化，代表着历史。中国意味着“天下”，普天之下的中心。中国是崇尚和平、不具有侵略性的。中国，是美德的象征。或许，上述说法中要加上“曾经”两个字，不过辉煌的历史终将有重现的时刻。

如今，习近平主席已经为中国描绘了一张绚烂的图景：中华民族的伟大复兴。这场复兴将让中国重现昔日的辉煌，到目前为止，中国已经取得了不少令人惊叹的成就。昔日中国之独特，在于她的传承与延续，而今日中国之独特，在于前所未有的高速发展与前所未有的稳定；昔日中国之卓越在于她的创新能力，如今的中国正逐步赶超西方国家的高科技水平；昔日中国孕育了古老的人类文明，而今日的中国正创造着一种新型文明，一种极具包容性的、具有中国特色的世界文明。昔日的中国塑造了人类历史，而如今的中国正在历史变革的汪洋中破浪前行；昔日之中国曾是普天之下的中心，而今日的中国已然成为世界的经济中心，拥有最雄厚的财政资产；昔日的中国崇尚和平，不干涉他国内政，不侵略、不殖民，如今的中国依然奉行着和平共处的信条，中国人的血脉中没有称王称霸的基因；昔日的中国象征着美德：和谐、道德、稳定，今日中国仍然致力于构建和谐、富强、公正的社会。

从古老而强盛的昔日中国，到改革开放后逐步复兴的今日中国，在这段时期内，中国经历了两个历史性的阶段：第一，近百年的屈辱期，在这一时期里，中国战乱不断，惨遭列强凌辱；第二，“文化大革命”时期，猛烈的革命运动瓦解了独特的古中国文化，催生了一种全新的革命文化。

可以说，中国是在一场沉重而屈辱的、猛烈而极具破坏性的运动中实现了文化转型，于是才出现了中华民族复兴的呼声、产生了关于未来的共同愿景。与此同时，中国提出了 2049 年的百年战略目标，计划在新中国百年之际，将中国建设成文明、富强、和谐、民主的社会主义国家。

正如前文所说，文化在中国政治（不论是国内政治还是国际政治）中发挥了极为重要的作用，因此有必要就文化对当代中国政治的影响，开展更为深入而具体的探究。中国文化的源头何在？五千多年的传承史，是否能证明中国文化具有坚强的生命力、具有优于其他文化的特质？

任何一个群体的文化均具有稳定性和独特性，往往在几年、几十年乃至几百年都不会发生变化，这是否意味着，标榜某种理念和习惯的文化，与新生事物或外来的文化理念格格不入？通常情况下，外来文化会遭到内部守旧文化的排斥，那么，引入先进的外部文化是否能够促进社会的革新与发展？此外，深层文化（同样在社会构建过程中形成）默默地塑造着人们的行为、观念、认知、日常习惯以及传统，故在其本性中已经深深地刻上深层文化的烙印。那么，在充满变数的日常社交环境、物理环境、政治环境、经济环境和安全环境中，深层文化将如何发挥影响？简言之：一个群体的文化，是否会受到新的行为方式的影响？比如，是否会受到更加开放的、更加高效的文化影响？在国际环境发生根本性变化时，强势文化群体是否会坚守其文化阵地并且不顾这种文化带来的消极影响？

二 军事文化

以上几个基本问题都会在接下来的讨论中有所涉及。为了让论述更有针对性，本文论题的范围缩小至战争与和平层面，换句话说，将讨论集中在文化策略或军事文化层面。“文化”这一概念向来存在争议，文化策略也不例外。弗兰克·霍夫曼博士在近期发表的《战略文化与战争形态》一文中指出：“政策制定者或军事策划者应尽可能深入地去了解，潜在对手的战略文化如何对其决策造成影响。”

然而学术界一直将文化策略视作军事科学和政治科学的分支，有关文化策略的定义也不尽相同，其中最重要的两种定义为：第一，文化策略指这样一种现象：尽管国家决策者面临着多重选择，其最终决策往往与某种政治路线密不可分。阿拉斯泰尔·伊恩教授的定义为：文化策略是指决策者表现出的宏观战略上的倾向性，这种倾向性来源于决策者对冲突的性质以及敌人的性质做出的普遍性假设。

致力于中国军事文化研究的著名学者——托马斯·G. 曼肯指出，文化策略包含三个层面：1. 国家文化策略（国家的定位，包括对内和对外定位）2. 军事战略文化（如何作战）3. 军事制度及组织文化（军事机构的组成方式）。

我们可以根据曼肯提出的三个层面来构建操作与分析框架，针对以下问题进行讨论：在文化策略的影响下，国家如何对威胁进行判定；最可能采用何种方式来应对威胁。在此基础上，我们可以提出以下假设：

1. 文化策略往往会受到世界秩序的支配。

2. 强国受到文化策略的影响较小，弱国受到的影响较大。

三 世界秩序与单极属性

首先，我们要对世界秩序这一概念进行界定。通常来讲，世界秩序是政治家、学者以及新闻界人士所引用的概念。亨利·基辛格曾做出过这样一番著名论断：“真正的世界秩序并不存在，每一种文明对于秩序的定义都是不同的。”（亨利·基辛格：《世界秩序》）曼肯将世界秩序理解为“围绕权利分配而形成的世界架构”。

以下，将从广义的概念出发，对世界秩序的内涵展开探讨。波茨·汉森指出，根据最新提出的“单极理论”来定义世界秩序（该理论以肯尼思·华尔兹的结构现实主义理论为基础）可以增强这一概念的学术性、操作性和说服力（波茨·汉森：《单极属性与世界秩序：理论及意义》）。汉森将世界秩序定义为“极性（单极、双极、多级）与大国政治（争夺政治领导权、推行政治议程）的结合体。”

这种定义的缺点主要在于表述不够明晰。单极属性通常被视作贬义词，且与当前世界格局的联系不大。如果将当前世界体系描述为“一国独霸的体系”，那么这种表述与许多国家领导人和学者的论调并没有太大的差别。习近平和普京都曾用“一国独霸”来描述当前国际体系。

简言之，汉森的单极理论主要以一系列的假设为基础：

“一国独霸”的体系意味着均衡与对称的缺失，意味着在这样一个体系之内，不存在势均力衡的两个大国，其余各国只能两者择其一。该体系的内部动态体现为三种形式：对超级大国进行簇拥、依附或反抗，其中的反抗极具危险性。此外，单极属性还意味着，各国要为确保国家生存、捍卫根本利益付出艰辛的努力。

该理论将国际体系的形态结构与单极化的政治议程结合一处，将世界秩序定义为：国际体系的总体结构加单极政治工程。从这个角度出发，我们可以对超级大国——美国的政治议程进行思考。美国的基本政治议程是什么？是推广市场经济、宣扬民主、人权、个体自由，倡导国际法律与秩序。如果中国、印度或俄罗斯成为唯一的超级大国，各自推行的政治议程定然会有所不同。令人惊讶的是，多数国家对美国在全球推行的政治议程表现出赞成与附和。

然而在特朗普时代，这样的政治议程是否能够持续下去？在特朗普的政治话语中，很少听到“自由、民主、人权”等字样。不过，这种情况总有一天会发生变化，特朗普最终会回归美国最基本的政治议程。

现在回到前文提出的假设——文化策略往往会受到世界秩序的支配。针对这点假设，笔者采用曼肯提出的三个层面作为分析框架。首先从国家战略层面，即国家的外部定位和内部定位层面，审视中美两国的文化策略。

四　国家文化战略

1. 美国

美国进入世界政坛较晚，文化、历史称不上源远流长，东西则濒临两大洋，便于在全球扩张势力。其综合国力位居世界之首，经济实力、军事实力、政治实力和文化实力均具有全球性的影响力。从这一角度来讲，不论对拉丁美洲、欧洲、亚洲还是太平洋地区而言，美国都算得上是超级大国。美国与邻国——加拿大和墨西哥这两个一般意义上的大国保持着长期而紧密的友好关系。作为曾经的殖民地，美国在理论层面是反殖民主义和反干预主义的，至少在涉及本土环境时如此（门罗主义便是绝佳的例证）。从本质上讲，美国属于移民国家，崇尚自由、民主和机会平等，与之前欧洲的独裁、专制、阶级主宰的社会形成鲜明对比。这里是美国梦的发源地，鼓励个人通过努力奋斗来取得成功。

2. 中国

中国是世界上最古老且历史从未间断的文明国家。作为典型的大陆强国，中国与 14 个国家接壤，且这些邻国并非全都是最友好的国家。受地理环境影响，中国的海上通路颇为局限，因而一直奉行“大陆强国”的政策。中国的综合国力位居世界第二，虽然积极融入世界，却没有争霸世界的野心。鉴于曾经遭受过殖民与侵略，中国向来反对干涉别国内政，注重国家主权和领土完整。作为发展中国家，中国致力于实现全面发展，因而可以长期保持崛起态势。中国的目标在于构建和谐社会，力争在民族复兴和实现中国梦的过程中恢复其昔日辉煌的历史地位。

对于定位不尽相同的两个国家，文化策略会在哪些层面影响两国对于威胁的感知?

美国自我标榜为独特而杰出的发达国家。

总体而言，美国感受不到常规意义上的安全威胁，其地理优势和常规军事优势能够将威胁控制在最低水平。尽管目前仍有遭受核威胁的可能，但与冷战时期相比，这种威胁的程度已经大幅降低，且美国拥有强大的核武器震慑力和防御能力。另外，美国对恐怖主义的防御相对较为严密。目前为止，美国面临的主要威胁是全球霸主地位受到挑战且使其无法凭借政治、经济、军事优势达到主宰世界的目的。第二个威胁在于，美国作为“希望的国度”，可能会失去对其他国家的吸引力，被世界各国视为以模仿见长的国家。

从文化策略视角来看，中国将自身定位为——在历史、文化、传统、延续与传承方面无可匹敌的国家。中国历史上从未出现过扩张主义、殖民主义和霸权主义，始终奉行和平共存的理念。由于中国曾在相当时期内遭受过威胁、剥削和侵略，因而在文化传统上历来存在着一种根深蒂固的“危机感”——对于主权遭到威胁、控制和侵害的危机感等。

3. 如何评估世界秩序对国家文化策略造成的影响

主流观点认为，从理论角度来看，当前世界秩序由世界体系的总体架构和美国的政治议程构成，因此，美国的国家战略与世界秩序大体相吻合，不仅自我标榜为世界主宰，更不容许任何国家争夺其军事霸主和科技霸主的地位。目前为止，美国的目标仍然在于塑造关键国家的未来选择，企图向全世界昭示，美国为推广民主、市场经济、个体自由、人权、国际法律与秩序做出了巨大贡献。尽管特朗普政权在短期内不会重拾昔日的论调，但美国的积极行动却在当前世界秩序中占据重要位置。

对中国而言，世界秩序对国家文化策略的影响体现在以下几个方面：首先，中国承认美国在世界秩序中占据优势地位，但却无意与之争锋，无意挑战美国支配下的世界秩序，只要美国不对亚洲的安全和稳定造成破坏，中国甚至不会去挑战美国在亚洲的领导权。从这种意义上来说，中国并不排斥美国主导的世界秩序。但与此同时，中国对美国干预世界秩序的方式表现出不满，曾反复提到中国人的血脉里没有称王称霸的基因，以此批判美国的干预行为。对中国而言，战争不仅耗费财力，而且有可能造成内部分化，因而要尽量避免战争，但前提是国家核心利益——主权、领土、国家统一不受外部威胁。

由于国际政治环境、经济环境、军事环境关系到中国产品的生产与出口，关系到中国能否从全球化进程中获利，因而世界秩序对中国文化策略的影响体现在国际环境的塑造上。

概括而言：美国的国家文化策略基本与当前世界秩序相符，而中国的国家文化策略则与其国家战略高度相关，但民族复兴的愿景却在显示，中国在未来有可能成为全世界最强大的国家，这与当前的世界秩序并不相符。因此，前文做出的假设并不适用于中国的国家文化策略。

五　结语

每个国家都有各自的身份，而文化则是这重身份中根深蒂固的一部分，它涉及风俗习惯和价值观，具有连贯性和聚合性。但文化常常会在内部动力或外来文化的压力下发生改变。是否存在永恒不变的深层文化？我对此表示怀疑。文化是值得珍视的，但同时它也具有负面影响，关于这一点，我们只需审视历史中的暴力行径便可知晓。暴力是用来维持秩序的必要工具，人类不但使用暴力，甚至还会赞扬暴力。值得庆幸的是，“几个世纪以来，特别是自冷战结束后，人类使用暴力的频率正逐步下降。”（史蒂芬·平克，《人性面面观：暴力史与人性》2012）

与其他文化相比，军事文化更加依赖那些根植于历史传统的惯例和风俗。正如一位美国政治科学家所说：“文化能把战略当成午餐吃掉。”

本文旨在审视世界秩序对于文化策略造成的影响，将世界秩序定义为国际体系的总体架构与独霸大国的政治议程的结合体，所谓的政治议程是指市场经济、民主体制、个体自由、人权以及国际法律和秩序的推行。

我们通过对美国军事文化的分析，可以得出这样一个结论：美国的军事制度与各国军事制度一样，转型的过程十分缓慢。军事文化属于深层文化。自第二次世界大战结束以后，美国军方便开始在全世界范围内部署军事力量，在冷战期间更是凭借强势军事手段对“苏维埃共和国”进行围堵。冷战后，世界格局由唯一的超级大国所主宰，而美国则从此成为世界秩序中最重要的一部分，这不仅直接影响了美国自身的文化策略，也间接地对中国的文化策略造成影响。在某些重要领域内，甚至改写了中国的军事文化及其文化策略。

因世界秩序而改写的中国军事文化主要体现在以下几个方面：

中国的文化自信和军事自信正逐步得到增强，与此同时，在军事战略层面，中国正不断向美国学习。中国正在融入世界，参与国际事务、参与国际秩序的建构。

主要结论：第一，中国的文化策略已经适应了冷战后形成的世界秩序；第二，中国文化策略中最重要的一些层面被世界秩序所改写；第三，世界秩序催生了中国的新型文化策略。

Culture and World Order

Bertel Heurlin / Denmark

Jean Monnet Professor of European and International Security, Department of Political Science, UCPH and Director of China Security Studies, Centre for Military Studies, UCPH, Co-founder and coordinator of UCPH's Think Tank on China,ThinkChina.dk.

I. Introduction

China is unique. China is exceptional. China is civilization. China is culture. China is history. China is centrality: tian xia, All under heaven. China is peace, non-aggression. China is virtue.

Or, rather, was. History has to return. Xi Jinping has more than any Chinese leader declared a glorious vision for China: The great revival of the Chinese nation. The rejuvenation is a return to the mighty past. But also the current China has achieved marvellous results. China was unique due to its continued existence. China is now unique due to its unprecedented fast and stable development and growth. China was exceptional due to its innovation capacity; China is now on the verge to close the gap to Western technological superiority. China was the continuing source of civilization; China is now on its way to build up a new inclusive worldwide civilization yet with Chinese characteristics. China was shaping history; China is now riding on the waves of historical evolution. China was centrality, tian xia; China is already now the economic centre of the world with the greatest amounts of financial assets. China was peace, non-intervention, non-colonialist, non-aggression; the current China is still preaching peaceful co-existence and is emphasizing that hegemony is not part of the Chinese DNA. And finally: China was virtue, harmony, moral, stability; China today is aiming at developing a harmonious, prosperous and just society.

But between times of the old mighty China, The Middle kingdom, Tian Xia and the China at the recent time from the beginning of the rejuvenation prepared by the Deng-Open-up policy, there are two historical periods. First, the hundred years of humiliation era, which implied external coercion, occupation and war and second, the "Cultural Revolution" era, which introduced an enforced ongoing revolution that in its full consequence meant a destruction of the ancient unique Chinese culture enabling a new revolutionary culture to emerge.

So, China has experienced heavy, humiliating, disruptive, tumult like, up-side-down cultural transitions, now eventually presented as the background for a plea for a rejuvenation of the past in form of a common vision for the future. At the same time there is a strategic idea at play in the shape of the 2049 objectives for the Chinese nation to be achieved, commemorating the 100 years of the PRC. The aim is to have a socialist, civilized, prosperous, harmonious and democratic country.

So, realizing the fundamental role of culture in Chinese politics, domestic as well as international, based on the observations and considerations in the introduction, it is an obvious task in more detail to examine the concise impact of culture in contemporary Chinese politics. What are the roots of Chinese culture? Is Chinese culture generally superior, due to is more or less unabridged existence during 5000 yeas, proving its robustness and strength?

And, is culture-looked upon as a constant, unique for a society, remaining unchanged through years, decades, centuries, a force upholding values and habits apparently not in tune with new developments and insights from the outside world, which however, in a given situation will be rejected as a reaction to the society′s own obsolete culture and there by opening up for valuable inputs from other cultures giving visions of renewal for the society?

Oris the deep culture, the forces (also shaped through social construction) that in a benign way structure our behaviour, beliefs, perception, and also our daily habits and customs so deeply ingrained in our nature that it affects us more than our immediate social, physical, political, economic, security related environment loaded with often fundamental changes? More simply expressed: Can a society′s culture be influenced by new ways of behaving – for example by a more forward oriented, more effective culture or will a society with a strong culture stick to this culture despite counterproductive effects in relation to fundamentally changed international conditions?

II. Military Culture

This is the basic question I will present today. In order to strengthen and also constraining the scope of the argument I choose to focus on the realm of peace and war. In other words: to aim at having a closer look at Strategic Culture or Military Culture. Just as “culture” as a notion is contested, certainly strategic culture is. In his recent essay (“Strategic Culture and Ways of War: Elusive Fiction or essential Concept?”, Naval War College Review, Spring 2017), dr. Frank Hoffman concludes, that “Policy makers and military planners should want to know more about the strategic culture of potential opponents and how it influences their decision makers, not less” (p.141).

Strategic culture is however a fully recognized scholarly sub discipline in Military Science and Political Science. There are numerous definitions: Two are central: “Military culture is the phenomenon that national decision makers despite having a row of different choices at their disposal tend to make decisions, which are tied to a certain political line." (NN. XX). Professor Alastair Iain Johnston's definition is the following, "Strategic culture is ranked grand strategic preferences derived from central paradigmatic assumptions about the nature of conflict and the enemy and collectively shared by decision makers".

The famous scholar dealing with Chinese military culture Thomas G. Mahnken is unfolding the concept to include three levels: 1. National Strategic culture (What is the position of the country, externally and internally). 2. Military strategic culture (How to fight wars) and finally, 3. Military instrumental, organizational culture. (How is the institution organized.)

By using Mahnken's three levels and by focussing on what the individual states perceive as threats through the lenses of strategic culture and on what tools they are most likely to use to counter the threat one can construct an operational analytical framework.

On this basis we now can formulate a controversial hypothesis: 1) Strategic culture has a tendency to be overruled by the existing world order. 2) For greater powers to a lesser degree, for smaller powers to a higher degree.

III. World Order and Unipolarity

First we have to determine the concept of world order. The world order notion is generally used by politicians, scholars, journalists. Henry Kissinger has famously stated that there never has been a true world order. Civilizations are defining their own concept of order. (Kissinger, Henry, 2015, *World Order*.) In Mahnken´s understanding World Order is how the world is organized according to distribution of power.

I will take a widening point of departure. According to a new theory on unipolarity, elegantly and convincingly argued, based on Kenneth Waltz structural realism, world order can be defined in a more operative and scholarly more persuasive way. (Hansen, Birthe, 2011, *Unipolarity and World order: A theory and its implications*). She defines world order as "a combination of polarity (unipolarity, bipolarity or multipolarity) and the political project undertaken by the great powers that create the direction for political leadership and constitute the political agenda." (Hansen, p.92).

The problem with the theory is mainly the name. Unipolarity is generally seen as a negative and irrelevant notion out of tune with the current world situation. If you are describing the current world system as a "one superpower system" or may even be are adding "system in transition", you will be in accordance with an overwhelming amount of state leaders and scholars worldwide. Xi Jinping and Vladimir Putin are explicitly referring to the current international system as a one superpower system.

Briefly Hansen's Unipolarity theory is based on a set of assumptions.

A system with one superpower means absence of global symmetric balance. Some states attempt to balance asymmetrically, but it is risky business. It means a system where the countries only have one option. No choice between two superpowers. The dynamics in the system are demonstrated in three ways: countries can "flock" around the superpower (bandwagon). They can be free riding or they can oppose the superpower, which could be extremely dangerous. Finally, unipolarity means "hard work" for the individual countries in order to secure their vital interests, primarily survival.

The theory combines the structural condition in the international system with the political project of the unipole. The sum of structure plus project is the definition of World order. But what is the fundamental project of the superpower USA? It is the promotion of market economy, democracy, individual freedom, human rights and international law and order. If China, India or Russia were the lonely superpower the global project would have been different. Nevertheless, it is surprising and convincing to see that most countries adhere to the objectives of the US- global project.

But is it also true in these Trump-times? In his proclamations and statements, you hardly hear the notions of freedom, democracy and human rights. In due time, however, this will change.Also a Trump will eventually adhere to the fundamental US-global political project!

Returning to the overarching hypothesis, that strategic culture tends to be overruled by the world order, defined according to the unipolarity theory, we will use the Mahnken three level analytical framework.

First we have National Strategic culture, i.e. the position of the country, externally and internally. Two countries will be examined, the US and China.

IV. National Strategic Culture

1. The United States

The US is the newcomer in world politics with rather limited old culture of its own. The US is the ultimate sea power, surrounded by the two biggest oceans worldwide and in this way reaching out to the entire globe. The US is number one in the world assessed by combined capabilities and as such a status quo power, and the US is present globally economically, militarily,politically and culturally. The US is in this way a Latin American power, a European power, an Asian power, an African power, and a Pacific power. In the immediate environment the US is having long lasting close and friendly relations with its only two less powerful neighbour countries, Canada and Mexico. As a former colony the US is in theory traditionally anti-colonialist and anti-interventionist, at least when it comes to the US´s own environment as is demonstrated in the Monroe doctrine. Internally the US is the immigration country per se, the land of freedom, democracy, opportunities contrary to the former European absolute, autocratic, class dominated societies. It is the country of the American Dream opening up for the individual rising possibilities.

2. China

China regards itself as the world´s oldest unabridged still existing civilization.

China is the typical land power, surrounded by 14 countries, certainly not the friendliest ones. Its access to the oceans is geographically restricted and its policy of becoming a land power AND a sea power is challenged by geopolitical realities. China is number two in the world in combined capabilities and a rising power. China is also going global, but having no desire to manage the world. As a country exposed to aggression and attempts to colonialism in the past it is anti-interventionistic and is emphasizing sovereignty and national integrity. Internally China is a one party system, which strives – as a developing country, for full development status and thus for a long time being a rising power. Its aim is a peaceful and harmonious society and a world where China can regain its position during a rejuvenation, "Chinese Dream"- process.

Two countries, two different position. What are the implications of their National Strategic culture focussing at threat perception?

The US is considering itself superior, outstanding, exceptional.

All in all, the US is not perceiving any conventional security threat. Positioned geographically secure having conventional military superiority the threat is minimal. A nuclear threat exists, but still to a much lesser degree than during the cold war, and the US has the strongest nuclear deterrent and protection. Also the US has a relative strong protection against terrorism. The main threat is a future development tending to weaken the American capability to global dominance, to reign the waves, to disseminate its political, economic and military superior forces in a way enabling it to maintain global reach in order dominate the world. Add to this a threat to lose the global attraction as a land of opportunities and as such also a land by many countries regarded as a country subject to imitation.

China is, according to the National Strategic culture, considering itself as an outstanding country with a history, a culture a tradition, a coherent, long lasting entity in the middle of the world second to none. It is a country having no tradition for expansionism, colonization, hegemony believing in peaceful coexistence. But

China has experienced a shorter period of being threatened, exploited, occupied. So there traditionally exists a threat perception historically well-founded, pointing to the threat of being contained, encircled and attacked on sovereignty.

3. How to assess the impact of the world order on the national strategic culture?

The main claim is that the world order- in the theoretical understanding consisting of the structural position plus the US political project- as regards the US is identical with its general national strategy. The US is signalling to be the inevitable world leader; the US is warning any peers to refrain competing with the US as regards military-technological superiority; the US still has the aim to shape the future choices of key states. The US is signalling to the world that it pays to adhere to democracy, market economy, personal freedom, human rights and international law and order. Although the Trump administration for the time being is reluctant to propagate missionary activities, this active part of the world order is an important part.

To China the world order is impacting the National Strategic Culture in the following way: China is regarding the US be the dominant, superior, inevitable lonely superpower. China has no desire to take over world leadership; it does not aim at challenging the American world order. Even it does not want to challenge the US-leadership in its own part of the world, Asia, as long as the US is taking care of Asian security and stability. In this way China is demonstrating to be included in the US-world order. China however, also is signalling that it certainly not is approving the way in which the US is managing the world order. China has several times emphasized that the Chinese does not have the gene of aggression and intervention or exerting hegemony, tacitly accusing the US for its managing activities. To China war is costly, not to be waged. War also tends to lead to internal separation. But there is a limit: war is a possibility if the Chinese core interests are fundamentally threatened. They have to do with sovereignty, integrity and unification.

Also the world order is influencing the Chinese National Strategic culture by shaping a political, economic and military global environment making it possible for China to produce and sell goods globally and thus to exploit the globalization process, which is a fundamental part of the liberal economic order.

To sum up: The world order content is more or less identical with the fundamental US National Strategic culture. To China the situation is interesting enough not far from the US-situation. The way in which China displays its National Strategic culture is in many ways similar to its National Strategy. The greater exception is rejuvenation vision, which hints at a future where China is the most powerful civilization and country in the world, certainly not in accordance with the current world order. So- a certain identity, but we are not seeing a World Order overruling process is at play. So, the hypothesis does not apply when we are assessing the Chinese National Strategic Culture.

V. Conclusion

Culture is an ingrained part of every society′s identity. It is about customs and values and it is about coherence and cohesion. But culture is also victim to constant change, from inside or from outside through imitation of or pressure from other cultures. Is there an unchangeable deep culture? I doubt. Culture is cherished, but culture can also be considered negative. Let us for example look at use of violence through history. Violence on all levels has been used and praised as an absolute necessity to uphold order. Professor Steven Pinker shows that use of violence is being constantly reduced during the centuries, and not least since the end of the cold war. (Pinker, Steven 2012, *The Better Angels of Our Nature: A History of Violence and Humanity*, Penguin Books.)

Military culture seems more than any other realms to rest on deep historically and traditionally rooted values and customs. So some will claim as an American political scientist: "Culture eats strategy for lunch".

I have however tried to examine the role the world order in influencing the strategic culture. World order is here theoretically determined as the overarching structural organization of the international system according to the combined capabilities of, in this case, the lonely superpower PLUS the political project of the lonely superpower, which is promotion of market economy, democracy, personal freedom, human rights and international law and order.

Looking at the US the result is that it, just like all military organizations are very slow transformers. The military culture is deep culture. The US-military however, has since WWII been used to be present and active worldwide- during the cold war with the exception of the Soviet Empire, which the US contained with heavy military means. And after the cold war the structural situation changed to a lonely superpower superiority. From then the US became the most important part of the world order, influencing directly the strategic and military culture in the US itself and indirectly the strategic culture in China. In some important areas the influence overruled the Chinese strategic and military culture.

The main area where Chinese military culture has changed according to the influence from the current world order is the following:

China is considering itself culturally superior–also in the military realm–but is increasingly imitating the US-military.

Again the main conclusion is that China also as concerns strategic culture has adapted to the conditions of the World Order, which reign from the end of the cold war. The most important areas of Chinese strategic culture are overruled by the current world order. A new Chinese military culture inspired by the world order is born.

国有企业相关国际规则：中国方案与全球治理

田丰[1]　【中国】
中国社会科学院世界经济与政治研究所研究员 /《国际经济评论》编辑部主任

国有企业作为国民经济的中坚和“一带一路”建设的主力军，其在“十三五”时期的改革发展情况好坏，直接关系到“一带一路”建设的推进速度和建设成果、全面建成小康社会新目标的顺利实现、中国经济的顺利转型升级以及中国基本经济制度的巩固完善。在既往中国国有企业改革的历程中，主要采取的方式是根据内部需要进行自主改革，对于外部规则的约束则相对较少考虑，其原因在于当时国有企业相关国际规则发展的程度以及中国国有企业跨境活动活跃的程度较为有限。随着经济全球化的发展，国有企业的运作、治理及其规范越来越成为国际经济规则体系变革与发展中一个绕不开的议题。与此同时，中国已经进入对外开放的新阶段，在此阶段坚持统筹国内国际两个大局，用好国内国际两个市场、实现市场深度融合，用好国内国际两种资源、实现资源高效配置，用好国内国际两类规则、实现规则有机衔接，是中国如期实现全面建成小康社会奋斗目标、推动经济社会持续健康发展必由之路。[2]《中共中央国务院关于构建开放型经济新体制的若干意见》特别提出，要大力培育开放主体，完善国有资本对外开放的监管体系，鼓励各类所有制企业发挥自身优势，深度参与国际产业分工协作。国内外形势的

1　原载于《国际经济合作》2016 年第 5 期。

2　中共商务部党组：《实现开放发展必须坚持统筹国内国际两个大局》，《求是》2016 年第 2 期。

新变化意味着，深入研究国有企业相关国际规则的趋势及影响、并就此提出针对性的建议刻不容缓。本文首先简要介绍了国有企业相关国际规则的基本框架与主要特点，随后重点介绍了国有企业相关国际规则的新发展，在第三部分，系统评估了新规则对于中国国有经济发展可能的影响，最后是作者的对策建议。

一　国有企业相关国际规则：基本框架与主要特点

国有企业相关国际规则是现行国际经济秩序的重要组成部分之一[1]，然而不同于一般贸易、原料及初级商品贸易、国际货币和发展援助、工业化以及运输等领域，国有企业或国有经济方面并没有建立全球性协调机构或形成全面制度安排，即处于“无核心”状态，其基本治理框架由多个维度、多个领域的相关规则交织而成。以世界贸易组织（WTO）的有关规定为例，WTO没有专门规制国有企业的协定，相关多边贸易规则散见于《关税与贸易总协定》（GATT）、《服务贸易总协定》（GATS）、《补贴与反补贴措施协定》（SCM）及特定成员的入世议定书或承诺中。总体看，国有企业相关国际规则涉及多边、区域、双边和单边等多个维度以及贸易、投资、竞争政策、补贴、倾销、公司治理、金融等多个领域，相互交织，形成规则网络体系。[2]

1. 国有企业相关多边贸易规则的主要特点

多边贸易规则主要指世界贸易组织及其涵盖协定确立的规则框架，其涉及国有企业的规定主要具有以下特点：

1　据1974年第六届特别联大《关于建立新的国际经济秩序宣言》及其《行动纲领》为核心的有关国际法文件，国际经济秩序所涉及的领域包括原料及初级商品、粮食、一般贸易、运输和保险、国际货币和发展援助、工业化、技术转让、跨国公司、发展中国家间（南南）合作、自然资源主权、联合国系统在国际经济合作中的作用等。原料及初级商品、粮食的贸易曾经或仍由相应国际协定规约或组织协调；一般贸易由WTO及管辖的一系列货物贸易协定协调；运输领域已有海上或国际航空运输组织及其诸多公约；国际货币和发展援助方面已有国际货币基金组织（IMF）与世界银行集团等组织及其有关协定；工业化方面已有旨在促进和加速发展中国家工业化的联合国工业发展组织；发展中国家间（南南）合作方面也有77国集团、海湾合作委员会等。但是，在技术转让、跨国公司、自然资源主权等国际经济秩序领域尚无多边国际条约。参见张乃根，《试论国际经济法律秩序的演变与中国的应对》。《中国法学》2013年第2期。

2　刘丁、姚梅镇、陈安等老一辈开创中国国际经济法学科的学者以及余劲松、曾华群、曹建明等中青年国际经济法学者都认为广义的国际经济法渊源包括国际法规范（国际条约、国际惯例）、国际组织重要决议、国内涉外经济法等。参见张乃根《试论国际经济法律秩序的演变与中国的应对》。《中国法学》2013年第2期。因本文篇幅有限，并未纳入关于国有企业的国内涉外立法。

总体上秉承所有制中性原则。WTO 的基本职能是组织制定和管理多边及诸边贸易协定，而这些协定的谈判、签署和履行由成员政府负责，WTO 对各成员的贸易政策和法规进行监督和管理，以保证其合规性。WTO 协定因而显著区别于其他以企业为约束对象的制度，尤其是基本上没有系统的制度设计以针对不同所有制企业进行分类监管。

WTO 部分协议中包含了一些与国有企业相关或部分重合的概念，例如国营贸易企业、公共垄断、公共机构等，但这些概念并不等同于国有企业。在 GATT/WTO 文本中，并没有"国有企业"这一词汇，仅有一些规则涉及特定非政府实体的行为，其中部分特定非政府实体与一般意义上的国有企业密切相关。例如，GATT 第 17 条规定，WTO 成员须确保其"国营贸易企业"（State Trading Enterprises）在商业考量的基础上运行，在进出口方面的活动遵守非歧视原则，对其他缔约方的贸易给予公平公正待遇。但对于什么是"国营贸易企业"，WTO 并没有给出清晰的定义，从而影响了协定的适用性。并且，可以确认的是，WTO 国营贸易企业条款仅适用于国有企业中涉及"贸易"功能的企业，具有生产、主权投资、提供公共服务等其他功能的国有企业不在此条的规范领域内。而"公共机构"是否是国有企业则取决于国有企业与政府之间的关系，如果没有证据表明政府对国有企业及其行为实施了有意义控制，国有企业不能被认定为"公共机构"。

在普遍的所有制中性基础上部分 WTO 规则对国有企业规制性更强。例如，SCM 并非专门针对国有企业，但国有企业经常被认为获得了或更有可能获得资金转移、税收减免、贷款等多种形式的补贴。一般情况下，WTO 要求成员履行国民待遇义务和市场准入义务，禁止偏袒本土企业，无论其为公有或私有企业。由于服务部门通常国有企业参与度较高，后者自然成为 GATS 的重要规制对象。

2. 国有企业相关区域经贸规则的主要特点

区域经贸规则是探索新领域国际规则的重要场所。在关于国有企业的规定方面，一些区域协定比多边贸易规则更为明确广泛，主要体现在以下几个方面：

明确的国有企业定义。例如美国—新加坡自由贸易协定规定，如果国家持有一家企业的股份超过 20%，那么这家企业就应被视为国有企业。

明确适用于国有企业的条款以及为国有企业提供的例外。美国—秘鲁贸易伙伴协议的投资章节规定，国有企业与私人投资者一样享有获得投资保护、参与投资争端解决的权利，同时成员国承担的条约义务同样适用于国有企业或者其他行使规制、行政或政府职权的实体。美国—新加坡自由贸易协定规定，针对行使政府职能、既非基于商业基础也非竞争性的服务，新加坡保留如下权利：允许政府控股企业成为唯一服务提供商；对于提供涉及公共健康、公共福利、安全、关键经济基础等服务的企业，新加坡政府可以限制外资总体持股比例（不超过 49%）、限制高管和董事会组成等。[1]

明确国有企业在竞争政策等领域的特定义务。这些义务主要包括：国有企业在进行货物交易、服务交易或投资等商业行为时，应与商业考虑相一致；国企不能从事反竞争的行为，不能滥用市场支配地位；国有企业从事商业行为应遵行非歧视原则；国有企业行使规制、行政或其他政府权力时，国企的行为方式应与缔约国承担的条约义务相一致。例如美澳自由贸易协定在“国有企业与相关事项”中规定，国有企业不得对贸易与投资造成阻碍；国有企业在行使政府授予的管理、行政职能时，不得与本条约相违背；在货物或服务的销售上奉行非歧视待遇。在一些区域协定中，缔约方还进一步明确要求特定成员减少其国有企业或削弱对国有企业的实质性控制。例如美国—新加坡自由贸易协定就求新加坡承诺“以基本消除为目标，继续减少对国企行使有效控制的所有权或其他利益”。

3. 国有企业相关专业领域经贸规则的主要特点

如前所述，国有企业相关国际规则涉及贸易、投资、竞争政策、补贴、倾销、公司治理、金融等多个领域，大部分领域在多边或区域规则中已经有了较为详尽的阐释，本处主要介绍公司治理和主权财富基金这两个多边或区域规则较少涉及的领域。在公司治理领域，OECD 多年来一直致力于推动建立与完善全球性公司治理与国有企业公司治理规范，特别是 2005 年出台了《OECD 国有企业公司治理指引》，代表了 OECD 国家国有企业公司治理的发展趋势，也为世界其他国家的国有企业公司治理提供了重要参考。在主权财富基金领域，2008 年国际上 26 个主权财富基金在美国华盛顿成立了“主权财富基金国际工作组”，工作组经过广泛的协商后发布了主权财富基金《公认的原则和实践》（圣地亚哥原则），在主权财富基金法人治理结构、信息披露、风险管理三个方面提出了规范性要求。这些指引与原则具有以下特点：

包括诸多对于细节的规定和详细建议。这是专业领域经贸规则与多边或区域规则最为显著的区别。例如 OECD 国有企业公司治理指引规定了国有企业董事自

1　李振宁：《论国有企业的国际贸易法规制》，《中国物价》2015 年第 10 期。

由权、国有企业公共职能和商业运作间的差别等事项，“硬化”了国有企业财务约束，对其投资回报水平作市场化要求。

缺乏约束力。《OECD 国有企业公司治理指引》和主权财富基金《公认的原则和实践》不是国家间签署的条约或协定，是否遵守其规范性要求取决于自愿，规则本身没有强制约束力，也没有专门的监督机构就成员执行规则的情况进行定期评估。

二 国有企业相关国际规则的新发展

国有企业相关国际规则的调整是全球金融危机以来国际经济规则调整的重要组成部分。目前美国、欧盟等发达国家致力于综合利用多边、区域、双边和专业领域等诸多平台，试图在经合组织、TPP 和跨大西洋贸易与投资伙伴协议（TTIP）等谈判框架下，确立其国际规则谈判的主导地位，引领国有企业相关国际规则的发展方向。

1. 国际投资便利化与投资促进

2016 年 2 月 26 日，联合国贸易与发展会议发布了《投资便利化和投资促进：全球行动指南》讨论稿（第二版）。[1] 该行动指南主要分为两部分：投资便利化行动以及支持有利于发展的投资促进和便利化行动。其中有关投资便利化的行动主要包括七项措施：（1）提升与投资者相关的投资政策、法规和程序制定的可获得性和透明度；（2）提高投资政策实施中的可预测性和一致性；（3）提高投资管理程序的效率和有效性；（4）建立建设性利益相关方关系；（5）就投资争端解决、相关立法监管等事项任命投资监察员 / 协调员牵头机构；（6）就投资便利化建立监管和审查机制；（7）通过国际投资协定条款等方式加强投资便利化国际合作。支持有利于发展的投资促进和便利化行动主要包括三方面措施：（1）就投资便利化加强发展中国家合作伙伴的努力，为建立透明有效高效的行政程序、解决投资争端、提高相关机构能力提供支持和技术援助；（2）就投资政策和积极主动的投资促进加强发展中国家合作伙伴的努力，为设计有效的投资促进策略、组织投资促进论坛、建立和维护适宜的投资促进机构等事项提供支持和技术援助；（3）通过国际投资协定条款等方式就有利于发展的投资促进和便利化事项加强国际合作。

1 UNCTAD. INVESTMENT FACILITATION AND PROMOTION: A Global Action Menu UNCTAD Discussion Note，*UNCTAD's Investment Policy Hub, Version 2-26 February 2016.*

2. TPP

国有企业是 TPP 谈判的关键领域之一。2012 年，美国正式提出在 TPP 中就国有企业进行谈判，而且力主将国有企业作为谈判的关键内容。2016 年 2 月 4 日，美国、日本、澳大利亚、文莱、加拿大、智利、马来西亚、墨西哥、新西兰、秘鲁、新加坡和越南 12 个国家在奥克兰正式签署了 TPP 协议。尽管特朗普上任美国总统后宣布退出 TPP，但由于 TPP 已经达成的文本根植于相关领域国际规则的新实践、新发展基础上，有可能代表国有企业相关规则未来部分发展趋势，深入理解 TPP 中关于国有企业的规定对于中国把握国有企业相关国际规则未来走向具有重要意义。与此前达成的多边或区域协定相比，TPP 中关于国有企业的规定具有以下特点：

独立成章。TPP 中，国有企业议题不再散见于竞争、补贴等多个部分，而是单独作为一章，明确列出。此举既在结构上体现了对国有企业规则的重视，也从内容上强化了国有企业方面的纪律。

重新定义国有企业。TPP 中国有企业指主要从事商业活动的企业，且同时满足下述三种条件之一：（1）股权条件，政府直接拥有 50% 以上的股本；（2）投票权条件，政府通过所有权益行使 50% 以上的投票权；（3）任命权条件，政府拥有任命董事会或其他类似管理机构大多数成员的权力。这一定义通过明确国有企业的类别和股权、投票权或任命权等政府控制企业的方式，严格界定了国有企业，为 TPP 中国有企业规则重心的转移提供了基石。

创设了对非商业援助的约束。TPP 约束的对国有企业的"非商业援助"主要来自三个方面：缔约方本身对国有企业、国有企业对国有企业以及缔约方对另一缔约方境内的国有企业投资。TPP 规定，缔约方不能通过对国有企业的"非商业援助"损害其他缔约方及其国内产业的利益。

拓展了对国有企业的约束范围。以补贴为例，在现有世贸规则中，《补贴与反补贴措施协定》仅规范货物贸易，而 TPP 在国有企业新定义下创设的对非商业援助的约束实际上覆盖了货物贸易、服务贸易和国际投资等领域，拓展了对国有企业的约束范围。关于国有企业和非商业援助的清晰而广泛的界定更为缔约方认定国有企业获得补贴、并采取相应救济措施提供了巨大的便利。

主张限制国有企业的管辖豁免。TPP 国有企业规则要求，对于在缔约方境内从事商业活动的外国拥有或通过所有权益控制的企业，缔约方应规定本国法院就对该企业提起的民事诉讼拥有管辖权。根据美国贸易代表办公室对TPP的解读，在缔约方境内经营的外国国有企业，不能通过主张国家豁免而规避对其商业活动的法律诉讼。而中国一贯的立场是一国政府及其财产不受任何外国法院的管辖，即享有绝对豁免。如果依据美国贸易代表办公室的解释，TPP将实施相对豁免，这样政府在从事商业活动而非履行政府职责时，应接受外国法院的管辖，从而实际上限制国有企业的管辖豁免。[1]

3. 公司治理

公司治理失效被认为是全球金融危机爆发的重要微观基础。围绕着金融危机暴露的公司治理问题，OECD、国际金融公司、国际清算银行巴塞尔银行监督委员会等机构发布了一系列加强公司治理的指引与原则。OECD在2015年9月发布了国有企业公司治理指引的更新稿，强调参与市场公平竞争的国有企业应该同等对待不同所有制类型的股东。由于金融危机中暴露的公司治理缺陷主要表现为内部控制和风险管理的失效、薪酬制度错位、董事会未能充分履职以及股东权利的缺失，关于公司治理国际规则的调整也主要围绕以下几点展开：

（1）董事会改革：明确基础目标、提高履职能力和增加责任

纽交所公司治理委员会[2]认为董事会的基础目标应该是为公司创造长期的、可持续增长的股东价值，并且董事会须就目标的实现情况向股东负责。董事会有职责领导企业制定相关政策，以支持股东价值的长期可持续增长。为此，董事会须清楚理解，"为追求短期股价增长而鼓励过度承担风险的公司政策，是与良好的公司治理相悖的"。董事会和管理层应"制定适当的薪酬计划，并与不同阶段的长期价值目标挂钩"。

为提高董事会履职能力，巴塞尔银行监督委员会[3]要求各国银行业监管部门对拟任董事和高管人员进行资质审查。董事和高管的任职资格包括具备相应的经验、能力和个人素质，如职业精神和个人诚信。OECD要求董事会采取措施确保股东在提名董事中发挥作用。董事会应有专门委员会负责识别潜在的董事会成员是否具备专门的技术、知识和经验以增加公司的价值。

新的规则还明确，董事会在制定公司战略、选拔高管人员、监控高管人员绩

1 韩立余：《TPP国有企业规则及其影响》。《国家行政学院学报》。2016年第1期。

2 http://www.nyse.com/pdfs/CCGReport.pdf.

3 Basel Committee on Banking Supervision, "Principles for Enhancing Corporate Governance", 2010. http://www.bis.org/publ/bcbs176.pdf.

效、决定高管人员薪酬水平、管理风险、制定税收计划、进行内部审计以及确保财务信息真实可靠等方面负有责任。一些国家针对参与政府救援计划的金融机构公布了限薪措施，同时还规定董事会应收回基于出现严重错误而赋予高管的奖金红利和激励性报酬，即要求这些公司披露相应的追回条款。

（2）风险管理改革：设立首席风险官、明确董事会和高管的风险管理职责以及加强信息披露

首席风险官主要负责企业范围的风险管理框架，具体包括：识别企业的主要风险，评估此类风险并计量相应的风险敞口，持续对风险敞口进行监控并确定相应的资本规划，对接受特定风险的决定是否与董事会确定的风险政策相符进行评估，并向高管层和董事会汇报风险管理信息。首席风险官享有充分的地位和权威，可以向首席执行官或董事会直接报告，对企业风险敞口决策有直接的影响力。

董事会及高管应积极参与操作风险管理框架的管理。所有风险评级和估值过程的重要方面都必须得到董事会和高管层的批准。董事会有责任确定企业对风险的承受能力，确保管理层建立一套评估各类风险的框架，并详细了解与评级相关的管理层报告。高级管理层应深入了解风险评级体系的设计和运作，掌握企业所承担风险的性质和程度，确保风险管理程序的规范，并及时向董事会提供重大风险变化的报告。

为使投资者能够更好地评估董事会和高管层在风险管理和内部控制的角色和效果，董事会有责任在年度股东大会上向股东提供详细的风险控制报告并汇报公司的风险控制状况，特别需要向股东说明的是，面对公司特有的风险，董事会和管理层采取哪些应对措施。

（3）薪酬管理改革：薪酬结构应与风险匹配、提高股东参与、加强信息披露与监管机构的权力

机构浮动薪酬的规模以及其在机构内的分配应考虑所有当前和潜在的风险。企业遭遇重大财务损失时，也应相应缩减甚至取消浮动薪酬。可考虑采取“薪酬追回”和“薪酬惩罚”等措施。高管奖金中的现金比例不得超过 50%，40%~60% 的奖金要延期 3-5 年发放。如果公司业绩随后表现不佳，延期发放部分将下调等。

上市公司至少每三年进行一次不具约束力的股东投票表决，以批准所任命高管人员的薪酬方案。若公司的金降落伞方案之前并未经过高管薪酬方案投票表决，则公司在就未来所有的收购、兼并、整合或出售方案寻求股东批准时须同时进行

此项表决。

及时对外披露薪酬年报，具体内容应包括确定整个机构薪酬政策的决策程序，衡量绩效和调整风险的标准，递延支付政策，决定薪酬以现金或其他形式分配的参数等。

对上市公司基于错误财务信息发放的高管薪酬，美国证监会拥有追索权，该追索权的行使不需要证明高管任何行为错误，只要发行人被要求重述以及已经支付的报酬超出会计重述后所应付的报酬即可，并且未赋予董事会任何裁量权（即使所能追回的报酬将小于追回所需要的成本）。

三　国有企业相关国际规则：影响与评估

推进国有企业改革是中国加快培育参与和引领国际经济合作竞争新优势的形势所需。中国正在积极构建开放型经济新体制，推进对内对外相互促进、“引进来”与“走出去”更好结合，促进国际国内要素有序自由流动、资源高效配置、市场深度融合，企业在全球范围内配置资源、参与国际竞争将成为常态。

重新规划现存国际经济规则或制度，在国有企业和非国有企业之间实现公平竞争，完善公司治理，加强风险管控，是近来部分国际规则调整的主要趋势。其背后的基本逻辑在于一些人看来国有企业具有特殊优势，实行了不合理的企业行为。综合来看，关于国有企业享有哪些特殊优势的观点主要包括：政府支付补贴；政府及政府金融机构提供有利的融资和信用担保；监管上的特别优惠（例如不适用信息公开义务或反垄断法）；保证垄断及现有企业的优势；政府稳定持股；免除破产和获取信息优势。关于国有企业进行哪些不合理企业行为的观点主要包括：公司治理、生产效率和经营效率需要提高；反竞争行为，例如限制出口、要求当地采购等；实施国家政治和战略意图，例如中国对非洲资源的投资，中国国家外汇管理局、新加坡淡马锡控股公司等主权财富基金在资源和基本设施等领域的投资。[1]

上述观点有其偏颇之处，主要在于未能准确评估国有企业的效率和国有企业的权责。首先，有研究表明，2002 年之后，中国国有绝对控股和国有相对控股企业的效率高于其他内资非国有企业。这种变化反映了“抓大放小”下国有企业整体效率的改善。从技术进步的角度看，国有独资和国有混合所有制国企的 TFP 增

1　川濑：《TPP 谈判与制定限制国有企业的规则》，RIETI 电子信息 No.130（2014 年 4 月）。

长率都比其他各类非国有企业更快。[1] 其次，上述观点过多考虑了国有企业获得的利益，而对其负担估计不足。例如，与一般市场经济国家的国有企业相比，中国国企承担额外八个方面职能：承担了国家对经济运行进行宏观调控的部分职能；承担了国家应对和处理突发事件的部分职能；承担了维护地区和社会稳定的职责；承担了确保国家大型活动成功举办的职能；承担了支援新疆青海西藏等地区经济社会建设的职能；承担了参与国际竞争和合作的部分职能；承担了国家对外交往和维护国家安全的部分职能；承担了很重要的部分政治职能。[2]

即使如此，我们仍然应该看到，当前国有企业相关国际规则的一系列与中国目前正在进行的国有企业改革有一致性。自改革开放以来，中国一直致力于通过剥离不良资产、股份制改造、股权分置等举措（如）以加强国有企业的市场化程度，同时放开竞争性产品市场，使得国企和私企都可以参与公平公正的市场竞争。当前，在新的国内外形势下，中国政策思路从总量上实施宽松宏观政策，调整为更注重采取各种措施激发微观主体活力；从放松财政货币政策从需求端发力，调整为更注重简政放权从供给端发力。在国企改革方面，致力于使得市场在资源配置中起决定性作用，以“市场化、专业化、国际化”为导向，通过分类改革、完善现代企业制度、增强活力和强化监管相结合，增强国有经济整体的“活力、控制力、影响力、抗风险能力”。因此，国有企业相关国际规则的发展方向与中国国有企业改革的进程有着契合的一面，实现两者的协调发展是提高主体活力、构建开放型经济新体制的形势客观所需。

然而竞争中立并不等同于制度中性，即便表面上平等适用于所有对象的规则，不同阶层、集团或个人从中的受益和受损状况也不尽相同。近来关于国有企业的一系列新规有可能对中国国有经济的发展、战略布局，尤其是国有企业参与国际竞争形成了强大的外部压力。

首先，国有企业在规则项下享有的国民待遇有可能被减损。TPP 国有企业条款将国有企业参与境外市场投资的审查阶段提前到进入行为发生之前，并把限制要求（如披露信息等）仅与国有企业身份挂钩而与市场行为割裂，大大增加了国有企业境外投资的成本与难度，可能对大规模走出国门的国有企业造成准入阶段

1 刘小鲁、聂辉华：《国企混合所有制改革：怎么混？混得怎么样？》，人大国发院年度报告[NPE2015S01]。

2 季晓南：《中国国企承担额外八个方面职能》，2015 年网易经济学家年会。

的投资壁垒。[1]

其次，国有企业跨境活动有可能面临更高的经营风险。例如TPP要求缔约方"不通过向在别国领土内生产、销售产品的国有企业提供非商业帮助损害另一缔约方国内产业"，如果该规定在其他国际规则中被推广采纳，那么在中国国有企业投资东道国的同行业企业认为其损害了自身利益的情况下，中国国有企业有可能被提起诉讼，并且由于TPP相关规定排除了关于补贴认定的多重障碍，在类似规则框架下中国国有企业更有可能因为接受非商业援助而成为东道国实施救济措施的对象。此外，尽管OECD指引只是一个非强制性规则，但其影响不可小觑。如果中国国有企业打算对OECD成员进行投资或在其境内经营企业，就必须参照OECD关于国有企业的指引，从而面临如何有效控制海外分支机构的问题。

最后，国有企业跨境活动有可能面临更高的交易成本。TPP要求缔约方应向其他缔约方提供有关国有企业或政府垄断实体的详细信息，如政府及国有企业持有的股份比例；对持有的特殊股票或投票权说明；在国有企业任职的政府官员的职务；过去3年的年度收入及总资产；依法从中受益的例外或豁免；年度报表及第三方审计报告等。这些关于透明度的要求广泛而具体，不仅客观上加大了企业的经营成本，还有可能成为继"国家安全审查制度"之后，拒绝中国企业进入市场的另一有效政策工具。例如2012年美国对中国企业华为、中兴的并购案件提起了国家安全审查，华为、中兴在回应调查委员会提出的"中国共产党与企业的关系"这一问题时，拒绝披露公司架构、党委在决策中的作用等信息，最终美国以这两家企业的并购活动违反国家安全为由，拒绝予以批准。

四　中国的对策

实现国有企业相关国际规则与国内国有企业改革协调发展是新形势下构建开放型经济新体制的客观要求。为此，相关工作应主要从两个方面开展：一方面对国有企业相关国际规则进行跟踪研究和评估，把握规则的前沿和发展趋势，明确国有企业相关国际规则的新发展对中国国有企业的影响，积极参与相关规则的构建；另一方面深入推进国有经济布局调整，打造适合国际化发展需要、更富效率的企业组织新形式，完善国资监管体制。

1　毛志远：《美国TPP国企条款提案对投资国民待遇的减损》，《国际经贸探索》2014年1月第30卷第1期。

国家间经济实力的重大变化和原有规则体系内在缺陷的显露是国际规则体系调整的内在原因，其实质是国际事务主导权的转移与争夺。如果任由少数国家主导国际规则体系调整，结果只能是以新的不公正取代旧的不公正，不仅各方很难取得共识，也会影响全球经济持续健康发展。国际规则的调整应切实考虑不同国家发展水平和发展能力的差异，在综合平衡基础上公平对待和反映各方利益，客观评估各国可以承担的责任，以使各方拥有的权利、履行的义务和承担的责任相匹配。

在未来一个时期，抢抓“创始红利”“参与红利”“改革红利”应成为我国参与构建更加公平公正国有企业相关国际规则的总体目标，具体应做到以下几点：

抢抓“创始红利”，完善多边规则。国有企业相关多边规则目前处于缺位状态，多边规则涉及我国根本利益，也是我国有所作为最具潜力的方面，多边规则所秉持的制度中性原则同样应被运用于国有企业领域。

抢抓“参与红利”，全面参与多层面、多领域的国有企业规则谈判。国有企业跨境活动涉及的商品、资本和组织管理形式多种多样，既有货物贸易，也有服务贸易；既有机器设备、商品等实物资本，也有商标、专利、生产诀窍等无形资本，还有债券、股票、衍生证券等金融资本；既有竞争政策、知识产权保护、专业技术标准、政府采购和补贴等“硬”领域，也有劳工、环境等“软”领域。我国应广泛参与各种谈判，争取在每一张谈判桌上都有自己的代表，并根据进展情况，选择重点予以支持。

抢抓“改革红利”，推动国有企业规则改革。特朗普出任美国总统后决定退出 TPP，虽然澳大利亚和新西兰等签署国表示不排除“TPP 减一”协定，但是 TPP 协定的未来尚存在较大不确定性。WTO 项下涉及的国有企业相关规则迄今为止仍在不断明晰中。尽管如此，中国仍应加强对相关规则的跟踪、研究和评估，制定风险预警机制和应对预案，并在多边、区域和双边等多个平台推动国有企业相关国际规则改革，当前的重点平台包括 WTO、APEC、RCEP、中日韩 FTA、中美 BIT、中欧 BIT 谈判等。此外，中国还需要在深入实施一带一路倡议基础上，加强与沿线国家合作，完善双边 FTAs 和 BITs，开拓构建国有企业相关国际规则的新空间。

以开放倒逼改革、推动国内制度与国际规则接轨是中国经济建设取得巨大成就的宝贵经验。同理，国有企业相关国际规则应成为中国推动国有经济改革发展的动力。归根结底，改革要处理好政府与市场的关系，致力于提高国有经济活力和竞争力，实现国有资本合理布局，分类推动国企改革，完善国有资产管理体制，即做到三个“管好”。

一是管好资本。资本是市场化资源配置中的核心要素。中国的经济体制改革是一个渐进的转轨过程，与此相应，国有资产管理体制也经历了从以“管企业”为主、向以“管资产”为主、再向以“管资本”为主的转变。资本对应所有者，与“管企业”和“管资产”相比，“管资本”更强调所有者的权责，更强调管理对象的价值形态而不是组织形态，更强调管理对象的流动性而不是实物资产。以“管资本”为主完善国有资产管理体制意味着在监管主体性质上，更加突出政府层面的出资人代表性质，在监管职责上，更加体现以产权为纽带，立足符合法律规范和公司治理基本原则的股东定位，围绕管好资本落实出资人责任。“管资本”重新界定了国资监管机构的职能，反映了从出资人角度加强国有资产监管的内在要求，意味着出资人管理职能重心的转变，即从以往“管人、管事、管资产”的相对全面的管理职能，转向以管资本为主的、管理重点更加突出核心性管理职能。

二是管好“为”与“不为”的边界。政企分开、政资分开的关键是处理好“为”与“不为”的边界，“该为”的决不推诿，决不缺位，积极主动，科学管理，“不该为”决不越位，决不揽权，该放的坚决放到位，把该给的坚决给到位，大力精简优化相关职能。首先，企业董事会应充分行使职权。董事会在公司治理中具有重要的核心作用，但受现有体制机制以及董事会自身治理水平和规范化程度影响，董事会权能尚未充分落实。随着国资监管改革的推进和董事会运行日益健全规范，可考虑下放一批本应由监管企业行使的经营自主权，以最大程度激发企业活力。其次，推进分类改革，充分保证竞争性企业行使经营自主权。除涉及重要子企业合并、分立；战略规划、主营业务发生重大调整；股权转让致使国有股失去控制地位，有可能造成国有资产流失的重大事项，需经国资委批准外，其余事项应交还一级企业管理。对于涉及国有资本权益，影响国有资本安全等确需国资监管机构管理的事项，也要改变现有监管的思路和方式，以更加市场化的机制和手段，通过完善机制、引导激励、股东问责等来实现管理目标。最后，移交一批非出资人事项由政府公共管理部门和社会组织行使。目前国有企业和国资监管部门客观上承担着大量公共管理职能，如：节能减排、安全生产、知识产权管理等。这些职能不仅导致国有企业和国资监管部门核心职能淡化，客观上还造成与其他政府管理部门职能重合，浪费了政府资源，也加重了企业的负担。在下一步改革中，对国有企业和国资监管部门目前承担的公共管理职能，应逐步移交给政府相关行业管理部门和社会组织。

三是管好制度规范与能力建设。改革重在落实。在实施过程中尤其需要注意将权力放进“制度的笼子里”，实行依法监管；同时该着重加强能力建设，避免在政策执行过程中的无谓效率损失。在制度规范方面，一方面可考虑制定完善一批核心制度，例如国有资本产权制度、国有资本运营管理制度、国有资本经营预算制度和国有资本风险管理风险防范制度；另一方面可考虑建立与强化一系列配套制度，例如政府购买公共服务制度规范，市场化购买资金安排操作手册，公私伙伴关系、公共服务外包、母基金模式、BOT 模式等的操作指引。在能力建设方面，需要提高国资监管和运营的统一性和专业性，推进经营性国有资本监管全覆盖，形成规则统一、权责明确、分类分层、规范透明、全面覆盖的经营性国资监管框架；需要依法依规放开各种准入限制，建立国有资本按市场规则有序进退、合理流动的机制；需要完善推进量化的考核指标体系和第三方评估机制。

Applicable International Rules for State-owned Enterprises: China's Solutions and Global Governance[1]

Tian Feng / China

Researcher of the Institute of World Economy and Politics at the Chinese Academy of Social Sciences, Director of the Editorial Department of *International Economic Review*

Since state-owned enterprises are the backbone of the national economy and the main force in the construction of the "Belt and Road" Initiative, the development of state-owned enterprises in the period of the "13th Five-Year Plan" is directly related to the speed and results of the construction of the "Belt and Road" Initiative, the smooth realization of the new goal of building a moderately prosperous society in all respects, the successful transformation and upgrading of the Chinese economy, and the consolidation and improvement of China's basic economic system. During the course of the reform of the state-owned enterprises in the past, the main approach adopted was independent reform according to internal needs, and the constraints on external rules were relatively considered, thanks to limited development of relevant international rules in relation to state-owned enterprises

1 Originally published in *International Economic Cooperation*, May 2016.

and the inactive cross-border activities of Chinese state-owned enterprises at that time. With the development of economic globalization, the operations, governance and regulation of the state-owned enterprises have become more and more important issues in the reform and development of the system of international economic rule. At the same time, China has entered a new stage of opening up to the outside world. At this stage, we should keep in mind both the domestic and international situations, make good use of the domestic and international markets and achieve thorough market integration, make full use of domestic and international resources and achieve efficient distribution of resources, take good advantage of domestic and international rules and realize the organic cohesion of those rules, which is the only way for China to achieve the goal of building a moderately prosperous society in all respects and promoting sustainable economic and social development.[1] The *Several Opinions of the CPC Central Committee and the State Council on Establishing a New Open Economic System* specifically points out that we should earnestly foster and open the subjects, improve the supervisory system for the opening up of state-owned capitals, encourage all kinds of ownership enterprises to exert their own advantages, and fully participate in international industrial labor division and collaboration. The new changes in the domestic and international situation imply that it is urgent to conduct an in-depth study of the trends and impacts of the relevant international rules of state-owned enterprises and bring forward pertinent suggestions accordingly. This article first briefly introduces the basic framework and the main characteristics of the applicable international rules for state-owned enterprises, and then focuses on the new development of the applicable international rules for state-owned enterprises. In the third part, the author systematically evaluates the possible influence of the new rules on the development of China's state-owned economy. Finally, the author puts forward countermeasures and suggestions.

---

1 Party Leadership Group of the Ministry of Commerce of the People's Republic of China, Considering Both Domestic and International Situations to Realize the Development of Opening up, *QIUSHI*, February 2016.

I. Applicable International Rules for State-owned Enterprises: Basic Framework and Main Characteristics

The applicable international rules for state-owned enterprises are an important part of the existing international economic order.[1] However, different from general trade, raw material and commodity trade, international currency and development assistance, industrialization, transportation and other fields, state-owned enterprises or state-owned economies have been in the "coreless" state with the absence of a global coordination agency or comprehensive institutional arrangement. The basic governance framework consists of related rules in multiple dimensions and areas. Let's take the relevant provisions of the World Trade Organization (WTO) as an example. The WTO does not have agreements specifically regulating state-owned enterprises, and relevant multilateral trade rules are dispersed in the *General Agreement on Tariffs and Trade* (GATT), the *General Agreement on Trade in Services* (GATS), the *Agreement on Subsidies and Countervailing Measures* (SCM) and the accession protocol or commitment of specific members. On the whole, the applicable international rules for state-owned enterprises involve multilateral,

1 According to the documents regarding the relevant international law of the 6th Special Session of the UN General Assembly in 1974, such as the *Declaration on the Establishment of a New International Economic Order* and its *Program of Action*, the areas covered by the international economic order include raw materials and primary commodities, foods, general trade, transportation and insurance, international currency and development assistance, industrialization, technology transfer, transnational corporations, developing countries (south-south) cooperation, natural resource sovereignty, the role of the UN system in international economic cooperation, etc. The trade of raw materials, primary commodities and foods was or is still regulated or organized and coordinated by corresponding international agreements; general trade is coordinated by the WTO and a series of goods trade agreements under its jurisdiction; the maritime and international air transportation organizations and their conventions have already been made available in the transportation field; there are organizations such as the International Monetary Fund (IMF) and the World Bank Group and their related agreements in terms of international currency and development assistance; in the field of industrialization, there is the United Nations Industrial Development Organization aimed at promoting and accelerating the industrialization of developing countries; in the field of the cooperation of developing countries (south-south), there are also G77, the Gulf Cooperation Council, etc. However, no multilateral international treaties exist in the areas of international economic order such as technology transfer, transnational corporations, and natural resource sovereignty. Refer to Zhang Naigen, Evolution of International Economic and Legal Order and China's Response, *China Legal Science*, 2013(2):180-191.

regional, bilateral and unilateral dimensions, as well as trade, investment, competition policy, subsidies, dumping, corporate governance, finance and other fields, which are intertwined to form a regular network system.[1]

1. The main characteristics of applicable multilateral trade rules for state-owned enterprises

Multilateral trade rules mainly refer to the framework of rules established by the WTO and its covered agreements. The regulations concerning state-owned enterprises mainly present the following characteristics:

As a whole, the principle of ownership neutrality is upheld. The basic function of the WTO is to organize the formulation and management of multilateral and plurilateral trade agreements. It is the responsibility of the member governments for negotiation, signing and performance of these agreements. The WTO supervises and manages the trade policies and regulations of all members to ensure compliance. Hence, the WTO agreements significantly distinguish themselves from other rules aimed at business constraints. In particular, the WO basically has no systematic system design to classify and supervise enterprises of different forms of ownerships.

Some WTO agreements include the concepts that are related to or partially overlap with state-owned enterprises, such as state trading enterprise, public monopoly, and public institution. However, these concepts are not equivalent to state-owned enterprises. In the GATT/WTO texts, the term "state-owned enterprise" does not exist, and only some rules involve the behavior of specific non-governmental entities, some of which are closely associated with state-owned

1 Scholars who created the subject of China's international economic law, such as Liu Ding, Yao Meizhen and Chen An, and the young and middle-aged scholars of international economic law, such as Yu Jinsong, Zeng Huaqun and Cao Jianming, all believe that the broad sources of international economic law include the norms of international law (international treaties and international conventions), important resolutions of international organizations, domestic foreign-related economic laws, etc. Refer to Zhang Naigen, Evolution of International Economic and Legal Order and China's Response, *China Legal Science*, 2013(2):180-191. Due to the limited space of this article, the domestic foreign-related legislation on state-owned enterprises is not included.

enterprises in the general sense. For example, Article 17 of the GATT stipulates that WTO members must ensure that state trading enterprises operate on the basis of commercial considerations, adhere to the principle of non-discrimination in import and export activities, and give fair and just treatment to the trade of other parties. However, the WTO does not make a clear definition of "state trading enterprise", which further affects the applicability of the Agreement. Moreover, it can be confirmed that the terms of the WTO on state trading enterprises are only applicable to the enterprises involved in the "trade" function in state-owned enterprises, rather than the state-owned enterprises that have other functions, such as production, sovereign investment and supply of public services. However, whether a "public institution" is a state-owned enterprise depends on the relationship between the state-owned enterprise and the government. If no evidence shows that the government has exercised meaningful control over the state-owned enterprise and its behavior, the state-owned enterprise cannot be identified as a "public institution".

Based on the neutrality of universal ownership, some WTO rules are more regulated for state-owned enterprises, for example, SCMs are not specifically targeted as state-owned enterprises. However, state-owned enterprises are often considered to have obtained or are more likely to receive various forms of subsidies, such as fund transfers, tax deductions and loans. Under normal circumstances, the WTO requires members to fulfill their national treatment obligations and market access obligations, and prohibits the favor of local enterprises, regardless of whether it is a public or a private enterprise. As state-owned enterprises usually have a high degree of participation in the service sector, the service sector naturally becomes an important regulatory object of GATS.

2. The main characteristics of applicable regional economic and trade rules for state-owned enterprises

Regional economic and trade rules are the important places for exploring international rules in new fields. In terms of the regulations on state-owned enterprises, some regional agreements are more explicit and extensive than multilateral trade rules, which are mainly manifested in the following aspects:

The concept of state-owned enterprise is clearly defined. For instance, the US-Singapore Free Trade Agreement stipulates that if a country holds more than 20% of the shares of an enterprise, the enterprise should be regarded as a state-owned enterprise.

The provisions clearly applicable to state-owned enterprises and the exceptions provided for state-owned enterprises are made available. The investment chapter of the US-Peru Trading Partnership Agreement stipulates that state-owned enterprises enjoy the same rights as private investors to obtain investment protection and participate in the settlement of investment disputes. At the same time, the treaty obligations of member states also apply to state-owned enterprises or other entities exercising regulatory, administrative or governmental functions. The US-Singapore Free Trade Agreement stipulates that to exercise the governmental functions and the noncommercial-based or non-competitive services, Singapore reserves the right to allow government-controlled enterprises to become the only service providers; for the enterprises that provide public health, public welfare, security, key economic foundations and other services, the Singapore government can limit the total shareholding proportion of foreign capital (up to 49%), and the composition of senior executives and the board of directors, etc.[1]

The obligations of state-owned enterprises in the policy regarding competition and other fields are made clear. These obligations mainly include: State-owned enterprises should comply with commercial considerations when conducting commercial transactions such as goods transactions, service transactions or investments; state-owned enterprises should engage in anti-competitive behavior and not abuse the position of market dominance; state-owned enterprises should adhere to the non-discrimination principle in the course of commercial activities; state-owned enterprises should exercise regulatory, administrative or other governmental

1 Li Zhenning, Discussion of International Trade Regulations of State-owned Enterprises, *China's Price*, 2015(10).

powers in a manner consistent with the treaty obligations of the contracting states. For example, concerning "state-owned enterprises and related matters", the US-Australia Free Trade Agreement stipulates that state-owned enterprises must not impede trade and investment; state-owned enterprises must not violate this Treaty when exercising state-mandated administrative and administrative functions; state-owned enterprises should uphold non-discriminatory treatment during the sale of goods or services. In some regional agreements, the contracting parties further explicitly request specific members to reduce their state-owned enterprises or weaken their substantive control over state-owned enterprises. For example, the US-Singapore Free Trade Agreement requires Singapore to promise to "aim at basic elimination and continue to reduce the ownership or other interests in the exercise of effective control over state-owned enterprises".

3. The main characteristics of economic and trade rules in the professional fields related to state-owned enterprises

As mentioned above, the applicable international rules for state-owned enterprises cover many fields, including trade, investment, policies regarding competition, subsidies, dumping, corporate governance, and finance, and most of which have been explained in more detail in multilateral or regional rules. This article mainly introduces the fields where corporate governance and sovereign wealth funds are less involved than the two multilateral or regional rules. In the field of corporate governance, the OECD has been working to promote the establishment and improvement of global corporate governance and corporate governance standards for state-owned enterprises for many years. In particular, the *OECD Guidelines on the Corporate Governance of State-Owned Enterprises*, released in 2005, reveals the developmental trend of the governance of state-owned enterprises in OECD countries and provides an important reference for the governance of state-owned enterprises in other countries. In the field of sovereign wealth funds, the 26 international sovereign wealth funds were established at the "International Working Group on Sovereign Wealth Funds" in Washington, U.S.A. in 2008. After extensive consultations, the working group issued the *Recognized Principles and Practices* of the Sovereign Wealth Funds ("San Diego Principles"), stipulating normative requirements in three aspects, namely, corporate governance structure, information disclosure, and risk management of sovereign wealth funds. These guidelines and principles have the following characteristics:

Many detailed provisions and recommendations are made available, which is the most significant difference between the economic & trade rules in the professional field and the multilateral or regional rules. For example, the *OECD Guidelines on the Corporate Governance of State-Owned Enterprises* stipulate the right of the freedom of the directors of state-owned enterprises, the public functions of state-owned enterprises, and the differences among commercial operations, which "harden" the financial constraint of state-owned enterprises and require market-oriented investment returns.

The force of constraint is missing. The *OECD Guidelines on the Corporate Governance of State-Owned Enterprises* and the *Recognized Principles and Practices* of the Sovereign Wealth Funds are not agreements or conventions signed among countries. Since the rules themselves are not binding, the compliance with the normative requirements of the rules is voluntary. In addition, no special supervisory agency conducts a regular evaluation for the implementation of rules by the members.

II. New Developments in International Rules Relevant to State-owned Enterprises

The revision of relevant international rules for state-owned enterprises has been an important part of the revision of international economic rules since the outbreak of the global financial crisis. At present, the United States, the European Union and other developed countries are committed to comprehensively utilizing multilateral, regional, bilateral and professional fields and other platforms, attempting to establish their dominant position in the negotiation of international rules under the framework of the OECD, TPP and the Transatlantic Trade and Investment Partnership Agreement (TTIP), and leading the developmental direction of relevant international rules for state-owned enterprises.

1. International investment facilitation and investment promotion

On February 26, 2016, the United Nations Conference on Trade and Development issued a discussion draft, *Investment Facilitation and Investment Promotion: A Guide to Global Action* (second edition).[1] The action guide is mainly divided into two parts, namely, the investment facilitation actions and the support actions conducive to investment promotion and facilitation. The former mainly includes seven measures: (1) increasing the availability and transparency of investor-related investment policies, regulations, and procedures; (2) improving the predictability and consistency in the implementation of investment policies. (3) raising the efficiency and effectiveness of the investment management processes; (4) establishing a constructive stakeholder relationship; (5) appointing an investment ombudsman/coordinator leading agency on investment dispute resolutions, related legislative supervision and other matters; (6) developing mechanisms of supervision and review for investment facilitation; (7) enhancing international cooperation for investment facilitation through international investment agreements. The latter mainly includes three measures: (1) strengthening the efforts of developing country partners in terms of investment facilitation, establishing transparent, efficient and effective administrative procedures, resolving investment disputes, and increasing relevant institutional capacity to provide support and technical assistance; (2) making more efforts at developing country partners on investment policies and proactive investments to provide support and technical assistance for the design of effective investment promotion strategies, organization of investment promotion forums, and the establishment and maintenance of appropriate investment promotion agencies; (3) strengthening international cooperation on investment promotion and

1 UNCTAD. INVESTMENT FACILITATION AND PROMOTION: A Global Action Menu UNCTAD Discussion Note, *UNCTAD's Investment Policy Hub, Version 2 – 26 February 2016.*

facilitation issues conducive to development through the international investment agreements.

2. TPP

The state-owned enterprise is one of the key factors in TPP negotiation. In 2012, the United States formally proposed to negotiate state-owned enterprises in the TPP, and urged the state-owned enterprise to be a key part of negotiation. On February 4, 2016, the United States, Japan, Australia, Brunei, Canada, Chile, Malaysia, Mexico, New Zealand, Peru, Singapore and Vietnam (12 countries) officially signed the TPP agreement in Auckland. Although Trump announced the withdrawal from the TPP after he took office as President of the United States, the documents signed by TPP may represent the future developmental trend of relevant rules of state-owned enterprises, because they are deeply rooted in the new practices and developments in international rules in related fields. The in-depth understanding of the TPP regulations on state-owned enterprises is of great significance for China in grasping the future direction of the relevant international rules for state-owned enterprises. Compared with the multilateral or regional agreements previously reached, the regulations on state-owned enterprises in the TPP own the following characteristics:

Independent chapters are established. In the TPP, the issues concerning state-owned enterprises are no longer scattered in many fields of competition, subsidies, etc., and instead, they are separately listed as one chapter. This measure not only reflects the importance attached to the rules of state-owned enterprises in terms of structure, but it also strengthens the discipline of state-owned enterprises in terms of content.

The concept of the state-owned enterprise is redefined. In the TPP, the state-owned enterprise mainly refers to the enterprise mainly engaged in commercial activities and which meets one of the following three conditions: (1) in terms of equity condition, the government directly owns more than 50% of the equity; (2) in terms of the right to vote, the government exercises more than 50% of the voting rights through all its rights; (3) in terms of appointment power, the government has the power to appoint a majority of the board or other similar regulatory organization. The definition clearly specifies the types of state-owned enterprises and governmental control methods of enterprises such as stock rights, voting rights or appointment power to strictly define the concept of state-owned enterprise, thus providing a cornerstone for the transfer of the focus of state-owned enterprise rules in the TPP.

The constraints on non-commercial assistance are established. The "non-commercial assistance" for state-owned enterprises regulated by the TPP comes mainly from three aspects: investment from contracting parties in state-owned enterprises, from state-owned enterprises in state-owned enterprises, and from contracting parties in state-owned enterprises in the territory of another contracting party. The TPP stipulates that the contracting parties must not harm the interests of other contracting parties and their domestic industries through "non-commercial assistance" to state-owned enterprises.

The scope of constraint on state-owned enterprises is expanded. Let's take subsidies as an example. In the existing WTO rules, the *Agreement on Subsidies and Countervailing Measures* only regulates trade in goods. However, the constraints on non-commercial assistance created by the TPP under the new definition of state-owned enterprise actually cover the trade in goods, trade in services, international investments and other fields, which further expands the scope of constraints on state-owned enterprises. The clear and extensive definition for state-owned enterprise and non-commercial assistance provides a huge convenience for the contracting parties in subsidizing the state-owned enterprises and taking corresponding remedial measures.

The constraints on the jurisdictional immunity of state-owned enterprises are proposed. The TPP state-owned enterprise regulations require that, for the enterprises that are owned by foreign capital or controlled by foreign capital through ownership equity in the territory of the contracting parties, the contracting parties should stipulate that their domestic courts have jurisdiction over civil actions brought against the enterprise. According to the interpretations of USTR Office in TPP, foreign state-owned enterprises operating within the territory of the contracting parties should not evade legal proceedings against their commercial activities through claim of state immunity. However, China's consistent position is that a country's government and its property are not subject to the jurisdiction of any foreign court, and that it enjoys absolute immunity. According to the interpretations of the USTR Office, the TPP will implement relative immunity. As a result, when the government engages in commercial activities rather than performing governmental duties, the government should accept the jurisdiction of a foreign court, thereby effectively limiting the jurisdictional immunity of state-owned enterprises.[1]

3. Corporate governance

The failure of corporate governance is considered as an important micro foundation for the outbreak of the global financial crisis. Regarding the issue of corporate governance exposed by the financial crisis, the OECD, the International Finance Corporation, the Bank for International Settlements, the Basel Committee on Banking Supervision and other institutions issued a series of guidelines and principles for strengthening corporate governance. In September 2015, the OECD issued an updated version of the guidelines on the corporate governance of state-owned enterprises, and emphasized that the state-owned enterprises involved in fair competition on the market should treat different ownership patterns of shareholders equally. The defects in the corporate governance exposed during the financial crisis are mainly manifested in the failure of internal control and risk management, the dislocation of the compensation system, the failure of the board of directors to fully perform their duties, and the lack of shareholder rights. The revision to the

1 Han Liyu. The TPP Rules of State-owned Enterprises and Their Impacts, National Academy of Governance, 2016(1).

international rules of corporate governance centers on the following points:

(1) Board reform: clarifying basic goals, improving performance capabilities and increasing responsibilities

The NYSE Corporate Governance Committee[1] believes that the primary goal of the board of directors should be the creation of long-term and sustainable growing shareholder value for the company, and that the board of directors must be accountable to shareholders for the achievement of the goal. The board of directors has the responsibility of leading the company in formulating relevant policies in order to support the long-term sustainable growth of the shareholder value. To this end, the board of directors must clearly understand that "the company policy that encourages excessive risk-taking for the pursuit of short-term stock price growth is contrary to good corporate governance." The board of directors and management should "develop appropriate compensation plans and link them with the long-term value goals at different stages".

In order to improve the capacity for duty performance of the board of directors, the Basel Committee on Banking Supervision[2] requires the banking supervisory authorities of various countries to conduct qualification inspection on the proposed directors and senior executives. The qualifications of directors and senior executives include appropriate experience, capabilities and personal qualities, such as occupational spirit and personal integrity. The OECD requires the board of directors to take measures to ensure that shareholders exert their functions in nominating the directors. The board of directors should have a special committee responsible for identifying potential board members with specific skills, knowledge, and experience in a bid to increase the value of the company.

The new rules also clearly specify that the board of directors should be responsible for the development of the corporate strategy, the selection of senior

1 http://www.nyse.com/pdfs/CCGReport.pdf.

2 The Basel Committee on Banking Supervision, "Principles for Enhancing Corporate Governance", 2010. http://www.bis.org/publ/bcbs176.pdf.

executives, the supervision of senior executives' performance, the determination of senior executives' compensation level, the management of risks, the formulation of tax plans, the implementation of internal audit, and the authenticity and reliability of the financial information. Some countries have published the measures for restriction on wages for financial institutions participating in government rescue program, and stipulated that the board of directors should recoup the bonuses and incentive payments granted to senior executives based on serious mistakes, which means these companies should disclose the relevant recovery clauses.

(2) Risk management reform: establishing the chief risk officer, clarifying the risk management responsibilities of the board of directors and senior executives, and strengthening information disclosure

The chief risk officer is mainly responsible for the enterprise-wide risk management framework, which specially includes: identifying the company's major risks, assessing such risks and measuring the corresponding risk exposures, continuously monitoring the risk exposures and determining the corresponding capital plans, evaluating whether the decision of a specific risk acceptance is consistent with the risk policy determined by the board of directors, and reporting the risk management information to the senior management and the board of directors. The chief risk officer enjoys full status and authority to report directly to the CEO or the board of directors, and has a direct influence on the decisions regarding the exposure of enterprise risks.

Both the board of directors and the senior management should actively participate in the management of the operational risk management framework. All important aspects in the process of risk rating and evaluation must be approved by the board of directors and senior management. It is the responsibility of the board of directors for determining the enterprise's ability to bear risks, ensuring the establishment of a framework for evaluation of various risks by the management, and thoroughly understanding the management reports related to risk rating. The senior management should have an in-depth understanding of the design and operations of the risk rating system, master the nature and degree of risks assumed by the enterprise, ensure the standardization of risk management procedures, and provide reports to the board of directors on major risk changes promptly.

In order to enable investors to better evaluate the role and effect of the board of directors and senior management in risk management and internal control, the board of directors is responsible for providing shareholders with detailed risk control reports, and reporting on the enterprise risk control status at the annual general meeting of shareholders, and specially explaining to shareholders what measures the board of directors and management should take in response to the specific risks of the enterprise.

(3) Reform of remuneration management: matching the structure of remuneration with the risk, and increasing the shareholders' authority of participating in and strengthening information disclosure and supervising the organization

The scale and distribution of the variable compensation within an organization should take into account all current and potential risks. When an enterprise suffers major financial losses, the variable compensation should be reduced accordingly or even cancelled. It is proper to consider the measures of "compensation recovery" and "compensation penalty", etc. The percentage of cash in the bonuses for senior management must not exceed 50%, and 40%-60% of the bonuses must be delayed by 3-5 years for distribution. In the event of poor enterprise performance subsequently, the deferred portion of payment will be lowered.

A listed company should conduct a non-binding shareholder vote at least every three years to approve the remuneration package of the appointed senior management. If the remuneration package for the senior management has not been voted before the enterprise's Gold Parachute Plan, the enterprise must also vote on it when seeking shareholders' approval for all future acquisitions, mergers, consolidations or sales.

The annual report on remuneration should be promptly disclosed, which specifically includes the determination of the decision-making process for the entire organization's remuneration policy, the criteria of performance measurement and risk adjustment, the deferred payment policy, and the determination of the parameters for the distribution of the remuneration in cash or other forms.

The USSEC (United States Securities and Exchange Commission) enjoys the right to recourse to the remuneration paid by listed companies to senior management based on erroneous financial information. The exercise of the right to recourse does not need to prove any misconduct by the senior management as long as the issuer is required to make a restatement and the remuneration already paid exceeds the payable amount after accounting restatement, and the board of directors is not granted any discretionary power (even if the recoverable remuneration is less than the cost required for recovery).

III. Applicable International Rules for State-owned Enterprises: Impact and Assessment

Promoting the reform of state-owned enterprises is urgently needed by China to accelerate the formation of new advantages over participating in and taking the lead in the competition for international economic cooperation. China is actively building a new system of open economy, promoting better integration of domestic and foreign mutual promotion, better combining "bringing in" with "going global", promoting the orderly and free flow of international and domestic factors, allocating resources efficiently, and achieving deep market integration. It will be normal for enterprises to allocate resources and participate in worldwide international competition.

In recent years, the major trends of revision of some international rules have been to re-plan the existing international economic rules or systems, achieve fair competition between state-owned and non-state-owned enterprises, improve corporate governance, and strengthen risk management and control. The underlying basic logic is the irrational corporate behavior of state-owned enterprises with special advantages, as believed by some people. On the whole, the views on the special advantages enjoyed by state-owned enterprises mainly include: government payment subsidies, favorable financing and credit guarantees provided by the government and government financial institutions, special preferences on supervision (such as obligations regarding inapplicable information disclosure or anti-trust laws), guarantee of monopoly and existing enterprise advantages, stable governmental shareholding and exemption of bankruptcy and information acquisition. The views on unreasonable corporate behaviors of state-owned enterprises mainly include: need for improvement in corporate governance, production efficiency and operational efficiency; anti-competitive behavior, such as export control and local procurement; implementation of national political and strategic intentions, such as China's investment in African resources, and investment of the State Administration of Foreign Exchange, Singapore Temasek Holdings and other sovereign wealth funds in resources and infrastructure.[1]

Due to the failure to accurately evaluate the efficiency, rights and responsibilities of state-owned enterprises, the forgoing views are biased to some extent. First, studies have shown that after 2002, China's state-owned absolute holding and state-owned relative holding enterprises have been more efficient than other domestic non-state-owned enterprises, revealing the improvement in the overall efficiency of state-owned enterprises under the principle of "invigorating large enterprises while relaxing control over small ones". From the perspective of technological progress, the wholly state-owned enterprises and state-owned mixed-ownership enterprises have faster TFP growth rates than other types of non-state-owned enterprises.[2] Second, the foregoing views take into consideration the benefits of state-owned enterprises excessively, and underestimate the burdens of state-owned enterprises. For example,

1 Chuan Lai, TPP Negotiations and Formulation of Rules for Constraints on State-owned Enterprises, *RIETI Electronic Information,* No.130 (April 2014).

2 Liu Xiaolu, Nie Huihua, *Mixed Ownership Reform of State-owned Enterprises: How to Mix? What about the Mixing Result?* An annual report of the National Academy of Development and Strategy, RUC, [NPE2015S01].

compared with the state-owned enterprises in general market economy countries, Chinese state-owned enterprises assume an additional eight functions, as follows: partial function of national macroeconomic control over economic operations, partial function of the state to respond to and deal with emergencies, maintenance of regional and social stability, guarantee of successful holding of large-scale national events, support of economic and social development in Xinjiang, Qinghai, Tibet and other regions, partial function of participation in international competition and cooperation, partial function of national external exchange and national security and partial important political functions.[1]

Even so, we should still verify whether the current series of applicable international rules for state-owned enterprises are consistent with the current state-owned enterprise reforms in China. Since the reform and opening up, China has been engaged in strengthening the marketization of state-owned enterprises by disposal of non-performing assets, joint-stock reform, equity division and other measures, and liberalizing the market for competitive products to enable both state-owned enterprises and private enterprises to participate in fair and just market competition. Under the new domestic and international situation nowadays, China's idea regarding the policy has been adjusted from implementation of loose macroeconomic policies to more attention on stimulation of the vitality of micro-subjects by means of various measures; the loosening of fiscal and monetary policy on the demand side has been adjusted to streamline the administration and delegate power from the supply side. In terms of reform of state-owned enterprises, China is trying its best to make the market play a decisive role in the allocation of resources, and improve the "vigor, control, influence, and risk resistance capability" of the state-owned economy through the combination of classified reforms, the improvement of the modern enterprise system, the enhancement of vitality, and strengthening of the supervision based on "marketization, specialization, internationalization". Therefore, the developmental direction of applicable relevant

1 Ji Xiaonan. The Additional Eight Functions of Chinese State-owned Enterprises, NetEase Annual Economist Conference 2015.

international rules for state-owned enterprises coincides with the progress of the reform of China's state-owned enterprises to some extent. The coordinated development among them is an objective requirement for improving the vitality of the subjects and constructing a new open economic system.

However, neutrality of competition is not equivalent to institutional neutrality, and even if superficially, the rules are applied equally to all objects, the benefits and damages of different classes, groups or individuals are not the same. The recent series of new regulations on state-owned enterprises are likely to have strong external pressure on the development of China's state-owned economy and strategic layout, especially the participation of the state-owned enterprises in international competition.

First of all, the national treatment enjoyed by state-owned enterprises under the rules may be derogated. The TPP state-owned enterprise clauses advance the examination stage of the state-owned enterprises participating in overseas market investment ahead of their behavior upon entry behavior, and link the restriction requirements (such as disclosure of information) only with the state-owned enterprise identity and separates them from the market behavior, thus greatly increasing the cost and difficulty of overseas investment of the state-owned enterprises. Consequently, this may cause investment barriers in the entry stage of the state-owned enterprises that have gone abroad on a large scale.[1]

Second, cross-border activities of the state-owned enterprises may face higher business risks. For example, the TPP requires that the contracting parties should "not damage the domestic industries of the other party by providing non-commercial assistance to the state-owned enterprises that manufacture and sell products in the territory of other countries". If this regulation is promoted and adopted in other international rules, lawsuits may be brought against Chinese state-owned enterprises

1 Mao Zhiyuan, Impairment of American TPP State-owned Enterprise Clause Proposal on the Treatment of Nation and People Investment, *International Economics and Trade Research*, Vol. 30, No. 1, January 2014.

under the condition that the same industry enterprise located in the host country of investment of China's state-owned enterprises believes that its own interests are harmed. In addition, since the TPP regulations rule out multiple obstacles to subsidy determination, China's state-owned enterprises are more likely to be relief objects of the host country under the framework of similar rules, thanks to the receipt of non-commercial assistance. In addition, although the OECD guidelines are only non-mandatory rules, the impact of their influence cannot be underestimated. If a Chinese state-owned enterprise intends to invest in OECD members or run business in the territory of OECD members, it must refer to the OECD guidelines for state-owned enterprises and face the issue of how to effectively control the overseas branches.

Finally, cross-border activities of state-owned enterprises may face higher transaction costs. The TPP requires that the contracting parties should provide other entities with detailed information on state-owned enterprises or government-monopolized entities, such as the proportion of shares held by the government and state-owned enterprises, explanations of the special shares or voting rights held, the position of government officials serving in state-owned enterprises, annual income and total assets in the past three years, beneficial exceptions or exemptions according to law and annual reports and third-party audit reports. These transparency requirements are extensive and specific, which not only objectively increase the operating costs of the enterprise, but may also become another effective policy tool for refusing Chinese enterprises to enter the market after the "national security review system". For example, the United States filed a national security review on the merger and acquisition of the Chinese companies Huawei and ZTE in 2012, and Huawei and ZTE declined to disclose the structure of the enterprise and the role of the Party Committee in decision-making in response to the issue "the relationship between the Chinese Communist Party and enterprises" raised by the investigation committee. Ultimately, the United States refused to give approval on the grounds that the merger and acquisition of Huawei and ZTE violated national security.

IV. China's Countermeasures

In order to realize the coordinated development between the applicable international rules for state-owned enterprises and the reform of domestic state-owned enterprises is an objective requirement for the establishment of a new open economic system under the new situation. To this end, relevant work should mainly be carried out in two aspects: on the one hand, follow-up research and assessment are conducted for the relevant international rules of state-owned enterprises to grasp the frontiers and developmental trends of these rules, clarify the impact of the new development of these rules on Chinese state-owned enterprises and actively participate in the construction of relevant rules; on the other hand, the layout of the state-owned economy is further adjusted to create a new and more efficient corporate organization that is suitable for the needs of international development, thereby improving the supervision and management system of the state-owned assets.

The major changes in the economic strength among countries and the inherent defects in the original system of rules are the internal reasons for revision of the system of international rules. The essence is the transfer and contention of the dominant rights in international affairs. If a few countries are free to lead the revision of the international system of rules, it only ends with the replacement of the old injustices by new injustices, which not only makes it difficult for the parties to reach a consensus, but it also affects the sustained and healthy development of the global economy. The revision of the international rules should effectively consider the differences in the level of development and capabilities for development of different countries, treat and reflect the interests of all parties on an equal basis, and objectively assess the responsibilities of all countries, so that all parties may have the matched rights, obligations and responsibilities.

In the future, grasping the "founding dividends", "participating in dividends" and "reforming dividends" should become the overall goal of China's participation in the establishment of fairer and more just state-owned enterprise-related international rules. To be specific, the following work should be accomplished:

Grasp the "founding dividends" and improve the multilateral rules. Currently, the relevant multilateral rules of state-owned enterprises are in a state of absence. Multilateral rules are most potential in China, which involves China's fundamental interests. The principle of institutional neutrality upheld by multilateral rules should also be applied to the state-owned enterprises.

Grasp the "participating dividends" and fully participate in the multi-faceted and multi-field negotiations regarding state-owned enterprise rules. The cross-border activities of the state-owned enterprises involve a variety of goods, capitals and organization management modes, including trade in goods and services, physical assets such as equipment and commodities, intangible capitals such as trademarks, patents, production, and financial capitals such as bonds, stocks and derivative securities; "hard" areas such as competition policy, intellectual property protection, professional and technical standards, government procurement and subsidies, and "soft" areas such as labor and the environment. China should participate extensively in various negotiations and strive to have its own representatives at each negotiation table, and choose the focus on which to give support according to progress.

Grasp the "reform dividends" and promote the reform of the state-owned enterprise rules. After Trump took office as the President of the United States, he decided to withdraw from the TPP. Although signatories such as Australia and New Zealand stated that they would not rule out the "TPP minus one" agreement, the future of the TPP agreement remains relatively uncertain. The relevant rules of the state-owned enterprises involved in the WTO have been increasingly clarified so far. Even so, China should continue to strengthen the tracking, research and evaluation of relevant rules, formulate risk warning mechanisms and response plans, and promote the reform of relevant international rules for the state-owned enterprises on multilateral, regional and bilateral platforms. The current key platforms include the WTO, APEC, RCEP, China-Japan-Korea FTA, Sino-US BIT, China-EU BIT negotiations, etc. In addition, China should further strengthen its cooperation with the countries along the “Belt and Road” route on the basis of in-depth implementation of the “Belt and Road” Initiative, improve bilateral FTAs and BITs, and open up a new space for the construction of relevant international rules for state-owned enterprises.

It is an invaluable experience for China to achieve tremendous success in economic construction through forcing reform by opening up, and promoting the integration of domestic systems with international rules. Similarly, the relevant international rules of the state-owned enterprises should become the driving force for China to promote the reform and development of the state-owned economy. In the final analysis, the reform must handle the relationship between the government and the market, strive to improve the vitality and competitiveness of the state-owned economy, realize the rational distribution of the state-owned capital, classify and promote the reform of the state-owned enterprises, and perfect the state-owned assets management system, that is, achieve “good management” in three aspects.

The first is aspect is managing the capital well. Capital is the core element of market-based resource allocation. The reform of China’s economic system is a gradual process of transition. Similarly, the state-owned asset management system has also experienced changes from “company management” to “asset management” and then “capital management”. Capital corresponds to the owner. Compared with “company management” and “asset management”, the “capital management” focuses more on the rights and responsibilities of the owner, the value forms of the management objects rather than the organizational forms, and the liquidity of the management objects rather than physical assets. The improvement of the state-owned asset management system based on “capital management” means that the nature of the investor representative becomes more prominent at the government level on the basis of the nature of the regulatory body. In terms of supervisory responsibilities, it further embodies the use of property rights as the link, and sets foot in the shareholder position of compliance with legal norms and the basic principles of corporate governance and centers on the capital management to implement the responsibilities of the investors. The "capital management" redefines the functions of the state-owned assets supervisory agency, and reflects the internal requirements for strengthening the supervision of the state-owned assets from the perspective of the investor. This means that the transformation of the focus of management functions of investors from the past comprehensive management functions of "people management, affairs management and asset management" to capital-based key management functions with more prominent management priorities.

The second aspect is managing the boundaries between "do" and "not do." The key to the separation of government from enterprise and the separation of government and capital is to handle the boundary between "do" and "not do". What should be "done" is never shirked, meaning no absence, active action and scientific management. What should "not be done" means no redundant intervention nor excessive authority. What should be done is done completely and what should be given is given thoroughly. Related functions should be vigorously streamlined and optimized. First, the corporate board should fully exercise its authority. The board of directors plays an important role in corporate governance. However, due to the influence of the existing institutional mechanisms, the level of governance and the standardization of the board of directors, the powers of the board of directors have not been fully implemented yet. With the advancement of reform of the state-owned asset management and the increasingly sound and standardized operation of the board of directors, decentralizing a group of business autonomies that should be exercised by regulatory agencies in order to maximize the vitality of the enterprise may be considered. Second, the classified reform is promoted to fully ensure the exercise of business autonomy by competitive companies. Other than the merger and acquisition involving major subsidiaries, the significant change in strategic planning and the main business operations, and the loss of the control status of the state shareholding due to the transfer of stock rights, major issues that may result in loss of state-owned assets should be subject to the approval of the State-owned Assets Supervision and Administration Commission. The remaining issues should be returned to Class I enterprises for management. For matters that need to be managed by state-owned assets regulatory agencies due to involvement in the rights and interests of the state-owned capital and influence on the safety of the state-owned assets, it is necessary to change the existing regulatory ideas and methods. More market-oriented mechanisms and means, such as mechanism improvement, incentives guidance and shareholder accountability should be adopted to achieve management goals. Finally, a batch of non-investor-related matters should be managed by public government administrations and social organizations. At present, state-owned enterprises and state-owned assets supervision departments objectively undertake a large number of public management functions, such as energy conservation and emission reduction, safety production, and intellectual property management. These functions not only weaken the core functions of the state-owned enterprises and state-owned assets supervision departments, but they also objectively overlap with the functions of other government management departments, which waste government resources and aggravate the burden on enterprises. In the next reform, the public management functions currently undertaken by state-owned enterprises and state-owned assets supervision departments should be gradually handed over to government-related industry management departments and social organizations.

The third aspect is managing system standardization and capacity building. The key to reform lies in implementation. During the process of implementation, it is particularly necessary to pay attention to putting power into the "cage of the system" and implement supervision according to the law; at the same time, it is important to focus on strengthening the building up of capacity in order to avoid unnecessary loss of efficiency in the implementation of the policy. With respect to system standardization, on the one hand, consideration may be given to formulating and improving a number of crucial systems, such as the state-owned capital property rights system, the state-owned capital operations management system, the state-owned capital operational budget system, and the state-owned capital risk management risk prevention system; on the other hand, consideration may be given to establishing and strengthening a series of supporting systems, such as a public service system for government purchases, market-based purchase fund operation manuals, public-private partnerships, public service outsourcing, the FOF (fund of funds) model, the BOT (build–operate–transfer) model and other operational guidelines. In terms of building up capacity, it is necessary to improve the uniformity and professionalism of the state-owned assets supervision and operations, promote the full coverage of the operational state-owned capital supervision, and form a standardized and transparent operational state-owned regulatory framework with unified rules, clear rights and responsibilities, hierarchical classification, and comprehensive coverage. It is absolutely necessary to loosen all kinds of access restrictions in accordance with the law, establish a mechanism for the state-owned capital to allow for an orderly access, exit and reasonable flow according to market rules; it is also necessary to improve the system of the quantitative assessment index and a third-party assessment mechanism.

“一带一路”对于全球经济治理的贡献

杜大伟 【美国】

美国布鲁金斯学会约翰·桑顿中国中心资深研究员

一　中国为基础设施建设贡献了大量资金

近几年，中国逐渐成为发展资金的供给大国，尤其为基础设施建设提供了大量资金。在受到世界各国普遍欢迎的同时，中国可以进一步提高贷款项目的透明度：指明针对哪些国家提供贷款、针对哪个行业、明确利率和偿还条款。目前为止，中国提供的资金主要有两个来源：中国国家开发银行及中国进出口银行。亚投行的重要性正逐渐凸显，但最开始提供的资金额度较小，这点是无可避免的。在亚投行成立后的前两年中，该行实施的投资、融资项目共计 16 个，金额约 25 亿美元，其中四分之三的资金由该行与世界银行等多边机构联合融资。截至 2016 年底，中国开发银行和中国进出口银行的对外贷款总额达到 6750 亿美元。几乎所有贷款项目都是在过去十年中实施，据此计算，中国每年对外投资高达 600—700 亿美元，多数资金都被用于发展中国家的基础设施建设。

然而这不过是“一带一路”做出的部分贡献。根据习近平主席的规划，随着“一带一路”的不断推进，连接中国、中亚与欧洲的古丝绸之路也会随之复兴。事实上，陆上丝绸之路的潜力颇为有限，因为相比陆路运输，海运成本更低。因此，中国又提出了“海上丝绸之路”的构想，此举的现实意义可谓不言自明：亚洲地区的多数经贸活动都是沿着自北向南的“海上丝绸之路”开展——从中国经由日本、东南亚、南亚，穿过苏伊士运河抵达欧洲。然而需要指出的是，目前为止，中国提供的发展资金中，只有一小部分流向“一带一路”沿线国家，根据中国开发银行及中国进出口银行报告所示，流入“一带一路”沿线国家的贷款总计2390亿美元，仅占中国对外贷款总额的35%。

当然，“一带一路”沿线国家的贷款总额较少，这点不足为奇，因为中国金融机构的主要借贷国均不在“一带一路”沿线。近年来，中国为拉美国家基础设施建设提供的贷款已经超过世界银行和美洲开发银行提供的贷款总额。拉美国家的主要借贷国包括：委内瑞拉、巴西、阿根廷以及厄瓜多尔。此外，中国在非洲国家投放了大量贷款，主要借贷国包括：安哥拉、埃塞俄比亚、苏丹、肯尼亚及刚果（金）尽管肯尼亚属于“一带一路”沿线国家，但其他借贷国则很难被归入沿线国家范畴。换言之，中国提供的发展资金具有全球性特征，并不受“一带一路”的区域限制。

鉴于非洲基础设施异常薄弱，中国向非洲国家提供的开发贷款受到热烈欢迎，近年来对非洲贷款总额占该区外部（基础设施建设）资金总额的三分之一，其余三分之二来自西方国家以及民间资本（PPI）。各类资金形成了鲜明的“劳动分工”，参与基础设施建设的民间资本几乎全部集中在营利性的电信产业，西方的援建资金用于修建供水及卫生设施，而中国提供的资金则十分均衡地分布在发电及运输（公路及铁路）行业。

二　环境与社会风险

中国在为基础设施建设贡献资金的同时，也引发了关于全球治理的一些争论。中国在采矿及基础设施工程领域投放的资金较大，但此类行业通常会引发环境风险以及大量搬迁居民的安置问题。目前为止，在环境及社会问题层面，中国尚未遵循国际标准，只遵循当地法律法规，诚然，这与中国不干涉别国内政的一贯立场相符，但问题在于，在治理能力较弱的国家，环保及社会法规很难得到严格贯彻。

自20世纪90年代起，以世界银行为首的多边开发银行曾经出台过严格的安全标准，其主要目的在于应对发达国家的民间群体施加的压力，以此缓解多边银行投资国与借贷国（发展中国家）之间的矛盾。为协调发展中国家的金融及发展问题，24国政府间组织于1971年成立，在一份研究报告中，该组织曾对安全标准的贯彻不力以及由此造成的代价进行了强烈谴责。

此类安全标准带来的负面影响在于，世界银行或多边开发银行在参与基础设施建设过程中，要付出较高的时间成本的资金成本，因而发展中国家只得从其他途径寻求资助。基础设施贷款本是世界银行的核心业务之一，曾在20世纪50—60年代，占据贷款总额的70%，自进入21世纪后，逐渐下降至30%左右。因此，中国提供的基础设施贷款受到多数发展中国家的欢迎。如前文所述，中国金融机构在拉美国家投放的贷款总额已经超过世界银行和美洲开发银行提供的贷款总额。对于借贷国而言，中国不仅贷款政策较为灵活，且“官僚作风”较轻，工程交付相对迅速，能够较快实现收益。然而，遵循当地法律法规并非没有风险。中国计划投资的拉美项目，如尼加拉瓜运河项目、巴西–秘鲁两国铁路（穿越亚马逊地区和安地斯山）项目等，均会造成环境风险及社会风险，需要在发展需求和环境风险之间权衡斟酌。

发展与环境工作组（由美洲多所高校组成的）曾就中国贸易与投资是否会造成环境退化这一问题开展调查，得出的结论为：“21世纪以来，中国在拉美开展的贸易与投资是造成当地环境退化的主要因素，以及社会冲突的来源之一。”此外，调查组指出：“中国投资商有能力执行高于当地法规的标准，但由于各国政府的法律法规差异较大、投资企业之间也存在经验上的差别，因而在环境标准的贯彻上表现出较大差异。拉美政府与民间团体应积极提高贯彻标准，实行企业负责制，促使投资企业相互学习。”

中国商务部于近期针对中国对外投资中的环境与社会风险下发了多份指导性的文件，在提高环境与社会风险管理方面迈出了重要一步。根据这些指导文件的规定，参与海外投资的中国企业必须开展环境影响评估并出台减缓措施，配合当地政府，对投资可能造成的负面影响进行鉴定。随着投资企业开始贯彻、执行这些指导性文件，中国正朝着国际标准不断靠近，这一点是值得肯定的。

早在亚洲基础设施投资银行（AIIB）成立之初便出现过关于环境风险与社会风险的争论。然而中国成立亚投行的部分原因在于，货币基金组织、世界银行以及亚洲开发银行等金融机构的改革速度过于缓慢。此外，通过亚投行，中国可以采用多边形式利用剩余储蓄，为对外投资提供支持。美国反对亚投行的主要原因在于治理问题，此外也包括环境与社会安全标准问题。而其他西方国家，如英国、德国、法国、澳大利亚等，对亚投行的态度表现出较大分歧。

从亚投行公布的官方文件来看，该行公布的环境及社会安全标准与世行标准极为相近：开展环境及社会风险评估、及时向群众公开关键信息、与利益相关方进行磋商、根据风险要素进行决策等，唯一的区别在于，亚投行没有就具体过程做出详细描述。据该行官方网站所示，应“根据风险等级”实施、贯彻环境及社会风险条例。亚投行的领导层所期望的，是在满足国际标准的同时，能够节约时间成本和资金成本。能够顺利贯彻这些指导条例，要通过时间的检验，更要靠实地经验的支持。随后，亚投行以多边开发银行的身份与安第斯开发公司（CAF）开展合作，由于亚投行的多数股东均为发展中国家，因此该行在发展中国家颇受青睐。值得注意的是，在开展项目的过程中，安第斯开发公司执行的环境与社会安全标准，大多以借贷国的法律法规为准，亚投行也表现出同样的倾向。或许这会带来一定程度的积极影响：既然投资与增长已经转移到发展中国家，如果开发银行能够按照借贷国的意愿开展工程，则可以极大提高效率。如果亚投行能够对世界银行以及区域开发银行造成足够压力，迫使其简化流程、加快基础设施建设进度，全球体系都有望从中国促成的积极改变中受益。

三 债务风险及可持续性

中国对外投资为全球治理带来的另一个问题涉及债务风险与债务可持续性。发展中国家可以借助一定量的外部资金发展基础设施建设，但有可能出现过度依赖外部资金的倾向。国外债务与国内债务不同，不仅要偿还本息，偿还能力还取决于出口状况。过量的外债可能会降低债务的可持续性。发展中国家在作出借贷决策之前，往往对本国的经济增长、外贸增长以及出口产品价格抱有乐观态度，但这些层面时常会遭受不可预计的冲击。例如，近年来许多发展中国家受到商品价格大幅下跌的影响，因而债务状况并不似前几年那样乐观。

目前为止，中国的对外借贷似乎并没有将风险指数考虑在内。民间投资者大多参考常规风险指数，即规管质量指数和法制指数，这两项在全球治理指数中指代平均治理水平。以这两项标准来衡量中国在拉美的两大借贷国，可以发现委内瑞拉的治理指数远远达不到区域平均值，相比之下，巴西的治理指数则高于区域平均水平。同样，安哥拉、刚果（金）以及苏丹的治理指数低于非洲平均值，而埃塞俄比亚、肯尼亚两国的治理水平显然要高得多。从这个角度来看，中国的对外投资不具有歧视性，且没有考虑到风险程度。

因此，中国在高风险环境下的投资并非总能带来令人满意的结果，这实属意料之中。目前，中国在委内瑞拉投资的一些项目已经陷入困境，有些项目已经搁置。为此，中国调整了对委贷款政策，但几乎可以确定的是，委内瑞拉无法做到全额偿还。从表面看，这些债务并不会带来过高的风险，因为委内瑞拉盛产石油，但原油价格一旦下跌，石油出口收入则不足以弥补债务缺口。安哥拉也面临着同样的问题。受油价下跌影响，安哥拉经济陷入困境，偿债负担沉重，所占政府财政比率高达60%，这意味着债务不具有可持续性。国际货币基金组织发布的《2017年非洲经济展望报告》显示，除安哥拉外，许多非洲国家同样面临着外债不可持续的负担。当然，多数非洲国家在偿债问题上表现良好，因此主要问题在于，如何鉴别各国的债务承担能力，确保投资能在基础设施建设和推动经济增长层面得到有效运用。

四　结语

对于“一带一路”沿线国家和发展中国家而言，中国已经成为开发资金、特别是基础设施建设资金的主要来源。不少证据表明，中国做出的贡献与全球经济治理形成了良性互动。在环境与社会安全层面，中国金融机构在学习全球标准的同时，能够根据发展中国家的意愿，努力提高投资项目的进度和效率，这对全球标准的改革树立了优秀的典范。在债务可持续性问题上，中国从对委内瑞拉投资以及对高风险国家的投资中吸取了教训，对外投资日趋理性。中国资金若能得到有效而合理的运用，定然能够极大促进发展中国家的经济发展。

How China's "Belt and Road" Initiative Can Support Global Economic Governance

David Dollar / United States of America

Senior Fellow in the John L. Thornton China Center at the Brookings Institution

I. China as Major Funder of Infrastructure

China has emerged in recent years as a major provider of development finance, especially funding for infrastructure. Since this development is largely welcomed around the world, China could help itself by being more transparent about its loans: which countries are receiving them, in what sectors, and with what interest and repayment terms. The two big sources of finance up to now have been China Development Bank and China EXIM Bank. The Asian Infrastructure Investment Bank may eventually become important, but it inevitably starts out small: in its first two years it committed 2.5 billion $ to 16 projects, three-quarters of which were co-financed with other multilateral development banks such as the World Bank. CDB and EXIM report aggregate external loan portfolios totaling 675 billion $ at end-2016. Virtually all of this has occurred in the past ten years, so China is lending 60-70 billion $ per year, mostly for infrastructure construction in developing countries.

Some of this is part of the "Belt and Road" Initiative. This is Xi Jinping's vision of restoring the ancient Silk Road stretching West from China through Central Asia to Europe. In truth, the overland route has limited potential as it is much more economic to moves goods by sea. So, it was practical for China to add the "maritime road" to the concept. Most economic activity in Asia occurs along the maritime route that goes South from China and Japan past Southeast Asia and South Asia and through the Suez Canal to Europe. It should be noted, however, that up to now, only a minority of China's development finance has gone to belt and road countries. CDB and EXIM report 239 billion $ of cumulative lending to BRI countries, that is, about 35% of the total.

It should not be a surprise that BRI plays a modest role because some of the well-known borrowers from China are not along the belt and road. In recent years China has been financing more infrastructure in Latin America than the World Bank and the Inter-American Development Bank combined. The big borrowers in Latin America are Venezuela, Brazil, Argentina, and Ecuador.[1] China has also been lending a significant amount to African countries. The big borrowers are Angola, Ethiopia, Sudan, Kenya, and DR Congo.[2] Kenya can be considered part of the belt and road, but it is hard to see how the other countries could be considered as part of BRI. In other words, China's development finance is global; it is not geographically limited by the belt and road.

The infrastructure funding in Africa is very welcome, given the continent's serious infrastructure deficiency. In recent years China has been providing about one-third of the external financing of infrastructure in Africa, along with Western donors and Private Participation in Infrastructure (PPI). An efficient division of labor has emerged in which PPI goes almost exclusively to telecom, a sector that can be organized on a commercial basis; Western aid finances water supply and

1 David Dollar, 2016, "China's investment in Latin America" , Brookings Institution, https://www.brookings.edu/wp-content/uploads/2017/01/fp_201701_china_investment_lat_am.pdf

2 David Dollar, 2016, "China's Engagement with Africa. From Natural Resources to Human Resources" , John L. Thornton China Center, Brookings Institution, https://www.brookings.edu/research/chinas-engagement-with-africa-from-natural-resources-to-human-resources/

sanitation; and Chinese funding is divided, fairly evenly, between power generation and transport (roads and rail).

II. Environmental and Social Safeguards

China's emergence as a major funder of infrastructure raises some issues of global governance. China is a major funder of mining and infrastructure projects that typically carry significant environmental risks and involve the involuntary resettlement of large numbers of people. China so far has been reluctant to subscribe to any international standards for environmental and social safeguards. Its position is that it follows the laws and regulations of the host country. This is a reasonable point of view, consistent with China's general position that countries should not interfere in each other's internal affairs. The problem, however, is that the implementation of environmental and social regulations is often weak, especially in the countries with weak governance.

The multilateral development banks that fund infrastructure in the developing world have developed stringent standards. Led by the World Bank, these standards have been developed since the 1990s, primarily in response to pressure from civil society groups in wealthy countries. The safeguards are an area of tension between the rich countries that fund the multilateral banks and the developing countries that borrow from the banks. For example, a 2015 study by the Intergovernmental Group of Twenty-Four, which was established in 1971 to coordinate the positions of developing countries on monetary and development issues, sharply criticizes the cost and delays associated with these safeguards.[1]

One unintended consequence of these safeguards is that it is time-consuming and expensive to do infrastructure projects with the World Bank or the other development banks. As a result developing countries have turned to other sources

1 Humphrey, Chris.(2015).*Infrastructure Finance in the Developing World: Challenges and Opportunities for Multilateral Development Banks in 21st Century Infrastructure Finance*. Retrieved from Intergovernmental Group of Twenty-Four Website:http://g24.org/wp-content/uploads/2015/06/MARGGK-WP08.pdf. 19.

of funding. Infrastructure was the original core business of the World Bank, accounting for 70% of lending in the 1950s and 1960s. That has steadily declined to about 30% in the 2000s. Given this situation, the emergence of China as a major funder of mining and infrastructure projects has been welcomed by most developing countries. As noted above, Chinese banks are financing more infrastructure in Latin America than the World Bank and the IADB combined. China is seen as more flexible and less bureaucratic. It completes infrastructure projects relatively quickly so that the benefits are realized sooner. However, China's approach of relying on a recipient country's own laws and regulations has its own risks. Some of the infrastructure projects that China has proposed in Latin America, such as the Nicaragua Canal or the Brazil-to-Peru rail across the Amazon and the Andes, carry serious environmental and social risks. Such projects call for carefully balancing development needs with environmental risks.

The Working Group on Development and Environment in the Americas, a multi-university effort, carried out case studies for eight countries on the question of whether Chinese trade and investment had led to environmental degradation. On the one hand, they conclude that "Chinese trade and investment in Latin America since the turn of the 21st century was a major driver of environmental degradation in the region, and was also a source of social conflict."[1] On the other hand, they find evidence of positive evolution: "Chinese investors show an ability to exceed local standards, but their performance varies widely across different regulatory regimes and between more experienced and newer firms. There is an important role for Latin American governments and civil society to raise the performance level across the board, through holding firms accountable and facilitating learning between firms."[2]

---

1 Ray, Rebecca, Kevin P. Gallagher, Andres Lopez, and Cynthia Sanborn. (2015). *China in Latin America: Lessons for South-South Cooperation and Sustainable Development*. Retrieved from Boston University Website:http://www.bu.edu/pardeeschool/files/2014/12/Working-Group-Final-Report.pdf. 2.

2 Ibid., 3.

An important recent development is that MOFCOM has issued guidelines on environmental and social policies for Chinese firms investing abroad.[1] The guidelines require Chinese companies operating overseas to conduct environmental impact assessments, develop mitigation measures, and work with local communities to identify potential negative impacts of investments. While implementation of the guidelines is left to individual investing countries, this is still an encouraging example of China evolving in the direction of global norms.

The issue of environmental and social safeguards was a key factor in the controversy around the founding of the Asian Infrastructure Investment Bank (AIIB). China proposed the new bank partly in response to its frustration with the slow pace of reform at existing institutions, including the IMF, World Bank, and ADB. The new bank is also a way for China to put its excess savings to use through a multilateral format, to complement (and perhaps provide some competition with) its bilateral efforts. The U.S. opposed the effort primarily due to concerns over governance, including the issue of environmental and social safeguards. Other major Western nations such as the United Kingdom, Germany, France, and Australia all chose to fight these battles from the inside.

AIIB has promulgated environmental and social policies which on paper are similar to the principles embodied in World Bank safeguards: environmental and social assessments to analyze risks; public disclosure of key information in a timely manner; consultation with affected parties; and decision-making that incorporates these risks. The AIIB approach, however, differs from that of the World Bank by avoiding detailed prescriptions for how to manage the process.
AIIB's website indicates that its environmental and social guidelines should be implemented "in proportion to the risk." AIIB's leadership hopes that the bank can meet international standards but be more timely and cost-effective. This is largely

1 Leung, Denise and Yingzhen Zhao. (2013). *Environmental and Social Policies in Overseas Investments: Progress and Challenges for China*. Retrieved from World Resources Institute Website: http://www.wri.org/sites/default/files/pdf/environmental_and_social_policies_in_overseas_investments_china.pdf.

a matter of implementation and it will take time and experience on the ground to see if the effort is a success. AIIB joins the Andean Development Corporation (CAF) as a multilateral bank in which developing countries have the majority of the shareholding, so it follows that the preferences of the bank align more with those of developing countries. It is interesting that CAF relies on borrowing countries' own environmental and social regulations in implementing projects. AIIB is evolving in the same direction. This could be a very positive innovation: since most investment and growth now take place in developing countries, it would be more efficient if development bank activities reflected the preferences of those countries. If AIIB's activities can put pressure on the World Bank and the regional development banks to streamline their procedures and speed up their infrastructure projects, then this would be a positive change to the global system that emanated from China.

III. Risk and Debt Sustainability

Another global governance issue raised by China's development finance concerns risk and debt sustainability. Countries can make use of a certain amount of external finance in order to build up infrastructure, but it is risky to rely too much on external finance. External debt, unlike domestic debt, has to be serviced and repaid through exports. Hence taking on too much debt entails risks that the debt will become unsustainable. Countries often make their borrowing decisions based on rosy forecasts about growth of the economy, growth of exports, and prices of key export commodities. All of these factors are subject to unpredictable shocks. In recent years, for example, many developing countries have been hit by the big decline in commodity prices, making their debt situations look much less favorable than just a couple years earlier.

One of the characteristics of China's development lending so far is that it has not paid much attention to risk indicators. A common risk indicator used by private investors is the quality of property rights and the rule of law. The World Governance Indicators include an index of property rights and the rule of law that is an average of all available such indicators.[1] Looking at China's two big clients in Latin America, Venezuela is far below the median on this measure while Brazil is above the median for the region. In Africa, Angola, Dr Congo, and Sudan are below the median for the continent, while Ethiopia and Kenya have reasonably good governance. Chinese funding in this sense is *indiscriminate,* going to high-risk and low-risk environments alike.

Not surprisingly, the Chinese lending to high-risk environments is not always working out well. Venezuela is struggling to complete projects financed by China and some have been abandoned. China's loans to the country have been rescheduled and it will almost certainly not be repaid in full. Upfront, the loans may have seemed low-risk because they are secured by oil, but with the drop in the oil price the revenue from oil is not sufficient to service the loans. Angola is struggling with a similar problem. Because of poor performance of the economy and the drop in the price of oil, the debt servicing burden for the country has increased to the point at which it takes up 60% of government revenue, a level that is not sustainable. The IMF's *Africa Regional Outlook 2017* finds that Angola and some other countries face unsustainable external debt burdens.[2] Much of Africa is doing fine in terms of debt service so the issue really is to distinguish among countries in terms of their ability to take on debt and to use it productively to build infrastructure and grow the economy.

IV. Conclusion

China has become a major source of development finance, especially for infrastructure, both for Belt and Road countries and for the developing world more generally. There is already evidence of positive interaction between global economic governance and Chinese practice. In the important area of environmental and social safeguards, Chinese banks are learning from existing global practices, while at the

1 The World Bank, Worldwide Governance Indicators (WGI), 2014, http://info.worldbank.org/governance/wgi.

2 International Monetary Fund, *Africa Regional Economic Outlook 2017,* available at: https://www.imf.org/en/Publications/REO/SSA/Issues/2017/05/03/sreo0517.

same time trying to make them more efficient and more in line with developing country preferences. This is potentially a positive evolution in global norms. In the area of debt sustainability, Chinese banks have learned from their indiscriminate lending to Venezuela and other high-risk countries and have shown more caution in recent lending. Used wisely and in appropriate amounts, Chinese financing can provide a very helpful boost to the developing world.

冷淡与狂喜：历史视角下的“一带一路”接受研究

希霍 【以色列】
希伯来大学荣休教授/海法大学荣休教授

一 引言

在长达五十多年的中国研究中，笔者尚未发现任何一项比“一带一路”倡议更受拥护的政策。自从习近平主席提出“新丝绸之路”建设的愿景以来，这项倡议在短短一段时期内便迅速成为国内外媒体的焦点及国际会议的议题。更具长远意义的是，各国大学相继成立了“一带一路”研究学会、研究中心。尽管这一倡议仅仅在4年之前，即2013年提出，但目前为止，相关主题的文章数量已经达到数百篇，专著数十本。不论就中国社会还是国际社会而言，“一带一路”引发的强烈反响可谓一种史无前例且值得关注现象，其强烈程度即便构不成“歇斯底里”，也可算作一种“狂喜”。然而值得注意的是，与中国的其他政策或战略（如中国主导的亚亚投行）相比，“一带一路”的内涵尚未得到清晰的界定，缺乏一定的组织性和系统性，且具有某种程度上的模糊性。在这种情况下，应如何解释“一带一路”倡议引发的“狂喜”热潮？以下，笔者将针对“一带一路”在中国以及国际社会的“接受史”而不是“一带一路”本身进行重点讨论。本文分为以下几个部分：第一，笔者将指出“一带一路”的模糊性；第二，分析“一带一路”在中国国内以及国际社会的接受情况；第三，在宏观历史语境下，探讨引发“狂喜”反响的种种原因；最后，笔者将针对“一带一路”的未来实施路径提出一些建议。

二 模糊性与挑战

必须指出的是，“一带一路”的最初含义并非是各大媒体或学术界所提到的“战略”、“工程”或“计划”，而是一项“倡议”（字面意思为proposal或initiative），这个词语的含义较为模糊，往往暗示着“行动的成分较少”“初始阶段”等意味，听起来更像是一句口号。“一带一路”倡议提出之后，人民日报使用的新闻标题为“习近平提议，由中国与中亚共建丝绸之路经济带”总体而言，中国官方媒体较为谨慎，大多使用“倡议”二字，而非官方媒体以及学术界（包括国外媒体及学术界）通常使用“战略”或“计划”等字眼。

与含义明确且作为一个正式组织而存在的亚投行不同，“一带一路”倡议的“口号”成分更明显。中国政府在发布对内、对外政策时，偶尔会使用口号而非平淡的文字阐释，但口号往往具有“求简”的特性，这种简化主义倾向会导致将复杂问题简单化，从而造成含义模糊，解读空间较大。自毛泽东主席之后，中国历任领导人都会在各自的任期内提出鲜明的口号，有时甚至是多个口号。从历史上看，许多国家（包括西方国家在内）的政党提出的口号大多含义模糊，且持续时间较短，如美国政府提出的“亚洲转向”、“亚太再平衡”以及“跨太平洋伙伴关系”等口号（其合法性和有效性往往令人生疑）。

“一带一路”这句“口号”的背后缺乏足够的信息支撑。2015年3月28日，在习近平主席提出“一带一路”倡议半年之后，中国国家发改委（NDRC）、外交部及商务部在国务院的授权下，联合发布了《推动共建丝绸之路经济带和21世纪海上丝绸之路的愿景与行动》，迄今为止，这份长达16页的文件是有关“一带一路”倡议最为详尽的阐述，但文件中依然缺乏足够的细节及详情，内容虽多但实质内容不足。因此，“一带一路”这一概念太过宽泛，似乎可以涵盖任何普遍意义上的国际经济关系，但关于“一带一路”的建设构架却很少提及，只提到依靠现有机制推进“一带一路”建设，如“中国–阿拉伯国家合作论坛”、“上海合作组织”（SCO）、“中国–东盟峰会”（十加一）、亚太经合组织（APEC）、“亚欧会议”（ASEM）、“亚洲合作对话”（ACD）以及中国-海湾合作委员战略对话等，很少或几乎没有提及任何关于融资、具体参与国等方面的信息，甚至没有提供官方地图。

从这个角度来讲，“一带一路”的模糊性可能会掩盖或忽视种种潜在的挑战。

在《推动共建丝绸之路经济带和21世纪海上丝绸之路的愿景与行动》中，出现频率最高者要数“合作”一词（14页，出现98次），中国政府认为，“一带一路”能够取得成功的关键在于各方间的紧密合作，认为“只要沿线各国和衷共济、相向而行，就一定能够谱写建设丝绸之路经济带和21世纪海上丝绸之路的新篇章。”然而在“一带一路”的决策过程和实施过程中，需要各国、中国的各个省份以及各方机构的参与，必须对所涉及的项目及活动进行有效的协调和管控，此乃挑战。

三　国内及国际反响

尽管“一带一路”倡议的内涵仍不明晰，且面临诸多挑战及风险，但这项倡议不仅在中国得到了积极响应（作为政府提出的倡议，国内自然会积极响应，这一点是可以理解的），更在全世界各个地区引起强烈反响。许多国家将自身视为中国“一带一路”倡议的“十字路口”、“关键位置”或“交通枢纽”。

据CNKI数据库显示，自中国提出“一带一路”以来，中国学术杂志上发表的相关文章数量达到数百篇。2015年12月13日，相关词条搜索结果达到2735条，这从侧面反映出“全国各界正掀起一场‘一带一路’热潮”。有些文章的下载数量高达数千次，读者群体规模成倍激增。除大量文章、专著及编著得以出版外，中国的许多大学相继成立了研究中心及研究所，如青岛大学的“一带一路”研究院，北京外国语大学的丝绸之路研究院，西安交通大学的丝绸之路经济带研究协同创新中心等。此外，中国国内举办了多场以“一带一路”及“新丝绸之路”为主题的会议。笔者本人也有参与到其中一场会议的组织工作，正是在这场会议上，中山大学珠海校区的中东研究前沿中心正式挂牌成立。

2017年1月2日至4日期间，中东研究国际研究班（学员均来自中国国内或中东地区）正式开课，研修重点集中在中东语境下的“一带一路”倡议。2016年10月15日，国际研讨会——“中国‘一带一路’发展战略：过去、现在和将来”在诺丁汉孔子学院宁波分院举行。2015年9月，中国与全球化研究中心（CCG）“一带一路”研究所举办了以“一带一路”与“跨太平洋伙伴关系”为主题的研讨会。以上列举的只是“一带一路”相关会议及研究机构中的一小部分。2017年5月14—15日，“一带一路”国际合作高峰论坛于北京召开，29位国家及政府领导人以及来自130个国家、70个国际组织的代表参与了本次论坛，掀起了“一带一路”建设的高潮。“一带一路”倡议在中国受到热捧不难理解，但在国际社会引起如此强烈的反响可谓不同寻常。

事实上，不论是在中国国内还是国际社会，“一带一路”带来的影响都是极其广泛的。对此，中国香港地区的响应最为积极。2016 年 5 月 10 至 11 日，香港理工大学物流及航运学系组织召开了“‘一带一路’海运物流国际会议”；同年 5 月 18 日，“‘一带一路’高峰论坛”于香港会展中心召开；2016 年 12 月 2 日，《南华早报》组织并召开‘一带一路’中国年会。需要指出的是，对“一带一路”的强烈关注并不仅限于中国。2015 年 11 月 19—20 日，“‘一带一路’与非洲经济发展”高级别研讨会在德班理工大学召开；2016 年 12 月 1—2 日，“一带一路：运输与全球供应链”国际研讨会在墨尔本的维多利亚大学召开；2017 年 1 月 19—20 日，“‘一带一路’国际战略：意义、前景及局限”国际研讨会在丹麦的奥尔堡大学召开。此外，据亚马逊统计数据显示，截至 2017 年 7 月，全世界范围内出版的‘一带一路’相关论著达 120 种，而谷歌学术统计的相关文章发表数量达到数百篇。

尽管如此，一些国家对于“一带一路”所持的看法却不尽相同。例如，俄罗斯的表现似乎不够积极，俄罗斯学者发表的相关文章、专著以及评论相对较少。“俄罗斯国内的一些媒体曾反复强调，‘一带一路’倡议会给俄政府提出的‘欧亚倡议’造成威胁，中国有可能借此机会取代俄罗斯在中亚的地位。”尽管中亚各国对中国经济力量的渗透表示担忧，但同时也急于摆脱来自俄罗斯的直接影响。俄罗斯在格鲁吉亚、克里米亚、乌克兰等地的政策，令中亚诸国更为担心。最新证据表明，中亚正试图摆脱俄罗斯的影响，对斯拉夫字母的使用和俄罗斯族逐渐表现出排斥情绪。

事实上，对于中国的经济渗透，特别是劳动纠纷以及中国劳动力的涌入，中亚地区的许多国家都表现出一种“中国恐惧症”以及“过于警惕”的态度，认为中国的“一带一路”会与俄罗斯主导的欧亚经济联盟（EEU，2015 年成立）相冲突，因为哈萨克斯坦正是该联盟的五个成员国之一。尽管如此，对中国的忌惮并不意味着“一带一路”倡议不被这些国家所接受。毋庸置疑的是，不论是哈萨克斯坦的民众观点还是官方政策，从本质上讲，都对“一带一路”持积极态度。“与对中国的忌惮相比，这种积极态度更占上风，因为所谓的忌惮不仅毫无来由，而且缺乏充分的依据。”中亚各国的普遍观点是，“一带一路”倡议带来的潜在利益，远远超过对中国影响带来的忧虑。

最开始，美国、西欧以及日本等国对于“一带一路”倡议的态度比较积极，但这种积极却逐渐转为批判。最近几个月发表的文章和评论中，均指出了“一带一路”倡议所面临的困境、局限以及挑战。

四 历史视角

既然“一带一路”倡议具有一定程度的模糊性和不确定性，且面临着种种挑战和风险，那么各国——特别是亚非国家——对于该倡议所采取的、近乎“狂喜”的态度又如何解释？很显然，这种积极的支持态度反映出亚非国家“取胜”的渴望。相比之下，位于“一带一路”终端的西欧国家，以及美俄两国则对该倡议表现出质疑及保守态度，认为该倡议所面临的重重挑战有可能为失败埋下隐患。笔者认为，两种态度的差异不仅仅在于“取胜”与否，因为中国曾反复强调，该倡议的宗旨在于促进共同发展、互利共赢。事实上，“一带一路”倡议是首个“东方”国家所提出的、极具建设性的全球倡议。从本质上看，该倡议的宗旨在于促进经济发展，代表着建设性的力量。自古以来，亚洲为西方的发展进步做出了重大贡献，包括印欧语言的使用、沿用至今的种种发明等。此外，在17—18世纪的“启蒙时代”里，亚洲思想对欧洲的哲学家、政客以及日常生活造成了巨大影响，丝绸之路贸易的贡献更可谓居功甚伟。然而与“一带一路”倡议带来的巨大效益相比，这些贡献都是微不足道的。

作为唯一的“东方”强国，日本的优势主要在于其经济实力。20世纪70、80年代，日本的经济发展达到顶峰，成为仅次于美国的世界第二大经济强国，与今日中国的世界地位相仿。但日本却从未提出过任何类似于“一带一路”的倡议，从未推行过大规模、跨区域的经济计划，至多在一些零星的计划中提供过些许帮助。尽管由日本掌舵的亚洲开发银行在某些层面类似于“一带一路”倡议，但作为多边金融机构，该行所反映出的，主要是以美日为首的、西方国家的利益。印度的经济力量虽然崛起迅速，但却缺乏足够的经验和意愿，无法提出一个类似于“一带一路”的倡议。阿拉伯国家虽然能源资源丰富，但却从未试图利用本国的能源资源为他国经济发展谋福利，更不用说中东国家。

“一带一路”的重要意义不仅仅在于它的规模和目标，因为具体规模尚不清楚，而目标尚且有待实现，而在于它所处的历史语境。“一带一路”在促进经济发展的同时，并不附带任何政治或军事条件。遗憾的是，西方观察人士及学者，特别是美国、俄罗斯学者（大多供职于高校及科研机构），往往按照其最熟悉的思维方式，即冷战思维来解读中国政府的“能动”倾向。因此，西方媒体和“专家”常常将“一带一路”倡议错误地称为“计划”、“战略”、“工程”或“政策”，认为中国正积极寻求政治控制、支配力及影响力，企图通过在国外修建“海军基地”和铁路来获取战略地位。可以说，是对中国历史、文化、军事能力以及中国意图的严重误解。因此，必须从历史的视角来审视“一带一路”倡议。

五 未来路径

尽管昔日的亚非殖民地国家通过各自的民族解放运动相继取得独立，但这些国家在经济层面仍然依附于昔日的殖民者，直接或间接地受到西方国家主导的国际金融机构（世界银行、亚洲开发银行、国际货币基金组织）的支配。从这重意义上来说，“一带一路”倡议的提出，以及亚洲基础设施投资银行的建立，为一场“国际性的解放运动”吹响了号角，为打破依附西方经济的现状做出了巨大贡献。作为这场运动的领导者，中国做出了史无前例的努力，而且没有附加任何条件。

这番人类史上前所未有的壮举，必然受到世界各国的珍视。中国不会重蹈殖民主义霸权的覆辙，更不会陷入冷战思维，在全世界范围内扩张军事力量、修筑军事基地。经济发展永远是重中之重，而且要摆脱政治的束缚。2005年，前任美国常务副国务卿罗伯特·佐利克曾表示，中国应该成为“一个负责任的大国”，在国际政治中扮演更加重要、更加积极的角色。这番言论曾引起多方解读，但不论从哪个角度阐述，这些解读者的立场都是与政治紧密相连的。持这种观点的人并非只有佐利克，许多西方国家和第三世界国家也能听到类似的呼声，许多学者，特别是在美国受教育知识分子，都持有类似的看法。

此类学者或知识分子大多经历过冷战时期，因此有意无意间接受了冷战思维——国际地位依赖于对他国的干涉、军事恐吓及压迫。然而这种思维方式并不正确，这不仅仅是因为冷战基本上已经结束，冷战思维已经遭到摒弃（俄罗斯的立场便是绝佳的例证），而是因为中国遵循着自身独特的思维方式，依靠自身的历史经验、文化价值以及外交模式。此外，中国实行改革开放政策已经证明，中国可以通过更加具有建设性而非破坏性的方式，实现其国际、国内目标。

“一带一路”倡议得到各国积极响应，特别是受到第三世界的热捧，这种现象反映出世界各国对于中国的期待，期待中国在世界舞台上发挥更大的影响力，但这种影响力未必一定要体现在国际政治层面。从历史经验来看，中国向来游离在世界政治问题的边缘，这是睿智的体现。中国不愿介入国际纷争，认为冲突应该由相关各方去解决，毕竟介入纷争便意味着要表明立场。基于种种考虑，中国政府从未站在国际冲突的任何一方。尽管自 20 世纪 70 年代后，中国成为了联合国安理会成员国、建立了广泛的外交关系网、加入了许多国际组织，但却从未直接地介入任何一场重大的政治纷争。

相反，中国向来只是通过直接而有效的方式，参与各类经济活动，“一带一路”倡议便是最具希望且最有力的证明。中国并非墨守成规，只不过采取的是更为中国化而非西方化的手段。这不仅仅是中国传统价值复兴的表现，更是遵循马克思主义原理的体现：经济发展和经济增长会造成一定的社会政治问题，但若想解决这些问题，不能仅凭直接的政治手段或军事手段，而是要借助经济发展本身来解决问题。中国若想确保“一带一路”倡议取得成功，必须要坚持走中国道路。

Qualified Ecstasy: Diversified Response to China's "Belt and Road" Initiative in Historical Perspective

Yitzhak Schihor / Israel

Professor Emeritus at the Hebrew University, Professor Emeritus at the University of Haifa

I. Introduction

Studying China for well over fifty years, I have never seen such an enthusiastic welcome to any Chinese policy or idea as the "Belt and Road" initiative. Within a short time the New Silk Road vision (as it has also been called) was captured by the international media (and the Chinese as well) and discussed in scores of conferences all over the world. Even more significant and of longer value, Belt and Road research institutes and centers have been set up in many universities. Although this initiative was launched only in late 2013, less than four years ago, by now hundreds of articles and dozens of books have already been published on this topic. This response, truly an ecstasy if not hysteria, is an unprecedented and intriguing phenomenon, not only with regard to China but also worldwide. Intriguing because unlike other Chinese policies and strategies, such as the Beijing-sponsored Asian Infrastructure Investment Bank, Belt and

Road is not well-defined, not well-structured, not institutionalized and is (perhaps deliberately) ambiguous. So, under these circumstances, how can we explain the ecstatic reaction to the Belt and Road initiative? In this paper I am going to deal less with Belt and Road itself and more with its reception in China and abroad (the German term is *Rezeptionsgeschichte*, or history of ideas reception). To begin with I shall underline Belt and Road's fuzzy nature, and then I shall offer some examples of the ways it has been received in China, around China and in the world. I shall then try to explain the reasons behind the enthusiasticresponse – though not always positive –to Belt and Road and to point to the broad historical perspective that provides the context for the various responses (both positive and negative). Finally I shall make some suggestions as to how Beijing should handle its Belt and Road initiative in the future.

II. Ambiguity and Challenges

It should be underlined at the very beginning that Belt and Road is not a "strategy", "project" or a "plan" – as it usually appears in many, or indeed most, media and academic references – but is a *changyi* (倡议),[1] literally an "initiative" or a "proposal", a term that implies less commitment, a vague meaning and no more than a first and initial step. It is little more than a slogan. When this initiative was announced, the *People's Daily* headline said that "Xi *Suggests* China Central Asia Build Silk Road Economic Belt"[2]. Official Chinese sources are careful to use the term "initiative", but whereas non-official sources and academics (also outside China) often use the terms "strategy" or "plan"[3].

1 Xie Tao, "Is China's 'Belt and Road' a Strategy?" *The Diplomat*, December 16, 2015.

2 September 8, 2013, at: http://english.peopledaily.com.cn/90883/8393079htm.

3 For the Chinese usage, see: Michael D. Swaine, "Chinese Views and Commentary on the 'One Belt, One Road' Initiative," *China Leadership Monitor*, Issue 47 (July 14, 2015) and "'One Belt, One Road': China'sGreat Leap Outward," *China Analysis* (European Council on Foreign Relations, June 2015). For Western sources, see, for example: Shannon Tiezzi, "China's Prescription for Troubled Xinjiang: the New Silk Road," *The Diplomat* (November 19, 2014), where she repeatedly uses the term "plan" ; Jiayi Zhou, Karl Hallding and GuoyiHan, "The Trouble with China's 'One Belt One Road' Strategy," *The Diplomat*, June 26, 2015.

Unlike the AIIB which is a well-defined and formal organization – the Belt and Road initiative is mainly a slogan. Occasionally, slogans are being employed instead of plain words when Beijing launches new policies, both domestic and foreign. Slogans represent attempts to simplify complicated issues in reductionist manners which remain vague and, therefore, open to diverse interpretations. To be fair, other countries (notably authoritarian – both on the right and on the left) use slogans, as well as Western countries (e.g. Washington's recent use of "pivoting" or "rebalancing" to East Asia, or the Trans Pacific Partnership – slogans whose validity is also doubtful), but not on the Chinese scale.

Behind the Belt and Road slogan there is very little information. On March 28, 2015, a year and a half *after* Xi Jinping's Belt and Road initiative introduction, the NDRC (National Development and Reform Commission), the Ministry of Foreign Affairs and the Ministry of Commerce – as authorized by the State Council – published a document entitled "Vision and Actions on Jointly Building Silk Road Economic Belt and 21st Century Maritime Silk Road." Covering 16 pages, this official document is the most detailed so far to be published on the Belt and Road initiative, although it is short on specifics.[1] It is a work of rhetoric art as it uses so many words to say so little. Exceptionally broad and general, Belt and Road covers whatever ordinary international economic relations cover anyway. It offers nothing about Belt and Road structure, except that it will use existing mechanisms such as the China-Arab States Cooperation Forum, Shanghai Cooperation Organization (SCO), ASEAN plus China (10+1), Asia-Pacific Economic Cooperation (APEC), Asia-Europe Meeting (ASEM), Asia Cooperation Dialogue (ACD), China-Gulf Cooperation Council Strategic Dialogue and a few more. It gives little, or practically no, precise information about financial commitments and fails to identify precisely the countries involved – or to provide official maps. But this is not all.

Belt and Road's ambiguity hides or down plays considerable challenges. A key

1 See: http://en.ndrc.gov.cn/newrelease/201503/t20150330_669367.html, accessed May 28, 2016.

word that appears most frequently in the document is "cooperation"(98 times in 14 pages).Many nations, perhaps too many, and Chinese provinces and agencies – are supposed and expected to become involved in Belt and Road's decision-making and implementation processes. It may lead to difficult and frustrating efforts to control and coordinate Belt and Road's activities, regarded by the Chinese as a precondition for Belt and Road's success: "*As long as* all countries along the Belt and Road make concerted efforts to pursue our common goal, there will be bright prospects for the Silk Road Economic belt and the 21st-Century Maritime Silk Road."[1]

III. Reactions at Home and Abroad

Despite Belt and Road's ambiguity, challenges and risks, this initiative has been enthusiastically applauded not only in China itself (which is understandable as an expected response to any government initiative) but also in the region and all over the world. It is somewhat funny to watch how many countries consider themselves as a "crossroad", a "key", or a "hub", in China's Belt and Road initiative.

Since the Belt and Road initiative had been announced, hundreds of articles appeared in Chinese academic journals according to CNKI (China National Knowledge Infrastructure). In 2015, "an astonishing 2,735" entries were published (as of December 13, 2015), an expression of a "nationwide craze over the Belt and Road."[2]Whereas these articles were published once, some of them had thousands of downloads which multiplied their readership on a huge scale.[3]In addition to the

1 *Ibid*.

2 Xie Tao, "Is China's 'Belt and Road' a Strategy?" *The Diplomat*, December 16, 2015.

3 For example, an article by Kong Qingfeng and Dong Hongwei, "Trade Facilitation and Trade Potential of Countries along the 'One Belt One Road' Route" ["一带一路" 国家的贸易便利化水平测算与贸易潜力研究],*GuojiMaoyiWenti* [Problems of Foreign Trade], No. 12 (2015), pp. 158-168, was downloaded 8,038 times; Lin Minwang's article, "Indian Perceptions of 'One Belt One Road' and China's Policy Choices" [印度对 "一带一路" 的认知及中国的政策选择], *ShijieJingjiyuzhengfa* [World Economics and Politics], No. 5 (2015), was downloaded 12,375 times. Source: CNKI.

articles, scores of books[1]and chapters in edited volumes which were published, a number of research centers and institutes were established in Chinese universities, such as Qingdao University's Belt and Road Research Institute; the Silk Road research Institute at Beijing Foreign Studies University;the Silk Road Economic Belt Research Center Collaborative Innovation set up at Xi'an Jiaotong University Center of Silk Road Economic Belt Research, and a few more. Many "Belt and Road" and "New Silk Road" conferences were held in China. I helped organize one of them which became the launching event of the new Middle East Center at Guangzhou and Zhuhai Campus of Sun Yat-sen University. Held in January 2-4, 2017, this Middle East Studies International Workshop (in which all the participants came from the Middle East and China) focused on the Belt and Road initiative in a Middle East context. An international conference on "China's One Belt One Road Initiative: Past, Present and Future" was held on October 15th, 2016,at the Nottingham Confucius Institute China Ningbo Branch, organized by the University of Nottingham Ningbo China. The "One Belt, One Road" Institute of the Center for China and Globalization (CCG) in Beijing held a seminar on November 9, 2015, on the relations between "One Belt, One Road" and TPP (Trans-Pacific Partnership) initiatives.This is just a small sample of

1 For example: Li Ping and Liu Qiang, *One Belt And One Road Strategy: Development of Energy Infrastructure And Integration of Energy Market in Asia-Pacific Region* (Beijing: China Social Sciences Press, 2015); Feng Bing, *One Belt and One Road: The Chinese Logic for Global Development* (Beijing: China Democracy & rule of Law Publishing House, 2015);Liu Wei, *The Belt and Road Initiative*(Shanghai: Jiao Tong University Press, 2015); Li Xiaopeng, *From Yellow River Civilization to The Belt And Road Initiative*, Vol.1 (Beijing: China Development Press, 2015); Yang Yiwei, *The Belt and Road Initiatives (Opportunity and Challenge)*(Beijing: People's Publishing House, 2015); Lin Yifuand JinLiqun, *One Belt One Road* (Beijing: China Literature and History Press, 2015); Zhao Jianglin, *The 21st Century Maritime Silk Road:Target,Implementation and Policy Suggestions* (Beijing: Social Science Academic Press, 2015);Yang Yiwei, *The Belt and Road: What Will China Offer the World in Its Rise* (Beijing: New World Press, 2016);Wang Yiwei, *The World Is Connected: The Logic of The Belt and Road Initiative* (Beijing: The Commercial Press, 2016); Liu Weidong,Tian Jinchen andOuXiaoli, *The Belt and Road Initiative Strategy Research/ Monographic Study on 'the Belt and Road Initiative'* (Beijing: The Commercial Press, 2017); Zhao Lei, *The Annual Report on One Belt One Road 2017* (Beijing: The Commercial Press, 2017); Ding Yani, Huang Mengting and Huang Rong, *A Data-Based Explanation of One Belt One Road* (Beijing: The Commercial Press, 2016). This is a small sample of Chinese books on the Belt and Road initiative.

conferences and institutes set up to study the Belt and Road initiative. This wave reached its high tide in May 14-15, 2017,when China convened "The Belt and Road Forum for International Cooperation" in Beijing. More than 29 heads of state and government in addition to representatives from over 130 countries and 70 international organizations participated. Such a welcome for Belt and Road in China is understandable and, in fact, expected. Apparently, it is less understandable and expected abroad.

As it turned out, external interest, both regional and far away, in the "Belt and Road" initiative was equally widespread. Hong Kong, actually a part of China, has been one of the leaders of this interest. For example, a conference on LMS on "Belt and Road" was held by the Department of Logistics and Maritime Studies of the Hong Kong Polytechnic University in May 10-11, 2016; a "Belt and Road Summit" was held at the Hong Kong Convention and Exhibition Centre in May 18, 2016; and a China Conference – One Belt One Road was hosted by the *South China Morning Post* on December 2, 2016. But interest has been high also far away from China. Thus, a conference on "One Belt, One Road" (OBOR) and a prosperous Africa was held at Durban University of Technology (South Africa) in November 19-20, 2015; an International Conference on "The Silk Road Economic Belt and the 21st Century Maritime Silk Road for Transportation and Global Supply Chain", was held at Victoria University, Melbourne, in December 1-2, 2016; Aalborg University in Denmark held an International workshop on China's "'One Belt, One Road' Global Strategy: implications, Prospects and Constraints", in January 19-20, 2017. According to Amazon data, by this month (July 2017),and in less than four years – actually too soon to judge its success (or failure) – 120 books on the Belt and Road initiative have been published all over the world and hundreds of articles – according to Google Scholar.

However, there are differences in the way the "Belt and Road" initiative has been received. Russia appears to be less than enthusiastic about China's "Belt and Road" initiative. In fact, compared to the multitude of articles, studies and commentaries on this issue published elsewhere, relatively few have been in Russia. "Some Russian media also have been highlighting the dangers of the Belt and Road program conflicting with Moscow's Eurasia initiative and helping China overtake Russia for influence among Central Asian countries.[1] Although the Central Asian republics have displayed concern about China's economic penetration in the region, they still remember the much longer and the directly coercive Soviet rule. Russia's aggressive policy in Georgia, the Crimea and Ukraine, has further alarmed Central Asia. Recent indications show that Central Asia is trying to get rid of the remnants of Russian influence, including the Cyrillic script and the presence of ethnic Russians.[2]

As a matter of fact, many Kazakhs display Sinophobic feelings and alarmist views about China's economic penetration, primarily regarding labor disputes and the influx of better paid Chinese workers. Also, some believe that the Belt and Road would compete with the Russian-sponsored Eurasian Economic Union (EEU, inaugurated in early 2015) – of which Kazakhstan is a member along with four other countries. Nevertheless, EEU membership and the public resentment against Beijing by no means imply that the Belt and Road initiative is rejected. Kazakhstan's public attitude toward the Belt and Road and – needless to say – Astana's official policy, are fundamentally positive. "The positive attitude is dominant in spite of the presence of Sinophobic sentiments in Kazakhstan, which

---

1 Saibal Dasgupta, "China's Ambitious 'Silk Road' Plan Faces Hurdles," Voice of America, April 15, 2015. See also: Casey Michel, "Putin's Eurasian Union Doomed to Irrelevance by China's Silk Road," *WorldPolitics Review*, October 5, 2015; Catherine Putz, "China's Silk Road Belt Outpaces Russia's Economic Union," *the Diplomat*, March 10, 2016. According to Alexander Cooley of Columbia University's Harriman Institute, these two projects are "conceptually incompatible" . See also: Sebastien Peyrouse, "The Evolution of Russia's Views on the Belt and Road Initiative," Roundtable: "China's Belt and Road Initiative: Views from along the Silk Road," *Asian Policy*, No. 24 (July 2017), pp. 96-102.

2 "Latin Alphabet Will Help Kazakh Language to Shake Off Russian Media Influence, Public Figure," March 17, 2016, at: https://www.interfax.kz/?lang=eng&int_expert_opinions&news_id=1395. See also: "After Ukraine, Kazakhstan Wary of Ethnic Russians Broaching Autonomy," March 3, 2016, at: http://www.reuters.com/article/us-kazakhstan-russia-idUSKCN0W51MY; "Strength of Russian Military Base in Tajikistan Expected to Be Reduced," *Asia Plus*, February 1, 2016. See also: NargisKassenova, "China's Silk Road and Kazakhstan's Bright Path: Linking Dreams of Prosperity," *ibid*., pp.110-116.

in turn do not have a solid ground and mostly based on myths".[1] This is typical of Central Asia whose prospective benefits from the "Belt and Road" initiative overshadow their concerns about China's influence.

US, Western Europe and Japanese attitudes toward the "Belt and Road" initiative – which seemed to have been more positive, welcoming and even enthusiastic at the beginning, tend to become increasingly more critical as time goes on. In recent months, many articles and commentaries underline the difficulties, hurdles and bumps on the "Belt and Road" initiative.[2]

IV. Historical Perspective

Given the Belt and Road initiative's ambiguity, uncertainties, obstacles and risks, how its ecstatic reception – primarily by Asian-African countries – could be explained? Obviously, Asian-African mostly enthusiastic support reflects the expectation that these are the countries that stand to win. Western Europe – Belt and Road's ultimate target – as well as Russia and the US, reflect more skepticism and reservations while underlying the problems and Belt and Road's seeds of failure. But to me, the roots of these different receptions are much deeper than just "winning" – especially since, as the Chinese underline, *everyone* is going to win. As a matter of fact, "Belt and Road" is the first worldwide constructive initiative by an "eastern" nation ever. The Chinese "Belt and Road" initiative, aims at, by and large an *economic* enterprise and is constructive. Asia had made some noteworthy contributions to the West. These include the Indo-European languages, inventions that are still in use, and influences on Europe's philosophers, statesmen and daily life during the 17th and 18th Age of Enlightenment centuries – not

1 This paragraph draws on: Azhar Serikkaliyeva, "Public Perception of the 'One Belt One Road' Initiative in Kazakhstan," Eurasian Research Institute (AkhmetYassawi University, February 23, 2016). See also: K. Syroezhkin, "China's Presence in Kazakhstan: Myth and Reality," *Central Asia's Affairs*, Vol. I, No. 42 (2011).

2 The Economist Intelligence Unit, "Prospects and challenges on China's 'one belt, one road': a risk assessment report" (2015); Moritz Rudolf, "China's 'Silk Road' Initiative Is at Risk of Failure," *The Diplomat*, September 24, 2015.Shen Laijin [申来津] and Huang He, "Japan's Cognition of The 'One Belt and One Road' Initiative andIts Enlightenment to China" [黄河，日本对"一带一路"倡议的认知及其对中国的启示], *Socialism Studies* [社会主义研究], No. 2 [232] (2017), pp. 149-153.

to mention Silk Road trade. But all these could be dwarfed by the tangible effects of the Belt and Road initiative.

Japan, the only other "eastern" great power whose credentials were primarily economic very much like China's today, and which reached its apex in the 1970s and the 1980s as second only to the US, very much like China is today, has *never* introduced an initiative or any large-scale multiregional economic plan, of the Belt and Road proportions. Instead, it has offered assistance on a piecemeal basis at best. Though associated with Japan, the Asian Development Bank, which could have been the source of an initiative similar to Belt and Road, is a multilateral enterprise which often reflects the interests of Western powers headed by the US,and primarily Japan.[1]India, the next upcoming economic power, never had the resources nor the will or experience to come up with an Belt and Road-like initiative. Likewise, none of the Arab energy-rich nations has ever tried to use their abundant resources to promote the economic development and growth of other nations – least of all their kin in the Middle East.

What is so significant about the "Belt and Road" initiative is not just its size and goals – still unclear and still to be accomplished – but its *historical context*. "Belt and Road" offers economic benefits without political and military involvement. However, Western observers and academics, in particular American scholars but also Russian and even Chinese– mainly those educated in American universities and research institutions – tend to interpret Beijing's activism abroad in Cold War terms, the only terms they are familiar with. Thus, Western media and "experts" frequently associate the Belt and Road initiative (often referring to it wrongly as a "plan", "strategy", "project" or "policy" – which is not) with Beijing's alleged pursuit of political control,predominance and influence, a strategic foothold accomplished by a buildup of

1 For example: Jonathan R. Strand, "State Power in a Multilateral Context: Voting Strength in the Asian Developing Bank," *International Interactions*, Vol. 25, No. 3 (1995), pp. 265-286; Christopher Kilby, "Donor Influence in Multilateral Development Banks: the Case of the Asian Development Bank," *Review of International Organizations*, Vol. 1, No. 2 (2006), pp. 173-195; Daniel Yew Mao Lim and James Raymond Vreeland, "Regional Organizations and International Politics:Japanese Influence over the Asian Development Bank and the UN Security Council," *World Politics*, Vol. 65, No. 1 (January 2013), pp. 34-72.

"naval bases"and railroads abroad. These reflect a gross misunderstanding of China's history, culture, military capabilities and even more so – intentions.

V. Future Course

Although most formerly colonized Asian-African nations did win *political* independence through successful struggles of their *national* liberation movements, many of them still depend *economically* on their former colonizers either directly or indirectly – subjected to international financial organizations such as the World Bank, the Asia Development Bank and the International Monetary Fund, all controlled by Western countries. Belt and Road, and the Asia Infrastructure Investment Bank,could be a spearhead of an "*international* liberation movement", leaders of a large-scale attempt – the first of its kind in history – to release these countries (many of them rich in natural resources) from their economic dependence on the West, no strings attached.

This unique precedent in human history should by no means be wasted. China should not repeat the mistakes of colonial powers of the past and avoid the Cold War mentality of expanding its military presence and spreading military bases all over the world. Economic development is the key and it should be divorced from politics. In 2005 Deputy Secretary of State Robert Zoellick, said that China should become "a responsible stakeholder" and play a more important, and active, role in international politics.[1]Various interpretations have been offered for the precise meaning of this term, but whatever they are – they have to do with politics. He is not alone. His views have been echoed not just in the West, as well as in Third World countries, but also among some Chinese scholars, especially those educated in the US.[2]

1 Julia Bowie, "China: A Responsible Stakeholder?" *The National Interest*, May 10, 2016.

2 For example: Yan Xuetong, "From Keeping a Low Profile to Striving for Achievement" , *The Chinese Journal of International Politics* 2014, pp. 153-184; Ling Shengli [凌 胜 利], "From 'Participant' to 'Constructor' – An Analysis of China's Participation in International Political and Security System" [从 "参与者" 到 "建设者" ——中国参与国际政治安全体系的进程分析], *Heping yu Fazhan* [Peace and Development, No. 4 (2016), pp. 7-17;He Kai and Huiyun Feng, "Debating China's Assertiveness: Taking China's Power and Interests Seriously," *International Politics*, No.49 (2012), pp. 633-644.

Most of them, who lived their adult life during the Cold War and, willingly or unwillingly, absorbed its ethos – that global predominance relies on intervention, military presence and coercion. However, this is not necessarily the right way to do it – not only because the Cold War is practically over and its ethos may have proved a failure (certainly from Moscow's standpoint) but primarily because China has its own ethos. And it relies on its own historical experience, cultural values and diplomatic models. Furthermore, China's modern experience, especially since the launch of reform, shows that China's international (as well as domestic) goals could be achieved in different ways which are more constructive and less destructive. Behind the warm welcome, especially in the so-called Third World, there is the expectation that China indeed should play a greater role in the world, yet not necessarily in politics. Indeed, China's record in contributing to the solution of international political issues is quite marginal – and for good reasons. China does not want to become involved in international conflicts, which should be solved by the parties concerned. Willingly or not, participating in conflict settlement implies taking sides. So, despite the tools Beijing has acquired since the early 1970s (permanent membership in the UN Security Council, an extensive network of diplomatic relations, and membership in many international organizations – including recent leadership positions), it has not been directly involved in settling outstanding *political* conflicts. However, Beijing has been directly and effectively involved in a variety of *economic* ventures,with the "Belt and Road" initiative being the most promising. Contrary the commonly held conventional wisdom, Beijing in Chinese rather than Western ways. This is not just a reincarnation of traditional Chinese values. It also conforms to a basic Marxist- principle: economic development and growth creates socio-political problems but might also help overcome them – rather than relying on direct political or, least of all, military intervention. If Beijing wants to guarantee the future success of "Belt and Road" initiative, it should rely on Chinese ways.

关于全球治理赤字和中国全球治理原则的思考

金灿荣 【中国】
中国人民大学国际关系学院副院长 / “长江学者”特聘教授

2015 年 12 月 18 日，联合国安理会一致决议通过开启叙利亚的和平进程，在当前混乱的世界形势中显得尤为珍贵。中东地区，美国两场反恐战争造成的破坏尚未得到有效恢复，延续了近五年的叙利亚内战又加剧了中东的动荡，恐怖主义行为带来严重的人道主义灾难的同时，也使得世界主要大国卷入中东的动乱。亚洲地区，日本解禁集体自卫权为海外用兵破除了法律障碍，美国高调介入菲、越与中国在南海的海洋权益争端使南海局势更加复杂。欧洲地区，北约东扩不断挤压俄罗斯的战略空间，俄格战争、乌克兰危机使得俄罗斯与欧洲的紧张关系加剧。在欧盟内部，恐怖主义袭击、难民问题向欧洲的治理乃至欧盟内部的稳定提出了新的严峻挑战。在全球范围内，极端恐怖主义活动出现向全球扩散的现象，安理会的五大常任理事国均面临着恐怖主义的威胁，伊斯兰国的横空出世使恐怖主义活动达到了一个新的高潮。在经济发展方面，欧洲经济尚未完全摆脱欧债危机的影响，美国经济刚刚开始出现复苏的迹象，美联储 10 年来首次加息。但是，世界银行的数据表明 2007 年以来世界经济整体 GDP 的平均增长率约为 2.18%[1]，这表明世界经济总体的发展并不乐观，尤其是中国经济的增速——世界经济的火车头——也在逐步放缓。世界形势总体展现出三大特点：一是世界经济继续低迷，

1 http://data.worldbank.org.cn/indicator/NY.GDP.MKTP.KD.ZG/countries/1W-A5?display=graph 2015/12/22 2007 年开始次贷危机逐渐发酵，计算近八年数据的平均数值为 2.175%

二是大国的地缘政治博弈更加严重，三是恐怖袭击的威胁上升。面对当前日益复杂、失序的国际局势，基辛格先生严肃的提问：“当今时代能建立世界秩序吗？”[1] 相比基辛格先生略显悲观的看法，本文认为：第二次世界大战后建立的世界秩序依旧在有效的发挥着作用，之所以世界展现出诸多乱象其原因在于世界秩序的弱化，而导致世界秩序弱化的根本原因在于全球治理赤字。

一 全球治理赤字的含义与成因

治理作为一种实践方式普遍存在于国家、区域乃至全球三个层次之中。国际社会的无政府状态天然地具备实践治理行为的土壤，尤其是在贸易领域的治理行为为全球治理理论提供了重要启示[2]。美国北伊利诺斯大学教授劳伦斯·S.芬克尔斯坦较早的尝试对“全球治理”的概念进行界定，芬克尔鲜明的提出，治理首先是一种实践，一种并非仅以政府为主体的实践，制度（institution）只是治理的重要方式之一。全球治理是在无最高权威条件下对跨越国家边界关系的治理，某种程度上全球治理表现出各国政府内部行为的国际化[3]。从统治（government）到治理（governance）转变被包括俞可平教授在内的部分学者认为是“人类的政治生活正在发生的重大的变革”之一，这种转变在国际关系方面则反映为“从民族国家的政府统治走向全球治理”[4]。俞可平教授认为，“大体上说，所谓全球治理，指的是通过具有约束力的国际规制（regimes）解决全球性的冲突、生态、人权、移民、毒品、走私、传染病等问题，以维持正常的国际政治经济秩序”[5]。相比前述突出实践、规制，更有一种观点认为全球治理概念是“一个为便于理解全球生活的高度复杂性和多样性而设计的有益视角”[6]。精确定义“全球治理”的概念从理论到实践都是一个非常具有挑战性的任务，华东政法大学发布的《全球治理指数 2015 报告》中具体的做法是以国别为基本单元，通过一个三级指标体系的指数集来测

1 【美】基辛格：《世界秩序》，胡利平等译，中信出版社 2015 年版，第 473 页。

2 John Gerard Ruggie, “Global Governance and ‘New Governance Theory’: Lessons from Business and Human Rights”, *Global Governance* 20(2014),PP5-17.

3 Lawrence S.Finkelstein, “What is global governance ？”, Global Governance,Vol,1,No.3 (Sept.—Dec. 1995), pp368-369.

4 俞可平：《全球治理引论》，载《马克思主义与现实》，2002 年第 1 期。

5 同上书，第 25 页。全球规制（global regimes）就是维护国际社会正常的秩序，实现人类普世价值的规则体系。

6 【美】马丁·休伊森、蒂莫西·辛克莱著，张胜军编译：《全球治理理论的兴起》，载《马克思主义与现实》，2002 年第 1 期。

量一国参与全球治理的程度[1]。全球治理跳出了传统国际关系理论的国家中心视角，以人类社会的共同利益为着眼点。从各种理论学说到具体操作的指标体系设计，全球治理的核心内容都是围绕保护人类社会的共同利益、满足人的共同需求而展开，因此全球治理的实质就在于全球性公共产品的供给。对全球治理赤字含义的理解需要透过碎片化的各种现象去把握实质，故全球治理赤字的含义即指全球治理实践中公共产品的供给不足。

第二次世界大战后所建立起来的世界秩序仍在发挥着作用，并不能以当前的诸多乱象去完全否定战后世界秩序的设计，全球治理赤字产生的基础性原因在于全球性公共产品的供给能力下降。供给能力的下降并非是由战后世界秩序引起的，而是由多方面客观因素综合发挥作用的结果。包含三个主要方面：第一，传统的全球公共产品供给者的供给能力下降；第二，全球经济整体处在一个下行的周期，缺少保障稳定供给能力的经济支撑；第三，既有的治理结构难以有效应对以网络问题、恐怖主义意识形态问题为代表的新问题。

美国、欧洲作为两大传统的全球性公共产品的供给者的供给能力下降，其中美国、欧洲能力的下降又各自具有不同的总体特点。美国供给能力下降的总体特点为“有力无心”，欧洲供给能力下降的总体特点为“有心无力”。两场反恐战争消耗了美国大量的战略资源，截至 2014 财年，反恐战争支出近 1.6 万亿美元，“超过 6000 名美军和 2300 名美国承包商丧生”[2]，除去这些直接的损失之外，还有许多潜在影响无法统计，例如战后士兵心理障碍造成的损害。但代价高昂的反恐战争并未带来理想的结果。反恐战争的十年间，中国经济飞速发展，在庞大经济规模的支撑下，中国已经成为对美国霸权地位最具挑战性的战略对手。因此，美国通过实施亚太再平衡战略将整个战略的重心重新调整回传统的国家间竞争，集中主要战略资源来应对中国的崛起，未来甚至极有可能实施彻底的遏制战略，故而在提供全球性公共产品事务上表现出“有力无心”。欧洲主要指以法、德为领导核心的欧盟地区，近年来该地区的情况发生了一些重大的变化。2014 年俄罗斯的新版军事学说将北约视为头号军事威胁，从地缘政治角度看，欧洲地处北约与俄罗斯军事对抗的前沿，将直接承受俄罗斯日益强化的军事压力。接连爆发的欧债危机、难民危机对当前欧盟的内部治理提出了严重的挑战，特别是在对待欧盟内部移民的问题上，法、德与英

1 高奇琦：《国家参与全球治理的理论与指数化》，载《社会科学》2015 年第 1 期。

2 【美】沃森国际问题研究所：《十年反恐战争的代价》，周诗文译，载《国际资料信息》2011 年第 9 期。

国之间出现裂痕，"法国总统奥朗德和德国总理默克尔就警告，英国必须尊重欧盟容许自由迁徙，非歧视等原则"[1]。法、德是欧盟内部核心的引导力量，然而当前法、德内部都面临着棘手的问题需要解决。发生在巴黎的恐怖袭击事件造成了上百人的死亡，法国内部的民族主义情绪受到了严重的刺激，受此影响，极右翼政党"国民阵线"在法国大选首轮投票中获得胜利。从长期的角度看，恐怖主义袭击的结果将极有可能成为内部族群分裂的导火索。人口的老龄化是未来德国必须面对的战略问题，其人口老龄化程度仅次于日本位居全球第二。这不仅意味着未来国家财政开支的进一步加重，而且意味着需要从外部引进充足的劳动力。单纯地从满足劳动力的客观需求看，接受难民对德国是有利的，但在如何对待难民的问题上，默克尔政府内部也出现了较大的分歧[2]，这与德国经济增长的持续低迷、国内日渐抬头的新纳粹主义有着密切的关系。作为殖民历史遗产主要继承者的老牌欧洲国家在提供公共产品方面有着特殊的优势，但是欧洲地区内部治理的挑战以及核心国家内部问题的凸显，使得欧洲在全球治理中显得"有心无力"。

全球性公共产品的持续有效供给离不开繁荣的经济来提供物质支撑，当前全球经济增长的总体状况处在一个低迷的状态，尤其是作为全球性公共产品传统供给者的欧、美大国经济增长乏力。中国——作为新的全球性公共产品供给者——的经济增长也开始放缓，2012—2014 年连续三年的中央经济工作会议提到"经济下行压力"，虽然今年的中央经济工作会议没有使用这一说法，但是市场是否认同还有待进一步观察。

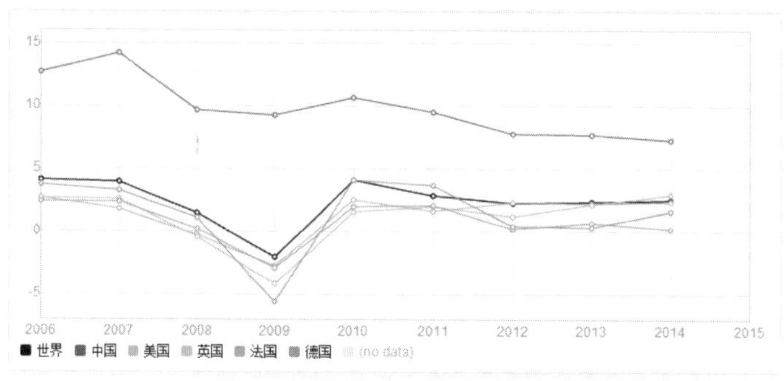

图 1：世界总体与主要大国 GDP 增长率图示[3]

1 http://phtv.ifeng.com/a/20151219/41526389_0.shtml 2015/12/24

2 http://epaper.gmw.cn/gmrb/html/2015-10/24/nw.D110000gmrb_20151024_10-05.htm 2015/12/25《光明日报》2015 年 10 月 24 日 05 版

3 http://data.worldbank.org.cn/indicator/NY.GDP.MKTP.KD.ZG/countries?display=graph 根据世界银行网站提供的数据自动生成图表的截图。2015/12/25

经济增长乏力，影响到作为供给主体的大国在意愿、能力方面均出现下降，公共产品供给的赤字逐渐增大并形成赤字累积，当前世界爆发的各种热点问题某种程度上就可以归结为赤字累积形成的效应。依照康德拉季耶夫的长周期理论，有数据统计研究证明，当社会经济处在大循环周期的上升段时，社会更容易发生战争、革命动荡等不稳定因素。当前全球经济处在经济大循环下行周期的后半段，正在向一个新的上升段周期过渡，伴随着向上升周期运动的过程发生冲突的频率必然会相对增加。长周期理论表明，不稳定现象的增多有其深刻的经济原因而非是文明冲突的必然结果。

表 1　　战争、革命动荡与康德拉季耶夫周期关系的表格[1]

		战争次数	革命动荡次数	总计
第一个大周期	上升段	11	7	18
	下降段	1	4	5
第二个大周期	上升段	7	11	18
	下降段	2	2	4
第三个大周期		11	11	22

以网络问题、环境问题、恐怖主义意识形态问题为代表的一系列新问题的出现对当前的全球治理结构提出了挑战。当前全球治理的结构是一种“由国家中心治理与超国家中心治理组成的一种复合结构”，该结构是一个非对称结构，国家中心治理占据主导地位[2]。而新问题存在的范畴已经远远超越了单一主权国家治理的空间范围，进而产生了治理实践中的结构困境。以互联网为例：互联网作为联通不同地区和世界的全球性基础设施，在人类生活的各个方面都发挥着基础性作用。自由、平等、开放的互联网特性在给人类生活带来诸多便利的同时也被不法分子用作实施犯罪的平台，“互联网的开放性使得网络犯罪呈现出跨国性、流动性的特点”[3]。英国国际战略研究所最新发布的《网络领域的衍变：对国家与全球安全的影响》战略档案，分析网络领域在影响全球安全环境以及国家间权力动态中起到

1　Yury V. Yakovets, “The Kondratieff’s Waves and Cyclic Dynamics of the Economy and Wars: Theory and Prospects” [A]. In Tessaleno .Devezas, Kondratieff Waves, Warfare and World Security,[C] Washington, DC, ect. T.C.Devezas(ED.) IOS Press, 2006.PP3—9.

2　【日】星野昭吉:《全球治理的结构与向度》，载《南开学报（哲学社会科学版）》2011 年第 3 期。

3　http://it.gmw.cn/2015-09/29/content_17210274.htm 2015/12/26。

怎样的作用以及正在起怎样的作用，处于研究该档案的核心地位[1]。该档案列出的影响网络领域衍变的十大因素第一项到第三项之间就展示了这种治理困境：一方面在人类对互联网的依赖不断增长，而脆弱的互联网系统又很容易被犯罪分子所利用；另一方面，美国在互联网方面的雄厚实力给了美国及其盟友不公平的战略优势，其倡导的网络自由与开放被很多政府视为不遗余力的暗中破坏[2]。如果想对这些新的问题得到有效治理，就必须要分散权力、平衡“国家中心治理”与“超国家中心治理”的结构，而这种分权与平衡在客观上势必会受到霸权与国家权力的天然抵触，致使全球治理赤字的累积无法得到有效处理。

二 全球治理赤字的危害

全球治理赤字的首要危害是对人权的危害。全球治理赤字对人所造成的各种直接危害是显而易见的，从疾病的扩散到环境的污染再到战争的难民等等。尤其是疾病传染与战争，如果无法有效遏制相关治理赤字的累积，最终带来的将是大规模的人道主义危机。根据联合国难民署的 2014 年的报告，仅仅排名前三的叙利亚、阿富汗和索马里三国的难民总数就超过了 750 万人[3]。联合国艾滋病规划署 2015 年的报告显示，2014 年全世界大约有 3690 万艾滋病病毒携带者，约 200 万新增感染者以及近 120 万人死于与艾滋病毒相关的疾病[4]。更让人难以想象的是，今天世界上仍有 7.95 亿人在忍受着饥饿，亚洲饥饿人口占全球总数的三分之二，其中南亚地区约 2.81 亿人营养不足[5]。贫困是饥饿的根源，中国“按每天 2 美元衡量，还有 1.7 亿多贫困人口，其中 1.3 亿人在农村，4500 万在城镇”[6]。人身安全、生存权与发展权均是最根本的基础人权，纵容全球治理赤字的累积就是对人权最大的侵犯。

全球治理赤字第二重危害是冲击战后形成的国际秩序，威胁这一保持世界各大国利益平衡的根基。战后的国际秩序是维系世界整体处于一种长和平状态的重

1 http://www.iiss.org/en/about%20us/press%20room/press%20releases/press%20releases/archive/2015-4fe9/december-20ab/cyber-dossier-dd72 2015/12/26

2 http://www.iiss.org/en/about%20us/press%20room/press%20releases/press%20releases/archive/2015-4fe9/december-20ab/cyber-fact-sheet-891a 2015/12/26

3 http://www.unhcr.org.hk/unhcr/sc/useful_resources/reports.html 2015/12/28

4 http://www.unaids.org/en/resources/presscentre/pressreleaseandstatementarchive/2015/november/20151124_LocationPopulation 2015/12/28

5 http://www.un.org/sustainabledevelopment/zh/hunger/ 2015/12/28

6 http://www.stats.gov.cn/tjzs/tjsj/tjcb/dysj/201509/t20150902_1239121.html 2015/12/28

要基础，即使是被部分战略分析人士认为正在试图重构当前世界体系的中国也没有改变这一秩序意图，习近平主席在联大一般性性辩论的讲话中庄重的向世界各国（尤其是美国）宣示："中国将始终做国际秩序的维护者，坚持走合作发展的道路。"[1]全球治理赤字对战后国际秩序破坏主要表现为三点：1.在治理领域侵蚀战后国际秩序；2.在安全领域将核大国卷入暴力冲突前沿；3.在意识形态领域极端主义思潮兴起。公共产品的供给维系着每个具体行为体对组织合法性的认知，"从规范意义上认定一个机构是合法的，也就意味着该机构拥有统治的权力"[2]。公共产品的供给不足将导致行为体对组织的合法性产生怀疑，甚至否定组织存在的意义。全球治理赤字与当前国际社会权力碎片化的现象重叠在一起对国际秩序形成了双重效应的挑战，针对联合国、国际货币基金组织等一些重大国际机构的改革要求就是对来自这种挑战的反映。大国特别是核大国在战后的长期和平中发挥了关键性作用，即使是大国之间的角力也多是以代理人方式进行，从而确保避免大国间直接的对抗。但在乌克兰危机、叙利亚危机的问题上，普京领导下的俄罗斯不仅走上了冲突对抗的前台，而且频频向外界展示核武力量。尤为需要注意的是，美国为首的北约在叙利亚上空划设了禁飞区，俄罗斯则在叙利亚布设S400防空导弹系统，在美、俄直接对抗性力量共存的情况下，双方具备了陷入"胆小鬼博弈"的必要条件，一旦双方之间出现与土耳其击落俄罗斯战机的相类似事件，其后果的严重性将难以预测。全球化的进程中，南北差距进一步拉大，全球治理赤字的增大不仅加剧了财富在南北国家之间分配不均，而且也放大了分配不均所造成的消极影响。贫困与怨恨的共振为极端主义思潮的兴起提供了社会基础，互联网技术更是将原本分散在不同地区的极端主义思潮在虚拟世界里实现了整合。特别是具有宗教色彩外衣的极端主义思潮，通过互联网能够在世界范围内进行快速、广泛的传播。伊斯兰国的出现是一个值得引起关注的现象，这种宗教极端主义思想不再是一种单纯的意识形态，已经成为建立实体政权的政治纲领。换言之，这种极端的宗教思想已经成为宗教极端主义者所推崇的一种类比于民主的"普世价值"。这种以互联网为依托的极端主义思潮的传播已经成为全球公害，然而各大国之间围绕着互联网治理的政治斗争仍旧在以邻为壑。

1 《携手构建合作共赢新伙伴 同心打造人类命运共同体》，习近平主席在第七十届联合国大会一般性辩论的讲话，2015年9月28日，纽约。

2 【美】布坎南、【美】罗伯特·基欧汉：《全球治理机制的合法性》，载《南京大学学报（哲学、人文科学）》，2011年第2期。

全球治理赤字的第三重危害是对中国利益的具体危害。2000 年前后，"走出去"政策上升为中国的国家发展战略之一，在"走出去"政策深化的过程中，中国与整个国际社会之间的利益也日益密切。大量的人员、资本、物资分布在海外，一旦国际或地区局势发生动荡，中国的利益就将会受到损伤。例如：在利比亚战争中，中国紧急组织撤回侨民以及其他人员 35800 多人，严重受损的在建工程项目价值更是高达 180 多亿美元[1]。中国走出去的规模越来越大，但是走出去政策所面临的"单兵突进困境"以及外部防范心理尚未得到根本改善[2]。从外交角度看，中国新近提出的"一带一路"倡议是对中国"走出去"策略的一次战略优化，从而改善自身庞大海外利益所面临的不利处境。

表 2　　与"走出去"策略相关指标的变化（2010—2014）[3]

项目 时间	外汇储备（亿 / 美元）	国内居民出境人数（万 / 人次）	进出口总额（亿 / 美元）	对外直接投资净额（亿 / 美元）
2010 年	28473	5739	29728	688.1
2011 年	31811	7025	36421	746.5
2012 年	33116	8318	38668	878
2013 年	38213	9819	41600	1078.4
2014 年	38430	11003	43037	1231.2

从国际关系的角度看，当前的战后国际秩序本身就是中国的重要利益。首先，中国实施改革开放战略的主要途径就是积极融入美国主导下的国际秩序。对其不合理部分的改革倡议不应当视为对秩序整体的否定，因为中国是当前国际秩序的主要受益者之一。其次，中国的大国地位为战后国际秩序所确立。作为安理会常任理事国，中国可以凭借联合国在处理全球事务中高度的合法性在维护世界整体利益的同时来更好地维护中国自身的利益。欧、美在全球治理赤字问题上的"有心无力"与"有力无心"直接影响到中国在海外利益的安全，但更具全局性影响力的是战后国际秩序合法性因全球治理赤字累积而受到的挑战。

1　http://finance.ifeng.com/news/special/zgqybly/ 2015/12/30

2　金灿荣：《"走出去"战略十年回顾：成就与挑战》，载《现代国际关系》2011 年第 8 期。第 3—4 页。

3　该表格依据近五年来《国家统计局的年度公报》以及《中国对外直接投资统计公报》所公开的数据制作，其中 2014 年进出口总额的数据为人民币计算，并未使用美元计算。为了便于制作表格，本文依据 2014 年人民币的平均汇率换算成美元计数。

此外，美国将战略重心转变为遏制中国的和平崛起将使得中国面临更为严峻的外部压力，但遏制中国将成为美国在21世纪最大的战略败笔。一个关键理由就在于当今世界的主要大国在战后的国际秩序都有着广泛的利益分布，没有任何一个大国在试图否定整个二战后美国为首的西方主导下的国际秩序。

三 引领治理——中国角色的新定位

在当前的全球治理体系中，欧洲和美国是主要领导者，中国是重要的参与者。在世界愈发连接成为一个整体的背景下，恐怖袭击、难民增多、气候变化问题、金融市场不稳……这些涉及人类命运的共同问题日益突出，与此相伴对全球治理的需要也日渐广泛、深入。现实中，美、欧“普世价值”优先的全球治理哲学和治理政策在实践中遇到挑战，“普世价值”的道德光环掩盖了现实政治的残酷，直到3岁的小男孩艾兰·库尔迪[1]死亡在海滩上的照片被媒体发布出来，中东地区的大规模人道主义危机才引发世界舆论的普遍关注。近年来，中国外交格外重视全球治理，中共中央政治局第二十七次集体学习的主题就是：全球治理格局和全球治理体制，这标志全球治理问题在中国对外战略视野中地位获得了重要提升。中国的全球治理实践涵盖了大国、周边与全球三个层次以及两条具体的操作路径：原有的治理机制的再激活与新治理机制的创建。

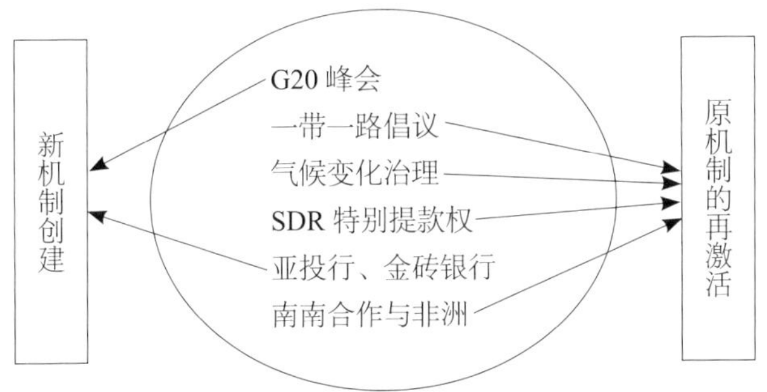

图2：中国全球治理的路径

首先，以新型大国关系为重心，稳定全球治理的基础。中、美两国是当今世界最具全球影响力的两个核心大国，因此中美关系的稳定是全球治理能够持续开展的根本保障。新一代领导集体当选后，立即着手构建中美新型大国关系，并逐

1 艾兰·库尔迪，一名来自叙利亚的儿童难民，在跟随家人乘坐一艘超载的小船偷渡的过程中遇难，除库尔迪外还有另外4名儿童也同样遇难。

渐将中美新型大国关系中的实践原则扩展到与其他大国的关系之中。其次，以构建“一带一路”战略经济带的宏大构想连接南北。从整个欧亚大陆的版图来看，欧洲一侧尤其是西欧部分的国家属于发达的北方国家，而亚洲一侧尤其南亚则属于比较落后的南方国家，经济上具有良好的互补性。一旦能够实现欧亚大陆内部的联通，降低交易成本，势必释放出巨大的经济潜力，为实现亲诚惠容的周边外交提供物质支撑。再次，中国以积极的行动使原有的全球治理机制再现活力。例如，中国推动人民币加入 SDR 特别提款权在为它国减少美元霸权的风险的同时也强化了该机构的合法性，进而稳固了国际货币金融体系。此外，中国在 20 国集团峰会上提出中国方案、在巴黎气候变化大会的庄重承诺以及对南南框架下的中非合作都是中国全球治理实践的组成部分。由于传媒话语的缺失和西方媒体固有的偏见以及部分信奉现实主义学者的宣扬，中国的全球治理行为被解读为意图取代美国谋求世界霸权。

在全球治理中，中国必须逐步完成从参与者到引导者的角色转变。这种转变不仅仅是中国海外利益受损的客观反映，更是当下复杂时代背景提出的客观要求。据统计，2014 年国内居民出境超过一亿人次，对外直接投资存量达到 8826.4 亿美元，对外直接投资净额达到 1231.2 亿美元[1]。在可见的未来，这一数字将继续提升。大规模海外利益存在以及数量庞大公民在境外出行要求中国不能再局限于参与者的角色，竞争必须跳出产品、技术的竞争而进入到规则制定权、话语权的竞争[2]。经济进入下行周期、全球化进程减缓、中等国家群体性、全球性问题恶化、各国政府领导力的弱化，让当前的世界面临着更多的不确定性[3]，未来的全球治理极有可能面临一个“G0 时代”。美、欧“普世价值”优先的全球治理哲学和全球治理实践所面临的困境引起了中、西学界的深刻反思，“西方需要从固有的道德优越感和中心主义话语中走出来”[4]从意识的深处告别西方中心主义。中国作为一个具有全球视野与时代抱负的大国，在面对一个充满不确定性的世界时有明确的关于自身和人类未来前途的定位，它需要通过引领全球治理对人类文明做出新的贡献。“明者因时而变，知者随事而制”，绵延数千年不绝的中华文明，特别是崇

1 参见《2014 年度中国对外直接投资统计报告》，中华人民共和国商务部 中华人民共和国国家统计局 国家外汇管理局，2015 年 9 月。

2 http://theory.people.com.cn/n/2015/0907/c40531-27550319.html 上网时间：2016/1/2

3 金灿荣、马鑫：《未来十年世界六大忧思》，载《国际关系学院学报》2012 年第 1 期。

4 金灿荣、刘世强：《告别西方中心主义——对当前国际格局及其走向的反思》，载《国际观察》2010 年第 2 期。

尚“和合”的中国哲学以及受到汤因比博士高度认可的“天下主义”世界观[1]为中国的全球治理提供着丰富的思想资源。习近平主席在第七十届联合国大会的一般性辩论使用了“打造人类命运共同体”的表述[2]，向世界表明了中国在看待全球治理问题上的世界观——人类共同命运。新的世界观下的治理思维，让中国形成了与美、欧截然不同的全球治理理念与实践。

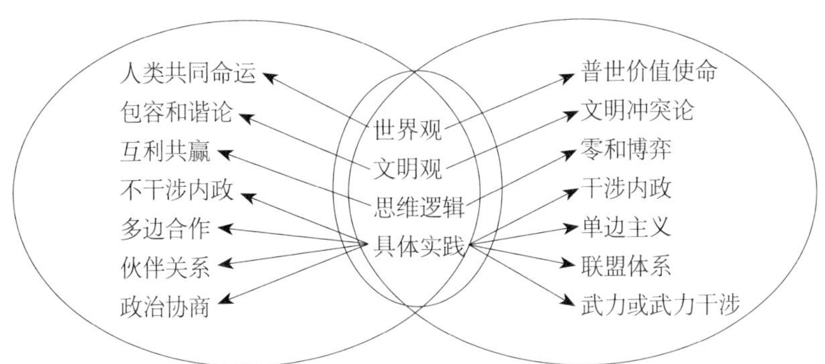

图 3：两种世界观下的全球治理范式

正如王毅外长所言：我们的国家从来没有像今天这样接近世界舞台的中央[3]，新的历史起点、新的时代形势，以及伟大民族使命的自觉共同要求中国必须要向全球治理的引领者转变。此外，中国将一部分力量投入全球治理赤字的解决中也有利于通过公共产品的供给来摆脱美国对中国的遏制。

未来，中国引领下的全球治理将会呈现出与以往不同特点。首先，中国的全球治理将以联合国为轴心。联合国既是整个战后世界秩序的核心，又是当今世界最具有世界代表性的国际组织。在国际事务中，联合国具有最广泛的影响力其工作已经影响到人们日常生活的许多方面，尤其是联合国安理会是世界上唯一具有合法性授权行使武力干涉的机构。如习近平主席指出的那样，“全球治理体系是由全球共建共享的，不可能由哪一个国家独自掌握”，“（中国）一直维护以联合

1 【英】汤因比，【日】池田大作：《展望 21 世纪：汤因比与池田大作对话录》；荀春生等译，国际文化出版公司 1997 年，第 283 页。

2 http://politics.people.com.cn/n/2015/0929/c1024-27644905.html 2016/1/3

3 http://politics.people.com.cn/n/2014/0902/c70731-25589955.html 2016/1/3

国为核心，以联合国宪章宗旨和原则为基础的国际秩序和国际体系”[1]。中国是联合国的创始国之一，也是安理会常任理事国与第三大会费来源国，联合国在全球事务中的合法性与中国在联合国的地位都促使中国的全球治理须以联合国为轴心。其次，在治理中强调发展优先。和平与发展这一当今时代的主题始终没有变，尤其是在落后的发展中国家和地区更急需通过发展来为社会问题的解决提供稳定的物质支撑。中国是世界上最大的发展中国家，强调发展优先是中国对自身成功经验总结的一个结论。在中国共产党的十八届五中全会上，对发展的认识更加深化，提出了“创新、协调、绿色、开放与共享”五大发展理念。强调发展优先有助于跳出意识形态问题的陷阱，有助于为解决现实中的问题寻找大最大的公约数。再次，强调全球伙伴体系。目前，中国已近建立起了一个庞大的、具有不同层次的伙伴关系网[2]。相比联盟关系，伙伴关系更凸出成员国之间的平等关系，其运行的目的不在于对付一个共同的外部敌人，而是基于维护伙伴国家内部的共同利益。伙伴关系的灵活性与包容性使其比联盟关系更能够有效应对全球治理内容碎片化的挑战。最后，坚持不干涉内政为原则。中国对于内政被侵犯有着沉痛的历史记忆，深谙“已所不欲，勿施于人”的道理，迄今为止除中国外其他安理会常任理事国都有粗暴干涉他国内政的行为记录。他作为主权原则的延伸，不干涉内政原则是由联合国宪章所确立的处理国际关系的一项基本原则，同时也是和平共处五项原则之一，中国政府多次在不同场合突出强调不干涉内政原则。例如，2014 年中国高调纪念和平共处五项原则发表 60 周年，第二届世界互联网大会上习主席讲话中首要强调尊重网络主权不干涉他国内政。由于战后新获得独立国家民族意识、主权意识的觉醒，这些国家对干涉内政十分敏感，只有严格遵守不干涉内政原则，才能够在全球治理中凝聚最大的共识形成治理的合力。

四 结语

中国参与、引领全球治理有利于世界的和平与发展，有助于维护中国的国民利益与国家利益。而且美国更应当清醒地认识到，如果在美国霸权出现衰落的过程中没有中国这样的大国来维系国际制度的有效性才是对美国利益的根本挑战。对内而言，中国的国民不能仅仅看到参与、引领全球治理的积极作用，更要客观

1 http://news.xinhuanet.com/world/2015-09/22/c_1116642032.htm 2016/1/4

2 在习主席 2015 年 10 月访问英国时，在双方发表的联合声明中首次使用了“面向 21 世纪全球全面战略伙伴关系”这一用“全球”加以修饰的伙伴关系提法。

清晰地意识到，参与全球治理特别是扮演引领者的角色需要付出一定的代价，同时要对治理的过程有一定的耐心，全球治理的作用效果表现出来不是一个短期见效的事情。因为从治理哲学到具体路径再到具体治理政策，全球治理将是一个复杂的系统工程。

Thinking on the Global Governance Deficit and China's Principles of Global Governance

Jin Canrong / China

Deputy Director of the School of International Relations at Renmin University of China, "Cheung Kong Scholar" Distinguished Professor

On December 18, 2015, the United Nations Security Council voted unanimously to usher in the peace process in Syria, which is particularly valuable under the current chaotic world situation. In the Middle East, the destruction of two U.S. wars against terrorism has not been effectively restored yet. However, the Syrian civil war, which has lasted for nearly five years, has exacerbated the turmoil in the Middle East. The terrorist acts of the Islamic countries have not only given rise to serious humanitarian disasters, but they have also brought the world powers to become involved in the turmoil in the Middle East. In Asia, the lifting of the ban in the right of collective self-defense by Japan has eliminated the legal obstacles for the operation of overseas troops. The high-profile intervention by the United States in the dispute among the Philippines, Vietnam and China over the maritime rights in the South China Sea has further complicated the situation in this area. In Europe, NATO's eastward expansion has squeezed the strategic space of Russia. The

Russia-Uganda war and the Ukrainian crisis have aggravated the tension between Russia and Europe. Within the European Union, terrorist attacks and the refugee issues are posing new and severe challenges to the governance of Europe and even to the stability of the European Union. In a global context, the extreme terrorist activities are spreading throughout the world, and the five permanent members of the UN Security Council are all facing the threat of terrorism. The emergence of the Islamic State has led to a new upsurge of terrorist activities. In terms of economic development, the European economy is still being haunted by the European debt crisis. The US economy is now beginning to show the signs of revival, and the Federal Reserve has raised its interest rates for the first time in over 10 years. However, the data of the World Bank show an average growth rate of about 2.18% in the overall GDP of the world economy since 2007, revealing the pessimistic overall development of the world's economy. In particular, the growth rate of China's economy - the locomotive of the world's economy, is also gradually slowing down. The situation in the world presents three major characteristics: First, the world's economy remains depressed; second, the geopolitical game of the great powers is becoming more serious; third, the threat of terrorist attacks is rising. Under the increasingly complicated and disordered international situation today, Mr. Kissinger solemnly put forward: "Can the world order be established in the present era?" In contrast with the pessimistic view of Mr. Kissinger, this article believes that the world order established after the World War II is still working effectively. The great number of chaos in today's world is due to the weakening of the world order, and the root cause of the weakening is the global governance deficit.

I. The Meaning and Causes of the Global Governance Deficit

Governance, as a practice method, generally exists in the three levels, i.e., country, region and world. The anarchy of the international community naturally possesses the soil for the practice of governance. In particular, the governance in the field of trade provides an important inspiration for the theory of global governance.

Lawrence S. Finkelstein, a professor at Northern Illinois University in the United States, made an earlier attempt to define the concept of “global governance”. Finkelstein clearly pointed out that “governance” is a practice first, a practice not centered on government, and “institution” is only one of the important approaches of governance. Global governance is the governance beyond the relations within the national border without any kind of highest authority, which shows the internationalization of the internal behaviors of various national governments to a certain extent. The transition from government to governance is considered to be “one of the major transformations that are occurring in the political life of human beings” by some scholars, including Prof. Yu Keping; this is reflected in international relations as “global governance from national state governments.” Prof. Yu Keping believes that, “Generally speaking, global governance refers to the solution to global conflicts, ecology, human rights, immigration, drugs, smuggling, infectious diseases and other issues through binding international regimes in order to maintain a normal international political and economic order.” Compared with the foregoing emphasis of practice and regime, there is another view that considers the concept of global governance: it is “a beneficial perspective designed to facilitate the understanding of the high complexity and diversity of global life.” It is a very challenging task to precisely define the concept of “global governance” from theory to practice. As shown in the *2015 Report of the Global Governance Index* issued by the East China University of Political Science and Law, the specific approach is to measure the degree of a country’s participation in global governance through a three-level index system with the country as a basic unit. Global governance jumps out of the state-centered perspective in the traditional international relations theory, and focuses on the common interests of human society. The core content of global governance is to protect the common interests of human society and meet the common needs of human beings from various theoretical theories to a specific system design of operational indicators. Therefore, the essence of global governance is the supply of global public goods. To understand the meaning of a global governance deficit, it is important to grasp the essence through various fragmented phenomena. Hence, the meaning of global governance deficit refers to the shortage of public goods in the practice of global governance.

The world order established after World War II is still working. It is improper to completely deny the design of the post-war world order with the current chaos. The fundamental reason for the global governance deficit is the decline in the supply capacity of global public goods. The decline in the supply capacity is the result of a combination of objective factors in many aspects, rather than the post-war world order. There are three main aspects: first, the supply capacity of traditional global public goods suppliers is declining; second, the global economy is in a downward cycle on the whole, and lacks the economic support to guarantee stable supply capacity; third, it is difficult for the existing governance structure to effectively respond to new issues represented by cyberspace and terrorist ideology.

As the traditional suppliers of global public goods, the United States and Europe, at the moment have a declining supply capacity, and present different overall characteristics of decline. The former is "strong in power but weak in will", while the latter is "strong in will but weak in power". The two wars against terrorism have consumed a large quantity of the strategic resources of the United States. By the end of the fiscal year 2014, the expenditure for the war against terrorism was nearly USD 1.6 trillion, and "more than 6,000 American soldiers and 2,300 American contractors lost their lives". In addition to these direct losses, there are still many potential impacts that cannot be counted, such as the damage caused by the psychological disorders of post-war soldiers. However, the costly war against terrorism has not brought about the desired result. In the ten years of the the war against terrorism, China's economy has developed rapidly, and under the support of a large economic scale, China has become the most challenging strategic rival to the hegemonic status of the United States. Therefore, the United States focusing its overall strategy back to the traditional inter-state competition through the implementation of the Asia-Pacific rebalancing strategy, and is concentrating its major strategic resources on coping with the rise of China. In the future, it is very likely that the United States will put its strategy of complete containment into practice. So, the United States is showing its attitude of "strong in power but weak in will" towards the supply of global public goods. Europe mainly refers to the European Union region with France and Germany as the core of leadership. In recent years, some major changes have taken place in the region. The new military doctrine of Russia in 2014 considered the North Atlantic Treaty Organization (NATO) as the first military threat. From the geopolitical perspective, Europe, located at the frontier of the confrontation between NATO and Russia, will directly bear the increasing military pressure from Russia. The outbreak of the European debt crisis and the refugee crisis in succession have posed a serious challenge to the current internal governance of the European Union. In particular, there has been a rift among France, Germany and Britain on the issue of the internal migration in the European Union. "French President Hollande and German Chancellor Merkel warned that Britain must respect the principles of the European Union in free migration and non-discrimination." France and Germany are the guiding forces of the internal core of the European Union. However, both France and Germany are now facing tough issues that need to be resolved. The terrorist attack in Paris caused the deaths of hundreds of people. The nationalist sentiment in France was severely stimulated, and as a consequence, the far-right "National Front" Party won in the first round of the French elections. From a long-term perspective, the result of terrorist attacks will most likely become the trigger of internal ethnic division. In Germany, the aging of the population is a strategic issue that Germany must face in the future, which is second only to Japan and ranks 2nd in the world. This means not only the further increase in national financial expenditures in the future, but also the need for introduction of sufficient labor force from the outside. Simply to meet the objective needs of the labor force, it is favorable for Germany to accept refugees. However, great differences exist in Merkel's government on the issue of how to treat refugees. This is closely associated with the continued downturn in German economic growth and the growth of Neo-Nazism. As the main successors to the colonial historical heritage, old European countries own special advantages in the supply of public goods. However, the challenges of the internal governance in Europe and the emergence of key state-level internal issues have made Europe become "weak" in global governance.

The sustained and effective supply of global public goods is inseparable from the prosperous economy which provides material support. Currently, the overall situation of the global economic growth is in a state of depression, especially the sluggish economic growth of the major European and American countries as the traditional suppliers of global public goods. As a new supplier of global public goods, China's economic growth has also begun to slow down The "downside pressure on economy" was mentioned at the Central Economic Working Conference for three consecutive years, from 2012 to 2014. Although it was not mentioned at the Central Economic Working Conference this year, the market response remains to be further observed.

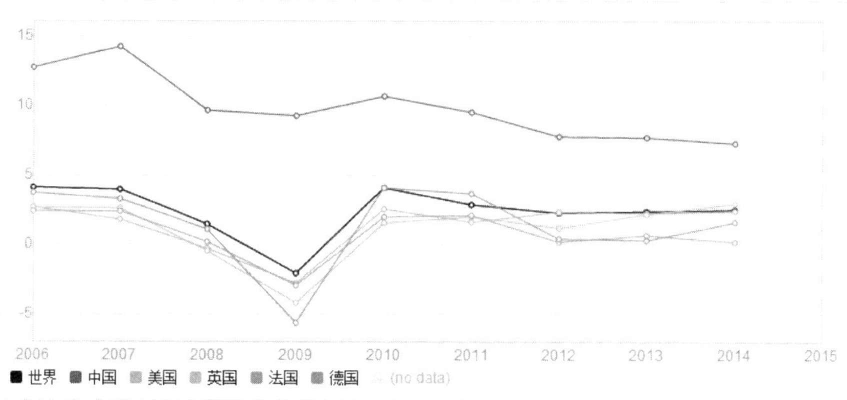

Figure 1 The Growth Rate of the World's GDP and that of the Major Powers

The sluggish economic growth leads to the decline of the willingness and capability of the great powers as main suppliers, further resulting in the gradual increasing deficit in the supply of public goods and forming the cumulative deficit. All the hot issues that are currently arising in the world can be attributed to the effect of the cumulative deficit to some extent. According to Kondratiev's theory of the long cycle, statistics of data and studies show that society is more prone to unstable factors, such as war and revolutionary turbulence, when the social economy is in the ascending stage of the period of a long cycle. The global economy is currently in the latter half of the downward period of the long economic growth cycle and is moving to a new ascending period. The frequency of conflicts will inevitably increase during the process of movement toward the ascending cycle. The long cycle theory shows that the increase of instability is due to profound economic reasons rather than the inevitable result of a clash of civilizations.

Table 1 Relationships among War, Revolutionary Turmoil and the Kondratiev Cycle

		Number of wars	Number of revolutionary turmoils	Total
First long cycle	Ascending stage	11	7	18
	Descending stage	1	4	5
Second long cycle	Ascending stage	7	11	18
	Descending stage	2	2	4
Third long cycle		11	11	22

The emergence of a series of new issues represented by network, environmental protection, and terrorist ideology poses a challenge to the current global governance structure. The current structure of global governance is a kind of "compound structure that consists of state-centered governance and supranational-centered governance". This structure is an asymmetric structure, where the state-centered governance occupies a dominant position. The scope of the new issues has gone far beyond the scope of governance of a single sovereign state, resulting in structural difficulties in governance practice. Let's take the Internet as an example: The Internet, as a global infrastructure connecting different regions, it plays a fundamental role in all aspects of human life. The free, equal, and open features of the Internet have not only brought many conveniences to humans but have also been unlawfully used by criminals as a platform for crimes. "The openness of the Internet makes cybercrime more transnational and mobile." The strategic archive, *Evolution of Cyberspace: Impact on National and Global Security*, released recently by the International Institute for Strategic Studies, analyzes the roles that the network has played or is playing in the global security environment and the power dynamics of various countries, which is the focus in the study of the archives. Among the top ten factors that affect the evolution of the network listed in the archives, the first to the third factors show the governance dilemma: On the one hand, the dependence of human beings on the Internet is growing, and the fragile Internet system is easily exploited by criminals; on the other hand, the strong strength of the United States on the Internet gives unfair strategic advantages to it and its allies, and the network freedom and openness advocated by the United States are considered as unfailing destruction by many governments. To effectively address these new issues, it is necessary to decentralize power and balance the structure of the "state-centered governance" and "supranational-centered governance". That decentralization and balance will inevitably suffer from the resistance to hegemony and state power, resulting in the impossibility to effectively deal with the cumulative deficit of global governance.

II. Hazards of the Global Governance Deficit

The primary hazard of a global governance deficit is the harm to human rights. It is apparent to see the direct harm of the global governance deficit to human beings, such as the spread of disease, environmental pollution and war refugees. Especially for the spread of disease and war, if the accumulation of related governance deficits is not curbed effectively, a massive humanitarian crisis will eventually take place. According to the 2014 Report of the United Nations High Commissioner for Refugees (UNHCR), the total number of refugees in the top three regions, i.e., Syria, Afghanistan and Somalia, exceeded 7.5 million. According to the 2015 Report of UNAIDS, there were approximately 36.9 million HIV carriers, about 2 million newly-infected patients and nearly 1.2 million people died of HIV-related diseases in 2014 in the world. It is hard to image that 795 million people are still suffering from hunger in the world today, and the number of hungry people in Asia accounts for two-thirds of the global total, of whom about 281 million people in South Asia are undernourished. Poverty is the root cause of hunger. In China, "according to the criterion of $ 2 per day, there are more than 170 million poverty-stricken people, including 130 million rural inhabitants and 45 million urban inhabitants". The right to personal security, the right to survival and the right to development are fundamental human rights. To indulge the accumulation of deficits of global governance is the greatest violation of human rights.

The second hazard of the global governance deficit is its impact on the international order established after war, which threatens the foundation for maintaining the balance of interests among the world's great powers. The post-war international order is an important basis for maintaining the long and peaceful state of the whole world. Even though some strategic analysts consider that China is trying to reconstruct the current world system, China has no intention of changing the order. During the general debate in the General Assembly of the United Nations, President Xi Jinping delivered a speech and solemnly declared to all countries (especially to the United States) in the world that "China will always be the defender of the international order and hold on to the path of peaceful development". The destruction that the global governance deficit caused to the post-war international order is mainly manifested in three aspects: 1. Corruption of the post-war international order in the area of governance; 2. Involvement of nuclear powers in the forefront of violent conflicts in the field of security; 3. The rise of extremist ideas in the ideological field. The supply of public goods sustains the recognition of each specific actor in the legitimacy of the organization. "If an institution is authenticated as a legal institution from the normative meaning, it means that the institution has the power to govern." The insufficient supply of public goods will cause the actors to question the legitimacy of the organization and even deny the significance of the existence of the organization. The overlapping of the global governance deficit with the existing fragmented power of the international community poses a double challenge to the international order, which is reflected precisely in the reform requirements for the major international organizations such as the United Nations and the International Monetary Fund. The great powers, especially the nuclear powers, play a crucial role in the post-war long-term peace. Moreover, the struggle among great powers is mostly carried out by agents so as to ensure the avoidance of direct confrontation among them. Regarding the Ukrainian crisis and the Syrian crisis, however, Russia under the leadership of Putin has not only embarked on the front of conflict confrontation but it has also frequently demonstrated its nuclear power to the outside world. It is particularly important to note that NATO led by the United States has set the no-fly zone over Syria and Russia and has deployed the S400 air-defense missile system in Syria. With the coexistence of direct confrontational forces between the United States and Russia, both sides have fallen into the necessary condition of the "game of cowards". Once both sides encounter an incident similar to the shooting down of a Russian fighter plane by Turkey, it would be difficult to predict the severity of the consequences. In the process of globalization, the gap between the North and the South is further widened, and the increase in the global governance deficit not only aggravates the uneven distribution of wealth between Northern and Southern countries, but it also amplifies the negative effect of an uneven distribution. The resonance of poverty and resentment provides a social foundation for the rise of extremist ideology. Moreover, the Internet technology integrates the extremist thoughts in the virtual world, which were originally scattered in different regions. In particular, the extremist thoughts under the cloak of religion can be rapidly and widely spread throughout the world by means of the Internet. The emergence of the Islamic State is a phenomenon worthy of attention. The religious extremist ideology is no longer a simple ideology, but it has become the political program for the establishment of a real government. In other words, the extreme religious thought has become a kind of "universal value" similar to democracy worshipped by religious extremists. The spread of the Internet-based extremist ideology has become a global public hazard. However, the political struggle among the great powers about Internet governance is still benefiting itself at others' expense.

The third hazard of the global governance deficit is the specific harm to China's interests. Around the year 2000, the "going global" policies was one of China's national policies of development. In the process of expanding the "going global" policy, China's interests have become increasingly closed to the entire international community. A large number of people, capitals and materials are distributed abroad. Once any international or regional unrest occurs, China's interests will be damaged. For example, during the Libyan War, China's emergency organization withdrew more than 35,800 expatriates and other people, and the value of seriously damaged projects under construction was as high as more than USD 18 billion. The scale of China's "going global" is getting bigger and bigger. However, the "dilemma of marching forward by individual soldiers" and the external defensive psychology faced by the "going global" policy have not been fundamentally improved yet. From the perspective of diplomacy, the "Belt and Road" Initiative newly proposed by China is a optimization of China's "going global" policy, which can further improve the unfavorable situation of China in the huge overseas interests.

Table 2 Change in the Indicators Related to the "Going Global" policy (2010--2014)

Item / Time	Foreign exchange reserves (billion/USD)	Number of domestic residents exiting the country (million/person-time)	Total import and export (billion/USD)	Foreign direct investment (billion/USD)
2010	28473	5739	29728	688.1
2011	31811	7025	36421	746.5
2012	33116	8318	38668	878
2013	38213	9819	41600	1078.4
2014	38430	11003	43037	1231.2

From the perspective of international relations, the existing post-war international order itself is an important interest of China. First of all, the main approach for China to use to implement the strategy of reform and opening up is to actively integrate itself into the international order under the leadership of the United States. Since China is one of the major beneficiaries of the existing international order, the unreasonable part of the reform initiative should not be regarded as a negation of the whole order. Second, China's status as a great power is established by the post-war international order. As a permanent member of the Security Council, China can better safeguard its own interests and safeguard the overall interests of the world by using the high degree of legitimacy of the United Nations in handling global affairs. The security of China's overseas interests is directly affected by the "strong in will but weak in power" attitude of Europe and the "weak in will but strong in power" attitude of the United States on the issue of the global governance deficit. However, what really has global influence is the challenge posed to the legality of the post-war international order due to the accumulation of global governance deficits.

In addition, the transition of the strategic focus of the United States to the peaceful rise that contains China will make China face more severe external pressures. However,, containing China will become the biggest strategic failure of the United States in the 21st century. One of the key reasons is that the great powers in the world today have a wide distribution of interests in the post-war international order. None of the great powers is attempting to negate the international order led by the United States and dominated by the West after World War II.

III. Leading Governance–New Positioning of China's Role

In the existing global governance system, Europe and the United States are the main leaders, and China is an important participant. In the context of an increasingly connected world, terrorist attacks, the increase in the number of refugees, climate change, and unstable financial markets... these common issues concerning the destiny of human beings have become increasingly prominent. At the same time, the need for global governance is also becoming wide and profound. In reality, the philosophy of global governance and the governance policy that give priority to the universal values of the United States and Europe are challenged in practice. The cruelty of the real politics has always been concealed by the moral halo of "universal values" until the photo of the death of the 3-year-old boy Aylan Kurdi on the beach was released by the media. Since then, the massive humanitarian crisis in the Middle East has given rise to widespread public attention in the world. In recent years, China's diplomacy has attached great importance to global governance. The theme of the 27th collective learning of the Political Bureau of the CPC Central Committee is: the pattern of global governance and the system of global governance, marking the important promotion of the global governance issue in China's external strategic vision. The practice of China's global governance covers three levels, namely, great power, periphery and global, and two specific operational paths, namely, reactivation of the original governance mechanism and creation of a new governance mechanism.

Figure 2 China's Path to Global Governance

First, it is important to focus on the relations among the new great powers, which is the foundation of global governance. China and the United States are the two core powers with the most global influence in the world today. Therefore, the stability of Sino-American relations is the fundamental guarantee for a sustainable development of global governance. After the election of a new round of leadership collectives, it is proper to set about establishing a new type of Sino-American relations, and gradually extend the principle of practice in Sino-American relations to the relations with other great powers. Second, the grand vision of constructing the "Belt and Road" strategic economic zone is used to connect the north and the south. From the entire map of Eurasia, the countries on the European side, especially Western Europe, are the developed northern countries, while the countries on the Asian side, especially South Asia, are the relatively backward southern countries. As a result, they are economically complementary. Once it is possible to achieve interconnectivity within Eurasia and reduce transaction costs, the huge economic potential will undoubtedly be released, thereby providing material support for the realization of neighborhood diplomacy characterized by amity, sincerity, mutual benefit and inclusiveness. Third, China has revitalized the existing global governance mechanism with positive actions. For example, China's promotion of the RMB accession to the Special Drawing Rights (SDR) has not only reduced the risk of USD hegemony in other countries but it also strengthened the legitimacy of the institution, thus stabilizing the international monetary and financial system. In addition, China's proposal of China's program at the G20 summit, the solemn commitments at the Paris Conference on Climate Change, and China-Africa cooperation under the South-South cooperation framework are all integral parts of China's global governance practices. Due to the lack of media discourse, the inherent prejudices in the Western media and the advocacy of some realist scholars, China's global governance behavior is interpreted as an attempt to replace the United States in seeking world hegemony.

In global governance, China must gradually transform its role from participant to leader. The transformation is not only an objective response to the damage of China's overseas interests, but also an objective requirement proposed against the current complex historical background. According to statistics, the number of domestic residents exiting the country exceeded 100 million, the stock of foreign direct investment reached USD 882.64 billion and the net amount of foreign direct investment reached USD 123.12 billion in 2014. In the foreseeable future, these figures will continue to increase. The presence of massive overseas interests and the exit of a great number of citizens require China not to be limited to the role of participant any longer, and in addition, China needs to jump out of the competition for products and technologies and devote itself to the competition for the power of rulemaking and speech. The downward cycle of the economy, the slowdown of the process of globalization, the deterioration of mass and global issues in the middle powers, and the weakening of the leadership of various national governments make the current world more uncertain. Future global governance is likely to face a "G0" era. The Chinese and Western academic circles are seriously reflecting on the dilemma faced by the philosophy and practice of global governance which give priority to the "universal values" in the United States and Europe. "The West needs to come out of the inherent moral superiority and centralist dialectics" to bid farewell to Western centralism. As a large country with a global vision and era ambitions, China has a clear idea of its position and of the future of human beings faced with a world full of uncertainty. China should make new contributions to human civilization through leading global governance. "Intelligent people tend to change strategies and methods according to different periods of time, and wise people tend to develop proper management methods based on the different developmental direction of different things". The Chinese civilization of thousands of years, especially the Chinese philosophy advocating "harmony and cooperation" and the "globalism" worldview highly recognized by Dr. Toynbee, provides a wealth of ideological resources for the global governance of China. During the General Debate of the 70th Session of the UN General Assembly, President Xi Jinping stated: "Creating a community of a shared future for mankind" to show the world China's world outlook on the issue of global governance – a community of a shared future for mankind. The governance idea under the new world outlook has enabled China to develop the concept and practice of global governance that are completely different from those of the United States and Europe.

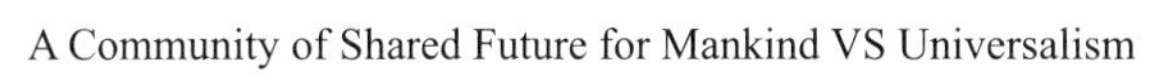

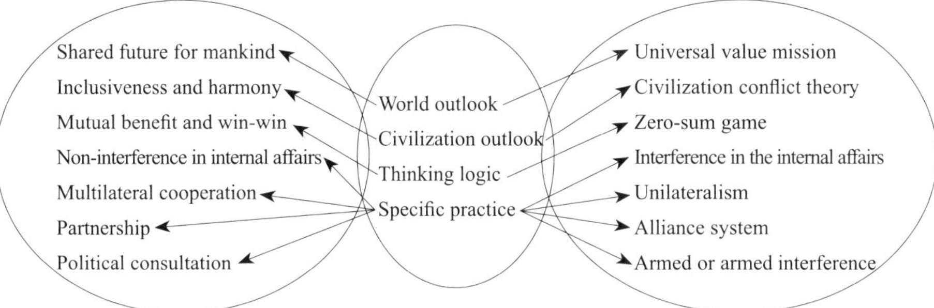

Figure 5 A Global Governance Model of Two World Outlooks

As Foreign Minister Wang Yi said, "our country has never been so close to the center of the world stage as it is today", and the new historical starting point, the new era, and the consciousness of the great nation mission all require that China must transform itself into a leader in global governance. In addition, China is taking some efforts to address the global governance deficit, which is conducive to getting rid of the United States' containment to China through the supply of public goods.

In the future, the global governance led by China will present different characteristics from the past. First, China's global governance will center on the United Nations. The United Nations is not only the core of the post-war world order but also the most representative international organization in the world today. In international affairs, the United Nations has the most extensive influence, and its work has affected many aspects of people's daily lives. In particular, the UN Security Council is the only body in the world with legal authority to engage in military intervention. As President Xi Jinping pointed out, "the global governance system is jointly established and shared by the world and cannot be controlled by one country alone." "(China) will always maintain the UN-centered international order and international system based on the purposes and principles of the Charter of the United Nations". China is one of the founding nations of the United Nations, a permanent member of the Security Council, as well as the third largest source country of membership dues. The legitimacy of the United Nations in global affairs and the status of China in the United Nations all force the global governance of China to be centered on the United Nations. Second, developmental priority is emphasized in governance. The themes of the era, peace and development, have never changed. It is urgently needed to provide stable material support for addressing social issues through development, especially in backward developing countries and regions. China is the largest developing country in the world, and the emphasis on developmental priority is a conclusion drawn from China's own successful experience. At the Fifth Plenary Session of the 18th Central Committee of the Communist Party of China, the understanding of development was further expanded, and the five developmental concepts of "innovation, coordination, greenness, openness, and sharing" were proposed. The emphasis on developmental priorities helps to escape from the trap of ideological issues and find the largest common divisor for solving practical problems in the real world. Third, the system of global partnerships is emphasized. Up to now, China has established a huge network of partnerships at different levels. Compared with a relationship of alliances, a partnership highlights the equal relations among member countries. The aim is not to deal with a common external enemy, but to safeguard the common interests within the partner countries. Compared with that, the flexibility and inclusiveness of partnerships make it more effective than alliance relationships in tackling the challenges in the fragmentation of global governance. Finally, the principle of non-interference in internal affairs is upheld. China has a painful historical memory of invasion of internal affairs and profoundly understands the truth of "do not do unto others what you would not have them do unto you." The permanent members of the UN Security Council, other than China, have had acts of gross interference in the internal affairs of other countries. As an extension of the principle of sovereignty, the principle of non-interference in internal affairs is a basic principle established by the Charter of the United Nations in dealing with international relations. It is also one of the five principles of peaceful coexistence. The Chinese government has repeatedly highlighted the principle of non-interference in internal affairs on different occasions. For example, China made high-profile commemoration for the 60th anniversary of the Five Principles of Peaceful Coexistence in 2014, and President Xi in the Second World Internet Conference emphasized the respect for internet sovereignty and the non-interference in internal affairs. Due to the awakening of the national consciousness and sovereignty consciousness of the new independent countries after war, these countries are very sensitive to the interference in internal affairs. Only by strict adherence to the principle of non-interference in internal affairs can we gather the greatest consensus in global governance to form a joint force for governance.

VI. Conclusion

China's participation in and guidance of global governance is conducive to world peace and development and helps to safeguard the interests of China's people and national interests. Moreover, the United States should clearly realize that the fundamental challenge to the interests of the United States is the absence of such a big country as China in maintaining the effectiveness of the international system in the decline of an American hegemony. Domestically, the Chinese people can not only see the active role of participating in and leading global governance, but also objectively and clearly realize the costs arising from the participation in global governance, especially the role of the leader. In the meanwhile, since global governance may not take effect in a short time, China should be patient in the process of governance. After all, from the philosophy of governance to a specific path and concrete governance policies, global governance will be a complex systematic project.

中国如何可能为世界提供一种新的文化选择

郑永年 【新加坡】
新加坡国立大学东亚研究所所长、教授

中国正在崛起，但崛起的标志是什么？这里不可避免要涉及文化问题。一个国家崛起的最主要标志就是文化的崛起。这种文化不仅能够支撑国家其他方面的崛起，而且也能够为这个世界提供另一个文化选择。就中国崛起而言，这里涉及至少三个相关的问题，第一，中国需要文化崛起吗？第二，中国需要一个不同于西方的文化吗？第三，中国能够创造一个不同于西方文化的文化吗？

一 中国能否为世界提供一种新的文化选择

第一个问题比较简单。尽管大多数人在谈论中国崛起的时候强调的是经济崛起，但很多人也开始涉及文化方面。越来越多的人意识到，没有文化的崛起，单一的经济崛起并不能说是真正的崛起。经济崛起大多是以 GDP 来计算的。一个国家的 GDP 很重要，但 GDP 只是其中一个主要指标，并不能涵盖其他方面。举例来说，根据经济学家安格斯·麦迪森（Angus Maddison）的估算，在 19 世纪 20 年代，中国的 GDP 占到了世界 GDP 的三分之一还多。从现在的角度来说，这不能不说是大国的象征。但很可惜的是，20 年之后，中国就被英国所打败，在著名的第一次鸦片战争中。当时包括英国、法国、德国和意大利在内的西欧 8 国的 GDP 只占世界 GDP 总量的 12%，而日本是 3%，美国是 1.8%。

中国是一个具有数千年传统的文明古国。为什么在一个新兴国家面前不堪一击？表面上看，英国的胜利在于其拥有当时世界上最庞大的海军和洋枪洋炮。但如果光从军事武器来看问题，就会过于肤浅。再深入一步，人们可以看到当时中国和英国的不同国家形式。在西方来到中国之前的很长历史时间里，中国拥有世界上先进的政治体制，尽管皇权体制和世界上的其他帝国差不了多少，但中国的文官制度或者官僚制度是最为先进的。但是这个体制一旦遇到产生于近代西方的国家体制，就变得不堪一击。传统中国皇权尽管理论上非常集权，但实际上往往是无比分权，“无为而治”，或者“统而不治”。人们常用“天高皇帝远”来形容这个体制。也就是说，这个体制没有很多制度建设，没有动员能力。皇权所拥有的动员能力主要是维持皇朝尤其是皇室服务的。因此，尽管当时中国拥有那么高比例的 GDP，但这些资源并不能有效组织起来，转化成为政府力量，尤其是军事力量。而英国呢？当时的英国所拥有的是一种全新的国家政权形式，即主权国家。这是一种高度集权的国家政权。之前，英国所有的是极其分散化的城堡政治。君主政治消灭了城堡政治，国家政治权力才能集中。尽管当时的英国的 GDP 并不算高，但国家能够有效动员资源和使用资源。英国是一个海洋国家，当时的英国具有世界上最强大的海军。

那么问题在于近代国家形式先崛起于西欧？这里就涉及文化的崛起。西欧近代国家的崛起是中世纪后期西欧理性文化崛起的产物。简单地说，这是一种最初源自地中海地区，后又逐渐容纳了包括中国文化在内的世界先进文化。文化的崛起自下而上，文化最后的政治结晶便是近代国家形式。当然这种文化还具有更广泛和深刻的内容，涵盖各个领域。因此，我们可以看到，西欧国家自 15 世纪之后，不断产生着有利于中央集权制度建设的政治文化。尤其对英国来说，因为是海洋国家，英国便根据自己的经验发展出了“自由贸易”理论。在很大程度上说，如果当时英国的船坚炮利是其硬实力的话，那么“自由贸易”便是其软实力。

无论从哪一方面来看，文化崛起的重要怎么说都不会过分。从这一角度来说，我们今天强调文化崛起和文化创新是一个正确的方向。

对前面的问题，即文化崛起的重要性，人们不会有很多疑义。但是对接下来的两个问题，就不好回答。我们需要创造一个不同于西方的文化吗？这个问题一旦提出，中国社会马上就会分化。在很大程度上说，自五四运动以来，中国是要消灭自己的文化的。当时的人们看到了西方的崛起是文化崛起所致，因此认为中国如果要强大起来，就要学西方的文化，消灭自己的文化。在亚洲，日本是一个例子。日本的明治维新是"去日本化"而"欧化"，即仿照欧洲国家（主要是英国和德国）来建设国家。当然，西欧文化或者西方文化因为中国共产主义运动的崛起而消失。中国共产党所接受的是马克思和列宁主义。这种选择当时是符合历史现实的。西欧是发达国家，社会经济政治各方面已经发展到很高的水平。人们可以向往这种文化，但很难搬用到落后的发展中国家。以苏俄为代表的共产主义文化崛起于较为落后的国家，对中国比较适应。也应当指出，当时欧洲发生了第一次世界大战，这对中国的知识和政治精英的影响很大。

把文化再造或者崛起等同于文化的西方化，或者说把西方的看成是共通的，都过于简单。上面说过，西方近代文化的崛起本身就吸收了很多非西方的文化。所有文化或者文明，因为都是人类社会创造和积累起来的，都存在有共同性的东西。的确，自近代以来，西方的文化话语一直占据强势，但这既不是说西方文明和其他文明没有相关性，更不是西方文明是普世的论据。中国文化和文明中的很多因素也可以是普世的。

日本一般被视为是属于西方国家。但日本并非真正是西方国家，而是一个假装西方的东方国家。日本接受了西方的工业化和民主化的制度形式，但无论是经济制度还是政治制度，其运作规则还是保留着浓厚的日本传统。可以说，日本是一个把西方形式和日本传统内容结合得很好的国家。同样，中国共产党在中国的成功也并非直接照抄照搬了苏俄模式，而是对苏俄模式进行了中国式的改造，也就是当时所说的"马克思主义中国化"。日本政治制度是西欧自由主义日本化的结果，而中国共产党政权是较为落后国家马克思主义中国化的结果。也就是说，不管是哪一种外来文化，如果要成功，都必须和本土文化结合起来。任何一种文化都是长期历史演进的产物，其可以变化，但不可以被取代。

因此，人们可以说，中国需要一个不同于西方文化的文化。如果中国单纯接受西方文化，那么中国就不能算是崛起。当今在中国盛行的各种"主义"都是西方的舶来品，尽管在中国因为加入了中国要素而变形，但很难对西方发生任何影响力。西方可能因为中国接受了他们文化而高兴，但这并不是说我们的文化具有吸引力。很多年前，笔者读过美国记者 James Fallows 写的一本书，书名叫《非常像我们》（*More Like Us*），就是说亚洲国家随着发展越来越像西方国家了。这当然是西方的胜利，西方的崛起，而不是亚洲的崛起。亚洲通过学习西方而崛起。

这是大多数西方学者的解释，也为亚洲大多数人所认同。在这个背景下，亚洲当然不是除西方之外的另外一个选择，亚洲只是西方的延伸。

显然，第三个问题更难回答，那就是，我们基于中国文化之上，有能力创造一个和西方不同的文化但又可以成为除西方之外的另一个选择的文化？产生一种不同的文化比较容易。这个世界上存在着不同的文化，一些文化比较强势，而另一些文化比较弱势。强势文化具有话语权，为比较多的人所接受，而弱势文化稍有话语权，甚至没有话语权，不为人所接受。也就是说，要创造一种不同于其他文化圈但同时又可以被其他文化圈的人所接受的文化，这是一件艰巨的任务。历史上，宗教文化，包括基督教、伊斯兰教和佛教文化是这样的文化。中国传统文化也是这样一种文化，至少在东亚文化圈里是这样。

造就这样一种文化很难，但不是不可能。这里举“东亚模式”的例子来说。1994 年世界银行出版了一本题为《东亚奇迹》（*The East Asian Miracle*）的书，肯定了亚洲的发展模式，并指出东亚模式不同于西方模式。这个研究项目的出台是一个很艰难的过程。当时的西方主流经济学并不承认有东亚模式，因为他们认为东亚模式没有什么了不起，因为东亚是向西方学习的。是西方因素促成了东亚模式。当然，东亚经济体，日本和亚洲四小龙都认为自己的发展和西方的不同。这些经济体成功了，当然可以开始说话，开始建立自己的话语权。尽管遭西方主流学者的反对，但这个研究项目最后是在日本银行的大力支持下成功推出。今天尽管也仍然有人不认同东亚模式，但东亚模式已经为西方主流所接受。当然，东亚模式也是很多发展中国家所模仿和接受的经济发展模式。实际上，在知识界，人们围绕着东亚发展模式已经发展出一套相对完整的知识体系，这套体系由各种亚洲要素组成，包括儒家文化、国家和政府的经济角色、社会因素例如高储蓄率，强调教育，家庭的作用等。

和东亚的经济话语相比，东亚国家和地区的政治话语就没有那么幸运了。在这方面，即使是亚洲的主流话语都是从西方进口而来。亚洲国家和地区没有自己的政治话语权，很多政治体系即使在实际运作过程中和西方的非常不同，但也都伪装成西方政治体系。日本是很典型的，韩国也差不多。实际上，即使是民主政体，亚洲国家的组织方式和西方很不相同，除了形式上的定期选举之外。比如，日本被视为是西方式民主，但自民党一党独大模式和西方民主大相径庭。当然，也有一些西方学者看到了这种不同。可以说，亚洲的政党、政府、社会等方面的组织有它们自身的规律。在形式上虽套上了西方政治形式但并没有改变其文化性质。

那么，中国的情形又是怎样呢？不能说中国没有文化。中国有数千年古老文明，是文明古国。在历史上，中国文明也曾经为西方文明作出了很大的贡献。西方启蒙时代哲学吸取了很多中国的理性主义。我们常常强调“四大发明”，这些是技术上的事情。即使在思想和实践领域，中国文化的影响力早已远远超出东亚地区，而达至西方。这里举两个例子。

一是中国的文官制度。传统上，中国发展出了世界上最为庞大、也最有效的文官体系。那么大的中华帝国靠什么来统治？建立帝国的是武力，但统治帝国的是发达的文官体系。西方也经过帝国时代，但没有发展出类似中国的文官体系。西方从近代国家的产生到后来的民主政治的转型和运作，没有文官体系是不可想象的。隐含在中国的文官体系里面的几个原则对西方产生了很大的影响。

一是皇权和治权的分离。天下是皇帝打下来的，国家的所有权属于皇帝，但是治理天下的权力，即治权或者相权（宰相）是向社会开放的。中国发展出了一套中央集权式的考试制度来录用官员。这和西方历史上的家族统治构成了鲜明的对照。西方引入了中国式的文官制度。在民主化发生之后，最终演变成为现在的政治和行政的分离。而政治和行政的分离是近代以来民主政治运作的制度前提条件。

二是文官的中立性。政治是要变的，但如何保证一个国家的政策的连续性呢？如何保证治权不会因为政治的变化而中断呢？中立的文官制度就是关键。西方，政治人物受民主规则的制约，但文官制度的运作具有其自身的规律，不受民主政治的影响。这一点任何西方一本教科书都会有论述。

三是文官轮流掌管不同部门的制度。中国历史上，文官一般不能在一个地方长期掌权，皇帝会把他们进行调动，也就是现在人们所说的“干部交流制度”。有两个目标，一是防止地方主义和地方势力的形成，二是为了让官员积累治理不同地区的经验，便于他们升迁，治理整个国家的事务。这一点也对近代西方国家政权制度也很重要，更不用说在亚洲了。

传统中国也是等级制度，有“士、农、工、商”等，但中国没有像其他文明那样的等级制度，例如基于宗教、种姓、民族等之上的等级制度。对中国的儒家来说，人只有“接受过教育”和“没有接受过教育”之分，而每一个人都是可以

"被教育好的"。西方传统教育制度是精英教育制度，能够接受教育的是贵族和富裕家庭的子女。在近代之前，教育权利为社会的绝少数人所垄断。中国的"有教无类"思想对西方后来的"大众教育"影响很大。尽管中国传统社会，儒家往往垄断知识，中国本身并没有发展出大众教育制度，但"有教无类"的思想则在西方演变成为"大众教育"制度。近代以来，西方各国政治制度逐渐民主化，而大众教育则构成了大众民主有效运作的最重要的一环。

二 文化创新的三个"解放"

那么，中国的文化创造和创新如何可能呢？这里我要强调讲三个"解放"，即从"思想和思维"的殖民地状态中解放出来，从权力状态中解放出来，从利益状态中解放出来。

首先是解放思想，就是从思想和思维的"殖民地状态"解放出来。中国自清末在军事和政治上被西方类型的国家打败之后就对自己的文化失去了信心。很多人把中国落后的终极原因归诸文化。"五四运动"的核心主题可以说是"去中国化"。当然，发展了数千年的传统文化并不是想去就能去掉的。20 世纪 30 年代蒋介石政权的"新生活运动"就是要复归传统文化。毛泽东尽管是反传统文化的先锋，但他也意识到传统文化的实际功能。在革命战争年代，他提倡马克思主义"中国化"。新中国成立后，很多运动表面上看是反传统的，但实际上是要复归传统。

不过，应当说明的是，所有这些运动中的中国因素已经退居到这些人的"潜意识"之中。反传统是中国革命的主线。自"五四运动"之后，学习西方变成了向西方追求真理。因为西方成为真理，那么包括中国本身在内的非西方就变成了不是真理了。向西方学习成为政治上的正确，否则就是不正确。当然，这里的西方既包括自由主义，也包括马克思主义等一切来自西方的东西。

学习西方并没有错，但把西方视为是真理则大错特错了。中国并不拒绝其他文明和价值，但中国文化本身必须成为主体。在学习西方过程中，因为没有中国的主体意识，中国文化就失去了自己的主体低位。问题在于，西方文化主导下的西方话语解释不了中国的一切。今天，越来越多的人已经意识到西方话语不能说明自己。（这一点，我在其他场合多次强调过。就是说，如果西方是苹果，中国是橘子的话，那么苹果的话语是解释不了橘子的。同样，橘子可以学习苹果，因为大家都是水果，但是必须明白，橘子学习苹果的目标不是把自己变成苹果，而是要把自己变成更好的橘子。）但是，很少有人去创造，去发明。不用说中国数千年的历史传统，中国改革开放以来有那么多的经验。中国为什么不能产生自己的话语呢？不能产生自己的概念和理论呢？大部分人一如既往地选择用西方来解释自己。这种情况不改变，中国永远不会有自己的话语、自己的概念和自己的理论，当然更不用说是文化软力量了。因此，我们尤其是知识分子必须花大力气从长达一个多世纪的思维和思想被“殖民”的状态中解放出来。西方继续要学，但中国的主体地位也必须得到确立。

第二个解放是要从政治权力中解放出来。中国传统数千年，主流文化是一种依附性文化，一种以王权为核心的文化。王权文化本身只是王权体制的结果。但我这里要强调的是中国文化的依附性质有效阻碍了文化的创新和扩张。

传统上，我认为中国的知识分子可以分为政治知识分子和非政治知识分子，分别由儒家和道家为代表。儒家是入世的，道家是出世的。也就是说，儒家是关心社会政治的，而道家则根本不关心现实社会的，道家往往对现实世界失去信心，因此往往崇尚自然，扎根到深山老林。道家讲清静，本来应当有很多时间来思考问题的。但因为与现实社会和政治无关，道家对中国的知识体系的贡献很有限。道家提倡人与自然的合一，不知道主客体之分，犹如庄子和蝴蝶的关系，不知道谁是主体，谁是客体。这种人与自然合一的哲学在一个层面来说具有相当的合理性，但很难演变成为一套科学思维和研究的体系。中国没有出现近代自然科学，和道家的态度是有关联的。

中国社会政治知识体系的主体是儒家。不过，儒家依附王权，为权力服务，往往变成权力的奴隶。这里有自觉的“奴隶”和被“奴隶”两种含义。有人说，“儒”这个字由“人”和“需”组成。从儒家的角度看，主要是为了解决“人”的“需要”问题，而这种“需要”是通过服务于王权而获得。从王权的角度看，主要是为了解决服务于自己的“人”的问题，也是一种“需要”。历史上，王权需要获得两种绝对的忠诚，一是知识的忠诚，即儒家，二是太监的忠诚。这两种忠诚保证王权的绝对性，儒家管理的是国家事务，太监管理的是王权内部事务。对儒家的忠诚又可以分为两种，一种是讲真话的忠诚，一种是讲假话的忠诚，即愚忠。尽管历史上不乏讲真话的忠诚，但大多都是“愚忠”，自私的“愚忠”，为了自己的利益，不惜说假话。从知识的角度来看，中国传统上的王权的统治术远比其他文明发达，这是儒家的功劳。西方人强调法治，中国人强调人治。有了法治和一套有效的国家制度，平常人也可以统治一个社会。但在中国，儒家是不提倡法治的。没有一套有效的国家制度，必须有一个非常聪明的人来做皇帝，否则天下就很难治理。我是研究政治学的，中国没有发展出一套国家制度建设学说来，和儒家仅仅服务于王权是有很大关系的。

儒家没有能够发展出有关中国社会政治的知识体系还有一个很重要的原因，那就是儒家垄断了知识。传统中国被视为是儒家社会，但是社会上到底有多少人可以成为是儒家呢？比例非常之少。人人可以成为“儒”，也就是说“儒”这个阶层是开放的，人人可以通过自己的努力，尤其是通过考试制度而成为“儒”，但开放性并没有导致“儒”和整个社会的关联。儒家垄断了知识，并没有努力把知识传播到整个社会，用今天的学术语言来说，就是儒家没有社会化的过程。服务于王权，这一本质决定了儒家对社会现实不那么感兴趣，自然也就没有关于这个社会的知识。上面说过，儒家的“有教无类”思想为西方所用，对西方的大众教育制度的建立产生了很大的作用，但这一思想在中国本土并没有发挥如此的作用。

与传统相比，中国社会现在已经大变样了。但是，中国知识阶层的权力依附性有没有变化呢？我的判断是，不仅没有变化，反而强化了。就对权力的关系来说，今天中国的知识分子可以分成三类，一类是为权力服务的，一类是反权力的，这两类是主体，第三类的是那些对政治和权力不关心人，类似于传统的道家。为权力服务的知识分子似乎不用加以详细讨论，大家都有认识，就是那些御用文人，光会说好话，为现政权辩护的人。第二类知识分子是反权力、反现存体制的人。实际上，这些人也是在追求权力，就是想用他们的知识去影响实际政治甚至得到实际政治权力。他们因此往往自觉地站在权力的对立面，也为了反对而反对。就是说，他们是要通过反权力而得到权力。

无论是为权力服务还是反权力都很难产生有关中国的知识体系。知识分子的权力哪里来？在中国，人们往往把那些经常讨论实施政治、关心现实的知识分子称为公共知识分子。这个概念来自西方，但在中国已经变形了。知识分子首要的任务是解释世界。在解释世界的基础上，知识分子才会拥有权力。如果你把世界解释好了，知道了社会实际上是如何运作的，问题在哪里，如何解决问题和改进社会，那么即使你没有任何权力职位，你也会得到权力。一些政治人物可能会采用的判断、诊断等来改革社会。所以，马克思说，哲学家有两件任务，即认识世界和改造世界，而认识世界又是改造世界的前提。在没有认识世界之前，你是不会有改造世界的权力的。中国的知识分子显然不是这样，总是没有能力去解释世界，但有巨大的野心去改造世界。结果是可想而知的，那就是导致权力和知识之间的恶性互动。知识想挑战权力，权力想遏制知识。知识和权力两者之间没有任何边界，两者都想互相渗透，结果两边都不专业。权力不专业，没有信心，总想控制一切。知识界不专业，解释世界的事情不做，但要干预政治。可以想见，如果这个恶性互动模式不改变，中国文化或者知识体系的创造还是没有希望的。

第三个解放是要从利益中解放出来。在很大程度上说，在今天的中国社会，物质利益对文化创新所产生的负面影响远远大于权力所带来的负面影响。我一直强调，我们这个文明已经经历过政治上的考验，但还没有经过商业文明的考验。从秦始皇的“焚书坑儒”到50年代的“反右运动”，中国的很多知识分子还是保持了其对自己坚持的知识的认同，体现出了抵抗权力和反抗权力的勇气。但是，改革开放以来的商业革命已经彻底冲垮了知识分子对知识的应有的信念，向物质利益投降了。为“五斗米折腰”是当代知识分子的常态。我记得一位领导人曾经感叹过，中国为什么没有穷人经济学家。其实，这非常容易理解。中国现在所拥有的是大量的利益知识分子，就是为各种利益说话的知识分子。为穷人说话没有利益可图，穷人当然不会有自己的知识分子。中国不存在一个民族、一个国家所应当有的“有机知识分子”，如果用意大利马克思主义者葛兰西的概念的话。有机知识分子能够超越具体的利益，而为民族、国家的整体利益说话。我们甚至可以说，执政党也没有这样的有机知识分子。谁都想从执政党那里分得一块利益，但就是没有人为这个组织的长远利益考虑。从知识供应的角度来说，中国目前所面临的诸种问题例如收入分化、社会不正义和道德衰落等等，知识分子是要负起责任来的。知识分子只有能超越自身的利益才能够为改革政策提供有用、有效的知识。

知识分子不能超越自己的利益，视追求私利为己任。这一特点更使得政治权力轻易吸纳和消化知识分子。这一点，我们可以举现在的科研制度的设计作为例子来说明。随着国家的财力的增加，国家对大学、研究机构的投入也越来越多。但是，我们并没有任何迹象可以回答这些年大家谈论的“钱学森之问”，即为什么中国没有大师级学者？道理很简单，因为中国没有培养大师的制度设计。中国的制度设计是用来控制知识发展的，而不是用来推动知识发展的。在中国的科研评审制度下，教授学者们活得很辛苦，整天要为发表论文发愁。中国的制度迫使人写很多的文章，但阻碍人们尽心作研究。哪有教授每年都能发表优秀论文呢？即使在西方优秀的大学，如果一位教授一生中能够发表几篇高质量的文章，就很不错了。举我们政治学领域。哈佛大学教授亨廷顿是大家熟悉的。但是他写过多少篇名著呢？没有多少。现在的评审制度要求我们的教授每年都能写出大文章来？这有可能吗？做研究和写文章完全是两码事情。好文章是建立在长期的研究基础上的，把时间都用来写文章了，哪有时间来做研究呀！

中国大学和研究机构的工资制度的设计也扼杀着知识的创造和创新。教授、教师和研究者们的基本工资都非常低，这要求他们把很多时间都花在申请研究经费，用各种变相的途径把研究经费转化成为自己的收入。这里就产生了很多负面结果。在西方，教授、教师和研究者 90% 以上的收入都来自基本工资，工资可以给他们带来体面的生活，这就会使他们有充分的时间来从事科研和教育。中国现在的情形如何？对很多人来说，可能不到一半的收入来自基本工资，其余的来自其他资源。在基本工资不能维持一个体面生活的情况下，谁有时间来做严肃的研究呢？如果也像西方那样，把工资制度调整一下，让 90% 的收入来源于基本工资，那么结果就会很不一样。那么，为什么不可以进行改革呢？

更令人担忧的是，中国的整个教育体系从幼儿园到博士后都被利益化了。这个非常漫长的教育链条，被各种利益所分割。那么多寄生于教育的机构，为了追求自己的利益设计了无数的项目，通过正式的制度和非正式的社会压力，施加于受教育者及其家庭之上。教育的目标是传授知识和生产知识。但现在中国教育的各个环节除了钱，似乎毫无目标。改革开放三十多年了，教育的投入也越来越多，但中国产生了一个像样的学者吗，更不用说是大师了。现在连两院院士都成为各种组织争取利益的工具。中国的教育者应当看看西南联大时期的情况，在那么恶劣的情况下培养出如此多的大师。可以说，钱越多，教育就越腐败。中国应避免陷入这样的恶性循环中去。否则牺牲的是受教育者及其家庭。因为接受教育是文化发展和创新的前提，在这样的情况下，才谈得上生产和创新知识和文化体系。

现在大家都在讲文化创新，知识创新。但如果所有这些制度不能得到改革，那么文化知识创新只会是幻想罢了。正如开头所讲到的，尽管越来越多的人看到了文化创新和文化“走出去”的重要性，有关方面也开始有具体的政策来追求这些目标，但没有基于自身的文化创造和创新，拿什么“走出去”呢？能够向世界销售什么呢？

三　新的文化选择

实际上，如果从国际的角度来看，中国文化的客观形势不容乐观。简单地说，两种主要的宗教文化，即西方文化正在急剧扩张，而中国文化则越来越处于守势。

西方文化，也就是地中海产生和开始兴起的文化仍然占据世界文化的主导地位，并且越来越具有进攻性和侵略性。这个文化从地中海开始一路扩张，先占据了大西洋两岸，现在又扩展到太平洋和印度洋。西方文化基于宗教之上，具有使命性。这种宗教使命一直是推动其无限扩张的巨大动力。同时，也需要注意到的是，这种文化尽管还具有宗教性质，但很多方面已经被世俗化，也就是不再具有原先的原教旨主义色彩。在亚洲尤其是东亚，这种变化更有利于其传播。

和这种宗教文化相比，中国尽管有经济崛起，但文化则处于守势。这种守势，即使在中国国内也很明显。原因很简单，正如上面所讨论的，中国人的思维本身就已经相当西方化了。我们现在所进行的文化推广活动，尽管声势浩大，但不会对中国文化的扩张具有任何实质性的意义。中国缺少的是一套核心价值 (core value)，也缺少一套可以和其他文化分享的共享价值 (shared value)。很显然，中华文明如果不能发展出一套自己的核心价值并在此基础上发展出共享价值，那么就会被前面两种文化逐步消解和融化。不过，从历史上看，中国的世俗文明成功地消解了其他的宗教文化，包括佛教文化和犹太教文化。我相信，中国可能也能够再次发展出一种新的文化范式，一种能够容纳和整合其他宗教文化而又能保持自己的世俗文化性质的文化。要不被消解，要不再次重生，中国的选择并不多。如果不想看到前一种情形，那么就必须重生。这就是我们今天讨论中国文化创新的全部意义。

How Can China Provide a New Culture Choice for the World?

Yongnian Zheng / Singapore

Professor and Director of the East Asian Institute at the National University of Singapore

China is rising, but what is the sign of its rise? Here, the cultural issue is inevitably involved. The most outstanding sign for the rise of a country is the rise of culture. Culture can not only support the rise of a country in other aspects, but also make another cultural choice available to the world. As far as the rise of China is concerned, at least three related questions arise. First, does China need the rise of culture? Second, does China need a culture different from Western culture? Third, is it possible for China to create a culture different from Western culture?

I. Can China Provide a New Cultural Choice for the World?

The first question is relatively simple. When it comes to the rise of China, many people begin to turn their attentions to culture, even though most people are highly concerned about the rise of the economy. An increasing number of people realize that, without the rise of culture, merely a rise of the economy is not a true rise. The rise of the economy is mostly based on the GDP. For a country, the GDP is of paramount importance. However, as a matter of fact, the GDP is only one of the main indicators and does not cover other aspects. For instance, according to the estimate by the economist Angus Maddison, China's GDP accounted for more than one-third of the world's GDP in the 1820s. Given the current situation, this is absolutely a symbol of a great country. Unfortunately, 20 years later, China was defeated by Britain in the famous first Opium War. At that time, the GDP of eight Western European countries, including Britain, France, Germany and Italy, accounted for only 12% of the world's total GDP. For Japan and the USA, the ratio was 3% and 1.8% respectively.

China is an ancient civilization with thousands of years of tradition. Why is it so vulnerable as an emerging country? On the surface, the world's largest navies, guns and cannons contributed to the victory of Britain. However, it is superficial to think it was simply due to military weapons. Moreover, people could see the different national forms of China and Britain at that time. In the long history before the Western countries set foot in China, China owned the the world's most advanced political system. In spite of almost no difference from other empires in the world in terms of a system of imperial power, China's civil service system or bureaucratic system was the most advanced. However, when facing the state system that emerged from the modern West, the system is not able to withstand a single blow. Theoretically, traditional Chinese imperial power was very centralized. However, in fact, it had always turned out to be decentralized, becoming "control by doing nothing" or "reigning but not governance." China itself often uses the saying "the emperor is as far away as the sky" to describe the system. In other words, the system has neither much capacity for institutional building nor mobilization. The capacity for mobilization possessed by the imperial power was mainly aimed at maintaining the dynasty, especially the royal service. Hence, although China had a high proportion of GDP at that time, those resources could not be effectively organized and transformed into government capabilities, especially military capabilities. What about Britain? At that time, Britain owned a completely new form of state power, namely, a sovereign state, a highly centralized form of state power. Previously, the extremely decentralized "castle politics" prevailed in Britain. The monarchy eradicated "castle politics", leading to the concentration of national political power. Britain was able to effectively mobilize and use resources, despite its low GDP at that time. As a maritime country, Britain had the most powerful navy in the world at that time.

So, the problem is: did the modern state form rise in Western Europe first? This involves the rise of culture. The rise of modern Western European countries was an outcome of the rise of the rational culture in Western Europe in the late middle ages. Simply put, it was a culture which originated from the Mediterranean region and later it gradually accommodated the world's advanced cultures, including the Chinese culture. The rise of culture starts from the bottom and goes to the top, and the final political fruit of culture is the form of the modern state. Surely, culture has also more extensive and profound contents covering all areas. Therefore, it can be seen that the political cultures conducive to the construction of a centralized system have constantly sprung up in Western European countries since the 15th century. Especially for Britain, as a maritime country, it has developed a "free trade" theory based on its own experience. To a large extent, if the strong ships and armaments were Britain's hard power at that time, "free trade" was its soft power.

It is impossible to overstate the importance of the rise of culture in any respect. From this perspective, our emphasis on cultural rise and cultural innovation is the right direction to take.

There will not be much doubt regarding the first question, that is, the importance of the rise of culture. However, it is not easy to answer the next two questions. The second question is: Do we need to create a culture different from Western culture? Once the question is raised, social differentiation would take place soon in China. Since the May 4th Movement, China has been eliminating its own culture to a large extent. At that time, people saw that the rise of culture contributed to the rise of the

West. Hence, they wrongly believed that China had to learn Western culture and eliminate its own culture to become stronger. In Asia, Japan is an example. The aim of the Japanese Meiji Restoration was to “de-Japanese” and “Europeanize”, meaning that Japan built its nation by following the European countries (mainly Britain and Germany). It is certain that the Western European culture or Western culture vanished because of the rise of the Chinese communist movement. What the Chinese Communist Party accepts is Marxism and Leninism, which conforms to historical reality. Western Europe, made up of developed countries, has developed into a very high level in all aspects of society, economy and politics. People may yearn for this kind of culture, but it is difficult to follow it in the backward developing countries. The communist culture, represented by Soviet Russia, emerged from relatively backward countries, and was relatively adaptable to China. It should also be noted that the First World War in Europe exerted a great influence on China’s intellectual and political elites. Both the Chinese Kuomintang and the Chinese Communist Party have accepted Soviet Russian culture, especially in politics.

It is too simple to re-shape a culture or make a culture rise up to equal Western culture, or view western culture as a universal culture. As shown above, the rise of modern Western culture itself has absorbed many non-western cultures. As all cultures or civilizations are created and accumulated by human society, they have universal things. Indeed, Western cultural discourse has always occupied a powerful position since the beginning of modern times. However, this neither means that Western civilization is independent from other civilizations nor that it serves as the universal argument of Western civilization. Many factors in Chinese culture and civilization can also be universal.

Japan is generally viewed as a Western country. However, in fact, Japan is an Eastern country that pretends to be a Western country, rather than a real Western country. Japan accepts the institutional form of Western industrialization and democratization. However, the operating rules of both the economic system and the political system still retain a strong Japanese tradition. It can be said that Japan is a country that combines the Western form with Japanese traditions well. Similarly, the success of the Chinese Communist Party in China is attributable to the Chinese-style transformation of the Soviet Russian model (known as the "Sinification of Marxism"), rather than the direct copy of the Soviet Russian model. The Japanese political system is the result of the Japanization of Western European liberalism, while the regime of the Chinese Communist Party is the result of the Sinicization of Marxism in the relatively backward countries. In other words, no matter what kind of foreign culture, it is a must to integrate with the local culture in order to achieve success. Any kind of culture is the product of a long-term historical evolution, which may be changed but cannot be replaced.

Therefore, people can say that China needs a culture that is different from the Western culture. If China simply accepts the Western culture, China cannot be considered as being on the rise. The various "isms" prevalent in China today are imported from the West, and it is hard for them to exert any influence on the West despite transformation due to integration with Chinese elements in China. The West may be pleased to see that China accepts the Western culture, but this does not mean that our culture is attractive. Many years ago, the author read a book entitled *More Like Us* written by James Fallows, an American journalist. The title of the book means that Asian countries are more and more like Western countries. It is, of course, the victory of the West, and the rise of the West, rather than the rise of Asia. Asia has risen by learning from the West. This is the interpretation of most Western scholars, and also that recognized by most people in Asia. In this context, Asia is not an alternative to the West, but just an extension of the West.

Obviously, it is more difficult to answer the third question, i.e., "Do we have the ability to create a culture that is different from the Western culture and serves as an alternative to it based on Chinese culture?" It is relatively easy to create a different culture. Different cultures exist in the world. Some cultures are relatively strong while others are relatively weak. Strong cultures have power of discourse and are accepted by more people, while weak cultures have little or no power of discourse, and are not accepted by people. In other words, it is a daunting task to create a culture that is different from other cultural circles but can be accepted by other cultural circles. Historically, religious cultures, including Christianity, Islamic culture and Buddhist culture, are exactly such kinds of cultures. Traditional Chinese culture is also such a culture, at least in East Asian cultural circles.

It is difficult, but not impossible, to create such a culture. Here below we give an example of the "East Asian Model". In 1994, the World Bank published a book entitled *The East Asian Miracle*, affirming the Asian developmental model, and pointing out the differences of the East Asian model from the Western model. The introduction of the research project was a very difficult process. At that time, Western mainstream economists did not recognize the East Asian model because they believed that the East Asian model learned from the West and was nothing extraordinary. The Western factors contributed to the East Asian model. Surely, the East Asian economies, Japan and the Four Asian Tigers (known as Hong Kong, South Korea, Singapore and Taiwan) all believed that their own developmental models varied from the Western model. These economies have succeeded, so they can speak and begin to build their own voices. Despite the opposition of Western mainstream scholars, the research project was finally successfully launched with the strong support of the Bank of Japan. Even though some people still do not agree with the East Asian model today, the East Asian model has already been accepted by the mainstream West. Certainly, the East Asian model is also an economic developmental model that has been imitated and accepted by many developing countries. In fact, a relatively complete knowledge system has been developed around the East Asian developmental model in the intellectual community. The system consists of various Asian elements, including Confucian culture, the economic role of the state and government, and social factors such as high savings rates, an emphasis on education and family role.

The political discourse of East Asian countries and regions is not as lucky as the economic discourse of East Asia. In this regard, although the mainstream Asian discourse is imported from the West, Asian countries and regions do not have their own political power of discourse. In terms of actual operations, many political systems vary greatly from the Western political systems, but they all disguise themselves as Western political systems. Japan is a typical example and the same is true for South Korea. In fact, even in terms of democracy, Asian countries have greatly different organizational modes from the West, except for formal periodic elections. For example, Japan is considered a Western-style democracy, but the one party dominance, the Liberal Democratic Party, is in stark contrast to Western democracy. Some Western scholars, of course, have seen that difference. It can be said that Asian organizations in political parties, governments, societies and other fields have their own laws, and copy the Western political forms, without changing their own cultural natures.

So, what is the situation in China? Since China is an ancient civilization with thousands of years of history, it is improper to say that China has no culture. In history, Chinese civilization has also made great contributions to Western civilization. For instance, the philosophy of the Western Enlightenment era has drawn on a lot of Chinese rationalism. We often emphasize the "four major inventions", which are technical things in fact. However, even in the field of thought and practice, the influence of Chinese culture goes far beyond East Asia and extends to the West. Here below are two examples.

The first example is the civil service system in China. Traditionally, China has developed the world's largest and most effective civil service system. What did the big Chinese Empire rely on to rule? Establishing an empire requires military force; however, ruling an empire requires a developed civil service system. The West has also experienced the age of empires, but it did not develop a civil service system similar to the Chinese one. It is inconceivable that no civil service system exists in the West from the birth of modern countries to the transformation and operation of later democratic politics. Several principles embedded in the civil service system in

China have exerted a great influence on the West.

First, the separation of imperial power and governing power. The empire is seized by the emperor, and the ownership of the empire belongs to the emperor. However, the power to govern the empire, that is, the power of governance or the power of the prime minister (the prime minister), is open to society. China has developed a centralized examination system to recruit officials, which contrasts with the family rule in Western history. The West introduced the Chinese-style civil service system, and after democratization took place, it eventually evolved it into the current separation of political power and administration power. The separation of politics and administration is the institutional prerequisite for the operation of democratic politics in modern times.

Second, the neutrality of civil officials. Politics is to change, but how can the continuity of a country's policies be ensured? How can it be ensured that the power of governance will not be interrupted by political changes? The neutral civil service system is the key. In the West, politicians are restricted by democratic rules; the operation of the civil service system has its own rules and is not affected by democratic politics, which has been discussed in many Western textbooks.

Third, the rotation of civil officials in charge of different departments. In Chinese history, civil officials generally could not hold power in one place for a long time because the emperor tended to mobilize them, which is known as the "cadre exchange system." There are two reasons for this: first, to prevent the formation of localism and local influence; second, to allow officials to accumulate experience in governing different regions, facilitate their promotion, and govern the affairs of the entire empire. This is also very important to the regime of power in modern Western countries, not to mention Asia.

The second example is the Chinese traditional thought of "education for all people without discrimination". Traditional China also has a hierarchical system, that is, "scholar, farmer, artisan and merchant", but, it does not have a hierarchical system based on religion, caste and ethnicity, as do other civilizations. For Chinese Confucians, people only have the distinction of "education" and "no education", and everyone can be "educated". The traditional Western educational system is an elite educational system, meaning that education is only accessible to the children of aristocrats and wealthy families. Before modern times, the power of education was monopolized by a few people in society. The Chinese thought of "education for all people without discrimination" has a great influence on the later "mass education" in the West. Though Confucianism often monopolized knowledge in the traditional Chinese society, China itself did not develop a system of mass education. However, the idea of "education for all people without discrimination" has evolved into a system of "mass education" in the West. Since modern times, the political systems of various Western countries have gradually become democratized, and mass education has constituted the most important part of the effective operation of democracy of the masses.

However, what is the situation in contemporary China? In this regard, we can begin it by discussing the Chinese cultural movement of "going global" that is in full swing. With the rise of the economy, China has realized the importance of cultural soft power. Own to no culture "going global", China's "going global" in other aspects has encountered great resistance. For example, enterprises "going global" are often regarded as a threat to the outside world, and military modernity as a threat to the safety of the world. Since recent years, China has been trying to push Chinese culture abroad, including the Confucius Colleges and a variety of "media going global" programs.

A harsh reality is that everybody knows that Chinese culture needs to "go global", but nobody knows what cultural things in culture need to go global. It is just like merchants marketing. If you want to sell a product, you must have the product first. Marketing is just a matter of packaging and strategy. Proper marketing can change people's perception of your product and even establish a sense of identity with your product. However, in any case, high-quality products must be made available first.

For low-quality products, marketing is like water off a duck's back, no matter how good it is.

China has neither its own product of cultural knowledge nor its power of discourse. The West has learned a lot from Chinese traditions and has greatly surpassed China in many aspects. It is difficult for China to rely on tradition to sell itself. It is irresponsible to only seek things from tradition, without seeking progress. More importantly, tradition is not able to explain contemporary China. Although China today has one aspect of traditional heritage, it is no longer a traditional cultural China. Over the past 30 years of reform and opening up, China has experienced great change. Of course, the great change can be traced back to 30 years before the reform and opening up, and even to the history since the late Qing Dynasty. This requires us to generate a new knowledge system and pursue a new kind of discourse. Without these, a new culture is out of the question.

The key to the problem is: Can we accomplish this task? Can the new culture become an alternative to Western culture? In words, can this culture not only be accepted by the Chinese, but also by people in countries and regions in other cultural circles.

This is obviously not the case now, at least we are far from this goal. A culture that needs to be a "soft power" requires at least three conditions. First, the culture, whether produced locally or combined with factors from the external "inputs", must be able to explain itself. If a culture cannot explain itself, how can the "others" understand it? Second, the culture must be able to convince and receive trust from "others". If the culture is not convinced and trusted by "others", the culture would have no soft power. Third, and more importantly, the "others" can voluntarily accept the culture. This is the essence of soft power. With these three conditions, the culture does not need to be promoted. In the Tang Dynasty, no government made efforts to promote culture, but its culture reached every corner of East Asian society. The spread of Western culture in modern times is basically not dependent on governmental power. I said previously that the values of democracy and freedom in the West are the core of the soft power of Western politics. However, if Western governments had used various means to introduce these values to other countries and force other countries to accept them, these values would have been the opposite of soft power, instead of the soft power.

Now, China still does not have such a culture, so all kinds of "marketing" actions are very laborious. What China owns now is a kind of dependent knowledge system, which either attaches itself to its own historical tradition or to Western culture. Culture contains traditional factors, or Western cultural factors, or a combination thereof, which brings about advantages rather than disadvantages. However, this culture must meet the first condition, that is, whether it can explain itself. What China lacks is a cultural product that can explain itself. All our products are now replicas with a strong sense of "knockoff". In the process of the so-called "cultural innovation", many people either copy Western things blindly or apply Western technologies by using Chinese materials. In many respects, China often uses the words of others to explain itself, so the result is apparent. As a large country, it is difficult for China to dress itself up in Western words, as small countries do. China tries to boycott Western-style political systems rather than pretending to be a Western country just like Japan and other countries. China strongly opposes the West in imposing Western logic on itself. However, what is China's logic? No one can give a clear answer.

The government and the people have been calling for "cultural innovation" for many years. However, what is the result? These calls often become simple policy slogans and policy campaigns. Now, the country has flourished, and everybody wants to split a piece of the cake. Can the money gained be used for cultural innovation? Nobody knows the answer. However, the past experience tells people that once the money has been earned, the final result tends to end up with nothing definite. Even if the money obtained can be used in the field of "cultural innovation", it does not necessarily guarantee cultural innovation.

In fact, money is not a prerequisite for cultural innovation from the perspective of history. The rich culture of Europe does produce enormous economic value, but money is the result rather than the premise. Many cultural creations happen under conditions of poverty. In fact, once the individual or the creator of a culture falls slave to money, it is rarely associated with cultural creation. To achieve culture creation or innovation, we must seek another approach.

II. Three "Liberations" of Cultural Innovation

How can China's cultural creation and innovation become possible? Here, I must emphasize three "liberations", that is, liberation from the colonial state of "thought and thinking", liberation from the state of power, and liberation from the state of interests. Let's discuss them separately.

The first is to liberate minds, meaning liberation from the "colonial state" of thought and thinking. After being defeated by Western countries in the military and political fields since the end of the Qing Dynasty, China has lost its confidence in culture. Many people attribute the ultimate cause of China's backwardness to culture. The core theme of the May 4th Movement can be described as "desinicization." It is surely not easy to eliminate the traditional culture that has developed over thousands of years. The "New Life Movement" of the Chiang Kai-shek regime in the 1930s was aimed to recover traditional culture. Although Mao Zedong was a pioneer of anti-traditional culture, he also realized the actual functions of traditional culture. In the era of the revolutionary war, he advocated the "Sinification of Marxism." After the founding of the People's Republic of China, many sports were anti-traditional on the surface, but in fact they were to return to tradition. For example, the "Movement of Learning from Lei Feng" advocated absolute political loyalty. Some of the things Mao Zedong did during the "Cultural Revolution", such as "personal worship", were more like traditional expressions.

However, it should be noted that all of the Chinese factors in these movements have been retreated to people's "subconscious". Anti-tradition is the main line of the Chinese revolution. Since the May 4th Movement, learning from the West has turned to pursuit of the Western truth. Because the West becomes the truth, non-western things, including China itself, become non-truthful. It is correct to learn from the West politically. In other words, it is wrong not to learn from the West. Of course, the West here includes liberalism, Marxism and everything from the West.

It is not wrong to learn from the West, but it is really a mistake to view the West as truth. China does not reject other civilizations and values, but Chinese culture itself must be the subject. In the process of learning from the West, Chinese culture has lost its own dominant position because of no Chinese subjective consciousness. The problem is that Western words dominated by Western culture cannot explain everything in China. Today, more and more people have realized that Western words cannot explain China. (I have emphasized this point on many other occasions. To be specific, if the West is an apple and China is an orange, the words for apple cannot explain orange. Similarly, the orange can learn from the apple because both of them are fruit. However, it must be made clear that the goal of orange by learning from the apple is to turn itself into a better orange rather than becoming an apple). However, few people devote themselves to creation and invention. With thousands of years of historical tradition, and much experience since China's reform and opening up, why can China not produce its own words? Why can China not produce its own concepts and theories? Most people, as always, choose to use the words of the West to explain themselves. If this situation does not change, China will never have its own words, its own concepts and its own theories, let alone cultural soft power. Therefore, we, especially the intellectuals, must take great efforts to liberate ourselves from the "colonial" state of thought and thinking that has lasted for more than a century. It is acceptable to continue to learn from the West, but China's dominant position must be established.

The second is to liberate from political power. For thousands of years of Chinese traditions, the mainstream culture is a kind of dependent culture and a kind of culture centred on royal authority. The kingship culture itself is only a result of the royal power system, which should not be blamed. It is just like the idea that the cultures of Christianity and Muslim are centred on religion. However, what I want to stress here is that the dependent nature of of Chinese culture greatly hinders cultural innovation and expansion.

Traditionally, I think Chinese intellectuals can be divided into political intellectuals and non-political intellectuals, represented by Confucianism and Taoism, respectively. Confucianism focuses on going into the society, while Taoism highlights standing aloof from the society. In other words, Confucianism is related to social politics, and Taoism does not care about the real society at all. Taoism often loses confidence in the real world, and advocates nature and tends to be rooted in mountains and forests. Taoism emphasizes tranquility. Despite much time to think about questions, Taoism's contribution to China's knowledge system is limited because of its irrelevance to the real society and politics. Taoism advocates the unity of man and nature, and has no distinction between subject and object. It is like the relationship between Chuang Tzu and the butterfly, where whoever is the subject and whoever is the object are unknown. The philosophy of unity of man and nature is quite reasonable on one level, but it is hard to evolve into a system of scientific thinking and research. The absence of modern natural science in China is associated with the attitudes of Taoists.

The subject of China's social political knowledge system is Confucianism. However, Confucianism, dependent on kingship and power, often becomes a slave to power. There are two meanings of active "slave" and being "slaved". Some people say that the term "Confucianism" consists of "human" and "need". From the viewpoint of Confucians, it is mainly to solve the "need" problem of "human", and the "need" is obtained by serving the royal power. From the perspective of royal power, it is mainly to solve the problem of serving "human", and it is also a kind of "need". Historically, royal power needs to obtain two absolute loyalties, namely, loyalty of knowledge (that is Confucianism), and loyalty of eunuchs. The two loyalties guarantee the absolute nature of royal power. The Confucians manage the affairs of the state, while the eunuchs manage the internal affairs of the royal power. The loyalty of Confucianism can be divided into two types. One is loyalty in telling truths, and the other is loyalty in telling lies, known as blind loyalty. Although there is no lack of loyalty in telling truths in history, most of them are "blind loyalties" and selfish "blind loyalties". They do not hesitate to tell lies for their own sake. From the perspective of knowledge, the tactics of Chinese traditional royal power are far more developed than other civilizations, which can be attributed to Confucianism. Westerners emphasize the rule of law, while Chinese people emphasize the rule of man. With the rule of law and an effective national system, ordinary people can also rule a society. However, in China, Confucianism does not promote the rule of law. Without an effective national system, it is necessary to have a very intelligent person as the emperor. Otherwise, it would be very difficult to govern the world. I am specialized in the study of political science. Why China has not developed a theory of construction of a national institution is largely because Confucianism only serves royal power.

Another important reason for Confucianism's failure to develop a knowledge system about Chinese social politics is that Confucians monopolize knowledge. Traditional China is regarded as a Confucian society, but how many people in society can become Confucians? The proportion is very small. Everyone can become a "Confucian," which means the class of "Confucian" is open to the society. Everyone can become a "Confucian" through efforts, especially through the examination system, but the openness does not generate an association between "Confucianism" and the whole society. Confucians monopolize knowledge and do not strive to spread knowledge to the whole society. In today's academic language, there is not a process of socialization of Confucianism. The nature of serving the royal power determines that Confucianism is not concerned about social reality, and naturally, there is no knowledge about the society. As mentioned above, the Confucian idea of "education for all people without discrimination" has been used by the West and has played a major role in the establishment of the Western system of education of the masses. However, the idea has not played such a role in China.

Compared with the traditional situation, the Chinese society has changed dramatically. However, is there any change in the dependence on power of the Chinese intellectual class? In my opinion, it has no change, and instead, it has been strengthened further. As far as the power relationship is concerned, Chinese intellectuals can be divided into three categories. The first category is for power, the second category is for anti-power, where Chinese intellectuals are the subject. The third category is those who do not care about politics and power, similar to traditional Taoists. The intellectuals who serve the power are not discussed in detail, and as everybody knows, they are scholars used by the emperor and aimed at saying good things and defending the current regime. The second category of intellectuals is those who oppose power and the existing system. In fact, these people are also pursuing power, and they want to use their knowledge to influence actual politics and even gain actual political power, so that they often consciously stand on the opposite side of power and carry out opposition for the sake of opposition. In other words, they strive to gain power through anti-power.

Whether intellectuals serve or oppose power, it is very difficult to produce a knowledge system for China. Where does the power of intellectuals come from? In China, people often call the intellectuals who often discuss the implementation of politics and concern about reality as public intellectuals. The concept comes from the West, but it has been transformed in China. The primary task of intellectuals is to explain the world. Based on the interpretation of the world, intellectuals have power. If you explain the world well, you will know how the society actually works, what problems there are, how to solve the problems and how to improve society. Even if you do not have any position of power, you will get power. Some politicians may use judgment, diagnosis and other means to reform the society. Therefore, Marx said that philosophers have two tasks, that is, understanding the world and changing the world, and the former is the prerequisite for the latter. Before you understand the world, you will not have the power to change the world. This is obviously not the case for Chinese intellectuals. They are always unable to explain the world, but they have a great ambition to change the world, which leads to a vicious interaction between power and knowledge. Knowledge wants to challenge power, and power wants to restrain knowledge. There is no boundary between knowledge and power. Both want to infiltrate each other, resulting in undesirable results on both sides. The unprofessional power has no confidence and always wants to control everything. Insufficient knowledge is unable to explain the world, but tries to intervene in politics. It can be imagined that if the model of vicious interaction were not changed, the creation of Chinese culture or knowledge system would still be beyond hope.

The third is to liberate from the interests. To a large extent, the negative impact of material interests on cultural innovation is far greater than the negative impact of power in today's Chinese society. I have always stressed that our civilization has passed the political test, but failed to pass the commercial civilization test. From the "burning of books and burying of scholars" of the First Emperor of Qin to the "anti-rightist movement" of Mao Zedong, many intellectuals in China have maintained their recognition of knowledge and have demonstrated the courage to resist and oppose power. However, the commercial revolution since the reform and opening up has completely destroyed the inherent beliefs of intellectuals in knowledge and made them surrender to material interests. It is the normal situation for the contemporary intellectuals to "make curtsies for the salary of five bushels of rice". I remember Premier Wen Jiabao once complained about why there are no poor economists in China. In fact, this is very easy to understand. What China now possesses is a large number of interest intellectuals, who speak for various interests. It is not profitable to speak for the poor, so the poor do not have their own intellectuals. In China, there is no "organic intellectual" that a nation and a country should have. As said by Gramsci, an Italian Marxist, organic intellectuals can transcend specific interests and speak for the overall interests of a people and a country. We can even say that the ruling party does not have those organic intellectuals. Everyone wants to share an interest from the ruling party, but no one is concerned about its long-term interests. From the perspective of knowledge supply, the intellectuals must take responsibility for various issues that China currently faces, such as income differentiation, social injustice, and moral decline. Intellectuals fail to provide useful and effective knowledge for reform policies beyond their own interests.

Intellectuals fail to transcend their own interests and make the pursuit of personal interests their own missions, which makes it easier for political power to absorb and digest intellectuals. We can illustrate it with the design of the system of current scientific research as an example. With the increase in the amount of national financial resources, the national investment in universities and research institutions also becomes increased. However, there is not any sign to answer the "Qian Xuesen's Question" discussed in the past years, i.e., "Why does China have no scholar master?" The reason is very simple, that is, China has no institutional design available for the training of a master. China's institutional design is aimed at controlling the development of knowledge, not to promoting the development of knowledge. Under China's system of scientific research and evaluation, professors and scholars are living hard, and they have to worry about publishing papers all day long. The Chinese system has forced people to write many articles, and hindered people from dedicated research. How is it possible for a professor to publish excellent papers every year? Even in a good university in the West, if a professor can publish several high-quality articles throughout his life, it is very good. For instance, in the political field, we all know Harvard University professor Huntington, but how many famous works has he written? Not a lot. China's evaluation system requires our professors to write several meaningful articles every year. Is it possible? The result is that no one can write an imaginary article for a lifetime. Doing research and writing articles are two things. A good article is based on long-term research. With a waste of much time in writing articles, how can professors set aside time to conduct research?

The design of the wage system in Chinese universities and research institutions is also related to the creation and innovation of knowledge. In China, professors, teachers, and researchers have a low basic salary without extra income, leading to a difficulty in surviving. This requires them to spend a lot of time on applying for research funds and trying every means to convert research funds into their own income, which leads to many negative consequences. In the West, more than 90% of the income of professors, teachers, and research comes from the basic salary, which is adequate for them to have a decent life, so that they have enough time to engage in scientific research and education. What is the current situation in China? For many people, less than half of their income comes from their basic salary, and the rest comes from other sources. Who has the time to engage in serious research carefully if the basic salary cannot maintain a decent life? If the salary system could be adjusted as it is in the West to enable the basic salary to account for 90% of the income, the results would be greatly different. Why not reform the salary system?

What is more alarming is that China's entire educational system has benefited from kindergarten to postdoctoral education. The long educational chain is divided by various interests. Many parasitic institutions in education have designed countless projects in pursuit of their own interests, and have imposed them on the educated people and their families through formal institutions and informal social pressures. The goal of education is to impart knowledge and produce knowledge. However now, all links of China's education are aimless, except money. In more than 30 years of the reform and opening up, more and more funds have been invested in education, but China has not produced a decent scholar, let alone a master. Now, even the academicians of the Chinese Academy of Sciences and the Chinese Academy of Engineering have become the tools for various organizations to fight for their interests. Chinese educators should look at the situation during the survival of the National South-West Associated University, where so many masters have been cultivated under bad circumstances. It can be said that more money leads to more corrupt education. China has fallen into a vicious cycle. The victims are the educated people and their families. Since the premise of cultural development and innovation is to receive education, it is impossible for China to produce and create knowledge and cultural systems in such a circumstance.

Now, everyone is talking about cultural innovation and knowledge innovation. However, if these systems are not reformed, cultural innovation and knowledge innovation will only become an illusion. As mentioned at the beginning, although more and more people have realized the importance of cultural innovation and cultural "going global", and relevant parties have also developed specific policies to strive to attain these goals, they have not carried out creation and innovation on their own culture. What can "go global"? What can be sold to the world?

III. New Culture Choice

As a matter of fact, the objective situation of Chinese culture is not optimistic from a global perspective. Simply put, the major religious culture, namely, the Western culture, is rapidly expanding, while the Chinese culture is mostly on the defensive.

Western culture, also known as the culture that emerged in the Mediterranean and flourished gradually, still occupies a dominant position in world culture and is increasingly offensive and aggressive. Western culture started its expansion from the Mediterranean Sea, and occupied both sides of the Atlantic Ocean, and now is expanding into the Pacific and Indian Oceans. Western culture, based on religion, has its missions. The religious mission has been a huge driving force for its unlimited expansion. Meanwhile, it should also be noted that although Western culture is religious in nature, many of its factors have been secularized, so that it no longer has its original fundamentalism. This change is more conducive to its spreading in Asia, especially East Asia.

Compared with the major religious culture, the Chinese culture is on the defensive despite the rise of the economy. The defensive status, even in China, is very obvious. The reason is very simple. As discussed above, the Chinese people's way of thinking has become quite Westernized. In spite of great momentum, the activities of cultural promotion that we are conducting now will not generate any substantive significance for the expansion of the Chinese culture. What China lacks is a set of core values and a set of shared values that can be shared with other cultures. If the Chinese civilization failed to develop its own set of core values and a set of shared values on such a basis, it would be gradually assimilated and melted by the previous two cultures. However, historically, China's secular civilization has successfully assimilated other religious cultures, including the Buddhist culture and the Jewish culture. I believe that China will once again develop a new cultural paradigm, a culture that can accommodate and integrate other religious cultures and that maintains its secular cultural nature. Assimilation or rebirth, there are not many choices available for China. To avoid assimilation, the Chinese culture must be reborn. This is the full significance of our discussion of Chinese cultural innovation today.

“一带一路”推进与中国战略思维方式

黄仁伟 【中国】
上海社会科学院原副院长 / 世界中国学论坛秘书长

古代中国有两个伟大基础工程，一个是万里长城，是当时国家安全的基础设施；另一个是南北大运河，是当时经济流通动脉的基础设施，它们影响了上千年的中国历史走向。“一带一路”就是当代中国与当代世界发展的基础设施网络，它和中国历史与现实的发展经验一脉相承的，也可能影响数百年甚至更长时间的世界历史走向。为此，需要了解中国战略文化的思维方式，有助于理解中国提出和推进“一带一路”倡议的动机和行为方式。

“要想富，先修路”，是当代中国的一句流行语。基础设施是发展的先决条件，尤其是交通基础设施网络，更是市场联结和产业经济带的纽带。中国经济和社会的发展变化，是与全国范围的基础设施革命紧密结合的。仅仅 15 年左右的时间，中国就基本形成了覆盖各省的高速公路、高速铁路、远距离输变电、无线通信、油气管线、港口机场、全球定位等立体交叉网络体系。在此过程中，中国逐渐形成和具备为整个欧亚大陆提供基础设施网络的经验和能力。在 2 至 3 倍于中国的时间里，可能实现欧亚大陆的全面联结即“五通”，这不是一句空话。

“积小胜为大胜”，这是中国战略文化的重要思想方法。这么一个巨大工程并不是在短时期内可以完成的，它需要 30 年至 50 年时间来实现其宏伟目标。同时，它又分解为一个又一个具体项目，由一个个地区和不同阶段组合而成的。这就是当代中国的“渐进主义”方法，中国改革开放和现代化的重要成果都是采取渐进方式取得的。中国老百姓的俗语说“一口吃不成胖子”，就是这个道理。

“量力而行”是中国人在工作中一贯倡导的稳健务实、实事求是的方法。“一带一路”倡议的目标非常宏大，不可能由中国一家来“包打天下”。要根据中国的能力、实力和东道国的可接受度，来逐步推进“一带一路”的具体项目。例如，中东欧国家非常欢迎“一带一路”项目到他们的国家落地，于是形成“16+1”模式。但是16个国家一起上有困难，只能从捷克、匈牙利、塞尔维亚等几个国家开始，从改造陈旧铁路系统入手，见效后可以形成更大范围、更多领域的项目。

“有所为而有所不为”，就是抓住重点、兼顾一般。“一带一路”倡议的空间范围覆盖60多个国家，与中国的距离远近不同，合作伙伴的密切程度也不同。这需要选择一批国家作为战略支点，重点建设“一带一路”项目。目前的重点地区主要是东南亚、中亚等地区；重点国家主要有俄罗斯、巴基斯坦、印尼和哈萨克斯坦等。如果我们不分轻重、一哄而上，势必出现项目成功率很低的混乱局面。

“两相情愿”原意是指男女之间谈恋爱需要双方都有内心的倾慕。在“一带一路”的项目合作中更是需要双方、甚至是多方自愿，绝不能出现强加于人的单边主义甚至强权主义的做法。中国方面要根据当地的实际需要选择项目，东道国也要根据中国的能力和利益相关度来进行选择。目前中国与一些国家本身的基础设施战略规划结合，形成良好的互动关系，为重大项目落地奠定了基础。

“预则立，不预则废”，是指对重大事件的战略前景要进行预测和预判，做好预案，才能确定其取得成功的路径。毋庸讳言，“一带一路”在其实现过程中将面对各种风险，包括安全风险、政治风险、经济风险、社会风险、文化风险、生态风险等等。每一个大类下面，还可以细分若干专项风险。而且每种风险都不会单独存在，而是各种风险交织共生、相互作用。中国应和东道国合作伙伴共同分析预测大项目可能遇到的各种风险，制定防范措施和危机反应机制。一个重大项目的建设周期长达几年甚至十几年，使用周期长达几十年甚至几百年，进行战略预测是保证重大工程取得长期效应的前提条件。

“由乱而治”是中国政治文化理念的一个总结，讲的是“乱”与“治”的辩证关系。“一带一路”沿线地区不乏动乱甚至局部战争，他们对“一带一路”的推进肯定有消极影响。动乱需要治理，一带一路沿线地区恰恰可以成为国际合作进行全球治理或地区治理的实验区。例如，国际合作共同打击恐怖主义，在“一带一路”沿线地区必然是一个不可回避的课题。它不是“一带一路”倡议的直接内容，却是其中的必要条件。打击毒品、非法移民、洗钱等跨国犯罪活动，都可能在“一带一路”推进过程中形成必要的国际合作机制。

“自上而下”与“自下而上”，这是政府与民众、政府与市场、国企与民企等几种互动关系的概括。在“一带一路”倡议提出以来，国外朋友总是有人问起，“一带一路”究竟是市场行为还是政府行为，国内学者也有人质疑这是政府大包干。我认为是政府倡导和推动的市场和产业一体化进程，其最终主体是企业。因为一个巨大的基础设施网络，需要极大的协调组织机制，在这方面中国政府的能力是举世公认的。“一带一路”倡议要在几十个国家中落实，更需要政府间的合作机制。然而，项目竞标、投资建设、经营管理等微观主体是企业，依据的是市场规则，政府不可能充当主体。因此，自上而下和自下而上，二者缺一不可。

“有容乃大”“兼容并蓄”，这是中国文化形成过程的主要特征，在“一带一路”推进过程中就体现为“开放、包容”。中国倡导“一带一路”，不等于中国一家单干，更不是排挤其他大国或制度、价值观不同的国家。中国不主张搞排他性的盟国体系，也不会在“一带一路”进程中扩张势力范围。中国文化提倡“己所勿欲，勿施于人”。中国长期受到超级大国及其盟国体系的排挤，深受其害，不会再去重复那一套。相反，中国欢迎西方国家包括美国、日本等都来参与“一带一路”进程，成为亚投行成员，具体投入有关项目中来。

“海内存知己”“四海之内皆兄弟”，中国古代把世界看作“天下”，把周围地区看作“海内”，天下和海内构成了中国文化的空间概念。“一带一路”继承和发扬这种空间观，在“一带一路”沿线实行“早期收获计划”，结成各种类型的战略伙伴关系，构建长期稳定的战略支点。这种战略支点，不是传统意义上的军事基地或盟国关系，而是利益结合点、网络枢纽点、金融中心点、文化汇集点、产业链接点、资源交换点、安全保障点。这些战略支点撑起整个“一带一路”网络，是各国共享的公共产品。

“欲取之，必先予之”、“多予少取、只予不取”，这是中国的传统义利观，前提是“取之有道”。在此基础上，通过共同利益、合作共赢而建构的新义利观，是“一带一路”利益结构形成的伦理基础。君子并非只讲“义”而不讲“利”，关键在于讲“道”。这个道就是共同利益，越是深厚的共同利益，则越符合道义，就越有持续的生命力。中国企业要警惕自己的行为过于把盈利作为第一考虑，造成“竭泽而渔”的后果。但是，中国和各国政府也要防止把“一带一路”看作是政府援助项目，对成本、盈利等基本核算手段置之不顾，造成另一种“竭泽而渔”。二者都是不可持续的。

简言之，“以天下为己任”是中国历代志士仁人的最高价值追求。“一带一路”是以人类命运为己任的当代中国责任体现和价值追求。我们要通过“一带一路”的推进，把利益共同体、责任共同体和命运共同体落到实处，从抽象概念转化为沿线地区实现共同发展、共同安全、共同治理的实践平台，使中国文化的精神价值内涵就在“一带一路”项目上得到物质体现和社会体验。

The Advancement of the "Belt and Road" Initiative and China's Strategic Thinking Mode

Huang Renwei / China

Former Vice President of the Shanghai Academy of Social Sciences, Secretary-general of the World Forum on China Studies

There were two great projects in ancient China, namely, the Great Wall of China, an infrastructure of national security at that time, and the North-South Grand Canal, an artery of the infrastructure for economic circulation at that time. They affected the trend of Chinese history over the past thousands of years. The "Belt and Road" is a network of infrastructure for the development of contemporary China and of the contemporary world. It is in line with the developmental experience of Chinese history and reality and may also affect the direction of world history for centuries or even longer. To this end, it is necessary to understand the way of thinking of China's strategic culture, which would help understand the motivation and behavioral pattern of China in proposing and promoting the "Belt and Road" Initiative.

"If you want to be rich, build roads first" is a popular saying in contemporary China. Infrastructure, especially the network of transportation infrastructure, is a prerequisite for development, which is the link between market linkage and the industrial economic belt. The change in the development of the Chinese economy and society is closely integrated with the nationwide revolution in infrastructure. In just 15 years or so, China has basically formed a three-dimensional intersecting network system of expressways, high-speed railways, long-distance power transmission and transformation, wireless communications, oil and gas pipelines, ports and airports, and global positioning covering all of the provinces. In the process, China has gradually developed and gained the experience and capabilities of providing networks of infrastructure for the entire Eurasian continent. With a double or a threefold period of time, it would be absolutely possible to realize the full connection of the "five links" of the continent of Eurasia.

"Many small victories add up to one big one." This is an important way of thinking in China's strategic culture. It is impossible to complete such a huge project in a short period of time. It will take 30 to 50 years to achieve that ambitious goal. At the same time, the "Belt and Road" Initiative is subdivided into many concrete projects, consisting of combinations of different regions and stages. This is contemporary China's "gradualistic" approach. The significant achievements of China's policy of reform and opening up and modernization have all been achieved in a gradual manner. As the old saying of the Chinese people goes, "One meal won't make a man fat".

"Act according to one's ability" is a steady, pragmatic and realistic approach that Chinese people have consistently advocated in their work. The "Belt and Road" Initiative has very ambitious goals, which are impossible to be "accomplished" by China alone. It is necessary to gradually implement the specific projects of the Initiative in accordance with the capability and strength of China, and the acceptability of the host countries. For example, the countries of Central and Eastern Europe look forward to the implementation of the "Belt and Road" Initiative in their territories, thus forming a "16+1" model. However, it is hard for 16 countries to take actions in concert simultaneously. So, it is proper to only start from several countries such as the Czech Republic, Hungary, and Serbia. After obtaining the desired result from the reconstruction of the old railway system, a larger range of projects may be established in more areas.

"Some things must be done and some things must not be done" means the concentration on crucial points with general factors taken into consideration. The "Belt and Road" Initiative covers more than 60 countries, and the levels of intimacy with partners are varied with the different distances from China. This requires the selection of a number of countries as strategic fulcrums to focus on the implementation of the "Belt and Road" Initiative. The current key areas are mainly Southeast Asia, Central Asia and other regions; key countries are mainly Russia, Pakistan, Indonesia and Kazakhstan, etc. If we take actions blindly in the absence of priorities, the chaotic situation with a very low rate of success of projects will surely occur.

"Consensual" originally means that love between men and women requires the admiration of both sides. The cooperation on the "Belt and Road" Initiative requires the voluntary consent of two or more sides. Imposed unilateralism or even power politics is absolutely prohibited. China should select projects according to the actual needs of the local area, and the host country should also make choices based on China's capabilities and interest relevancy. At present, China integrates with the infrastructural strategic planning of some countries to form a good interactive relationship, laying the foundation for the implementation of major projects.

"Being prepared ensures success and not being prepared spells failure" means that the success of a major event depends on the predication and preparation of the strategic prospects of that major event. Undoubtedly, the "Belt and Road" Initiative will face various risks during implementation, including a security risk, a political risk, an economic risk, a social risk, a cultural risk, and an ecological risk, etc. Each major category of risk may be subdivided into a number of special risks. In addition, each risk will not exist alone. As a matter of fact, many risks coexist and interact with each other. China should work with the host country partners to analyze and predict various risks that may be encountered during the large projects, and formulate preventive measures and crisis response mechanisms. A major project may have a construction period of several years or even more than ten years, and a cycle of use of several decades or even hundreds of years. Strategic foresight is a prerequisite for ensuring the long-term effects of a major project.

"Governance out of chaos" is a summary of China's political and cultural concepts, and stresses the dialectical relationship between "chaos" and "governance." In the areas along the route of the "Belt and Road" Initiative, turmoil or even local warfare exists, which surely exerts a negative impact on the implementation of the Initiative. The turmoil needs to be managed. The areas along the route can be precisely the experimental areas for international cooperation to conduct global governance or regional governance. For example, international cooperation in the fight against terrorism is an unavoidable issue in the areas along the route of the "Belt and Road" Initiative. Instead of a direct content, it is a necessary condition of the Initiative. In the process of implementation of the "Belt and Road" Initiative, the necessary mechanism of international cooperation may be formed to fight against transnational criminal activities, such as anti-drugs, illegal immigration and money laundering.

"From top to bottom" and "from bottom to top" are the generalization of several kinds of interactive relations between the government and the people, between the government and the market, and between state-owned enterprises and private enterprises. Since the "Belt and Road" Initiative was proposed, foreign friends have always questioned whether the "Belt and Road" Initiative is a market action or a government action. Some domestic scholars have also questioned whether it is a government contract. In my opinion, it is the integration process of market and industry advocated and promoted by the government, and the ultimate subject is the enterprise. A huge network of infrastructure requires a mechanism of extensive coordination and organization. In this regard, the capabilities of the Chinese government are universally acknowledged. The "Belt and Road" Initiative will be implemented in dozens of countries, which requires a mechanism of inter-governmental cooperation. However, the enterprise is the micro subject in project bidding, investment and construction, and it is during operations and management when the market rules prevail. The government cannot serve as the main subject. Therefore, both "from top to bottom" and "from bottom to top" are indispensable.

"A wide heart embraces all" and "all-inclusive" are the main features in the process of the formation of Chinese culture. "Open and inclusive" are embodied during the implementation of the "Belt and Road" Initiative. China's promotion of the Initiative does not mean that China is solely responsible for all things excluding other countries with different systems and values. China will neither advocate a system of exclusive allies nor expand the sphere of its influence in the implementation process of the "Belt and Road" Initiative. Chinese culture advocates "Don't do to others what you don't want others to do to you." As China has suffered a great deal from its exclusion by the superpowers and their allies for a long term, China will by no means exclude others. On the contrary, we welcome Western countries, including the United States and Japan, to participate in the process of the "Belt and Road" Initiative and become members of the Asian Infrastructure Investment Bank to specifically invest in related projects.

As the old saying goes, "Long distance does not separate bosom friends" and "Within the four seas all men are brothers", the world is regarded as the "land under heaven", and the surrounding area was regarded as "the four seas" at the time of ancient China. The land under heaven and the four seas form the spatial concept of the Chinese culture. The "Belt and Road" Initiative inherits and promotes precisely that spatial concept. The "Early Harvest Plan" is put into practice in the regions along the route of the Initiative to form various types of strategic partnerships and establish a long-term stable strategic fulcrum. The kind of strategic fulcrum is a combination of a point of interests, a network hub, a financial center, a cultural gathering point, a point of industrial linking, a resource exchange point, and a security guarantee point, rather than a military base or ally relationship in the traditional sense. These strategic fulcrums prop up the entire "Belt and Road" network and are common products shared by all countries.

"Giving is the prerequisite of receiving," and "giving more and receiving less, and only giving without receiving" are China's traditional views of justice and profit, and the premise is to "make profit in proper ways". On this basis, the new concept of justice and profit developed through common interest and win-win cooperation is the ethical foundation for the structural formation of the benefits from the "Belt and Road" Initiative. A man of noble character does not attach importance to "justice" only, without "profit." The key lies in "morality." The morality is the common interest. The deeper common interest leads to more compliance with morality and more lasting viability. Chinese companies must be careful of not considering profitability as their first priority, causing the consequences of "draining the pond to get all the fish". However, the governments in China and other countries should also not view the "Belt and Road" Initiative as a government aid project, without consideration of cost, profit and other basic accounting methods, resulting in another sense of "draining the pond to get all the fish". Both of these situations are unsustainable.

In summary, "taking the world as its own duty" is the highest value pursuit of the Chinese people with lofty ideals. The "Belt and Road" Initiative is the reflection of the responsibility and value pursuit of "taking the fate of mankind as its own duty" of contemporary China. We must take advantage of the "Belt and Road" Initiative to really achieve the community's interests, the community's responsibility and the community's fate, and transform the abstract concept into a practical platform for the realization of common development, common security and common governance in the regions along the route. As a result, the connotations in the spiritual values of Chinese culture enjoy material reflection and social experience in the "Belt and Road" Initiative.

中国、肯尼亚以及全球治理

吉迪恩·马切里亚·穆内 【肯尼亚】
内罗毕美国国际大学历史与国际关系教授

本文将从四个切入点来解释中国与肯尼亚当前所处的地缘政治状态。第一，作为全球治理单位，中肯两国所处的国际语境；第二，中国与肯尼亚的建国；第三，中国与肯尼亚的地缘政治价值；第四，国际“竞技场”中的中国与肯尼亚。

一　中肯两国所处的国际语境

目前，世界各国人民是通过地缘政治单位——定义了疆界的国家——开展自发性的组织，因而国家似乎是自然形成的，存在的合理性是不言自明的。作为管理人民、开展社会经济活动的工具，国家若想生存下去、保持其存在的合理性，则必须面临“利益”和“安全”等种种挑战。在捍卫国家“利益”方面，各国、各地区的能力存在不同程度的差异，这种能力体现为：从多种渠道获取资源，或阻碍潜在对手获得资源。

利益是区分不同国家的标志，是国民身份的组成部分。从这个角度来看，国家是一种“核心价值观”，核心价值观的存亡标志着国家和民族的存亡。因此，所有组织机构——不仅是政府机构——必须确保国家的存在。为了对各类组织机构进行有效管理，国家必须具备这样一种能力：能够将（国内及国际）政治、资源、空间、地理以及战略等关键概念运用于实践，并让这些因素产生交互作用。若想成功地运用这种能力来捍卫国家利益，领导人应该对以下几点有所认识：1. 本国的思想观念。2. 相关各国的思想观念。3. 本国与他国的异同点。

以上三点认识，有助于国家捍卫其地缘政治利益。地缘政治在很大程度上可以归为一种知识性的实践活动，主要涉及地理与政治两个概念。地理涉及区域与环境，而政治则涉及向人民与组织机构投射并施加权力的能力。因此，地缘政治的内涵在于，通过对他人空间施加权力、通过操纵他人的空间来实现某种政治目的。从国际视角来审视，这意味着要通过操纵他国政治来实现本国的既定目标。将本国统治权强加给他国人们的行为，被称作帝国主义。

从本质上讲，帝国主义就是施加给他国人民的强权统治。如何实现或避免这种强权，则需要实施相关的战略，需要一套审度方法。针对地域进行的审度被称作地缘战略，它决定着采用什么样的手段实现地缘政治目标。因此，地缘政治是服务于地缘政治利益的工具。

二　中国与肯尼亚

以上关于“国家”的分析同样适用于中国和肯尼亚。两国都是全球治理、国际权利游戏中的新进选手，都试图在最新一轮权利体系重组中获得一席之地。在不同历的历史阶段中，两国的形象均遭到欧洲帝国主义的固化，近现代时期的国家形象均具有双重性：先是欧洲强权的附庸，后转为推翻强权的“革命者”。作为第三世界国家，两国都曾遭到欧洲国家的摆布，又同样通过革命的方式获得解放，开始在世界舞台崭露头角。两者的区别在于，历史、地理、人口规模以及治国理政的方式有所不同。

1. 中国

不论从概念角度还是地理角度来看，中国都拥有着最古老的地缘政治身份，而且这种身份具有极强的辨识度和延续性。15—16 世纪，当中国放弃海洋霸权、将目光转向内陆时，欧洲殖民者开始凭借种种借口进行殖民扩张，而中国的地缘政治身份曾一度令欧洲帝国主义者感到迷惑。19 世纪，中国与欧洲（西欧）及其帝国主义子嗣——美国的碰撞，造成了中国传统领土的部分流失，从此进入“百年屈辱”阶段。这段屈辱史从 1840 年的中英鸦片战争开始，当时英国为了扭转对华贸易逆差，不惜向中国输入大量鸦片。因此，今日中国的疆界很大程度上是在欧美日俄等外部帝国主义势力的作用下形成的。

2. 肯尼亚

同样，肯尼亚大体上也是外部帝国主义势力达成一致的结果。在官方描述中，肯尼亚的诞生几乎是由帝国主义战略上的意外事件所致，因为英国曾一度宣称，是为了防止欧洲国家染指印度利益，才被迫占领肯尼亚。1888 年，英国皇家东非公司（IBEAC）获得英国皇家特许，代表英国政府管理肯尼亚地区。1895 年，该公司破产后，英国政府接管肯尼亚，开始修建连接印度洋与乌干达的“疯狂快线”——乌干达铁路，1901 年，该线路修至维多利亚湖附近的基苏木。此后，肯尼亚掀起反殖民斗争，于 1963 年取得独立，以其“白人之国”和“茅茅之国”的双重形象引发了世界关注。

在“白人之国”这重形象中，非洲人失去了主权、合法的自由权，甚至失去了被“归属为人类”的权利。英德意三国签署的协约以及地理因素决定了今日肯尼亚的疆界。在非洲人失去种种合法权的同时，在伦敦、巴黎、罗马、柏林、布鲁塞尔、里斯本等地，欧洲各国却敲定了对非洲的“合法”殖民权。根据在柏林签订的协约，各国应对占领区域进行有效管理，而这种管理则是通过士兵、行政管理者与传教士来实现。其中，传教士肩负的使命较为特殊——削弱非洲人的意志，使其甘心接受卑微的从属地位。士兵负责军事占领，而行政管理者则与传教士联手，在合力抹杀非洲历史的同时，培植“欧洲崇拜”的意识。在肯尼亚，英国殖民者剥夺了人民的土地，将这片土地粉饰成“白人之国”“人间天堂”的假象，将肯尼亚的主人变为白人（mzungu）的奴仆。

三 革命的国度

中国与肯尼亚的共同点在于都以“革命者”的形象推翻了帝国主义者的政治统治并引起世界关注。两国在摆脱外部控制的过程中，共产主义者与民主主义者之间展开了漫长的斗争，而革命者的形象正是在这场斗争中形成。共产主义者取得最终胜利，并于 1949 年 10 月向全世界宣布，中国从此不再屈从于外部势力。这场胜利震惊了帝国主义世界，标志着一名踌躇满志的新选手从此走入国际竞技场。因此，中国向来与其他反帝国家（多数为第三世界国家）保持着紧密而友好的关系。

中国革命的胜利在世界地缘政治舞台产生了强烈影响，三年之后，1952 年，激愤已久的非洲终于爆发了“茅茅运动”，反殖民的呼声由此传遍全球。在肯尼亚“革命”运动的激励下，非洲各殖民地纷纷掀起武装斗争，从而造就了“茅茅”这一令殖民者闻风丧胆的形象，肯尼亚因而被描绘为革命者的“茅茅之国”。

“茅茅运动”在非洲各地以及世界各地产生了深远的影响。在“茅茅”理念的启发下，北罗得西亚（赞比亚旧称）开始向政府施压、迫使其让步。2012 年 10 月，罗伯特·穆加贝（津巴布韦前总统）表示：“在坚韧的茅茅战士身上，我们看到了自己的影子。”在南非，纳尔逊·曼德拉抛弃了甘地的主张，凭借基马蒂的“茅茅”理念创立了军事组织“民族之矛”。其他非洲殖民地，特别是安哥拉、莫桑比克及罗德西亚，武装斗争几乎成为一种“潮流”。既然“茅茅运动”能在肯尼亚取得成功，定然也适用于其他地区，甚至包括美国。美国黑人运动领袖马尔克姆曾表示，“茅茅革命”同样适用于非裔美国人。

四　中国与肯尼亚的地缘政治价值

对其他国家而言，中肯两国均具有一定的战略价值。作为制造大国，中国产出的商品几乎远销各个国家。在崛起的过程中，中国逐渐赶超日本，成为仅次于美国的世界第二大经济体。当然，这种赶超不仅体现在经济成就上，更体现在国际形象上。中国已经成为全球经济引擎，全球的经济中心。因此，当中国经济放缓时，世界各国都不可避免地受到冲击，对中国市场和投资依赖性较强的区域尤其如此。

对于新兴经济体而言，中国已经成为“不言自明”的领导人，成为金砖国家（巴西、俄罗斯、印度、中国、南非）经济体的中坚力量。在国际事务上，金砖国家正在挑战欧洲七国集团的统治地位。

随着更多经济体的加入，七国集团逐渐演变为二十国集团，这无疑稀释了七国集团的垄断力量。

中国对于其他国家的价值主要在于市场和投资等经济层面。肯尼亚或多或少也具备一定的地缘政治价值。首先，肯尼亚正逐渐成为东非区域的经济中心，虽然与中国并不在同一层次，但在某种程度上也可以算作是非洲大陆的经济中心。对于邻国而言，肯尼亚是东非的区域经济引擎；对于乌干达、卢旺达、布隆迪、南苏丹、刚果东部乃至埃塞俄比亚等地区而言，肯尼亚是内陆地区的出海通道；对于中国、日本、印度等亚洲大国而言，肯尼亚是获取东非资源的入口。另外，由于赤道贯穿中部，肯尼亚的区位优势有利于卫星发射，拥有世界上唯一的海上航天发射场——圣马科发射场以及马林迪航天监控站。与此同时，作为东非区域的金融中心及通讯中心，肯尼亚也是除北美和西欧外，联合国在非洲的主要活动中心，许多国家都在肯尼亚设有大使馆。

五 国际“竞技场”中的中国与肯尼亚

在全球权力体系深度重组的过程中，多数国家都在新的现实中寻找着适合各自的地位。曾经影响力较大的组织机构正逐渐丧失地位，因为许多强国对这些组织机构的信心正在衰减。它们曾经是强国谋求地缘政治利益的工具，用于分裂或控制其他国家。联合国与国际刑事法院便是被强国利用、随后又遭抛弃的典型。

随着西方创造的全球性组织机构逐渐“失势”，权力体系重组也造成了西方国家在全球范围内的“失势”。在这一过程中，许多国家进行了自发性的改革，有些国家则被迫改革，还有一些介乎两者之间。这些不仅发生在美、中、英、俄、德、日、法等大国，也发生在巴西、土耳其、印度、南非、伊朗、以色列以及墨西哥等中等国家。一些国土面积虽小、但却逐渐崭露头角的国家也进行了类似的改革。作为正在崛起的小国，肯尼亚在改革过程中克服了来自内部和外部的重重阻力。

在中肯两国的“后解放”时期以及交往期间，共同利益与共同的挑战要求两国开展互利合作。中肯关系曾经历过一段起伏，进入21世纪后，两国在掀起全球性影响的同时，各自的地缘政治地位正不断上升。在革命后代的领导下，两国互敬互谅，不再任凭自诩为“世界利益捍卫者”的帝国主义/殖民主义国家所驱使。两国都曾遭到欧洲国家的侵略，特别是在19世纪，致使中国经历了“百年耻辱”、使肯尼亚沦为殖民地。

两国都是在伟大领袖和政党的领导下，成功地摆脱了欧洲的殖民统治。1949年10月，当毛泽东主席在北京的天安门广场宣布新中国成立时，中国已经通过自身的奋斗，走出了“百年屈辱”的历史。20世纪50年代，肯尼亚通过“茅茅战争”摆脱了英国的殖民统治，而这场运动的支持者就是乔莫·肯雅塔。肯雅塔是20世纪30年代的反殖民斗士，第二次世界大战前后倡导非洲主义，最后从“茅茅战争”中脱颖而出，于1964年领导肯尼亚成立了共和国。其子乌胡鲁·肯雅塔正是肯尼亚的现任总统。

中肯两国相互友好，肯尼亚独立后，高度重视肯中关系，内罗毕最初建立的六个外交使团中，便包括驻北京大使一职。尽管在20世纪60–70年代，两国关系曾一度“遇冷”，但自80年代中国开展“体育场外交”以来，两国一直保持着紧密而友好的外交关系。中国援建的现代体育场馆，象征着在冷战正式结束前，中国已开始对内罗毕产生巨大的影响。随着冷战的结束，隐藏在地缘政治“伪装”下不断变幻的权力关系开始显现。当西方国家沉浸在必胜的信念中、日益疏远昔日盟友时，非洲国家对亚洲、特别是对中国的好感与日俱增。

1. 中国

中国与其他大国的竞争日益激烈，并逐渐改变着全球的权力结构。作为幅员辽阔、人口众多的大国，中国与蛮横自大的美国不同，始终遵循着邓小平同志“韬光养晦”的外交战略，收敛锋芒，只通过软实力施加影响。中国之所以始终不渝地奉行这一战略，主要因为以下三个原因：减少他国的威胁感，同时降低中国的负面形象；第二，有助于中国团结遭受欧洲剥削的第三世界国家，形成全球政治杠杆优势；第三、“韬光养晦”有助于中国通过软实力渗透并改变世界格局。

在跻身全球强国之列的同时，中国也在积极消除自身崛起带来的威胁感。通过这种方式，中国正改变着世界格局，并构建起一种新型全球治理秩序。之所以能够做到这一点，是因为中国对其他国家始终奉行友好外交，而不是以武力相逼，从不炫耀军事实力，始终坚持公道与理性。

在某一段历史时期内，中国的邻国和竞争对手——印度与日本——曾一度在经济和地缘政治上占据优势。作为亚洲的经济强国，日本曾在南非实行种族隔离制期间跻身欧洲经济强国之列，被给予白人国家的殊荣。作为地缘政治大国，印度曾在挑战欧洲统治地位方面位居第三世界前列。但中国逐渐超过了日本和印度，不仅在经济成就方面，也包括对第三世界国家的经济影响和政治影响方面。

与此同时，中国也超越了许多欧盟成员国，在某些方面，特别是在全球形象上，正在超越美国。从表面看，美国似乎正逐渐淡出全球治理，唐纳德·特朗普正试图进行一次彻底的重组，他似乎认为奥巴马/克林顿的“救世”情结导致了利比亚战争与叙利亚战争，而正是这两场战争造成了美国国际地位的下滑。相比之下，中国正以最低的地缘政治成本和经济成本，逐渐成为全球经济的引擎。

与日益衰落的西方相比，中国的国际地位正日益崛起，这点并非偶然，特朗普更是心知肚明。执迷于“救世情结”的美国学者和决策者正在鼓吹“文明的冲突”，甚至有人鼓吹中国是美国的头号劲敌。布什与奥巴马在“救世宣言”中不断推广所谓的民主体制，呼吁各国要“站在历史正确的一面”，最终导致了西方世界的移民危机，这可谓自食其果。

在中国深入推进“一带一路”倡议的同时，美国的反应可谓不乏敌意。然而随着中国的和平理念深入人心、占据国际市场的份额不断扩大、默默无闻地提供着全球治理的方案，中国在以下三个方面的表现远远超出了欧洲诸国。第一，根据协定，以合理的价格出售高质量产品和服务；第二，准时交付，不像欧洲各国以诸多怪异的借口进行拖延；第三，尊重贸易伙伴国的意愿，增进双方互信。相比之下，欧洲对待非洲国家的态度却截然相反：价格过高，延迟交付且寻找诸多借口，通过无谓的说教侮辱贸易伙伴国。

2. 肯尼亚

在权力重组的过程中，肯尼亚恰好抓住了历史机遇。在世界各国（不论大小）采取一切手段谋求本国利益时，作为东非地区的重要国家，肯尼亚正不断提升自身的全球地缘政治身份。所谓的一切手段是指，符合国家利益的、所有可用的手段。这些国家利益往往与商贸、外交、完全乃至国家形象紧密相连。

尽管东非存在着一定的不安因素，但相对来说较为稳定，发展前景较好，因此具有较高的地缘政治价值。的确，东非地区的许多国家之间存在着激烈的竞争和敌对关系。比如，肯尼亚和坦桑尼亚，两国都是19世纪英德在东非地区（从印度洋到刚果东部）开展殖民争霸的结果。不同的殖民经验和后殖民经验塑造了两国的不同身份，给人造成一种互为“天敌”的印象。殖民地身份以及后殖民时期选择的不同道路，导致两国间互不信任，从这个角度便可以解释两国之间的政治问题。

作为一个逐渐崭露头角的小国，肯尼亚正竭力化解地区纠纷，至少在东非区域如此。尽管曾短暂地迷失在奥巴马带来的陶醉感中（奥巴马的父亲来自肯尼亚），但肯尼亚很快便清醒过来，在全球权力体系重组的过程中，以现实的态度面对国际关系，以务实的行动捍卫其全球利益。肯尼亚从未与华盛顿的特朗普、莫斯科的普京、北京的习近平、伦敦的特丽莎・梅、特拉维夫的内塔尼亚胡、东京的安倍晋三、安曼的侯赛因、达累斯萨拉姆的马古富力、比勒陀利亚的雅各布・祖马、新德里的纳伦德拉・莫迪、朱巴的萨尔瓦・基尔、阿布贾的穆罕默德・布哈里、马尼拉的杜特尔特等人发生过争吵。肯尼亚了解这些国家的利益所在，但只关心本国的利益，只关心在权力重组的过程中，各国的意图何在。

在全球治理秩序重组的过程中，中国与肯尼亚应相互借鉴，找到彼此的位置。

两国的区别在于，作为全球重组的领导者，中国能够迫使昔日的强国接受这一现实，在这一点上，肯尼亚也不甘落后。在很长一段时间内，中国一直强调其经济的全球影响力、注重为快速崛起的工业寻求原材料，这说明，中国已经停止了向内探求，转而向外寻求利益。

在这个过程中，中国在全世界范围内掀起了向第三世界寻求石油等原材料的风潮。东非地区的“原材料”储备丰富，所以欧洲各国才会如此焦虑，不断指责中国在非洲扩张势力。因此，昔日的强国似乎也参与到在整个东非区域“发现”石油、天然气、煤炭及其他材料的竞争中来，或许此举是为了遏制中国发展。但与此同时，中国已经深度参与到非洲及其他区域的社会经济工程以及安全工程中来。

肯尼亚属于中国新战略的组成部分，而与中国合作可以帮助肯尼亚在世界权力重组的过程中确立自身地位。美国与肯尼亚签署的拉穆港–南苏丹–埃塞俄比亚交通走廊 (LAPSSET) 工程极有可能改变东非的社会经济及安全状况。目前，中国已经按时完成了从蒙巴萨港至内罗毕的准轨铁路，且该线路正不断向西延展。此外，中国最大的媒体电视台——中央电视台在内罗毕设立了非洲分台，可以将电视节目传送到非洲乃至世界的各个角落。中肯两国均认为，这会给两国的经济和政治带来积极影响。

China, Kenya, and Global Governance

Gideon Macharia Munene / Kenya

Professor of History and International Relations, United States International University in Nairobi

I would like to approach my presentation in terms of four, probably overlapping, phases that help to explain China's and Kenya's current geopolitical status and positions. These are first the context of "state" as the global administrative unit. Second is the creation of the Chinese and the Kenyan states. Third is the geopolitical value of China and Kenya to other states. Fourth is China and Kenya in the international arena.

I. The Context of State as Global Administrative Unit

Peoples in the world presently organize themselves through geopolitical units that have defined borders called states that have acquired a self-justification that makes them appear to be natural. As the instruments through which to administer people and conduct their socio-economic affairs, states struggle to survive as viable entities in the midst of many challenges among them being "interests" and "security". The ability of a country or region to secure interests varies with its capacity to access multiple resources or to deny access to potential rivals. It is a power game that not all play with the required finesse.

Interests distinguish one state from the others. It is part of the identity of particular people. In this sense, a state is a "core value" whose survival implies the survival of those people. All institutions, not just government organs, therefore, should ensure the survival of the state. To manage the institutions properly, each state needs to have capacity for interplay and application of such key concepts as politics, resources, space or geography, and strategy at the domestic and global levels. For successful interplay and application, those running a state should be conceptually tuned to three types of knowledge that help to safeguard the interests. These are knowledge of the national philosophy and ideals, knowledge of the national ideals and philosophies in other countries that a state interacts with, and knowledge of the points of convergence and divergence that a state has with those other states.

The command of the three types of knowledge safeguards a state's geo-political interests. Geopolitics is mostly an intellectual exercise handling two concepts, geography and politics. While geography deals with territories and the environment, politics is the ability to exercise and project power over other people, institutions, and countries. This makes geo-politics an exercise of power over other people's space by manipulating space to achieve political ends. At the international level this implies one country politically manipulating others to achieve its purported desires. That is imperialism, the forcing of foreign governance on a people.

In itself, imperialism is forced governance on a people. This necessitates strategy, a calculated method of how to get or avoid something. Calculation over territory is geo-strategy which is the rationale behind techniques used to achieve certain geopolitical objectives. Geo-strategy is thus an instrument for serving the interests of geopolitics.

II. The Creation of Chinese and the Kenyan States

The above concerns relating to states are at play in both China and Kenya as states. Both countries are recent entrants into the modern global governance power games, each trying to find its niche in the emerging power realignment. At different times, each was a fixation in the minds of Euro-imperialists. Each has had two modern times global images; initial subservience to Euro-power dictates followed by a "revolutionary" overthrow of those dictates. Both were victims of Euro manipulation, in the Third World, liberated themselves through revolutions, and are assertive at the global stage. Their differences include history, geographic and demographic size, and style of governance.

China

China boasts of being the oldest identifiable and continuous geopolitical entity, conceptually and geographically. It mesmerized Euro-imperialists who made it one of their excuses for expanding outside Europe in the 15th and 16th Centuries at the very time that China started looking inward and abandoning maritime imperial adventures. In the resulting clash between the *Euros*, meaning Western Europe and its imperial offspring called the United States of America, China lost parts of its historical territories. It lost to competing imperial forces in the 19th Century and entered what it later termed a "Century of Humiliation". It dramatically began in the British Opium War of the 1840s when Britain decided to turn the Chinese into drug addicts in order to shift the balance of trade with China in British favour. To a large extent, therefore, the official borders of the Peoples Republic of China were determined by external imperial powers such as the Europeans, the Americans, the Japanese, and even the Russians.

Kenya

On its part, Kenya is a creation of mainly external imperial agreements. Officially, Kenya was almost a strategic accident in that the British claim they were forced to acquire it in order to keep other Europeans from interfering with British interests in India. In 1888 Britain gave a charter to the Imperial British East African Company, IBEAC, to run the territory on the behalf of the government. The collapse of the company in 1895 forced the government to take over and start building a railroad to link the Indian Ocean and Uganda, the Uganda Railway nicknamed the *Lunatic Express* which reached Kisumu on Lake Victoria in 1901. Thereafter, it embarked on a dream of creating a colonial state that, up to 1963, produced two overlapping imageries that captured global attention. These are the "White Man's Country" and the revolutionary "Mau Mau Country."

In the white man's country image, Africans lost sovereignty, legitimacy freedom, and the right to be human. Subsequent agreements between the British, the Germans, the Italians, and Geography, determined Kenya's present international boundaries. As such, the new source of legitimacy in Africa was lodged in such European capitals as London, Paris, Rome, Berlin, Brussels, and Lisbon. As agreed at Berlin, each was expected to show effective occupation of claimed territories and they did it using three tools of soldiers, administrators, and missionaries. The Missionaries were particularly tasked to soften Africans to accept their new subservient status. While the soldiers conquered, the administrators ruled and worked hand in hand with the missionaries destroy the African past while creating a new consciousness that admired things European. In Kenya, Britain dispossessed people of their lands and created the image of white man's country that was paradise on earth which turned the owners of the land into servants for the *mzungu*.

III. Revolutionary Countries

China and Kenya have in common the image of being "revolutionary", capturing global attention by throwing away imperial political control in dramatic ways. The revolutionary image came from the prolonged internal struggle between the Communists and the Nationalists as it sought to liberate itself from external control. The Communists won and in October 1949 proclaimed a new China that would not be subservient to external interests. This success was a shock to the imperial world and it marked the entrance of a new serious player in the world arena. It sought to identify itself with other anti-imperial players that were mostly found in the Third World.

Three years after "revolutionary" China forced its presence on the world geopolitical stage, the outbreak of the Mau Mau War in 1952, a result of built up African resentments, sent anti-colonial reverberations across the globe. Natives in colonial Kenya mounted a "revolution" that became an inspiration to other African colonies to mount anti-colonialism through armed struggle. The war created a startling Mau Mau image that was as an alternative to the white man's country image. In the process, Kenya acquired the image of a revolutionary "Mau Mau Country".

The Mau Mau impact was felt in the rest of Africa and beyond. In Northern Rhodesia, anti-colonialists used "Mau Mau" as inspiration and pressure to the government to give concessions. "We see ourselves in those resilient Mau Mau fighters," Robert Mugabe of Zimbabwe remarked in October 2012. In South Africa, Nelson Mandela abandoned the Gandhi ways and adopted Kimathi's Mau Mau ways by forming Umkhonto we Sizwe, Spear of the Nation. And armed struggle became the in-thing especially among the settler colonies of Angola, Mozambique, and Rhodesia. If it worked in Kenya, it can work elsewhere, maybe even in the United States where Malcolm X was talking of the Mau Mau as an appropriate "revolution" for African Americans.

IV. Value of China and Kenya to Others

As countries, China and Kenya have gained strategic value to others, near and far. China emerged as the place for almost every country to turn to for manufactured items of different qualities. In the process, China surpassed Japan as the second most powerful economy that is second only to that of the United States. The surpassing of Japan was not just on economic performance, but also in terms of global image. China became the global economic engine, the global hub. As a result, when the Chinese economy slows down, the rest of the world feels the effect. Among those affected by any slow-down in the Chinese economic performance are various world regions that have increasingly come to rely on Chinese markets and investments.

With time, China acquired image as the undeclared leader of emerging powers. It was the main force of the BRICS movement involving Brazil, Russia, India, China, and South Africa, that started challenging the dominance of the mainly Euro G7 in global affairs. As a consequence, the monopoly that the G7 used to have on deciding global agenda was partly eroded by the expansion of the club of economic powers to become G20 for annual meetings to deliberate on global trends.

While the value of China to the others is mostly economic in the form of markets and investments, Kenya has geo-strategic value to the others, big and small. Kenya has also emerged as an economic hub, not on the same scale as China, but in the East African region and to some extent the African continent. To its immediate neighbours in Eastern Africa, it is the region's economic engine and also the gateway to the sea for the land locked states of Uganda, Rwanda, Burundi, South Sudan, Eastern Congo, and even Ethiopia. To Asian power houses such as China, Japan, and India Kenya is the entry point to the resources of the region. Besides, located on the Equator it has satellite value which explains the satellite station, San Marcos, near Malindi which tracts global weather patterns. It is also the financial and communication hub of Eastern Africa, hosts the only UN agency outside North America and Western Europe, and has some of the largest embassies in Africa.

V. China and Kenya in the International Arena

There is serious global realignment taking place with most countries trying to find out where they fit in the new realities. In the evolving realignment, institutions that were previously held in high regard increase their irrelevancy mainly because the powerful and the assertive countries have been losing faith in them. In part, this is because those institutions allowed themselves to be misused to promote the geopolitical interests of some powers in fixing purported rivals or imposing controls on those who should remain as *client states.* Among institutions with diminishing relevancy are the United Nations and the International Criminal Court that big powers use, misuse, and ignore at will.

With its created global institutions losing relevance, the *Conceptual West* is in global decline as a power as realignment takes place. In that realignment, some countries are reorganizing themselves, others are being reorganized, and a third group is caught in-between. It is happening to powerful countries like the United States, China, Russia, Britain, Japan, Germany, and France as well as to medium size powerhouses like Brazil, Turkey, India, South Africa, Iran, Israel, and Mexico. The realignment is also there in small and increasingly assertive countries. It is in the category of small assertive countries that Kenya finds itself, fending off internal and external distractions.

In their post-liberation period and engagements, China and Kenya share concerns and interests which demand that they collaborate. The two countries appear to have fluctuating relationship and are both, in the 21st Century, on the geopolitical upswing as they assert their global presence forcefully. Currently led by sons of "revolutionaries", they have grown to respect each other, extend hands of understanding, and reject insulting instructions from imperial/colonial centres that pretend to be the custodians of world interests. Both were victims of Euro aggression with Britain in the lead, particularly in the 19th Century, that led to a "Century of Humiliation" for China and to colonialism in Kenya.

Both, inspired by dreams of strong leaders and parties, successfully fought their way out of the Euro-imposed condition. China was the first to fight its way out of its "Century of Humiliation" when in October 1949 Mao Zedong proclaimed the New Era at Tiananmen Square in Beijing and started building a New China. Similarly, Kenya fought its way out of British colonialism in the Mau Mau War of the 1950s and one of those accused of masterminding it was a "revolutionary" named Jomo Kenyatta. An anti-colonial intellectual giant of the 1930s and a promoter of Pan-Africanism before and after World War II, Kenyatta emerged from the Mau Mau War to lead Kenya into its Republican status in 1964. His son, Uhuru Kenyatta, is now president of Kenya.

Both countries found attractions to each other. At independence, Kenya considered China to be so important that Beijing was one of the original six diplomatic posts that Nairobi established. The two countries had their "downs" in the late 1960s and 1970s but this changed in the 1980s as China embarked on stadia diplomacy. The construction of modern stadia became signals of Chinese presence in Nairobi, long before the official end of the Cold War. The end of the Cold War removed the geo-political blind covering shifting global power relations, As the West indulged in triumphalism and became excessively hostile to its former friends, many African countries found Asia very attractive and China was in the forefront of that attraction.

China

China is in big time competition with other big powers and is shaping global realignment. A huge country geographically and demographically, it struggles to hide power even when it is physically difficult to do so and has adopted a *soft* way of projecting power. Unlike the United States which is often very noisy about its power and self-importance, China refrains from announcing its power even when it is visible to others. It adheres to Deng Xiaoping's *geopolitical last will and testament* or *farewell address* to the Chinese in which he advised them to hide power. This advice has been religiously followed for three good common sense reasons. First, it reduces both the appearance of being a threat to other states and also the likely negative reactions towards China. Second, it helps China to identify with the *Euro* exploited Third World countries that it needs for global political leveraging. Third, the avoidance of bragging enables China to infiltrate and revolutionize the world *softly*.

Particularly conscious of its rise to global prominence and going out of its way to minimize public awareness of that rise, China is deliberately reorganizing the world and creating a new world governance order. It does this by adopting friendly policies that attract rather than threaten other countries. It tends to be self-effacing and to appear to be reasonable at all times.

There was time when its global competitors were neighbouring India and Japan which were below the top tier in terms of economic and geopolitical prestige. Japan was economic giant in Asia, doing so well that it was admitted into the club of the Euros to become, in the days of apartheid in South Africa, an honorary white country. India was the geopolitical Third World giant that seemed to lead in challenging Euro dominance in global governance. With time, China outpaced both Japan, in terms of economic performance, and India in terms of projecting itself in the Third World as a force of economic and political liberation.

China also outpaced the Europeans individually or as part of the European Union entity and is outdoing the United States in selected areas, particularly in the global image area. The United States is seemingly retreating from global engagement, especially with Donald Trump trying to recast everything because, he seemingly believes, the Obama/Clinton *messianism* had led to disasters in Libya and Syria that eroded American global stature. This was in contrast with China which emerged as the global economic engine, with minimal geopolitical and economic costs, to its standing.

The Chinese global dominance, rising in proportion to the decline of the *Conceptual West*, is not by accident and Trump knows it. As American thinkers and policy makers got themselves lost in *messianism* and preparing for *clashes of civilisation,* a few thinkers kept on insisting that China was the real challenge to American power. At the time, George W. Bush and Barack Obama made messianic pronouncements about forcing democracy or being on the right side of history that boomeranged and produced the immigration crisis in the West.

The Americans sounded bellicose at the very time that China was increasing engagement with its “Belt and Road” initiative. It was pushing its global peaceful agenda and capturing the world market and also seeming to offer solutions without making noise. This enabled China to succeed by doing three things better than any Euro power. These are first offering reasonable prices for quality goods and services as agreed in the discussions. Second is ability to deliver on time without attaching strange excuses for failure to perform, as the Euros do. Third is by showing respect to the wishes of other countries that it deals with which ends up cultivating confidence. The reverse is the case when the Euros deal with particularly African countries: their prices are excessive, they do not deliver and find excuses for not delivering, and they insult other countries through dubious lectures.

Kenya

Kenya fits right in the midst of that realignment. It is a key country in the East African region that is of growing importance in global geo-politics as various countries, big and small, strive to promote their interests through all means possible. All means implies what each can get away with as long as it is perceived to be in its national interests. Those interests are commercial and trade related, diplomatic, security, and even image.

Although the region has its share of turbulence, it is comparatively stable and prosperous and attracts a lot of geopolitical attention. Various countries compete and at times the rivalry is intense. Kenya and Tanzania, for instance, are products of late 19th Century German and British imperial rivalry in Eastern Africa that stretched from the Indian Ocean eastwards to eastern Congo. The two had different colonial and post-colonial experiences which shaped their identities and give the impression of being natural rivals. Suspicion rooted in lingering colonial identities and experiences and attempts to chart separate post-colonial paths explain some of the political difficulties that are to be found between Kenya and Tanzania.

Kenya is doing its best as one of the small but assertive zonal powerhouses, at least in the Eastern Africa region. Temporarily caught up in the Obama euphoria, it has since come out of the stupor and is entrenching its global interests by dealing realistically with all the other players in the global realignment. Kenya, having no quarrel with Trump in Washington, Putin in Moscow, Xi Jinping in Beijing, Teresa May in London, Netanyahu in Tel Aviv, Shinzo Abe in Tokyo, King Hussein in

Amman, John Pombe Magufuli in Dar es Salaam, Jacob Zuma in Pretoria, Narendra Modi in New Delhi, Salva Kirr in Juba, Mohammed Buhari in Abuja, or Duterte in Manila, has opportunity to place itself in the midst of their perceived interests while being clear as to what its own interests are despite what others may want. This entails examining what each of realigning countries is up to.

China and Kenya need looking into as each tries to find its niche in global governance realignment. The difference between the two is that China is the leader of that global realignment, forcing other powers to accept that reality, and Kenya does not want to be left behind. For a long time, China had been asserting its economic global presence as it sought raw materials for its rapidly growing industries. It stopped being inward looking and went out to the world to safeguard its interests.

In the process, China became a world-wide catalyst for "discovery" of strategic raw materials such as oil in the Third World. Eastern Africa featured high in these discoveries and thereafter, Euro-powers seemed worried as they complained about Chinese presence in Africa. As a result, big powers appeared to compete for the "discovery" of oil, gas, coal, and other minerals throughout East Africa probably in order to stop China from "discovering" them. To compound the situation, China also became involved in socio-economic and security infrastructural projects for Africa and other regions.

Kenya was part of that new thinking and linking up with China is a way of claiming its place in a realigned world. The LAPSSET undertaking stretching from LAMU to Juba and probably to Duala is potentially transformative in terms of socio-economic and security. China already completed the SGR railway line from Mombasa to Nairobi on time and is extending it westwards. It has also set up its biggest media outreach station in Nairobi, CCTV-Africa, from where it can reach any corner of Africa and the world. Both sides, China and Kenya, consider the development to be economically and politically positive.

新丝绸之路上商品、人员和资本交换

维特·沃伊达 【捷克】

VIT 顾问公司执行董事 / 拉瓦克（上海）有限公司副董事长 / 律师、中文公证译员

2015 年 3 月 28 日，中国国家发展改革委、外交部、商务部联合发布了《推动共建丝绸之路经济带和 21 世纪海上丝绸之路的愿景与行动》。

新丝绸之路使得中国从防御性重商主义（保护国内市场）转向主动性重商主义（在海外获得市场份额，并打开国外市场），中国以往所有贸易倡议的整合，提高其贸易政策的效率，防止各类活动者在出国时互相伤害．另外中国对获取原材料和出口的关注；继续出口劳动密集型制造业产品；扩大其在高端制成品和不同服务领域的市场份额；同时投资外汇储备（因中国贸易顺差导致）需有利于增强中国在国际市场的影响力。这些政策为中国市场提供了众多机遇也势必对欧洲市场造成挑战。

一　东西方沟通的差异

东西方沟通的差异表现如下：

公开讨论的形式限制——中国的好客、礼貌、面子传统。

中国的沟通目标是组织好会议，不发生任何意外，保持“和谐”，维护“正确的政治方向”。关键是“政治正确性”——强烈的爱国主义，政府领导，官员“总是对”。

欧洲的方法：批判主义和自由思想——受社会正确性的限制（矫枉过正），自由竞争带来了创新发明，对于这个问题我们可以通过公开讨论以达成新的理解、认知及改善的能力（更优异的功能：高效且更简单的方案）。

二　中欧贸易问题

欧盟为中国第一大贸易伙伴（连续12年）中国为欧盟第二大贸易伙伴（连续13年）：

- 中欧双边货物贸易额36115.9亿元（同比增长3%）；
- 中国向欧盟出口22369.3亿元（同比增长1.3%）；
- 欧盟进口13746.6亿元（同比增长5.9%）；
- 对欧贸易顺差8622.64亿元（同比下降5.4%）。

综上所述，平衡中欧货物贸易还需15–20年时间。中欧贸易有很显著的三个特点，对外贸易结构不断优化；双向投资合作不断加深；经济技术合作逐步体制化。我们也可以看到中欧贸易在持续增长的同时也遭遇了很多问题，这里先谈三个主要问题。

1. 贸易失衡/平衡问题：中方存在大规模的贸易顺差

欧洲限制对华高科技出口；欧盟对于中国是否能够有效保护知识产权。

中国正在逐步加强法治与知识产权保护；但相关的法律法规来保障知识产权不够，整个社会法律意识正在得到改变。高关税。"中国制造2025"将对内、外资企业一视同仁，届时关税会得到相应解决。

2. 在货物贸易上存在大量顺差，而服务贸易上是长期逆差

双方一旦发生内部问题（比如欧债危机），欧中保护主义势力抬头，将限制他国对自己的出口。

贸易救济措施：反倾销措施、反补贴措施、保障措施和特殊保障措施。利用技术贸易壁垒。

对此，根据《中国加入世界贸易组织协定书》第15条规定进行讨论，欧盟应履行条约义务，致力于找到符合WTO规则、对各国一视同仁、对中国非歧视性的解决方案。

3. 中国对外主要出口低附加值的初级产品，处于产业分工的下游，行业利润率低；欧中经贸关系常常受到官方政策的影响，经济要求和政治企图之间的摇摆

不定是其主要原因。具体表现如下：

• 在“一带一路”的环境下，欧中的商业合作结构开始有所拓展；

• 基础设施的建设合作，之前一直有限制的金融合作；

• 欧盟主要金融强国加入亚投行，亚投行的经营运作也需要借助欧盟国家在国际金融机构的经验和人才的优势；

• 中国主要支持最大规模的企业进中国市场。

因此，中国正在积极建立扶持欧盟中小企业对华直接投资的政策体系，创造更多的优惠条件，例如：市场准入条件，国内融资条件，优惠的税收条件以及较低的土地出让金等。进而慢慢解除中小企业来华投资在信息来源，资本规模和融资条件等多方面因素的限制。

三　资本贸易

1. 首先，从欧盟角度看存在五个问题：

• 以“一带一路”为例，中国投资的项目标准不公开，未公开招标，基本由中国团队来实施。

• 中国的外商投资环境却越来越差。

• 服务业几乎对外资封闭，外资银行在中国的市场份额已从 2% 下降到 1%，保险业几乎没有外资参与。

• 在汽车制造这样的行业，外资要进入中国必须通过与中国企业建立合资企业，而且往往与技术转让挂钩。

• 中国的产业政策应该具有更多的法律保障性，而不能依靠随意更改的行政决策。

2. 其次，从中国角度，正在采取一系列措施：

• 自 2017 年 7 月 1 日起实施《金融机构大额交易和可疑交易报告管理办法》。

• 监管机构参考发达国家经验后完善监管制度的正常行为。

• 外资并购国内企业后，政府保持对并购行为的规制。

• 符合以下两个条件的产业，都应是允许跨国并购的领域：第一，不涉及中国国民经济命脉的主要行业和关键领域；第二，中国缺乏国际竞争优势领域（电子、制药、航空、新技术等）。

New Silk Road: Problems on Mutual Exchanges of Goods, Services, People and Capital

Vit Vojta / Czech Republic

Executive Director of VIT Consulting Ltd., Vice Chairman of RAVAK (Shanghai) Co. Ltd., Lawyer and Certified Chinese Court Interpreter

The National Development and Reform Commission, the Ministry of Foreign Affairs and the Ministry of Commerce jointly issued the "Vision and Action to Promote the Economic Development of the Silk Road and the Maritime Silk Road in the 21st Century" on March 28th, 2015.

The New Silk Road points China's shift in direction from passive mercantilism (protection of domestic market) towards active mercantilism (to gain market shares abroad and unlock foreign markets), Integration of all China's previous trade initiatives makes its trade policy much more efficient and prevents different actors from undermining each other when they go abroad. China has begun to focus on accessing raw materials and on exports, to continue exporting labor-intensive manufactured goods, to expand its market shares in high-end manufactured goods and other services and also in the foreign exchange reserves resulting from China's trade surplus needing to be invested in a way that gives China more influence on the international market. Those not only provide a lot of opportunities for China, but at the same time also bring challenges and threats for Europe.

I. the Communication Problem between East and West

Limits of open discussion (form): Chinese hospitality, politeness, face-giving tradition

China's goal of Communication is to organize a hold a well-organized conference, without any accidents and to stay in "harmony" while keep a correct political orientation. Key approach is "political correctness" – strong patriotism, paternalism, government leaders and staff are "always right".

European approach is based on criticism and liberal thinking–limited by social correctness (hypercorrectness), while free competition brings innovation, inventions.

For this problem, open discussion may achieve new understandings, new knowledge and the ability to make things better (better functionality: difficulty lessens with efficiency).

II. Key Problem: EU–China Goods Exchange

EU is China's largest trade partner (12 consecutive years); China is EU's second largest trade partner (13 consecutive years):

- The trade volume of EU-China amounts to 3.61159 trillion RMB (year-on-year growth of 3%);
- China's exports to EU are 2.23693 trillion RMB (year-on-year growth of 1.3%);
- EU's imports to China are 1.37466 trillion RMB (year-on-year growth of 5.9%);
- The trade surplus to EU is 862.264 billion RMB (year-on-year decline of 5.4 %).

Above all, it can be concluded that 15-20 more years needed to balance EU-China trade development. There are three main characteristics of EU-China goods exchange: continually optimize the structure of foreign trade; constantly deepen the mutual investment cooperation; gradually systematize the economic and technical cooperation. We can also witness that EU-China trade is continuously increasing but at the same time it causes a lot of problems.

1. Trade imbalance/balance: China has a large trade surplus

Europe restricts high-tech exports to China; EU cannot effectively protect China as per intellectual property rights.

China is gradually strengthening the rule of laws and protecting intellectual property rights. It is not enough to protect intellectual property rights only with relevant laws and regulations. It is necessary to change the law consciousness of the whole society. High tariff. “Made in China 2025” will treat domestic and foreign enterprises equally, and until the tariff will be accordingly solved.

2. A large surplus in goods trade and a long-term deficit in service trade

In case of domestic problems of the two parties (such as the European Debt Crisis), protective force in EU-China will arise and limit other countries' exports.

Trade remedy measures: anti-dumping measures, countervailing measures, supporting measures and special supporting measures.

Make use of technical trade barriers.

Therefore, the EU should fulfill its obligations in accordance to Article 15 of the “Protocol on the Accession of the People's Republic of China”. They are committed to finding solutions that conform to WTO rules, treat all countries equally, and uphold non-discriminatory to China.

3. China exports mainly low value-added primary products in downstream of the industrial division and with low profit margins, and the EU-China economic and trade relations are often influenced by official policies. The main reason is the unsteadiness in economic demands and political attempts.

Such as:

• Under the circumstances of "Belt and Road", the business cooperation mode of EU-China starts to develop;

• The cooperation in infrastructure construction and previously restricted financial cooperation;

• The major financial powers of EU have joined the Asian Infrastructure Investment Bank (AIIB). The operation of AIIB also requires the experience and talents in international financial institutions from EU countries;

• China supports mainly largest companies in entering the Chinese market – easy to manage.

Therefore, China is actively establishing the policy system to support the direct investment by small and medium-sized EU enterprises in China. Creating more favorable conditions: market entry requirements, domestic financing conditions, preferential tax policies and lower land rent, etc. This way it is possible to gradually remove restrictions of small and medium-sized enterprises' investment in China in as a source of information, capital scale and financing requirements, etc.

III. Exchange of Capital

1. Five problems from the perspective of EU, they are:

• Take the "B&R" as an example, the projects invested by China lack open standards or public bidding and the projects are basically carried out by the Chinese team;

• The foreign investment environment in China is getting worse;

• The service sector is almost closed to foreign investment. Foreign banks' market share in China has dropped from 2% to 1%, and there's almost no foreign involvement in the insurance industry;

• In industries like automobile manufacturing, foreign investments in China require establishing joint ventures with Chinese companies as well as technology transfer;

• China's industrial policy should have more legal guarantees and cannot rely on arbitrary administrative decisions.

2. From the perspective of China, some measures are being carried out:

• Launch "Measures for the Administration of Financial Institutions' Reporting of High-Value Transactions and Suspicious Transactions" on July 1st, 2017;

• The regulators will improve regulatory systems after learning from developed countries' experience;

• After the acquisition of domestic enterprises by foreign companies, the government keeps regulating merger and acquisition behavior;

• The business that meets the following two conditions are entitled to cross-border mergers and acquisitions: first, the major industries and key sectors that do not involve the lifeblood of China national economy; second, the sectors that China lacks international competitive advantages (electronics, pharmaceuticals, aviation, new technology, etc.).

人类命运共同体：世界治理新方案

薛力 【中国】
中国社会科学院世界经济与政治研究中心国际战略研究室主任

一　人类命运共同体提出背景

与冷战刚结束到2008年全球金融危机时期相比，当前的世界格局具有若干新特点。

首先，西方国家的全球影响力相对下降，发展中国家的影响力提升。明显标志是七国集团从讨论全球政治经济文化议题的“富国俱乐部”，变成主要聚焦政治与社会问题的西方大国论坛。经济议题被边缘化后，政治议题难以达成共识，更无法操作，社会问题重要性稍显逊色，这使得七国集团受关注程度大大下降，影响力明显减弱。

其次，发达国家对全球经济的贡献下降，新兴经济体的贡献明显上升。典型标志是，2008年国际金融危机重创发达国家后，二十国集团从财长会议升格为领导人峰会，成为国际经济合作主要论坛。其主要使命是：在发达国家和新兴市场国家之间就实质性问题进行开放及有建设性的讨论和研究，寻求合作并促进国际金融稳定和经济的持续增长。许多金融、财政议题先在二十国集团会议上达成共识，再提交相关国际机构落实执行。由于新兴经济体在二十国集团中占多数，因此，他们的具体经济主张，有望通过这一途径产生全球影响力，甚至成为国际经济规制的一部分。

再次，全球化进程遭遇挫折，甚至出现“逆全球化”趋势。关贸总协定与世界贸易组织的主要任务是推进全球自由贸易，可旨在推进全球贸易的多哈回合2001年启动后迟迟没有大进展，2009年后实际上已经被搁置。许多国家转而推进区域整合，一些发达国家纷纷以“公平贸易”为旗号，推行贸易保护主义。

最后，中国的全球角色地位凸显。中国经济总量在全球坐二望一，贡献了全球经济增量的三分之一，但在全球产业链分工中，整体上依然处于中下游。推进经济全球化符合包括中国在内的新兴经济体的利益，也符合发达国家服务业、先进制造业等行业部门的主张。和平崛起依然是中国的坚定信念与现实选择。

在上述背景下，中共十八大报告首次提出“要倡导人类命运共同体意识”。此后，习近平主席在一系列双边和多边重要外交场合多次强调树立人类命运共同体意识，提出共建中国—东盟命运共同体、中国—巴基斯坦命运共同体、亚洲命运共同体等，表明中国愿同世界各国共同致力于促进世界的和平、稳定、繁荣与进步。2015年9月，习近平在第七十届联合国大会一般性辩论时，首次提出要继承和弘扬联合国宪章的宗旨和原则，构建以合作共赢为核心的新型国际关系，打造人类命运共同体，并阐述打造这一共同体的途径：建立平等相待、互商互谅的**伙伴关系**；营造公道正义、共建共享的**安全格局**；谋求开放创新、包容互惠的**发展前景**；促进和而不同、兼收并蓄的**文明交流**；构筑尊崇自然、绿色发展的**生态体系**。

可见，构建人类命运共同体，是中国提出的全球治理新方案，旨在打造政治、安全、经济、文化、生态“五位一体”的全球共同体。

二　人类命运共同体与中国智慧

各国都希望给世界打上属于本国的烙印，大国尤然，而且具有更大的可能性。提出自己的主张是实现上述目标的第一步。打造人类命运共同体的主张，既体现了中国传统文化的智慧，也深受革命文化与社会主义建设文化的熏染。

文化包括普遍性成分与特殊性成分。前者使得不同文化间的沟通与共识成为可能，后者体现文化差异性并构成文化特色。中国传统文化一早便拥有“和羹之美，在于合异”的思想与胸怀，儒家文化与道家文化作为中国传统文化的主流，主张“礼”“和而不同”“道法自然”。人类命运共同体理念与之遥相呼应：彼此以礼相待的世界显然是一个有序而和平的世界，奉行“和而不同”理念的国家互为伙伴，个人与国家的发展需要符合生态要求，不同文明都拥有独特魅力和深厚底蕴，相互碰撞交融，各美其美。

中国共产党在革命战争年代，把来自西欧的马克思主义、来自苏联的列宁主义，与中国国情相结合，创造性地提出了“农村包围城市、武装夺取政权”，“统一战线、武装斗争、党的建设”成为中国革命的三大法宝。其中，统一战线思想在我国后来的外交实践中具有特殊指导意义。20 世纪 80 年代，确立了党在社会主义初级阶段的基本路线，为此在外交上确定了独立自主的和平外交路线。这一外交路线在 90 年代演化为“在全球推行伙伴外交”的外交原则。

中国特色社会主义建设文化基于改革开放以来中国发展的经历。在经济社会高速发展的背景下，中国深切体认到构建与强化社会价值观体系的重要性，因此在十八大提出积极培育和践行社会主义核心价值观。这些核心价值观涵盖了个人、国家、社会三个层面，大致上体现了现阶段不同族群、阶层对价值观认知的最大公约数，也体现与折射了全人类共同的文明成果和“共同价值”。而人类命运共同体概念，则是中国反哺世界的表现。

三　人类命运共同体：一种新的外交理念

人类命运共同体作为一种外交理念，与西方的外交理念有着明显不同。世界文化呈现多样性，没有孰是孰非或者高下之分，但有强大硬实力支撑的文化更容易对外产生影响。西方文化在过去几百年里就是一种强势文化，以至于肇始于哥伦布发现新大陆时期的全球化，在相当程度上被等同于西方化，第二次世界大战以后，则被一定程度上等同于美国化。无疑，西方外交理念主导下的全球化以及与之相关的现代化，在多方面具有积极意义，但也存在明显缺陷：其一，民族国家体系的建立，对于发展经济、推动国家现代化起到了巨大的推动作用，但也成为国家间冲突的一大原因，并放大了国家间冲突的规模，两次世界大战就是证明。其二，基督教（以及犹太教、伊斯兰教）所代表的一神论及其彼岸性，对于扩大族群规模、强化族群的文化认同起到了积极作用，但也导致了不同宗教之间发生冲突的概率与冲突的烈度上升，十字军东征是典型案例。其三，西方文化中的二元对立思维、对法治的单一偏好，固然有助于深化人们对自然世界与人类世界的认识，稳定社会秩序、促进商品经济发展，但也强化了人类世界与自然世界以及人类世界内部不同部分之间的鸿沟。这都与外交理念有关。

在西方外交理念的主导下，世界分为“我们”与“他们”，“我们”是进步的、正义的、代表了普遍的价值观和人类的发展方向，"他们"是落后的、非正义的、只能代表特定的价值观，因此，必须被"同化"到西方主导的世界中。这一点在第二次世界大战以前通过战争、殖民、传教等实现。在第二次世界大战后这些方式或者不能用，或者不好用，或者效果不佳，因此，"国际规范"就成了特别有用的手段："我们"主导建立一系列清晰的国际规范（国际制度、国际机构、"国际"成文法，辅之以"国际习惯"法），以此规范、约束、引导"他们"的行动与利益诉求。对于不接受者，则软硬兼施进行制裁、孤立、污名，乃至发动武力"惩罚"。这种外交理念并没有达到预期的效果，反而导致了大量的冲突与局部战争。

人类命运共同体则体现了中国的传统价值取向：世界是"无外"的，即没有"我们"与"他们"的鸿沟，因此，不同文明可以坦然共存。在此前提下，聚焦绿色发展、实现安全共享既是必然的、也是可能的。

因此，人类命运共同体中的成员，是互商互谅的伙伴关系，可以共享安全。不同文明间相互交流但不同质化，没有高下之分。同时，这一主张也吸收了西方文明对平等、正义、合作等因素的强调。可见，人类命运共同体所体现的外交理念、所主张的世界治理方案具有相当的比较优势。

四 人类命运共同体的全球影响

在融入世界体系的过程中，中国经历了三十年的快速发展，综合国力大幅提升，从而得以在2008年世界金融危机后，在全球凸显自己的角色定位，在本地区与全球治理中发挥更大的作用，世界也期待中国承担更大责任。

在和平时期，大国影响世界既需要硬实力也需要软实力，一种能被外界接受的理念主张，既能引导自己的外交行为，也有助于向外扩展自己的硬实力。在人类命运共同体外交理念的指导下，中国通过一系列外交举措落实这一主张，展现中国的大国责任，同时也希望其能为世界所接受、产生浸润性影响，引领世界治理新方向。

"一带一路"倡议是构建人类命运共同体的组成部分。就目前而言，中国属于"有全球影响力的地区大国"，有潜力发展成为"综合性全球大国"。构建人类命运共同体，周边国家与亚欧大陆无疑属于优先方向，这也正是"一带一路"的主要辐射范围。目前已经有100多个国家和国际组织参与到"一带一路"倡议中来，40多个国家和国际组织同中国签署合作协议，20多个国家参与国际产能合作计划。“一带一路”成为中国提出的全球影响力最大的倡议之一。

建立新型大国关系是构建人类命运共同体的重要环节。在“无政府但有秩序”的国际社会中，大国关系一直是国际政治的重要影响因子。中国提出的新型大国关系，特别是中美新型大国关系，主张“不冲突、不对抗、互相尊重、合作共赢”，这一理念普遍为世界各国所接受。此前，奥巴马政府几乎不用“新型大国关系”这一表述，而美国新任国务卿蒂勒森近日来华访问，虽然没有提到“新型大国关系”，却明确以“不冲突、不对抗、相互尊重、合作共赢”来界定中美关系。这表明特朗普政府对“新型大国关系”的接受度高于奥巴马政府。当然，确认这一点还需要持续关注中美关系的走向。

中国为构建人类命运共同体所做的努力也表现在应对气候变化方面。2015年，习近平在气候变化巴黎大会上提出，将于2030年左右使二氧化碳排放达到峰值并争取尽早实现。2016年，中国在联合国总部签署了《巴黎协定》，向国际社会发出了中国愿与各国共同抵御全球变暖的积极而有力的信号，这更是中国践行绿色发展、推动世界构筑绿色发展生态体系的生动实践，展示了中国的大国责任。

五　形塑人类命运共同体所面对的挑战

改革开放以来，中国集中精力谋发展，这是基于对自身发展水平与人口数量的判断，也源于中国自身发展就是对世界的最大贡献，改变自己、影响世界的理念。但是，人类命运共同体作为一种构建人类未来命运的新主张，要被全球主要国家接受，还面临不少挑战。

首先，理论上需要进一步完善。逻辑上的严密与内涵上的清晰事关理论的生命力与影响力。人类命运共同体内“和而不同”的界限是什么？只包括国际社会发展、各国家国际组织的责任和利益，还是也包括国际成员的安危？人类命运共同体是否是大同世界的现代版？如何让不同政治信仰、宗教信仰的群体和谐共处于一个共同体当中？这些都有待于进一步研究。

其次，实践中的操作问题。要引领国际关系新走向，有赖于具体的实践成就。发展可以协同、责任可以分担，利益可以共享，但不同国家、不同文明各自秉持独具特色的政治体制、经济体制、文化认同，如何就政治权利达成共识？如何就经济发展方式和全球化达成共识？如何就人类命运共同体的文化内涵达成共识？这些均需在实践中进一步摸索。

再次，中华文明是一种区域文明，其影响力主要限于中国及其周边。中国的发展道路具有特殊性，中国也强调自己在政治价值观上的独特性，反对普世价值。那么，如何构建一套系统的价值观，在阐述各自发展道路的同时，与“人类命运共同体”的主张协调起来，也值得我们思考。

总之，未来，中国的国际影响力将进一步上升，实现从“有全球影响力的地区大国”向“综合性全球大国”的转变。人类命运共同体的提出，显示了中国的自信与能力：既努力对自己、对世界有所作为，也具有求同存异、和而不同的大国风范。构建人类命运共同体，正是为了找到利益支点，以共同发展让更多人共享美好未来。

Community with a Shared Future for Mankind: A New Solution for Global Governance

Xue Li / China

Director of the International Strategy Division under the Institute of World Economy and Politics at the Chinese Academy of Social Sciences

I. Background for Proposing the Community with a Shared Future for Mankind

Compared with the period from the end of the Cold War to global financial crisis in 2018, the current world pattern presents several new characteristics. **First, the global influence of Western countries has been relatively reduced, while the influence of developing countries has increased.** It is clearly marked by the transformation of the Group of Seven (G7) from the "rich-country club" that discusses global political, economic and cultural issues to the Western great powers forum that focuses on political and social issues. After economic issues have been put aside, it is difficult to reach a consensus on political issues, and it is even more difficult to deal with them. The social issues are slightly less important. This leads to a significantly decreasing amount of attention and influence on the part of the G7.

Second, the contribution of developed countries to the global economy

has declined, while the contribution of emerging economies has significantly increased. The typical sign is that, after great loss to the developed countries by the 2008 global financial crisis, the Group of Twenty (G20) has been upgraded from a meeting of finance ministers to a summit of leaders, becoming a main forum for international economic cooperation. Its main mission is to conduct open and constructive discussion and research on substantial issues between developed countries and emerging market countries, and to seek cooperation and promote international financial stability and sustained economic growth. At the G20 meeting, a consensus is reached on many financial and fiscal issues before submission to relevant international agencies for implementation. Since emerging economies account for a majority of the G20, their specific economic ideas are expected to generate a global influence through this approach and even become a part of international economic rules.

Third, the process of globalization faces setbacks and even the trend of "reverse globalization". The primary task of the GATT and the World Trade Organization is to promote global free trade. However, the Doha Round, which aims at promoting global trade, has not made much progress since its launch in 2001, and has actually fallen into abeyance since 2009. As a matter of fact, many countries have pushed for regional integration. Some developed countries have promoted the implementation of trade protectionism under the banner of "fair trade".

Finally, the global role of China becomes prominent. China's total economic aggregate is ranked second in the world, contributing one-third of the global economic growth. However, China is still at the middle and lower reaches on the whole in the global industrial chain division. The promotion of economic globalization not only complies with the interests of emerging economies, including China, but also conforms to the propositions of industrial sectors of developed countries, such as the service industry and the advanced manufacturing industry. The peaceful rise remains to be China's firm belief and realistic choice.

Against such a background, the report of the 18th National Congress of the Communist Party of China proposed for the first time that "it is necessary to advocate the awareness of the community with a shared future for mankind." Since then, President Xi Jinping has repeatedly stressed the idea of establishing the awareness of the community with a shared future for mankind on a series of important bilateral and multilateral diplomatic occasions, and proposed the joint establishment of the community with a shared future for China-ASEAN, the community with a shared future for China-Pakistan, and the community with a shared future for Asia, etc., showing China's willingness to promote world peace, stability, prosperity and progress by working together with other countries in the world. At the general debate of the 70th UN General Assembly in September 2015, Xi Jinping proposed for the first time to inherit and carry forward the purposes and principles of the UN Charter, develop a new type of international relations centering on win-win cooperation, build a community with a shared future for mankind, and elaborate the following approaches to building that community: establishing a partnership of equal status, mutual negotiation and mutual understanding; setting up a safe pattern of fairness and justice, common construction and sharing; seeking a developmental prospect of openness, innovation, inclusiveness and mutual benefit; promoting a harmonious, diversified and all-embracing cultural exchange; and building an ecological system that respects nature and green development.

It can be seen that building a community with a shared future for mankind is a new global governance solution proposed by China. It aims to create a "five-in-one" global community with politics, security, economics, culture and ecology.

II. Community with a Shared Future for Mankind and Chinese Wisdom

All countries, especially great powers, hope to mark the world with their own national identity. The great powers are more likely to present their own ideas as the first step to attaining the foregoing goal. The idea of building a community with a shared future for mankind is not only an embodiment of the wisdom of traditional

Chinese culture, but it is also deeply influenced by a revolutionary culture and a culture of socialist constructionism.

Culture includes a universal component and a special component. The former makes it possible for there to be communication and consensus among different cultures. The latter reflects cultural differences and includes cultural characteristics. Chinese traditional culture has the ideology and main ingredient of the idea of a “delicious soup is made by combining different ingredients” in the early days. As the mainstream of traditional Chinese culture, Confucian culture and Taoism culture advocate “etiquette”, “harmony in diversity” and “law from nature”. The idea of the community with a shared future for mankind echoes with them: the world where everyone treats each other with due respect is clearly an orderly and peaceful world, countries that pursue the concept of “harmony in diversity” are cooperation partners, and the development of individuals and nations needs to meet ecological requirements; each with a unique charm and a profound background, different civilizations collide with each other and show their beauty respectively.

During the revolutionary war, the Chinese Communist Party combined Marxism from Western Europe and Leninism from the Soviet Union with China’s national conditions, and creatively proposed the road of “encircling the cities from the countryside and seizing political power by the armed forces.” The “united front, armed struggle, and party construction” became the three magical weapons of the Chinese revolution, among which, the idea of the united front had special significance in the later diplomatic practice in China. In the 1980s, the Party established the basic route of the primary stage of socialism. For this reason, an independent peaceful diplomatic policy was formulated in terms of diplomacy. The diplomatic policy evolved into the diplomatic principle of “partnership diplomacy in the world” in the 1990s.

The socialist constructionist culture with Chinese characteristics is based on the experience of China’s development since the reform and opening up. Against the background of rapid economic and social development, China has deeply realized the importance of building and strengthening the social values system. Therefore, the 18th National Congress of the Communist Party of China witnessed the proposal of actively cultivating and implementing socialist core values. Covering the three dimensions of the individual, the country and the society, these core values roughly represent the greatest common denominator of the cognition of values by different ethnic groups and classes at the present stage, and also embody and reflect the achievements of the common civilization and the "common values" of all human beings. The concept of the community with a shared future for mankind is the manifestation of China's feeding the world back.

III. Community with a Shared Future for Mankind: A New Diplomatic Concept

The community with shared future for mankind, as a diplomatic concept, is distinctly different from the Western diplomatic concept. The world cultures show diversity without the distinction between correctness and incorrectness and between superiority and inferiority. However, the cultures with strong hard power are more likely to exert an external influence. Western culture has been a dominant culture in the past few centuries. As a consequence, globalization is considerably equivalent to Westernization after Columbus discovered the new world, but also equivalent to Americanization to some extent after World War II. Undoubtedly, the globalization led by the Western diplomatic concept and its related modernization have positive significance and apparent shortcomings in many aspects: First, the establishment of a nation-state system plays a huge role in promoting economic development and national modernization, but it also becomes a major cause of conflict among nations, and amplifies the scale of those conflicts, as evidenced by the two world wars. Second, the monotheism and its paramitality represented by Christianity (as well as Judaism and Islam) play a positive role in expanding the scale of ethnic groups and strengthening the cultural identity of those groups, but they also lead to the rising probability and intensity of conflicts among different religions, with the Crusades as a typical case. Third, the dualistic opposition and the single preference for the rule of law in Western culture help deepen people's understanding of the natural world and of the human world, stabilize social order and promote the development of a commodity economy, but they also strengthen the gap between the human world and the natural world, and among different parts of the human world. This is related to diplomatic concepts.

Under the leadership of Western diplomatic concepts, the world is divided into "we" and "others". "We" are progressive, just, and represent universal values and a human developmental direction. "Others" are backward, unjust and only represent specific values, and therefore must be "assimilated" into the world dominated by the West. This had been achieved through war, colonialism, and missionary work before World War II. However, these methods could not be used or are not easy to use or ineffective after World War II. Therefore, "international norms" become the particularly useful means: "we" guide the establishment of a series of clear international norms (international systems, international institutions, and "international" statutory law, supplemented by "international customary" law) to regulate, restrict, and guide the actions and interests of "others". Those who do not accept international norms are subject to carrot-and-stick sanctions, isolation, stigma, and even the "penalty" of the use of "force". This diplomatic concept has not achieved the desired results, but it has led to a large number of conflicts and local wars.

The community with a shared future for mankind embodies China's traditional value orientation: the world is "shared" without the gap between "we" and "others". Therefore, different civilizations can coexist calmly. Under this premise, it is inevitable and possible to focus on green development and achieve safe sharing.

Therefore, the members of the community with a shared future for mankind are partners of mutual negotiation and mutual understanding, who can share security. Without the difference between superiority and inferiority, different civilizations communicate with each other and are not homogenized. At the same time, this concept also absorbs the emphasis of Western civilization on equality, justice, and cooperation, etc. It can be seen that the diplomatic concept embodied in the community with a shared future for mankind and the world governance solution advocated have considerable comparative advantages.

IV. Global Influence of the Community with a Shared Future for Mankind

In the process of integration into the world system, China has experienced rapid development for 30 years, and its comprehensive national strength has been greatly improved. This has enabled China to highlight the position of its role in the world after the 2008 global financial crisis and to play a more important role in regional and global governance. The world also expects China to take on greater responsibilities.

In times of peace, the great powers need both hard power and soft power to make an effect on the world. An idea that can be accepted by the outside world can not only guide diplomatic behavior, but also help expand hard power. Under the guidance of the diplomatic concept of the community with a shared future for mankind, China strives to implement the concept through a series of diplomatic measures, demonstrating China's responsibilities as a great power. At the same time, China also hopes that the concept will win the recognition of the world, produce invasive influence, and lead the global direction of new governance.

The "Belt and Road" Initiative is an integral part of building the community with a shared future for mankind. For the time being, China is a "regional great power with a global influence" and has the potential to develop into a "comprehensive global power". To build a community with a shared future for mankind, the priority is undoubtedly given to the neighboring countries and the Asia-Europe continent, which fall precisely into the main scope of radiation of the "Belt and Road" Initiative. So far, more than 100 countries and international organizations have been involved in the Initiative. More than 40 countries and international organizations have signed cooperation agreements with China, and more than 20 countries have participated in international capacity cooperation programs. The "Belt and Road" Initiative has become one of the most influential global initiatives proposed by China.

Building a new type of great power relationship is an important link in building a community with a shared future for mankind. In the "anarchic but orderly" international community, great power relationships have always been a critical factor in international politics. The new type of great power relationship proposed by China, especially the new Sino-American relationship, advocates "no conflict, no confrontation, mutual respect, and win-win cooperation", which have generally been accepted by all countries in the world. Previously, the Obama administration hardly ever used the expression "new type of great power relationship". However, during the recent visit to China, Tillerson, the new U.S. Secretary of State, clearly defined the Sino-American relationship as "no conflict, no confrontation, mutual respect, and win-win cooperation", despite no reference to a "new type of great power relationship". This shows that the Trump administration is more receptive to the "new type of great power relationship" than the Obama administration. To verify this point, we surely still need to constantly pay attention to the trend of Sino-American relation.

The effort of China in building a community with a shared future for mankind is also reflected in its response to climate change. In 2015, Xi Jinping proposed at the Paris Conference on Climate Change that we will make carbon dioxide emissions achieve the peak around 2030 and strive to realize it as soon as possible. In 2016, China signed the *Paris Agreement* at the UN Headquarters. This not only sends the international community the active and powerful signal of China's willingness to work together with other countries to fight against global warming, but it also reflects the practice of China to implement green development and promote the building of a green developmental ecosystem in the world, showing China's responsibility as a great power.

V. Challenges Faced by Shaping the Community with a Shared Future for Mankind

Since the reform and opening up, China has concentrated on the pursuit of development, which is based on the judgment of its own level of development and the number of its population, but it also originates from China's own development as the greatest contribution to the world and the idea of changing itself and influencing the world. However, the community with a shared future for mankind, as a new idea to build the future destiny of mankind, faces many challenges in winning the recognition from major countries in the world.

First of all, further improvement is needed theoretically. The strictness of the logic and the clarity of the connotation concern the vitality and influence of the theory. What is the boundary of "harmony in diversity" in the community with a shared future for mankind? Does it only include the development of the international community, the responsibilities and interests of the international organizations of various countries, or the safety of international members? Is the community with a shared future for mankind a modern version of the world of universal harmony? How can we make different groups of political beliefs and religious beliefs coexist in a community? These issues require further study.

Second, the operation issue in practice. To lead the new direction of international relations depends on concrete achievements in practice. Development can be coordinated, responsibilities can be shared, and benefits can also be shared. However, different countries and civilizations have their own unique political systems, economic systems, and cultural identities. How can a consensus on political rights be reached? How can we reach a consensus on a mode of economic development and globalization? How can we reach a consensus on the cultural connotation of the community with a shared future for mankind? These need to be further explored in practice.

Furthermore, the Chinese civilization is a regional civilization, whose influence is mainly limited to China and its surroundings. China’s path towards development is unique, and China also emphasizes its uniqueness in political values and opposes universal values. So, how can we construct a set of systematic values to coordinate with the concept of “the community with a shared future for mankind” in the elaboration of respective paths towards development? It is worth our consideration.

To sum up, China’s international influence will further increase in the future to successfully achieve the transition from a “regional power with a global influence” to a “comprehensive global power”. The proposal of the community with a shared future for mankind shows China’s self-confidence and ability: strive to make contributions to itself and the world, and seek common ground while reserving differences, and pursue harmony in diversity. To build a community with a shared future for mankind is precisely finding the fulcrum of benefits, thereby allowing more people to share a better future by virtue of common development.

土耳其在“一带一路”倡议中扮演的角色

哈桑·坎波拉特 【土耳其】
安卡拉政策研究中心董事会主席

陕西历史博物馆的大厅门口矗立着一尊石狮雕像，雕像后方是一幅瀑布浮雕。瀑布代表着悠久的中国历史，而狮子则代表着力量与文化。事实上，狮子的形象正是通过丝绸之路由西方传入中国的。

奥斯曼帝国的历代苏丹偏爱中国陶瓷器，因为比起金银器具，陶瓷器不存在中毒的风险。15 世纪初，中国的制瓷理念深深地影响了奥斯曼帝国的陶瓷艺术家，伊斯坦布尔曾一度成为世界第二大中国青白瓷集散地。

在长达数千年的历史长河中，中国从西方所学颇为有限，反倒是中国向西方提供了诸多借鉴。

中土两国都有着悠久的文化传统，都位于同一块大洲，而且两国是近邻。中土两国均为亚洲重要国家，前者位于亚洲最东端，后者位于亚洲最西端。因此，两国间的战略合作对于亚洲的安全稳定具有至关重要的意义。比起土耳其与其他国家的高层次合作，中土两国的战略合作更为独特，不仅成立了联合研究团队，而且制定了应急预案。两国战略合作的宗旨在于，通过高层对话及共同行动来推动两国关系发展。近年来，土—中关系发展迅速，从这个角度来看，中国的维吾尔族与土耳其的伊斯兰教应被视作两国友好关系的共同基础，而不是冲突的来源，双方应该用建构和互补来替代竞争。为了维持和平稳定、维护国家统一、实现民族富强，两国应进一步深化合作。

两国应从长远着眼，倾力打造中—土关系。2002 年，两国双边贸易额达到 16 亿美元，2017 年第一季度增至 280 亿美元。遗憾的是，两国所占贸易额比例极不平衡（1：13），且中国游客数量正在逐渐减少，2015 年达到 10 万人，而在 2016—2017 年间，该数字大幅下降。为此，土中两国各方机构将大力推广“2018 土耳其中国旅游年”。

由于现代丝绸之路的主要线路并不穿过土耳其，因此“一带一路”倡议尚未成为影响两国经济关系的首要因素。此外，横亘两国之间的国家和地区存在安全问题，这给两国的外贸规模造成了一定的限制。

“一带一路”的重要意义不仅局限于中国与欧洲的联通，而是一项包含多个维度、多个层面的宏伟工程。因此，如果土耳其只是中国商品通往西方的“中转站”，两国深化合作的空间会比较有限。所幸的是，中国的一些投资项目极大拓展了两国的合作空间，比如安卡拉—伊斯坦布尔高铁项目、盐湖地下天然气储库项目等。更重要的是，土耳其可以成为中国大宗商品生产基地，从而避免高额运费对中国商品的需求造成限制。

Turkey's Role in the "Belt and Road" Initiative

Hasan Kanbolat / Turkey

Ankara Policy Center, Chairman of the Board

At the entrance of Shaanxi Museum of History, there stands a large statue of lion. Behind the statue of lion, there is a picture of waterfalls. Waterfalls represent long history of China. Lion represents power and culture. The figure of Lion comes from the West through Silk Road.

Ottoman sultans preferred to use Chinese porcelains rather than golden and silver ware, due to fear of toxication. Chinese porcelains affected artistic understanding of Ottoman ceramic artists in the beginning of 15th century. So that, the second largest Chinese blue-white porcelain collection was formed in Istanbul.

Through the thousand years, China has learnt couple of things from the West and the West had learnt so many things from China.

Both Turkey and China has rooted traditions. Both belong to same lands. They are neighbours. Turkey is a great power at the westernmost side of Asia whereas China is the great power at the easternmost-side. Because of that reason, the strategic cooperation between Turkey and China is vital for the security and stability in Asia.

Turkish-Chinese strategic cooperation is unique than most of Turkey's other high level inter-state partnerships. It consists a joint study group and contingency planning for strategic cooperation. It aims to improve relations by high-level meetings and common actions. For last two years, Turkish-Chinese relations have improved swiftly. In this aspect, issues on Uigur and Islam should be considered as common ground for promoting friendship and cooperation, rather than being considered as an axis of tension. Structurism and complementariness should replace competition. For peace, unity, prosperity and stability, both nations should be in more collaboration.

Turkish-Chinese realtion should be elaborated in long perspective. In 2002, the foreign trade volume between two countries was 1.6 billion USD, whereas in the first quarter of 2017, it became 28 billion USD. Unfortunately, the trade between two countries are in against of Turkey with the ratio 1:13. In addition to this, the number of Chinese tourists visiting Turkey has declined from three hundred thousand in 2015, to much less in years between 2016 and 2017. The year of 2018 will be celebrated in China as Turkish Tourism Year.

Turkey doesn't stand on the main route of designated modern silk road. That's why, the role of Silk Road won't be prioritized in developing Turkish-Chinese economic relations. Moreover, most of the countries among Turkey and China pose security issues and insufficient capacity for trading.

"Belt and Road" initiative not only connects China to the West. It is also a multi-dimensional and it has variety of aspects. Because of this, Turkish-Chinese relations cannot be improved only by sending Chinese goods to the West via Turkey. This relation can also be improved with Chinese investment projects like Istanbul-Ankara High Velocity Train, Chinese investment on Salt Lake Natural Gas Refinery. Most of all, what is important is that, the production of heavy and large Chinese goods in Turkey in order to prevent fall of demand upon Chinese products due to freight costs.

中国传统智慧与全球治理

李永辉 【中国】
北京外国语大学国际关系学院院长 / 中国国际关系学会理事

首先，有两点需要说明，第一，这里所说的中国智慧，指的是中国传统智慧，而所谓传统本身，还可以再分为古典传统、近代传统与当代传统，因此，这里要说的更多的是建立在中国几千年历史基础之上的古典传统智慧。第二，中国古代的传统内容十分丰富，不可一概而论，就国家间关系而言，有儒家的理想主义、法家的现实主义、墨家的和平主义、道家的自然主义等。当然，主流是儒家和法家的，关于这一点的最经典、最权威，我认为也是最接近事实的表述是汉宣帝所说的："汉家自有制度，本以霸王道杂之，奈何纯任德教，用周政乎？"这段教训太子的话虽然主要是讲内政的，但也适用于对外政策。因此，对中国古典传统的现代理解有可能产生两个误解，一是过于理想化的儒家理解，只讲和、德、仁这些正面的东西，二是过于现实的法家式的理解，这在当代国际关系学者中比较普遍。事实也许是在两者之间。

传统的中国的东西与现代的世界的东西之间似乎是风马牛不相及的，但这些古老的传统的智慧，也许会对当代世界有重要的启示。

第一，中国传统的国际观是开放的、普世的天下主义，而不是狭隘的民族主义。民族主义起源于近代欧洲，传统中国秉持的是普世主义的天下观。古代中国的所谓夷夏之分，也主要是文化的而非种族的。

南宋哲学家陆象山说："东海有圣人出焉，此心同也，此理同也；西海有圣人出焉，此心同也，此理同也；南海北海有圣人出焉，此心同也，此理同也；千百世之上有圣人出焉，此心同也，此理同也；千百世之下有圣人出焉，此心同也，此理同也。"（《陆九渊集》）

因此，超越吉卜林式的东方与西方的对立，提倡文明对话，寻求心灵的共振点。建立人类命运共同体，应该成为我们共同的追求。

第二，张弛有度的发展节奏。《礼记》里面记载了孔子与他的学生子贡的一段对话，当时他们在看祭礼（狂欢节，那时候中国人是比较开放的），孔子问子贡说："赐（子贡的名字）也乐乎？"子贡答道："一国之人皆若狂，赐未知其乐也。"孔子说："张而不弛，文武弗能也；弛而不张，文武弗为也；一张一弛，文武之道也。"（《礼记·杂记下》）当前我们面临的全球治理的一大问题是，自 20 世纪 70 年代以来的这一轮全球化的无节制的扩张及其不可持续。因此，我们需要更加平衡的经济发展、全球化与全球治理。同时，我想，这也是理解中国发展的文化密码之一。当前，中国的经济发展也在经历这样的转型，即从过于强调经济发展到注重更加平衡的发展。

第三，天人合一，实现人与自然和谐的可持续发展。可持续发展是当今世界的重要发展理念，也是世界各国的共识，巴黎气候变化大会通过的《巴黎协定》就是很好的证明。

中国传统文化强调人与自然的和谐，这在道家的思想中表现得最为突出，儒家也讲天人合一。这些思想无论是对于中国自身的发展，还是对全世界的可持续发展，都有十分重要的意义，也是中国对世界的重要思想贡献。

第四，由内及外。两年前，新加坡李显龙总理在拉惹勒南讲座上阐述新加坡的外交哲学时指出，要用修齐治平的道理，他形容这是永恒的智慧结晶（a timeless piece of wisdom）。对一个人而言，修身是最根本的事，由此推之，对一个国家而言，根本就是在搞好内政，内政是外交之本，缺少坚实的内政做后盾，就谈不上推行成功的外交政策。

第五，王道与国际秩序。王道是一种制度安排和价值体系。当今世界正面临权力转移与格局转型，在国际秩序的变革中，王道思想可以提供文化资源。这样说并不是要重建传统的王道，实际上，王道是时代的产物，是周公所创立的周王朝的价值体系与制度安排的体现。随着周王室的衰微，王道作为一种政治秩序已不复存在，在孔子的时代已经无法恢复，更不要说今天了。也不是要恢复所谓的华夷秩序或所谓朝贡体系。今天，这也是不可能的。但如果我们将其理解为道德价值和某种道义合法性，还是有其现实意义的。在国家层面上，王道可以被理解为软实力。

王道思想所提倡的天下体系与西方国家所构建的现代主权国家体系最大的不同是：王道思想认为国际社会本来就存在强弱与尊卑间的不对等，对此不能视而不见，反而要正视其道德意涵。因此，王道思想强调，对强者、居上位者应该负有更高的道德责任，居上位者要修德文、以大事小、多予少取、济弱扶倾、薄来厚往。用今天的话来说，就是要承担国际责任，提供公共产品。这也反映在习近平主席提倡的基于这一传统智慧的正确的义利观之中。

Chinese Traditional Wisdom and Global Governance

Li Yonghui / China

Director of the School of International Relations and Diplomacy at Beijing Foreign Studies University, Council Member of the China National Association for International Studies

First of all, there are two points to be explained. First, the Chinese wisdom described here refers to Chinese traditional wisdom, and the so-called tradition itself can be divided into classical tradition, modern tradition and contemporary tradition. Therefore, what we want to talk more about here is the classical traditional wisdom based on thousands of years of the history of China. Second, the traditional content of ancient China is very rich, and it cannot be generalized. In terms of relations among countries, there are Confucian idealism, Legalist realism, Mohist pacifism, Taoist naturalism, and so on. Of course, the mainstream is Confucianism and Legalism. With respect to this, the most classic and authoritative, which I think is the closest to the fact, is what Emperor Xuan of the Han Dynasty said: "The Han Dynasty has its own system; we govern the country with the combination of Confucianism and Legalism. How can our country be governed by pure Confucianism? Isn't it naïve to implement the political system of the Zhou Dynasty which has perished?" Although this paragraph targeted the prince, mainly on internal affairs, it was also applicable to the foreign policy. Therefore, there may be two misunderstandings regarding the modern understanding of Chinese classical tradition; one is the overly idealized understanding of Confucianism, which only focuses on positive aspects, such as harmony, virtue and benevolence. The second is the too realistic and legalist understanding, which is common among the scholars of contemporary international relations. The truth may lie between the two.

Traditional, Chinese aspects and global modern aspects seem to be unrelated to each other; however, these ancient traditional wisdoms may have some important enlightenment for the contemporary world.

First, China's traditional international outlook is an open and universal cosmopolitanism rather than a narrow nationalism.

Nationalism originated in modern Europe. Traditional China holds the view of universal cosmopolitanism. In ancient China, the so-called division of Yi and Xia was mainly cultural rather than racial.

Lu Xiangshan, a philosopher of the Southern Song Dynasty, said: "If there is a saint in the East China Sea, he will share the same morality and ethics; if there is a saint in the West China Sea, he will share the same morality and ethics; if there are saints in the South China sea and the North China Sea, they will also share the same morality and ethics; if there were saints thousands of years ago, they would share the same morality and ethics; if there are saints thousands of years later, they will also share the same morality and ethics." (*Collection of Works of Lu Jiuyuan*)

Therefore, we should transcend Kipling's opposition between the East and the West, advocate dialogue between civilizations and seek the the soul's point of resonance. The establishment of a community of a shared future for mankind should be our common pursuit.

Second, it is the proper pace of development. *The Book of Rites* contains a dialogue between Confucius and his student Zigong. When they were watching the sacrificial rites (a kind of carnival; the Chinese people at that time was very open-minded), Confucius asked Zigong: “Ci (the name of Zigong), are you happy too?” Zigong replied: “Even if the people of the whole country are crazy happy, I don’t know what they are happy about.” Then Confucius said: “As far as governing the country is concerned, if you keep on straining tightly without relaxation, even the Emperor Wen and Emperor Wu of the Zhou Dynasty could not do that; if you keep relaxing without tension, even the Emperor Wen and Emperor Wu of the Zhou Dynasty would not do that. Tension and relaxation is the approach of governing a country adopted by Emperor Wen and Emperor Wu of the Zhou Dynasty.” (*The Book of Rites · Miscellany II*). One of the major problems we are facing regarding global governance at present is this round of unrestrained expansion and unsustainability of globalization since the 1970s and the 1980s. Therefore, we need more balanced economic development, globalization and global governance. At the same time, I think this is also one of the cultural codes through which one can understand China’s development. At present, China’s economic development is undergoing such a transformation from overemphasizing economic development to a more balanced development.

Third, the harmony between man and nature means to achieve the harmonious development of man and nature. Sustainable development is an important concept of development in today’s world and the consensus of all countries across the globe. The *Paris Agreement*, adopted by the Paris Conference on Climate Change, is good proof.

Chinese traditional culture emphasizes the harmony between man and nature, which is most prominent in Taoist thought. Confucianism also stresses the unity of heaven and man. These ideas are of great significance to the development of China itself and for the sustainable development of the whole world. It is also the important ideological contribution of China to the world.

Fourth, it is from inside to outside. Two years ago, Li Xianlong, Prime Minister of Singapore, described Singapore's diplomatic philosophy in a lecture at the Rajaratnam School of International Studies, pointing out the importance of using the principle of self-cultivation, family harmony, country management and world peace; he described it as a timeless piece of wisdom. For an individual, cultivating one's moral character is the most fundamental thing. For a country, it is fundamental to do a good job in internal affairs, and the internal affairs are the basis of diplomacy. Without a solid stable internal political environment as the backup force, we are not eligible to talk about conducting a successful foreign policy.

Fifth, it is the kingcraft and the international order. Kingcraft is an institutional arrangement and system of values. Nowadays, the world is facing power transfer and pattern transformation. In the transformation of international order, kingcraft thoughts can provide cultural resources. This is not to rebuild traditional kingcraft. In fact, kingcraft is the product of the times. It is the embodiment of the system of values and the institutional arrangement of the Zhou Dynasty founded by the Emperor Zhou. With the decline of the Zhou royal family, kingcraft ceased to exist as a political order. It cannot be restored in the era of Confucius, let alone today, nor is it necessary to restore the so-called Sino-foreign system or the so-called tributary system. It is not possible today. However, if we regard it as moral value and some moral legitimacy, it still has its practical significance. At the national level, kingcraft can be understood as soft power.

The biggest difference between the world system advocated by kingcraft and the system of a modern sovereign state constructed by Western countries is: Kingcraft advocates that there originally exists inequality between the strong and the weak and the superiors and the inferiors, so we could not turn a blind eye to it. Instead, we should face up to its moral meaning. Therefore, kingcraft thoughts stress that the powerful and high-ranking people should shoulder more moral responsibilities. People with high positions should cultivate themselves in morals and culture, bear in mind the overall interests, give more and ask for less, and help the weak and aid the needy. In today's words, it refers to assuming international responsibility and providing public goods. Kazan Stan: surface inequality and fact equality, superficial equality and de facto inequality. It also reflects the correct concept of righteousness and profit advocated by President Xi Jinping based on this traditional wisdom.

“一带一路”倡议：以中国软实力促全球发展

贝赫扎得·沙哈德 【伊朗】
德黑兰大学荣休教授

两千多年前，在西汉使臣张骞的帮助下，中国开辟了一条连接中亚与西亚的商贸之路——“丝绸之路”。“丝绸之路”得名于丝绸，中国最主要的出口商品。在随后的两百多年里，沿线区域一直受到丝绸之路的影响。

2013 年，中国国家主席习近平提出建设现代丝绸之路的倡议，即“一带一路”倡议，通过连接沿线 60 个国家、6 条走廊，实现中国与中亚、西亚以及南亚部分区域的联通。所谓“联通”并不局限于地理意义上的相通。

经过三年的倾力打造，“一带一路”倡议已经进入更加细化、更加全面的发展阶段。各方将通力合作，构建六大经济走廊，包括新亚欧大陆桥、中蒙俄、中国–中亚–西亚、中国–中南半岛、中巴以及孟中印缅六条线路。通过铁路、公路、水路、石油管道、信息高速公路的联通，六大经济走廊将成为六条能源工业带。

中国希望通过新丝绸之路实现沿线国家的联通、提高各国生产力，从而促进互利合作、增进友好关系。

“一带一路”倡议的宗旨在于打造世界上最大的合作平台，包括经济合作、政策联通、经贸金融合作、社会与文化交流等各个层面。

倡议提出后，沿线 60 多个国家（GDP 总额高达 21 万亿美元）均对参与“一带一路”倡议的行动计划表现出兴趣。

目前，各方的努力已经取得一定成效。中国与匈牙利、蒙古、俄罗斯、塔吉克斯坦以及土耳其等国签署了双边合作协议，一大批工程即将上马，其中包括连接中国东部沿海（义乌）、途径伊朗并通往欧洲的铁路线（首次班列已经抵达伊朗，从义乌至德黑兰，运送货物只需要平时的一半时间）此外还包括连接老挝、泰国的铁路项目。

目前，宁波航运交易所正与波罗的海交易所共同开发中国—地中海—中东—欧洲航运线路的集装箱运价指数。200多家企业签署了参与“一带一路”沿线项目的合作协议。

据估计，“一带一路”累计投资总规模或高达6万亿美元。

“一带一路”倡议致力于弥合亚洲各国在基础设施建设水平上的差异，未来十年内的资金需求高达9000亿美元。这意味着亚洲基础设施建设所需资金还存在50%的缺口。

中国于2015年宣布，投资总额超1万亿人民币（1600亿美元）的基础设施工程正相继上马或即将提上日程。亚投行成立后，初始资本达到1000亿美元，其中75%来自亚洲及大洋洲，中国拥有26%投票权，成为亚投行第一大股东。

自邓小平[1]时期掀起改革开放浪潮以来，中国经济形通过基础设施建设实现了持续快速的发展，形成了独特的中国模式。正如“世界养老基金委员会”（WPC）的学者指出，“一带一路”是中国经济发展模式走向世界的必然结果。这一倡议最终将重塑欧洲经济格局，乃至改变整个世界的经济秩序。

中国“一带一路”的真正价值在于软实力的提升。新丝绸之路的两条线路，丝绸之路经济带以及21世纪海上丝绸之路，均通过基础设施建设实现中国与欧洲、中亚、波斯湾、南亚以及非洲的联通，其目的在于推动丝绸之路沿线国家的自由贸易和经济发展。

因此，“一带一路”倡议是一种双赢战略，能够将中国在过去三十年中取得的改革成就和经济奇迹推广至世界各国。

“一带一路”所面临的挑战在于，推广中国模式是一项浩大而艰巨的工程，涉及各国众多私人企业和国有企业，正如经济学家智库2016年年度报告中所示，“一带一路”沿线的65个国家均存在不同程度的政治风险，合作伙伴国的社会稳定性各有差异……高速铁路等工程现今仍然处于规划和招标阶段，尚未产生预期

1 中国改革开放的总设计师。自改革开放以来，中国创造了当代历史上前所未有的社会经济发展奇迹。

的效益。连接东南亚、柬埔寨、老挝、缅甸、泰国、马来西亚以及新加坡的铁路线便是例证。泰国等国家已经表示愿意承担修筑成本，但目前中国尚未提供相应的技术支持。

由于基础设施工程耗时较长，政治格局的变换会带来种种风险，导致各方无法按照既定协议向前推进。政治的不确定性会造成项目延迟，例如，对于投资总额高达 460 亿的中巴经济走廊项目而言，可能面临的风险包括恐怖主义、极端主义等难以调和的政治难题。新建交通线路涉及 1500 名职员，巴基斯坦能否保证线路安全及员工的人身安全？自印度和巴基斯坦取得独立后，两国的冲突一直持续不断，有鉴于此，新建线路只能避开敏感区域。

尽管在实施“一带一路”过程中会遇到重重困难与挑战，但这并不意味着沿线项目会失去持续推进的动力。需要强调的是，“一带一路”倡议的真正价值在于为国际社会带来共同利益、扫清政治分歧、改善沿线各国之间的关系。

正如查塔姆学会于 2017 年发表的一份报告所示，尽管“一带一路”倡议可能遭遇重重挑战，然而鉴于中国软实力的不断提升，新兴经济体均对该倡议表现出相似的热情，因此中国取得成功的可能性很大。

“丝绸之路”本身便是软实力的某种隐喻，它象征着昔日的辉煌、开放、联通以及和平贸易。

“一带一路”倡议强调的软实力曾在前任主席胡锦涛执政期间得到反复强调，在中国政治议程中占有重要地位。软实力的核心在于“联通性”，这与目前基于地缘政治和伙伴关系的概念、原则、规则形成鲜明的对比，能够为中国带来明显的战略优势。这也解释了为何 34 个国家均与中国签署了合作协议。

亚洲正迅速变成世界政治中心和经济中心，而中国已经成为全球经济增长的引擎。中国的中产阶级人数由 2000 年的 500 万激增至 2.5 亿，这是当代历史中前所未有的巨大跨越。

通过“一带一路”的实施，参与国能够吸取中国经验、复制中国的成功模式。2017 年，中国对外直接投资额高达 1830 亿美元，这恰恰证明了中国对于发展全球经济的决心。此外，中国外汇储备高达 3.3 万亿美元，位居世界第一，这充分说明中国已经成为世界经济增长的引擎。然而中国在寻求国家富强的同时，并没有忘记与世界其他区域——那些国家安全系于经济状况的国家——分享成功经验。对于中国而言，国家关系的本质在于开放与交流，在于通过互利合作推动全球经济发展。

丝路基金初始规模为400亿美元，加上亚投行的法定资本金1000亿美元，总计1400亿美元，这为“一带一路”建设提供了撬动更多资金的杠杆，确保为“一带一路”沿线国家和地区提供资金支持，为世界经济增长带来新动能。

与此同时，“一带一路”倡议也被视做亚洲为实现东西方的联通所做出的努力。仅在2015年，中国发往欧洲的货运班列便高达815列（作为中国与欧洲的中转站，伊朗自然会喜不自胜）

国际产能合作是“一带一路”倡议的一大亮点，因为过剩产能可以分配到“一带一路”沿线国家。其中“六大经济走廊”沿线国家的GDP占据世界30%，具有强大的产能消化能力。

除此之外，中国正与美国和欧盟商讨三边协议（中国与欧盟的合作正稳步推进，但由于特朗普政府采取孤立主义立场，中美合作尚无进展），与非洲、拉美进一步深化合作，尽管两者都不是“一带一路”沿线国家，但却能让中国的影响力超越国界、走向全球。这正是世界大国所独有的特征。

中国经济取得的成就、创造的增长奇迹都为“一带一路”倡议的成功奠定了基础，增强了世界各国“复制中国成功模式”的信心。

“一带一路”注重国家与国家之间的联通，而不是全球性的规则，贸易和经济的持续增长是推进“一带一路”工程的主要动力。未来的合作将会扩展至光纤和电信领域，涉及贸易便利化及货币政策协调等多个方面。这会进一步促进沿线国家之间的合作。

曾被一些国家视为“空谈”的“一带一路”倡议已然明显表现出成功的迹象，尽管在实施过程中会遇到更多挑战。中国开发银行与中国进出口银行在工业、基础设施建设、能源、贸易融资以及金融服务等领域提供了强有力的资金支持。

如前文所述，中国正在加紧步伐提高自身软实力，以每年100亿左右的成本促进国家软实力的提升，通过海外新闻机构以及孔子学院推动文化交流、促进国家之间的对话。“一带一路”是中国政府的长期性规划，为了推进该规划的实施，中国不惜斥资万亿，在全球范围内兴建铁路、公路网等基础设施。第二次世界大战后，沦为废墟的欧洲通过马歇尔计划实现了复兴，而“一带一路”的规模及意义远远超越了马歇尔计划。

The "Belt and Road" Initiative: Chinese Soft Power Initiative for Global Development

Behzad Shahandeh / Iran

Professor Emeritus, Tehran University

More than 2000 years ago China's imperial envoy Zhang Qian helped to establish the "Silk Road", a network of trade routes that linked China to Central Asia and West Asia. The name came from China's most important export- silk, the road itself influenced the development of the entire region for hundreds of years.

In 2013 China's President Xi Jinping proposed establishing a modern equivalent of the Silk Road, networks linking China to Central Asia, West Asia and parts of South Asia. "One Belt One Road" (Yi Dai Yi lu) as the name prescribed for the initiative , specifically aims at creating a network of development across six corridors encompassing 60 countries- comprising more than physical connection.

Three years in the making, "Belt and Road" Initiative has entered a new stage of more detailed and comprehensive development. The work will see the development of six major economic corridors including the "New Eurasian Land Bridge"– China-Mongolia-Russia-Central Asia-Western Asia, Indo-china Peninsula, China-

Pakistan- Bangladesh, China- India-Myanmar. These corridors will be the sites of energy industrial clusters and will be created through the use of rail, roads, waterways, oil pipelines and information highways.

By both connecting and enhancing the productivity of countries along the new Silk Road, China hopes the benefits of cooperation can be shared and the circle of friendship can be strengthened and expanded.

“Belt and Road” Initiative aims to create the world’s largest platform for economic cooperation, including policy coordination, trade and financing, and social and cultural cooperation.

More than 60 countries with a combined GDP of 21 trillion US dollars have expressed interests in participating in “Belt and Road” Initiative action plan.

The efforts have already made some practical achievements. China has signed bilateral cooperation agreements with Hungry, Mongolia, Russia, Tajikistan and Turkey. A number of projects are underway, including a train connection between Eastern China (Yiwu) and Iran that is planned to be extended to Europe (the train from Yiwu arrived in Tehran in half time it usually took for merchandise to reach Iran. There are also new rail links to Laos, Thailand, and high-speed rail projects in Indonesia.

China’s Ningbo Shipping Exchange is collaborating with the Baltic Exchange on a container index of rates between China- Mediterranean- the Middle East – and Europe. More than 200 enterprises have signed cooperation agreements for projects along “Belt and Road” Initiative, routes.

The accumulative anticipated investment over indefinite time scale is estimated at 6 trillion US dollars.

“Belt and Road” Initiative aims to bridge the infrastructure gap of Asia(less China) needing over 900 billion US dollars over the next ten years. This means that there is a 50% shortfall in infrastructure spending in the Asia continent.

As of 2015, China announced that over one trillion Yuan

(160 billion US dollars) of infrastructural projects were in planning or construction. The Asian Infrastructure Investment Bank has authorized an initial capital of 100 billion US dollars – 75% of which will come from Asia and Oceania. China will be the largest stake holder with 26% of voting rights.

The crux of the matter as the "World Pension Council"(WPC) experts have argued, is that the "Belt and Road" initiative constitutes a natural international extension of the infrastructure –driven economic development framework that has sustained the rapid economic growth of China since the adoption of the Chinese economic reform under Deng Xiaoping, which could eventually reshape the Eurasian economic continuum and more generally the international economic order.

China's "Belt and Road" Initiative real value rests with soft power. The two routes: Silk Road Economic Belt and the 21st Century Maritime Silk Road link China to Europe via Central Asia – Persian Gulf , South Asia and Africa, through building infrastructure and networks , high speed train , university backup (Xi'an Jiaotong University), with the main aim of boosting free trade and development en route Silk Road.

The initiative has been branded as a win –win project duplicating Chinese great success of reforms in its three decade of miracle development.

The challenge for "Belt and Road" Initiative as massive transformation of the new Silk Road akin to Chinese model is the difficulties beset by all similar projects. The vastness of the initiative with numbers of private, public and international institutions involved is the main obstacle in implementing the huge undertaking. As pointed out by 2016 annual report of Economist Intelligence Unit, connections are rather tenuous since 65 countries involved in the initiative bring the baggage of their own political risks, the stability of partners involved and … large proportion of projects remaining in planning and tendering stage, like for example high –speed rail projects, which are yet to produce concrete developments envisioned. A visible example is the rail link with Southeast Asia crawling through Cambodia, Laos, Myanmar, Thailand, Malaysia and Singapore. Some like Thailand have agreed to bear the costs, but technology from China must arrive which has yet to be realized.

As infrastructure projects are time consuming, risks are accompanied with the change as the political climate forces its way to affect the implementations of the agreed agendas. The delays arising out of political uncertainties as for example the carrying out of China-Pakistan Economic corridor, a giant 46 billion US dollars undertaking confronted with terrorism, extremism and political challenges are obstacles to be reckoned with. Can Pakistan maintain security of the new transportation routes with 1500 personnel involved? The routes bypass sensitive territories with India raising protest to its construction. There have been three conflicts between Pakistan and India since independence of the two states in South Asia ...

The difficulties and challenges lurk behind the initiation of “Belt and Road” Initiative, but that does not mean that “Belt and Road” Initiative will be crowded by them and lose its momentum. It must be stressed that “Belt and Road” Initiative real value and benefit is the international clout it stands to gain as it attempts to spearhead international policy and improves relations with “Belt and Road” Initiative partner countries.

In the recent Chatham House report published in 2017, it is dully stated that China’s soft power push with emerging economies grappling with similar aspirations towards deployments of the initiative is likely to succeed amid all the difficulties that will and could arise.

The metaphor of Silk Road is itself a sort of soft power, conjuring images of the past age, openness, connectivity, and peaceful trade.

The “Belt and Road” Initiative stressing on soft power as stated by former

President Hu Jintao back in 2007 with soft power occupying an important position in China's agenda, relies on connectivity with clear strategic advantages for China. This contrasts sharply with existing treaty-based concepts where geographical scope, partner countries, strategy, principles and rules are clearly defined at the outset. Thirty four countries have already signed cooperation agreements with China.

Asia is rapidly becoming the world's political and economic gravity. China middle class comprising five million people back in 2000 has been boosted to 250 million people, a giant leap not seen in contemporary history.

"Belt and Road" Initiative banks on the success of China abound with experiences that can be duplicated by the partner countries and communities. Outbound direct investments reaching 183 billion US dollars in 2017 is just an example of Chinese persistence in developing global economy. The recent recovery of the Chinese economy with the foreign assets of the country topping 3.3 trillion US dollars as the world's number one holder of these assets is another testimony that China can indeed become the vehicle for world's growth. This clout has furthered China's desire in seeking to establish its identity as world power bent on sharing its success with the rest of the world where security dependent on economic well-being has become the stand for all. The Chinese vision of major power relations where it is equal to other great powers opens up more activities for China to enhance its desire to pursue its global development agendas with "Belt and Road" Initiative as its engine.

Forty billion US dollars Silk Road Fund to be increased one hundred billion US dollars as "Belt and Road" Initiative gains momentum has been staked out to leverage the eventual one trillion and four hundred billion US dollars envisioned for the overhauling the designated "Belt and Road" Initiative operations.

China's grand plan though depicted by some as Asian endeavor looks both to the East and West. In 2015 alone, 815 freight trains from China reached Europe.

International capacity cooperation is the catch word for "Belt and Road" Initiative, whereby some manufacturing capacity (excess capacity) is being relocated to "Belt and Road" Initiative partner countries in the "Six Economic Belt" comprising two-third of world populace with 30% of GDP and world consumption.

To add to the above endeavors, China is going in for tri-lateral agreements with the United States and the European Union (the cooperation with the latter is gaining momentum due to US isolationist postures under president Donald Trump) in Africa and Latin America, where its interests are not directly involved but giving it a global reach and influence beyond its immediate borders- the hallmark of a global power.

The "Belt and Road" Initiative has the Chinese economic viability, "exceptionalism" of China's growth story with the firm believe that its success can be re-duplicated across the globe.

China sees connectivity rather than global rules leading to increased trade and continuing growth as the main driver of "Belt and Road" Initiative .The areas of cooperation in future will consist of fiber optics, telecommunications, trade facilitations, monetary policy coordination…which will raise the stakes for collaborations along the "New Silk Road".

The success of "Belt and Road" Initiative which some decline as mere talking shop is clearly visible given all the difficulties it has faced and will face in future. The first and foremost is the institutional link of China Development Bank(CDB) and the Export –Import Bank of China (Cexim) with "Belt and Road" Initiative in the field of industry, infrastructure, energy , trade finance and financing services.

As dully stressed above, China has stepped up its soft power offensive. China is now spending around 10 billion US dollars annually on a plan to boost its global soft power. The efforts include the expansion of China's foreign language media abroad, establish more Confucius Institutes and promote culture as a vehicle of dialogue. "Belt and Road" Initiative fits into this as Beijing aims in spending some 1 trillion US dollars to create vast network of road and rail infrastructure across the globe. "Belt and Road" Initiative in its spending is larger than the famed Marshall Plan which rescued Europe from the ruins of World War Two.

“一带一路”倡议和行动为全球治理树立了一个积极的榜样

邵峰 【中国】
中国社会科学院世界经济与政治研究所国际战略研究室研究员、硕士生导师

随着全球化的深入进展给人类社会的未来发展带来了严峻的挑战。为此，国际社会提出了全球治理的概念和理论，形成了学术界的持久热点之一。然而，由于全球问题的性质复杂，造成了公用地的悲剧与集体行动的困境两种现象。[1] 在实践中，全球治理总是雷声大雨点小，国际社会面对多种挑战似乎显得无从下手或者力不从心。在这种情况下，习主席提出的“一带一路”倡议和稳步推进，可以说是为全球治理树立了一个榜样。

习主席在“一带一路”高峰论坛的主旨演讲中把这些国际关系的无情现实总结为“三大赤字”，即和平赤字、发展赤字、治理赤字，是摆在全人类面前的严峻挑战。为此，习主席提出了明确的解决方案，即通过“一带一路”倡议实现政策沟通、设施联通、贸易畅通、资金融通、民心相通，构建以合作共赢为核心的新型国际关系，实现共同繁荣。

一　“一带一路”倡议是对全球治理模式的创新

在全球治理理论中，根据治理主体在国际体系中的不同地位，一般可分为三种不同的治理模式：一是国家中心治理模式，即以主权国家为主要治理主体的治

1　王小民:《全球问题与全球治理》，载《东南亚研究》，2004 年第 4 期。

理模式。具体地说，就是主权国家在彼此关注的领域，出于对共同利益的考虑，通过协商、谈判而相互合作，共同处理问题，进而产生一系列国际协议或规制。二是有限领域治理模式，即以国际组织为主要治理主体的治理模式。具体地说，就是国际组织针对特定的领域（如经济、环境等领域）开展活动，使相关成员国之间实现对话与合作，谋求实现共同利益。三是网络治理模式，即以非政府组织为主要治理主体的治理模式。

然而，全球治理在理论和实践中存在很大的局限，由于利益、力量、地位、战略的不同，以及国际权威的缺乏导致的国际社会无政府状态，难以达成治理主体的一致集体行动。作为最重要治理主体的国家是力有余而心不齐，而其他的治理主体是心有余而力不足。

中国的“一带一路”倡议，大致可以归为国家中心治理模式的范畴，但是在设计和组织运作上却具有重大的开创性意义，也可以说是一种对全球治理模式的创新。这个创新体现在两个方面：首先，以一个负责任的大国为核心倡议者和推动者，同时欢迎和争取所有具有参与意愿的国家参与进来，并一直保持非排他性和开放性，秉承共商、共建、共享的原则，以和平合作、开放包容、互学互鉴、互利共赢的丝绸之路精神为指引，以打造命运共同体和利益共同体为合作目标，更好造福有关各国人民。其次，如李向阳教授所指出的，如果说其他国际合作机制更多的是以规则为导向，那么“一带一路”倡议则是以发展为导向，倾向于在发展的过程中探讨双边或多边更多新的合作可能性。[1]

有学者认为，“和谐世界”论的提出为陷入理论和实践困境的全球治理论开辟了另一条反思的蹊径。当今全球问题的关键不在于建构某种全球共同价值观，而在于如何达成求同存异的全球共识。相比全球治理论的高深和理想，和谐世界论显得更为务实，内涵也更为丰富。全球治理论主张价值共识是基本，而和谐世界论则求同存异，认识到不同并给予包容，不强求形成一致的价值观，确实为我们解决当前全球问题提供了一个很好的认识平台。我们可以把“和谐世界”看作中国对于“全球治理”理论的一种官方理论回应。[2]

习主席提出的“一带一路”战略倡议，应该说是对胡锦涛主席提出的“和谐世界”理论的进一步深化和具体实践，体现了中国外交的继承性、一致性和与时

1　陈湖：《专家：“一带一路”建设不划小圈子、不走寻常路》，中国新闻网，2017 年 4 月 27 日，http://www.chinanews.com/cj/2017/04-27/8210181.shtml。

2　陈承新：《国内“全球治理”研究述评》，载《政治学研究》，2009 年第 1 期。

俱进、不断创新的品质。

二 习主席为“一带一路”倡议和全球治理提出了重要的指导思想

习近平主席多次提出，人类已经成为你中有我、我中有你的命运共同体，“一带一路”倡议以共赢为目标，核心理念是共商、共建、共享，并总结出和平合作、开放包容、互学互鉴、互利共赢为核心的丝路精神。

2016 年 4 月 29 日，习主席在中共中央政治局第三十一次集体学习时的讲话中指出：“一带一路”倡议，唤起了沿线国家的历史记忆。古代丝绸之路是一条贸易之路，更是一条友谊之路。在中华民族同其他民族的友好交往中，逐步形成了以和平合作、开放包容、互学互鉴、互利共赢为特征的丝绸之路精神。在新的历史条件下，我们提出“一带一路”倡议，就是要继承和发扬丝绸之路精神，把中国发展同沿线国家发展结合起来，把中国梦同沿线各国人民的梦想结合起来，赋予古代丝绸之路以全新的时代内涵。

2017 年 1 月 18 日，习主席在联合国日内瓦总部发表题为《共同构建人类命运共同体》的演讲，回答了“世界怎么了、我们怎么办”这一困扰世界的问题。习主席说：“在‘一带一路’建设国际合作框架内，各方秉持共商、共建、共享原则，携手应对世界经济面临的挑战，开创发展新机遇，谋求发展新动力，拓展发展新空间，实现优势互补、互利共赢，不断朝着人类命运共同体方向迈进。这是我提出这一倡议的初衷，也是希望通过这一倡议实现的最高目标。”“一带一路”就是中国为解决当前世界面临问题和挑战而提供的一条解决之道、破局之道。

中国外交部前副部长何亚非认为，习主席的讲话为解决全球化的发展带来的问题和挑战提出了重要的指导思想。中共十八大以来，习主席针对全球治理提出了一系列新的思想。从 2013 年秋提出的“一带一路”倡议，到中国更加重视多边主义、支持 G20 成为全球治理的首要平台，再到提出全球伙伴关系而不是相互对抗的军事同盟，以及共同构建人类命运共同体。习主席在“一带一路”论坛的系列讲话，从现实、历史两个维度给出了中国对今后世界发展方向的看法，特别是对全球治理观念提出了创新的看法。“和平合作、开放包容、互学互鉴、互利共赢”，这就是中国为新的全球化给出的指导思想。

从习主席的讲话我们可以深切地体会到，中国政府对全球治理的思想已逐步形成了一套系统的方案，对今后世界的发展和全球治理具有重要的理论和现实意义。

三 “一带一路”倡议为经济全球化和自由贸易拓展了新的路径和空间

“一带一路”倡议的理论基础并不复杂，也没有标新立异，仍然是国际贸易的核心理论即自由贸易理论，其核心主张就是自由贸易可使参与贸易的双方均获得贸易利益。“一带一路”倡议的宗旨之一就是致力于维护全球自由贸易体系和开放型世界经济。4 年来，“一带一路”建设从无到有，从理念变为行动，由点成线，由线及面，改变了全球经济合作的方式，开拓了国际合作新空间。

习主席讲，这是贸易畅通不断提升的 4 年。中国同“一带一路”参与国大力推动贸易和投资便利化，不断改善营商环境。2014 年至 2016 年，中国同“一带一路”沿线国家贸易总额超过 3 万亿美元。中国对“一带一路”沿线国家投资累计超过 500 亿美元。我们要打造开放型合作平台，维护和发展开放型世界经济，共同创造有利于开放发展的环境，推动构建公正、合理、透明的国际经贸投资规则体系，促进生产要素有序流动、资源高效配置、市场深度融合。

当前全球化面临诸多挑战，可以说是站在一个十字路口，面对两股不同力量的作用。一股是将它向后拉的保护主义力量，尤其是某些发达国家贸易保护主义、孤立主义等倾向加剧，使经济全球化的不确定性上升；另一股则是继续坚持自由化的力量，以西方国家的有识之士和新兴市场国家为主要代表。当美国表现出逆全球化的态势后，很多继续支持全球化的国家期待着中国能够在全球治理中发挥更多、更大的作用。

“一带一路”倡议的提出和实践，为经济全球化和自由贸易拓展了新的路径和空间。

首先，“一带一路”倡导的开放、包容、非排他性等新理念和丝路精神为经济全球化增添了新的平台和新的活力。

习主席在讲话中提出了和平合作、开放包容、互学互鉴、互利共赢为核心的丝路精神。“一带一路”倡议反对贸易保护主义，提倡构建开放、包容、共享、均衡的全球经济，承载着以构建自由贸易区网络为目标、促进全球自由贸易进程的新使命，为经济全球化带来了新的理念，将成为经济全球化的新主角。我国也将以“一带一路”为总抓手，加快形成对外开放的大平台、大通道、大布局，进一步赢得国内经济转型和国际市场竞争的主动。[1]

---

1 迟福林：《“一带一路”：引领新的经济全球化》，载《光明日报》，2017 年 5 月 19 日。

其次，"一带一路"倡议打造的宏大网络极大地拓展了经济全球化和自由贸易的空间。

"一带一路"倡议本质上属于开放性地区主义。传统区域性贸易安排明显具有排他色彩，其自由化措施大多仅限于成员内部，对域外非成员采取歧视性待遇。而开放性地区主义在强调区域内合作的同时，也不排斥区域外合作，倡导对内开放和对外开放达到平衡，不仅要求区域成员之间相互开放、相互平等、消除歧视、减少区域内障碍，也支持区域成员与非区域成员的交往，力争实现在开放中推动各成员共同进步、促进各地区共同发展。[1]"一带一路"的开放性和非排他性完全符合开放性地区主义的要求。

"一带一路"的参与者以亚欧国家为主，非洲、美洲、大洋洲等其他域外国家只要愿意都可参与，这是一个真正的开放型的国际合作平台和机制。国务院发展研究中心副主任隆国强教授认为，"一带一路"倡议的目标宏大，内容丰富，覆盖且超过了以往几乎所有的自贸安排。习主席提出的政策沟通、贸易畅通、资金融通、设施联通、民心相通的"五通"，几乎囊括了国际经贸合作交流的所有内容。相比之下，现有的任何一个自贸安排内容都显得逊色很多。[2]

国外也有学者认同这一点。美国《福布斯》的文章分析指出，中国"一带一路"倡议的魅力在于，打造了一个多样化和相互连接的网络：这是一个连接中欧的升级版运输线路和新贸易枢纽网络，一个加强版覆盖整个欧亚地区的经济体系。与传统的"线路"相比，这样的"网络"更高效、安全和健康，或将成为世界贸易的转折点。英国《经济学人》也预测说，中国的"一带一路"将在未来10年内改变世界贸易的格局。[3]

四 "一带一路"倡议为沿线发展中国家的现代化进程提供了巨大的机遇

"一带一路"倡议重视中国与发展中国家的合作，为发展中国家的现代化进程提供了巨大的机遇和发展手段。

1 秦治来:《准确理解地区主义的"开放性"——以东亚地区合作为例》，载《世界经济与政治》，2008年第12期。

2 《中国经济报告》记者独家专访:《隆国强谈"一带一路"：现有的任何一个自贸安排与之相比都逊色很多》，新浪财经，2017年5月9日，http://finance.sina.com.cn/wm/2017-05-09/doc-ifyexxhw2976250.shtml。

3 转引自《中国的"一带一路"倡议，外媒是这么看的》，中国新闻网，2017年5月15日，http://www.chinanews.com/cj/2017/05-15/8224571.shtml。

分布在"一带一路"沿线的大多数国家均属于发展中国家，也是"一带一路"建设的薄弱环节。"一带一路"建设的难点和重点都在发展中国家，只要在发展中国家实现了突破，"一带一路"就取得了实质性进展。自新中国成立以来，中国就形成了一系列永远与第三世界同呼吸、共命运的独特外交传统。发展中国家在中国外交全局中的战略基础地位更加重要，"一带一路"也是中国与发展中国家共同发展之路。[1]

一方面，发展中国家的经济发展和现代化进程一向是国际社会的棘手难题，另一方面，在当前中国发展的重大机遇期，中国外交大有作为需要新的着力点。目前，面向发展中国家的国际合作平台严重不足，"一带一路"倡议有力地弥补了发展中国家在公共平台和资源上的缺陷。经过多年的外交实践，中国外交在21世纪形成了"大国是关键，周边是首要，发展中国家是基础，多边是重要舞台"的全方位外交布局。"一带一路"倡议以及高峰合作论坛的举行，凸显了中国对发展中国家的重视和多边外交的作用，正是中国全方位外交布局的完美体现。

林毅夫认为，"一带一路"建设以推动发展中国家共同发展为目的，以发展中国家最需要的基础设施建设为抓手。为此，中国发起成立亚洲基础设施投资银行和丝路基金，受到广泛欢迎。"一带一路"所关注的基础设施建设，可以帮助发展中国家解决基础设施瓶颈问题。不仅如此，中国劳动密集型产业对外转移以及国际产能合作，能够帮助发展中国家实现快速发展。第二次世界大战以来的经验表明，哪个发展中国家能够抓住劳动密集型产业国际转移的窗口机遇期，哪个国家就能实现二三十年的快速发展，摆脱贫困，进入中等收入甚至高收入国家行列。"一带一路"倡议之所以能得到这么多国家的响应，最主要的原因在于它不仅符合中国的利益，也会给其他发展中国家带来千载难逢的发展机遇，助推其实现工业化、现代化的梦想。[2]

这个历史性机遇主要表现在三点：

一是投资。截至2016年底，中国企业已在"一带一路"沿线20多个发展中国家建设56个经贸合作区，累计投资超过185亿美元，为东道国创造了近11亿美元税收和18万个就业岗位。

二是援助。习主席在"一带一路"高峰论坛开幕式讲话中宣布，中国将在未

1 赵可金：《发展中国家为"一带一路"助力》，中国网，2015年6月23日，http://opinion.china.com.cn/opinion_83_132183.html。

2 林毅夫：《"一带一路"助推发展中国家现代化》，载《人民日报》，2015年9月18日。

来3年向参与“一带一路”建设的发展中国家和国际组织提供600亿元人民币援助，建设更多民生项目。我们将向“一带一路”沿线发展中国家提供20亿元人民币紧急粮食援助，向南南合作援助基金增资10亿美元，在沿线国家实施100个“幸福家园”、100个“爱心助困”、100个“康复助医”等项目。我们将向有关国际组织提供10亿美元落实一批惠及沿线国家的合作项目。

三是人才培养。从一个具体的小例子也可看出中国对帮助发展中国家的善意和真诚。在欠发达的发展中国家，除了资金和技术瓶颈外，人才短缺也是发展乏力的基础性原因之一。中国有句古话，“授之以鱼不如授之以渔”，中国政府为发展中国家培养人才也是尽了最大努力。过去4年，中国政府每年向相关国家提供1万个政府奖学金名额，地方政府也设立了丝绸之路专项奖学金，鼓励国际文教交流。这是一个相当可观的数目。事实上，中国每年也有大批年轻人赴海外学习，公派的名额很少。比如，根据教育都的统计，2015年，我国有52.37万人出国留学，其中国家公派2.59万人，单位公派1.60万人，自费留学48.18万人，占90%以上。中国的父母用自己辛苦大半辈子的积蓄供孩子到国外留学深造，而“一带一路”沿线国家每年却有这么多的机会来中国免费学习，足见中国人的厚道和政府的诚意。当然，从长远看，为了促进民心相通，为夯实“一带一路”的人力资源基础，这些付出还是值得的。

五 “一带一路”倡议以及中国的后续行动表明中国将在全球治理领域发挥更大作用

对于“一带一路”倡议对全球治理的价值和重要意义，国际社会也给予了充分肯定。2016年11月17日，第71届联合国大会协商一致通过关于阿富汗问题第A/71/9号决议，呼吁国际社会进一步凝聚援阿共识，在政治、经济、安全领域向阿富汗提供援助。决议欢迎“一带一路”等经济合作倡议，敦促各方通过“一带一路”倡议等加强阿富汗及地区经济发展，呼吁国际社会为“一带一路”倡议建设提供安全保障环境。这是联合国大会决议首次写入“一带一路”倡议，得到193个会员国的一致赞同，体现了国际社会对推进“一带一路”倡议的普遍支持。

2017年4月25日，联合国教科文组织总干事博科娃接受《人民日报》记者采访时说，当亚欧多国被极端主义蹂躏的时候，我们认识到，塑造多元包容的世界是多么重要。中国正在通过“一带一路”倡议在其中发挥关键作用。博科娃表示，当今世界需要更多像“一带一路”这样的倡议，以促进跨地区经贸合作和跨文化沟通交流，实现地区和世界的繁荣与和谐。

5 月 13 日，来华出席“一带一路”国际合作高峰论坛的联合国秘书长古特雷斯在与中国外交部长王毅会谈时表示，中国是全球经济增长的重要引擎，在促进可持续发展和全球治理方面发挥着重要引领作用。习主席提出的“一带一路”倡议和联合国 2030 年可持续发展议程方向一致，有助于推动经济全球化更加平衡、包容、和谐发展，对于通过国际合作解决当今世界面临的诸多挑战具有重大意义。中方倡导并主办此次“一带一路”国际合作高峰论坛，体现了中国在世界上独具一格的长远战略眼光。

随着中国的发展和世界格局的变化，中国与世界的互动关系也在发生更加积极的变化。中国一贯主张在国际关系上大小国家一律平等，同时，作为一个大国，应该为维护世界和平、促进共同发展发挥更大作用，这是中方的真诚愿望和实际行动。中共十八大以来，中国的主场外交好戏连台，成为中国外交的一大亮点。2014 年，中国主办了亚太经合组织领导人非正式会议，2016 年主办了二十国集团杭州峰会，2017 年又主办了“一带一路”国际合作高峰论坛，并且承诺下一届论坛继续在中国举办，这意味着中国的外交将采取更加积极的姿态，中国将在全球治理领域发挥更大作用。

当前，人类社会正处在一个大发展、大变革、大调整的时代。一方面，人类已经成为你中有我、我中有你的命运共同体；另一方面，和平赤字、发展赤字、治理赤字是摆在全人类面前的严峻挑战。“一带一路”倡议呼唤世界和平、追求合作发展、践行综合治理，是中国对全球问题开出的一剂药方，是一种蓝图宏伟而又实实在在的解决方案。虽然前方还会有各种各样的困难和挑战，但我们相信“一带一路”倡议一定会取得成功，不仅有益于中国的发展，而且将造福于沿线国家的人民。

The "Belt and Road" Initiative and Action Set a Positive Example for Global Governance

Shao Feng / China

Researcher and Master Instructor of the International Strategy Division under the Institute of World Economy and Politics at the Chinese Academy of Social Sciences

The expansion of globalization has posed severe challenges to the future development of human society. For this reason, the international community has brought forward the concepts and theories of global governance, forming one of the persistent hot spots in the academic community. However, the complicated nature of global issues leads to two phenomena, namely, the tragedy of public land and the predicament of collective action.[1] In practice, global governance has always witnessed lots of talk and little action, and the international community seems to have no way of or has become unable to deal with these various challenges. In this case, the "Belt and Road" Initiative proposed by President Xi and its steady progress can be said to set an example for global governance.

During the keynote speech in the Belt and Road Forum for International

1 Wang Xiaomin, Global Issues and Global Governance, *Southeast Asian Studies*, 2004 (4).

Cooperation, President Xi summed up the ruthless reality of international relations as "three deficits," namely, the deficit in peace, the deficit in development, and the deficit in governance, which are serious challenges faced by all mankind. For this reason, President Xi proposed a clear solution: to achieve policy coordination, connectivity of infrastructures, unimpeded trade, financial integration and closer people-to-people ties by virtue of the "Belt and Road" Initiative to further build new international relations centering on win-win cooperation and realizing common prosperity.

I. The "Belt and Road" Initiative is an innovation to the global governance model

In the theory of global governance, there are normally three different governance models according to the different statuses of governance subjects in the international system, that is, the state-centered governance model, the limited-field governance model and the network governance model. The state-centered governance model is a governance model with the sovereign state as the main governance subject. Specifically, in the fields of common concern and for the consideration of common interests, the sovereign states cope with issues together through consultation, negotiation and mutual cooperation, further generating a series of international agreements or regulations. The limited-field governance model is a governance model with international organizations as the main governance subjects. Specifically, international organizations carry out activities in specific fields (such as the economic and environmental fields) to enable relevant member states to achieve dialogue and cooperation in order to strive for their common interests. The network governance model is a governance model with non-governmental organizations as the main governance subjects.

However, global governance has great limitations in theory and practice. It is difficult to achieve consistent and collective actions of the governance subjects, because of different interests, strengths, statuses and strategies, and the state of anarchy caused by the absence of an international authority. The countries that serve as the most important governance subjects are strong in power but weak in will, while other governance subjects are strong in will but weak in power.

The "Belt and Road" Initiative proposed by China can be broadly classified as a state-centered governance model. However, it has an important pioneering significance in strategic design, organization and operation, so it can be considered as an innovation to the global governance model. The innovation is reflected in two aspects. First, China, a responsible and powerful country, serves as the key initiator and promoter to welcome and strive for the participation of all countries with participative willingness; China has always displayed a non-exclusive and open-minded attitude, it adheres to the principles of mutual consultation, construction and sharing and to the Silk Road spirits of peace and cooperation, openness, inclusiveness, mutual learning, mutual benefit and win-win results in order to benefit the people of all countries with the cooperation goals of building a community of a shared future for mankind and a community of shared interests. Second, as Professor Li Xiangyang pointed out, if other international cooperation mechanisms are more rule-oriented, the "Belt and Road" Initiative is development-oriented and tends to explore further new bilateral or multilateral cooperation possibilities in the process of development.[1]

Some scholars believe that the proposal of the "harmonious world" theory has opened up another way of thinking regarding the global governance theory trapped in the dilemma of theory and practice. The key to current global issues is not the construction of some common global values, but how to reach a global consensus that seeks a common ground while reserving differences. Compared with the profoundness and ideal of the global governance theory, the harmonious world theory is more pragmatic and profound in meaning. The global governance theory advocates value consensus as its basis. By contrast, the harmonious world theory seeks common ground while reserving differences, recognizes differences and

---

1 Chen Su, *Experts: Not Dividing Small Circle and Not Taking Usual Path in the Construction of the "Belt and Road" Initiative*, 2017-04-27, http://www.chinanews.com/cj/2017/04-27/8210181.shtml

shows tolerance, without striving for consistent values. Therefore, the harmonious world theory indeed provides us with a good platform for understanding the current global issues. We can regard the "harmonious world" as one of China's official theoretical responses to the "global governance" theory.[1]

The "Belt and Road" Initiative proposed by President Xi should be seen as a further expansion and concrete practice of the "harmonious world" theory proposed by former President Hu Jintao, reflecting the inheritance, consistency and an advancing with the times, and the constant innovation of China's diplomacy.

II. President Xi Put Forward Important Guiding Idea for the "Belt and Road" Initiative and Global Governance

President Xi Jinping has repeatedly stated that mankind has become a community of a shared future in which you have me and I have you. With the aim of achieving win-win results, the "Belt and Road" Initiative has the core ideas of mutual consultation, construction and sharing, and sums up the Silk Road spirits of peace and cooperation, openness, inclusiveness, mutual learning, mutual benefit and win-win results.

On April 29, 2016, President Xi pointed out, in his speech at the 31st Collective Learning of the Political Bureau of the CPC Central Committee: The "Belt and Road" Initiative evokes the historical memory of the countries along the route. The ancient Silk Road was a road for trade, as well as a road of friendship. In the friendly exchanges between the Chinese nation and other countries, the spirits of the Silk Road, characterized by peace and cooperation, openness, inclusiveness, mutual learning, mutual benefit and win-win results, have been gradually formed. Under the new historical conditions, we put forward the "Belt and Road" Initiative to inherit and carry forward the spirits of the Silk Road, combine the development of China with the development of the countries along the route and combine the Chinese

1 Chen Chengxin, A Review of Research on Domestic "Global Governance", *Political Science*, 2009(1).

dream with the dreams of the people of the countries along the route to grant new time connotations to the ancient Silk Road.

On January 18, 2017, President Xi published a speech entitled *Work Together to Build a Community with a Shared Future for Mankind* at the United Nations Office in Geneva, and answered the question haunting the world: "What's wrong with the world and what can we do about it?" President Xi said: "In the framework of international cooperation of the 'Belt and Road' Initiative, all of the parties uphold the principles of mutual consultation, construction and sharing to work together in order to meet the challenges faced by the world economy, create new opportunities of development, seek new developmental momentums, and expand new developmental space in order to achieve complementary advantages, mutual benefit and win-win results, thereby moving towards the community of shared future for mankind. It is the original intention of my initiative and the highest goal that I hope to achieve through this initiative." The "Belt and Road" Initiative is a solution provided by China to the existing global issues and challenges.

He Yafei, former vice minister of the Ministry of Foreign Affairs of the People's Republic of China, believes that the speech of President Xi has provided important guidelines for addressing the problems and challenges brought about by the development of globalization. Since the 18th National Congress of the Communist Party of China, President Xi has put forward a series of new ideas for global governance, such as the "Belt and Road" Initiative proposed in the autumn of 2013, greater emphasis by China on multilateralism, support of the G20 as the primary platform for global governance, proposal for a global partnership rather than confrontational military alliances, and working together to build a community of a shared future for mankind. The series of speeches that President Xi delivered at the Belt and Road Forum for International Cooperation express China's views on the future direction of the world's development from two dimensions, reality and history, and in particular, propose innovative views on the concept of global governance. "Peace and cooperation, openness, inclusiveness, mutual learning, mutual benefit and win-win results" are China's guiding ideologies for the new globalization.

From President Xi's speech, we can completely realize that the Chinese government has gradually formed a systematic plan for global governance, which is of an important theoretical and practical significance for the world's future development and for global governance.

III. The "Belt and Road" Initiative has Opened up new Paths and Space for Economic Globalization and Free Trade

The theoretical basis of the "Belt and Road" Initiative is neither complicated nor new. It is still the core theory of international trade, that is, the free trade theory. The core idea is that free trade can enable both parties involved in trade to gain trade benefits. One of the purposes of the "Belt and Road" Initiative is to safeguard the global free trade system and the open world economy. In the past four years, the construction of the "Belt and Road" Initiative started from scratch, from idea to action, from point to line and from line to face, changing the way of global economic cooperation and opening up new space for international cooperation.

As said President Xi, these have been the four years of continuous improvement in trade. China cooperates with the participating countries of the "Belt and Road" Initiative to vigorously promote trade and investment facilitation, and constantly improve the business environment. From 2014 to 2016, China's total trade volume with the countries along the "Belt and Road" route exceeded 3 trillion USD. China's investment in the countries along the route amounted to over 50 billion USD. We must build an open cooperation platform to maintain and develop an open world economy, jointly create an environment conducive to openness and development, promote the establishment of a fair, rational, and transparent international system of rules for economic and trade investment, and promote the orderly flow of production factors, the efficient allocation of resources, and the complete integration of the market.

At present, globalization is facing many challenges. It can be said that it stands at a crossroads and faces the influence of two different forces. One is the protectionist force that pulls it backwards, and particularly, the intensified tendency of some developed countries to adopt trade protectionism and isolationism which increases the uncertainty of economic globalization; the other is the power to adhere to liberalization, mainly represented by insightful people of Western countries and emerging market countries. When the United States shows an anti-globalization trend, many countries that continue to support globalization, expect China to play a greater role in global governance.

The proposal and practice of the "Belt and Road" Initiative has opened up new paths and space for economic globalization and free trade.

First of all, the new concepts and spirits of the Silk Road, that is, openness, inclusiveness, and non-exclusivity, advocated by the "Belt and Road" Initiative have added new platforms and new vitality to economic globalization.

In his speech, President Xi proposed the spirits of the Silk Road, characterized by peace and cooperation, openness, inclusiveness, mutual learning, mutual benefit and win-win results. The "Belt and Road" Initiative opposes trade protectionism and advocates the establishment of an open, inclusive, shared and balanced global economy. With the goal of building a network of free trade areas and the new mission of promoting the process of global free trade, the "Belt and Road" Initiative brings about a new concept to economic globalization and in the future, it will become the new protagonist of economic globalization. China will also proceed from the "Belt and Road" Initiative to accelerate the formation of a large platform, a large channel, and a large layout for opening up to the outside world, and further gain the initiative in domestic economic restructuring and international market competition.[1]

1 Chi Fulin, The "Belt and Road" Initiative: Leading a New Economic Globalization, *Guangming Daily*, May 19, 2017.

Second, the huge network created by the "Belt and Road" Initiative has greatly expanded the space for economic globalization and free trade.

The "Belt and Road" Initiative is essentially an open regionalism. Traditional regional trade arrangements clearly have an exclusive color, and most of their liberalization measures are limited to the members and discriminate against non-members outside the region. Open regionalism emphasizes cooperation within the region without exclusion of cooperation outside the region, advocates internal and external opening up to achieve a balance. Open regionalism not only requires open and equal status of the regional members, elimination of discrimination, and reduction of barriers in the region, but it also supports the exchanges between regional members and non-regional members, so as to strive to promote common progress among all members and common development in all regions.[1] The openness and non-exclusivity of the "Belt and Road" Initiative fully comply with the requirements of open regionalism.

The participants in the "Belt and Road" Initiative are mainly Asian and European countries; other countries in Africa, the Americas and Oceania may participate as much as they wish. It is a truly open international cooperation platform and mechanism. Professor Long Guoqiang, deputy director of the Development Research Center of the State Council, believes that the "Belt and Road" Initiative is ambitious in its goal and rich in its content, covering almost all of the free trade arrangements of the past. The "Five-Pronged Approach (policy coordination, connectivity of infrastructures, unimpeded trade, financial integration and closer people-to-people ties)" proposed by President Xi involves almost all of the aspects of international economic and trade cooperation and exchanges. In contrast, the contents of any existing free trade arrangement are greatly inferior.[2]

---

1 Qin Zhilai, Accurately Understand the "Openness" of Regionalism – Take the Cooperation with East Asian Countries as an Example, *World Economics and Politics*, 2008(12).

2 An exclusive interview by the reporter of *China Policy Review*, Long Guoqiang Talks about the "Belt and Road" Initiative: Superior to Any Existing Free Trade Arrangement, 2017-05-09, http://finance.sina.com.cn/wm/2017-05-09/doc-ifyexxhw2976250.shtml

Some scholars abroad also agree with this point. An article in the American *Forbes* magazine points out that the charm of China's "Belt and Road" Initiative lies in the establishment of a diverse and interconnected network, which is an upgraded version of a transportation route and a new network of trade hubs connecting China and Europe, as well as an enhanced version covering the entire Eurasian economic system. Compared with the traditional "route", this "network" is more efficient, safe and healthy, and will become a turning point in world trade. The British *Economist* magazine also predicts that China's "Belt and Road" Initiative will change the pattern of world trade in the next 10 years.[1]

IV. The "Belt and Road" Initiative Provides Tremendous Opportunities for the Modernization of the Developing Countries along the Route

The "Belt and Road" Initiative attaches importance to the cooperation between China and the developing countries, and provides tremendous opportunities and means of development for the process of modernization of the developing countries.

Most countries located along the "Belt and Road" route are developing countries and are also the weak link in the "Belt and Road" Initiative. The difficulties and priorities in the construction of the Initiative all lie in the developing countries. As long as breakthroughs have been achieved in the developing countries, substantial progress can be made in the "Belt and Road" Initiative. Since the founding of New China, China has formed a series of unique diplomatic traditions that will always share the breath and common destiny with the Third World. The strategic foundation of the developing countries is even more important in the overall situation of China's diplomacy. The "Belt and Road" Initiative is also the common path towards development for China and developing countries to venture down.[2]

On the one hand, the process of economic development and modernization of

1 Quoted from View of Foreign Media in China's "Belt and Road Initiative" , 2017-05-15, http://www.chinanews.com/cj/2017/05-15/8224571.shtml

2 Zhao Kejin: Developing Countries Help the "Belt and Road" Initiative, 2015-06-23, http://opinion.china.com.cn/opinion_83_132183.html

the developing countries has always been a thorny problem for the international community. On the other hand, in the major developmental period of China's development, China's diplomacy needs a new focus to make substantial progress. At present, the international cooperation platforms for the developing countries are in short supply. The "Belt and Road" Initiative has made up for the shortcomings of the developing countries in terms of public platforms and resources. After many years of diplomatic practice, China's diplomacy has created a comprehensive diplomatic arrangement: "Great powers are the key, periphery is the priority, the developing countries are the foundation, and multilateralism is the important stage" in the 21st century. The "Belt and Road" Initiative and Cooperation Summit Forum has highlighted the importance attached by China to the developing countries and the role of multilateral diplomacy, which are the perfect embodiment of China's comprehensive diplomatic arrangement.

Lin Yifu considers that the construction of the "Belt and Road" Initiative is aimed at promoting the common development of the developing countries, which proceeds from the construction of infrastructures most needed for them. To this end, China's launch of the Asian Infrastructure Investment Bank and the Silk Road Fund has been widely welcomed. The infrastructure construction of the "Belt and Road" Initiative can help the developing countries solve infrastructure bottlenecks. Moreover, China's external transfer of labor-intensive industries and the cooperation on international capacity are favorable to the developing countries in achieving rapid development. According to the experience since World War II, the developing country that can grasp the window of opportunity for the international transfer of labor-intensive industries will achieve rapid development for 20 to 30 years and eliminate poverty, and further enter the ranks of middle-income or even high-income countries. The main reason why the "Belt and Road" Initiative is popular in many countries is that it not only meets the interests of China, but also brings golden development opportunities to other developing countries, conducive to the realization of their dreams of industrialization and modernization.[1]

These historic opportunities are mainly reflected in three points:

The first one is investment. By the end of 2016, Chinese enterprises had built 56 economic and trade cooperation zones in more than 20 developing countries along the "Belt and Road" route. The accumulated investment exceeded 18.5 billion USD, creating the tax revenues of nearly 1.1 billion USD and 180,000 jobs for the host countries.

The second one is assistance. In the opening speech of the Belt and Road Forum for International Cooperation, President Xi announced that China would provide assistance in the amount of 60 billion RMB to the developing countries and international organizations participating in the "Belt and Road" Initiative in the following three years and build more projects for people's livelihood. We would also provide 2 billion RMB in emergency food aid to the developing countries along the "Belt and Road" route, increase the investment of 1 billion USD in the South-South Cooperation Assistance Fund, and implement 100 "happy homes", 100 "love aids", 100 "rehabilitation medical aids" and other projects in the countries along the route. We would provide 1 billion USD to relevant international organizations to implement a number of cooperation projects benefiting the countries along the route.

The third one is talent training. From a small concrete example, we can also see the goodwill and sincerity of China in helping the development of the developing countries. In underdeveloped developing countries, the shortage of talents is one of the basic reasons for the lack of development in addition to capital and technological bottlenecks. There is an old saying in China that goes: "It's better to teach a man to fish than to give him fish." The Chinese government has also done its utmost to cultivate talents for the developing countries. In the past four years, the

1 Lin Yifu: The "Belt and Road" Initiative Promotes the Modernization of Developing Countries, *People's Daily*, September 18, 2015.

Chinese government provided 10,000 government scholarships to relevant countries each year. Local governments also established special Silk Road scholarships to encourage international cultural and educational exchanges. In this regard, that is a considerable number. In fact, China also has a large number of young people studying abroad every year, including a few of government-sponsored people. For example, according to statistics from the Ministry of Education, 523,700 Chinese people studied abroad in 2015, of which 25,900 people were sponsored by the government, 16,000 people were sponsored by their affiliations, and 481,800 people studied at their own expense, accounting for more than 90%. Chinese parents use their hard-earned savings for their children to study abroad. The countries along the "Belt and Road" route have so many opportunities for their children to study in China for free every year, which shows the kindness of the Chinese people and the sincerity of the Chinese government. To promote closer people-to-people ties and consolidate the human resource base of the "Belt and Road" Initiative, there is no doubt that these efforts are still worthwhile in the long run.

V. The "Belt and Road" Initiative and China's Follow-up Actions Show that China will Play a Greater Role in Global Governance

The international community has fully recognized the value and significance of the "Belt and Road" Initiative for global governance. On November 17, 2016, the 71st General Assembly of the United Nations unanimously adopted No. A/71/9 resolution on the Afghanistan issue and called on the international community to further build up a consensus on the aid to Afghanistan and provide assistance to Afghanistan in the political, economic and security fields. The resolution welcomed the "Belt and Road" Initiative and other economic cooperation initiatives and urged all parties to strengthen economic development in Afghanistan and the region through the "Belt and Road" Initiative and called on the international community to provide a safe and secure environment for the construction of the Initiative. The "Belt and Road" Initiative was included in the resolution of the General Assembly of the United Nations for the first time, which was unanimously agreed to by 193 member states, reflecting the universal support of the international community for advancing the “Belt and Road” Initiative.

On April 25, 2017, UNESCO Director-General Bokova said, during an interview with a reporter from the *People's Daily,* that when many Asian and European countries were paralyzed by extremisms, we realized how important it is to create a multi-dimensional and inclusive world. China is playing a key role with the “Belt and Road” Initiative. Bokova also said that today's world needs more initiatives like the “Belt and Road” to promote cross-regional economic and trade cooperation and cross-cultural communication and exchanges in a bid to achieve regional and global prosperity and harmony.

On May 13, the UN Secretary-General Guterres, when attending the Belt and Road Forum for International Cooperation held in China and talking with Chinese Foreign Minister Wang Yi, said that China is an important engine for global economic growth and plays an important leading role in promoting sustainable development and global governance. The “Belt and Road” Initiative proposed by President Xi is consistent with the *Transforming Our World: The 2030 Agenda for Sustainable Development* and is conducive to promoting a more balanced, inclusive and harmonious development of economic globalization, so it is of great significance in solving the many challenges facing the world through international cooperation. China advocates and hosts the Belt and Road Forum for International Cooperation, reflecting China's unique long-term vision in the world.

With the development of China and changes in the world pattern, the interaction between China and the world is also undergoing more positive changes. China has consistently advocated the equality of large and small countries in international relations. At the same time, China, as a big country, should play a greater role in safeguarding world peace and promoting common development, which is China's sincere desire and practical action. Since the 18th National Congress of the Communist Party of China, China's home-country diplomacy has gained remarkable achievements, becoming a highlight of China's diplomacy. China hosted the Annual APEC Economic Leaders' Meetings in 2014 and the G20 Hangzhou Summit in 2016. In the current year, China also hosted the Belt and Road Forum for International Cooperation and promised to host the next forum, too. This means that China will adopt a more positive attitude in diplomacy and play a greater role in the field of global governance.

At present, human society is in an era of great development, great change and major adjustment. On the one hand, mankind has become a community of a shared future in which you have me and I have you; on the other hand, the deficit in peace, the deficit in development, and the deficit in governance are the serious challenges faced by all mankind. The "Belt and Road" Initiative calls for world peace, and pursues cooperative development and the practice of comprehensive governance. It is a prescription for China on global issues, a grand blueprint and a realistic solution. In spite of many difficulties and challenges ahead, we believe that the "Belt and Road" Initiative will surely succeed, which will not only boost the development of China, but it will also benefit the people of the countries along the route.

全球文化中的“中国角色”

罗树雅 【墨西哥】
国际巴洛克博物馆馆长

在过去的50多年里，国际环境似乎始终不能令西方国家，特别是富裕而强盛的北美国家、北欧国家以及日本满意。尽管这些国家占据科技领先地位、享有丰厚的经济福利，然而在如何应对当前世界面临的“深刻而普遍的危机”这一问题上，这些国家的民众有着极大的分歧。

墨西哥知名学者海梅·托雷斯·博德在担任联合国教科文组织干事期间，曾提出这样一个构想——构建不同文明之间的新型对话关系，从而推动国际社会朝着更加平等的方向迈进。但由于各国存在意识形态层面的差异，强权大国对这一构想始终不屑一顾。

在1980年的联合国大会上，多名国际专家在匈牙利学者欧文·拉兹洛和我本人的领导下，提交了一份全球形势研究报告，报告中指出未来国际形势将充满不确定性，这一点主要表现在，西方理念指导下的全球治理会引发普遍的不满情绪，而强权大国却以想当然的态度看待西方治理模式的合理性。这份报告提出了多项建议，试图改变这种状况，但始终没有引起重视。

继越南战争和苏联解体之后，全世界经历了一场严重的金融危机，恐怖主义势力开始抬头，种种迹象表明，如果我们想继续以积极的态度去接纳全球化的现实，则必须尽快培养一种全新的、具有创造性的思维方式和行为模式。

一

随着经贸交流和技术交流的不断深化，我们时常会与其他国家的陌生人交往，这就要求采用最具创意的方式来构建跨文化关系，让双方能够进行深层的、个性化的交流，而这便意味着对一些传统的价值观和价值理念提出质疑。

美国杰出人类学家爱德华·T. 霍尔曾指出，跨文化关系极为复杂，因此在构建国际关系的过程中，文化中的许多重要层面往往被忽略。此外，霍尔认为，致力于了解自我、了解异国文化的专家学者，通常会遭遇本国文化体系中不存在的种种状况。专家学者尚且如此，可以想象商人、经济学家、律师或是政客受到的影响有多么强烈！[1]

如果没有中国的积极参与，根本不会出现新型全球秩序这个概念。中国人民创造了灿烂的文明，中国的经贸规模正日益扩大，中国所处的战略位置使得科技交流与军事交流变得异常迅速，种种实例可以证明这一点。

当然，中国并非首次引领世界。1776 年，苏格兰著名经济学家亚当·斯密曾指出，中华帝国之富足，远远超过欧洲各国之总和。早在 19 世纪初，中国便已经成为世界头号制造大国。英国学者李约瑟指出，在欧洲文艺复兴时期，中国的科学技术已经达到十分先进的水平。

二

尽管如此，在具有欧洲中心主义色彩的历史编纂中，现代发展往往被归功于欧洲文化的先进性，中国及东方文化则被贬斥为落后的文化。在 19 世纪，欧洲的进步往往被描述成一种独特的进化过程，而亚洲社会却被贴上“封闭、僵化、专制”的标签，这显然是受到西方历史相关分类模式的影响。在这种叙事中，欧洲文明在文化、技术、社会以及地理曾各个层面均具有进步性，而其他国家或地区的历史则不具有进步元素，甚至被视为阻碍进步的障碍。为此，彭慕兰、王国斌、杰克·A. 戈德斯通以及马凯硕等杰出思想家正试图构建一种新型的世界性的历史话语，在这一话语体系内，中国和东亚将扮演属于他们的中心角色。

1 ［美］爱德华·霍尔：《超越文化》，1976。

三

在这一背景下，“一带一路”倡议的提出可谓正逢其时。习近平主席提出的这一倡议，目的在于确保中国能在复杂而危险的全球化语境中引领世界的发展方向。中国外交部长王毅认为，“一带一路”并非是中国的“独奏”，而是各方参与的“交响乐”。新华社则称其为“振兴世界经济的‘中国方案’”。很显然，交响乐的隐喻更受国际社会的青睐。

“一带一路”的关键目标在于扩大经贸范围及基础设施建设，这些地理经济学意义上的目标若想顺理实现，则需要构建一个无比庞大和复杂的外交体系，从而创造一种新型的多边机制。这一过程具有极其重要的意义，它暗示着一种以中国和亚洲的和平观、幸福观为基础、以增进不同国家和地区间的相互理解为使命的新型外交体系的出现。

因此，“一带一路”所秉持的“和平共处五项原则”（互相尊重主权和领土完整、互不侵犯、互不干涉内政、平等互利、和平共处）至关重要，但必须注意的是，在当代语境下，“一带一路”的实施仍然面临重重挑战。尽管中国政府的官方文件中反复指出，“一带一路”倡导文明宽容、提倡不同文明间的交流与互鉴，然而目前为止，国际社会尚不具备实施这一伟大构想的工具。

四

“一带一路”将掀起新一轮全球重组的浪潮，在这个过程中，旅游及学术交流将扮演重要角色。此外，艺术展、书展、电影、广播以及电视项目正在规划当中，疾疫防控、医学交流、公共卫生突发事件应对、重大传染病防治等合作项目也被列入议程。值得注意的是，“一带一路”也为中医药合作提供了机遇。

拉美国家对“一带一路”给予了高度关注。2017 年 5 月 14—15 日，联合国拉美加勒比经济委员会（CEPAL）在北京参加了“一带一路”国际合作高峰论坛，委员会执行秘书阿莉西亚·巴尔塞纳认为，“一带一路”倡议与拉美国家的根本价值观高度契合，这将进一步增进中国与拉美的互动与交流，为双方经贸投资带来绝佳的机遇。此外，巴尔塞纳还表示，习近平主席 2016 年 11 月对委员会总部的访问具有重大意义。

今年 6 月 30 日，太平洋联盟总统峰会在哥伦比亚的西部城市卡利举行。在本次会议上，墨西哥、哥伦比亚、智利及秘鲁四国总统达成一致，将“扩大跨洋自由贸易”确立为外交政策的核心内容之一。许多人认为，通过新丝绸之路建设，太平洋联盟有望扩大与亚洲经济体、特别是与中国的经贸合作。

五

目前，智利和秘鲁两国已经与中国签署自由贸易协定，鉴于中国与墨西哥的双边贸易总额于 2016 年达到 749.28 亿美元，两国签署贸易协定的可能性很高。

中国与墨西哥的经贸合作可以追溯到 17—18 世纪的第一轮贸易全球化浪潮。当时，作为“新西班牙”殖民地的墨西哥通过“中国大帆船贸易航路”与中国保持着紧密的商业往来。在这段墨西哥人引以为傲的历史时期内，墨西哥为“巴洛克时期”的文化及艺术创新做出了重要贡献。

墨西哥的历史名城普埃布拉曾是当时的商贸中心，控制着通往马尼拉的太平洋航路以及经由古巴通往西班牙的贸易路线。为了纪念这些文化成就和技术成就，普埃布拉市成立了一座巴洛克国际博物馆，并于 2016 年 2 月首次开放。首次当代艺术展便是以“中国大帆船贸易航路”为主题。

六

中国正在重新规划政治体系，对此，世界各国正怀着浓厚的热情，盼望从中国汲取经验，在批判和重评的基础上，将文化传统发扬光大。以荷兰学者罗布・里曼为代表的国际学者指出，在当前世界政治利益的驱使下，各国自然而然地接受了一种“伪商业价值理念”，这种价值观以满足原始欲望和基本欲望为表征，缺乏内在质量和超越性。这点是令人遗憾的，因为它排斥了文化、教育、智慧的重要意义。

我们正盼望着中国能够提出一个更好的选择，通过“一带一路”建设，实现各大洲、大洋彼此联通的梦想。目前，中国的儒家思想正逐步适应当代的挑战，或许在这些思想理念的基础上，中国的知识精英可以构建起全新的中国政治模式，为解决当前四处蔓延的信心危机做出巨大贡献。

The Role of China in the Emergence of a Global Culture

Jorge Alberto Lozoya / Mexico

Director of International Museum of the Baroque

For at least fifty years, the Western world has felt uncomfortable with international circumstances. This is specially true in the case of powerful and rich North American and Northern European countries. Japan often shares the perception. In spite of the huge technological and scientific advancement they enjoy and the economic welfare shared by vast majorities, the members of these societies openly express disagreement with the handling of what is nowadays perceived as a deep universal crisis.

Created after the Second World War and when directed by the renowned Mexican intellectual Jaime Torres Bodet, the United Nations Educational, Scientific and Cultural Organization (UNESCO) intended to build a new dialogue amongst civilizations, as a means to advance in the construction of a more egalitarian planetarian community. Already involved in their ideological confrontation, the winning superpowers did not even consider the possibility of such an endevour.

The 1980 General Assembly of the United Nations received a global Report prepared by a large number of international experts lead by the eminent Hungarian scholar Ervin László and myself, in which we informed the Organization of the widespread uncertainty about the future. A main expression of uneasiness referred to an overall dissatisfaction with Western theories and practices of good governance, the universal validity of which was taken for granted by dominating powers. None of the many suggestions we made in order to overturn this phenomenon was ever considered.

The Vietnam War and the disappearance of the Soviet Union, followed by a gigantic financial crisis and the reemergence of terrorism,confirmed the urgent need for new creative thinking and acting, if globalization is to be a welcomed reality.

I

As economic and technological exchanges advance, we are constantly interacting with strangers, people from other nations. This process demands the most creative approach to transcultural relations, exposing each one of us to very deep and personalized experiences, that provoques the questioning of basic values and attitudes.

As the brilliant American anthropologist Edward T. Hall pointed out, the complexity of the procedure may explain why the more significant aspects of culture are persistently brushed aside in international relations. He remarked that those of us who professionally embark onthe task of understanding ourselves and others abroad, encounter situations not at all similar to what our own culturally conditioned projective systems led us to expect. If this happens to experts, imagine the surprise all the new impacts imply for traders, economists, lawyers or politicians![1]

The new global order cannot be conceived without the active participation of China. The wonderful cultural heritage of the Chinese people, the ever-increasing size of their economy and trade, the strategic site of the nation in a planet where technological, scientific and military interactions are being built at enormous speed:

1 Hall, Edward T., *Beyond Culture*, New York, Anchor Press/Doubleday, 1976.

everything points in that direction.

Of course there is nothing new about the fact that China commands a leading role in the world. In 1776, the famous Scottish economist Adam Smith stated that China was a richer Empire than all European countries together. At the beginning of the 19th Century China was the number one manufacturing power. The science historian Joseph Needham demonstrated how at the time of the European Renaissance, China was already a highly advanced technological society. The French Illustration recurrently payed deserved homage to Chinese philosophy, education and political practice.

II

Nevertheless, Eurocentric historiography tended to perceive modern development as a process in which European cultural superiority was taken for granted. China and other Eastern powers were thus submitted to regressive analysis. At the same time, 19th Century descriptions of progress were built upon purely Western historical categories and presented as a unique evolutionary process. Consequently Asian societies were portrayed as closed, immobile and despotic. According to this approach cultural, technical, social and geographic factors made Western civilization unique, while other national or regional histories missed facilitating elements or presented obstacles that prevented industrial developments. Kenneth Pomeranz, R. Bin Wong, Jack A. Goldstone or Kishore Mahbubani– among other brilliant thinkers – intend to create a new global historical discourse in which China and East Asia play the important role they deserve.[1]

1 Ollé, Manuel, "Los espejos de la historia en el presente de China: reflejosy percepciones" , *Análisis y pensamiento iberoamericano sobre China,* 23, 2nd. Semester 2017, pp. 4-20. www.politica-china.org See Pomeranz, Kenneth,*The Great Divergence. China, Europe and the Making of the Modern World Economy,* Princeton, Princeton University Press, 2000; R. Bin Wong, *China Transformed. Historical Change and the Limits of European Experience,* Ithaca, Cornell University Press, 1997;Goldstone, Jack A. *The Rise of the West – or Not? A Revision to Socio-economic History,*2001 http://www.hartford-hwp.com/archives/10/114.html; Mahbubani, Kishore, *The New AsianHemisphere. The Irresistible Shift of Global Power to the East*, New York, PublicAffairs, 2008.

III

In this context, The Belt and Road Initiative (B&R) is an exciting and very timely initiative of President Xi Jinping, designed to guarantee China a leading role in the complex and risky developments of globalization.Foreign Minister Wang Yi interestinglydescribed the project as "a symphony of all relevant parties". Xinhua News agency called it "the Chinese solution to global economic blues."[1] Needless to say that the musical metaphors are most welcome.

The recovery of legendary historical sea routes and the construction of overland corridors connecting China with Europe, Central and West Asia, the Middle East and West Africa imply a protomagical understanding of planet Earth that must be recognized as such.

The geoeconomics of broadening trade and building infrastructure as key B&R strategic goals, will need the netting of one of the largest and most complex diplomatic systems ever designed, in order to generate a new kind of multilateralism. This extremely significant process suggests the appearance of a new diplomacy based upon Chinese and Asian perceptions of peace and happiness, fostering understanding among different peoples and cultures.

The upholding by B&R of the Five Principles of Peaceful Coexistence (mutual respect for each other's sovereignty and territorial integrity, mutual non-agression, mutual noninterference in each other's internal affairs, equality and mutual benefit, and peaceful coexistence) is significant. However one should keep in mind that such an undertaking has never been effectively exercised during the contemporary era.

Chinese government documents claim that the Initiative advocates tolerance among civilizations and supports their dialogue, while shelving differences and drawing on each other's strengths. As of today, the international community lacks

1 https://www.theguardian.com/world/2017/may/12/the-900bn-question-what-is-the-belt-and-road-initiative

the tools to undergo such a magnificent task.

IV

We learn from the proposal that tourism and student exchange will be essential factors in the process of this new global integration. Art festivals, book fairs, films, radio and television programs are also being considered. Epidemic prevention, medical exchanges and coordinated address of public health emergencies and major infectious diseases are in the agenda. Please notice that cooperation on traditional medicine is offered.

Latin America followed with great interest the announcement of B&R. May 14 and 15, 2017 the United Nations Economic Comission for Latin America and the Caribbean (CEPAL by its Spanish initials)attended in Beijing a significant international Summit to welcome the Initiative. Secretary General Alicia Bárcena considered B&R a profound agreement with fundamental values, that will strengthen the interconnection between China and Latin America providing new and exciting opportunities for trade and investment. Secretary Bárcena also acknowledged the great significance of the visit President Xi Jinping payed to CEPAL headquarters in Santiago, capital city of Chile in November, 2016.

During the recent Pacific Alliance Summit held June 30 in Cali, Colombia, the Presidents of the four member countries–Mexico, Colombia, Chile and Peru-confirmed their conviction of expanding Transpacific free trade as a key element of their foreign policy. It is widely believed that the Pacific Alliance represents a key opportunity to enlarge and diversified trade with Asian economies and especially with China, through an organic link with the new Silk Road. In any event,

V

Chile and Peru already have a Free Trade Agreement with China and the possibilities of Mexico signing one are large, since bilateral trade in 2016 was of

74.928 billion USD.[1]

Historically, Mexico's links with China are part of the first trade globalization, that took place during the 17th and 18th Centuries. Mexico –then known as New Spain- maintained very strong commercial links with China, regularly navigating the Pacific Ocean following what was then known as The China Galleon Route. We Mexicans are very proud of this period, when our ancestors played a significant role in the innovative cultural and artistic movement known as the Baroque era.

The Mexican city of Puebla was the commercial center of the trade, controlling both the Transpacific Route to Manila and the trade links with Spain through Cuba. Today we in Puebla have the International Museum of the Baroque to celebrate these cultural and technological achievements. The Museum opened in February 2016 and its first temporary exhibit was devoted to The China Galleon.

VI

China is rethinking its political system; that is a well-kept open secret. World expectations on the matter are enormous. We want to learn from China's self-critical reevaluation of its inheritance while looking towards a better future.[2] Global intellectuals, like Dutch scholar Rob Riemen, describe and regret how around the world political interests propel the automatic acceptance of a pseudo-commercial attitude, that promises instant satisfaction of primitive and elemental desire, lacking quality and transcendence. All of that against the role of culture and education,

1 León de la Rosa, Raquel Isamara, "La Ruta de la Seda Marítima en el siglo XXI:¿Oportunidades para América Latina?" ,*Explorando espacios para la integración entre América Latina y Asia Pacífico,* pp. 177-198.Observatorio América Latina-Asia Pacífico,ALADI, CAF, CEPAL. www.observatorioasiapacifico.org
Gómez Tamez, Alejandro, "La relación comercial de México y China" , Aduanas,julio 13,2017. http:// www.aduanasrevista.mx/la-relacion-comercial-de-mexico-y-china/

2 Bell, Daniel A., *China's New Confucianism. Politics and Everyday Life in a Changing Society,* Princeton, Princeton University Press, 2208.

obliterating wisdom and beauty.[1]

We all wish that China will provide a better option, navegating the oceans and carving new routes across several continents. Probably a well conceived Chinese political system, based upon re-emerged Confucian values adapted to contemporary challenges, will soon be admired all over the world as a significant contribution to help overcome the prevailing universal crisis of confidence.

1 Riemen, Rob, *Para combatir esta era. Consideraciones urgentes sobre el fascismo y el humanismo(To Fight Against this Age. On Fascism and Humanism),* Mexico, Penguin Random House, 2017.

基础设施建设、中国发展经验和全球经济治理

——以张培刚的一个理论创见为中心

钟祥财 【中国】

上海社会科学院经济研究所研究员 / 中国经济思想史学会常务理事

面对世界经济陷入萧条以来的复苏乏力，中国提出的“一带一路”倡议是广受关注的应对方案之一。这个方案从何而来？它对未来的全球治理影响如何？本文拟通过对中国经济学家张培刚一个理论创见的回顾分析，谈谈自己的看法。

一

张培刚（1913—2011），湖北红安人。1934 年毕业于武汉大学经济系，进入中央研究院社会科学研究所任助理研究员。1941 年赴美留学，于 1943 年和 1945 年在哈佛大学获得硕士、博士学位。1946 年回国，任国民政府资源委员会经济专门委员、武汉大学经济系教授、系主任。1947 年被聘为中央研究院社会科学研究所通讯研究员。1948 年任联合国亚洲及远东经济委员会顾问及研究员。1949 年以后历任武汉大学校委会常委兼总务长、经济系主任、代理法学院院长，华中工学院建校规划办公室主任、基建办公室主任、政治经济学教研室主任，华中工学院社会科学部主任、经济研究所所长，华中理工大学经济管理学院名誉院长、经济发展研究中心主任，华中科技大学经济学院名誉院长，中华外国经济学说研究会名誉会长等。著作有《清苑的农家经济》（1936）、《广西粮食问题》（1938）、《浙

江省食粮之运销》（合著）（1940）、*Agriculture and Industrialization*（1949）、《宏观经济学与微观经济学》（合著）（1980）、《微观宏观经济学的产生和发展》（合著）（1986）、《发展经济学通论第一卷——农业国工业化问题》（1991）、《新发展经济学》（主编）（1993）、《发展经济学教程》（主编）（2001）、《发展经济学》（主编）（2009），论文被编成《张培刚经济论文选集》（上、下卷）（1997）、《张培刚经济文选》（2011）。

在经济学界，张培刚被誉为发展经济学的创立者之一。20世纪40年代后期，他的博士论文《农业与工业化》（*Agriculture and Industrialization*）在哈佛大学被评为经济学专业最佳论文奖并获得“威尔士奖金”，作为《哈佛经济丛书》第58卷，1949年由哈佛大学出版社出版，1969年再版。该书1951年被译成西班牙文，在墨西哥出版。在这本著作中，张培刚提出了若干具有原创价值的理论观点，主要包括：1. 关于农业与工业的相互依存关系，以及农业对工业乃至对整个国民经济的贡献和基础作用；2. 关于“工业化”的定义和涵义——包括农业的现代化和农村的工业化；3. 关于基础设施和基础工业的“先行官”作用；4. 关于工业化的发动因素与限制因素；5. 关于工业化对农业生产和对农村剩余劳动力的影响；6. 关于工业化过程中利用外资和开展对外贸易的问题。而本文所要分析的就是上面提到的第3个观点。

在阐述工业化和产业革命的问题时，张培刚写道：“参照以往两个世纪的历史，我们就能够清楚地看到，‘基要的’创新（‘Strategical’innovation）怎样带来，又怎样加强我们所谓‘工业化’的过程。其中最显著的是：铁道的建立、钢制船舶的使用及运输的摩托化（Motorization），蒸汽引擎的广泛应用及动力工业的电气化（Electrification），在制造业及农业上机器的发明和应用，以及机器工具的制造和精细化。这些基要的创新或基要的生产函数的变化，更进一步加强了伴随现代工厂制度、市场结构及银行制度之兴起而来的‘组织上的’变化（‘Organization’changes）。这一切变化，都曾经对农业及制造工业的生产结构发生巨大的作用，因之曾经构成，而且将继续构成，工业化过程的主要特征。”[1]在分析工业化的速度问题时，他强调：“工业化的特点，只能以制造工业的扩张表现一部分。其他生产部门的扩张，尤其是视为具有战略重要性的生产部门如

1　张培刚：《农业与工业化（上卷）：农业国工业化问题初探》，华中工学院出版社1984年版，第71—72页。

采矿及运输，虽不说应该予以更多的注意，至少也应该予以等量齐观。”[1]在这里，张培刚把运输、能源、制造等视为实现工业化的战略性产业，其中铁路又居于首要的位置。

20世纪70年代末，中国经济开启了社会主义市场化改革的进程，张培刚对发展经济学的研究也步入了一个新的提升和丰富的阶段，关于基础设施的重要性，他的认识更为清晰了。1993年，由他主编的《新发展经济学》一书指出："基础设施是现代工业建立和发展的基本条件。由于基础设施投资规模巨大，资金回收周期长，因而，基础设施的缺乏往往成为发展中国家工业化过程中的"瓶颈"，结果既浪费了资源，又贻误了发展时机。因此，发展中国家要实现工业化和经济起飞，必须注重和发挥基础设施的先行作用。"[2]何为基础设施？张培刚定义说："基础设施（或称社会分摊成本），是指为直接生产部门和人民生活提供共同条件和公共服务的设施和机构"，它有广义和狭义两种理解，前者包括教育、科研、环境和公共卫生、司法、行政管理等，后者"一般包括运输、仓储、通讯、发电和输变电、供气、供水和排污等城市设施，以及与农业有关的灌溉系统等等"[3]。

关于基础设施在经济发展中的重要性，张培刚从三个方面进行了分析。首先，"基础设施是直接生产部门赖以建立和发展的基本条件。基础设施的发展水平，直接和间接地影响生产部门的成本和效益，影响其供给的数量和质量。例如，发达的运输和通信系统，有助于各种生产要素和产品的空间转移，降低生产部门的转移成本；有助于在生产部门和市场之间建立广泛的联系，保持供给和需求的平衡，降低交易成本。又如，完善的仓储设施可以保证工业物资和各种农产品的有效供给，减少其在流通过程中的损耗，增加供给的数量并提高其质量。再如，充分的电力供应可以为生产部门和人民生活提供高效和廉价的能源，有助于降低生产成本和提高人民的生活质量。还有，城市公用设施的发展可以通过对生产部门职工生活和福利的重大影响，进而降低生产部门的工资成本和提高职工的劳动效率；农业水利设施的建设，为农业科学技术的进步，为化肥、良种等现代生产要素的

---

1 张培刚：《农业与工业化（上卷）：农业国工业化问题初探》，华中工学院出版社1984年版，第115页。

2 张培刚主编：《新发展经济学》，河南人民出版社1993年版，第184页。

3 同上书，第184页。

利用，创造了条件，有助于农业生产率的提高"[1]。

其次，"基础设施具有外部经济的作用。现代工业是建立在专业化分工基础上的大规模生产，规模经济会导致生产部门和企业的平均成本降低，基础设施为专业化分工创造了要素和产品空间转移以及市场交易的便利。因此，基础设施的建设为工业集中和规模经济创造了前提条件。经济活动在地理上的集中，反过来也使基础设施本身的利用效率得到提高"[2]。

第三，"基础设施的建设还能够推动经济结构和社会结构的变革，并且提高城乡人民的生活水平。国际上用来衡量一国社会经济发展水平的指标，有许多是用基础设施的发展水平来衡量的。例如人均电力消费，职业人口中有电、水、煤气的人的百分比，大众传播媒介的水平，每百人电话机数，等等。这些指标构成一国社会经济发展目标的重要内容"[3]。

据此，他明确提出："如何满足工业化过程中对基础设施投资的巨大需求，如何协调基础设施与直接生产部门投资之间的优先次序和投资比例，是发展中国家工业化过程中必须认真作出的政策选择。我们认为，根据基础设施在经济发展中的作用及其特点，基础设施应该超前建设。"[4]

2009 年，由张培刚和张建华主编的《发展经济学》出版，作者强调："工业化战略运用的一个重要领域是基础设施的投资，而基础设施在工业化中又具有特殊的地位和作用。"[5]"基础设施是涉及经济增长、环境保护、生活质量和社会可持续发展的基础性产业。基础设施的状况如何，决定着一个国家和地区经济结构的优劣，进而决定其经济发展的水平和速度以及现代化的进程。然而，由于基础设施的资本系数高，技术上具有不可分性，建设周期较长，投资规模大，具有基础性和先行性，许多发展中国家的基础设施投资往往滞后，从而在一定程度上制约了经济发展。因此，发展中国家要加快经济发展，就必须注重基础设施的建设，发挥基础设施的作用。"[6]

不难看出，在张培刚的发展经济学理论中，基础设施建设一直居于重要的位置，他对这一问题的研究，不仅起步时间早，而且持续了 60 多年，反复强调，不

1 张培刚主编：《新发展经济学》，河南人民出版社 1993 年版，第 185 页。
2 同上书，第 185 页。
3 同上书，第 185—186 页。
4 同上书，第 189 页。
5 张培刚、张建华主编：《发展经济学》，北京大学出版社 2009 年版，第 343 页。
6 同上书，第 345—346 页。

断深化。落后国家的经济起飞需要具备多种条件，基础设施并非唯一的前提，但由于张培刚的这一理论创见是基于中国的历史条件和国际的经验比较而提出的，尤其是在当代中国的改革开放中付诸实践，得到验证和丰富，对中国经济的发展产生了显著的影响，因而值得加以进一步的分析。

二

前面提到，张培刚在分析基础设施重要性的同时，已经注意到问题的另一面，即发展中国家在进行基础设施建设的过程中必然面临的瓶颈。这些瓶颈往往是与基础设施的本身特点和发展中国家的经济状况联系在一起的。

关于基础设施的本身特点，《新发展经济学》列举了三点：其一，“规模大、配套性强、资金密集、技术上具有不可分割性，因而一开始就需要有最低限度数量的投资作为其创始资本”；其二，“与直接生产部门比较，建设周期长，投资资金难以在短时期内得到回收”；其三，“它不仅要求建设时间上适当超前，在投资上优先保证，而且还具有技术先行的含义”。[1] 关于发展中国家存在的相关问题，也大致有三点：1.“发展中国家国土辽阔，资源分布分散，既要保证基础设施与直接生产部门在总体上和地区分布上协调发展，又要保持各区域之间工业发展的相对平衡。这是特别困难的问题”；[2] 2.“在实行计划经济的发展中大国，国家不仅承担对基础设施的投资，也承担直接生产部门的投资。集权体制下对保持经济高增长的内在冲动，分权体制下地方政府对发展制造业的偏好，加之国有企业本身预算软约束导致的低效率，都会使基础设施的投资得不到保证”；3. 基础设施具有“公共物品”的特性，价格被控制在低水平，“这种政策的直接后果是刺激了对基础设施的不合理需求，使本来就紧张的基础设施国家短缺”，而且，“发展中国家政府出于政治上的原因或者为了控制工资，即使基础设施的成本提高也很少相应地提高其使用价格。这样，基础设施部门的自身积累的能力由此而大大削弱”。[3]

这些瓶颈问题是如何被破解的？当代中国的改革实践提供了一个成功案例。

张培刚曾在其博士论文中写道：“我们可以依据工业化是由政府或由个人先行发动，将工业化分为三种类型：1. 个人或私人发动的，2. 政府发动的，3. 政府

1 张培刚主编：《新发展经济学》，河南人民出版社 1993 年版，第 186—187 页。

2 同上书，第 191—192 页。

3 同上书，第 192 页。

与私人共同发动的。在历史上，我们很难将任何国家明确地划归第一类型或第二类型，因为在这种过程开始时，总是包括政府和个人两方面的努力。但是如果象进行任何分类一样，允许有一定的误差或含糊范围存在，我们仍然可以将英国、法国及美国归入第一类型，苏联归入第二类型，德国及日本归入第三类型。苏联所发生的工业化过程可以称之为‘革命的’（revolutionary）类型，以与当前在其他国家所发生的‘演进的’（evolutionary）类型相区别。”[1] 应当指出，在张培刚撰写此书的时候，中国的工业化还处在酝酿阶段，虽然中国的学者和政治家早在20世纪20年代开始就围绕着中国是否要走西方国家工业化道路的问题展开讨论[2]，但进入30年代以后，日本对华侵略客观上阻碍了中国经济发展的进程。1949年以后，社会主义计划经济使工业化基础初步建成，但正如张培刚所说，一方面国有经济效率不高，另一方面，政治运动频繁，导致了中国经济发展不充分。这种情况直到1978年才出现根本改变，以中共十一届三中全会为标志的当代中国改革开放，使中国经济的工业化和城市化步入了一个快速推进的时期。从类别上说，中国的这种工业化既不是“革命的”，也不是“演进的”，而是“改革的”。之所以说它是“改革的”，是因为这一进程既保留和发挥了社会主义经济的制度优势，又融入了现代市场经济的效率、开放和创新等特点。

毋庸讳言，在改革开放的初期，“究竟是直接生产活动优先增长，还是基础设施优先增长”，或者说“鸡和蛋哪个先出现”的困惑[3] 确实是存在过的。因为经济改革的直接起因是有效供给短缺，而一旦改革有了成效，基础设施落后的问题就凸显出来了，例如，“在1983年以后，随着食品供应的增加，政府开始允许没有城市户口的农民进城。当时，沿海地区的出口产业能够吸收大量进城务工希望过上好日子的农村青年。在中国历史上，有过战乱和饥荒导致数百万人迁徙的现象，但从未达到1978年以后那样的迁徙规模”[4]。北京、上海等大城市中的住房难、乘车难，山西等省向外运输煤炭的铁路车皮紧缺，农民工春节回家的“一票难求”，都说明在较长一段时间里中国的基础设施建设跟不上经济发展的要求。在这种情况下，中国政府采取的做法一是坚持改革，激发市场活力，提高经济效益，为改

1 张培刚：《农业与工业化（上卷）：农业国工业化问题初探》，华中工学院出版社1984年版，第97页。

2 钟祥财：《二十世纪二十至四十年代立国之争及其理论影响》，《社会科学》2003年第11期。

3 张培刚、张建华主编：《发展经济学》，北京大学出版社2009年版，第347页。

4 [美]傅高义：《邓小平时代》，冯克利译，香港中文大学出版社编辑部、生活·读书·新知三联书店编辑部译校，生活·读书·新知三联书店2013年版，第651页。

善和发展基础设施提供必要的前提；二是扩大开放，积极引进外资和采用国际先进技术，加快国内的基础设施改造，例如，1978 年基础产业和基础设施投资的资金来源基本上都是国家财政资金，而在 2007 年基础产业和基础设施投资的资金来源中，国家预算内资金占 8.4%、国内贷款占 23%，利用外资占 1.8%，自筹资金占 59.9%。投资主体分经济类型看，国有投资占 62.3%，外资占 4.8%，私营个体占 5.8%。[1]；三是制定科学规划，逐渐加大对基础设施的投入。在社会经济和综合国力具备了必要的条件时，果断地整合各方面的优势，全面推进基础设施的现代化建设。

根据权威部门的统计资料[2]，从 1979 年到 2007 年的 30 年间，全国基础产业和基础设施方面的投资累计达到 297985 亿元，占同期全社会投资的 38.4%，年均增长 19.9%，比同期国民经济年均增幅高 4.2 个百分点[3]。其中，交通运输业的发展尤其快速，累计完成投资 74246 亿元，年均增长 19.9%。具体来看，铁路营业里程由 1978 年的 5.2 万公里增至 2007 年的 7.8 万公里，增加了 2.6 万公里，新增里程大部分是采用先进技术和设备的电气化铁路营业里程，1978 年我国国家铁路电气化里程仅为 1000 公里，2007 年达 2.4 万公里；2007 年，公路通车里程由 1978 年的 89 万公里增至 358 万公里，增长了 3 倍，其中高速公路由 1988 年的 0.01 万公里增至 5.39 万公里，增长了 538 倍，“五纵七横”国道主干线初步形成，公路等级明显提高；到 2007 年底，已有民用航班飞行机场 148 个，比 1985 年增加了 66 个，航线 1506 条，比 1990 年增加了 1069 条，民用航空运输线路长度为 234 万公里，比 1990 年增加 183 万公里；2007 年，沿海主要港口货物吞吐量达 38.82 亿吨，是 1980 年的 17.9 倍；管道输油（气）里程 5.45 万公里，是 1978 年的 6.6 倍，上海港口已成为全世界最大港口，年吞吐量近 5 亿吨。

近十年来，我国基础设施建设的步伐持续加快。以高速铁路为例，正如有一篇新闻报道所写的那样，“就在 2007 年以前，中国还没有一条可以称为‘高速’的铁路，短短几年间，随着一列列翩若游龙的高铁列车贴地飞行，中国已经是世界上高速铁路系统技术最全、集成能力最强、运营里程最长、运行速度最高、在

1 《基础产业和基础设施建设成绩斐然——改革开放 30 年我国经济社会发展成就系列报告之四》，中央政府门户网站 www.gov.cn, 2008 年 10 月 30 日。

2 本段所引资料均来自《基础产业和基础设施建设成绩斐然——改革开放 30 年我国经济社会发展成就系列报告之四》，中央政府门户网站 www.gov.cn, 2008 年 10 月 30 日。

3 这里的基础产业是指农业、能源、原材料供应等，基础设施主要是指交通运输、邮电通讯，还包括水利环境、教育文化卫生体育设施。

建规模最大的国家。从无到有。6年间，中国高铁飞速发展。条条高铁，不仅筑就着祖国大地上的钢筋铁骨，也悄然改变着人们的生活”[1]。2008年，我国第一条高速铁路（北）京（天）津城际铁路开通运营。2009年，世界上一次建成里程最长、工程类型最复杂时速350公里的武（汉）广（州）高铁开通运营。2010年，世界首条修建在湿陷性黄土地区，连接中国中部和西部时速350公里的郑（州）西（安）高速铁路开通运营。2012年，世界上第一条地处高寒地区的哈（尔滨）大（连）高速铁路通车运营，时速200公里，将东北三省主要城市连为一线。截至2012年底，中国高速铁路总里程达0.9356万公里。2013年以后，随着宁（南京）杭（州）、杭（州）甬（宁波）、盘（锦）营（口）高铁以及向（塘）莆（田）铁路的相继开通，高铁新增运营里程0.1107万公里，中国高铁总里程达到1.2万公里。2014年，中国铁路新线投产规模创历史最高纪录，铁路营业里程突破11.2万公里，高速铁路营业里程超过1.6万公里，居世界第一。2016年，连接京广高铁与京沪高铁两大干线的郑（州）徐（州）高铁开通运营，设计时速350公里，一批拥有自主知识产权、达到国际先进水平的科技成果得到应用。2017年6月，具有完全自主知识产权、达到世界先进水平的“复兴号”动车组列车投入使用，7月，打通中国高铁横贯东西“最后一公里”的宝（鸡）兰（州）高铁正式运营。按照最新发布的《中长期铁路网规划》，到2025年，我国铁路网规模将达17.5万公里左右，其中高铁3.8万公里左右，比2015年底翻一番。到2030年，基本实现内外互联互通、区际多路畅通、省会高铁连通、地市快速通达、县域基本覆盖。

20世纪90年代初，张培刚在谈到发展中国家如何化解基础设施建设的难题时提出了如下对策：（1）有效控制直接生产部门的需求，使之与基础设施的供给能力相适应；（2）适度保护与有效竞争相结合，使直接生产部门提供较多的盈余；（3）对投资体制进行改革，政府主要承担基础设施的投资，直接生产部门的投资则主要由企业承担；（4）提高基础设施的产品和劳务的价格，使其具备一定的自我发展能力；（5）制定切实可行的长期发展规划，在正确预见工业发展需要的基础上，使基础设施建设适当超前。[2]事实证明，以高速铁路为代表的中国发展经验已经极大地丰富了发展经济学中的基础设施理论，坚持改革开放，发挥制度优势，

1 《高铁之“变”——近年来我国高铁发展成就综述》，财新网，2012年9月13日。
2 张培刚主编：《新发展经济学》，河南人民出版社1993年版，第192-193页。

依靠科技创新，基础设施的优先发展有力助推了中国经济的跨越式迈进，而且为未来全球经济治理提供了值得探索的思路。

三

如果把张培刚的理论创见作为中国智慧的体现，那么它在全球化背景下的价值除了能为中国带来发展，还可以在走出国际经济萧条方面发挥应有的作用。事实上，张培刚在撰写博士论文时，已经注意到世界经济的长周期问题。他指出，在"演进的"工业化过程中，"企业创建精神及生产技术"是"使工业化开始的重要发动力量"，[1]但他还提到，"从历史的记载看来，有人认为，战争除了曾经对于许多国家起过破坏和阻碍经济发展的作用外，也曾经对于有些国家起过引进并加速工业化过程的刺激作用"。[2]在介绍以战争解释经济扩张的相关理论时，张培刚特地分析了康德拉季耶夫（N. D. Kondratieff）和汉森（Alvin H. Hansen）等人的观点，然后总结说："战争对于经济扩张的影响可以从三方面来考察。首先，战争创造需要，因而刺激新产品的出现，并刺激那种在国内生产较为有利的代替品的应用。其次，战争刺激就业，而且不论在节省劳动力方面或在节省原料方面，都表现出必须进行生产技术的革新。最后，战争有助于涤除若干制度上的阻碍，以免其妨碍有关收入分配及财产所有权的社会改革。"[3]

在张培刚的博士论文中，康德拉季耶夫的观点只是被用来解释决定工业化进程和速度的原因，2008年国际金融风暴发生后，苏联经济学家康德拉季耶夫的理论再次引起人们的讨论。在发表于1925年的《经济生活中的长期波动》一文中，康德拉季耶夫写道："资本主义社会制度经济生活的运动不是简单的、直线的，而是复杂的、周期的"，"我们确实有理由设想：在资本主义经济中存在着平均长约50年的长期波动。这个事实使经济动态问题更加复杂了"。[4]相对于这种长期波动，资本主义经济还出现过7-11年的中间波动，在有些学者看来，导致这两种周期性波动的原因并不相同，具体而言，中间波动产生于资本主义制度的内部原因，而长期波动则是由于偶然的、超经济的环境和事件造成的，如技术的改变、战争

1 张培刚：《农业与工业化（上卷）：农业国工业化问题初探》，华中工学院出版社1984年版，第98页。

2 同上书，第99—100页。

3 同上书，第101页。

4 ［苏］尼·康德拉季耶夫：《经济生活中的长期波动》，李琮译，《现代国外经济学论文选》第十辑，商务印书馆1986年版，第1页。

和革命、新的国家被纳入世界经济、黄金生产的波动等。对此，康德拉季耶夫予以驳斥。

他认为：“技术的改变无疑对资本主义的发展进程有非常重大的影响”，“生产技术的改变意味着：1. 有关的科学技术发现和发明已经完成；2. 它们的应用在经济上是可能的”，但是，“科技发明本身并不足以给生产技术带来真正的变化。只要有利于采用它们的经济条件还不具备，它们就没有用。这可以用下述实例来说明：十七世纪和十八世纪的科技发现和发明，只是到十八世纪末的产业革命时期才得到大规模的应用。如果这是正确的，那么，认为技术的改变带有偶然性而实际上并非来源于经济需要的想法，就大大逊色了”，显然，“技术发展本身是长期波动的节奏的一部分”。[1] 他写道：“战争和革命也非常有力地影响着经济发展的进程。但是，战争和革命不是凭空而来的，它们不是由个别人物的任意行为造成的。它们产生于实际的，特别是经济的环境。认为战争和革命是由外部因素造成的并能造成长期波动，会引起这样一个问题：为什么它们有规则地一个接一个地发生，并且只发生在长期波动的高涨时期？有一种设想很可能是正确的，即战争起源于经济生活步伐的加速和紧张程度的加强，起源于争夺市场和原料斗争的加剧，而社会动荡则在新的经济力量的压力下最容易发生。”[2] 至于新国家的开发，也只是“新的高涨使得有必要和可能去开发新国家、新市场和新的原料来源，从而加速资本主义发展的步伐”[3]。

由此可见，在康德拉季耶夫的研究中，资本主义经济有它自身的发展周期，它与科技进步密切相关，它对新技术的需求和采用构成了周期的一个阶段，而战争和革命则是经济周期中若干矛盾无法解决所造成的，如经济生活步伐的加速，紧张程度的加强，争夺市场和原料斗争的加剧，等等。康德拉季耶夫的长周期理论得到了熊彼特的肯定，后者认为，“假如我们看看经济活动的长波，相同的事实更为明显，对它的研究能把资本主义的性质和机制看得比什么都清楚”[4]，但是他进一步指出：战争、革命、人口、资本、货币等常常是产业改变的条件，但还不是推动产业改变的主要力量，“来自资本主义企业创造的新消费品、新生产方式

1　[苏]尼·康德拉季耶夫：《经济生活中的长期波动》，李琮译，《现代国外经济学论文选》第十辑，商务印书馆1986年版，第15页。

2　同上书，第16页。

3　同上书，第16页。

4　[美]约瑟夫·熊彼特：《资本主义、社会主义和民主》，杨中秋译，电子工业出版社2013年版，第65页。

或运输方式、新市场、新产业组织形式，才是开动和保持资本主义发动机运动的根本推动力”[1]。

借鉴康德拉季耶夫和熊彼特的经济周期理论，韦森认为眼下世界经济面临的问题既具有相似性，也增加了一些新的变动要素。他指出：“在过去20多年世界经济的全球化大潮中，大量外资和制造业新技术流入了改革开放过程中的中国。外资的流入和新制造业技术的引进，加上中国丰裕的低成本劳动力这一要素禀赋，在全球化的分工体系中，就自然地形成了中国出口导向型的经济增长模式。中国的这种增长模式，又与前几年美国金融市场的虚拟繁荣和资产泡沫化形成互补，使得美国人一方面能够在虚拟经济部门繁荣的条件下享受从中国和其他发展中国家进口的廉价商品，另一方面又可依靠国际资金的大量流入来弥补国内储蓄不足对美国政府财政支出以及大企业融资短缺所可能产生的经济增长制约”，这“也在世界经济的整体上延缓了处在全球化分工链条另一端的美国和其他西方发达国家早就该发生的经济衰退”。[2]

既然经济全球化一方面使中国经济获得了快速增长，另一方面也推迟了发达国家经济衰退的到来，那么人们就有理由期待，中国的发展经验和成果如能惠及其他发展中国家，全球经济治理会出现新的解决方案。根据前述张培刚的分类，个人或私人发动的工业化经历时间长，依赖市场的基础设施建设周期缓慢，熨平经济波动的机制比较刻板、建构；政府发动的工业化虽然快速，但包括基础设施在内的经济运行总体效率低；而政府与私人共同发动的工业化由于赶超目的性强，在国内经济达到一定发展程度后，往往具有对外扩张性。这解释了20世纪上半期世界经济长周期为何与战争或革命相伴随。相比之下，当代中国的经济发展道路是有独特性的，得益于张培刚等中国经济学家的理论创见，邓小平先生抓住了难得的历史机遇，启动了中国经济由计划向市场的改革进程，原有的工业基础和国有经济在改革中获得新的生命力，市场竞争使整个社会经济充满活力，对外开放给中国发展创造了“引进来”和“走出去”的巨大空间，中国的基础设施建设所取得的成就，中国经济所出现的增长，都与此相关。基于这一发展经验和全球

1 ［美］约瑟夫·熊彼特：《资本主义、社会主义和民主》，杨中秋译，电子工业出版社2013年版，第78页。

2 韦森：《目前世界经济衰退的深层原因与中国的合宜宏观政策选择——从熊彼特的商业周期理论看目前的世界经济衰退》，张晖明、邓霞主编：《金融危机的马克思主义解读》，复旦大学出版社2009年版，第184页。

经济挑战，中国政府提出了“一带一路”倡议，力求通过各国合作，扩大经济交往，以推进基础设施建设为重点，加快发展中国家的工业化进程，同时为世界经济强劲复苏提供助力。本文认为，这是一个值得关心和平发展的人们深入思考、促成实践的中国方案。

The Construction of Infrastructure, China's Development Experience and Global Economic Governance

— With the Original Theory of Zhang Peigang as the Focus

Zhong Xiangcai / China

Researcher of the Institute of Economics at the Shanghai Academy of Social Sciences, Managing Director of the Association of the History of Chinese Economic Thought

Faced with sluggish recovery since the depression of the world's economy, the "Belt and Road" Initiative proposed by China is one of the solutions that have attracted great attention. Where does the solution come from? How does it affect global governance in the future? In this article, the author talks about his own views by review and analysis of the original theory of Zhang Peigang, a Chinese economist.

I

Zhang Peigang (1913-2011), born in Hong'an, Hubei Province, graduated from the Department of Economics of Wuhan University in 1934 and then worked for the Institute of Sociology, Academia Sinica as an assistant researcher. He studied abroad in the United States in 1941, and earned a master's degree and a doctoral degree from Harvard University in 1943 and 1945, respectively. Then, he returned to China in 1946 to serve as a professional economic member of the Resources Committee of the National Government, and a professor and dean of the Department of Economics of Wuhan University. In 1947, he was appointed communication researcher of the Institute of Sociology, Academia Sinica. In 1948, he served as a consultant and researcher for the U.N. Economic Commission for Asia and the Far East (ECAFE). Since 1949, he has served as a standing committee member and dean of general affairs of the School Council, dean of the Department of Economics, and acting dean of the Law School of Wuhan University; director of the School Planning Office, director of the Civil Construction Office, and director of the Political Economics Teaching and Research Office of Huazhong University of Science and Technology; director of the Social Science Division, and director of the Institute of Economics of Huazhong University of Science and Technology; honorary dean of the School of Economics and Management and director of the Economic Development Research Center of Huazhong University of Science and Technology; honorary dean of the HUST School of Economics, and honorary president of the China Foreign Economics Research Association. His works include *Farming Economy of Qing Yuan* (1936), *Food Problems in Guangxi* (1938), *Transportation and Sales of Food Grains in Zhejiang* (co-author) (1940}, *Agriculture and Industrialization* (1950), *Macroeconomics and Microeconomics* (co-author) (1980), *Emergence and Development of Micro-Macroeconomics* (co-author) (1986), *General Theory of Development Economics, Vol. 1 - Industrialization of Agricultural Countries* (1991), *New Development Economics* (Editor-in-Chief) (1993), *Course of Development Economics* (Editor-in-Chief) (2001) and *Development Economics* (Editor-in-Chief) (2009). His papers are compiled into the *Collection of Economic Papers of Zhang Peigang* (Volume I and II) (1997) and *Economics Anthology of Zhang Peigang* (2011).

In economic circles, Zhang Peigang is known as one of the founders of development economics. In the late 1940s, his doctoral dissertation, *Agriculture and Industrialization*, won the Best Paper Award for Economics at Harvard University and received the "Welsh Prize", it was compiled into the 58th Volume of *Harvard Economics Series*, published by Harvard University Press in 1949 and reprinted in 1969. The book was translated into Spanish in 1951 and published in Mexico. In the book, Zhang Peigang put forward a number of theoretical viewpoints with original value, mainly including: 1) the interdependence of agriculture and industry, and the contribution to and basic role of agriculture in industry and even in the entire national economy; 2) the definition and connotation of "industrialization", including the modernization of agriculture and the industrialization of rural areas; 3) the "pioneer" role of infrastructure and basic industries; 4) the mobilization factors and limiting factors of industrialization; 5) the influence of industrialization on agricultural production and the rural surplus labor force; 6) the problems of using foreign investments and engaging in foreign trade in the process of industrialization. What this article intends to analyze is the third viewpoint mentioned above.

When explaining the issues of industrialization and industrial revolution, Zhang Peigang wrote: "With reference to the history of the past two centuries, we can clearly see how 'strategical' innovation brings about and strengthens the so-called 'industrialization' process. The most notable points are: the establishment of railways, the use of steel ships and the motorization of transportation, the widespread use of steam engines, and the electrification of the power industry, the invention and application of machines in the manufacturing industry and in agriculture, and the manufacturing and refinement of machine tools. These strategical innovations or changes in basic production functions have further strengthened the 'organizational' changes with the rise of the modern factory system, the market structure and the banking system. All these changes have played a dramatic role in the structure of production in agriculture and in the manufacturing industry, which have constituted and will continue to constitute the main features of the process of industrialization."[1] When analyzing the speed of industrialization,

1 Zhang Peigang, *Agriculture and Industrialization (Volume I): A Preliminary Study on the Industrialization Issue of Agricultural Countries*, Huazhong University of Science Technology Press, 1984, pp.71-72.

he stressed: "The characteristics of industrialization can only be represented in part by the expansion of the manufacturing industry. The expansion of other production sectors, especially the production sectors of strategic importance such as mining and transportation, should be given at least equal attention."[1] Here, Zhang Peigang regards transportation, energy, and manufacturing as strategic industries for the realization of industrialization, of which, railway occupies first place.

In the late 1970s, the Chinese economy started the process of the reform of socialist marketization. The research of Zhang Peigang on development economics also entered a new stage of improvement and enrichment, leading to a more profound understanding of the importance of infrastructure. In 1993, the book, *New Development Economics*, edited by him, pointed out: "Infrastructure is the basic condition for the establishment and development of modern industry. Due to the huge investment in infrastructure and the long cycle of fund recovery, the lack of infrastructure often becomes the 'bottleneck' in the process of industrialization in developing countries, resulting in a waste of resources and a delay in development opportunities. Therefore, developing countries must focus on and give play to the antecedent role of infrastructure in achieving industrialization and economic development in leaps and bounds."[2] What is infrastructure? Zhang Peigang defined it as follows: "Infrastructure (or social sharing cost) refers to the facility and institution aimed at providing common conditions and public services for direct production sectors and people's lives." It has broad and narrow senses. The former includes education, scientific research, environment and public health, justice, and administrative management, etc. The latter "generally includes urban facilities such as transportation, warehousing, communications, power generation, transmission and transformation, gas supply, water supply, and drainage, as well as irrigation systems related to agriculture, etc."[3]

1 Zhang Peigang, *Agriculture and Industrialization (Volume I): A Preliminary Study on the Industrialization Issue of Agricultural Countries*, Huazhong University of Science Technology Press, 1984, p.115.

2 Zhang Peigang (ed.), *New Development Economics*, Henan People's Publishing House, 1993, p.184.

3 Zhang Peigang (ed.), *New Development Economics*, Henan People's Publishing House, 1993, p.184.

As to the importance of infrastructure in economic development, Zhang Peigang made an analysis of three aspects. First, "infrastructure is the basic condition indispensable to the establishment and development of direct production sectors. The level of development of infrastructure directly and indirectly affects the cost and effectiveness of production sectors, as well as the quantity and quality of supply for the production sectors. For example, the advanced transportation and communication system is conducive to the spatial transfer of various production factors and products, and the reduction of the transfer costs of the production sector; and it helps establish extensive links between the production sector and the market, maintain a balance between supply and demand, and reduce transaction costs. For another example, complete storage facilities can ensure the effective supply of industrial materials and various agricultural products, reduce losses in the circulation process, increase the quantity of the supply and improve the quality. Moreover, a sufficient supply of electricity can provide efficient and cost-effective energy for the production sectors and for the people, which is favorable to reducing production costs and improving the quality of people's lives. Furthermore, the development of urban public facilities exerts a significant impact on the lives and welfare of the employees in the production sectors, thereby reducing the wage costs of production sectors and improving the labor efficiency of workers; the construction of agricultural water conservation facilities creates conditions for the progress of agricultural technology and the use of modern production elements such as fertilizer and improved varieties, which contributes to the improvement of agricultural productivity."[1]

Second, "infrastructure has the role of external economy. Modern industry is the large-scale production based on the specialized division of labor. The economy of scale will lead to lower average costs of production sectors and enterprises. Infrastructure brings convenience to spatial transfer and to the market transaction of factors and products for the specialized division of labor. Therefore, the construction

---

1 Zhang Peigang (ed.), *New Development Economics*, Henan People's Publishing House, 1993, p.185.

of infrastructure creates the preconditions for industrial concentration and the economy of scale. The geographical concentration of economic activities has, in turn, improved the efficiency of the utilization of infrastructure itself."[1]

Third, "the construction of infrastructure can also promote the transformation of economic structures and social structures, and improve the living standards of the people in both urban and rural areas. Many indicators used to measure the level of a country's social and economic development are based on the level of development of its infrastructure, such as per capita electricity consumption, percentage of electricity, water, and gas users in the occupational population, the level of the mass media, and the number of telephones per 100 people, etc. These indicators (185) constitute an important content of the level of a country's social and economic development ."[2]

Based on this, he clearly stated: "How to meet the huge demand for the investment in infrastructure in the process of industrialization, and how to coordinate the priorities and investment ratios between infrastructure and investment in the direct production sector must be taken seriously in the process of industrialization in developing countries. We believe that infrastructure should be constructed ahead based on the roles and features of infrastructure in economic development."[3]

The *Development Economics* edited by Zhang Peigang and Zhang Jianhua was published in 2009. The authors stressed: "An important area for the utilization of the industrialization strategy is investment in infrastructure, and infrastructure has a special status and role in industrialization."[4] "Infrastructure refers to the basic industry that involves economic growth, environmental protection, living

1 Zhang Peigang (ed.), *New Development Economics*, Henan People's Publishing House, 1993, p.185.

2 Zhang Peigang (ed.), *New Development Economics*, Henan People's Publishing House, 1993, pp.185-186.

3 Zhang Peigang (ed.), *New Development Economics*, Henan People's Publishing House, 1993, p.189.

4 Zhang Peigang, Zhang Jianhua (eds), *Development Economics*, Peking University Press, 2009, p.343.

quality and sustainable social development. The status of infrastructure determines the strength and weakness of the economic structure of a country and a region, and further determines the level and speed of economic development and modernization. However, since infrastructure has the features of a high capital coefficient, technology inseparability, a long construction period, large investment, fundamentality and antecedence, the investment in infrastructure always tends to lag behind in many developing countries, and this restricts economic development to a certain degree. Therefore, if developing countries want to accelerate economic development, they must pay attention to the construction of infrastructure and bring the role of infrastructure into full play."[1]

It is easy to see that, in the theory of Zhang Peigang in development economics, the construction of infrastructure has always occupied an important position. His research on this issue not only started early, but also lasted for more than 60 years with repeated emphasis and intensification. The economic development of backward countries needs a variety of conditions, and infrastructure is not the only prerequisite. However, the original theory of Zhang Peigang was proposed based on China's historical conditions and the comparison with international experiences, and was put into practice, verified and enriched in the reform and opening up of contemporary China especially, generating a significant impact on the development of China's economy. Hence, it deserves further analysis.

II

As mentioned earlier, while analyzing the importance of infrastructure, Zhang Peigang noticed the other side of the issue, that is, the bottlenecks inevitably faced by the developing countries in the process of the construction of infrastructure. These bottlenecks are often associated with the inherent characteristics of infrastructure and the economic conditions of developing countries.

1 Zhang Peigang, Zhang Jianhua (eds), *Development Economics*, Peking University Press, 2009, pp.345-346.

As to the inherent characteristics of infrastructure, the *New Development Economics* lists three points: First, "due to large scale, high support, intensive capital, and inseparable technology, a minimum amount of investment is required to be used as starting capital"; second, "due to a long construction period, investment funds are difficult to recover within a short period of time in comparison with the direct production sector"; third, "it not only requires the proper advancing of the construction schedule, but it also gives priority to investment which has the meaning of a technology pioneer."[1] There are roughly three points related to the issues existing in developing countries: 1. "As developing countries have a vast territory and scattered resources, it is particularly difficult to ensure the coordinated development of infrastructure and of the direct production sectors in overall and regional distribution, and maintain the relative balance of industrial development among the various regions";[2] 2. "A large developing country that implements a planned economy should undertake investment in infrastructure and in the direct production sector. The investment in infrastructure cannot be guaranteed due to the internal impulse of high economic growth under a centralized system, the local governmental preference for the development of manufacturing industries under the decentralized system, and coupled with the inefficiency of soft budget constraints of the state-owned enterprises"; 3. With the characteristic of "public goods", infrastructure has the price controlled at a low level. "The direct consequence of the policy is to stimulate the irrational demand for infrastructure, causing further shortage of infrastructure in the country with a tense state of infrastructure." In addition, "the government of the developing country scarcely increases the utilization cost of infrastructure for political reasons or control of wages, despite an increase in the cost of infrastructure. On this occasion, the ability for accumulation of the infrastructure sector is thus greatly weakened."[3]

---

1 Zhang Peigang (ed.), *New Development Economics*, Henan People's Publishing House, 1993, pp.186-187.

2 Zhang Peigang (ed.), *New Development Economics*, Henan People's Publishing House, 1993, pp.191-192.

3 Zhang Peigang (ed.), *New Development Economics*, Henan People's Publishing House, 1993, p.192.

How can the bottleneck problems be addressed? The practice of reform in contemporary China provides a successful case.

Zhang Peigang wrote in his doctoral dissertation: "We can divide industrialization into three types according to governmental or individual initiation of industrialization: 1. individually or privately initiated; 2. governmentally initiated; 3. governmentally and privately initiated. Throughout history, it has been difficult for us to clearly classify any country as either the first type or the second type, because both governmental and individual efforts are often involved at the beginning of the process. However, if certain errors or ambiguities are allowed to exist just like any classification, we can still classify the United Kingdom, France and the United States as the first type, the Soviet Union as the second type, Germany and Japan as the third type. The 'revolutionary' type that takes place in the course of the process of industrialization in the Soviet Union is distinguished from the 'evolutionary' type that currently occurs in other countries."[1] It should be pointed out that when Zhang Peigang wrote this book, the industrialization of China was still in the embryonic stage. Although Chinese scholars and politicians began to discuss whether or not China would take the path towards industrialization of Western countries in the early 1920s,[2] Japan's aggression against China after the 1930s impeded the economic development of China. After 1949, the socialist planned economy made the foundation of industrialization basically completed. However, as Zhang Peigang said, on the one hand, state-owned economic efficiency was low, and on the other hand, frequent political movements led to insufficient economic development in China. This situation did not fundamentally change until 1978. The reform and opening up of contemporary China marked by the Third Plenary Session of the 11th Central Committee of the Communist Party of China made the industrialization and urbanization of the Chinese economy step into a period of rapid progress.

1 Zhang Peigang, *Agriculture and Industrialization (Volume I): A Preliminary Study on the Industrialization Issue of Agricultural Countries*, Huazhong University of Science Technology Press, 1984, p.97.

2 Zhang Xiangcai: The Dispute over the Nation Establishment (1920s-1940s) and Its Theoretical Influence, *Social Science*, 2003(11).

In terms of category, China's industrialization is neither "revolutionary" nor "evolutionary". As a matter of fact, it is "reformatory." This is because the process not only retains and exerts the institutional advantages of the socialist economy, but also incorporates the characteristics of efficiency, openness, and innovation of the modern market economy.

Undoubtedly, the confusion[1] does exist over "whether to prioritize the increase of direct production activities or the infrastructure," or "regarding the chicken and the egg, which comes first" at the initial stage of the reform and opening up. Because the direct cause of economic reform is the shortage of effective supply, the problem of backward infrastructure becomes apparent once the reform gains results. For instance, "With the increase in food supply after 1983, the government began to allow rural workers without urban household registration to enter cities. At that time, the export industries in the coastal areas were able to absorb a large number of rural youths eager for living a good life in cities. Throughout the history of China, there have been wars and famines that caused the migration of millions of people. However, the scale of migration in 1978 was unprecedented."[2] The difficult housing and transportation in cities such as Beijing and Shanghai, the shortage of trains for coal transportation from Shanxi and other provinces, and the "hard-to-get ticket" for rural workers to return home for the Spring Festival, all showed that the construction of China's infrastructure was incapable of keeping up with the requirements of economic development in a longer period of time. In this circumstance, the actions taken by the Chinese government were first of all to insist on reform, stimulate market vitality and increase economic efficiency in order to provide the necessary prerequisites for the improvement and development of infrastructure; second, to expand opening up, actively attract foreign investment, and adopt international advanced technologies to speed up the reconstruction of domestic infrastructure. For

1 Zhang Peigang, Zhang Jianhua (eds), *Development Economics*, Peking University Press, 2009, p.347.

2 Ezra Vogel: *Deng Xiaoping and the Transformation of China*, translated by Feng Keli, and proofread by the Editorial Department of the Chinese University Press, and the Editorial Department of SDX Joint Publishing Company, SDX Joint Publishing Company, 2013, p.651.

instance, the sources of funds for investment in basic industries and infrastructure in 1978 were basically national fiscal funds. Among the sources of funds for investment in basic industries and infrastructure in 2007, national budget funds accounted for 8.4%, domestic loans 23%, foreign investment 1.8%, and self-raised funds 59.9%. According to the type of economic investor, state-owned investment accounted for 62.3%, foreign investment 4.8%, and private individuals 5.8%[1]; third, to formulate a scientific plan and gradually increase investment in infrastructure. When the social economy and comprehensive national strength have the required conditions, it is necessary to decisively integrate the advantages of all parties to comprehensively promote the modernization of the infrastructure.

According to the statistical data of authoritative departments[2], from 1979 to 2007, the investment in basic national industries and infrastructure totaled 29,798.5 billion RMB, accounting for 38.4% of the total social investment in the same period, with an average annual growth of 19.9%, which was 4.2 percentage points higher than the average annual growth of the national economy in the same period.[3] Among them, the transportation industry experienced particularly fast development, with a total investment of 7,424.6 billion RMB, an average annual increase of 19.9%. Specifically, the operating mileage of railways was increased from 52,000 kilometers in 1978 to 78,000 kilometers in 2007, an increase of 26,000 kilometers. Most of the new mileage was the electrified railway operating mileage with advanced technology and equipment. The mileage of railway electrification was only 1,000 kilometers in 1978, and reached up to 24,000 kilometers in 2007; the traffic mileage of highways was increased from 890,000 kilometers in 1978

1 Prominent Achievements in the Construction of Basic Industries and Infrastructures - Fourth Report on the Achievements of China's Economic and Social Development in 30 Years of Reform and Opening up, www.gov.cn, October 30, 2008.

2 Prominent Achievements in the Construction of Basic Industries and Infrastructures - Fourth Report on the Achievements of China's Economic and Social Development in 30 Years of Reform and Opening up, www.gov.cn, October 30, 2008.

3 The basic industries here refer to agriculture, energy, raw material supply, etc. The infrastructure mainly refers to transportation, post and telecommunications, and also includes water conservation environment, as well as educational, cultural, and health sports facilities.

to 3,580,000 kilometers in 2007, an increase of 3 times, of which the mileage of expressway was increased from 100 kilometers in 1988 to 53,900 kilometers, an increase of 538 times. The "five vertical and seven horizontal" national road trunk lines were initially formed, and the grade of the road was significantly improved; by the end of 2007, there were 148 civilian flight airports, an increase of 66 over 1985, and there were 1,506 air routes, an increase of 1,069 over 1990, the length of civil air transportation routes was 2.34 million kilometers, an increase of 1.83 million kilometers over 1990; in 2007, the cargo throughput of major coastal ports reached 3.882 billion tons, which was 17.9 times that of 1980; the mileage of oil (gas) pipeline was 54,500 kilometers, which was 6.6 times of that in 1978. Shanghai's port has become the largest port in the world with an annual throughput of nearly 500 million tons.

In the past decade, China witnessed the accelerated pace of the construction of infrastructure. With the high-speed railway as an example, as reported in a news report, "Before 2007, China did not have a railway that could be called 'high speed'. In just a few years, a series of high-speed railway trains have been traveling very quickly close to the ground. China has the most complete high-speed rail system technology, the highest integration capability, the longest operating mileage, the highest operating speed, and the largest construction scale in the world. Starting from scratch, the high-speed railways in China have achieved rapid development over a period of six years. The great number of high-speed railways not only builds up the reinforced steel frame on the motherland, but also quietly changes people's lives."[1] In 2008, China's first high-speed railroad, the Beijing-Tianjin inter-city railroad, was opened for operation. In 2009, the Wuhan-Guangzhou high-speed railroad with the longest built-in mileage and the most complex type of project at a speed of 350 kilometers per hour was opened for operation. In 2010, the Zhengzhou-Xi'an high-speed railroad at a speed of 350 kilometers per hour, which was the first in the world to be built in a collapsible loess area and connected central and western

1 Changes in High-speed Railroads: A Summary of China's Achievements in High-speed Railroad Development in Recent Years, www.caixin.com, September 13, 2012.

China, was opened for operation. In 2012, the Harbin-Dalian high-speed railroad, the world's first high-speed rail located in a high-altitude-cold area, was opened for operation, which linked major cities in the northeastern provinces to the front line at a speed of 200 kilometers per hour. By the end of 2012, the total mileage of China's high-speed railroads had reached 9,356 kilometers. After 2013, with the successive opening of the Nanjing-Hangzhou high-speed railroad, the Hangzhou-Ningbo high-speed railroad, the Panjin-Yingkou high-speed railroad, and the Xiangtang-Putian high-speed railroad, the operating mileage of high-speed railroads was increased by 1,107 kilometers, and the total mileage of China's high-speed railroads reached up to 12,000 kilometers. In 2014, the scale of operations of China's new railway line hit a record high. The operating mileage of railways made the breakthrough of 112,000 kilometers, and the operating mileage of high-speed railroads exceeded 16,000 kilometers, ranking first in the world. In 2016, the Zhengzhou-Xuzhou high-speed railroad linking the Beijing-Guangzhou high-speed railroad and the Beijing-Shanghai high-speed railroad was opened for operation at a design speed of 350 kilometers per hour. A number of scientific and technological achievements with independent intellectual property rights and at an internationally advanced level were applied. In June 2017, the "Renaissance" EMU train with independent intellectual property rights and an internationally advanced level was put into use. In July, the Baoji-Lanzhou high-speed railroad across the "last mile" for linkage between eastern and western China was officially put into operations. According to the newly released *Medium- and Long-term Railway Network Plan*, the size of China's railway network will reach 175,000 kilometers by 2025, including about 38,000 kilometers of high-speed railroads, which is the double of what it was by the end of 2015. By 2030, basic internal and external interconnections, inter-regional multiple access, provincial high-speed railroad connectivity, rapid access to prefectures and cities, as well as basic coverage of all counties will have been basically achieved.

In the early 1990s, Zhang Peigang proposed four countermeasures when he talked about how to address the problems of the construction of infrastructures in developing countries: (1) to effectively control the demand of the direct production sectors to adapt to the supply capacity of infrastructure; (2) to combine appropriate protection with effective competition to enable the direct production sectors to provide more surplus; (3) to carry out reform on the investment system so as to require enterprises to be mainly responsible for the investment in infrastructure, and enterprises to be mainly responsible for the investment in direct production sectors; (4) to raise the price of infrastructure products and services to allow them to have a certain self-developmental capacity; (5) to formulate practical long-term development plans to properly advance the construction of infrastructures on the basis of the correct prediction of industrial development needs.[1] Facts have proved that the developmental experience in China represented by high-speed railroads have greatly enriched the infrastructure theory in development economics. The adherence to the reform and opening up, the good use of institutional advantages, the reliance on scientific and technological innovation, and the preferential development of infrastructure effectively boosted the economy of China to achieve leap-forward development, thus providing ideas to explore for future global economic governance.

III

If Zhang Peigang's original theory is viewed as the embodiment of Chinese wisdom, its value in the context of globalization can not only facilitate the development of China, but also play its due role in recovering from the international economic depression. In fact, when Zhang Peigang wrote his doctoral dissertation, he had already noticed the long-cycle problem of the world's economy. He pointed out that in the process of "evolutionary" industrialization, "the innovative spirit and production technology of enterprises" are "the important driving force for the start

1 Zhang Peigang (ed.), *New Development Economics*, Henan People's Publishing House, 1993, pp.192-193.

of industrialization."[1] Besides, he also mentioned that, "According to the historical record, some people believe that war destroys and impedes economic development in many countries, but it also generates stimulating effects in the introduction and acceleration of industrialization in some countries."[2] When introducing related theories about the explanation for economic expansion through war, Zhang Peigang specifically analyzed the views of N. D. Kondratieff and Alvin H. Hansen, and then concluded that: "The impact of war on economic expansion can be reviewed from three perspectives: First, war creates need, and further stimulates the emergence of new products and the application of more favorable substitutes in the domestic production. Second, war stimulates employment, and shows the necessity for innovations in production technology in terms of saving labor or saving raw materials. Finally, war helps eliminate some institutional obstacles to avoid the interference with social reforms related to income distribution and property ownership."[3]

In Zhang Peigang's doctoral dissertation, the views of N. D. Kondratieff were only used to explain the reasons for determining the progress and speed of industrialization. After the international financial crisis took place in 2008, the theory of N. D. Kondratieff, an economist of the former Soviet Union, caused wide discussion among people once again. In the article, *The Long Waves in Economic Life,* published in 1925, N. D. Kondratieff wrote: "The economic life movement of capitalist social institutions is complicated and cyclical rather than simple and straight." "We really have reasons to assume that there is an average long-term fluctuation of about 50 years in the capitalist economy. This fact makes

1 Zhang Peigang, *Agriculture and Industrialization (Volume I): A Preliminary Study on the Industrialization Issue of Agricultural Countries*, Huazhong University of Science Technology Press, 1984, p.98.

2 Zhang Peigang, *Agriculture and Industrialization (Volume I): A Preliminary Study on the Industrialization Issue of Agricultural Countries*, Huazhong University of Science Technology Press, 1984, pp.99-100.

3 Zhang Peigang, *Agriculture and Industrialization (Volume I): A Preliminary Study on the Industrialization Issue of Agricultural Countries*, Huazhong University of Science Technology Press, 1984, p.101.

the dynamic economic issue more complicated."[1] Compared with the long-term fluctuation, the capitalist economy has also experienced the intermediate fluctuation for 7 to 11 years. Some scholars hold that the causes of the two types of cyclical fluctuations are varied. Specifically, the intermediate fluctuation is the result of the internal causes of capitalism. By contrast, the long-term fluctuation is the result of accidental and super-economic conditions and events of the environment, such as technological change, war and revolution, incorporation of new countries into the world's economy, and fluctuation in gold production. In this regard, N. D. Kondratieff refuted it.

N. D. Kondratieff believes that, "There is no doubt that technological change generates a very significant impact on the developmental process of capitalism." "The change of production technology means: 1. the related scientific and technological discoveries and inventions have been completed; 2. the applications are economically possible;" however, "scientific and technological inventions are not sufficient to bring about real changes in production technology. They are useless as long as the economic conditions conducive to their adoption are not made available. This can be illustrated by the following example. The scientific and technological discoveries and inventions of the 17th and 18th centuries were put into large-scale applications until the period of the Industrial Revolution in the late 18th century. If this is true, it is an awful idea that the change in technology is considered to be accidental and does not actually come from economic needs." Obviously, "Technology development itself is a part of the rhythm of long-term fluctuation."[2] He wrote: "War and revolution also produce a very powerful influence on the course of economic development. However, war and revolution don't come out of the air. They arise from actual reality, especially economic environment, instead of the arbitrary behavior of individual figures. It is believed that war and

1 N. D. Kondratieff, *The Long Waves in Economic Life*, translated by Li Cong, Volume X of *Anthology of Modern Foreign Economics Papers*, The Commercial Press, 1986, p.1.

2 N. D. Kondratieff, *The Long Waves in Economic Life*, translated by Li Cong, Volume X of *Anthology of Modern Foreign Economics Papers*, The Commercial Press, 1986, p.15.

revolution are caused by external factors and can cause long-term fluctuation. This raises a question: Why do they occur regularly one after another and only during the upsurge of the long-term fluctuation? An imagination is most likely to be true that war originates from the accelerated pace and increased tension of economic life, and the intensification of the battle for the market and raw materials. The social turmoil is most likely to occur under the pressure of new economic forces."[1] As to the development of a new country, "a new surge makes it necessary and possible to develop new countries, new markets and new sources of raw materials, thereby accelerating the pace of capitalist development."[2]

It can thus be seen that in the study of N. D. Kondratieff, the capitalist economy has its own cycle of development which is closely associated with scientific and technological progress. Its demand for and use of new technologies constitute a phase of the cycle. War and revolution are caused by several unsolvable contradictions in the economic cycle, such as the accelerated pace of economic life, a strengthened state of tension, and an intensified battle for markets and raw materials. The long-cycle theory of N. D. Kondratieff was recognized by Schumpeter. Schumpeter maintained that, "If we look at the long wave of economic activity, the same facts become more obvious. The relevant study can make the nature and mechanism of capitalism clearer than everything."[3] However, Schumpeter further pointed out that war, revolution, population, capital, currency and other factors were often considered as the conditions for industrial change, rather than the main force for industrial change. As a matter of fact, "New consumption goods created by capitalist companies, new modes of production or transportation, new markets, and new forms of industrial organization are the fundamental driving forces for starting and maintaining the movement of the engine

1 N. D. Kondratieff, *The Long Waves in Economic Life*, translated by Li Cong, Volume X of *Anthology of Modern Foreign Economics Papers*, The Commercial Press, 1986, p.16.

2 N. D. Kondratieff, *The Long Waves in Economic Life*, translated by Li Cong, Volume X of *Anthology of Modern Foreign Economics Papers*, The Commercial Press, 1986, p.16.

3 Joseph Schumpeter: *Capitalism, Socialism and Democracy*, translated by Yang Zhongqiu, Publishing House of Electronics Industry, 2013 Edition, p.65.

of capitalism."[1]

With reference to the economic cycle theory of N. D. Kondratieff and Schumpeter, Wei Sen considers that the problems faced by the world's economy at the moment have both similarities and some new varied elements. He points out: "Over the past 20 years of global economic globalization, a large number of foreign capitals and new manufacturing technologies have flowed into China in the course of the reform and opening up. China's export-oriented economic growth model has naturally been shaped according to the system of globalized division of labor, thanks to the inflow of foreign capitals, the introduction of new manufacturing technologies, and China's abundance of low-cost labor force. China's growth model is complementary to the previous years of virtual prosperity and asset bubbles of the US financial market, which enables Americans to enjoy cheap goods imported from China and other developing countries under the conditions of prosperous virtual economic sectors, and to rely on the big inflow of international funds to make up for the fiscal expenditures of the American government due to a lack of domestic savings and the possible economic growth constraints caused by short financing of large companies." "The economic recession ought to have occurred in the United States and other Western developed countries at the other end of the globalized division of labor chain should have been delayed in the world economy as a whole."[2]

Since economic globalization not only leads to rapid economic growth in China but it also delays the economic recession in developed countries; it is reasonable to expect that China's developmental experience and achievements can benefit other developing countries and come up with new solutions to the governance of the global economy. According to the foregoing classification of Zhang Peigang,

1 Joseph Schumpeter: *Capitalism, Socialism and Democracy*, translated by Yang Zhongqiu, Publishing House of Electronics Industry, 2013 Edition, p.78.

2 Wei Sen: The Deep Causes of the Current World Economic Recession and China's Choice of Appropriate Macroeconomic Policies: Viewing the Current World Economic Recession from the Business Cycle Theory of Schumpeter, Zhang Huiming, Deng Xia (eds): *The Marxist Interpretation of the Financial Crisis*, Fudan University Press, 2009, p.184.

individually or privately initiated industrialization experiences a long period of time. The market-dependent infrastructure has a slow cycle of construction. The mechanism for eliminating economic fluctuations is relatively rigid and constructive. In spite of fast development, the governmentally initiated industrialization, including infrastructure, has the low overall efficiency of economic operations; after the domestic economy reaches a certain degree of development, the governmentally and privately initiated industrialization tends to expand externally because of a strong sense of a purpose of forging-ahead. This explains why the long cycle of the world economy in the first half of the 20th century was constantly accompanied by war or revolution. In contrast, the path of economic development in contemporary China is unique. Deng Xiaoping seized a rare historical opportunity and initiated the reform of the Chinese economy from a planned economy to a market economy. As a result, the original industrial foundation and the state-owned economy gain new vitalities in the reform, market competition makes the entire social economy full of energy, and the opening up to the outside world creates tremendous space of "bringing in" and "going global" for the development of China. The achievements in the construction of Chinese infrastructure and the growth in the Chinese economy are all associated with this. Based on the developmental experience and global economic challenges, the Chinese government has put forward the "Belt and Road" Initiative to strive to expand economic exchanges through cooperation among various countries, focus on the promotion of the construction of infrastructure, accelerate the process of the industrialization of developing countries, and meanwhile, drive the strong recovery of the world's economy. This article believes that the "Belt and Road" Initiative is one of China's programs that is worthy of people concerned about peace and development to think deeply and promote practice.

共同发展与共同价值

Mutual Development and Common Value

在“汉学与当代中国”座谈会上的发言

萨米尔·哈巴什奈 【约旦】

前副首相/中国—约旦非政府文化科技理事会主席

首先，请允许我代表中国—约旦非政府文化科技理事会全体成员向中国政府以及为此次活动付出辛勤努力的工作人员表示感谢。

中国—约旦非政府文化科技理事会旨在加强阿拉伯国家和中国之间的联系，尤其是中国与约旦的关系。无论是在公共领域还是在社会领域，或者是在教育、经济、社会等方面，这些非政府组织都为中国和阿卜杜拉二世领导的约旦间的关系努力。

我想借此机会表达以下几点：

目前我们关注的主要问题是恐怖主义，它将使世界各地的国家平民成为受害者，迫使数百万人离开家园，最终成为难民。我们在约旦也遭受恐怖主义威胁，为了约旦公民和我们的国家安全，避免恐怖主义带来的结果，我们不得不遏制超过150万叙利亚难民在我们的土地上建避难所。这意味着反恐是一项全球性的责任，每个国家都应该为争取世界公平做出贡献。

我认为，世界上主要冲突的解决方案和首要问题是巴勒斯坦问题，并根据国际决议。因此，发达国家需要帮助发展中国家进行斗争，以保障他们的良好生活，贫困和失业可能对全球的发展带来极大的负面影响。

值得一提的是，“阿拉伯人的呼吁”是由100多名公众人物和非政府组织签署、并于 9 月在开罗阿拉伯联盟正式发布的一项活动，我对该活动将要实现的结果充满希望。最后，我也对中国政府提出的维护全球公平和期待世界和平方面的政策表示十分赞赏。

The Speech on the "Symopsium on China Studies" 2017

Samir Habashneh / Jordan

Former Deputy Prime Minister of Jordan, Chairman of the Cultural (Non Governmental) Dialogue Cooperation Committee Between Jordan and China

First allow me to thank the government of the People's Republic of China and everyone who contributed in making this event on behalf of all the Non-Governmental Committee for Sino-Jordanian Cultural Cooperation & the Jordanian Association for Science & Culture members.

This non-governmental entity seeks to enhance the ties between two brothers nation Arab & China especially with Jordan. In both public and civil society fields educationally, economically, socially, etc., where these association support and complete the Jordanian and Chinese official efforts led by the Chinese leader and his Majesty Kong Abdullah II.

I would like to take the opportunity to go through the followings:

The main topic that leads our concerns these days is terrorism, the agenda that targets each and every country around the world causing civil victims and forcing millions of people to leave their homes and ending up as refugees. We in Jordan have suffering terrorism threats targeting Jordanian citizens and our national security, where as a result of this terror we had to contain more than a million and a half Syrian refuge in our lands. That means that counter terrorism is a global responsibility every country shall contribute fighting it military and by a serious efforts to reach a fair.

Solutions for the main conflicts in the world and top of it all are the Palestinian issue and in accordance with the international resolutions. Therefore, it is significant that the developed countries need to backup the developing countries to fight in order to secure them a well human life, and poverty and unemployment can be part of the global destruction.

It is worth mentioning that the "Arab Call" was signed by over a hundred public figures and NGO's and will be launched at the Arab League in the Cairo coming September, full of hope to achieve real outcomes.

At last, we do admire the calm policy of the People's Republic of China which can look forward to world peace and global equity.

基于共同发展的周边命运共同体建设

赵江林 【中国】
中国社会科学院亚太与全球战略研究院国际经济关系研究室主任、研究员、经济学博士

周边命运共同体的概念首次提出是在2013年10月召开的中国周边外交工作座谈会上，习近平总书记特别强调“要让命运共同体意识在周边国家落地生根”。[1]命运共同体是和平发展、平等发展、开放发展、共同发展、可持续发展的集合理念，周边命运共同体是命运共同体概念在周边国家的实践，改变国与国之间传统的发展型态，最终形成有着共同价值认同的新型关系，为世界经济社会的全新发展提供一种新范式。

一 中国为什么要提出建设命运共同体

中国推出命运共同体概念的目的是通过倡导人类命运共同体意识，打破传统西方发达国家狭隘的发展路径和发展理念，将全人类的共同发展置于首要的位置上，换句话说，如果西方的发展属于“一部分人先富起来”的话，那么今天中国倡导的人类命运共同体意识则属于走“共同富裕”的道路。

第一，每一个人、每一个国家在发展面前人人平等。首先工业化成果本身就属于“公共产品”，不为哪个国家所专属，因此，任何国家都没有权利垄断工业

1 《习近平：让命运共同体意识在周边国家落地生根》，http://news.xinhuanet.com/2013-10/25/c_117878944.htm.

化成果。至于如何让每一个人都享有工业化成果需要通过可行的方式来解决，而不是武断地将一些国家排除在外。

第二，发展模式可以多样，不强求整齐划一。每个国家因资源禀赋，历史渊源、地理气候、人文特点等因素决定了即使在走工业化道路方面也可有自己的独特选择，只要适合本国国情，就是最佳的发展模式。中国改革开放近40年的发展成就足以证明模式、道路不必向西方看齐，每个国家都有决定自己命运的权利。

第三，不以意识形态来人为地将国家进行划分。在发展这一大问题上，意识形态不应起到主导作用，每个国家、每个人都不应受意识形态的制约而被“剥夺”发展机会。因此今天，中国积极倡导建设文化多元的价值观体系，目的是将世界各国的发展包容其中，不因经济发展水平的高低来评价一国的文明发展程度。

二　周边命运共同体：世界经济社会发展的新范式

基于上述，中国建立命运共同体的内涵是如何推进人类走共同发展、共同富裕的道路，具体包括：

第一，建立包容型的世界经济体系，即打破西方长期建立的狭隘的只允许少数国家“富裕”的世界经济体系，创建一个能够将发展中国家都被包容其中的世界经济体系，所有国家均享有平等的发展权。

第二，以共同发展为导向的发展模式。走共同富裕道路是中国建设命运共同体的出发点和落脚点。目前某些国家仍然怀疑中国提出的“一带一路”倡议，认为中国的目的是为了自身的发展，甚至蛊惑当地政府和民众反对中国的“一带一路”建设。事实已证明，中国的“一带一路”倡议不仅是惠及自身，更是惠及他国的倡议，将成为走共同富裕道路的践行手段。

第三，以可持续发展为终极目标的发展路径。可持续发展道路尚在摸索过程中，特别是在重大技术没有取得突破之前，可持续能否实现还是一个未知数，但是这一方向性的道路是确定的，中国在这方面发展具有的示范意义。

三　命运共同体建设的可行性

周边是中国外交、经济延伸的第一落脚点，也是中国命运共同体建设成功与否的关键点和实验区。在改革开放近40年的时间里，中国与周边国家关系获得了全方位的发展，也正是在这一基础上，为今天的周边命运共同体建设奠定了现实基础。

一是与绝大多数周边国家建立了良好的政治关系。中国已经同8个周边国家签署睦邻友好合作条约，正在同东盟商谈签署中国—东盟睦邻友好合作条约，并愿同所有周边国家商签睦邻友好合作条约，这将为双边关系发展和地区繁荣稳定提供有力保障，为周边命运共同体的推进打下了良好的基础，更容易在共同发展上达成共识。

二是与周边国家建立了密切的经贸关系。中国同绝大多数周边国家签有自贸区协定，在零部件、资本品等产业分工方面建立了密切的关系。目前中国已成为世界最大的进口国之一，与美国进口规模相当，凭借自身的市场，中国有能力协助周边国家完成工业化进程。数据表明，中国从周边国家进口的产品已从2005年的2829千亿美元上升到2015年的5761亿美元，其中包括消费品、资本品和零部件等具有国际分工含量的产品，进口规模同期从1587亿美元上升到3282亿美元。中国推出“一带一路”倡议表明中国已有一定的市场能力接纳周边国家的产品和服务。未来，通过“五通”建设，中国与周边国家将建立起新的供求平衡体系，率先完成经济共同体建设。

中国与周边国家的相互投资水平也较以往有较大幅度的提升，特别是近年来产能合作的推进、工业园区的建设进一步夯实了中国与周边国家的产业合作基础。据统计，2015年中国对外投资已经超过吸引外资的规模，2016年中国对外投资规模达到1700亿美元，成为世界对外投资规模第二大经济体，累计的对外投资规模正在比肩日本。由中国倡议的亚洲基础设施投资银行、金砖银行、丝路基金的建立正在努力为发展中国家提供以基础设施为主的资金，构筑全球互联互通体系，以解除基础设施瓶颈对经济增长的制约。据统计，2015年中国对周边国家投资存量914亿美元以上，未来中国还将继续加大对周边国家的投资力度。

三是基础设施互联互通工作得到顺利推进。中国有技术完成周边国家的“联通”建设，使周边国家成为“陆联国”，从而进一步激发周边国家的发展潜能。目前中国与周边国家正在建设的高速铁路、航空、港口等正在以前所未有的速度向前推进，部分设施已经对当地的经济发展起到不可小觑的作用，周边国家在与中国的交往过程中也越来越感受到中国发展模式的魅力和中国与周边国家建设共同体的务实性。

四是人文交流日趋便捷、活跃，为周边命运共同体推进提供了共同体意识确立的前提。目前中国与多个周边国家开展多层次的人文交流。在今年的“一带一路”高峰合作论坛上，中国进一步提出加强与周边国家人文交流合作的升级版。

五是“澜湄合作”成为中国周边命运共同体建设的案例典范，助推了中国和周边国家命运共同体建设的信心。“澜湄合作”是第一个由中国发起和主导的新型周边次区域合作机制。[1]今天的中国自身已成为全球产业价值链的重要组成部分，凭借中国上万亿美元的产业能力，使得周边国家有机会参与中国构筑的全球产业价值链中，从而迅速完成工业化任务。在合作机制方面，“澜湄合作”采取更为灵活的处理方式，体现了合作的包容性、发展的平等性以及共同富裕、共同发展的理念，极大地增强了周边国家参与合作、共建命运共同体的舒适度。也正因此，“澜湄合作”以前所未有的速度和质量增长，在短短的几年时间内取得了巨大的成效，为周边命运共同体建设提供了样板。[2]

1　刘均胜，《澜湄合作：示范亚洲命运共同体建设》，《中国经济周刊》2016年第4期。

2　余潇枫、王梦婷，《非传统安全共同体：一种跨国安全治理的新探索》，《国际安全研究》2017年第1期。

Building a Community with a Shared Future in Neighboring Areas Based on Common Development

Zhao Jianglin / China

Director and Researcher of the Division on International Economic Relations under the National Institute of International Strategy at the Chinese Academy of Social Sciences

The concept of a community with a shared future in neighboring areas was first proposed at the neighborhood diplomacy work conference of China held in October 2013. General Secretary Xi Jinping emphasized in particular that "it is necessary for the awareness of a community with a shared future to take root in neighboring countries".[1] A community with a shared future is a collective concept of peaceful development, equal development, open development, common development, and sustainable development. A community with a shared future in neighboring areas is the practice of the concept of a community with a shared future in neighboring countries, which changes the traditional pattern of development among countries, and eventually forms a new relationship with a recognition of shared values, thereby providing a new model for the new development of the world's economy and

1 Xi Jinping: Make the Awareness of the Community with a Shared future Rooted in the Neighboring Countries, http://news.xinhuanet.com/2013-10/25/c_117878944.htm.

society.

I. Why does China Propose to Build a Community with a Shared Future?

The reason why China proposes to build a community with a shared future is to break the traditional narrow path towards development and developmental concept of the American and Western developed countries and place the common development of all mankind in the first place through the advocacy of an awareness of a community with a shared future for mankind. In other words, if the American and Western development belongs to the model of "let some people get rich first", the awareness of a community with a shared future for mankind advocated by China today belongs to the model of "common prosperity".

First, every individual and every country are equal before development. The results of industrialization, in essence, belong to "public goods" and are not exclusive to any country. Therefore, no country has the right to monopolize the results of industrialization. The question of how to make everyone enjoy those results needs to be solved in a feasible way, instead of arbitrarily excluding some countries.

Second, the model of development can be varied without the requirement of uniformity. The unique resources, historical origins, geographical climates, and cultural characteristics of each country determine its own unique choice in the path of industrialization. As long as the developmental path is suitable for national conditions, it is the best model of development. The developmental achievements of China's reform and opening up in the past 40 years are enough to prove that the model and path need not be aligned with the American and the Western countries. Each country has the right to determine its own destiny.

Third, we do not divide countries by ideology. As to the major issue of development, ideology should not play a leading role. Every country and every individual should not be deprived of opportunities for development because of ideology constraints. Therefore, today, China actively advocates the construction of a culturally diversified system of values in a bid to incorporate the development of all countries in the world and not to evaluate the degree of development of the civilization of a country due to its level of economic development.

II. A Community with a Shared Future in Neighboring Areas: a New Model of World Economic and Social Development

Based on the foregoing information, the connotation of China's establishment of a community with a shared future is how to advance along the road of common development and common prosperity for mankind, specifically including:

First, building an inclusive world economic system. In other words, the narrow long-established world economic system that only allows a small number of countries to become "rich" in the United States and the West is broken to create a world economic system in which the developing countries can be incorporated and all countries can enjoy the equal right of development.

Second, following the developmental model of orientation towards common development. Taking the road of common prosperity is the starting point and foothold for China's establishment of a community with a shared future. At present, some countries still doubt the intention of China to propose the "Belt and Road" Initiative, they consider that China is aimed for its own development, and even deceive the local governments and people against China's "Belt and Road" Initiative. Facts have proven that China's "Belt and Road" Initiative is not only an initiative benefiting itself and other countries, but it also becomes a practical means for undertaking the road towards common prosperity.

Third, following the developmental path with sustainable development as the ultimate goal. The path towards sustainable development is still in the process of experimentation. It is still unknown whether sustainable development can be achieved before significant technological breakthroughs have come about. However, there is no doubt about the directional path and China will also become a model of development in this regard.

III. Feasibility of Building a Community with a Shared Future

The neighboring area is the first place in which China's diplomacy and economic development can expand, as well as a key point and experimental area for China to successfully build a community with a shared future. In the past 40 years of reform and opening up, China's relations with its neighboring countries have achieved all-round development, laying a realistic foundation for building a community with a shared future in neighboring areas today.

First, good political relations with the vast majority of neighboring countries have been developed. China has signed some treaties of good neighborliness and friendly cooperation with eight neighboring countries, and now, it is negotiating with the ASEAN countries on the signing of the China-ASEAN Treaty of Good Neighborliness and Friendly Cooperation. China is also willing to negotiate the treaties of good neighborliness and friendly cooperation with all neighboring countries. This will provide a strong guarantee for the development of bilateral relations and regional prosperity and stability, and lay a good foundation for advancing the idea of a community with a shared future in neighboring areas. As a result, it is easier to reach a consensus on common development.

Second, close economic and trade relations with neighboring countries have been established. China has signed free trade zone agreement with the vast majority of its neighboring countries and has established a close relationship in industrial divisions such as parts and capital goods. At present, China is one of the largest importing countries in the world, comparable to the United States. With its own market, China has the ability to assist neighboring countries in completing the process of industrialization. The data shows that China's imports from neighboring countries increased from USD 282.9 billion in 2005 to USD 576.1 billion in 2015, of which the volume of imported products with international division such as consumer goods, capital goods and parts was increased from 158.7 billion USD to 328.2 billion USD in the same period. China's launch of the "Belt and Road" Initiative shows that China has a certain capacity for a market in order to be able to accept the products and services from neighboring countries. In the future, through the "Five-Pronged Approach" (i.e., policy coordination, connectivity of infrastructure, unimpeded trade, financial integration and closer people-to-people ties), China will establish a new supply and demand balance system with neighboring countries to take the lead in completing the construction of an economic community.

The level of mutual investment between China and its neighboring countries has also been greatly improved compared with the past. In particular, the advancement of its capacity for cooperation and the construction of industrial parks in recent years have further consolidated the foundation for industrial cooperation between China and its neighboring countries. According to statistics, China's investment abroad in 2015 exceeded the scale of foreign investment that it attracted. In 2016, the scale of China's foreign investment reached up to 170 billion USD, enabling China to become the world's second largest foreign investment economy. Now, the scale of Chinese cumulative investment abroad comes up to that of Japan. The establishment of the Asian Infrastructure Investment Bank, the BRIC Bank, and the Silk Road Fund initiated by China is striving to provide infrastructure-based funds for developing countries and to build a global interconnection system so as to relieve the constraint of the infrastructure bottleneck on economic growth. According to statistics, China's investment in its neighboring countries in 2015 was more than 91.4 billion USD. In the future, China will continue to increase its investments in its neighboring countries.

Third, the infrastructure interconnection and intercommunication work has been smoothly advanced. Technologically, China is able to complete the construction of "interconnection" with its neighboring countries and make its neighboring countries become "land-linked countries", thereby further stimulating the developmental potential of those neighboring countries. At present, high-speed railways, airports and ports jointly constructed by China and its neighboring countries are advancing at an unprecedented speed. Some facilities have played an important role in the local economic development. In the process of exchanges with China, the neighboring countries have increasingly realized the charm of China's developmental model and the pragmatic approach of China's construction of a community with its neighboring countries.

Fourth, cultural and educational exchanges have become increasingly convenient and active, providing the preconditions for the establishment of an awareness of a community with a shared future in neighboring areas. So far, China has conducted multi-level cultural and educational exchanges with a number of its neighboring countries. At the Belt and Road Forum for International Cooperation in the current year, China further proposed an upgraded version of the strengthening of cultural and educational exchanges and cooperation with neighboring countries.

Last but not least, the Lancang-Mekong cooperation has become a model case of China in building a community with a shared future in neighboring areas, which has boosted the confidence of China and its neighboring countries in building a community with a shared future. The "Lancang-Mekong cooperation" is the first new peripheral sub-regional cooperation mechanism initiated and led by China.[1] Unlike the past, China itself is now an important part of the global industrial value chain. With China's trillions of dollars of industrial capacity, its neighboring countries have the opportunity to participate in the global industrial value chain built by China, thus quickly completing industrialization tasks. In terms of the mechanism for cooperation, the type of cooperation carried out in Lancang-Mekong adopts a more flexible approach, which reflects the inclusiveness of cooperation, the equality of development, and the concept of common prosperity

1 Liu Junsheng, Lancang-Mekong Cooperation: Demonstration of the Community with a Shared future in Asia, *China Economic Weekly*, 2016(4).

and common development, and it greatly raises the comfort of the neighboring countries in their participation in the cooperation and establishment of a community with a shared future. Hence, the Lancang-Mekong cooperation has developed with unprecedented speed and quality, and it has achieved tremendous results in just a few years, setting an example for building a community with a shared future in neighboring areas.[1]

1 Yu Xiaofeng, Wang Mengting, "Non-traditional Security Community: A New Exploration of Transnational Security Governance" , *Journal of University of International Relations*, 2017(1).

中国文化的对外影响：以越南—中国文化交流为例

阮玉长 【越南】
战略研究与国际发展中心主席

纵观越南和中国之间的关系，自古至今如何认识和解读中国，一直以来都是一个客观的要求，同时也是越南学术界不懈努力之工作，其目的是为了确定两国在历史上的相关性、互动性以及在某个特定的时间上两国的关系之内涵。此项工作既具有吸引力但也充满着挑战性，在过去中国曾经处于东方之“宗主国”的位置上，而现在的中国的综合影响力及辐射力也在不断地在全球范围内提升并扩大。

一

这里的文化可以从广义上加以解释，即“人在建构社会的相关活动及其产物的整体性中所建立和维持社会体系的秩序”。可见，此文化之影响是历史必然性，同时也可以指的是文化从其中心往周边散发的情况。

二

从19个世纪到殖民时期之前越南和中国都有着文化上的长期且深远的联系。这种关系之联系性通过文化上的渗透、折射、交流和引进后改变等直接或间接的方式。尽管两国在不同时期经历过时起时伏变化，但如果回顾一下就会发现，这整个过程却不曾间断过。中国前任国家主席胡锦涛曾用下面的几句简洁有力的话来概括此关系：“山水相连，文化想通，理想相同，命运相关。”

中华民族是一个伟大的民族，具有一个灿烂无比、可持续性的、承前启后的且十分发达的文化。中华文化是东方文化之精髓，对包括越南在内的许多东方国家的影响尤为深远。越南文化从中国文化中引进诸多精华元素以及越南文化所需的因素，符合于越南本土文化并能够从中创造出越南民族独特的文化特色。在此过程中，中国儒家思想对越南文化的影响至深，大部分都是从唐、宋、明这三个朝代之儒学引进来的，而最主要的是宋代儒学。儒学在越南的历史上不断得到巩固和提升。越南有选择性地引进、接纳并接受中国儒学中的一些长处并试图摸索如何解读这些长处以利于其封建国家政权、社会结构之建设。

在封建时代里，中国文化对越南文化之影响尤为明显，特别体现于社会的上层建筑或上层社会，然而在众多乡村社区——通常被俗称为与世隔绝的“乡村之竹丛”，其影响相对来说没有那么明显。虽然在进入一个组织结构已经十分紧密的村庄体系时，此影响已经被衰减了，但其仍然保存在一些婚丧嫁娶、节日庆贺等社会礼仪及风俗习惯中。

17 世纪以前，从北纬 16 度以北，中国文化之影响尤其显著。而从北纬 16 度往南的古代王国则较多受到印度文化之影响。从 17 世纪中期，当越南的领土渐渐地往南扩张，随之而来的是中国文化也慢慢渗透到南方。必须指出，在越南的历史长河中，称得上是“大儒”的人物往往来自于北方。而北方的知识分子常常号称“北河士夫”（北河指的是北越），或者被戏称为“深儒”。

我小时候在越南中部的一个贫困地区的一所乡村学校上学，从那时起，我就能够深深地感受到中国文化在我的家乡随处可见，王勃庙就在我家附近，文鹏庙在我家的后面，而一间孔庙就在我家前面的田野中间矗立着。庙里所供奉的是孔夫子，旨在鼓励当地的学习之风。我的曾祖父和我的外公均是 19 世纪中期至 20 世纪初“末儒”时期的儒者，当时已是法国教育体系开始在越南强制施行，他们最终都不得志。有关于儒学之最后一波科举考试是在 1918 年至 1919 年间举办的。

三

中华文化对越南文化之影响主要表现在以下四个方面：

其一，越南各个封建朝代在建立以儒家思想为治国原则的中央集权国家之时，尤其是黎氏皇朝（1428—1789）以及阮氏皇朝（1802—1884）都从中国封建的政权组织方式及法律体系等方面借鉴了许多相关内容。

其二，越南各个封建朝代主动引进并接纳儒家思想和伦理，以“三纲五常”为社会架构。汉字当时成为越南正式的国家文字。儒学被推广到国家教育体系、采用科举制度。成立于1070年的文庙——国子监被视为是越南最早的大学。在那里，矗立着孔子、周公的铜像以及儒家的七十二贤人画像，四季供奉，香火不绝。可以说，文庙称得上是越南最早成立的“孔子学院”。

其三，越南的文学艺术、建筑、干支年历、阴阳五行、术数、中医针灸等领域都跟中国息息相关。这些领域的相关知识被尽量地本土化以用于探索自然及社会和人类。越南诗人亦十分擅长古风诗（old style）及唐律诗（regulated verse）。而在科举制度的要求下，律诗的结构更加严格。越南的诸多文学作品或多或少采用一些直接从中国借用过来的语料、历史事迹、典故或地名。

其四，对世界观的认知。宇宙观（阴阳五行，阴阳历中的农历等）；人生观（“人身小宇宙”、干支五行体系被使用于算命，孔孟思想和伦理中的仁孝礼义、三纲五常被奉为标准）；社会社群的组织（重男轻女、重“士”轻“商”等）；利用和应付自然环境（衣食住行、生产活动等）；对于社会环境，宗教的解读（佛教、儒学、道教等）。

四

自然环境、国家诞生和形成的历史、民族自尊心、社会经济背景等因素已经塑造了越南民族文化之核心，同时在中国文化和儒家思想渐渐渗入到越南社会结构里之时，这些本土因素也与那些外来的价值观互相碰撞。

越南文化属于水稻文化。人们主要务农，相对来说，人们对自己村庄和国家会有一种十分强烈的亲切感和归属感。众所周知，种植水稻主要依靠水利，而水利工作显然不是一家一户能负担起的，而是要整个社群的人一起出力。再加上越南属于热带季风气候，故越南人也因应气候特点而创造出比例对称、与自然环境和谐的家园。

越南封建朝代主动引进和接受儒家思想的主要目的是能够从中借鉴和采用一些有关组织社会和管理国家的方法。

越南并非复制中国封建朝代的国家组织形式，而应该是说将之用以参考的目的，以符合自己国家背景以及适应一种几乎名不副实的诸侯国身份（对内称帝对中国则称王爵）。这不是一种政治上的隶属，而是对中华文化的敬仰，同时也是一个小国对于一个在亚洲地区最强大国家应有的态度。册封抑或是朝贡均为诸侯国明显的特征，但这并没有伤害到越南民族的自尊心。必须指出的是尽管名义上对外受中国册封，然而封建时代的越南在对内及对外事务都相当独立自主。

必须指出的是，儒家思想的一些基本概念传入到越南之时可能会有不同的解读方式。就像书写形式上同样是“忠”和“孝”，但是对于越南人而言，“忠”即“忠于国”，而“孝”则即“孝于民”，这与原本的“忠”和“孝”有所不同。

村庄是越南社会核心的行政单位，支配并决定越南人的文化交流与接受。村庄文化是越南文化核心的基础。任何一种新的文化价值务必要符合村庄和国家的传统价值观，其中村庄带有最高程度的自治性，即所谓的“王法比不过乡规”。

越南文学经典之作《金云翘传》(《翘传》)是一部根据中国明末清初原著小说《金云翘》用越南本民族文字喃字写成的叙事诗，这部书被不同时代的越南人所接受和喜爱，因为它的核心内容以及故事情节已经被越化了，充满着越南国魂和文化底蕴。我的母亲是一个土生土长的农民，但她对《翘传》十分熟悉，在我们小的时候她甚至把《翘传》当做摇篮曲来唱给我们听。与此同时，越南读者也已经分不出主人公翠翘到底是中国人还是越南人，变成读者普遍同情一个古代女子。同时，也因为阅读《翘传》，越南读者才对中国的一些地名、风俗习惯十分熟悉。

因为采取灵活的引进、接受方式及不断地创新，越南已经从中国文化及中华文明的精髓里吸收不少养分。越南文化是对中华文化价值的创新。中国文化与越南文化之间的交流，在很大程度上改变了越南文化的原本面貌，让越南文化变得更加丰富多样和完善，同时也使得两国之间的连接性变得更加紧密。在越南的外交文化上，对于中国天朝(封建时越南对中国的敬称)，越南所采取的外交策略是“和孝”，所谓的“和孝”指的是“和睦相处并孝于天朝”。

五

自1884—1945年间，法国一步步吞并越南，在全越境内实行殖民统治。尽管如此，中国对当时的越南的影响还是随处可见。

自1919年起，法国殖民已经管控越南各个学校体系，并开始废除深受中国文化影响的越南封建文化遗产，这一过程持续了近半个世纪。

1885年的《天津条约》是中法争夺对越南的影响的战争结束之后，法国殖民政府和清朝政府所签署的一份条约。据此条约，法国殖民政府要彻底地割除中国对越南的政治及文化的影响和联系，但是中国文化在越南渗透的过程出自于生活的需求同时也是自然而然的历史演进过程。

19世纪，大量的以越南喃字呈现的越南语翻译的中国小说以手抄或木刻版的形式在越南境内出现并广泛流行，与此同时，法国传教士也在提倡并推行使用拉丁拼音代替汉字及越南喃字。然而，这些传教士却未料到他们所提倡的拉丁文已经成为越南儒者和革命人士进行为国家的独立自主斗争的武器。此时，中国对越南的影响则通过以"三民主义"为核心的"辛亥革命"、"五四运动"、"南昌起义"等一些新兴思想和潮流表现出来。

越南拉丁国语字其时又恰巧成为将中国文化传播到越南的有效工具，而且规模空前地扩大，变得更加大众化。首次上百部中国小说被翻译成越南文并在20世纪前30年得以大量出版。与此同时，"鸳鸯蝴蝶"派为代表的中国言情小说在越南也大有市场并且十分盛行。

越南伟大思想家胡志明主席是继承越南传统文化和汉学的代表人物，他终生为搭建越南和中国的新时代文化交流之桥梁而努力。

胡志明主席高度评价一些儒家思想和伦理："儒家思想的优点乃是修身养性"。胡主席认为儒家思想的核心价值在于"正心修身"道德观。

从童年开始，胡志明主席就已经受到正宗儒家思想的熏陶了，并从中获得了全方位且充分的儒学道德教育。胡主席十分尊敬孔夫子，对儒家思想的名言佳句里面所包含的美好的、具有时代感的价值高度评价。1965年5月拜访孔子故居时，胡主席因触景生情，创作了《访曲阜》诗，这首诗寄托了他对孔夫子的缅怀之情：

五月十九访曲阜，
古松古庙两依稀。
孔家势力今何在，
只剩斜阳照古碑。

六

自从法国殖民统治越南起，越南和中国的文化联系曾经一度被中断，与此同时，在越南境内发生越南文化与法国、美国、苏联、中国（1911年起）等世界各大国文化相互交流与接触的现象。这些外来文化在进入越南之时都曾经过互相渗透、互相交流和改变以符合于越南的国情和核心价值。

在19世纪末和20世纪前期的越中文化交流的一个独特现象就是越南的很多西学家都对汉学了如指掌，融会贯通，进而产生了新一代越南现代文化的知识分子骨干。这一现象让我联想到目前中文在越南的许多高中和大学的普及，假以时日必将会大大有利于越南年青一代更加了解中国，并从中国文化精髓中吸收养分，特别是在语言方面。换言之，越南人将愈来愈了解越南语中的汉越词汇，进而使用起来更加标准。

在中国改革开放与越南更新事业期间，河内也常常观察和参考中国的改革开放的成功经验，如朱镕基总理时代的政府结构改革，特别是现在习近平主席推行的反腐倡廉和中国共产党建设等。

七

从小到大，我阅读了上百部中国历史小说和武侠小说。这些书籍现在在越南的各个书店都有售，很容易买到。

与此同时，在高科技时代背景下出现了一个颇为积极的文化交流现象，即只要有一部平板电脑或智能手机且可以连上无线网络，所有的越南人都可以下载中国的各种书籍到自己的设备以便阅读。更有不少越南的中文译者常常出于自己的兴趣爱好而去翻译中文书籍和各种综艺节目等。

中国历史小说或现代武侠小说以及中国的各种传说书籍之所以在越南如此受欢迎，是因为故事情节，被摆设在中国庞大的历史和文化空间。阅读时，故事给人们提供了极为丰富的知识，如关于中医、饮食、饮酒、种花、茶道、武术、治国平天下以及中国历史上的典故等。

我尽力阅读一切中国经典的历史、武侠小说，每次阅读时，我都对中国过去和现代作家的丰富想象力以及他们厚实的文化底蕴倍感敬佩和充满仰慕之情。

目前中国在世界各地成立越来越多的孔子学院，这当然是一件相当重要的事，然而这只是传播中华文化的一种方式。在当下的高科技时代，中国文化在与世界文化的交流与传播中如何扮演更重要的角色，带来更多、更强而有力的优势变得越来越重要。因此，中国或许要考虑如何充分利用高科技让中国与世界各国的文化交流过程变得更便利、顺畅。

八

中国文化的影响力不断扩大至全球范围内还是一种新的现象。不管是何种文化，人都是其中的主体。不管在中国境内还是在与世界交流、接轨的过程中，中国人尚需时间来适应并完善自己的心态，同时也能将自己适应并融入一个日新月异的文化时代里。如果说那些欧美工业国家需要花几百年的时间也能让其人民形成一种工业文化，那么现代中国可以采取许多其他方式，以缩短时间。中国的经济实力可以作为扩展软实力的一个支撑或引擎。“一带一路”倡议目前也正在如火如荼地进行当中，这必定能为中国文化的影响向亚、欧、非这三个大洲扩展提供更宽广的空间。

世界正在努力认识和解读中国。中国人不管是去国外旅游、学习进修还是做生意，都有更多的机会与其他国家的文化接触，所以中国人对于世界的认识也应随之加强。

越南人在近几年来很明显地感受到中国经济的崛起，但可惜的是人们尚未看到中国企业文化相较于其他国家的企业文化的优越性。

前不久香港《文汇报》曾探讨与分析中国企业前往越南投资的有利条件及挑战，文章指出中国企业必须先把自己的形象和商誉搞好，同时提高生产技术及环保意识。

中国驻胡志明市总领事馆商务参赞韦锡臣接受采访时曾称：“内地企业须努力把形象搞上去，因为越南现在对中资的印象就是商品质量低，技术水平低，设备落后和污染风险很大”。他同时指出中国人要把自己的商誉放在首位，这样才能慢慢转变越南对中国企业的态度。韦参赞还提到：“立足在这里，也是立足于全球的布局，而不是只看越南，这样才能成功。”

中国目前正在进入中华民族伟大复兴时期。世界也在期待中国经济、科技和文化的发展更上一层楼。不管怎样，中国的崛起是一个客观现实，能够为人类的进步以及中国与其他国家之间包括文化方面的相关合作作出积极而强有力的贡献。

如何认识和解读在新时代的中国，如何发挥并优化作为中国的周边邻国的优势，进而有效地引进中国文化的新兴价值以及高科技，这需要积极切实的思考。

External Influence of Chinese Culture: An Example of the Vietnam-China Cultural Exchange

Ngoc Truong Nguyen / Vietnam

Chairman of Center for Strategic Studies and International Development

With an overview of the relationship between Vietnam and China since ancient times, how to understand and interpret China has always been an objective requirement and a direction of efforts from the Vietnamese academic community. The purpose is to determine the historical correlation and interactivity, and the connotation of the relationship between the two countries at a particular time. This work is particularly attractive, but also full of challenges, as China was once in the position of "suzerain" in the East in the past, and the overall influence and radiation of China are also constantly increasing and expanding throughout the world.

I

Culture, here, can be interpreted in a broad sense, that is, "culture is the integrality of the relevant activities of the living people in the construction of society and the resulting products in order to establish and maintain the order of the social system"[1]. This shows that the influence of culture is a historical inevitability.

1 Ruan Shiqiang: Culture and Development, *Journal of Social Sciences*, 2001(2):48.

Meanwhile, it also means that culture emanates from its center to the periphery.

II

There was a long-standing and far-reaching cultural relationship between Vietnam and China in the past 19 centuries and before the colonial period. That relationship has changed directly and indirectly through cultural infiltration, refraction, exchange and introduction. Although the two countries have experienced ups and downs in different periods, the relationship between them has not been interrupted throughout the entire process. Hu Jintao, the former President of China, has always used the following simple and powerful four phrases to summarize this relationship:

> "Mountains and rivers being connected, cultures being interlinked, ideals being the same, and fates related to each other".

The Chinese nation is a great nation with a splendid, sustainable, inherited and highly developed culture, where men of talent come out in succession. Chinese culture is the essence of the Eastern culture, so that it is particularly far-reaching for many Eastern countries, including Vietnam. The Vietnamese culture introduced many essential elements from the Chinese culture, which are required by Vietnamese culture and are consistent with the Vietnamese local culture, thus creating unique cultural features of the Vietnamese nation. During the process, Chinese Confucianism exerted a far-reaching impact on Vietnamese culture. Most of Confucianism was imported from Confucianism in the Tang, Song, and Ming dynasties, especially Song Confucianism. In the history of Vietnam, Confucianism has continued to be consolidated and promoted. Vietnam has selectively introduced, received and accepted some advantages of Chinese Confucianism and tried to interpret these advantages in favor of its feudal state power and of the construction of its social structure.

In the feudal era, Chinese culture exerted a particularly obvious impact on Vietnamese culture, which was manifested in the superstructure of the society or the upper class. However, in many rural communities – commonly known as isolated "rural bamboo groves"[1], the influence was not apparent. In the village system with a close organizational structure, the influence was reflected, but still existed in some social etiquettes and customs such as weddings, funerals and holidays.

Before the 17th century, the influence of Chinese culture was particularly obvious to the north of the latitude 16°, while the ancient kingdoms were mostly influenced by Indian culture to the south of the latitude 16°N. Since the middle of the 17th century, Vietnam's territory gradually expanded southward, and accordingly, Chinese culture slowly penetrated into South Vietnam. However, it must be pointed out that the so-called "Great Confucians" have always come from North Vietnam during the long history of Vietnam, and the North Vietnamese intellectuals are often called "Northern River Scholar-bureaucrats"[2] (North River refers to North Vietnam), or jokingly called "Foresighted Confucians"[3] (Foresighted Confucians: a Vietnamese term, meaning foresight).

When I was a kid, I studied in a rural school in a poor area in central Vietnam. Since that time, I have felt the presence of Chinese culture deeply in my hometown. Wang Bo Temple is located near my house, Wen Peng Temple is behind my house, and a Confucian Temple is in the middle of the field in front of my house. The target of worship in the Confucian Temple is Confucius, with an aim to encouraging the local learning atmosphere. Both my great-grandfathers of the fifth generation and my grandfather were Confucians of the "Late Confucianism" period, from the middle of the 19th century to the early 20th century. Because of the historical background and the mandatory implementation of the French educational system in Vietnam, they were eventually not appreciated at any time. The last imperial

1 Original text: "Lũy tre làng", original meaning: "rural bamboo groves". It is a metaphor because rural areas in Vietnam are often surrounded by bamboo or bamboo groves. The "rural bamboo groves" means "village or countryside" .

2 Original text: "Sĩ phu Bắc Hà" (Northern River Scholar-bureaucrats), in ancient times, it means the Confucians from northern Vietnam.

3 Original text: "Thâm nho" (Foresighted Confucians), newly created Chinese-Vietnamese words. It means that because Confucianism was known as a very abstruse subject in the past, those who learned and understood Confucianist thoughts were often considered to have superb, profound and even foresighted thoughts.

competitive examination related to Confucianism was held in 1918 and 1919.

III

The influence of the Chinese culture on the Vietnamese culture is mainly reflected in the following four aspects.

First, when various feudal dynasties in Vietnam established a centralized state with Confucianism as the ruling principle, especially in the Lishi Dynasty (1428-1789) and the Ruanshi Dynasty (1802-1884), they drew on lots of relevant contents from organizational mode and legal system of the Chinese feudal regime.

Second, various feudal dynasties in Vietnam actively introduced and embraced Confucian ideas and ethics, and adopted the "the three cardinal guides and the five constant virtues" as their social framework. The Chinese characters became the official language of Vietnam at that time. Confucianism was promoted and extended to the national teaching & learning system and the imperial examination system. The Imperial College of Confucian Temple, established in 1070, is considered the earliest university established in Vietnam. There are bronze statues of Confucius, Zhou Gong, and also vivid portraits of the 72 Confucian sages, who are worshiped at all seasons, with an endless stream of pilgrims. It can be said that the Imperial College of Confucian Temple is the first Confucius College established in the world.

Third, Vietnamese literary arts, architecture, abacus, annual calendar, yin-yang and the five elements, divination, Chinese medicine, acupuncture and other fields are closely linked with China. The relevant knowledge in these fields is possibly localized for the exploration of human beings in nature and society. Vietnamese poets are also very proficient in old-style regulated verse and that of the Tang Dynasty. Under the strict requirements of the imperial examination system, the structure of regulated verse is further compacted. Many of Vietnam's literary works have adopted corpus, historical stories, allusions or place names more or less directly from China.

Fourth, the influence of the Chinese culture on the Vietnamese culture is also reflected in the cognition of the world view, including cosmology (yin-yang and the five elements, the average of yin and yang, even numbers and integers, the lunar calendar, etc.), in the outlook on life ("human universe", benevolence, filial piety, etiquette and righteousness, three cardinal guides and five constant virtues of the heavenly stems and earthly branches, and the five elements used in the study of astrology-telling, fortune-telling, Confucius and Mencius thoughts, and ethics), in the organization of social communities (privilege men over women, and privilege scholar-bureaucrats over merchants, etc.), in the utilization of and response to the natural environment (food, clothing, housing, travel and production activities, etc.) and in the interpretation of the social environment and religion (Buddhism, Confucianism, Taoism and character, etc.).

IV

The relation between the Vietnamese culture and the Chinese culture is exchange and trade-off, introduction and change.

The core of Vietnam's national culture has been shaped by the natural environment, the history of the birth and formation of the nation, national self-esteem, and the socio-economic background, etc. When the social structure of Vietnam is gradually penetrated by the Chinese culture and Confucianism, these local factors will collide with and refract the exotic values.

Vietnamese culture belongs to the rice culture, because most people are engaged in farming. Relatively speaking, people have a strong sense of intimacy and belonging to their own villages and countries. It is known that farming mainly depends on water conservation, but work on water conservation is obviously beyond the affordability of more than one household, and needs the concerted efforts of the entire community. Moreover, as Vietnam is home to a tropical monsoon climate, the Vietnamese people build their homes in symmetrical proportion with and harmony with the natural environment due to these climatic characteristics.

Why Vietnam feudal dynasties actively introduced and embraced Confucianism is mainly because they can draw lessons and adopt some advantages in the organization of society and in the governance of the nation.

Vietnam is not a national organization that duplicates the Chinese feudal dynasty; on the contrary, it is a feudatory state more in name than reality, which uses the Chinese feudal dynasty only for reference in order to conform to and adapt to its own national background (claiming to be an emperor domestically, but a king in China).[1] Instead of a political subordination, it shows the admiration for Chinese culture, and the due attitude of a small country towards the most powerful country in Asia. The conferring of titles or the paying of tributes is an obvious feature of the feudatory states, but this does not hurt the self-esteem of the Vietnamese nation. It must be pointed out that although Vietnam nominally accepts the conferring of titles by China, Vietnam was quite independent in its internal and external affairs at the time of feudalism.[2]

China, as a large country, executes great disorder under heaven, where there is no shortage of big families and wealthy families. Vietnam, as a small country, tends to "maintain affections"[3], and emphasizes the so-called "hometown feeling and village friendship"[4]). The size of the feudal imperial court in Vietnam is also quite small. The same is true for the scale of the construction of the court.

It must be pointed out that some basic concepts of Confucianism may have

1 Original text: "Trong đế ngoài vương" , original meaning: "claiming to emperor at home, but king in the world" , means that ancient Vietnam accepts the title conferred by China, so it is nominally a state tributary to China, but in fact Vietnam is relatively independent.

2 Li Chengkui: *History of Vietnam: From the Origin to the Middle of the 20th Century*, p.153, translated from Histoire du Viet Nam, des origines à 1858, Sud Est Asie, Paris, 1982.

3 Original text: "Một trăm cái lý không bằng một tí cái tình" , Vietnamese folk adage, original meaning: "One hundred strong words cannot take away a trace of affection." It means that the society advocates generosity and stresses friendship between people. It is always theoretically impossible to teach.

4 Original text: "Tình làng nghĩa xóm" , original meaning "hometown feeling and village friendship" . It refers to the mutual affection of fellow countrymen or fellow villagers, and the emotions among the neighbors.

different interpretations when introduced into Vietnam. By taking "loyalty" and "filial piety" as an example, for Vietnamese, "loyalty" means "loyalty to the country" and "filial piety" means "filial piety to the people", which are different meanings from the original meaning of "loyalty" and "filial piety".

As the key administrative unit in Vietnamese society, the village serves as a reference for governing and determining Vietnamese cultural exchanges and acceptance. Village culture is the foundation of the Vietnamese culture. Any new culture value must conform to the traditional values of the village and of the nation. The village has the highest degree of autonomy, as the old saying goes "rural rules prevail over national law"[1].

The *Jin Yunqiao Biography* – a classic of Vietnamese literature – is a narrative poem written in the Vietnamese national language Chu Nom according to the original novel *Jin Yunqiao* written by Qingxin Cairen in the late Ming and early Qing dynasties. This book has been widely accepted and favored by Vietnamese people from different ages because its core content and storyline have been localized and are full of Vietnam's national soul and cultural heritage. My mother is a native peasant, but she is also very familiar with the *Jin Yunqiao Biography*. In my childhood, she even used the *Jin Yunqiao Biography* as a cradlesong to sing to us and educate us by. At that time, Vietnamese readers were unable to tell whether the protagonist Cui Qiao was a Chinese or a Vietnamese. Instead, readers generally sympathized with the identity of an ancient woman. Because of reading that book, Vietnamese readers know some of the Chinese place names and customs well.

Due to a flexible introduction, acceptance, and continuous innovation, Vietnam has absorbed many nutrients from the essence and good value of the Chinese culture and civilization. The Vietnamese culture is a further unique innovation in the value of the Chinese culture. The exchange between the Chinese culture and the Vietnamese culture has changed the original appearance of the Vietnamese culture

1 Original text: "Phép vua thua lệ làng", Vietnamese idiom, original meaning: "rural rules prevail over national law". It means that rural customs are superior to national laws.

to a great extent since it was introduced, enabling the Vietnamese culture to become more diversified and further perfected, and making the connection between the two countries closer. For Chinese Celestial Empire (Vietnamese homage to China at the time of feudalism), the diplomatic strategy of Vietnam was “harmony and filial piety”[1] in Vietnam’s diplomatic culture. The so-called “harmony and filial piety” mean the “coexistence in harmony and filial piety to the Chinese Celestial Empire”.

V

From 1884 to 1945, French protectionism gradually annexed Vietnam and carried out colonial rule throughout Vietnam. China fought a war, but ultimately it was defeated and unable to protect its back garden in the south. Despite this, China’s influence on Vietnam could still be found everywhere at that time.

Since 1919, French colonialism has controlled various school systems in Vietnam and started the nearly semi-centennial process of abolishing Vietnam’s feudal cultural heritage that was deeply influenced by the Chinese culture.

The *Tianjin Treaty,* signed in 1885, is a treaty between the French colonial government and the Qing Dynasty after the end of the Qing-France war over the influence of Vietnam. According to the treaty, the Qing Dynasty had to withdraw its troops from Bac Ky[2], and recognize France’s sovereignty over Vietnam. The treaty ended the practice of the Vietnamese paying tribute to the Qing Dynasty in the position of the Celestial Empire.

However, the French colonists had to sign the two treaties of 1887 and 1895 with the Qing government to thoroughly remove the political and cultural influences and connections of China in Vietnam. However, the penetration of culture is boundless. The process of cultural infiltration comes out of the needs of life as well as from a very natural historical evolution.

---

1 Original text: “Hòa hiếu”, newly created Chinese-Vietnamese words. It means “coexistence in harmony and filial piety to Chinese Celestial Empire (ancient China)”.

2 Original text: “Bắc Kỳ”, old name for northern Vietnam.

In the 19th century, a large number of Vietnamese translations of Chinese novels into the Vietnamese Chu Nom appeared and spread widely throughout the Vietnamese territory in the form of handwriting or woodcarvings. Surprisingly, compared with Chinese characters, it was more efficient and concise to use the Latin alphabet just recently introduced to spell Vietnamese characters and express the Vietnamese language. During the process, French missionaries became the founders to advocate and promote the use of the Latin alphabet instead of Chinese characters and the Vietnamese Chu Nom. However, these missionaries did not realize that the Latin letters advocated became a sharp weapon of the Vietnamese Confucians and revolutionaries for the national independent struggle. At that time, China had passed some new ideas and trends to influence Vietnam, such as the 1911 Revolution with the Three People's Principles, the May Fourth Movement, and the Nanchang Uprising.

At that time, the Vietnamese Latin national language happened to be an effective tool for spreading the Chinese culture to Vietnam, and the difference lay in its unprecedented scale of expansion and more popularization. For the first time, hundreds of Chinese novels were translated into the Vietnamese language and published in large quantities in the first 30 years of the 20th century. At the same time, the Chinese romance novels with the story line of "mandarin ducks and butterflies" were commercioganic and very popular in Vietnam. According to legend, the Chinese opera was introduced to Vietnam as early as the 13th century after the defeat of the army of the Mongolia Yuan Dynasty in Vietnam, while the Chinese drama has been popular in South Vietnam since the 18th century.

President Ho Chi Minh, a great thinker and littérateur, is the representative who inherited the traditional Vietnamese culture and sinology. During his lifetime, he dedicated himself to establishing a cultural exchange bridge between Vietnam and China in the new era.

President Ho Chi Minh spoke highly of some Confucian ideas and ethics: "The advantage of Confucianism is self-cultivation."[1] President Ho Chi Minh believed that the core values of Confucianism are the "mind rectification and self-cultivation" morality, knowledge and studying hard.

Since his childhood, President Ho Chi Minh was edified by authentic Confucian thoughts, and received full and complete Confucian moral education.[2] President Ho Chi Minh respected Confucius as a world sage, and highly valued the fine and contemporary values in the famous quotes and phrases of Confucianism. During a visit to the former residence of Confucius in May 1965, President Ho Chi Minh wrote a poem called "A Visit to Qufu" from his feelings as an expression of his remembrance and honor to Confucius:

In the visit to Qufu on May 19,
I saw lonely and isolated ancient pines and ancient temples.
Where is the power of Confucianism?
Only the setting sun shines on ancient tablets.[3]

VI

Since the French colonial rule of Vietnam, the mainstream of the cultural connection between Vietnam and China has been interrupted. At the same time, Vietnamese culture made exchanges and contacts with the cultures of the powerful countries on the globe, such as France, the United States, the Soviet Union and China (since 1911). Before their introduction into Vietnam, these foreign cultures had all experienced the process of mutual refraction, exchange and change in order to conform to Vietnam's national situations and core values.

In the late 19th century and early 20th century, a unique phenomenon of Sino-

1 *Ho Chi Minh Thoughts and Vietnam's Revolutionary Route*, Vietnam National Political Press, Hanoi, 2000, p.51.

2 References from *Discernment of Ho Chi Minh*, Vietnam Culture and Communications Press, 1999, p.43.

3 The original text was written in Traditional Chinese:
五月十九访曲阜，古松古庙两依稀，孔家势力今何在，只剩斜阳照古碑。

Vietnamese cultural exchanges was that many Western scholars in Vietnam were well-versed in and thoroughly acquainted with sinology to generate a new generation of excellent and core intellectuals of modern Vietnamese culture. This phenomenon reminds us of the current popularity of the Chinese language in many Vietnamese high schools and universities. If achieved, it will greatly help the young generation in Vietnam to understand China better, absorb the nutrients from the essence of Chinese culture, and bring about more advantages than disadvantages in terms of the language. In other words, the Vietnamese people will become more and more aware of Chinese-Vietnamese words, and further use them in a more standard way.[1]

During the period of China's reform and opening up and Vietnam's renewal cause, Hanoi often explored, observed and drew lessons from the routes and successful experiences of China's reform and opening up, such as Premier Zhu Rongji's reform of the structure of the government, or President Xi Jinping proposed the anti-corruption strategy, the construction of the Communist Party of China, etc.

VII

Since my childhood, I have read hundreds of Chinese historical and martial arts novels. Today, these books are widely sold in various bookstores in Vietnam and are readily available. During the period of the Vietnam War, in the 1960s, if I wanted to read a book, I often had to walk about 50 to 70 kilometers to get it.

At the same time, a rather positive phenomenon of cultural exchange appears in the context of the high-tech era. As long as a tablet computer or smart phone with a Wifi connection is available, all of the Vietnamese people can download Chinese books to their own devices for reading. There are also many Vietnamese translators who often translate Chinese books and various TV shows out of their own interests.

1 According to incomplete statistics, Chinese-Vietnamese words account for 60%-70% of the Vietnamese vocabulary. The so-called Chinese-Vietnamese words are the general term derived from some Chinese root words or source words in Vietnamese language.

Why Chinese historical novels or modern martial arts novels and books about legends are so favored by the Vietnamese people is because the design of the story is vivid and lifelike, and is placed in China's huge historical and cultural space. While reading them, these stories give abundant extra knowledge to people. In addition to the traditional Chinese culture, we can also learn about Chinese medicine, diet, drinking habits, growing flowers, tea ceremonies, martial arts, country governance and military tactics, state harnessing, some events in China's history, changes of dynasties, and many thought-provoking truths.

I hardly miss reading any of the Chinese classical historical novels or modern martial arts novels. Every time I read one, I feel great respect and admiration for the abundant imagination and profound cultural heritage of Chinese writers, both of the past and modern ones.

In summary, the article assumes that China is currently sparing no effort to establish more and more Confucius Colleges around the world. This is of course a very important issue, but should only serve as a reference index for evaluating the degree of dissemination of the Chinese culture. What is more important is that the current high-tech era may play a more important role in the exchange and dissemination of Chinese culture and world culture, and bring stronger and more powerful advantages. Therefore, China may have to consider how to fully use high tech technology to make the process of cultural exchange between China and other countries much smoother.

VIII

After all, the continuous expanding influence of the Chinese culture on a global scale is a new phenomenon. No matter what kind of culture, people are the subject. The Chinese people should take some time to make adaptations and improve their own mentalities either in China or in the process of communication with the world. At the same time, the Chinese people should adapt and integrate themselves to the ever-changing cultural era. If the European and American industrial countries needed to spend hundreds of years to allow their people to develop an industrial culture, the modern China could take many other shortcuts to shorten the time. China may use its economic strength as support and an engine for expanding its soft power. The Belt and Road Initiative is currently in full swing, which will surely provide greater and broader space for the expansion of the Chinese cultural influence to Asian, European, and African continents.

The world is trying to understand and interpret China. The Chinese people have better opportunities to contact the world outside, regardless of traveling abroad, further study overseas or doing business. Therefore, the understanding of the Chinese people should also be improved to the entire world.

In recent years, the Vietnamese people have clearly felt the rise of China's economy. However, it is a pity that people have not yet seen the superiority of Chinese corporate culture over other corporate cultures.

In mid-June not long ago, an article in *Wen Wei Po* discussed and analyzed some favorable conditions and challenges for Chinese companies investing in Vietnam. The article pointed out that China's enterprises had to improve their image and goodwill first, and then increase production technology and environmental protection awareness.

During an interview, Wei Xichen, the Commercial Counselor of the Chinese Consulate-General in Ho Chi Minh City, said: "Inland enterprises must make great efforts to raise their images because Chinese enterprises leave the Vietnamese people with the impression of low-quality products, low technological level, out-of-date equipment and high risk of pollution". At the same time, he pointed out that the Chinese people must put goodwill first, so that the attitude of the Vietnamese people towards Chinese companies can be changed gradually. Counselor Wei also said incisively that: "To achieve success, it must be based on here, that is, based on the global layout, and not limited to Vietnam."

Now, China is stepping into a period of great rejuvenation of the Chinese nation. The world is also waiting for further development of China in economy, technology and culture. In any case, the rise of China is an objective reality, which can make positive and powerful contributions to human progress and related cooperation between China and other countries, including culture.

How to understand and interpret China in the new historical era, how to use and optimize our advantages as a neighboring country of China, and further effectively introduce the emerging culture value and high technology of China are the urgent needs of life.

共同发展与包容互鉴的文明观

许利平 【中国】
中国社会科学院亚太与全球战略研究院社会文化研究室主任兼东南亚研究中心主任

自2008年国际金融危机爆发以来，世界经济复苏乏力，如何促进经济增长，解决高企不下的失业率，成为各国政府工作的主要目标。但一个国家的发展，离不开其他国家的支持，特别是在宏观经济政策的协调方面。因此，加强各国政策沟通和协调是共同发展的前提。

另一方面，共同发展还面临着地区和全球性非传统安全的挑战，比如流行性疾病、粮食安全、能源安全等。各国政府应该在信息分享、经验交流等方面，开展集体行动，共同应对挑战，实施共同发展。

“一带一路”沿线国家发展程度不一，拥有各自文明。为了更好地推进共同发展，必须秉持包容互鉴的文明观，促进民心相通，构筑共同发展的社会基础和民意基础。与此同时，可以更好地挖掘共同发展的潜力。

世界是不同的文明组成的、多样性统一的世界，也是因文明的多元性、独特性而成为多姿多彩的世界。不同的民族，在长期的历史发展过程中经形成具有本民族特色的文化传统、伦理道德与民族精神，形成了各具特色的文明。任何一种文明都有自己的特点与优点，都是世界文明密不可分的一部分，都为世界文明的发展做出了贡献。“人类文明的发展，从茹毛饮血发展到现在的生物工程，从刀耕火种发展到现在的信息技术，其中不同民族和不同文明都作出了贡献。不同文明有历史长短之分，无优劣高下之别。”正是这些不同的民族、国家与文化，使人类文化愈加丰富多彩和意蕴深厚，使人类文化在人类历史的长河中形成了互鉴互补、互动、和持续发展的状态。“文明的多样性是人类社会的基本特征，也是人类文明进步的重要动力。”

文明在其过去、现在发展过程中，存在相互的冲突，而且在未来的发展过程中，也将不可避免地产生冲突。冲突虽然产生混乱与动荡，但也往往可能产生更优秀的文化混生物，形成文化在冲击中的交流、融合和生长。提出“文明冲突论”的亨廷顿认为，未来世界中国际冲突的根源将主要是文化的而不是意识形态的和经济的。……全球政治的主要冲突将在不同文明的国家和集团之间进行，文明的冲突将主宰全球政治，文明间的断裂带将成为未来的战线。国际政治的核心部分将是西方文明和非西方文明以及非西方文明之间的相互作用。国际冲突在经历了君主冲突、民族国家冲突和意识形态冲突之后，将进入文明冲突的阶段。亨廷顿指出了不同文明之间存在冲突，但是过分强调和凸显了冲突方面。冲突虽然是不同文明在发展过程中互动的一种方式和状态，但并不是文明唯一的发展模式，也不是文明发展的终极方向。“文明的差异不是世界冲突的根源，而应是世界交融的起点。海纳百川，有容乃大。这个世界应少一些对抗，多一些对话，少一些傲慢与偏见，多一些交流与沟通，这样才能共同发展和进步”。

文明在人类历史长河的发展与实践证明，更多的是不同的文明之间和谐共存。交流、互鉴、合作是文明发展的重要方式和常态，是文明持续发展和不断进步的路径。“多样文明的交往，并不能导致为单一文明，而是在交汇、融合中表现出独特性、差别性和差异性。人类文明的兴衰存亡与更替，始终受着多样性的统一规律的制约。”通过不同文明之间的对话、合作、交流，促进不同民族、国家之间的理解和信任。“文明交往的真谛在于由浅入深的理解，是理解因素的不断增强。理解赋予交往是理性、开放、和谐、自觉和创造力。交往追求的目标不仅是文明的自我理解和欣赏，而且是了解他人、理解他种文明、学会宽容和接纳多元理念，是和而不同”。

在当今急剧变化的国际形势中，文明多样性的凸现、文明交往的日趋频繁，是时代发展的主潮流。而傲慢与偏见已成为文明交流的最大障碍。文明之间缺乏理解、信任、尊重与包容，成为冲突的根源。因此，加强文明之间的交流与沟通，学习与合作非常重要。不同制度、不同文化的国家，应以平等的态度、以包容的胸怀、互信的理念，加强交流，互相借鉴，增强不同文明的活力，推进不同文明的和谐共进。

“一带一路”聚居着许多不同的民族和国家，汇集着不同的文化。“一带一路”沿线每个民族都有自己的优秀文化传统，都是世界文明的重要组成部分，都是推进世界文明发展与进步的动力。各民族、各国应摒弃傲慢与偏见，摒弃文明冲突的思维，促进文化交流与交融，构建多种文化和谐共存的局面。

习近平主席多次倡导文明之间的尊重、平等、互鉴、与和谐共生。他指出：“世界上没有放之四海而皆准的发展模式，各方应该尊重世界文明多样性和发展模式多样化”。“‘万物并育而不相害，道并行而不相悖。’我们要尊重文明多样性，推动不同文明交流对话、和平共处、和谐共生，不能唯我独尊、贬低其他文明和民族。人类历史告诉我们，企图建立单一文明的一统天下，只是一种不切实际的幻想。尺有所短，寸有所长。我们要倡导交流互鉴，注重汲取不同国家、不同民族创造的优秀文明成果，取长补短，兼收并蓄，共同绘就人类文明美好画卷”。

世界上没有单一的普世文明，是多种文明的统一体。每一种文明都是平等的，都应该得到尊重。“让文明交流互鉴成为增进各国人民友谊的桥梁、推动人类社会进步的动力、维护世界和平的纽带。我们应该从不同文明中寻求智慧、汲取营养，为人们提供精神支撑和心灵慰藉，携手解决人类共同面临的各种挑战。”各民族、各国应以开放的态度接受文明的多元性，推动不同文明之间的交流与交融。“一带一路”沿线国家，特别是亚洲各民族、各国应继续传承“和谐至上”传统文化思维，以包容互鉴、多元共进的文明观，以照顾各方舒适度的亚洲方式，加强交流、互鉴与合作，推进不同民族文化的交融与进步，增进彼此的理解与信任，实现多种文明的和谐共生。

Prospects of the Common Development of Civilization, Inclusiveness and Mutual Learning

Xu Liping / China

Director of the Department of Asia-Pacific Social & Cultural Studies and Director of the Center for Southeast Asian Studies under the National Institute of International strategy at the Chinese Academy of Social Sciences

Since the outbreak of the international financial crisis in 2008, the recovery of the world's economy has been sluggish. How to promote economic growth and solve the high unemployment rate has become the main goal of the governments in various countries. However, the development of a country is inseparable from the support of other countries, especially in the coordination of macroeconomic policies. Therefore, strengthening the communication on and coordination of national policy is the prerequisite for common development.

On the other hand, common development also faces challenges from regional and global non-traditional security, such as epidemics, food security, and energy security. Governments of all countries should act in concert in terms of the sharing of information and the exchange of experiences in order to jointly respond to challenges and implement common development.

The countries along the "Belt and Road" have different degrees of development and their own civilizations. To better promote common development, we must uphold the prospects of civilization of inclusiveness and mutual learning in order to promote the communication of popular sentiments and build the social foundation and public opinion foundation for common development. At the same time, it is also important to better tap the potential of common development.

The world is a diverse and unified world composed of diverse civilizations, as well as a colorful world thanks to the diversity and uniqueness of civilizations. Different nationalities have formed unique cultural traditions, ethical moralities and national spirits in the course of long-term historical development, and have further established distinctive civilizations. With its own characteristics and advantages, every civilization is an inseparable part of world civilization and has made contributions to the development of world civilization. "Different nationalities and civilizations have made contributions to the development of human civilization, either from the development of eating raw meat and drinking blood to current bio-engineering or from the development of slash-and-burn cultivation to the current information technology. Different civilizations have a distinction in length but no distinction between superiority and inferiority." It is these different nationalities, countries and cultures that have made human culture more colorful and profound in meaning. This has enabled human culture to form a state of mutual learning, complementation, interaction and sustainable development along the course of the long river of human history. "The diversity of civilization is a basic feature of human society, as well as an important driving force for the progress of human civilization."

Civilizations have mutual conflicts in their past and present development, and will inevitably produce conflicts in the future process of development. Despite the chaos and turbulence created by conflicts, it is also possible to produce more excellent cultural hybrids, leading to cultural exchanges, integration and growth during cultural shock. Huntington, the proposer of the theory of "Clash of Civilizations", believes that the root of international conflicts in the future world will be primarily culture rather than ideology and economics... The major conflicts in global politics will be carried out among nations and groups of different civilizations. The clash of civilizations will dominate global politics, and the fracture zone between civilizations will become the future front. The core of international politics will be the interactions between Western civilizations and non-Western civilizations, and those among non-Western civilizations. After experiencing monarchical conflicts, national conflicts and ideological conflicts, international conflicts will enter the stage of civilization conflicts. Huntington points out the conflicts among different civilizations, but overemphasizes and highlights those conflicts. Although conflict is a mode and state of interaction among different civilizations during the process of development, it is neither the only developmental mode of civilization nor the ultimate direction that development of civilization takes. "Instead of the source of conflicts in the world, civilization differences should be the starting point for the world to blend together into one. The sea can hold the water from thousands of rivers. Hence, the world should have less confrontation, more dialogue, less arrogance and prejudice, and more exchanges and communication, so that common development and progress can be achieved."

The development and practice of civilizations throughout the long history of human beings have proved a more harmonious coexistence of different civilizations. Exchange, mutual learning and cooperation are the important ways and normal states for the development of civilizations, as well as the paths for sustainable development and the progress of civilization. "Communications among diverse civilizations show the uniqueness, difference and distinction in the convergence and integration rather than leading to a single civilization. The rise, fall and replacement of human civilizations are always constrained by the unified law of diversity." Dialogue, cooperation, and exchange among different civilizations promotes the mutual understanding and trust among different nationalities and countries. "The essence of the exchange of civilizations lies in the understanding from the shallower to the deeper, and the ever-increasing comprehension of understanding factors. Understanding makes communication rational, open, harmonious, conscious and creative. In addition to civilization self-understanding and appreciation, communication is aimed at understanding others, comprehending other civilizations, learning to tolerate and accept pluralistic ideas, namely, harmony in diversity."

In today's rapidly changing international situation, the emergence of cultural diversity and the increasing frequency of exchanges of civilization are the main trends of the times. Now, the biggest obstacle to exchanges among civilizations is arrogance and prejudice. The lack of understanding, trust, respect and tolerance among civilizations has become the roots of conflict. Therefore, it is of paramount importance to strengthen the exchange, communication, learning and cooperation among civilizations. Countries with different systems and cultures should strengthen exchanges and mutual learning, and enhance the vitality of different civilizations with an attitude of equality, inclusiveness and mutual trust in order to promote the harmonious and common development of different civilizations.

The area covered by the "Belt and Road" is home to many different peoples and nations, where different cultures come together. Each ethnic group along the "Belt and Road" has its own prominent cultural traditions, which constitute an important part of world's civilization and they become the driving force behind the development and progress of world civilization. All nationalities and countries should abandon arrogance and prejudice and abandon the concept of the clash of civilizations to promote cultural exchanges and integration, thus achieving the harmonious coexistence of multiple cultures.

President Xi Jinping has repeatedly advocated respect, equality, mutual understanding and harmonious symbiosis among civilizations. He pointed out: "There is no universally-acceptable developmental model in the world. All parties should respect the diversity of world civilizations and the diversification of patterns of development." "As the old saying goes, 'all things can be cultivated without harming each other, and all roads are parallel and not contrary to each other,' we must respect the diversity of civilizations, promote exchange, dialogue and harmonious coexistence among different civilizations, rather than belittle other civilizations and nations. Human history tells us that the attempt to establish a unified single world of civilization is just an unrealistic illusion. Sometimes a foot may prove short while an inch may prove long. We must advocate exchanges and mutual learning, and attach importance to learning from the achievements of outstanding civilizations created by different countries and different nationalities to draw on the strong points of others to make up for its own weak points, thus jointly creating a beautiful picture of human civilization."

The world is the unity of multiple civilizations without a single universal civilization. Every civilization is equal and deserves to be respected. "We should make the exchanging of civilization and mutual learning a bridge to improve the friendship of peoples of all countries, a driving force to advance human society, and a link to safeguarding world peace. We should seek wisdom from different civilizations and absorb nutrition to provide spiritual support and comfort for people and work together to solve all kinds of challenges that all of mankind faces together." All ethnic groups and nations should accept the diversity of civilizations with an open attitude and promote the exchanges and integrations among different civilizations. The countries along the "Belt and Road", especially Asian nations and countries, should continue to inherit the traditional cultural concept of "harmony first", the strength of exchanges, mutual learning and cooperation, to promote the blending and progress of different ethnic cultures and increase mutual understanding and trust through the prospects of civilization that are inclusiveness and mutual progress and the Asian mode of consideration of all parties so as to realize the harmonious coexistence of multiple civilizations.

中国与变革中的国际秩序

袁正清 【中国】

中国社会科学院世界经济与政治研究所 研究员、博士生导师/《世界经济与政治》副主编

众所周知，中国的崛起是发生在当今世界的一场重大变革，理解中国与国际秩序的关系，有助于我们观察整个世界的变革轨迹。

关于中国与世界秩序的关系，我想用三个关键词来说明——参与、适应、完善。这三个词可以反映出中国与国际组织、与世界秩序的关系。

第一个关键词是“参与”。1978年改革开放之前，中国基本上很少与国际社会接触，改革开放之后，中国开始与世界银行、国际货币仅仅组织等国际机构进行接触，希望得到来自西方国家的资本、资金和技术，随后开始加入一些国际性的经济组织，并于1980年成为世界银行、国际货币基金组织的一员。此外，中国还加入了亚洲开发银行、联合国人权委员会、国际原子能机构等国际性组织，签署了《外层空间条约》等协议文件。对于中国而言，这是一段观察期和学习期，是学习国际组织规则的一个过程。

第二个关键词是“适应”。20世纪90年代中期，中国加入国际组织的比率达到相当高的水平，几乎与一些发达国家持平。从此之后，中国开始主动适应国际规则，在国际组织事务中扮演更为积极的角色。例如，自2001年加入WTO之后，中国开始以前所未有的速度推行市场经济改革。由于中国的经济发展已然与世界经济紧形势密联系在一起，从某种程度上来说，是外部的国际经济规则推动了中

国的内部改革。中国必须学会适应。在此期间，中国与整个世界发生了许多次摩擦，经历了惨痛的教训，但同时也获得了不少利益。

第三个关键词是“完善”。进入新世纪后，世界形势因三起事件而发生改变：9·11恐怖袭击、国际金融危机、中国成为世界第二大经济体。金融危机揭示了这样一个道理——以世界银行和国际货币基金组织为基础的国际金融体系是不完善且需要改革的。改革的重要动力来自于以中国为代表的新兴经济体的群体崛起，而原有的全球治理机制已无法容纳新的发展诉求，对于中国来说，一方面要继续在存量上对世界银行和国际货币基金组织进行改革，发挥G20的作用。在这一点上，人民币成为“特别提款权”篮子货币、国际货币基金组织份额公式改革便是绝佳的例证。另一方面，要在增量上补充和完善现有的全球治理及地区治理制度。按照国际标准和地区特色，通过金融制度的创新，弥补国际金融机构在亚洲基础设施上的盲点和不足。在中国的倡导和努力下，金砖国家新开发银行正式成立，该行是二战以来第一所由发展中国家自行创立的国际金融机构。

亚投行的成立也能很好地证明这一点。亚投行旨在为亚洲基础设施建设提供资金，其运作不仅符合国际标准和国际规则，更能与世界金融体系形成互补，与世界银行和国际货币基金组织之间，存在紧密的合作与联系。亚投行并非另起炉灶，而是秉持开放、包容的原则，欢迎包括美国在内的各国的参与。诚然，亚投行会给他金融组织带来竞争，但笔者认为，这种竞争是良性的、有益的竞争，能够促进国际金融组织的效率提升。

当然，最令人瞩目的莫过于2013年前提出的“一带一路”倡议，越来越多的国家正不断加入“一带一路”建设中来。2017年5月14—15日期间，中国举办了“一带一路国际合作论坛”，以此为契机，中国与各方一道，建设一个更加开放、更加高效的国际合作平台，以共商、共建、共享为原则，以开放包容为特征，以互利共赢为追求，从而构建更加紧密、更加坚实的合作关系。

笔者认为，以上三个关键词能够反映出中国与整个世界的关系。首先，中国在过去38年的改革开放进程中，与整个世界融为紧密的一体；其次，中国开始为全球经济治理做出贡献。中国的崛起是世界秩序中的重要变量，对于中国和世界而言，将来的挑战在于权力的过渡、利益的分配以及可能产生的摩擦与冲突。

有些学者认为，中美两国会陷入修昔底德陷阱，甚至可能引发两败俱伤的惨剧。此类预言或许会不幸言中，但这种结局却并非无可避免。未来局势如何，取决于我们能否以新智慧、新思维去应对新的世界秩序。

随着世界格局的不断变化，中美关系正日益复杂化。我们需要一种新的愿景，或是一轮理念上的革新。在构建新型国际关系方面，中国开创性地提出了“人类命运共同体”的理念，其核心内容在于合作共赢，而非零和博弈，在于伙伴关系而不是结盟，在于文明之间的沟通与对话，而非文明的冲突和碰撞，若想维持和平与发展，只有走开放、包容的道路，尽管这条路上会满布荆棘。崛起的中国需要更多地了解外部世界，而国际社会，特别是美国，同样需要了解中国。各方可以发挥自身优势，通过合作实现互利共赢。我们今天的讨论正是为实现这一目标而做出的努力。

China and International Institutions in a Changing World

Yuan Zhengqing / China

Researcher, Doctoral Advisor and Deputy Editor-in-Chief of the Editorial Office of *Journal of World Economy and Politics* at the Institute of World Economy and Politics at the Chinese Academy of Social Sciences

As we know, China's rising is the most important change in today's world. Understanding China's relationship with international institution is helpful for observing a changing world.

I want to express my understanding in three key words, namely participation、adaptation and complementation. These three words describe the relationship between china and international institutions, in some sense, relationship between China and the world order.

Now the first word participation, before 1978, China is basically away from international society. After reform and opening up, China began to engage in western countries and international organizations such as the World bank and IMF, China needed western capital、international organization loans and advanced technology. China participated in some economic organizations and became a member of council in the World Bank and IMF in 1980. China also entered some international agencies such as Asia Development Bank, UN human right committee and IAEA and signed Outer Space Treaty and so on. This period is an observing and learning process for China, a process of learning the institution rules in particular.

The second word adaptation, China's participation rate is very high in middle-1990's, close to levels of some major countries. China began to adapt to international rules, played some roles in institution affairs. For example, china entered the WTO in 2001.china's market-oriented reform is faster than before, China's economy is truly integrated with world economy system to some extent international economic rules push china to reform from outside. China must take an adaptation. In this process, there are many frictions and pains between china and the world. However, china benefited much from the world.

The third key word is complementation. Three events have changed the world in the new century. Namely September 11 attack, international financial crisis and China's becoming the second largest economy in the world. Financial crisis demonstrated that the international financial system based on World Bank and IMF has some flaws, this system needs reform, china's development has become one of the driving forces of world economic growth. These changes demand a new round of global governance. We see share reform in World Bank and IMF. As for China, on the one hand, it actively promotes the reform of international financial system and facilitates economic stability through G20. RMB was included in the SDR currency basket of the IMF. IMF quota reform plan and so on. These moves are stock reform; on the other hand, china takes incremental reform on global and regional governance. China is also an active participant in the establishment of new international economic and financial mechanisms which have complemented the current global economic governance system and international financial institutions. At China's initiative and with its efforts, the BRICS New Development Bank was formally set up, the first international financial institution independently founded by developing countries since World War II;

AIIB is another example. AIIB is set by international standards and rules. it makes up for lack of Asian infrastructure investment. This bank is a complementation to the financial system .it has many connections and cooperation with the World Bank and IMF. AIIB is not to set up a separate kitchen. It's open and inclusive; welcome the United States to join .certainly AIIB has competition with other financial agencies. In my opinion, this competition is good and healthy. It advances efficiency of international financial institutions.

We certainly notice the "Belt and Road" initiative .Since it was proposed in 2013. It has attracted more and more countries to join. The BRF was held in Beijing from May 14 to 15, 2017. China takes this forum as an opportunity to create a more open and more efficient platform for international cooperation; to build a closer and stronger partnership network by following the principle of wide consultation, joint construction and shared benefits, openness and inclusiveness and win-win cooperation.

In my perspective, three words above reflect the relationship between china and the rest of the world. First, China was integrated into the world through 38 years of reform and opening up, China has rapidly entered the world stage, Chinese is deeply embedded in the international community, and second, China has provided public goods for global economic governance.

China's rising is an important variable. power transformation、interest distribution and idea friction are challenges for china and the world. Some scholars argue that china and the US will fall in Thucydides trap, or tragedy of great power will come up. These predictions are probably the future for china and the US. These arguments maybe become self-fulfilled prophesy. However, this future is not inevitable. The future depends on whether we have new wisdom or new thinking about the international order in some sense. The world has changed. Relationship between China and US is very complex. We need a new vision or innovation of idea. China has pioneered a new type of international relations, and advocated to build a community of shared future for mankind. Its core content is win-win cooperation, not zero-sum game, partnership not alliance, civilization dialogue and communication not civilization clash. Openness and inclusiveness is a right and difficult road to peace and development. Rising china needs to more understand the outside world. The world, especially the US also needs to understand China. We can work together to get benefits by using our individual advantages. Our discussion today is a part of this effort.

中巴经济走廊建设的里程碑：2017“一带一路”国际合作高峰论坛印象

穆罕默德·伊克博·乔拉 【巴基斯坦】
巴基斯坦旁遮普大学艺术和人类学院院长、教授

2017年5月14—15日，具历史意义的“一带一路”国际合作高峰论坛在北京召开，来自世界各地的20多位国家元首及政府首脑出席了本次论坛。米安·纳瓦兹·谢里夫（巴基斯坦总理）就推进“中巴经济走廊”后续项目等问题与中方达成共识，这也是巴基斯坦历史上各位首席部长同时出席高峰论坛。中巴经济走廊将为巴方发展与富强带来绝佳的机遇，因而受到国内各派政党的欢迎，但关于走廊建设的可行性、路线、透明度、建设方案等问题引发了各方密切关注。本文试图从中巴关系的宏观视角切入，分析2017“一带一路”国际合作高峰论坛对中巴经济走廊建设造成的影响。笔者认为，本次论坛不仅是中国“一带一路”建设中的里程碑，更是巴基斯坦经济、社会、文化、战略等各层面取得历史性发展的标志性事件。此外，本文将对各派政党领导人对于中巴经济走廊建设的主要关注点进行分析。

一 “一带一路”与中巴关系

2013年底，习近平主席宣布了中国外交史及经济发展史上最具气魄的战略性工程，提出了构建丝绸之路经济带与21世纪海上丝绸之路的“一带一路”倡议，旨在通过基础设施建设，实现中国与周边国家及边境地区的联通。从这个意

义上看，“一带一路”可以视做现代历史上规模最宏伟的发展计划。陆上丝绸之路，即丝绸之路经济带，旨在促进中国欠发达地区与中亚、欧洲地区的沟通。21世纪海上丝绸之路则通过港口和铁路建设，实现中国南部省份与东南亚新兴经济体的连接。

“一带一路”倡议的实施恰逢中国外交锋芒渐露的历史时刻，这使，“一带一路”通常被解读为一种地缘政治战略，而并非纯粹的经济战略。尽管这种解读具有一定程度的合理性，但笔者认为，过度强调“一带一路”的地缘政治意图，会导致该倡议的主要层面——地缘经济层面被忽略。总体而言，“一带一路”倡议的出发点在于推动地缘经济发展，这与中国国内产业政策的变化颇为契合。

二　一带一路：地缘政治战略还是地缘经济战略？

2013年中共十八大召开前，中国的决策者与专家学者曾就国家外交政策——特别是周边政策的战略方向展开激烈讨论。2013年10月，“周边外交工作会”在北京召开，这次会议是2006年以来的首次大型外交政策会议，也是新中国成立以来的首次周边外交政策会议，参会者多为中国外交政策领域的决策者，包括中共中央政治局的全体常委。

习近平主席在会上指出，中国周边国家具有“极其重要的战略意义”，要进一步增进中国与周边国家的友好关系、加强经济交流、深化安全合作，“维护周边和平稳定是周边外交的重要目标，要积极参与区域经济合作，加快基础设施互联互通，建设好丝绸之路经济带、21世纪海上丝绸之路，构建区域经济一体化新格局”。

习近平主席清楚地意识到，中国丰富的经济资源在维护区域稳定、增强中国在周边国家中的影响力等方面发挥着关键作用。这次“周边外交工作会”被分析人士视做中国外交政策上的重要转折点。卡内基国际和平基金会副总裁包道格指出，这次会议象征着——中国领导层调整了邓小平的“韬光养晦”战略，转向更为主动的周边外交政策，因而“一带一路”的主要动因被解读为广泛的地缘政治战略。这种解读具有一定程度上的合理性，且与“一带一路”倡议的部分特征相吻合，中巴经济走廊便是绝佳的例证。该项目属于“一带一路”项目的“旗舰”工程，为此，中巴双方均投入了无限的热情与有力的支持。中巴经济走廊起点在中国新疆的喀什，终点在巴基斯坦俾路支省的瓜达尔港，由于瓜达尔港临近波斯湾，中国能源运输可以此作为中转站，不必穿过马六甲海峡，在东南亚局势紧张或发生武装冲突时期，中国可以凭借这条线路突破西方国家对中国的航路封锁，从此减少对印度洋航线的依赖。

1.“一带一路”高峰论坛与巴基斯坦的省级对接

纳瓦兹·谢里夫总理与各部部长的集体参会可谓一项盛举，这说明，巴基斯坦各省官员对中巴经济走廊的重要意义产生了一致性的认识。该走廊不仅能让巴方成为游戏规则的改变者，更能为双方带来互利。在此之前，巴基斯坦政界人士曾对中巴经济走廊建设深表担忧，然而信德省及开伯尔-普赫图赫瓦省的参与明确反映出巴方对这项伟大工程的一致态度，更证明了此前的种种顾虑不过是杞人忧天而已。

中方为扫清种种无谓的政治疑虑付出了巨大努力。中国政府多次发表声明，指出中巴经济走廊旨在为巴基斯坦全国各地而非某一地区带来利益。2014 年发生的游行示威与静坐事件曾导致中国主席访巴行程延迟，而此次巴方领导人集体参会的盛举无疑为消除该事件的消极影响做出了积极的贡献，更为巴基斯坦人民争得一份荣光。作为“一带一路”倡议的重要组成部分，“一带一路论坛”（BRF）旨在通过互利合作促进共同发展，同时也彰显了中国在世界舞台上的领导地位。

作为“一带一路”倡议的旗舰工程，中巴经济走廊不断遭到一些国内外势力的诋毁和抹黑，但巴方成功抵制了种种谣言，并且以前所未有的决心和信心完成这项工程。美国政府显然对这一工程持反对态度，美国国家情报总监丹尼尔·科茨声称，中巴经济走廊将会成为恐怖分子的最新目标。这番论断可谓奇怪之极，这无异于在宣称，为了避免恐怖分子袭击，所有重大开发工程都应该下马。在谣言纷起、种种阴谋论甚嚣尘上之际，巴基斯坦领导人能够以国家社稷为重，抛开党派分歧、达成一致意见，实属难得。结束访华后，信德省首席部长赛义德·穆拉德·阿里·沙以及开伯尔-普赫图赫瓦省首席部长卡塔克改变了之前对于中巴经济走廊的看法，将之描述为一项宏伟的发展计划，一项能够改变巴基斯坦前途与命运的计划。

作为巴基斯坦正义运动党（PTI）的代表人，卡塔克曾在党内势力的逼迫下，在游行示威中徒然浪费四年时间，此刻他已经意识到，政治煽动毫无益处，若想在下届大选中获胜，只能依赖中巴经济走廊。结束访华后，卡塔克对这项宏伟工程表现出明显兴趣，并且得到中方的积极回应。此后，卡塔克与总统在中巴经济走廊问题上完全达成了一致。

作为巴基斯坦人民党的代表，信德省首席部长——赛义德·穆拉德·阿里·沙曾对中巴经济走廊持保守意见，但并不像卡塔克表现得那样激进。自从结束访华行程后，阿里·沙抛开了之前的种种疑虑，并为信德省的多个项目争取到中方投资。俾路支省前任首席部长阿卜杜尔·马利克博士以及现任首席部长纳瓦布·萨那奥拉·泽瑞均未对中巴经济走廊表示反对。与其他区域相比，俾路支省会因瓜达尔港收获更多利益。该省已经建起多条公路网，将在中巴经济走廊建设中发挥关键作用。

2. 项目成果

新华社称，习近平主席号召双方尽快完成瓜达尔港相关项目，以及中巴经济走廊沿线的经济特区、工业园区的建设。谢里夫办公室表示，除价值 34 亿人民币（4.39 亿美元）的合作协议外，两国还签署了两份价值 23 亿人民币（3.33 亿美元）的合作协议，其中包括：

——在瓜达尔港西南部修建机场。瓜达尔港属于深水港，可以作为从新疆进入阿拉伯海的入海口。

——（巴基斯坦）哈维连陆港项目。

价值11亿人民币（1.6亿美元）的经贸技术合作项目，通过兴建东湾高速公路，将瓜达尔港与巴基斯坦当前的公路系统连接在一起。

据中国官方文件显示，2014—2016 年，“一带一路”相关国家新签对外承包工程合同额达到 3049 亿美元，其中一些项目将持续数年之久。

一些国家对中国投资可能造成的债务负担表示担忧，但巴基斯坦对此持乐观态度，巴方政府首席经济学家在接受路透社采访时表示，巴方债务持续到 2022 年，本息合计 50 亿美元，但交通走廊带来的中转费用，足以弥补债务缺口。

三 结语

“一带一路”的目的在于通过兴建新通路连接亚洲、欧洲及非洲。“一带一路”倡议主要关注经济发展，但同时也具有政治意义和战略意义。该倡议致力于实现共同发展、共同富裕以及能源安全，通过改善巴基斯坦的区域经济，能够从根源上消除恐怖主义，有助于中亚及中东局势稳定。对于这样一项能够给该区域带来共同利益、有助于区域稳定的倡议，美国本该表示支持。但美国对于“一带一路”的态度并不积极。但无可否认的是，在中国梦的大前提下，中巴经济走廊定然能为双方带来丰厚的回报。目前为止，针对能源及基础设施领域的投资高达460亿美元，项目建成后带来的利润将远远超过这个数字。在支持者的眼中，中国的“一带一路”将改变整个区域乃至全世界的游戏规则，关于这一点，目前尚未有人提出异议。中巴经济走廊预示着中巴双方以及周边国家的共同富裕与共同发展，将促进两国经贸合作、军事合作以及经济的进一步发展。但考虑到美、印两国对于“一带一路”的怀疑、对中巴经济走廊的保守态度，巴基斯坦应在项目开展的过程中，谨慎巧妙地处理各方面可能出现的问题。

CPEC Milestone: Some Impressions on the "Belt and Road" Summit 2017

Muhammad Iqbal Chawla / Pakistan

Professor & Dean, Faculty of Arts & Humanities, University of the Punjab, Lahore, Pakistan

A unique and historic International summit, "The Belt and Road Summit," was held in Beijing on 14-15 May 2017 where dozens of heads of state and governments from all over the world took part. Mian Muhammad Nawaz Sharif (Prime Minister of Pakistan) also actively participated in the Summit and re-insured the continuity and consolidation of the China-Pakistan Corridor project. This was the first time that Chief Ministers of all the four provinces of Pakistan also participated and deliberated on the Summit. Therefore, the entire major political parties welcomed (CPEC) for the development and prosperity of the country but they have serious concerns about some aspects, such as the route of the corridor, viability, transparency and execution of this project. Therefore, this paper will attempt to understand main objectives of the One Belt and Road Summit 2017 and its effects on CPEC from the overall perspective of Pakistan-China Relations. However, the present author believes this summit was a milestone not only for the advancement of One Belt one Road for China but also a historic development for the economic, social, cultural and strategic consolidation of Pakistan. This paper will also like to touch upon some concerns of the political leaders on the procedural matter adopted for the implementation of the CPEC by the Nawaz Sharif Government.

I. Belt and Road: Pakistan-China Ties

At the end of 2013 Chinese President Xi Jinping announced one of China's most ambitious foreign policy and economic initiatives. He called for the building of a Silk Road Economic Belt and a 21st Century Maritime Silk Road, collectively referred to as Belt and Road, which has also come to be known as the Belt and Road Initiative. Xi's vision is an ambitious program of infrastructure building to connect China's less-developed border regions with neighboring countries; in this regard, Belt and Road is arguably one of the largest development plans in modern history. On land, Beijing aims to connect the country's underdeveloped hinterland to Europe through Central Asia. This route has been dubbed the Silk Road Economic Belt. The second leg of Xi's plan is to build a 21st Century Maritime Silk Road connecting the fast-growing Southeast Asian region to China's southern provinces through ports and railways.

Xi has launched Belt and Road at a time when Chinese foreign policy shows signs of greater assertion. This has meant that Belt and Road is often interpreted as a geopolitical plan rather than a purely economic one. While there is a great deal of truth to this interpretation, this analysis argues that focusing on the geo-political dimensions of Belt and Road obscures its principally geo-economic drivers, in particular its connection to changes in China's domestic industrial policy.

II. Belt and Road: Geostrategy or Geoeconomics?

Before the 18th Party Congress in 2013, there were heated debates among Chinese policy-makers and scholars about the strategic direction of the country's foreign policy, especially in its neighboring areas. In October 2013, Beijing convened an important work-conference on what it termed 'peripheral diplomacy'.

It was reportedly the first major foreign policy meeting since 2006 and the first-ever meeting on policy towards neighboring countries since the founding of the People's Republic. It was attended by all of the important players in the Chinese foreign policy-making process including the entire Standing Committee of the Politburo.

At the Peripheral Diplomacy Work Conference, Xi said that China's neighbors had "extremely significant strategic value". He also said that he wanted to improve relations between China and its neighbors, strengthening economic ties and deepening security cooperation. "Maintaining stability in China's neighborhood is the key objective of peripheral diplomacy. We must encourage and participate in the process of regional economic integration, speed up the process of building up infrastructure and connectivity. We must build the Silk Road Economic Belt and 21st Century Maritime Silk Road, creating a new regional economic order."

Xi clearly sees China's considerable economic resources as a key tool in his efforts to maintain regional stability and assert China's leadership in the country's neighborhood. Analysts regard the work-conference as a significant turning point in the evolution of China's foreign policy. Douglas Paal of the Carnegie Endowment for International Peace argues that the conference saw the Chinese leadership effectively change Deng Xiaoping's famous policy, "hide your strength and bide your time". According to Paal, in its place, the new Chinese leadership advanced a more proactive diplomacy in surrounding regions. This new, more activist foreign policy has reinforced the impression that Belt and Road is primarily driven by broad geo-strategic aims. Certainly some elements of Belt and Road are consistent with such a characterization. The China–Pakistan Economic Corridor is a prime example. It is widely regarded as one of the flagship projects of Belt and Road with enthusiastic backing and active support of both Beijing and Islamabad. The proposed corridor is expected to connect Kashgar in Xinjiang in China's far west with the Port of Gwadar in the province of Baluchistan. Given the port's proximity to the Persian Gulf, it could be used as a trans-shipment point for China's energy supplies obviating the need to go through the Straits of Malacca, which can be effectively blocked to Chinese commercial shipping by the western powers in a period of rising tensions or an active armed conflict, in Southeast Asia. This could have a debilitating effect on Chinese sea-borne trade especially through the Indian Ocean.

1. Participation of Pakistani Provinces in Belt and Road Summit

The travel of all the chief ministers to China with Prime Minister Nawaz Sharif, which was a great sight to watch, materialized only after his opposing provincial chief executives fully realized that the China-Pak Economic Corridor (CPEC) is a real game-changer for Pakistan and will equally benefit their areas as well. The inclusion of chief ministers from Sindh and Khyber Pakhtunkhwa (KP) in the premier's entourage tremendously reflects the spirit of national harmony, cohesion and unity on the CPEC and is spectacular news from Pakistan to China, which had been worried over the spurious political bickering and point-scoring on these grand projects.

China had to work hard to remove the baseless misgivings and suspicions created about the CPEC for political reasons. More than once, it was compelled to issue clarifications so that everybody's doubts were dispensed and it to make clear to all that the CPEC was for the benefit of whole of Pakistan and not for any specific region. It had earlier disapproved the delay of the Chinese president's visit to Pakistan due to the chaos and mayhem generated by the 2014 sit-ins. The participation of such a high level Pakistani delegation in the Belt and Road Forum for International Cooperation in Beijing is a great honor for Pakistan. The Belt and Road Forum (BRF) is part of the "Silk Road Economic Belt and the 21st Century Maritime Silk Road" initiative launched by President Xi Jinping in 2013. The Forum aims at promoting common development through a win-win cooperation.

The CPEC is the flagship project of Belt and Road. The BRF is being attended by 27 other heads of state and government. It exposes the leadership role that China is playing. It is known that some influential foreign countries and certain domestic elements are hell-bent upon sabotaging the CPEC, but their efforts have been successfully countered by Pakistan as it has continued its strong determination and resolve to carry out that project. US National Intelligence Director Daniel Coats can only explain the logic what he has just stated. His remarks amply show the antipathy Washington has against the CPEC. He claimed that building of the CPEC in Pakistan would allow terrorist groups more targets for attacks. It is a very strange argument and is like saying that major development projects should not be undertaken for the sole reason that they will provide more targets to terrorists. At this time when conspiracies are being consistently hatched against the CPEC, the unanimity in Pakistan's political leadership belonging to different political parties, has been most sought after. These leaders thus proved that they have the guts to rise above their politics for national cause and progress. After their trips to China, Sindh Chief Minister, Murad Ali Shah, and Khyber Pakhtunkhwa (KP) Chief Minister, Pervez Khattak, changed their mind about the undertaking of the CPEC flagship, began supporting the prime minister and started describing it as a massive development plan that would transform the destiny and fate of Pakistan.

The KP chief minister belonging to the Pakistan Tehreek-e-Insaf (PTI) was forced by his party to waste almost four years in its protests. He understood, though very belatedly, that the politics of agitation was unproductive and useless and what would really pay him in the next general elections was the CPEC. Then, he started exhibiting interest in this gigantic project and received the expected positive response from China. After this healthy development, not much difference remains between his and the prime minister's pronouncements. Both are thus on the same page at least on this matter.

The Sindh chief minister, who belongs to the Pakistan People's Party (PPP), had also expressed reservations about the CPEC but in a rather low-key manner and was never as hard-hitting as Khattak had been. However, whatever concerns and doubts he had spoken about were removed after he paid a couple of visits to China and got promises of Chinese funding for several projects recommended by him. Obviously, there was no problem about the CPEC from the previous Balochistan chief minister, Dr Abdul Malik, and the incumbent, Sanaullah Zehri. Among the provinces Balochistan will benefit from the CPEC much more than any other area because of the Gawadar port. A sprawling network of roads has been completed in this province, which will play a key role in the CPEC.

2. Projects

Xi called for a swift completion of projects involving Gwadar Port and special economic and industrial parks along the corridor, the Xinhua state news service reported. Among the 3.4 billion RMB($493 million) in deals Sharif's office said were signed on Saturday were:

- Two cooperation agreements worth 2.3 billion RMB (333 million $) for an airport in the southwestern town of Gwadar, site of a deep-water port that is to provide an outlet to the Arabian Sea from the far western Chinese province of Xinjiang.

- Establishment of the Havelian Dry Port in Pakistan

- Agreement on economic and technical cooperation costing 1.1 billion RMB (160 million $) for the East Bay Expressway linking Gwadar to Pakistan's existing highway system.

China has stated that between 2014 and 2016, its businesses signed projects worth 304.9 billion $ in countries participating in "Belt and Road" projects. Some of the projects could be in development for years.

Some countries are wary of the debt burden that the Chinese financing could create. Pakistan, however, has expressed an optimistic view, with the government's chief economist telling Reuters this week that the repayments will peak at around 5 billion $ in 2022, but will be more than offset by transit fees charged on the new transport corridor.

III. Conclusion

The Belt and Road is destined to establish new routes linking Asia, Europe and

Africa. The idea of "One Belt and One Road" is based mainly on economy, but has political and strategic components and implications. It aims for joint development, common prosperity and energy security. Since improving the region's economy could weaken the root-cause of terrorism and help stabilize Central Asia and the Middle East, USA should be more positive about the initiative as a stabilizing force for common good in the region. According to Zhuang Jianzhong, Vice Director of Shanghai Jiao Tong University's Center for National Strategy Studies, so far, this has not been the case with the US. The China-Pakistan Economic Corridor will benefit greatly and reap great dividends from the overall Chinese dream. The benefits will go beyond the initial 46 billion USD investment in energy and infrastructure projects once they are completed. The Belt and Road has been perceived by Chinese planners and their well-wishers as a game-changer for the entire region and beyond; so far there seems no reason to have any doubts in this regard. The CPEC will be a harbinger of economic prosperity and well-being for Pakistan, China and the neighboring states. Both projects will work in tandem with trade and will result in heightened economic cooperation, strengthened military alliance and greater economic prosperity. But with increased skepticism over the Belt and Road by USA and India's reservations regarding the CPEC, Pakistan needs to tread carefully and skillfully.

共同发展、共同价值与国际新秩序

冯维江 【中国】
中国社会科学院世界经济与政治研究所国际政治经济学研究室主任、副研究员

共同发展是器物层面的要求；共同价值是观念层面的与共同发展相适应、并对发展进程中与共同价值出现偏差部分进行校正的参照系。中国历来讲究共同发展，“不患寡而患不均”，“老吾老以及人之老”，“一花独放不是春，百花齐放春满园”等，都体现了共同发展的要求。而和平、发展、公平、正义、民主、自由等全人类共同价值，也是中国不懈的追求。从中国方面看，共同发展的要求和共同价值的弘扬，集中体现在中国所主张并追求的更加公正合理的国际新秩序上。这方面，中国已经提出了清晰而具体的主张。

首先，国际新秩序要求把建立伙伴关系，而非民族国家兴起以来通常存在的种种针对第三方的结盟关系，确定为国家间交往的指导原则，并在伙伴关系的基础上构建总体稳定、均衡发展的大国关系框架，作为确保全球战略稳定、构建以合作共赢为核心的新型国际关系的基石。

其次，国际新秩序要及时充分反映世界格局的变化，增加新兴市场国家和发展中国家的代表性和发言权，将包容性全面体现到全球治理的过程和结果之中。世界格局正处在一个加快演变的历史性进程之中，新兴市场国家和发展中国家崛起已经成为不可阻挡的历史潮流。顺应这一潮流，才能更好调动广大新兴市场国家和发展中国家的积极性，携手为世界共同繁荣和普遍安全提供充足、高效和可

持续的国际公共产品。

再次，饱满完整的国际新秩序，不仅追求人与人、国家与国家之间的合作与共同发展，而且追求人与自然、人类社会与生态环境之间的和谐，追求天人合一。习近平总书记指出，“人与自然共生共存，伤害自然最终将伤及人类”，“我们应该遵循天人合一、道法自然的理念，寻求永续发展之路”，“建设一个清洁美丽的世界”。

最后，构建更加公正合理国际新秩序的终极目标，指向打造人类命运共同体这一宏大理想。中国方面为国际社会勾勒出一个持久和平、普遍安全、共同繁荣、开放包容、美丽清洁的新世界。人类命运共同体不是一个已经获得和正在享受着的世界，而是一种人们热切希望栖息、希望拥有的世界。人类命运共同体意识的萌生和树立，有望为世界各国走向合作共赢提供可信的理性与感性基础。

应看到，当前的世界距离国际新秩序的建立、距离人类命运共同体的理想境界还有巨大的差距。弥合这一差距，需要所有国家的共同努力，尤其需要大国采取切实可信的行动，发挥率先垂范的作用。这也是强调“共同”的原因所在。“共同”既是权利，也是责任。“世界的命运必须由各国人民共同掌握，世界上的事情只能由各国政府和人民共同商量来办”；“作为大国，意味着对地区和世界和平与发展的更大责任，而不是对地区和国际事务的更大垄断”。塑造国际新秩序所面临的很多问题不再局限于一国内部，很多挑战也不再是一国之力所能应对的，需要各国通力合作来解决和应对。

Common Development, Common Values and the New International Order

Feng Weijiang / China

Director and Assistant Researcher of the International Political Economy Division under the Institute of World Economy and Politics at the Chinese Academy of Social Sciences

Common development is a requirement of implements level. Common value is a frame of reference that is compatible with common development at a conceptual level which corrects the deviations from the concept of common values in the developmental process. China has always paid attention to common development. Many old sayings, such as "Inequality rather than want is the cause of trouble", "Expand the respect of the aged in one's family to that in other families", "One swallow does not make a summer", all reflect the requirement for the common development. The Chinese nation has never ceased to pursue the common values of all mankind, including peace, development, fairness, justice, democracy and freedom. From the perspective of China, the requirement for common development and the promotion of common values are basically embodied in the more just and equitable new international order that China advocates and pursues. In this regard,

China has put forward clear and concrete proposals.

First of all, the new international order requires the establishment of partnerships, rather than all kinds of alliances that have existed against a third party since the rise of nation-states, as the guiding principle for inter-state exchanges. In addition, it is necessary to build a stable and balanced framework of relationship among major countries on the basis of a partnership which should be the cornerstone of the new type of international relationship that ensures global strategic stability and centers on win-win cooperation.

Second, the new international order must reflect the changes in the world pattern promptly and adequately, increase the representation and voice of the emerging market countries and developing countries, and fully incorporate inclusiveness into the processes and results of the global governance. The world pattern is in a historical process of accelerated evolution. The rise of emerging market countries and developing countries has become an irresistible historical trend. Only by conforming to this trend can the enthusiasm of a large number of emerging market countries and developing countries be mobilized so as to work together to provide sufficient, efficient, and sustainable international public goods for the common prosperity and universal security of the world.

Third, a full and complete new international order not only pursues cooperation and common development between man and man, and between nation and nation, but also seeks harmony and unity between man and nature, and between human society and the ecological environment. General Secretary Xi Jinping pointed out, “Man coexists with nature, which means that any harm to nature will eventually come back to haunt man.” “We should follow the concept of harmony between man and nature and the law from nature, pursue the path of sustainable development” and “We should build a clean and beautiful world”.

Finally, the ultimate goal of building a more just and rational new international order is to set the ambitious ideal of building a community with a shared future for humanity. China has outlined a new beautiful and clean world of lasting peace, universal security, common prosperity, openness and inclusiveness for the international community. A community with a shared future for humanity is a world that people are eager to inhabit, rather than a world that has been made accessible to and is being enjoyed by human beings. The initiation and establishment of the consciousness of a community with a shared future for humanity is expected to provide a trustworthy rational and perceptual basis for the countries across the world in order to achieve cooperation and win-win results.

However, it should be noted that the current world still has a long way to go for the establishment of a new international order and an ideal realm of a community with a shared future for humanity. In order to close up the gap concerted efforts of all countries are required, and especially, great powers should take credible actions to set an example. This is also the reason for emphasizing "common". "Common" is not only a right, but also a responsibility. "The destiny of the world must be shared by all peoples. The world issues can only be handled by governments and people of all countries through consultation." "The status of a great nation means greater responsibility for regional and global peace and development, rather than a greater monopoly in regional and international affairs." Many issues faced during the shaping of the new international order are no longer limited to one country. Many challenges are beyond the capacity of a single country to cope with, and require all countries to work together to solve them and respond to them.

中国的“合作共赢”理念与哈中合作关系的新阶段

纳比坚·穆哈穆德汉 【哈萨克斯坦】

哈萨克斯坦共和国阿里·法拉比国立大学当代中国研究中心主任/东方学系汉学教研室主任

中国作为重要的世界主导性国家之一提出的内、外政策理念不仅对本国而且对世界，特别是对亚洲邻国产生极为重要的效应。哈萨克斯坦共和国是中亚大国，又是与中国山水相连的近邻，且与中国具有几千年交往历史的丝路沿线国家。1991 年 12 月 16 日哈萨克斯坦宣告独立，12 月 27 日中国宣布“承认哈萨克斯坦共和国独立”，并于 1992 年 1 月 3 日两国正式建立外交关系，发表《哈中建交公报》，确立了发展两国关系的基本原则。从此两国关系已经历了 25 年的合作发展历程。

一　中哈友好合作历史进程

我们认为 25 年的两国关系经历了三个发展阶段（中国学者也把两国关系的发展分三个阶段，但分期年份略有不同，认为 1992—1995 年为两国关系的第一阶段，1995—2004 年为第二阶段，2005 年至今为第三阶段）。

我们认为 1992—1998 年是哈中关系发展的第一阶段。在这一时期两国签署一系列的重要协议：1993 年双方签署了“关于哈中友好关系的联合声明”，使两国关系进入睦邻友好关系时期；1994 年中国政府阐述中国与中亚国家关系原则：“睦邻友好，和平共处，发展互利合作，促进共同繁荣，尊重各国选择，互不干涉内政，尊重主权和支持在地区稳定原则基础上建设相互关系";1996 年 7 月哈中两国发表"哈中联合声明",决心将哈中睦邻友好关系提高到面向 21 世纪的协作与伙伴关系;1996 年哈中两国在军事安全领域建立了合作关系;1997 年哈中两国建立石油天然气领域的合作;1998 年哈中两签署国家边界勘定协定。

1998 年至 2005 年为哈中关系发展的第二阶段。此阶段两国关系上升到战略伙伴关系阶段。2002 年 12 月 23 日哈中双方签署了"哈萨克斯坦共和国和中华人民共和国睦邻友好合作条约"以及 2003 年 6 月 3 日签署了"哈萨克斯坦共和国和中华人民共和国 2003 至 2008 年合作纲要"等重要文件,并建立上海合作组织框架下多边合作机制。

2006 年至 2015 年 9 月为两国关系发展的第三阶段。在这阶段:2005 年 4 月 7 日在阿斯塔纳两国元首签署了"哈萨克斯坦共和国和中华人民共和国关于建立和发展战略伙伴关系的联合声明",制定两国关系发展方向:加强政治互信,深化安全合作共同维护地区安全稳定,促进经济合作,谋求共同繁荣,扩大人文合作和民间交往,增进两国人民的传统友谊。2006 年 12 月哈中双方签署了"哈萨克斯坦共和国和中华人民共和国 21 世纪战略伙伴关系"文件。此阶段两国关系发展的主要表现在能源领域,石油和天然气管道的投入运营和两国贸易额的不断增长,因而哈萨克斯坦成为中国在中亚第一贸易伙伴和独联体第二贸易大国。

二 当代中国国际合作的新理念是"合作共赢"

习近平主席针对新的世情、国情,提出了一系列治国理政思想。在国际问题领域,习近平主席在各种不同的场合谈到:"我们要高举和平、发展、合作、共赢的旗帜,坚持在和平共处五项原则基础上同各国友好相处,在平等互利基础上积极开展同各国的交流合作,坚定不移维护世界和平、促进共同发展";"我们必须走出一条和衷共济、合作共赢的新路子";"什么是当今世界的潮流?答案只有一个,那就是和平、发展、合作、共赢"。可见,合作共赢已经构成当今中国奉行的新型国际关系新理念,也成为中国发展对外关系的新原则。

这种合作共赢的原则,是对当代国际关系基本原则的一个创造,它强调国际社会,不分国家的大小、强弱、贫富、社会制度和意识形态,面对共同的发展问题,面对全球性的挑战,各国只有合作,才能实现共同的发展,才能摆脱危机,实现生存。人类已经构成了一个命运共同体、利益共同体、责任共同体,任何国家都不能置身事外，独善其身，更不能以邻为壑、损人利己。它打破了过去国际关系中的零和游戏，真正将国际关系建立在平等互利基础上，实现了国际社会的共赢，从而为建立国际政治经济新秩序迈出了一大步。这种理念，体现了中国对国际社会关系的一种新的认识，也是对国际社会的一大贡献。

合作共赢的外交理念，对世界各国的发展，对实现人类的和平发展，对深化国际交往和合作，都具有十分重要的意义，因此，得到了国际社会的广泛认同和赞许。这一理念和外交原则顺应了各国发展的梦想和时代潮流。任何一个共同发展、共同受益的国际倡议和项目都会被国际社会接受，如果它有足够的实力和诚意引领诸国实现其目标的话。

三 “一带一路”促进中哈合作共赢进入新的阶段

2013 年 9 月，中国国家主席习近平首次访问中亚国家，他在哈萨克斯坦纳扎尔巴耶夫大学演讲时提出了共建“丝绸之路经济带”构想，引起很大的反响。2013 年 10 月，习近平主席在出访东南亚国家期间，提出共建“21 世纪海上丝绸之路”的重大倡议，得到国际社会高度关注。这些倡议，统称为“一带一路”。在一定程度上讲，这些倡议，不仅是合作共赢的理念的重要体现，也是合作共赢的重要成果。习近平主席将提出的“合作、共赢”新理念融入中国“一带一路”外交政策，赢得丝路沿线国家和参与国家的广泛赞许和认同。因为自从冷战结束以来许多发展中国家和发达国家，乃至国际社会都曾提出过发展“丝绸之路计划”，但至今都未见其显著效果。当然，这有其复杂的主客观因素，但最主要的原因是它们都没有把丝路沿线国家根本利益和未来发展与其项目紧密联系起来；也没有相应的资金和技术作保障。而中国提出“一带一路”倡议虽然比它们晚些，但有备而来，即有政治、经济和文化教育理论，又有资金、技术和实施规划。而且中国所制定的“政策沟通，道路联通，贸易畅通，货币流通，民心相通”原则，以及它所倡导的弘扬平等互信、包容互鉴、合作共赢精神和造就人类命运发展共同体意识，具有极大的感召力，实现了合作发展中保障本国利益是丝路沿线国家和发展中国家的共同愿望。

到目前为止，“一带一路”倡议及其“合作共赢”原则，赢得广泛的赞誉和积极回应，取得举世公认的丰硕成果。这在 5 月北京举行的“一带一路”国际合作高峰论坛上充分彰显。习近平主席在演说中总结：中国同 40 多个国家和国际组织签署了合作协议，同30多个国家开展机制化产能合作。本次论坛期间，我们还将签署一批对接合作协议和行动计划，同60多个国家和国际组织共同发出推进“一带一路”贸易畅通合作倡议。各方通过政策对接，实现了“一加一大于二”的效果。

中国对“一带一路”沿线国家投资累计超过500亿美元。中国企业已经在20多个国家建设356个经贸合作区，为有关国家创造近11亿美元税收和18万个就业岗位。本次论坛又签署了32个双边、多边合作文件以及企业合作项目。这些事实说明，中国建立新型国际政治、经济关系外交政策已经取得极大成功。

“一带一路”是中国在哈萨克斯坦共和国提出的，并促进了双方的合作共赢进程。2013年底，哈萨克斯坦总统纳扎尔巴耶夫在2014年度国情咨文中提出“光明之路”新经济政策，把发展交通运输基础设施、发展工业基础设施、发展能源基础设施和发展公共基础设施作为优先发展项目。并提出将其与中国倡议直接衔接。从此两国高层互访更加频繁，在“一带一路”框架下签订了一系列的合作协议。2014年12月中国总理李克强访问哈国，双边签署总额达140亿美元的30多项合作协议；签署“关于共同推进丝绸之路经济带建设的备忘录”，并就价值“180亿美元的哈中合作框架协议”达成共识。两国初步确定16个早期收获项目和63个前景项目清单，涉及水泥、钢铁、平板玻璃、矿业、化工、能源、电力等领域。2015年3月哈国总理马西莫夫访华期间，两国签署加强产能与投资合作备忘录和总金额为236亿美元的产能合作协议。2015年中国企业宣布了12个对哈萨克斯坦的“绿地投资”项目，总投资额约12亿美元，中国成为哈萨克斯坦对外直接投资的最大来源国。

2015年8月31日，哈国总统纳扎尔巴耶夫访华，哈中双方签署“哈萨克斯坦共和国和中华人民共和国关于全面战略伙伴关系新阶段的联合宣言”和加强产能与投资合作政府间框架协议，这是中国与外国签订的首个产能合作协议。为保证协议落实，中国还建立了部门间工作机制，同时设立产能合作基金，其中确定的52个项目并签订了总金额230亿美元的25项协议。其中汽车组装、聚丙烯项目、阿斯塔纳市轻轨项目已开工或竣工，而钢铁、冶炼、水泥等领域十余个项目正在启动之中。哈国总统纳扎尔巴耶夫在2017年度国情咨文中敦促政府优先实施哈中签署的合作项目。

2017年5月在北京召开的“一带一路”高峰论坛上，哈国总统纳扎尔巴耶夫发表讲话，他认为："一带一路"项目的付诸实施，必将使丝路沿线国家，其中包括中亚地区获得以崭新的发展模式而著称于世界的良好机遇。他称赞"光明之路"和"一带一路"衔接而取得的成就，并建议下一步在"科技创新领域加深合作"。因为他在本年度国情咨文中提出发展科技、教育创新，增强国人竞争力政策。由此可以看出哈国总统制定的新政策都有乘"一带一路"东风而推行之含义。

哈萨克斯坦驻华大使努雷舍夫说："哈萨克斯坦与中国在落实"一带一路"倡议的重要组成部分——"丝绸之路经济带"的问题上保持着密切协作。目前，我们与中方在产能合作领域共同实施 51 个总价值达 260 亿美元的项目。我相信，这些计划的成功实施不仅将推动哈萨克斯坦的发展，还将推动整个地区的发展。"

2015 年 8 月 31 日，哈中两国领导人签署"哈萨克斯坦共和国和中华人民共和国关于全面战略伙伴关系新阶段的联合宣言"。这是在中国"一带一路"新型外交关系背景下，哈中关系提升的标志。

可以说，自从合作共赢原则提出，中哈两国战略伙伴关系进入新阶段。新阶段的特点是，在新的国际形势下中国提出"一带一路"国际倡议及其新的合作原则，尤其是合作共赢新理念被哈国所接受和积极回应而制定"光明之路"新经济政策与"一带一路"构想相对接，从此出现两国关系更加迅速发展态势。正如哈国总统纳扎尔巴耶夫所说"从外资和贷款数额以及合资企业数量方面中华人民共和国成为哈国的主要经济伙伴之一"。在新的合作理念指引下，哈中两国合作共赢为基础的双边关系的发展前景非常宽阔。哈中在"一带一路"框架下新的合作共赢必将在中亚地区产生示范效应。

China's Concept of "Win-Win Cooperation" and the New Stage of Cooperation Between China and Kazakhstan

Muhametkhanuly Nabizhan / Kazakhstan

Head of the Department of Sinology, Al-Farabi Kazakh National University, Director for the Center of Modern China Studies

China, as one of the important world-dominating countries, puts forward internal and foreign policy concepts which exert extremely important effects on China itself and on the whole world, especially its Asian neighbors. The Republic of Kazakhstan is a large country in Central Asia, a close neighbor with the same landscapes as China's and a country along the Silk Road; it has a history of exchanges with China that is thousands of years long. On December 16, 1991, Kazakhstan proclaimed its independence. On December 27, China announced the *Recognition of the Independence of the Republic of Kazakhstan*. On January 3, 1992, the two countries formally established diplomatic relations and issued the *Communiqué of the Establishment of Kazakhstan-China Diplomatic Relations*, which determined the basic principles for the development of the relationship between the two countries. Since then, the relations between the two countries have experienced 25 years of cooperation and development.

I. The Historical Process of a Friendly Cooperation between China and Kazakhstan

We believe that 25 years of relationship between the two countries has undergone three stages of development (Chinese scholars have also divided the development of the relationship between the two countries into three stages, with a slight difference in the period of each stage. They believe that the period from 1992 to 1995 represents the first stage, the period from 1995 to 2004 represents the second stage, and the period from 2005 to the present represents the third stage).

We believe that the period from 1992 to 1998 is the first stage of the development of the relationship between Kazakhstan and China. During that period, the two countries concluded a series of important agreements. In 1993, the two countries signed the *Joint Statement on a Friendly Relationship between China and Kazakhstan*, enabling the relationship between the two countries to enter a period of a good-neighbor relationship. In 1994, the Chinese government explained the principles of the relationship between China and Central Asian countries: "Good-neighborly relationship, peaceful coexistence, development of mutually beneficial cooperation, promotion of common prosperity, respect for choices of the various countries, non-interference in internal affairs, respect for sovereignty, and support for the establishment of mutual relations based on regional stability". In July 1996, Kazakhstan and China published the *Kazakh-Chinese Joint Statement* and decided to upgrade the good-neighborly relationship between Kazakhstan and China to a relationship of cooperation and partnership in view of looking towards the 21st century. In 1996, Kazakhstan and China established a cooperative relationship in military security. In 1997, the two countries developed cooperation in oil and gas fields. In 1998, the two countries signed a national boundary demarcation agreement.

The period from 1998 to 2005 is the second stage of the development of the relationship between Kazakhstan and China. During that period, the relationship between the two countries rose to a strategic partnership. Kazakhstan and China signed many important documents, such as the *Treaty of Good-Neighborly and Friendly Cooperation between the Republic of Kazakhstan and the Republic of China* on December 23, 2002 and the *Outline for Cooperation between the Republic of Kazakhstan and the Republic of China (2003-2008)* on June 3, 2003, and established the multilateral cooperation mechanism under the framework of the Shanghai Cooperation Organization.

The period from 2006 to September 2015 is the third stage of the development of the relationship between the two countries. During that stage, the two heads of state signed the *Joint Statement of the Republic of Kazakhstan and the People's Republic of China on the Establishment and Development of a Strategic Partnership* on April 7, 2005 in Astana, and further formulated the direction for the development of bilateral relations: strengthening mutual political trust, intensifying safe cooperation, jointly maintaining regional security and stability, promoting economic cooperation, seeking common prosperity, expanding humanistic cooperation and non-governmental exchanges, and enhancing the traditional friendship between the two peoples. Besides, Kazakhstan and China signed the document entitled "Strategic Partnership between the Republic of Kazakhstan and the People's Republic of China in the 21st Century" in December 2006. At that stage, the development of bilateral relations was mainly demonstrated in the field of energy, the operation of oil and natural gas pipelines, and the continuous growth of bilateral trade volume. As a result, Kazakhstan became the first trading partner of China in Central Asia and the second largest trading country in the Commonwealth of the Independent States.

II. The New Concept of "Win-Win cooperation" in the International Cooperation of Contemporary China

After coming into power, President Xi Jinping brought forward a series of governing ideas in light of the new world situation and national situation. With regard to international issues, President Xi Jinping said, on various occasions, that, "We must hold high the banner of peace, development, cooperation and win-win situation, develop friendly ties with all the other countries on the basis of the Five Principles of Peaceful Coexistence, actively carry out exchanges and cooperation with all the other countries on the basis of equality and mutual benefit, unswervingly safeguard world peace and promote common development"; "We must venture down a new path with concerted effort, mutual cooperation and win-win"; "What is the trend of today's world? There is only one answer: peace, development, cooperation and win-win cooperation". This shows that the win-win cooperation has become a new concept of new international relations pursued by China today, and has become a new principle for China in developing foreign relations.

The principle of win-win cooperation is a creation of the basic principles for contemporary international relations. It emphasizes the international community, regardless of the size, strength, wealth, social system and ideology of the country. In face of common developmental issues and global challenges, all countries can achieve common development, overcome the crisis and achieve survival only if they cooperate with each other. Mankind has already formed a community of destiny, a community of interests, and a community of responsibility. No country may stay out and remain alone, or implement beggar-thy-neighbor policy or seek benefits for itself at the expense of other countries. It breaks the zero-sum game of the past international relations, truly establishes international relations on the basis of equality and mutual benefits, and achieves a win-win situation for the international community, thus taking a big step towards the establishment of a new international political and economic order. This concept reveals a new recognition of China in international community relations and is also a major contribution to the international community.

The diplomatic concept of win-win cooperation is of paramount significance to the development of all countries in the world, the realization of the peaceful development of mankind and the deepening of international exchanges and cooperation. Therefore, it has been widely recognized and praised by the international community. This concept and diplomatic principle are in line with the developmental dreams of all countries and the tide of the times. Any international initiative and project for common development and benefit will be accepted by the international community if they have enough strength and sincerity to lead all countries to attain their goals.

III. The New Stage of Sino-Kazakhstan Win-Win Cooperation under the Promotion of the Belt and Road Initiative

In September 2013, Xi Jinping, the President of the People's Republic of China, paid his first visit to the countries of Central Asia. In the speech at the Nazarbayev University in Kazakhstan, Mr. Xi proposed the idea of jointly building the "Silk Road Economic Belt", which caused great repercussions. In October 2013, during his visit to Southeast Asian countries, Mr. Xi put forward a major initiative to commonly build the "21st Century Maritime Silk Road" (hereinafter referred to as the "Belt and Road"), attracting great attention from the international community. The initiative is collectively referred to as the "Belt and Road". To some extent, the initiative is not only an important embodiment of the concept of win-win cooperation, but also an important result of win-win cooperation. President Xi Jinping integrated the new concept of "win-win cooperation" into the "Belt and Road" Initiative, which gained extensive praise and recognition from all countries along the Silk Road and the participating countries. Since many developing countries, developed countries and even the international community proposed the development of the "Silk Road" after the end of the Cold War, no significant results have been achieved so far. It is surely due to many complex subjective and objective factors. However, the main reason is that the fundamental interests and future development of the countries along the Silk Road are not closely linked; what's more, no sufficient funding and technology are made available as a guarantee. Although China put forward the "Belt and Road" Initiative later, China has made adequate preparations in political, economic, trade, cultural and educational theories, as well as funds, technology and plans for implementation. In addition, great charisma arises from the principles of "policy communication, road connectivity, unimpeded trade, currency circulation, and people-to-people links" formulated by China, the avocation of equality, mutual trust, inclusiveness and mutual learning, the win-win spirit of cooperation, and the awareness of creating a community of human destiny and development, which realized that safeguarding domestic interests in cooperation and development, is the common aspiration of the countries along the Silk Road and the developing countries.

So far, the "Belt and Road" Initiative and the principle of "win-win cooperation" have won extensive praise and positive responses, and they have achieved world-renowned fruitful results, which were fully demonstrated at the International Cooperation Summit for the "Belt and Road" Initiative held in Beijing in May, 2017. In his speech, President Xi Jinping concluded that "China has signed cooperation agreements with more than 40 countries and international organizations, and cooperated with more than 30 countries in the cooperation for institutionalized capacity. In this forum, we also entered into a batch of cooperation agreements and action plans, and promoted the 'Belt and Road' trade cooperation initiative jointly with more than 60 countries and international organizations. All of the parties have achieved the effect of 'one plus one is greater than two' through policy linkage." China's investment in the countries along the 'Belt and Road' has totaled over 50 billion USD. Chinese enterprises have constructed 56 economic and trade cooperation zones in more than 20 countries, creating nearly 1.1 billion USD in taxes and 180,000 jobs for the countries concerned. The forum witnessed the conclusion of 32 bilateral and multilateral cooperation documents and corporate cooperation projects. These facts show that China has achieved great success in the establishment of new diplomatic policies on international political and economic relations.

The "Belt and Road" Initiative was proposed by China in the Republic of Kazakhstan, which facilitated the cooperation and win-win progress between the two countries. At the end of 2013, Kazakh President Nursultan Nazarbayev put forward a new economic policy of the "Bright Road" in the *2014 State of the Union Address* to consider the development of transportation infrastructures, industrial infrastructures, energy infrastructures and public infrastructures as developmental priorities, and also proposed to link the policy directly with the Chinese Initiative. Since then, high-level mutual visits between the two countries have become more frequent and a series of cooperation agreements have been concluded under the "Belt and Road" framework. In December 2014, China Premier Li Keqiang visited Kazakhstan and signed over 30 bilateral cooperation agreements amounting to 14 billion USD; he signed the *Memorandum on Jointly Promoting the Construction of the Silk Road Economic Belt* and reached consensus on the Sino-Kazakhstan Cooperation Framework Agreement Worth 18 Billion USD. The two countries initially identified the list of 16 early harvesting projects and 63 prospective projects involving such fields as cement, steel, flat glass, mining, chemicals, energy, electricity and others. When Kazakhstan Prime Minister Massimov visited China in March 2015, the two countries signed a memorandum of cooperation on enhancing the capacity and investments and the agreement on the capacity for cooperation worth USD 23.6 billion. In 2015, Chinese enterprises announced 12 "greenfield investment" projects for Kazakhstan, with a total investment of approximately 1.2 billion USD. As a result, China became the largest source of foreign direct investment in Kazakhstan.

When the Kazakh President Nursultan Nazarbayev visited China on August 31, 2015, Kazakhstan and China signed the *Joint Declaration on the New Phase of the Comprehensive Strategic Partnership between the Republic of Kazakhstan and the People's Republic of China* and the agreement regarding an inter-governmental framework for strengthening their cooperation on capacity and investments, the first capacity cooperation agreement between China and a foreign country. To ensure the implementation of the agreement, China set up an inter-departmental working mechanism, established a capacity cooperation fund, and entered into 25 agreements worth 23 billion USD for 52 identified projects. The auto assembly project, polypropylene project, and the Astana light railway project have commenced or been completed, while more than ten projects in the fields of iron and steel, smelting and cement are ready to start. In the *2017 State of the Union Address*, Kazakhstan President Nazarbayev urged the government to give priority to the cooperation projects signed by and between Kazakhstan and China.

At the International Cooperation Summit for the "Belt and Road" Initiative held in Beijing in May 2017, Kazakh President Nazarbayev delivered a speech, and believed that the implementation of the "Belt and Road" Initiative would surely bring good opportunities known as the new developmental model to the countries along the Silk Road, including the Central Asian region. He praised the achievements from the connection of the "Bright Road" and the "Belt and Road" Initiative, and suggested intensifying cooperation in the field of "technology innovation" during the next step. The proposal of technological development, education innovation and the policy of the enhancement of national competitiveness in the *2017 State of the Union Address* reveals that the new policy formulated by the Kazakhstan President takes advantage of the "Belt and Road" Initiative for its implementation.

Nuryshev, a Kazakhstan ambassador to China, said that "Kazakhstan and China have maintained close cooperation on the implementation of the 'Silk Road Economic Belt', an important part of the 'Belt and Road' Initiative. At present, we are implementing 51 projects worth 26 billion USD in the field of cooperation on capacity in their cooperation with China. I believe that the successful implementation of these projects will not only promote the development of Kazakhstan, but also promote the development of the entire region".

On August 31, 2015, the leaders of Kazakhstan and China signed the *Joint Declaration on the New Stage of Comprehensive Strategic Partnership between the Republic of Kazakhstan and the People's Republic of China*. This is a sign of improvement in the relationship between Kazakhstan and China under the background of new Chinese diplomatic relations of the "Belt and Road".

It can be said that the strategic partnership between China and Kazakhstan has stepped into a new phase since the principle of win-win cooperation was proposed. The new stage is characterized by the fact that Kazakhstan has accepted and responded positively to the “Belt and Road” international initiative and new cooperation principles proposed by China under the new international situation, especially the new concept of win-win cooperation, and developed the new economic policy of the “Bright Road” and connected it with the concept of the “Belt and Road” Initiative; since then, the relationship between the two countries has presented a trend of rapid development. As Kazakh President Nursultan Nazarbayev said, “the People’s Republic of China has become one of the major economic partners of Kazakhstan in terms of foreign capital, loans and the number of joint ventures”. Under the guidance of the new concept of cooperation, there will be very broad prospects of development for the bilateral relations based on cooperation and a win-win relationship between Kazakhstan and China. This concept makes sure that the new cooperation and a win-win relationship between China and Kazakhstan under the “Belt and Road” framework will have a demonstration effect in Central Asia.

References

Discussion of Xi Jinping on Governing the Country and Dealing with Politics. Beijing: Foreign Languages Publishing House, 2014, pp. 30, 250, 266.

http://finance.sina.com.cn/wm/2017-05-14/doc-ifyfekhi7612864.shtml *Egemen Kazakhstan*, 2014-11-11.

China Becomes the Largest Source of FDI in Kazakhstan [EB/OL]. www.ft.com, 2016-08-18 (1).

Wang Zhimin: Sino-Kazakhstan Cooperation on Capacity and Its Spillover Effect in the Context of the “Belt and Road” Initiative. *Northeast Asia Forum*, 2017(1).

Nazarbayev: State of the Union Address. http://www.akorda.kz/kz/addresses/addresses_of_president/memleket-basshysy-nnazarbaevtyn-kazakstan-halkyna-zholdauy-2017-zhylgy-31-kantar

Nazarbayev: Initiative for Renewing Central Asia. *Aikyn*, 2017-05-16, page 1.

Nuryshev: Active Connection of the “Bright Road” and the “Belt and Road” Initiative Creates a Model of Cooperation. Http://finance.sina.com.cn/roll/2017-05-12/docifyfecvz1021606.shtml, accessed on 2017-05-12, 02:11.

Astana Expo: New Starting Point for Development. *Egemen Kazakhstan*, 2017-06-08.

我们如何发现共同的价值观

马丁·阿尔布劳 【英国】
英国社会学学会荣誉副会长 / 英国社会科学院院士、荣休教授

就在 G20 德国汉堡峰会召开前不久，美国总统特朗普曾在波兰对当地群众发表讲话。在讲话中，他呼吁美国人民、波兰人民以及欧洲人民“不惜一切代价”捍卫共同的价值观，认为个体自由和国家主权等价值理念，是定义“我们的国家共同体”（即西方国家）的种种要素。

此类呼声所强调的，是价值观对于共同体或社会的重要意义，但实际上，这种呼声所反映出的，正是 20 世纪西方社会和学术界话语中反复出现的一个主题。早在 20 世纪 60 年代，西方著名社会学家塔尔科特·帕森斯便提出过类似的看法：

> 在分析某一社会的体制结构和发展进程时，可以用社会成员所共有的价值取向作为主要参照点，这一方法可以作为现代社会学理论研究一个主要原则。

这番论断不仅在社会学领域，更在西方文化内部引发了一场旷日持久的激辩。这场论战从 20 世纪 60 年代持续至今，论辩双方就其中隐含的意义展开争论，甚至曾一度引发双方冲突。

辩论结果如何？从广义上来说，除了引发对于“价值观”这一概念的混乱、对于理论的怀疑外，尚未得出任何结果。

我们首先要意识到，共同的价值观未必一定会带来和平、和谐、合作，未必会提高人类生活的“可忍受”度，当然更谈不上“满意度”。因此，任何人都可

以得出这样的结论：特朗普希望“不惜一切代价”来捍卫共同价值观、指望此举能够增进西方国家的团结，但对于西方国家而言，这是一项不可能完成的任务。

帕森斯凭借敏锐的洞察力对美国社会进行了审视，并指出了美国价值观的定义。这番定义不但措辞谨慎，而且巧妙地避开了反对者的政治观点。他将美国价值观概括为：“对社会的外部态势表现出的一种‘工具能动主义’倾向或‘主动支配’的倾向”，所谓的外部态势包括“自然界以及除美国外的其他社会”（作者强调）。

这种“主动支配”的倾向或许很好地解释了，为何西方国家始终对美国价值观抱有一丝警惕心理。

当然，冲突并非仅仅由这种“本国至上”的态度所导致，因为即便最具普适性的价值观中往往也隐含着引发冲突的因素。法国大革命便是历史上的绝佳例证。这场革命宣扬自由、平等、博爱的价值观，但这是否意味着，我没有任何权利压迫你？是否意味着所有人的饮食量必须保持一致？是否意味着要把所有陌生人都当作自己的兄弟？

随着这类价值观逐渐变得神圣化，便不难理解为何积极拥护此类价值观的人，会将法国大革命从1793年的举国欢腾很快引入当年的“恐怖统治”。

当然，我的意图并不在于“污蔑”价值观，也不在于历数各国尊奉的价值观存在何种优点。美国梦与中国梦各有不同的起源，许多层面均具有不可迁移性。然而随着历史的发展，许多价值观的出现确实起到了稳定社会、促进友好关系的作用。

因此，本文讨论的重点在于，人民与国家如何去“发现”有助于和平相处、提高生活意义的价值观。这类价值观或许并不是人们早已秉持的价值观，而是需要人民在相互协作的过程中，主动去发掘、去认同的价值观，

正如习近平主席2014年3月在联合国教科文组织总部的讲话所示：

> “当今世界，人类生活在不同文化、种族、肤色、宗教和不同社会制度所组成的世界里，各国人民形成了你中有我、我中有你的命运共同体。
>
> 我们应该推动不同文明相互尊重、和谐共处，让文明交流互鉴成为增进各国人民友谊的桥梁、推动人类社会进步的动力、维护世界和平的纽带。”

这篇讲稿收录在《习近平谈治国理政》一书中，该书引述了中国历史、文化、

特别是近期改革开放中积累的经验，以示从合作中吸取经验能够帮助我们取得什么样的成就。此外，该书具有相当程度上的理论热情，试图将各类公共政策的理念梳理成完整而连贯的体系。

此外，《习近平谈治国理政》提出了一种将各类理念和政策融为一体的领导方式，这在西方国家是罕有其匹的。西方国家关于公共政策的论辩反映出价值观上的冲突，这些价值理念往往令人困惑、缺乏系统性的理论支撑。

20 世纪 70 年代，哈佛大学教授丹尼尔·贝尔写过一本社会学著作。在对未来的展望中，贝尔提到了“后工业社会”的来临。他准确地预测了服务业的崛起，甚至更加精准地预计到将来会出现民粹派与精英派的冲突。

当然，根据贝尔的推测，未来社会将会根据理论知识的精专程度来进行区分，这种推测显然十分离谱。尽管如今的民粹主义者或许会排斥他们眼中的“专家的权力”，但专家政治论者并不通晓理论，而通晓理论的学术界专家却往往莫衷一是，对于由标语、推特和名人引领的公众话语而言，几乎无法产生任何实质性的影响。

相比之下，中国对于理论建设的积极探索能够为“一带一路”相关政策提供强有力的支持，尽管这些政策尚未得到世界其他国家的广泛认可。关于这一点，王义桅教授已经在那本极为实用的《一带一路：中国崛起给世界带来什么？》一书中进行过精辟阐述。

王教授明确指出西方全球化构想的种种狭隘之处，同时对中国公共政策中近期反复出现的“共同体”的理念进行了详尽阐述。通过对中共十八大报告的分析，王教授指出，在国际事务中，“命运共同体”的理念超越了 1965 年欧共体提出的“共同体”，后者具有种种局限性，早已过时。

在西方话语中，共同体的概念中往往含有强烈的排他意味——使内部成员聚合一处，排除外部“他者”。但与此同时，它也暗示着这样一种可能：由共同经验构成的这种自发性的、非理性的基础，可以扩展到共同体外部的世界，而习近平提出的“命运共同体”所指涉的，恰恰是这重含义。在命运共同体中，并不存在外部的他者。

对于共同体概念中的这种“延展”含义，西方杰出社会学家——阿米泰·埃茨奥尼曾进行过探讨。他指出，东西方可以在价值观层面达成一致，从而创造一种新型全球秩序。如果将西方的个人主义与东方的社会责任融合一处，则可将共同体扩展至全世界。

当然，在寻求全世界共同价值观的过程中，或许会遇到各种阻碍，比如东方国家在价值观层面同样存在巨大差异，或许只比西方国家的差异略小而已。埃茨奥尼也曾坦然表达过这种顾虑。如果我们始终纠结于这一点，就会再次陷入帕森斯的中心价值观和社会整合理念所构成的争辩漩涡之中。如果价值观既能造成分歧又能促成共识，那么，我们在寻找具有向心力的价值观时，应遵循何种路径？

我们不妨变换一下视角，首先要接受这样一个事实，即不同文化、不同民族的价值观之间，存在着无可消解的差异，然后从“一带一路”的视角出发，探讨如何在推进“一带一路”的实践中克服种种潜在的冲突。

2017 年 1 月 18 日，伦敦巴金–达格纳姆区的居民在兴奋与惊叹中迎来了纵贯 7500 英里的义乌—伦敦班列。区委会委员长表示：“对于伦敦和本区而言，这是一则重磅消息。”

这便是合作共赢。所谓的共赢首先要能为双方带来利益，也就是说，双方要处于同一个利益共同体之中。

合作共赢与共同价值观之间，存在着多大的相关性？合作的基础是否取决于商品的使用价值？或许是，或许不是，因为中国生产的圣诞树装饰品，在西方市场中所占份额极为有限。交换价值则应当另作考虑。根据人类学提供的证据，交换在本质上属于一种普世性的价值，尽管交换以不同的形式开展。每一笔交易或购买背后，都是对交换价值的肯定。

然而东西文化、中英文化的根本差异仍然存在。我们是否应在两者间寻求更深层次的理解、找出一些差异之下的深层含义，以供我们分享？

寻求人类关系中的相互理解一直是西方思想中反复出现的主题，对此，德国社会哲学家尤尔根·哈贝马斯曾进行过广泛地探索。他指出：“人类所有的互动中，都隐藏着交际的合理性。”言语行为本身便是基于被听者所理解这一假设。可以根据这一初步基础，建立起一套价值体系，进而构建以对话为核心的制度性架构。

对于知识分子而言，这个理念无疑是具有吸引力的，笔者也不例外。然而不论相互理解有多么重要，“一带一路”的优势并不在于此，相互理解或许是最终取得的成果，而不是优势。即便我们可以将“相互理解”作为共同价值观，但这种价值观并不能为“误解”和“更深层次的冲突”提供解决方案。

每个社会在一开始都会假设，自身的价值理念具有普遍适用性。美国的《独立宣言》便是不言自明的一个例证。例如,《独立宣言》中谈到了“人人生而平等”，这或许是一种高贵的情感，但显然会造成矛盾。

每个人都有权施展自身的能力，坚持与众不同的自我，并超越他人。因此，平等和竞争必然成为帕森斯“工具能动主义”中的必然要素，其结果必然导致对自然和他人的支配。

西方的历史经验较为独特，一方面属于帝国的延伸，一方面建立在个人对权威的挑战上，因此，若将西方理念作为普世价值进行推广，其过程必然是无比痛苦的。相比之下，东方却学会了在同化西方关于市场和法律管理的理念同时，又不会造成自身价值体系的失衡。

“一带一路”的目的并不在于将东西方融合一处，更不会削弱沿线国家的文化差异意识。“一带一路”的宗旨在于促进各国互利合作，在保留原有价值观的基础上，寻求和发现新的价值观。这些被发现的价值观并不独属于某一个国家，而是全人类的共同财产。

在互利的基础上实现共同目标，这种意识才是最重要的，也是“一带一路”所积极倡导的。只有以共同的现实利益为前提，不同文化之间才有相互沟通和交流的可能。中国的四大发明——造纸术、火药、印刷术以及指南针——之所以传遍世界，并非由于各国认同中国的价值观，而是在于这些发明的实际用途。

共同目标可以克服而不是消除文化差异。这一点，在世界各地都能找到例证。以西方国家为例：2009 年 8 月，我有幸参观了阿塔卡玛大型毫米波天线阵，以及位于智利（海拔 5000 多米）沙漠地带的 ALMA 天文望远镜。

这项由欧洲、美国、东亚与智利联合开展的项目具有一个共同目标：建成由 66 个抛面天线组成的、全世界最大的射电望远镜。

每座天线的口径达 112 米，重 115 吨，三个国际团队负责修建各自部分的天线，修建方式各有不同。美国将天线分为两部分修筑，最后进行对接，而欧洲团队则分为四个部分。参观欧洲施工场地时，访客可以随处走动、将施工过程拍摄下来，而参观美国的施工场地时，访客只有 5 分钟时间，而且禁止拍照。东亚团队的施工场地则严禁访客进入。

众所周知，各国文化都十分重视安全问题，但关于安全的准则却不尽相同。对访客的限制可以视做文化准则的介入，即国际合作中遭遇的阻碍。然而从项目的整体进程看来，各国的确在共同目标的指引下，跨越了文化差异、成功地开展了合作。在各方的通力合作下，ALMA 于 2013 年 3 月 13 日正式运行并对外开放。

"一带一路"将为共同价值观的发掘和创造做出巨大贡献。这项工程建立在现实需求之上，因而能够唤起对技术和财富的共同渴望。在"一带一路"不断推进的过程中，各国的不同价值理念会产生相互碰撞、引发争论，但同时也为发现共同价值观提供了平台。"一带一路"的实施会让人们更加深刻地认识到，价值观并不是永恒不变的静态元素，而是一种不断发展的、现实需求的产物。

How Do We Discover Common Values?

Martin Albrow / United Kingdom of Great Britain and Northern Ireland

Honorary Vice-President of the British Sociological Association, Fellow of the Academy of Social Sciences, Emeritus Professor

Just before the recent meeting of the G20 nations in Hamburg, Germany the American President Donald Trump addressed the people of Poland and called upon Americans, Poles and Europeans to defend their values "at any cost".[1] He cited individual freedom and sovereignty as values defining "our community of nations", equated in his speech with "the West."

An appeal to values as central to a community or society echoes a recurrent theme both in public and academic discourse in the West over the last century.The dominant figure in Western sociology in the 1960s, Talcott Parsons declared:

> "That a system of value orientations held in common by the members of a social system can serve as the main point of reference for analysing structure and process in the social system itself may be regarded as a major tenet of

1 White House Press Office, "Remarks by President Trump to the People of Poland," July 6th 2017.

modern sociological theory."[1]

It would be only a slight exaggeration to say that the intensive debates, not just within sociology, but even within Western culture itself, from the 1960s onwards were a prolonged, often bitter, conflict between opponents and defenders of the implications of that statement.

What conclusion has been reached? Very broadly, I suggest, until now, nothing but confusion about values and scepticism about theory.

Let us be clear at the outset. Common values do not guarantee peace, harmony, co-operation or any of the other goods that make human life tolerable, let alone satisfying. Indeed one can say that President Trump gives the West an impossible task if he expects strength and solidarity to result from a defence of its values "at any cost".

Parsons, who was an acute observer of the United States, seeking to steer a path between rival political standpoints, offered a carefully crafted definition of American values. He summed them up as "instrumental activism", or "active mastery" toward what he called "the situation external to the society", and that included both "*nature and other societies*" (my emphasis).

That "active mastery" might well explain why the rest of the West does not always find American values reassuring.

But it is not just a "my nation first" attitude that creates conflict. Even the most universal values may have conflict built into them. The prime examples historically must be those of the French Revolution: liberty, equality and fraternity. Am I at liberty to oppress you? Can anyone demand we all eat the same amount? Is every stranger to be my brother?

When values like these are treated as sacrosanct, is it any wonder that their

1 Talcott Parsons, 1960, *Structure and Process in Modern Societies,* The Free Press, Glencoe, Ill. P. 172.

uncompromising advocates led the French Revolution from jubilation in 1789 to the Reign of Terror in 1793?

Now it is not my purpose to stigmatise values in general, or even to judge the respective merits of values that different countries revere most. The American Dream and the Chinese Dream have their unique origins and perspectives that are not transferrable. But some values do emerge over time that stabilise societies and foster good relations between them.

Consequently I want to dwell on the processes whereby people and nations find values that help them to live in peace with each other and find fulfilling lives. These may be values that will be held in common, but not necessarily ones they already hold. They will be discovered in the processes of working together.

It was in this spirit that President Xi Jinping spoke to UNESCO in March 2014:

> Today we live in a world with different cultures, ethnic groups, skin colors, religions and social systems, and all people on the planet have become members of an intimate community with a shared destiny.
>
> ... We should encourage different civilizations to respect each other and live in harmony, so as to turn exchanges and mutual learning between civilizations into a bridge promoting friendship between peoples around the world, an engine driving society, and a bond cementing world peace. (287-8)

This speech was reprinted in Xi's published collection entitled *Xi Jinping: The Governance of China*. It is a volume that draws on Chinese history and culture and especially its recent experience of opening out, as an example of what learning in co-operation with others can achieve. It is also driven by theoretical enthusiasm, a desire to bring ideas for public policy together in a coherent whole.

As such *Xi Jinping: The Governance of China* offers the kind of leadership, combining ideas and policies in a coherent whole, that has no effective Western equivalent. Public policy debates in the West mirror its value conflicts, are confused and lacking in comprehensive theoretical underpinning.

It is a contrast that reminds me of a book famous in the 1970s, also written by a Harvard Professor of Sociology, Daniel Bell. Looking to the future he wrote of the coming of post-industrial society.He correctly recognised the rise of service occupations and, for us today, even more presciently, the future conflict between populist and elitist tendencies.

But Bell was very wide of the mark in predicting that future society would be distinguished by the centrality of theoretical knowledge.[1]Populists today may reject what they see as the power of the experts, but these are technocrats without theory, and the babel of theoretical voices, within and across academic disciplines has little real influence on a public discourse that is led by slogans, tweets and celebrity.

By comparison the serious employment in China of theoretical ideas is a huge strength in its Belt and Road policies, largely unrecognised in the rest of the world. I can do no better than illustrate this by reference to Professor Wang Yiwei's exceptionally useful book *The Belt and Road Initiative: What will China Offer the World in its Rise.*[2]

Wang explicitly points to the deficiencies of Western ideas of globalization and describes current elaborations of the idea of community in Chinese public policy. Based on the report adopted by the 18th Congress of the Communist Party of the People's Republic of China, he points to the ways the idea of a community of common destiny in international affairs transcends the limitations of an older usage of community as conceived in the European Community of 1965.

In Western discourses the idea of community has often carried strong overtones of exclusion, binding members together and excluding others. Yet it can also express the spontaneous, non-rational basis of shared experience that can reach out to the wider world and it is this that the idea of a community of common human destiny

1 Daniel Bell, 1974, *The Coming of Post-Industrial Society,* Basic Books, New York, p. 20.

2 2016, Beijing, New World Press.

involves as Xi has developed it. For in it there are no outsiders.

This expansive sense of community was explored in the West by the eminent sociologist Amitai Etzioniwho argued for an East-West consensus on values to create a new global order.[1] A compromise between Western individualism and Eastern emphasis on social obligations could extend community to the whole world.

If we might have reservations on this route to shared values for the world it is that differences on values among different Eastern countries are just as great, if not greater than the differences between Western countries. To be fair, Etzioni acknowledges this but we are then on the downward slope to the unresolved debates that followed on from Parsons' doctrine on central values and social integration. If values in general can produce dissensus as much as consensus by what route can we find those that bind us together?

Let us take a different starting point. Let us accept there will be irreducible differences between cultures on national values and ask how Belt and Road can work in practice to overcome potential conflicts.

On the 18th January this year a crowd of excited residents of the London borough of Barking and Dagenham greeted the first freight train to travel direct the 7500 miles from the city of Yiwu in China. "This is great news for the borough and for London" said the leader of the borough council.

This was win-win co-operation. In the first instance it offered benefits to both sides. They share, in other words, a community of common interest.

How far did this depend on sharing values? Could it be the use-value of the goods? Possibly, possibly not. The market for Christmas tree ornaments that are manufactured in China for Western customers is rather limited where they are made. Exchange value, however, is another thing. Exchange in one form or another is, on all anthropological evidence, is a universal value even if it takes many forms. We

1 Amitai Etzioni, 2004, *From Empire to Community,* Palgrave Macmillan, New York, p. 211.

reaffirm that with every trading deal or purchase.

But the fundamental differences in culture, Western and Eastern, British and Chinese remain. Do we try then to compromise between them or seek a deeper understanding, an exploration of a profound meaning underlying the differences that we can then all share?

This quest for mutual understanding all human relations is a recurring theme in Western thought, examined most extensively by the German social philosopher Jürgen Habermas.He finds that the assumption of "communicative rationality" underlies all human interaction. The speech act in itself presumes the possibility of the other understanding it. Upon that elementary basis it is possible to erect a value system and on it institutional structures with dialogue as their pivotal concept.

This is an appealing notion for intellectuals, and I include myself among them, but I would suggest that the strength of Belt and Road does not depend on mutual understanding, however valuable that may be. It may be an outcome. But even if we accept that "mutual understanding" could well qualify as a universal value,in itself it offers no solution to misunderstandings or deeper conflicts.

Every society begins from the assumption that its own values have a universal applicability. The American Declaration of Independence speaks of self-evident truths, like "All men are created equal". It may be a noble sentiment but manifestly results in paradoxes.

Each person can claim the right to realise their own abilities, be different and aspire to be better than others. Equality and competition are then bonded in Parsons' "instrumental activism" with its outcome of mastery over nature and others.

The West is learning, painfully some would say, to temper its claims to universality for its special historical experience, built as it is so much on the extension of empire and the individual's challenge to authority in the idea of rights. The East by contrast has been learning to assimilate and adapt Western notions of markets and legal regulations without undermining its own values of harmony.

But Belt and Road is not offering to amalgamate West and East, still less to diminish the sense of difference between the many cultures along its routes. Belt and Road is based in bringing countries together, and in this way will create new values as well as drawing on old ones. They will belong to no country in particular but become part of a common human heritage.

More important than anything else is the perception of a shared interest in achieving a common goal. This is what Belt and Road offers in abundance. Nothing allows cultures to be bridged more than the recognition of a shared practical interest in results. The four great Chinese inventions, papermaking, gunpowder, printing and the compass spread worldwide not through an appreciation of Chinese values but because of their proven usefulness.

The pragmatic demonstration of the importance of a shared goal in overcoming cultural differences, without eliminating them, can be illustrated from anywhere in the world. Let me conclude with an example from the West when in August 2009 I had the privilege to visit the construction site of the Atacama Large Millimeter Array, the ALMA telescope,5000 meters high in the Chilean Desert.

This was a joint project of European, American and East Asian consortia in cooperation with Chilean agencies. They shared an aim, to build the world's largest radio telescope by combining 66 radio antennae to work together as a single telescope.

Each individual antenna dish was up to 12 meters in diameter and weighed 115 tons. Each of the three international teams assembled its quota of dishes on site. Each did it differently. The Americans proceeded by joining two halves of the dish, the Europeans four quarters. Visitors to the European site could observe this, being allowed to walk round freely and photograph the construction process. But to the American site visitors were allowed a 5-minute-stay only and photographs were forbidden. On the other hand access was not permitted at all to the East Asian site.

As we know, all cultures put a value on security, but their norms differ greatly. We may well view those access rules as the inevitable intrusion of cultural norms acting as impediments to international co-operation. Yet in the event the whole project also illustrated the triumph of co-operation around a shared goal over those cultural differences. ALMA proceeded to full operation and was opened officially on March 13th 2013.

Belt and Road will be an immense exercise in discovering shared values and creating common ones. Rooted in practical needs it can elicit common responses to technology and to wealth creation. The combination of its projects with multiple and diverse national statements of value will stimulate debate and create sites for finding common values. It will reinforce the view that values are not static elements existing in timeless perfection but pragmatic achievements in permanent course of development.

中国和法国：地方合作与交通公共设施的合作

多梅尼克·比瑟罗 【法国】

法国农业及渔业部前部长/法国运输部前副部长/法国滨海夏朗德省议会主席/全法国省议会联合会主席

一　前言

中国和法国分别在各自的区域是幅员最辽阔，经济最发达的国家之一。这两个国家都有着悠久的历史，省级和地区的行政管理都相对集中，都拥有可以从事对外贸易的海岸线，具有相当多的共同点。

中法两国已经建立了长期的外交关系的框架，而以2004年，即“中法文化年”为分水岭，中法之间的地方合作进入了一个蓬勃而持续发展的新阶段。

外交关系的质量可以从多个侧面体现，而地方合作就是其中之一。这种地方合作将地方置于交流的中心，因此产生了丰富的多样性，也更人性化。这不仅仅是北京和巴黎之间的对话，这是地区之间，中国人和法国人之间的相互交流，是促进彼此经济发展，造福两国人民的交流。

如何评价今天中法关系的质量，通过地方交流而产生的中法关系，其趋势又如何？

这种地方合作是属于我们两国之间积极而强有力的外交关系的一种表达方式，也就是说两国政府让地方合作成为两国外交关系一个重要的组成部分。而促进经济方面的合作，当然是合作的主要目标之一。

除了经济发展可以给地方和居民所带来的共同的好处之外，这一雄心壮志还得益于中法两国都是面向世界和经济成功转型的国家，都对外开放。而交通部门是能明确体现这种成功的领域之一。

二 中法地方合作

在中法文化年（2004年10月至2005年7月）期间，中法地方合作作为确认并深化中法全球战略伙伴关系的重要主题，得到了大力的支持。

2005年10月，中国人民对外友好协会和武汉市与法国地方当局对外行动代表处和波尔多市，在武汉共同召开了中法地区合作的第一次会议。此后，这类会议在法国和中国的地方政府以及其他相关团体之间定期召开。

会议的核心内容包括：人文交流、教育与高等教育、科学创新与科技、文化与文化遗产、体育、健康和旅游。

同时成立了中法地区合作联合委员会，其两位联席主席分别是Jacques Auxiette先生（法国卢瓦河大区前主席）和中国人民对外友好协会会长李小林女士。

法国59个地区政府和中国64个地方政府一起积极参与了147个地区合作项目（包括高校、文化、经济交流，区域可持续性发展和文化遗产提升项目）。这些项目分为**三个主题：教育和研究**（52个项目），**可持续性经济发展**（48个项目），**文化和遗产**（35个项目）。

包括：

- 与布列塔尼大区和卢瓦尔河大区以及滨海夏朗德省合作发展中国游艇业；
- 与新阿基坦大区在高科技（光学和激光）方面进行的合作；
- 与奥克西塔尼大区在农业、农村发展以及药学研究方面的合作；
- 与诺曼底大区在基础设施和设备问题上进行合作；
- 法国埃松省与其中国合作伙伴一起共同致力于环境的保护和管理。

法国大部分的大区委员会在中国设有代表处，**法国地方当局对外行动代表处（受法国外交部管辖）负责协调工作，并定义相关经济工作范畴。**

中法地区合作会议已经成为定期会议，第6次会议将于2018年10月在法国图卢兹市举行，工作重点将放在旅游和文化遗产，农业和农业食品以及可持续发展城市。

法国时任外交部长让−马克·艾罗和中国全国人大常委会副委员长吉炳轩出

席了在成都举行的上一次中法地区合作会议上，这标志着该会议是一个真正的中法交流时刻，体现了重大的意义。

双方共同确定的优先事项，了解双方地方政府的理想与期望；解释法国最新的行政区划改革情况；促进地区合作项目的均匀分布，并建立新的伙伴关系（特别是在大城市之间）；更好地平衡双方的关系（目前更倾向于中方的利益）。

三 在中法地区合作中省政府的地位

国际行动必须能够一起应对共同挑战：对抗全球气候变化，地方居民的国际开放，青年人的职业发展，遗产古迹保护……这些不同领域里，我们不是输出法国对这些问题的解决办法，而是通过相互交流，共同构建解决方案。因此，这些项目不仅对中方的合作地市有影响，对法方的合作地市也一样有意义。

例如，自 1988 年以来，法国的萨瓦省与塞内加尔的比尼奥纳省合作创办了“他者的社会行动”项目。这一举措的总体目标是将两国地方上的社会行动的经验和方法加以整合，以期加强双方社会政策的效果。更具体地说，对于法国的萨瓦省，要进一步让更多的公民使用社会资源；对于塞内加尔的比尼奥纳省，则是发展针对最贫困者的社区社会行动。

国际行动需要建立多方合作的伙伴关系，牵涉到具有多元化专业知识的多个合作伙伴（国家的地方服务机构、协会，社团和教育机构、企业、公民）。

例如法国的卢瓦尔大西洋省与摩洛哥的阿加迪尔省共同建立了一个合作平台，在该平台上，法国卢瓦尔大西洋省的协会和其在摩洛哥阿加迪尔省的姐妹协会联合起来，共同在社会工作领域发挥作用。该平台旨在加强协会的工作能力，协调使民众能够更好地获得社会服务的项目，推进和评估社会工作，以提高决策者的敏感度。

国际合作项目应该被视为地方政府的职能，是其所提供的公共服务的一种，而不是一种边缘化的项目。为此，国际合作项目应是跨部门的，涉及不同的服务类型，这非常重要。

例如，作为法国与加拿大魁北克省的合作框架项目的一部分，法国滨海夏朗德省的青年事务部与加拿大魁北克省国际发展部合作，促进国际间的青年交流。

为了产生实际效果，项目必须有长远目标，最好在已经有长期合作关系的地方之间开展合作。

例如，法国瓦尔图瓦兹省与日本有着悠久的合作历史，1987年就与日本大阪府签署了合作协议。这种合作关系是建立在双方在工业，经济，技术和学术领域的交流基础之上的，并以共同的发展愿景作为目标。

面对多重挑战时的策略，包括，财务挑战：中央政府转移支付分配比率下降，而地方政府支出（特别是社会支出）增加，所产生所谓的“剪刀效应”；法律挑战：法国最近进行了行政区划改革，省政府承担的职能有所变化，这使得开展国际合作项目的不确定性增加。

值得注意的是，法国新的地方政府组织法里删除了省政府和大区政府的一般管辖权条款。然而，省政府还是保留了开展任何类型的国际项目的可能性（包括其在法国国内已经失去管辖权的经济领域的项目）。因此，法国很多大区政府所开展的国际经济合作项目——特别是针对中国的国际经济合作项目——省政府也有权利开展。

政治挑战：面对市民和民选代表，必须证明国际开放能给地区带来好处。

尽管面对这些挑战，但没有一个省政府放弃发展国际合作。法国地方政府用于国际合作的预算下降是来源于整体经济的影响，而并非是地方政府有退出国际合作的意愿。

中法间合作项目其效率也不尽相同。孚日省和青岛的合作伙伴关系获得了2014年经济合作奖。但同样是开展中法地方合作，根据2014年法国《新共和国报》的一篇文章报道，“维恩省与深圳市（中国）之间的经济合作已经有20年的历史，但这种合作对该省所产生的经济效益几乎为零”。

四 滨海夏朗德省与中国东北地区合作的例子

“中国视野”项目是2012年由法国滨海夏朗省和中国东北地区一起发起的一项活动，该项目向滨海夏朗德省所有的组织开放，拓展全新的视野，并深化活动的内容。

这一项目的战略目标首先是为了在法国滨海夏朗省和中国吉林省和辽宁省之间围绕着旅游推广、农业食品、文化、高等教育和科研等优先主题建立一个横跨多领域的桥梁，并针对滨海夏朗德省的一些优势领域（**如游艇、水疗、马业**）进行深入合作。

由滨海夏朗省的民选代表、技术人员和国际专家一起，共同组成了一个指导委员会，为该项目提供指导方针。“中国视野”项目为滨海夏朗德省的所有单位提供所需的专业知识，并建立了一个包括所有与中国东北地区合作参与者的交流网络，以帮助他们实现合作项目的成功。

1.“中国视野”项目概况

4 年以来，有近 80 家公司在多个领域，多个主题（农业食品，游艇，马业，健康 / 保健）和中国开展了合作项目。有一些公司的营业额增长了高达 35%。到 2016 年底，由于这些项目所产生的商业交流，直接创造了 20 个工作岗位。

2. 省政府的服务工作

省政府主要通过两项服务工作使“中国视野”平台能行之有效地工作，切实加强中法关系。首先是 2014 年 1 月成立的“中国视野商业俱乐部”，目的旨在加强法国企业处理与其中国合作伙伴关系的技能。

第二项是 2013 年 9 月在辽宁省政府的协助下在沈阳开设的滨海夏朗德省驻中国代表处。该代表处通过其跨文化的能力，就近给在中国市场开展业务的“中国视野商业俱乐部”成员提供支持和帮助。这个代表处成为了滨海夏朗德省在沈阳的一扇窗口，有助于法国企业与潜在的中国合作伙伴建立相互信任关系，值得特别强调的是：该代表处也大大增强了参与法国企业在中国的信誉度。

3. 优势领域（如游艇、水疗、马业）

中国辽宁省具有漫长的海岸线，因此中法合作的第一步就是在游艇业上的合作。

2013 年，在锦州设立了帆船学校（园艺博览会）。锦州的帆船学校迁往大连，成为大连星海湾国际游艇俱乐部。2017 年夏天，该学校接待了来自法国拉罗谢尔帆船委员会的专家，工作包括培训帆船教员并为学员提供课程。 2017 年 9 月举行了帆船学校“法国方式（àlafrançaise）”的开幕典礼。

马业也是一个重要的合作领域。法国滨海夏朗德省与中国良运集团合作，共同发展中国的这个行业。在中国开设了一家马术俱乐部“法国方式（àlafrançaise）”，并向该俱乐部出售了 50 匹小马。即将在大连，上海和杭州开设两家新的小马俱乐部。马业是一个正在不断扩张的行业。每年都有 8 名中国马术教练在法国滨海夏朗德省接受马术高级培训。由法国滨海夏朗德省提供技术支持，为在中国建立一个良种马养殖和繁育中心的计划进行可行性研究。2017 年夏季，一群年轻的中国骑手在滨海夏朗德省鲁瓦扬地区参与马术活动，度过他们的假期。

滨海夏朗德省在温泉理疗和水疗行业也具有领先优势，在其省内有多家温泉理疗和水疗中心。在中国辽阳弓长岭区也有大量的温泉水疗中心。2015 年 9 月，滨海夏朗德省接待了中国辽阳市的一个代表团的访问，加深了双方之间的合作关系。滨海夏朗德省陪伴其中国合作伙伴共同开发温泉产品，更支持鼓励发展对温泉进行医疗层面的应用（温泉治疗、温泉水配送和健康安全问题）。

4. 从 2012 年的“中国视野”项目到 2017 年的“国际视野”项目

“中国视野”项目的方法已逐渐扩展到整个前普瓦图–夏朗德大区的公司。

为了正式确定这种互惠关系，2017 年 6 月 26 日，由滨海夏朗德省发起，和夏朗德省、德塞夫勒省、圣特市、昂古莱姆市、普瓦捷市和比利牛斯–大西洋省一起，成立了“国际视野”项目。

利用滨海夏朗德省“中国视野”项目所积累的经验，新阿基坦大区内有意愿参与“国际视野”项目的地方政府希望将这些宝贵的合作经验应用到其他相关和有前途的国际市场项目中去。

因此，“中国视野”项目发展成为了“国际视野”项目，目的在于在让现有合作伙伴关系结出丰硕果实的基础上，进一步扩大可能的国际合作范围。

五　交通基础设施的地方合作

法国和中国在交通领域有着悠久的合作历史。在航空和航天方面，两个国家在高科技产业领域有宽广的发展空间，在全球范围内有能力参与这个行业发展的国家，无论在过去还是现在，都相当有限。法国公司已经在这个领域表现出愿意合作的意向。

可持续发展是中法伙伴关系的重要组成部分之一。多个合作项目聚焦于交通运输领域。

六　在民航高等教育领域的合作：天津中欧航空工程师学院

从 2008 年到 2013 年，该项目由中国和法国共同资助其运营经费。法方由法国政府和法国大型航空企业（空中客车集团 Airbus，欧洲直升机公司 Eurocopter，赛峰集团 Safran 和泰勒斯集团 Thalès）一起提供资金支持。中欧航空工程师学院的法方院长 Michel Martin 先生由法国交通运输部通过法国民用航空总局（DGAC）

提供资金进行聘任。

三家法国航空高校共同组成了以法国国立民航大学（ENAC）为首的法国航空航天高校集团（GEA），该项目的成功有赖于他们的努力。项目每届招收100名工程师专业的学生。法国前交通运输部部长 Dominique Bussereau 先生资助了首届中欧航空工程师学院的学生，因此该届学生也被称为“2007 Bussereau 届”毕业生。

七 中法交通运输企业合作项目

中法交通运输企业的合作项目包括与空中客车（Airbus）合作项目、与赛峰集团的合作、与法国达飞海运集团的合作等。

2016 年冬，在天津设立了空客 A330 的完成中心。

经过多年的发展，空中客车公司已占据了中国市场 50%的份额。

赛峰集团（Safran）是中国民用航空市场和国防市场的主要参与者。自从1980年在北京开设办事处以来，赛峰集团与中国业内人士建立了紧密的合作关系。

赛峰集团在中国的业务可追溯到 20 世纪 70 年代初，中国海军刚刚收购了配备透博梅卡涡轮增压发动机的超级大黄蜂直升机。这是赛峰集团在中国的首个重大合同。 80 年代，随着与中国的进一步合作，赛峰集团和中国航空工业集团公司签署了关于 Arriel 1 航空发动机的许可生产和 Z9 直升机自动控制系统的协议。为了方便和中国的交流，赛峰集团决定在北京设立首家代表处。

此后，合作协议成倍增加，赛峰集团已经成为中国航空工业的重要合作伙伴。今天在中国飞行的客机中，超过一半的客机配备了赛峰集团的 CFM56 发动机，也就是说今天有 2800 台 CFM56 发动机正在中国运行。在中国运营的一半直升机装备了 Turbomeca 发动机。与此同时，赛峰集团的其他子公司也持续在中国取得进展，如今在中国，航线上运营的三分之一的客机使用了 Messier-Bugatti-Dowty 公司的产品。

2015 年达飞海运集团在其总部接待了中国国务院总理李克强，并积极加入了中国的“新丝绸之路”项目。

1992 年，法国达飞海运集团进入中国并在上海设立了达飞海运集团的第一家中国办事处。

法国达飞海运集团在中国的 25 个省份设有 60 个办事处。在中国有 76 条线路，停靠在 13 个不同的港口，每周 248 个班次，总共拥有 10%的中国市场份额。

巴黎地铁交通发展亚洲有限公司（RDTA）是第一个进入中国的法国交通运营商，2005 年在上海成立办事处，2007 年在北京成立地区总部，2015 年将巴黎地铁交通发展亚洲有限公司的总部迁往香港。

巴黎地铁交通发展亚洲有限公司在中国有多种经营方式，公司展示了法国在公共交通领域丰富的经验与知识。在负责运营和维护该市历史悠久的有轨电车系统（是世界上最古老的有轨电车系统之一），每天运送 20 万乘客。在南京和沈阳等城市也签署了城市交通运营合作协议，采用适应性的移动解决方案，开发未来城市。

在电动公共汽车领域，中国制造商宇通（法国 Dietrich Carebus 集团的合作伙伴）和中国企业比亚迪一起主导着整个中国的电动公共汽车市场。比亚迪宣布在法国瓦兹省阿隆市投资 1000 万欧元，从中国进口零部件，用于组装生产零排放公共汽车。

China and France: the Regional Cooperation and Cooperation in the Field of Transport Infrastructure

Dominique Bussereau / France

Former Minister of Agriculture and Fishing, Former Junior Minister for Transportation, President of the Charente-Maritime Departmental Council and President of the Assembly of French Departments

I. Introduction

China and France, having much in common, their own continents both are among the most extensive and more economically developed, with long history, during which the administration of the provinces and territories was very centralized.

China and France have already established for a long time in the context of the diplomatic relations, since 2004, the “Les Années Chine-France”saw a turning point at which the regional cooperation has been strenghened.

The quality of diplomatic relations can be indicated from many aspects, the cooperation is one. The trade cooperation is centred in areas and provides a wide variety of topics, and more. it is not only Beijing and Paris, which are, it is our territory, Chinese and English, which are to meet each other and find out what they can promote mutual economic benefits to their communities.

How to classify the quality of today's Sino-French relationship, as they are through their territories, and what, in the end, these relations will be?

If these regional cooperation relations are an expression of close diplomacy relationship between the two countries, in which the two states are to ensure that their territories are an essential part of the economic development, the cooperation is course, one of the major good objectives.

The economic success of the two countries has benefited from the fact that both China and France are countries that have successfully transformed the economy, and both have opened up to the outside world. The transport sector is one of the areas that can clearly reflect this kind of success.

II. Regional Cooperation between France and China

The French and Chinese cooperation was strongly encouraged as a focus for deepening relations between France and China, and the comprehensive strategic partnership was reaffirmed during the Sino-French Cultural Year (October 2004 - July 2005).

In October 2005, the Chinese People’s Association for Friendship with Foreign Countries and the External Representative Office of Wuhan, French local authorities and Bordeaux jointly held the first meeting on the Sino-French regional cooperation in Wuhan. Since then, such meetings have been held regularly between local governments in France and China and other related groups.

The core content of the conference includes: humanities exchange, education and higher education, scientific innovation and technology, culture and cultural heritage, sports, health and tourism.

There is a French-Chinese joint committee for regional cooperation, the two co-chairmen are Jacques Auxiette (former chairman of the Loire region in France), and Ms. Li Xiaolin, president of the Chinese People's Association for Friendship with Foreign Countries.

The 59 regional governments of France and 64 local governments in China have actively participated in 147 regional cooperation projects (including universities, cultural and economic exchanges, regional sustainable development and cultural heritage promotion projects). These projects are divided into three themes: education and research (52 projects), sustainable economic development (48 projects), culture and heritage (35 projects), such as,

• Cooperation with Brittany and the Loire region and Charente-Maritime to develop the Chinese yacht industry;

• Cooperation with New Aquitaine in high technology (optics and lasers);

• Cooperation with Oxitani in agriculture, rural development and pharmaceutical research;

• Cooperation with the Normandy area on infrastructure and equipment issues;

• Essonne Province, France and its Chinese partners work together to protect and manage the environment.

Most of the regional councils in France have representative offices in China and the French local authorities representative office (Under the jurisdiction of the French Ministry of Foreign Affairs) are responsible for external operations.

The Sino-French Regional Cooperation Conference has become a regular meeting and the 6th meeting will be held in Toulouse, France in October 2018. The work focus will be on tourism and cultural heritage, agriculture and agri-food and sustainable cities.

French Foreign Minister Jean-Marc Allen and Vice Chairman of the Standing Committee of China's National People's Congress Ji Bingxuan attended the Sino-French Regional Cooperation Conference held in Chengdu, which marked that the conference was a true Sino-French exchange and reflected a great significance.

The priorities identified by both parties were to understand the ideals and expectations of the both sides of the local governments; to explain the latest administrative reforms in France; to promote the even distribution of regional cooperation projects and establish new partnerships (especially between metropolises); and to balance the relationship between the two sides (at present, China's interests are more favorable).

III. The Status of the Provincial Government in the Sino-French Regional Cooperation

International actions must be able to address common challenges together, such as, confrontation of global climate change, international openness of local residents, professional development of young people, the protection of heritage sites... In these different areas, we are not exporting French solutions to these problems, but through interact with each other to build a solution together. Therefore, these projects not only have an impact on the cooperation of the Chinese cities, but also make sense for the French partner cities.

International action requires the establishment of multi-partnerships involving multiple partners with diverse expertise (national local service agencies, associations, associations and educational institutions, businesses, citizens).

International cooperation projects should be regarded as the functions of local governments, a kind of public service provided by them, not a marginal project. For this reason, international cooperation projects should be cross-sectoral and involve different types of services.

In order to make the practical sense, it is better to carry on the cooperation in the areas which have a long cooperation history.

Strategies in the face of multiple challenges, include,

• Financial challenges, the central government's declining transfer payment, distribution ratio and the increase in local government spending (especially social spending), resulting in the so-called "scissor effect";

• Legal challenge, France has recently conducted an executive zoning reforms that have changed the functions undertaken by the provincial government, which has increased the uncertainty of international cooperation projects.

It is worth noting that the French new local government organization law deleted the general jurisdiction clause of the provincial government and the regional government. However, the provincial government has retained the possibility of carrying out any type of international project (including projects in the economic field where France has already lost jurisdiction). Therefore, the international economic cooperation projects carried out by many French regional governments, especially those aimed at China's international economic cooperation projects, also have the right to carry out the provincial government.

• Political challenge: In the face of citizens and elected representatives, we must prove that international openness can bring benefits to the region.

Despite these challenges, none of the provincial governments gave up the development of international cooperation. The decline in the budget for French government's use of international cooperation is due to the impact of the overall economy, rather than the willingness of local governments to withdraw from international cooperation.

IV. The Cooperation between Charente-Maritime and Northeast China

The "China Vision" project is an event initiated co-sponsored by Charente-Maritime, France and the Northeast China region in 2012. The project is open to all organizations in Charente-Maritime and develops new horizons and deepens the content of the activities.

The objective of this strategy is, above all, to create a multidisciplinary bridge between the Charente-Maritime, and Jilin and Liaoning , northeast China. around priority issues such as the promotion of tourism and the agri-food sector, culture, higher education and scientific research research and make deepened cooperation in fields of Charente-Maritime's superiority (water sports, spas, and equestrian).

Together with elected representatives, technicians and international experts from the Charente-Maritime, a steering committee was formed to provide guidelines for the project. The "China Vision" project provides the necessary expertise for all units in Charente-Maritime and has established a communication network with all participants in cooperation with Northeast China to help them achieve the success of the cooperation project.

1. the general introduction of the "China Vision" project

In four years, nearly 80 companies have undertaken cooperations with Chinese companies in a multisectoral mission and theme (water sports, agr-food, equestrian, health / wellness). Some have seen their sales increased to 35%, and by the end of 2016, 20 jobs were directly created by the trade generated during these missions.

2. the service provided in the provincial governmental level

The provincial governments have worked together through two service projects to enable the "China Vision" project as a platform to work effectively and to strengthen Sino-French relations. The first is the "China Vision Business Club", which was established in January 2014. The purpose is to strengthen French companies' skills in dealing with their Chinese partners.

The second is the representative office of Charente-Maritime in China opened in Shenyang in September 2013 with the assistance of the Liaoning Provincial Government. Through its cross-cultural capabilities, the representative office provides support and assistance to members of the "China Vision Business Club" who conduct business in the Chinese market. This representative office has become a window of Charente-Maritime in Shenyang, which helps French companies to establish mutual trust with potential Chinese partners. It is worth emphasizing that this representative office has also greatly enhanced the participation of French companies. China's credibility.

3.areas of excellence (water sports, spas, equestrian)

Since Liaoning with a long coastal area, the first of the Sino-French cooperation is in the field of water sports.

In 2013, a sailing school (horticultural expo) was established in Jinzhou. The sailing school in Jinzhou moved to Dalian and became Dalian Xinghai Bay International Yacht Club. In the summer of 2017, the school hosted experts from the La Rochelle Yachting Commission in France. The work involved training sailors and provided courses for students. The opening ceremony of the sailing school "à lafrançaise" was held in September 2017.

Horse industry also is an important area of cooperation. Charente-Maritime, France partnered with Chinese Liangyun Group to jointly develop this industry in China. In China, an equestrian club "àla francçaise" was opened and 50 colts were sold to the club. Two new pony clubs will be opened in Shanghai and Hangzhou. Horse industry is a growing industry. Every year, eight Chinese equestrian instructors receive advanced equestrian training in Charente-Maritime, France. Technical support was provided by Charente-Maritime, France, and a feasibility study was conducted to establish a thoroughbred breeding and breeding center in China.

In 2017 a group of young Chinese riders participated in equestrian activities in the Royan area of Charente-Maritime and spent their holidays. Charente-Maritime also has a leading edge in spa treatments with many hot springs.

There are also a large number of hot spring spas in Liaoyang's Gong changling District. In September 2015, Charente-Maritime received a visit from a delegation from Liaoyang City, China, which deepened the cooperation between the two parties. Charente-Maritime is accompanied by its Chinese partners to jointly develop hot spring products, and it also supports the development of the application of hot springs to the medical level (thermal treatment, hot spring water distribution and health and safety issues).

4. from the “China Vision”project (2012) to“International Vision”project (2017)

The “China Vision”project has been gradually extended to the entire former Poitou-Charentes companies. In order to formalize this reciprocal relationship, on June 26, 2017, it was initiated by the Charente-Maritime, and in the provinces of Charente, Desèvre, Sainte, Angouleme, Poitiers and Together with the Pyrenees-Atlantic Province, the“International Vision”project was then established.

Based on the experience gained from the Chardonnay Coastal “China Vision”project, local governments in the New Aquitaine region who wish to participate in the “International Vision” project hope to apply these valuable cooperation experiences to other relevant and promising international Going to market projects.

Therefore, the “China Vision”project has developed into an “international vision”project aimed at further expanding the scope of possible international cooperation based on the achievements of the existing partnership.

V. Regional Cooperation in the Field of Transport Infrastructure

France and China have a long history of cooperation in the transportation sector. In aeronautics and astronautics, the two countries have a broad space for development in the field of high-tech industries. Countries that have the ability to participate in the development of the industry in the world are very limited, both in the past and in the present. French companies have demonstrated their willingness to cooperate in this area.

Sustainable development is one of the important components of China-France partnership. A number of cooperative projects focus on transportation.

VI. Sino-European School of Tianjin

From 2008 to 2013, the project was jointly funded by China and France for its operating expenses. France is funded by the French government together with major French aviation companies (Airbus, Eurocopter, Safran and Thales). Mr. Michel Martin, the French dean of the China-Europe Aviation Engineers College, was appointed by the French Ministry of Transport through the French Civil Aviation Administration (DGAC).

The three French aviation universities jointly formed the French Aerospace University Group (GEA) headed by the National Civil Aviation University of France (ENAC). The success of this project depends on their efforts. Each year, the project recruits 100 engineers and students. The former Minister of Transport of France, Dominique Bussereau, sponsored the students of the first Sino-European Aeronautical Engineers College. Therefore, this student is also called the "2007 Bussereau" graduates.

VII. Sino-French Transport Enterprises Cooperation Project

The Sino-French cooperation projects for transportation and transportation include cooperation with Airbus, cooperation with Saifran Group, and cooperation with France's CMA Group, etc.

In the winter of 2016, Airbus Manufacturer establishes Airbus A330 completion center in Tianjin. After years of development, Airbus has occupied 50% of the Chinese market.

Safran is a major player in the civil aviation market and defense market in China. Since opening its office in Beijing in 1980, Safran has established a close cooperation with Chinese industry professionals. The Safran Group's operations in China date can be traced back to the early 1970s. The Chinese Navy has just acquired a Super Hornet helicopter equipped with Turbomeca turbocharged engines. This was Safran's first major contract in China. In the 1980s, with further cooperation with China, Safran and China Aviation Industry Corporation signed an agreement on the licensed production of Arriel 1 aero engines and the Z9 helicopter automatic control system. In order to facilitate communication with China, Safran Group decided to set up its first representative office in Beijing. Since then, the cooperation agreement has multiplied, and Safran has become an important partner of China's aviation industry. Among the passenger planes flying in China today, more than half of the passenger planes are equipped with the Safran CFM56 engine, which means that 2,800 CFM56 engines are currently operating in China. Half of the helicopters operating in China are equipped with Turbomeca motives. At the same time, other Safran Group subsidiaries have continued to make progress in China. Today, in China, one-third of the passenger planes operating on the route use Messier-Bugatti-Dowty products.

In 2015, CMA received the visit of Premier Li Keqiang, at its headquarters and actively participated in the "New Silk Road" project in China. In 1992, CMA Group entered China and established the first China office of CMA Group in Shanghai. France CMA Group has 60 offices in 25 provinces in China. There are 76 lines in China, which are docked at 13 different ports and have 248 flights per week. In total, they have 10% of the Chinese market share.

RDTA is the first French traffic operator to enter China. In 2005, it established an office in Shanghai. In 2007, it established a regional headquarters in Beijing and in 2015, will be the headquarters of the Paris Metro Transportation Development Asia Ltd. Move to Hong Kong.

Paris Metro Transportation Development Asia Limited has a variety of management methods in China. The company has demonstrated France's rich experience and knowledge in public transportation. It is responsible for the operation and maintenance of the city's historic tram system, one of the world's oldest tram systems, delivering 200,000 passengers daily. In cities such as Nanjing and Shenyang, they also signed a cooperation agreement on urban traffic operations and adopted adaptive mobile solutions to develop future cities.

In the field of electric buses, the Chinese manufacturer Yutong (a partner of the French Dietrich Carebus Group) and the Chinese company BYD are leading the entire electric bus market in China. BYD announced that it will invest 10 million euros in Aaron, Oise, France to import spare parts from China for the assembly and production of zero emission buses.

考古发现中的古代丝绸之路基层社会根柢

——管窥丝绸之路古今共同发展与共同价值

刘海旺 【中国】

河南省文物考古研究院院长

中国是世界上最早发明养蚕缫丝，纺织丝绸的文明古国。自汉代开始，古代中国的丝绸大量运销至西亚和欧洲。1877 年德国学者李希霍芬将中国与亚欧之间以丝绸贸易为媒介的交通道路命名为“丝绸之路”。近年来中国与丝绸生产及丝绸之路相关的一些考古发现和文化遗产保护体现了丝绸之路的古今发展与共同价值。

一 汉代广泛的植桑养蚕是丝绸之路的基层社会支撑

蚕的主要食物是桑树的叶子，因此，野生桑树的选择利用，人工桑树的栽培种植是古代丝织业由起源到发展的主要条件之一。先秦时期桑树的种植历史文献多有记载，在考古出土的器物上也见有明确的桑树图像及采桑场景。到了汉代，中国的古代丝织业达到了一个很高的技术水平，丝绸之路沿线考古出土的各种精美丝织品数量众多，丝织品的大量生产，必然要求汉代的桑树种植更为广泛、普遍。汉代皇帝、官府在大力劝导、督促农耕大发展的同时，也一并要求、督导桑树种植的大发展。西汉初年文景时期大力提倡农桑的结果，是丝织品产量的空前增加。在汉武帝在元封年间（公元前 110—前 105 年）巡视四方途中，“所过赏赐，用帛百余万匹……”其时，桑弘羊主持全国财政税收，一年之中“均输帛五百万匹”，足见当时植桑养蚕丝织生产之盛。汉代地方官吏在皇帝的倡导下，更身体力行地加大植桑力度以为政绩：“陈晔为巫令，有惠政，桑生二万余株，民以为给。”

2003 年发现的属于西汉晚期的三杨庄汉代聚落遗址宅院周围人工植树数量较多，清理出的树叶遗存绝大多数为桑树叶，证明三杨庄汉代聚落遗址所发现树木多为桑树。另外，甘肃嘉峪关东汉至魏晋壁画墓中发现的相当数量的采桑图表明，植桑养蚕及丝绸生产随着丝绸之路的开通向西的大扩展。

三杨庄汉代聚落遗址桑树的普遍种植表明，每一个普通农民家庭种桑养蚕是汉代丝绸业高度发展的社会基础物质条件，也是“丝绸之路”这一历史动脉的末梢起点并获得基层社会的支撑。客观上，丝绸之路也为古代基层社会经济的发展提供了商品需求，有助于基层社会的共同发展。

二　隋唐宋“运河丝绸之路”促进了基层社会的全面发展繁荣

水路运输是古代长距离运量最大、最经济、最便利的交通运输方式。中国古代人工运河开凿历史悠久，但其中对当时社会发展功用最巨、影响最大的莫过于隋唐宋时期（581—1127）的中国大运河中的通济渠（汴河）。隋唐宋时期的大运河是陆上丝绸之路与海上丝绸之路的主要连接通道，可称之为“运河丝绸之路”。

考古发掘表明，通济渠（汴河）的堤岸均用土夯筑或堆筑。这是汴河有别于世界其他地区古运河形态的最主要特征之一。平原地区的运河固然由于落差较小而易于出现淤积，但水流较为缓慢也便于大小船舶的停靠，这就形成了十分便利的水上交通，唐宋时期通济渠（汴河）两岸合适的区段聚居了较多的工商户和包括丝织业在内的手工作坊与商铺市场等，形成了众多大大小小的“河市”。北宋熙宁年间（1072—1073），日本僧人成寻从台州北行沿运河前往五台山参佛，船行至南京应天府（今商丘），他在其日记中记到：“大桥上并店家灯火，大千万也。伎乐之声，遥闻之。……店家买卖，不可记尽。”北宋晚期画家张择端在其《清明上河图》中以运河和“河市”为中心，描绘了城市、运河和“河市”的面貌形态。

文献记载和考古发现表明，隋唐至北宋时期运河的便利交通，使得沿运河两岸形成了众多的大小规模不等的城镇“河市”，这类河市是开放式的，有别于隋唐时期城市封闭式的基层社会里坊制管理方式，并逐渐影响和瓦解了这类封闭式的管理模式。可以说，运河交通极大地改变了唐宋时期基层社会的经济文化面貌。而这些改变也带来了当时基层社会的空前繁荣和共同发展，支撑着以丝绸为代表的对外贸易。

三　丝绸之路等相关文化遗产保护的共同发展与共同价值

丝绸之路与中国大运河申报世界文化遗产极大地促进了相关文化遗产的保护与展示。丝绸之路世界文化遗产在中国境内有22处考古遗址、古建筑等遗迹，包括河南省4处、陕西省7处、甘肃省5处、新疆维吾尔自治区6处。中国大运河世界文化遗产涉及沿线8个省市27座城市的27段河道和58个遗产点。这些遗产点体现了世界文化遗产所共有的普遍意义和价值，同时，都得到了有效的保护并建成遗址公园，既改善了环境，遗产的完整性也得到了有效的保护，成为人民参观、学习、旅游、休闲、健身等的公共场所，特别深受当地人民的喜爱、支持和欢迎。

当今，中国的文化遗产保护出现了前所未有的热潮，正是基于这些文化遗产所具有的普遍的历史文化价值和所产生的社会共同发展前景和全方位影响。

四　结语

古代丝绸之路对当时沿线国家和社会发展所产生的积极影响是深刻而全面的，特别是给社会基层人民的生产和生活带来了更多的机会、条件、便利和改变；反过来，基层社会的人民为丝绸之路提供了丰富的源源不断的物质和精神产品。现在，我们社会大众仍然在享用古代丝绸之路所带来的财富和所具有的价值，又在“一带一路”新的共同发展实施中获得新的更多的收获。“惠及人民大众”是古今丝绸之路所具有的共同的最大价值。

The Basic Social Foundation of the Ancient Silk Road in Archaeological Discoveries

——Analysis of the Common Development and Common Value of the Silk Road in Ancient and Modern Times

Liu Haiwang / China

Director of the Henan Provincial Institute of Cultural Heritage and Archaeology

China was the first civilized country in the world to invent silkworm breeding, silk reeling and silk spinning. Since the Han Dynasty, a large amount of ancient Chinese silk has been sold to Western Asia and Europe. In 1877, Richthofen, a German scholar, named the road for the transportation of silk between China and Eurasia the "Silk Road". In recent years, some archaeological discoveries and cultural heritage protection related to the silk production and the Silk Road have been seen to reflect the common development and common value of the ancient and modern Silk Road.

I. Extensive the Breeding of the Silkworm during the Han Dynasty is the Basic Social Support for the Silk Road

The main food of the silkworm is the leaves of the mulberry tree. Therefore, the selection and utilization of wild mulberry trees and the cultivation of mulberry trees is one of the major conditions for the development of the ancient silk industry from its origin. The planting of mulberry trees in the pre-Qin period is documented not only in literature, but people have found clear mulberry images and scenes of collecting mulberry leaves on the excavated artifacts. During the Han Dynasty, the ancient silk industry in China had reached a high technical level. The number of fine silk fabrics unearthed along the Silk Road was large, and the mass production of silk was bound to require more extensive and universal mulberry planting during the Han Dynasty. During the Han Dynasty, the emperor and the government strongly urged the development of farming, while at the same time, they requested and supervised the great development of mulberry cultivation. In the early years of the Western Han Dynasty, during the Wenjing period, the result of vigorously promoting mulberry planting was an unprecedented increase in the output of silk fabrics. After Emperor Wu of the Han Dynasty settled the frontier issues, during the Yuanfeng period (110BC-105BC), he made an inspection tour across the country. Each place he visited, he granted silk as a reward, which came to a total of millions of pieces of silk. At that time, Sang Hongyang presided over the national fiscal revenue and taxes. In one year, "five million pieces of silk were transported to the silk market", which showed the flourish of the silk fabric through planting mulberry and raising silkworm at that time. Under the advocacy of the Emperor, the local officials of the Han Dynasty strengthened the planting of mulberry as a political achievement: "Chen Ye, who served as the county magistrate, implemented the preferential policy of that by which people who planted mulberry trees exceeding 20 thousand would be rewarded."

In 2003, a large number of artificially-planted mulberry trees around the residences of the Sanyang Village settlement site of the late Western Han Dynasty were found. Most of the leaves found were mulberry leaves which prove that most of the trees found there were mulberry trees. In addition, a large number of paintings of mulberry plantings were found in the Mural Tombs from the Eastern Han Dynasty to the Wei and Jin Dynasties in Jiayuguan, Gansu Province. This might indicate that the mulberry planting, silkworm breeding and silk production gradually expanded westward along with the opening of the Silk Road.

The widespread planting of mulberry in the Sanyang Village settlement site of the Han Dynasty shows that the mulberry planting and silkworm breeding of every ordinary peasant family was the basic material condition for the high development of the silk industry during the Han Dynasty, and it was also the starting point of the historical development of the "Silk Road" and the social support at the grass-roots level. Objectively speaking, the Silk Road had also provided commodity demand for the development of the ancient grass-roots social economy, which was conducive to the common development of the grass-roots society.

II. The "Canal Silk Road" during the Sui, Tang and Song Dynasties Promoted the All-round Development and Prosperity of the Grass-roots Society

Water transportation was the largest and most economical and convenient means of transportation in ancient times. The ancient Chinese artificial canals have a long history, but the most useful with the greatest influence on the social development at that time was the Tongji Canal (Bian River) during the Sui, Tang and Song Dynasties (581-1127) in China. The Grand Canal was the main connecting channel between the Silk Road and the Maritime Silk Road during the Sui, Tang and Song Dynasties, and it could be called the "Canal Silk Road".

Archaeological excavations show that the embankments of Tongji Canal (Bian River) were all rammed or stacked with earthland. This is one of the most important features of the Bian River, unlike the form of ancient canals in other areas of the world. Although the canals in the plain area are easy to silt up because of the small fall, the water flow is slow and convenient for the docking of large and small ships, which forms a very convenient kind of water traffic. A lot of industrial and commercial households and handicraft workshops and store markets, including the silk weaving industry, were gathered at the suitable sectors of the Tongji Canal (Bian River) during the Tang and Song Dynasties, forming a large number of big and small “river markets”. During the Xining period of the Northern Song Dynasty (1072-1073), the Japanese monk Chenxun went from Taizhou up to Mount Wutai along the canal to the warship Buddha. When the boat arrived at the Yingtian prefecture of Nanjing (now called Shangqiu), he noted in his diary that: “In the evening, there were thousands of shops along the banks of the canal with all of their lights on. Music could be heard from afar… the shop owners were busy with business.” During the late Northern Song Dynasty, Zhang Zeduan, a painter of the Northern Song Dynasty, took the canal and “river market” as the focal point of his painting, depicting the city, the canal and the “river market” in his *Riverside Scene at Qingming Festival*.

Therefore, documents and archaeological discoveries show that the convenient transportation of the canal from the Sui and Tang dynasties to the Northern Song Dynasty brought about numerous township river markets of different sizes and scales along the banks of the canal. This kind of river markets must have been open, unlike the closed Li-Fang unit managing system (The Li-Fang unit system is the complex of the basic unit of ancient Chinese urban and rural planning and the residential management system) of the grass-roots society in the cities during the Sui and Tang dynasties, and the open type gradually influenced and caused this kind of closed management mode to fade away. It could be said that canal traffic greatly changed the economic and cultural features of the grass-roots society during the Tang and Song Dynasties. These changes also brought about unprecedented prosperity and the common development of the grass-roots society at that time, supporting the foreign trade represented by silk.

III. The Common Development and Value of the Protection of the Silk Road and Other Related Cultural Heritage

With respect to the Silk Road and the Grand Canal, the application for a world cultural heritage has greatly promoted the protection and display of related cultural heritage elements. The world cultural heritage of the Silk Road has 22 archaeological sites and ancient buildings in China, including 4 places in Henan

Province, 7 in Shaanxi Province, 5 in Gansu Province, and 6 in the Xinjiang Uygur Autonomous Region. The world heritage site of China's Grand Canal involves 27 river courses and 58 heritage sites in 27 cities of 8 provinces along the route. These heritage sites reflect the special universal significance and value of the world's cultural heritage. At the same time, they have been effectively protected and built into the Heritage Park, which not only improves the environment, but effectively protects the integrity of the heritage, becoming a public place for the people to visit, study, travel, spend their leisure time, carry out fitness activities and so on. It is particularly popular with, supported and welcomed by the local people.

Today, the protection of cultural heritage in China has had an unprecedented upsurge, which is based on the universal historical and cultural value of these cultural heritage sites and the social common developmental prospect and overall impact generated by them.

IV. Conclusion

The ancient Silk Road has a profound and comprehensive impact on the development of the country and society along the route. Especially for the production and life of the people at the grass-roots level, it brings more opportunities, conditions, conveniences and changes. In turn, the people of the grass-roots community have provided a wealth of material and spiritual products for the Silk Road. Now, we are still enjoying the wealth and value of the ancient Silk Road and getting more new benefits from the implementation of the "Belt and Road" common development. "Delivering the benefits to the public" is the greatest common value of the ancient and modern Silk Road.

共同价值观是共同发展的关键

曾繁兴 【毛里求斯】

非盟统计评议机制委员 / 毛里求斯艺术和文化部前部长 / 联合国项目前协调员

一 前言

我们已经进入一个由网络引领的新时代。网络给人类社会造成了巨大影响，迫使人类对工作方式、生活方式、经营方式、娱乐方式进行重新审视，更影响到不同社会之间的交流与互动方式。的确，当今世界已经缩小成一个地球村，没有人可以生活在封闭与孤立中。

我们依然生活在 2008 年金融危机的余波之中，资本主义世界正在寻求新的发展计划和发展方向。我们的生活充满了不确定性。2017 年 1 月，美国正式退出跨太平洋伙伴关系协定，随后又于同年 6 月退出《巴黎气候协定》。种种迹象表明，美国对于领导现代世界的信心正在衰减。失去殖民地的欧洲各国更是计穷智竭，无力引领全球事务。与此同时，“华盛顿共识”达成的政策措施造成了全世界范围内贫富差距的不断扩大，引起发展中国家的强烈憎恶。突尼斯商贩布亚齐兹以自焚的悲剧率先发起反抗，随即北非、拉美、亚洲各地妇女纷纷涌上街头，高举锅碗瓢盆，呼吁改善民生。整个世界似乎失去了方向。

恰恰在这个对未来充着迷茫的时代，世界各国从一项全新的工程中看到了希望——一个可以引领世界前进的全球性工程。这便是习近平主席提出的“一带一路”倡议。2013 年 10 月 13 日，习近平主席在印度尼西亚国会发表重要演讲时，提出要构建东西方新型合作关系、建设“中国–东盟命运共同体”和21世纪“海上丝绸之路”。目前，“一带一路”的辐射区域主要集中在亚洲和欧洲，涉及沿线60多个国家。“一带”囊括了穿越中亚、西亚、中东及欧洲的“古丝绸之路”沿线国家；海上丝绸之路始于中国沿海地区，连接新加坡与地中海。除此之外，还有一条“被遗忘的”沟通南北、连接中国与西南印度洋群岛的丝绸之路。

二　什么是共同发展？

1. 共同发展中的合作方

“一带一路”所描绘的，正是“新一轮全球化”波澜壮阔的愿景，目的在于沟通和连接亚、非、欧三大洲的各个国家。很显然，这项工程的意义和吸引力在于，它能够为所有参与国带来利益，能够通过经贸交流和文化交流，促进共同发展。相关各方若想更好地达成一致，首先要确保对“共同价值观”和“共同发展”等理念的理解不产生偏差。

首先要指出的是，昔日殖民主义带来的世界贸易模式和贸易格局绝对不是互惠互利的。即便在当前世界格局下，发达国家和国际金融机构依然采用各种形式遏制发展中国家的经济发展。对此，我们见证过无数的例子。如今，世界各国所期待的，正是平等待遇、以平等的地位参与竞争。因此，在发展中国家领导人的眼里，“一带一路”正是通过经贸交流和文化交流促进共同发展的有效手段。

2. 受益方

然而共同发展的含义不仅局限于此，不仅仅意味着国与国之间通过互惠互利实现发展。国家由不同的区域、阶级、群体组成，并非所有人都能平等地分享国家财富。发展中国家的各个阶层，特别是贫苦阶层，急需改变他们的经济处境和生活环境。然而对于刚刚摆脱殖民统治的国家而言，这种改变很难实现。许多地区尚未通电，没有收音机，也没有电视，人民群众大多没有接受过教育，处于闭塞状态，他们喝不上纯净水，享受不到医疗保险和基本的教育，困守在贫困的现实中却无力逃脱，他们甚至想象不出摆脱贫穷后的生活是怎样一种状态，从来没有一种可以激励他们、使其摆脱贫困的模式。但如今，这种状况已经被彻底改变。不论生活在世界的任何一个角落，人们都可以了解外部世界发生着什么，知道那里的人们如何生活、吃什么、穿什么。电视、因特网、无线网等技术，可以让相隔千里的人们实时了解对方的状态。眼界开阔后，人们会进行对比，会对自身境况有着更深刻的认识，从此拒绝接受悲惨的社会处境。世界上的每个家庭都期望着能够喝上清洁水、吃上像样的食物、享受到医疗保险、让孩子接受教育、保护家人免遭虐待和不公。这是任何一个国家的人民所期待的而政府和领导人应该给予的基本需求。

然而发展中国家始终面临这样一种风险——“一带一路”倡议的主要受益者，最终会是那些政治权力和经济权力的支配者，即富有的统治阶级，而人民大众依然处于被伤害、被剥削、遭受贫穷的状态。这就要求建立一种有效的分配机制，确保社会弱势群体能够平等地享受国家财富。我们始终不能忘记，在 20 世纪刚刚摆脱殖民统治后，许多发展中国家的领导人取代了外国殖民者的地位，通过剥削本国人民、窃取国家财富来中饱私囊。

许多发展中国家的人民可能还从未听说过“一带一路”，因而还不知道他们有机会改善自身的生活，许多人每日的开销不超过 2 美元，没有电视，买不起报纸，对本国形势尚且一无所知，当然无法了解中国的国家主席对未来描绘的宏伟愿景。因此，当前最主要的任务在于，尽快让发展中国家的人民了解“一带一路”。

三　什么是共同价值观？

1. 共同的价值观

从一般意义上来讲，价值观是指个体、群体或群族所尊奉的一系列原则，包括社会或民族之形成、发展所依赖的准则和伦理。价值观通常以传统的形式代际相传，在以文化 / 文明冲突和融合为表征的现代语境中，价值观的有效性和重要性遭到质疑，于是便产生了“是否存在共同价值观”的追问。答案是不言自明的，不论个体差异如何、所处背景如何不同，没有人会否认，诚实、正值、宽容是多数人秉持的共同价值观，这些人会排斥谎言、谴责掠夺或谋杀行为。然而对于身处政治现实的各国而言，是否存在普适性的价值观或原则这一问题仍然有待探讨。概括而言，多数国家都会遵守联合国宪章的宗旨，或遵守签署的双边协议。然而总有某些国家会出于内部形势或自身利益的考量，弃邻国之价值观于不顾。

2. 冲突的价值观

不同的价值观会引起国内冲突，比如，当政府的宗教政策或民族政策与国民的价值观或原则发生抵触时，就会引发冲突。为了更好地说明这个问题，请允许我以我的祖国毛里求斯为例。目前，毛里求斯依然属于中等收入的发展中国家之列，但在半个世纪之前，情况并非如此。20 世纪 60 年代，蒂特马斯教授在一份报告中警告说，如果毛里求斯不能大幅降低出生率，则永远无法消除贫困。因此，政府开始推行生育控制政策，这一政策遭到了宗教团体和其他群体的抵制。印度同样面临着人口过剩的问题，且问题的严重性远远高于毛里求斯，甚至会导致经济发展瘫痪、造成世代贫穷的后果。拉吉夫・甘地总理的弟弟——桑贾伊・甘地曾试图推行绝育政策，最终导致总理遇刺的悲剧。然而圣雄甘地却将生育控制视作犯罪行为。

值得注意的是，印度的邻国——中国，同样面临着人口过剩的问题。但中国的计划生育却没有引起动乱，通过“一胎”政策大幅降低了人口数量，这也是中国能够取得经济飞速发展和高速增长的一个原因。从中国的例子中可以看出，民众做出的选择，是为了实现国家富强这个统一的目标。儒家倡导的“舍己为公”的精神早已深深刻入中国人的民族心态之中。

以上示例说明，国家与国家之间，国家的不同群体之间都可能发生价值观冲突的现象。若冲突发生在内部，政府可以借助民族价值观或政治文化进行调节。但问题是，在“一带一路”所倡导的共同发展、共同富裕的伟大愿景中，能否避免或调和国家之间的价值观冲突？在当代语境下，人类的共同价值观早已发生变化，共同发展的理念——饮食、医疗、教育、住房、安全等——对于秉持不同价值观的各个群体，是否具有足够的吸引力？

四 “西方”与“东方”的世界观差异

世界各国人民均对自身及他者有着明晰而具体的认识，这种认识构成了国民价值观，以及对本国在世界所处地位的认知。众所周知，历史和地理环境塑造并丰富了人类文明，几个世纪以来，个体及群体的价值观是在不同环境、不同生活模式的交互作用中产生并固定下来。这种世界观包括决定个体行为和国家行为的理念、信念以及宗教信仰。为了确保“一带一路”倡议的稳步推进，有必要对沿线国家及人民的世界观进行了解，从而判定沿线国家的世界观是否与“一带一路”的宗旨相符，两者间是否会发生文化或宗教层面的冲突。

1. 西方世界观

西欧的世界观是在“预言”与“科学”这两股相互冲突的洪流中逐渐形成的。首先，西欧人的祖先来自信仰“天启宗教”中东地区——三大“一神宗教”的发源地。西欧人的祖先自认为是亚当和夏娃的后代，祖先因为忤逆上帝而被逐出伊甸园，因此，为了死后重生或升入天国，他们的行为必须符合宗教规范，根据神的意旨有所为或有所不为。自上帝对亚伯拉罕进行开示后，先知宗教开始在中东沙漠地区流传开来，当地涌现出一批先知，最后一位便是创立伊斯兰教的穆罕默德。

这种信仰从中东传至巴勒斯坦，随后，基督教通过先知和传教士传至西欧。

在基督教传入西欧的几个世纪之前，希腊便已经产生了科学思想的萌芽，例如，德谟克里特斯当时便提出了奠定后世科学基础的“原子唯物论”，但先知宗教的传入阻碍了科学发展的进程。15世纪之前，希腊人的科学精神和独立批判的思想一直遭到神学的禁锢，先知宗教宣扬死后升入天国、永世享乐，以此慰藉信众。然而世人很难忘记，这些宗教并不反对奴役他人，反而鼓励宗教迫害、殖民扩张，为西方的帝国主义张目助威。

随着牛顿、达尔文、弗洛伊德等人的出现，西欧再次掀起了科学研究与探索的浪潮。一代代西方思想家开始排斥上帝信仰或先知信仰，以“无神论”或“不可知论”者自居。这些思想家的理念是，在此时、此地建造人间乐园，而不是等待死后升天，他们注重追求现世的美好生活，不会把希望寄托于遥远而不可知的未来。从这个角度而言，“一带一路”会对这一群体产生较强的吸引力。

2. 中国及东方国家的世界观

与西方世界观相比，东方世界观可谓截然不同。中国人并不信奉非唯一的上帝或阿拉伯国家的先知，他们的世界观是在孔子、老子等哲学家的影响下逐渐形成，其世界观中包含了儒、释、道三教的哲学理念。中国的哲人、思想家和智者注重对“道”的探求，注重人类存在的现世意义。

由于中国人并不接受“天启”思想，因而未曾受到希伯来人或阿拉伯人宗教圣典的影响。他们是伏羲和女娲的后代，而不是亚当和夏娃的子孙，没有对“天国、原罪、地狱”等概念的认知。哲人和智者宣扬的信条，大多关于如何经营现实生活，从不强迫人民崇拜天堂里的上帝，或为宗教服务。务实的中国人并不喜欢投机，虽然炼丹术源自中国，但炼丹的目的只是为了追求长生，并不指望上帝创造奇迹或企盼神的干预。因此，中国人的心灵是自由不羁的，其关注点在于面对和解决现实问题。为了改善现实生活，中国人民“在工程、科技、数学、战争、运输、音乐等各个领域”创造了无数的发明，“欧洲人正是从这些发明中得到灵感，从而拉开了工业革命的序幕。”在《中国科学技术史》中，英国人李约瑟对中国科学技术的成就与贡献进行了详尽地记述。从中国人的职业道德中可以看出，中华民族是一个自立自强的民族。中国人祭拜天地先祖，期待自身也能像先祖一般优秀，为后世敬仰。

简言之，中国人更注重现世的成功，注重个人与“道”的关系。中国人不信奉天堂的存在，只注重在现实生活中构建天堂。中国人的“三位一体”不是“圣父、圣子与圣灵”，而是能够在现实生活中获取的“福、禄、寿”。

3.“超自然”信仰与“一带一路”

总体而言，人类似乎可以划分为两大阵营：其中一个阵营信奉“先知宗教”，崇拜上帝或先知，另一个阵营信奉哲学理念，不存在神的意旨。前者大多集中在西欧和中东地区，以神的意旨或准则指导现实生活，期待来世和天堂的美好生活；后者集中在东方，寄希望于现世生活，并为改造现实而努力奋斗。除此之外，还有一大阵营，即信奉轮回转世的印度教徒。这些人认为，经过无数次轮回转世后，灵魂可以得到净化，从此不必回到人世间受苦，而是与无限和永恒融为一体。

目前亟待回答的问题是，这些关于上帝、来世或轮回的信仰，是否会影响“一带一路”倡议的推进，不同的信仰群体是否能够避免冲突、达成一致，通过各方协作来改善此时、此地的人类生活。

五　结语

“一带一路”倡议是中国领导人为新世界描绘的美好愿景，为中国、西方、中亚、中东、非洲、印度洋群岛之间的经贸交流和文化交流提供了前所未有的机遇。但与此同时，这一倡议也面临着重重阻碍和挑战。在“一带一路”得到沿线60个国家及人民的热烈支持和积极响应之前，有必要对各国的价值观、对共同发展的经济、社会、商业及文化目标进行梳理。在深入推进“一带一路”这一全球性的工程之前，各国必须就可能影响其参与积极性的价值观层面达成一致。

如果没有社会各个阶层——领导者、规划者、开发者、人民大众——的通力合作和大力支持，则无法实现发展。只有确保社会各个群体均享有平等的受益权，才能确保合作的顺利开展。

与此同时，为了确保各方有足够的动力开展持续合作，首先要实现思想上的统一，通过协调各方的理念、准则来增进互利互信，提高透明度，确保项目顺利开展；同时要秉持双赢的原则，确保平等互利，只有在双方实现共同发展时，才不会引发沮丧和嫉妒。的确，如果“一带一路”能够为各国企业开辟新市场，其贡献不仅仅在于改善落后国家或发展中国家人民的生活水平，更能为发达国家带来裨益，从而为构建一个更加美好的世界做出贡献。

当然，以上论述听起来不乏理想主义色彩，但人类的所有成就都起源于最初的梦想，难道不是么?

Common Values as a Key to Mutual Development

Tsang Fan Hin / Mauritius

Member of African Peer Review Mechanism Panel, Former Minister of Arts and Culture, and UN Program Coordinator

I. Introduction

We have entered a new world ushered in by the Internet that impacts considerably on human societies worldwide forcing mankind to rethink the ways they work, live, do business and enjoy themselves, and more important on how they interact with other societies in different parts of the world. Indeed, our world today has shrunk into a global village and no man can live in isolation.

We are still in the backlash of the 2008 crash and the capitalist world is now in search of new purposes and directions. We live in uncertainties. The US retreat from the Trans-Pacific partnership (TPP) last January and the Paris Agreement suggests loss of confidence in its leadership role of the modern world. Europe now stripped of its colonies and devoid of ideas is in no position to take a major lead in world affairs. At the same time, the developing world abhors the policies imposed by the Washington consensus, which have been widening the gap between rich and poor everywhere. The first protest was tragically expressed by Bouazizi, the Tunisian vendor's self-immolation, followed by housewives in Northern Africa, Latin America and Asia taking to the streets with pots and pans clamoring for a more decent life. The world seems to have no sense of direction.

It's during this period of uncertainties about the world's future that that for the first time after the first Afro-Asian led global economy[1]that the world was informed about a new global project to take the world forward. That was the Belt and Road project announced by PRC president Xi Jinping at the Indonesian parliament on 3 October 2013, proposing a new form of cooperation between East and West, to include all the countries in between, a Belt overland and a Road overseas. Today, the coverage area of the Belt and Road initiative is primarily Asia and Europe, encompassing around 60 countries. Essentially, the 'belt' includes countries situated on the original Silk Road through Central Asia, West Asia, the Middle East, and Europe. The Maritime Silk Road, runs from the Chinese Coast through Singapore to the Mediterranean. There is also the Forgotten North South Silk Road linking China and the South West Indian Islands[2].

II. What is Mutual Development?

1. The Partners in Mutual Development

Belt and Road today comes up with a mighty vision of a new globalization involving and connecting countries from different continents: Asia Europe and Africa. It is obvious that such a project to be meaningful and attractive must be beneficial to all countries participating and help in their development through the promotion of trade and cultural exchanges.To make sure that all the parties concerned are on the same wave lengths, there would be need for the countries involved first to have a shared understanding of expressions like *common values* or *mutual development.*

1 John M Hobson: *The Eastern Origins of Western Civilisation,* CUP, 2004

2 J Tsang Mang Kin: *The Forgotten Guangzhou-Indian Ocean Maritime Silk Route*, at World Maritime Silk Road merchants And The 21 Century Seminar, at World Hakka Meizhou, China, August 28, 2015; The paper has been translated into Chinese

We can start by saying that the former models or patterns of trade that the world has known with the rise of colonialism have been quite far from being mutually beneficial. Now in our own present century, we have witnessed numerous forms of economic subjugation of developing countries by advanced economies as well as international financial institutions. What countries want today is fair treatment and they need to know that they will be treated on an equal footing and operate on the same level playing field. Consequently, the leaders of developing countries view the Belt and Road project as a means of ensuring mutual development through trade and cultural exchanges.

2. The Beneficiaries

But there is more. II's not just a question of countries aiming to develop one another for their mutual benefit. A country is made up of different sections, classes or groups that do not equally and necessarily have access to a country's wealth. All these different groups, especially the poorer ones in the developing countries want a drastic change in their economic situation and life style. That was not possible immediately after the colonies achieved independence. There was no electricity, no radio, no TV. As a result, the masses were uninformed and uneducated. They had no access to clean water, medical care, proper education. They only knew they were poor and saw no way out of the tunnel. They could not imagine different living conditions outside of poverty and had no model to inspire them.But today, the situation has completely changed. It is now possible anywhere on the planet to know what is going on elsewhere, how people live, are dressed, what they eat and what they wear. There is the TV, internet, Wi-Fi, which means that people thousands of miles apart can be informed in real time. They can see what is going on around them. They compare, understand and refuse their miserable social situation. Every family on earth wants to have safe water, proper food, medical care, education for the children, shelter and protection from abuse or injustice. These are the basic and fundamental needs that populations anywhere expect of their governments and leaders.

There is always the risk in developing countries that those who command the levers of power, political and economic, mostly the wealthy and ruling classes end up being the main beneficiaries of the Belt and Road initiative to the detriment of the masses that are left exploited and poverty-stricken as before. This means that appropriate mechanisms need be put in place to ensure equitable sharing of the wealth among the more vulnerable sections of society. It should not be forgotten that in the last century immediately after attaining independence, we find leaders of several developing countries replacing the foreign colonisers and exploiting their own people, amassing and utilising the country's wealth to their own benefit.

Chances are that the masses in developing countries have never heard of Belt and Road and therefore do not know that it can improve their lives. In most countries where people live on less than 2 US$ a day, have no TV, and can't even buy a newspaper they remain uninformed about their own country and for sure cannot be expected to know about PRC President's great vision for the future. This means that informing the people in developing countries about Belt and Road is a major task that needs to be tackled urgently.

III. What do We Mean by Common Values?

1. Shared Values

Values are generally defined as the principles that inspire and guide an individual, a group or a nation. They are codes and ethics on which a society or a nation is founded and by which they stand. They are generally handed down by tradition and in the modern age there are sometimes questions about their validity or importance in the present age of convergence or confrontationbetween cultures and civilizations. So, the question is whether we have common values? Certainly, as far as individuals whatever the background is concerned. No one will deny that honesty, truthfulness, tolerance are common values that are shared by most people. They reject lies, condemn robbery or murder. But when it comes to countries practising real politic, the question arises as to whether there really are common values or principles accepted by all. In In general most nations abide by UN sponsored or bilateral agreements they have signed. But there are courses of action that one country can take in response to its own internal circumstances and for its own interests in complete disregard for the values of its neighbours.

2. Conflicting Values

Values can create conflicts in the same country when, for example, the Government makes choices that certain specific, ethnic or religious view as contrary to their own values or principles. To illustrate my point, allow me to refer to my own country Mauritius, which happens today to be listed amidst the middle income developing countries. That was not the case half a century ago, in the 1960's when a Report from Professor Titmuss warned us that if we did not considerably reduce our birth rate it would be impossible to put an end to poverty. In response, the Mauritian Government introduced birth control which met with resistance from religious and other bodies. India faced the same overpopulation problem but on a gigantic scale threatening paralyse economic development and keep generations of Indians in poverty all their lives. PM Rajiv Gandhi's brother Sanjay tried promoting birth control and even went to forced sterilization of the female population, which led to his assassination. In India, however, Mahatma Gandhi considered birth control criminal.

It is interesting to note here the case of India's next door neighbour China, faced with a similar overpopulation problem. The Chinese had no qualms about drastically halting population growth by limiting the birth rate to one child per family. This enabled them to achieve the rate of economic growth and development we know today. In the case of China, the objective of prosperity in the long-term dictated choices which the Chinese people readily accepted. Deep in their psyche the Chinese have always been conditioned since Confucius to put national interests before individual preferences.

The above examples show that countries or specific groups in any country may have different or conflicting values. If the problems are internal it seems that they can be managed by the local authorities according to each country's philosophy or political culture.But what about conflicting values opposing neighbouring countries? Are they manageable? Are they surmountable or reconcilable in the context of the grander objective which is to ensure progress and prosperity for all, as proposed by Belt and Road? Or will mutual development- providing access to food, medical care, education, housing and protection-be powerful or attractive enough to form part of a renewed set of the common values mankind would need today?

IV. What about World Views of East and West?

The different peoples of the world have their specific views of themselves and of others, which form their world view and their place in the world. As we all know, civilisations are shaped and enriched by history and geography. It's the interaction between the environment and the mode of life over the centuries that have moulded and nurtured the world view of individuals and societies.This world view includes the philosophies, beliefs and religions which dictate the behaviour of individuals and countries. It would be extremely useful if we try to predict the future or success of Belt and Road to know the world views of the peoples on the path of Belt and Road and whether these peoples have an agreed view of the aims and objectives of Belt and Road and whether the objectives of Belt and Road do not run counter to the world view, culture or religion of the societies or peoples concerned?

1. World Views in the West

Western Europe has a world view drawn by two contradictory currents, prophetic and scientific. First, they are heirs to the revelations from the Middle East that produced the three monotheistic religions. They believe they are the children of Adam and Eve thrown out of Paradise for disobeying God and must follow a certain course of action in order one day after they die, they will come back to life and live in Heaven. They have orders from above that tell them what to do or not to do; they have directions on how to behave on earth and get ready to live someday in heaven after they die. These are the teachings of prophetic religions born in the deserts of the Middle East when God spoke to Abraham and a string of prophets, the last one being Mohammed who founded Islam. This is the set of creeds that moved from the Middle East to Palestine and later brought Christianity to Western Europe, through the teachings of prophets and the work of missionaries.

As a result, the prophetic religions halted scientific research that had started centuries before Christin Greece when Democritus came up with his idea of the atoms that paved the way to our scientific age. The scientific spirit of the Greeks became submerged by fifteen centuries of creeds that made independent thinking and questioning impossible. The prophetic religions provide consolation and hope more specially to the damned of the Earth who nurture hopes of happiness in an after-life after they die. It's difficult, however, to forget that these religions did not stop slavery, encouraged religious intolerance, launched colonisation and backed western imperialism.

But today scientific research and enquiry have come back with Newton, Darwin or Freud. As a result, several generations of Westerners came to question religion or reject their faith in God and his prophets and call themselves atheists or agnostics. This means that these people want their Paradise on Earth, now, today, not tomorrow, in Heaven. It would also mean that this category of people would be more attracted to what Belt and Road has to offer, that is a better life now while they are still alive, not in the distant unknowable future.

2. World views in China and in the East

World views in the East are completely different. The Chinese have nothing to do with the personal Gods or the prophets from Arabia but owe their world view to philosophers like Confucius or Lao Zi whose combined teachings produced a combination of Confucianism, Daoism and Buddhism.They have philosophers, gurus and thinkers that think and meditate on the infinite, to find a meaning for human existence on Earth.

As non-recipients of revelations the Chinese remained untouched by the Hebrew or Arabic Sacred Books. They are the Children of Fuxi and Nuwa, not of Adam and Eve. They have no knowledge of Paradise, of Sin or Hell. They were spared all the commandments and directives from prophets on how to run their daily lives, with no obligation to run religious services, or to worship a personal God in Heaven. The Chinese were not inclined to speculation. For sure they invented alchemy, but this was dictated by the desire for immortality but they never sought life eternal or called for miracles or direct intervention from any God. So, they remained free and had all the time to address and solve all their everyday problems. Responding to challenges to their well-being, the Chinese came up with numerous solutions, inventions and discoveries "*in the fields of engineering, technology, maths, science warfare, transportation and music that helped inspire the European and industrial revolutions.*"[1] and are now recorder in the numerous volumes written by Joseph Needham. They relied on themselves, which perhaps explains Chinese work ethics. They worship Heaven and Earth plus their Ancestors, honour them by behaving honourably and trusting one day to be an Ancestor, honoured and worshipped by future generations.

In short, the Chinese are more concerned with a successful life on earth, considering one's relation with the infinite to be a personal and private affair. They have no heaven, they try to make their heaven on earth and they look to a trinity which tells them what to try to achieve on Earth: Fu Lu Shou 福禄寿 meaning Happiness, Financial security and Longevity.

3. The Supernatural and "Belt and Road"

It appears that Humanity can be divided into two major blocs, the three prophetic religions with a God and Prophets and the philosophical religions that has no God and no messengers from him. The first group mostly in Western and Middle Eastern has clear instructions on how to live their lives on earth, with commandments and

1 Robert Temple: *The Genius of China – 3000 years of Science, Discovery and Invention,* Andre Deutsch

codes of behaviour. They have hopes in an afterlife that will set things right and bring rewards in Heaven. The second Eastern group has no such certainties and pin their hopes on the present life and seems to have no alternative but to improve it. There is also a third bloc comprising mainly Hindus who believe in reincarnation and hope after successive incarnations to be purified and no longer required to return to Earth but absorbed in the Infinite.

The question to answer is whether the beliefs in God or in an afterlife or successive reincarnations has any impact on the degree of commitment to Belt and Road project and whether the two groups can reach some sort of Agreement, avoid conflicts and try to work together and improve the lives of mankind, here and now.

V. Conclusion

Belt and Road is a wonderful vision that points to a new world and opens new opportunities for trade and cultural exchanges for all countries that stand between China and the West, including Central Asia, the Middle East, Africa and the islands of the Indian Ocean. At the same time, it faces numerous obstacles and challenges. Before Belt and Road can be owned and promoted by all the peoples of the 60 countries, there is the need for them to clarify and harmonize their views and objectives in mutual development: economic, social, commercial and cultural. They will also have to agree on a set of the values that will govern their participation in the new globalization project.

There can be no development without the cooperation between all the segments in society, the leaders, planners and developers should have the support of the rest of the population and this cooperation will only be possible once there is agreement on the fair share of distribution of the wealth produced.

But as pointed out above, there should be shared vision to maintain interest and keep the momentum for going forward. Hence the need for a code of ethics to govern all the parties to ensure reliability, trust and transparency that will help the grand project thrive. We must ensure equity according to the win-win principle, for only by prospering thy neighbor will we prosper ourselves and stifle all feeling of frustration and jealousy. Indeed, if Belt and Road can help provide access to new markets for entrepreneurs and companies for all countries, Belt and Road's contribution towards building a better world will help realize the deep-seated longings for the populations not only of the least advantaged and developing countries but also those of the powerful and highly developed economies.

Of course, all this may sound idealistic, but has man done anything without first dreaming about it?

探寻共同发展的新路

欧阳向英 【中国】
中国社会科学院世界经济与研究所马克思主义世界政治经济理论研究室主任

"如果10多亿中国人有着与澳大利亚人或是美国人同样的生活模式，那么我们会处于一个不幸的时代，地球将无法承受。"这句话据说是美国前任总统奥巴马先生在接受澳大利亚广播公司（ABC）专访时讲的，谈的是气候问题。从经济学的角度看有一定道理，但从伦理的角度却深深刺痛了中国人的心。理性地说，美国希望中国找到一种与环境协调的新的经济发展模式，中国又何尝不希望如此?

中国渴望发展，中国人渴望过上富裕文明的生活，但地球只有一个，地球上的资源是有限的。如何解决人口—资源—环境的矛盾，使发展中国家与发达国家一起走上富裕之路，是我们这个时代的难题。

一　发展是发展中国家和发达国家的共同愿望

20世纪，世界经济增长速度和财富积累都达到了前所未有的水平，与此同时，由于经济增长的收益分配极不平等，南北收入差距也达到了一个前所未有的新高度。正如托马斯·皮凯蒂在其代表作《21世纪资本论》中所说，如果继续现在的趋势，21世纪将和19世纪一样，出现巨大的贫富落差和尖锐的社会矛盾，红旗到处飘扬，甚至引发社会动荡和战争。

贫富分化、南北差距是现存国际经济秩序中最持久和最令人不安的特征之一。

如何解决这一问题？不同国家的不同学者提出了不同的解决方案。有人认为全球化建立在发达地区与不发达地区的不平等交换基础上，因而主张反全球化或与发达地区脱钩；有人认为应建立全球性社会调节机制，通过工业化国家对发展中国家提供发展援助实现国际收入转移；有人认为应组织新的大规模社会运动，以抵抗对工人阶级不利的那些因素。中国学者大多认为，发展中出现的问题应该通过进一步的发展来解决，其中确立更合理的发展模式是关键。

可以说，世界各国处于不同发展阶段，意识形态千差万别，但发展是各国的普遍追求。从世界范围来看，排除热点涌动的地缘政治问题，则人口 - 资源 - 环境问题最为突出。这既是在历史中积淀下来的，又是在现实中不断加深的。解决它，有赖于人类创造新的发展模式，从传统的以自然为征服对象的发展观中解放出来。

二　五大发展理念是中国解决自身发展问题的唯一出路

改革开放 40 年来，中国取得了举世瞩目的发展成就，经济实力和综合国力明显上升，但人口多、底子薄、城乡和地区发展不平衡、生产力不够发达的状况并没有得到根本改变。尤其人口红利衰减，资源环境的承载能力受到挑战，生产要素总量约束正逐步显现，主要依靠低要素成本参与国际竞争的局面难以为继，公共服务质量和收入分配不公可能成为影响经济发展的新瓶颈。

科学制定适应时代要求和人民愿望的行动纲领，找到突破挑战的薄弱环节，更加奋发有为地工作，是解决上述问题的关键。中国从 20 世纪 90 年代中期实施可持续发展战略，鼓励从事对资源、环境有利的经济活动，摒弃不利的经济活动，标志着开始重视经济活动的生态合理性。然而，所谓"不利于资源和环境的经济活动"大多是基于贫困落后的社会现实开展起来的，骤然关停意味着亏损和失业，但不治理则意味着污染终将反噬人类自身。这时，在 GDP 增长和可持续发展间找到动态平衡点，稳步实现产业升级和结构转型，就成为至关重要的事情。

中国共产党十八届五中全会提出了"创新、协调、绿色、开放、共享"五大发展理念，集中了发展经济学和中国特色社会主义实践的优秀成果，既是中国解决自身问题的良策，也是中国拉动世界经济的良方。

"创新"是经济发展的不竭动力。目前，世界经济面临新一轮全球产业分工调整和第四次科技革命的重大机遇，科学统筹规划战略性新兴产业，使其成为我国参与国际经济技术合作和竞争发展的新优势，是关系民族崛起和国家复兴的百年大计。中国需要创新发展理论、创新体制机制、创新生产方式、创新工艺流程、创新思想观念，在全民创新、全面创新的基础上引领经济发展。

“协调”是各要素保持平衡。不仅要促进人口－资源－环境的协调，也要缩小城乡差距、地区差距和贫富差距，实现经济－社会综合平衡发展。

“绿色”强调将环境因素作为经济增长的成本考虑。不以对环境和资源的破坏性使用来换取经济增长，努力使经济活动按照“资源－产品－废弃物－再生资源”的反馈式循环流程，建设资源节约型和环境友好型社会。

“开放”是中国的基本国策。面对世界经济环境的新变化，应发展更高层次的开放型经济，加快转变外贸增长方式，调整进出口结构，加快中国企业“走出去”的步伐，提高对外投资质量，参与新一轮国际经济规则塑造。

“共享”是社会发展的内容。作为负责任大国，中国不仅要让本国的老百姓分享到经济发展的果实，切实提高普通居民的生活－生命质量，而且通过“一带一路”等顶层设计，与周边国家实现经济联动与成果共享。“一带一路”沿线有些国家或担心中国输出落后的产业，或担心中国掠夺资源并将自己变为附庸国，其实是不理解“一带一路”和中国发展阶段的关系所致。当初中国引进外国投资来改善就业、提高经济发展水平，却忽视了资源枯竭和环境污染给国家带来的危害，如今绝不会将此模式照搬到“一带一路”沿线国家去，就算个别企业想要照搬也行不通。随着时代的变迁，各国普遍重视清洁产业的发展，污染企业会为环境破坏而付出高昂的代价。同时我们也要看到，传统行业并非除了环境污染就一无是处，钢铁、煤炭、水泥、光伏、纺织、船舶制造等在经济发展的某一阶段不可或缺，只是需要从粗放转变到创新发展和绿色发展的轨道上来。

五大发展理念源于新中国独立自主、自力更生的发展思想，吸纳其他国家发展过程中的经验教训，是对世界发展观念的贡献。“一带一路”是中华文明复兴道路上的伟大倡议，它不局限于一国一地，而是构建利益、责任和命运共同体，需要世界各国基于共同价值，达成基本共识，付诸统一行动，为解决本国经济和世界经济的发展做出切实努力。

三　新发展模式对世界发展理念的贡献

现在，全球有10亿左右的人口生活极端贫困，每天平均收入不足1.25美元，还有10亿人口营养不良。根据美国国家情报委员会的预测，到2030年，由于经济发展、个人收入提高，极端贫困人口的数量将会下降约50%，但如果全球经济出现长期萧条，到2030年，那么减贫50%的目标就只能完成一半。到2030年，传染疾病造成的死亡预计将会减少30%，而非传染性疾病导致死亡的人数将增多。到21世纪中叶，根据人口与社会学家的预测，全球人口可能超过80亿，主要增长来自亚非发展中国家，人类将面临传统疾病及其变异传播、不可再生能源枯竭、环境承载力濒于极限的威胁。

国际社会迫切需要实现人口—资源—环境全面协调可持续发展，这有赖于人类创造新的发展模式。五大发展理念是新时期中国经济升级转型的指导思想，也吸纳了其他国家发展过程中的经验教训，对世界发展模式是个贡献。

首先，环境问题涉及发展中国家的贫困问题，而发展中国家的贫困问题又与现存的不公正、不合理的国际政治经济旧秩序有密切的联系。发展中国家在脱离西方殖民主义体系取得独立后，旧的国际垂直分工体系和经济结构并未相应改变。这种状况恶化了发展中国家谋求发展的条件，制约着发展中国家保护环境的努力。与发达国家相比，发展中国家的处境要困难得多。因此，国际社会要谋求环境保护的国际合作取得进展，首先要设法解决发展中国家的贫困问题，使发展中国家尽量摆脱对环境资源的依赖。而要做到这一点，就必须改变不公正、不合理的国际政治经济旧秩序。否则，人类很难实现环境保护的目标。

其次，经济增长不等于经济发展，而经济发展也不等于发展。基于一切生产和社会活动都应服务于人类自身，而人类发展主要体现在人的各种能力的提高上，所以发展理应包含人的全面发展和自由解放。中国作为最大的发展中国家，不仅在经济增长上有待持续，在全面发展与社会进步上更任重道远。

最后，作为地球村的一员，任何国家在追求自身发展的同时，必须兼顾到其他国家的发展，不能将自己的发展建立在损害他国利益的基础上。对于发展中国家和不发达国家来说，必须要做到全面协调，努力满足人民群众多层次的需求，也要协调好各个方面的发展，做到统筹兼顾。随着中国特色社会主义实践的不断深入，中国的发展模式必将引领中华民族走向伟大复兴。到那时，中国的发展观对各国探索更科学、更文明的发展道路，对人类探索一般社会发展规律，乃至对世界社会主义运动的复兴必将做出更大贡献，从而彰显出更重大、更深远的世界影响。

To Explore a New Road for Common Development

Ouyang Xiangying / China

Director of the Marxism World Political Economy Theory Division under the Institute of World Economy and Politics at the Chinese Academy of Social Sciences

"If over a billion Chinese citizens had the same living patterns as Australians and Americans do right now, then all of us would be in for a very miserable time, the planet just cannot sustain it", pronounced by U.S. President Barack Obama during the interview by the Australian Broadcasting Corporation (ABC) about the climate issue. From the perspective of economics, it makes sense to some extent. However, from the perspective of ethics, it deeply hurts the hearts of the Chinese people. Rationally, the United States expects China to find a new economic developmental model that is in harmony with the environment. China also expects it, doesn't it?

China is eager for development and the Chinese people are eager to live a rich and civilized life, but there is only one planet with limited resources. In our era, it is difficult to solve the population-resource-environment conflict and enable the developing countries and developed countries to embark on a path to prosperity.

I. Development is the Common Aspiration of Developing and Developed Countries

In the 20th century, both the speed of the world's economic growth and the accumulation of wealth have stepped into an unprecedented level. Meanwhile, due to the extremely unequal distribution of income from economic growth, the income gap between the North and the South has also reached an unprecedented new height. As Thomas Piketty said in his masterpiece, *Capital in the Twenty-first Century*, “If current trends continue, a huge gap between the rich and the poor, sharp social conflicts, fluttered red flags everywhere, and even social unrest and war would take place in the 21st century, just like in the 19th century”.

The disparity between the rich and the poor and the gap between the north and the south are one of the most lasting and disturbing features of the existing international economic order. How can this problem be solved? Different scholars in different countries have proposed different solutions. Some people believe that globalization is based on the unequal exchange between developed and underdeveloped regions, so they advocate anti-globalization or separation from developed regions; some people hold that a global mechanism for social regulation should be established to enable industrialized countries to provide developing countries with developmental assistance in order to realize the transfer of international income; some people maintain that a new large-scale social movement should be organized to resist the factors unfavorable to the working class. Most Chinese scholars believe that problems arising in the course of development should be solved through further development, and the key is to establish a more reasonable model of development.

It can be said that various countries in the world are at different stages of development, and their ideologies vary greatly. However, development is a common pursuit of all countries. Except the issue of a geopolitical hotspot, the most prominent issue is the issue of population-resource-environment from a global perspective. This has been both accumulated throughout history and intensified in reality. The solution depends on mankind's creating a new model of development, and becoming liberated from the traditional developmental concept of conquering nature.

II. The Five Developmental Concepts are the Only Way for China to Solve its Problems of Development

Over the past 40 years from the reform and opening up, China has obtained remarkable achievements in development, and has risen significantly in its economic strength and overall national strength. However, the conditions of a large section of the population, a weak foundation, unbalanced development in urban and rural areas, and underdeveloped productivity have not been fundamentally changed. In particular, the demographic dividend is declining, and the carrying capacity of the resource environment is being challenged, gradually revealing the constraints on total production factors. It is hard to continue the situation of relying mainly on low factor costs to participate in international competition. The quality of public services and the unfair distribution of income may become new bottlenecks to economic development.

The keys to addressing these problems are to scientifically formulate a program of action that meets the needs of the times and the aspirations of the people, find out the weak points for breakthroughs in challenges, and work harder and more productively. From the mid-1990s, China has implemented the strategy of sustainable development, encouraged the economic activities conducive to resources and environment, and abandoned unfavorable economic activities, marking the start of an emphasis on the ecological rationality of economic activities. However, the so-called "economic activities detrimental to resources and to the environment" are mostly based on the social realities of poverty and backwardness. Sudden closure means loss and unemployment, but non-governance means that pollution will eventually come back to haunt human beings. At this time, it is of paramount importance to find a dynamic equilibrium between the growth of the GDP and sustainable development and steadily achieve industrial upgrading and structural transformation.

The Fifth Plenary Session of the 18th CPC Central Committee put forward the five developmental concepts of "innovation, coordination, greenness, openness, and sharing", which focused on the outstanding achievements in the development of economics and the practice of socialism with Chinese characteristics. It is not only a good policy for China to solve its own problems, but also a good solution for China to drive the world economy.

"Innovation" is an inexhaustible motive force for economic development. At present, the world's economy is facing some great opportunities for a new round of regulation in global industrial division of labor and the fourth scientific and technological revolution. To strategically plan the new emerging industries in order to enable them to be a new advantage for China's participation in international economic and technological cooperation and competitive development is a fundamental task that is crucial for generations to come, and which is related to the rise and rejuvenation of the nation. China needs innovative theories of development, innovative institutional mechanisms, innovative production methods, innovative technological processes and innovative ideas to lead economic development on the basis of national innovation and comprehensive innovation.

"Coordination" means a balance among various factors. It is necessary to not only promote population-resource-environment coordination, but also to narrow the rural-urban divide, regional disparity and economic inequality in order to achieve an economical-social balanced development in all aspects.

"Greenness" emphasizes the consideration of environmental factors as the cost of economic growth. Instead of a destructive use of the environment and resources in exchange for economic growth, we will endeavor to build a resource-saving and environment-friendly society in accordance with the feedback-based recycling process of "resource-product-waste-recycling resource" in economic activities.

"Openness" is one of China's basic national policies. Facing the new changes in the global economic environment, we should develop a higher-level open economy, speed up the transformation of the growth of foreign trade, adjust the structure of imports and exports, accelerate the pace of Chinese enterprises' "going global", improve the quality of foreign investments, and participate in the establishment of a new round of international economic rules.

"Sharing" is a part of social development. As a responsible big country, China must not only allow its own people to share the fruits of economic development and effectively improve the quality of ordinary residents' lives and survival, but also to strive to achieve economic linkage and the resulting sharing with neighboring countries through the "Belt and Road" Initiative and other top-level projects. Some countries along the route of the "Belt and Road" Initiative may worry about China's output of backward industries or fear that China will plunder resources to turn them into vassal states. In fact, it is because of the lack of understanding of the relationship between the "Belt and Road" Initiative and China's developmental stage. Previously, China introduced foreign investments to improve employment and raise the level of economic development, but ignored the harm to the country caused by resource depletion and environmental pollution. Today, this model will by no means be copied in countries along the route of the Initiative, and even, it is impracticable for individual companies to copy it. With the changes of the times, countries generally attach importance to the development of a clean industry. Polluting companies will pay a high price for environmental destruction. At the same time, we must also realize that traditional industries are not but useless, environmental polluters. Steel, coal, cement, PV, textiles, shipbuilding are indispensable at certain stages of economic development. It is only necessary to shift from extensive development to innovative and green development.

The five developmental concepts originate from the developmental ideas of independence and self-reliance in New China, and learn lessons from the development of other countries. So, the five principles of development are the contribution to the concept of world development. The "Belt and Road" Initiative is a great initiative on the road to the revival of Chinese civilization. It is not limited to one country and one region, and instead, it is aimed at building a community of interest, responsibility and destiny. This requires the countries of the world to reach a basic consensus based on common values, take actions in concert, and make practical efforts to solve the problems of development of the domestic economy and the world's economy.

III. Contribution of the New Model of Development to the Concept of World Development

Nowadays, about one billion people around the world are living in extreme poverty, with an average daily income of less than 1.25 US$, and in addition, a billion people are suffering from malnutrition. According to the forecast of the U.S. National Intelligence Council, because of economic development and an increase in personal income, the number of people living in extreme poverty will decrease by about 50% by 2030. However, if the global economy suffered a long-term depression, only half of the goal of poverty reduction by 50% would be accomplished by 2030. By 2030, the number of deaths from infectious diseases is expected to decrease by 30%, while the number of deaths caused by non-communicable diseases will increase. According to the forecasts of demographers and sociologists, the global population may exceed 8 billion by the middle of the 21st century, with the main increase in the developing countries in Asia and Africa. Human beings will face many threats, including the spread of traditional diseases and their variability, the depletion of non-renewable energy, and the limit of the carrying capacity of the environment.

It is urgently necessary for the international community to realize the overall coordinated and sustainable development of the population, the resources and the environment. This depends on the establishment of a new model of development. With lessons learned from the development of other countries, the five concepts of development are the guiding ideology for China's economic upgrading and transformation in the new era, and are also the contribution to the world model of development.

First of all, the environmental issue involves poverty in developing countries, and the poverty in developing countries is closely linked to the existing unjust and unreasonable old international political and economic order. After the developing countries gained independence from the Western colonialist system, the old international system of vertical division and economic structure have not been changed correspondingly. This situation not only deteriorates the conditions for developing countries to be able to seek development, but it also restricts the efforts of developing countries to protect the environment. Compared with the developed countries, the developing countries are in a much more difficult situation. Therefore, to make progress in international cooperation regarding environmental protection, the international community must first of all try to solve the problem of poverty in the developing countries so that developing countries can get rid of their dependence on environmental resources as much as possible. To achieve this, it is necessary to change the unjust and unreasonable old international political and economic order. Otherwise, it will be very difficult for human beings to attain the goal of environmental protection.

Second, economic growth does not equal economic development, and economic development also does not equal development. All of the production and social activities are aimed at serving human beings, and human development is mainly reflected in the improvement of human capabilities. Hence, development should include the full development, liberation and freedom of human beings. As the largest developing country, China not only needs to continue its economic growth, but it also has a long way to go in terms of overall development and social progress.

Finally, while pursuing its own development, any country, as a member of the global village, must take into account the development of other countries, without harm to the interests of other countries. For the developing and underdeveloped countries, they should achieve overall coordination, strive to meet the multi-level needs of the people, and try to coordinate the development of all aspects to achieve overall planning and all-round consideration. With the expansion of the practice of socialism with Chinese characteristics, China's model of development will surely lead the Chinese nation towards a great rejuvenation. At that time, China's concept of development will make greater contributions for all countries to dig into a more scientific and more civilized developmental path, explore the laws of general social development and even rejuvenate the worldwide socialist movement, thereby exerting a greater and more far-reaching influence on the world.

印度国际大学中国学院：培育印中关系的先驱

阿维杰特 【印度】
印度国际大学中国学院院长、副教授

印度和中国这两个文明古国有着悠久的传统友谊。任何国家的文化都是在与另一个国家的文化交流和融合过程中得到发展和加强的。印度与中国的文化关系可以追溯到很早的时期。印度和中国之间的密切接触已经跨越了一千多年，使得印度文化在中国的传播取得了非常丰硕的成果。在梵语的经文中有多处提及“中国”——如印度史诗《摩诃婆罗多》就多次提到中国；还有两本印度的古籍《政事论》（Arthasastra）和《摩奴法典》也提到中国。人们可以从音乐舞蹈、文学、建筑、绘画和雕塑等领域找到印度对古代中国文化的影响。由于当时两国联系的纽带主要是佛教，所以当佛教在印度消亡后，两个国家之间的联系就被中断了。而随后几个世纪的政治发展更是阻碍了两者之间更进一步交往。

直到 1924 年罗宾德拉纳特·泰戈尔来到中国，印中两国的传统友谊才得以恢复。泰戈尔不仅是一个全球性国际社区构想的先行者，而且还将其一生过成了一个名副其实的世界公民。1921 年，泰戈尔成功建立印度国际大学，这个大学在其办学思路、教学目标和课程设置方面都是真正体现国际化思路的。由于泰戈尔的愿景与努力，20 世纪印中的文化复兴得以觉醒。泰戈尔对中国的访问不仅把高度的印度文明成就带到了中国，而且唤醒了中国人对东方文明成就的认知。在泰戈尔看来，印中文明的合作不仅与印度和中国的未来发展有关，而且与亚洲和整个世界的未来有关。他认为印中文明是东方文明的支柱。泰戈尔试图通过组织中印两国学者和许多其他国家学者一起共同开展各种“中印文化研究”的项目，从而复兴和加强这两个跨越喜马拉雅山的古代国家之间的历史渊源。正是在泰戈尔全球化视野的帮助下，1937 年“中国学院”成立，这在当时的印度是唯一的。

泰戈尔访问中国后，两国的文化互动无论是广度与深度都获得了持续不断的发展。在第一个阶段，中国把印度研究扩展到了哲学、历史、社会、语言和其他方面，并在大学也开设了这些领域的课程。在第二阶段，中国学者与学生开始访问印度，学习和从事相关研究，如曾圣谛、谭云山、徐志摩、许地山、高剑父和海维谅等。在第三个阶段，最杰出的成果是成立中印学会和中国学院，在中国有很多艺术和文学圈内的人自泰戈尔 1924 年访问中国以后就对泰戈尔感兴趣了。这样一来，研究人员就获得了在许多领域充分发展的机会。谭云山创造和建立的中国学院事实上是一个多元文化的学术机构，致力于把中国文化引进和介绍到印度。

1924 年，泰戈尔应北平演讲协会的邀请来到中国。他在中国各个城市发表了关于印度文化和文明的讲话。在访问期间，他与中国学术界进行广泛交流。泰戈尔也给中国人留下了深刻印象。泰戈尔从中国返回印度后，在法国知名学者西勒万・列维教授和中国学者林我江（音）的帮助下，于 1926 年在印度国际大学开设了中国研究的课程。1928 年，中国学院的创始人谭云山教授来到圣地尼克坦，经过他的不懈努力，在印度国际大学设立了中国研究部。谭云山回到中国后，与北京大学副校长蔡元培博士，国民政府文化部长戴季陶博士讨论了泰戈尔关于中国研究的理想和目标。所有这些中国人都热情回应了这一想法，1933 年，中印学会（中国）正式在南京成立，蔡元培为第一任会长，谭云山为第一任秘书长。中印学会的目的旨在唤醒人们对中印两国崇高精神文化的自觉，即对和平、友爱、自由和平等的关注，进而促进两国人民的文化交流与友谊。中印学会还计划捐赠书籍和资金，用于建造中国学院。1934 年，中印学会（印度）在圣地尼克坦（和平乡）成立，由文化教育界名人组成。中印学会设想要组织印度文化代表团到中国访问，中国代表团对印度进行访问，包括开展研究工作和关于印中两国的文化讲座；建议印度学生前往中国留学，中国留学生来到印度学习；在中国设立印度研究所，在印度设立中国大楼并且出版书刊等。中印学会在此期间的工作重点主要是建立中国研究中心，最后成立中国学院，其具体目标如下：

1. 推动印度的中国研究和汉语学习。

2. 促进印度和中国的文化交流。

3. 培育印度和中国两国之间的友谊和友爱。

4. 联合和团结印中两国人民。

5. 共同促进人类的普遍和平与和谐。

6. 协助建立全人类的“伟大团结”。

泰戈尔希望看到中国学院能在中印关系中发挥重要作用，这反映在他对中国学院的具体定位中，即：

> 成立中国学院的目标是要建立和促进中国和印度的文化交流，为中国学者研究印度语言、文学、历史、宗教和哲学等，为印度学者学习汉语、文学，宗教，哲学等提供便利……佛教被认为是所有这些研究的核心。

泰戈尔以极大的热情主持了这项工作，因为他将两国文化复兴的愿景变成现实，中国学院就象征着这个活生生的现实。印度前总理尼赫鲁派女儿英迪拉·尼赫鲁代表他来参加中国学院的开幕式。她代为转达了她父亲令人鼓舞人心的致辞：

> 这是我生活中非常难得的机会能来这里参加这样一个盛大的仪式。我满怀欣喜地承诺会来参加这个盛会。我坚信我必须来参加这个庆祝活动。因为这个仪式的伟大并不仅仅局限于过去这两个国家的永久记忆，也是对未来友谊的期待。因此，它将建立一个新的联系，这将使我们两国，印度和中国在适当的时候相互接近。

此外，印度国父圣雄甘地也对中国学院的成立发来了祝福的贺信，他在信中说：

> 我希望中国学院成为印度与中国之间重新建立友好关系的象征。

此外，在中国学院成立仪式上，泰戈尔发表演讲说：

> 这确实对我来说是美好的一天，长久盼望的一天，当我能够代表我们的人民赎回一个我们过去隐藏的古老承诺，承诺印度人民与中国人民之间保持文化和友谊的交往，这种互动是建立在我们祖先1800年以来一直保有的极大耐心和牺牲基础上。当我前几年去中国的时候，我感受到从印度的心脏涌出的伟大的生命之泉，充满了山脉和沙漠，进入到遥远的土地，滋润着人民的心脏。我想到那些伟大的朝圣者，那些高贵的英雄，他们为了自己的信仰，为了忠诚的信念，以及自我解放的理想，生发出对万物的热爱。他们冒着生命危险，被迫接受自己家里人去世

的坏消息，许多人消失了并没有在身后留下痕迹。只有几个人能够讲述他们的故事，这不是一个有关英雄主义或者任何浪漫借口职业的冒险故事，而是一个朝圣者将爱与智慧作为礼物的故事，一个留在他们主人记忆中难以磨灭的故事。我读到关于我被当作一个受人尊敬的族群代表时是深感自豪的，并对我们祖先取得的成绩留下了深刻印象。

今天要开放的中国学院大楼将同时作为随着时间的推移而增长的理解的象征和核心。这里的学生和学者将来自中国与我们一起生活，分享我们的生活也让我们分享他们的，通过他们对这项共同事业的投入，可以慢慢地重建我们两国人民之间伟大而富有成效的已经中断了10个世纪的友谊。对于印度国际大学来说，我也希望能够相信人类是团结一致的，愿意为了信仰而遭受苦难的东西方国家能够相聚在一起。我相信有这样的人，尽管他们的努力可能似乎太小，不能在历史上留下印迹……

泰戈尔的这些话清楚地表明了他对印度与中国文明交往的重视程度。

一 中国学院成立的初始阶段

自从中国学院成立以来，它一直是一个独特的研究机构，为中国学者研究印度的文化、哲学、宗教和语言，为印度学者学习中国的文化、历史、哲学、语言等提供便利。佛教是 印度—中国文化接口的重要媒介，中国学院特别关注佛教研究和佛典经卷的研究，并且将中国汉传佛教经典重新回译为梵文版本的经典。

该机构吸引了不少学生和学者，既有来自中国和印度各地的，也几乎包括所有亚洲、非洲、欧洲和美国的。外国留学生大部分来自斯里兰卡、日本、缅甸、泰国和尼泊尔。所有这些学者的研究成果以书籍出版或者论文形式发表在印度和国外的学术刊物上。除了进行大量的佛经翻译工作外，中国学院还开始出版期刊“中印杂志”。中国学院受到了许多来访的杰出人士以及给予中国学院财力支持的资助人的极大重视。

从1937年成立，直至1970年，被认为是中国学院学术活动的黄金时期。在中国学院成立的初期，除了中文外，中国学院还开设了藏文和梵文等各种语言课程。在此期间，中国学院还出版了许多书籍，组织了各种讲座，为那些前往中国学习和研究的学生提供了许多奖学金。所有这些学者所进行的研究都遵循了中国学院的学术理想即把早期的汉语类佛教经典翻译为英文，包括现代印度语翻译也是其中的重要领域。他们主要工作集中在佛教、印中关系、中国历史、中国艺术与比较研究等方面。一些中国学者也将泰戈尔的作品从孟加拉语翻译为中文。

后来，这些人都成为了该院中国研究的核心。此外，还有一些学者组成了中国文化艺术圈，如徐志摩、徐悲鸿、陶行知和张德谦等人，他们或访问过中国学院或在那里工作过。徐志摩与泰戈尔在圣地尼克坦建立了深厚的友谊。

二　中国著名学者在过去 75 年间对于印中学术和文化互动中的贡献

在谈论中国学院时，我们必须考虑到在印度–中国教育和文化交流发展方面做出巨大贡献的一批学者的成就。首先，中国学院的灵感和灵魂当然是泰戈尔，接下来的两位教授是谭云山和师觉月。谭教授的独特个性在于将儒家伦理与佛教教义相结合，诠释了儒家自我修养的仁、义与佛教教义怜悯（karuna）、智慧（Prajana）和忍耐（ksanti）的结合，从而体现了两国精神文化的最高价值。谭云山强调这是我们文化的精神基础，热切希望两国人民能为面临现代冲突的世界做个好榜样，让其他国家受到启发，进而仿效他们，因为这是消除冲突和迎接世界持久和平的最好办法。用这种方式，人类将给这个地球带来一个消除贪婪、不安全、仇恨和冲突的乌托邦（mahasamata），世界本身将成为一个幸福的居所（sukhavati dhame）——这是一个拥抱全人类幸福的愿景。

谭云山担负起恢复印度与中国之间中断近千年联系的责任。与玄奘来到印度学习并将其丰富的哲学财富带回祖国回馈自己同胞不同的是，谭云山不仅深入到印度文化的源泉，而且如同孔夫子一样充满了仁慈之心，他定居在圣地尼克坦，把印度当成了自己的第二个家，为印度人传授中国文化和文明的精华。作为一个热心的佛教学者，谭云山有着虔诚的宗教信仰，他的谦逊和安静是中华文明的象征。作为泰戈尔真正的门徒、朋友、合作者和同事，谭云山不仅是一个有思想远见的人，而且还是一位真正的行动者，因此，他无疑是印度国际大学最具魅力的人物之一。

师觉月博士是在印度从事中国研究的老前辈，而与他同时代的大多数受过教育的印度人对于中国多元文化遗产及其对印度历史的重要性是无动于衷的。从 1945 年至 1947 年的两年间，师觉月就与中国学院有了联系，后来又成为中国学院的教授。他也是印度国际大学的研究主任。他主要从事佛教研究，并在中国从事印度学的教学工作。他通晓古代汉语、梵语、藏语、尼泊尔语以及其他一些中亚语言。他主要研究印度与中国的佛教文化交流。师觉月关于中国文化全面科学的研究与其丰富的研究成果使得他在20世纪从事汉语学习的印度学者中具有非同凡响的分量。他也是世界上第一位撰写中印联系特别是历史调查的作者。《印度与中国：千年文化关系》这本书提供了有关印度与中国之间相亲相爱的信息。他对印度与中国这一阶段的兄弟关系进行了非常学术化和全面的调查。师觉月博士还收集和翻译了几本古代中国的年鉴，其中载有公元前印度的历史和地理学的基本信息。此外，他还翻译了中文中有关印度的纪录，如把公元7世纪（唐代）道宣编辑的《释迦方志》译成英文，这是从一个佛教徒角度出发的有关中亚和印度的系统地理知识，是对著名的玄奘记录（《大唐西域记》）不可或缺的补充。在工作和生活中，师觉月是一位完美的中印学专家。除了师觉月教授外，还有一批与中国学院有关的知名学者是Pandit Vidusekhara Sashtri、P.V. Bapat、V.V. Gokhale、Sujit Kumar Mukhopadhyaya、Santi Bhikksu Sastri、N.Aiyaswami Sastri 和 Prahlad Pradhan 等。年轻一代的学者还包括 Krishna Kinker Sinha、阿米坦德拉纳特·泰戈尔等人。

作为中国研究的学者，1942年，辛哈（Krishna Kinkar Sinha）教授加入印度国际大学的中国学院。他在谭云山教授的指导下，学习汉语和中国古典文献。在中国，辛哈教授是第一位被任命为教授印地语和印度文化的印度教授。他还把中文翻译成为印地语，他的一些作品包括：《现代中国》（1914）、《三民主义》（1948）和《中国的命运》。

从1937年至1971年谭云山主持中国学院的工作期间，中国学院各类学者的作品旨在突出佛教在印中文化互动中发挥的重要作用，包括在世界文化交流史上起到的特殊桥梁作用。在中国学院成立的初期，有很多热心学者进入中印研究领域。中国学院成为中国和印度学者的聚会场所。

三 中国学院在印度与中国文化交流中的先驱作用

自从中国学院成立以来，无论是官方和私人学者的访问量都增加了，其中一些访客是非常特别的。如圣雄甘地、尼赫鲁等都至少不止一次访问过中国学院。当尼赫鲁访问印度国际大学时，他就对中国学院产生了特殊的兴趣。当著名中国艺术家徐悲鸿于1939年来到印度国际大学时，还在中国学院担任了一年的中国艺术客座教授。在1941年，蒋介石和夫人访问了中国学院，并在泰戈尔在和平乡的住所（Uttarayana）进行了短暂停留。新中国总理周恩来由副总理贺龙元帅陪同访印也是印中关系史上的一件大事。1957 年 1 月 30 日，印度国际大学授予周总理名誉文学博士（Desikottama）学位，在他来访期间，向中国学院赠送了大量关于现代中国文学、历史、政治、经济学以及一些再版经典共计超过万册的图书，他还向泰戈尔的纪念馆捐赠了 6000 卢比。在此之前，1940 年国民政府的考试院长戴季陶也访问过中国学院，他用中文写作了一篇短文，追溯了印中两国的历史交往并祈愿两国能够重建友好关系，现在这篇文章就刻在中国学院大楼一侧的墙上。太虚大师率领的第一个中国佛教代表团也访问过国际大学。

法舫法师也是太虚大师的门下弟子，他于 1942 年来到印度国际大学中国学院专门研究佛教。在他留学圣地尼克坦期间，他学习巴利语、梵语和英语。1945 年，他去锡兰的南方学校学习，并于一年后应谭云山教授的邀请返回圣地尼克坦担任中国佛教的讲师。法舫法师为加强中印文化交流做出了巨大贡献。法师还撰写了《佛教人生观》《佛教秩序》和《印度文化》等著作。著名学者和政治家对中国学院的强烈兴趣一直激发着年轻一代学习印中的文化与文明，以及致力于中印之间的协作伙伴关系。

除了官方的学者交流外，从 1937 年至 1960 年代末期的中国学院还接受了印度、中国、日本和锡兰大约 40 名知名的研究人员或学生来访，他们在不同时期来到中国学院学习。所以，从中国来的大多数人还是回到中国继续从事学术研究。其中三人还被邀请到西方，在美国和加拿大的大学教授亚洲研究课程。

一些来自中国的知名访客如吴晓铃和夫人石真（1941—1945）、巫白慧（1942—1952）、史舒鲁（Shi Shulu）（1938—1942 和 1948—1956）、周达夫（1939—1947）、杨云彦（1944—1952）、常任侠（1944—1945）、徐虎（1944—1950）、于玉山（Yu Yusan）（1948—1950）、冉云华和他的妻子（1953—1970），金克木（1941—1945）等。除了来自中国的杰出访客外，还有来自其他国家，如斯里兰卡、德国、美国、日本、缅甸、泰国和尼泊尔等国的学者，他们也在不同时间访问了中国学院。如卡林顿·古德里奇（Carrington Goodrich）在 1953 年至 1954 年也任教于中国学院，苏门曼加拉牧师（1937—1941 和 1943—1944）和牧师潘纳西里（1941—1946）以及许多来自斯里兰卡的学者也都在中国学院任教和从事研究。

四　中国学院近年来的发展

近几年到中国学院访问的学者教授多以短期为主，他们举办讲座，对促进印度与中国的学术交流与友谊作出了重大贡献。包括魏凤江教授、耿引增教授、杜维明教授、周福成教授、林成杰教授、董友沉教授和白开元教授等都值得特别提及。2009 年 1 月，北京大学历史文献研究中心的两位教授来到中国学院进行为期两个月的工作，对中国学院保存在学院图书馆的古籍进行了编目。这就表明中国各大学的学者对来到中国学院从事研究工作很有兴趣。

鉴于印中两国学者日益增加的文化交流，现在正是探索中印大学之间学术和文化合作新途径的时候了。为了鼓励两国人民之间的接触与合作，2011 年 7 月，印度共和国印度国际大学和中华人民共和国云南大学在昆明签署了谅解备忘录。按照这个计划，来自这两所大学的大约 200 名学生访问了对方的研究机构。该计划的实现可能要归功于与中国学院有关的许多学术精英的终身学术奉献和成就。2014 年 11 月，中华人民共和国主席习近平授予印度国际大学中国学院“和平共处五项原则”奖，奖励中国学院在维护和平共处五项原则，加强中印人民之间的友谊和促进世界和平与发展方面的贡献。

2016 年 11 月 3 日，印度国际大学中国学院图书馆与中华人民共和国上海图书馆签署了“谅解备忘录”（MOA）。在两个图书馆之间签署这种备忘录对印中教育交流具有十分重要的意义。2016 年 12 月 31 日，印度国际大学与云南民族大学还在昆明市签署了“谅解备忘录”，旨在进一步推动各自机构的学术目标，促进印度国际大学和云南民族大学师生之间更好的了解。

印度国际大学中国学院一直致力于教师培训课程，由中国北京大学专家进行汉语教学新技术的授课，为全印各地从事汉语教学和研究工作的教师和研究者提供相应的培训工作。

中国学院的成就可以总结为以下三点：

1. 中国学院是一个印中文化对话的场所，目的在于促进思想交流，促进中印双方相互了解。

2. 中国学院是一个印中感情的摇篮。通过泰戈尔和谭云山的不懈努力，中国学院将印中友爱的情感传播到了印度的其他地区。

3. 中国学院是印中文化与教育互动的纽带。

中国学院的成立是印中文化交流史上的一个重大事件。自它成立以来，中国学院就为印中文化交流提供了一个稳定的平台，有助于加强各个领域的印中关系，已经并将继续吸引了来自世界各地的学者和学生。作为印度国际大学不可分割的一部分，中国学院已在培育印中文化关系方面发挥出了领头羊的作用。

Visva-Bharati Cheena Bhavana: Pioneer in Fostering India-China Relations

Avijit Banerjee / India

Associate Professor and Head of Department of Chinese Language and Culture (Cheena Bhavana) of Visva-Bharati University

India and China, the two ancient civilization of the World have a long traditional friendship. The culture of any nation develops and strengthens during the exchange and fusion with the culture of the other nation. The cultural relations between India and China can be traced back to very early times. The close contact between India and China spanning for more than one thousand years was extremely fruitful in the dissemination of Indian culture in China. There are numerous references to China in Sanskrit texts – India's epic *Mahabharata* refers to China several times, including a reference to presents brought by the Chinese at the Rajasuya Yajna of the Pandavas; also, two other ancient books of India *Arthasastra* and the *Manusmriti* mention China. One can find the cultural influence of India on Ancient China in the field of Music and Dance, Literature, Architecture, Painting, Sculpture etc. Since the link of the two countries at that time chiefly depended upon Buddhism, so when Buddhism died out in India, the one nation was severed from the other. The political development in the later centuries further prevented close intercourse.

This old friendship was not resumed until 1924 when Rabindranath Tagore came to China. Rabindranath Tagore was not only a forerunner in envisioning a globalized world community but also lived his entire life as a veritable citizen of the world. In his day, Tagore was a pioneer for successfully founding Visva-Bharati in 1921, a university that was truly international in its philosophy, goals and curriculum. The awakening of India-China cultural renaissance in the 20th century is mainly due to the vision and effort of Rabindranath Tagore. Tagore's visit to China not only brought home to the Chinese the high attainments of Indian civilization but also awakened in the Chinese minds the grandeur of the Eastern Civilization. In Tagore's view, the cooperation between Indian and Chinese civilization was not only related to the future development of India and China, but also related to the future of Asia and of the World at large. He felt that India-China civilization was the mainstay of the Oriental civilization. Tagore sought to revive and strengthen the historical relationship between the people of both these Trans- Himalayan ancient countries through various academic research projects on "Sino-Indian Cultural Studies" collectively undertaken by the scholars of China and India and by scholars of many other countries. It was Tagore's global vision that helped establish Cheena Bhavana (中国学院) in 1937, the only one of its kind in India at that time.

After Tagore's visit to China, cultural interactions between the two countries gained substantial developments both in dimension and in depth. In the first place, Indian studies in China expanded to philosophy, history, society, language and other fields. Universities began to have curricula in such subjects. Secondly, Chinese scholars and students began to visit India, studying and pursuing research on India. They included Zeng Shengdi, Tan Yunshan, Xu Zhimo, Xu Dishan, Gao Jianfu, Hai Weiliang etc. Thirdly, the most outstanding fruition was the establishment of the Sino-Indian Cultural Society and Visva-Bharati Cheena-Bhavana. A large number of people in China related to the field of art and literature gained interest about Tagore after his visit to China in 1924. Thus, the researchers got a huge opportunity of cultivating many rich fields. The Cheena Bhavana that was created and moulded by Tan Yun-shan was in fact a multi-national institution with an element of cultural infusion into India from china.

Rabindranath Tagore came to China in the year 1924 at the invitation of the Lecturer's Association of Peiping. He delivered speeches on Indian culture and civilization at various cities of China. During this visit, he discussed at large with China's academic circle on exchange of scholars and professors. Tagore made a deep impression upon the Chinese mind. After his return from China, Tagore started the programme for Chinese Studies in Visva-Bharati in 1926 with the help of the French savant Prof. Sylvian Levi and a Chinese scholar Lin Wojiang. Prof Tan Yunshan, the Founder Director of Cheena Bhavana came to Santiniketan in the year 1928 and made tireless efforts in setting up a Research Department of Chinese Studies in Visva-Bharati. Tan Yunshan went back to China and discussed the ideals and objectives of Gurudeva with the then Vice chancellor of Peking University Dr. Cai Yuanpei and Dr. Dai Jitao, Minister of culture in Kuomintang Government. All these Chinese personalities enthusiastically responded to the ideas and in the year 1933, the Sino-Indian cultural society was formally established in Nanjing with Cai Yuanpei as its first President and Tan Yunshan as its first secretary. The society was aimed at arousing the people's attention to the noble ideals of spiritual culture of the two nations, i.e. peace, universal love, freedom and equality; also to promote culture exchanges and friendship between the people of the two countries. The society also planned to donate books and manage funds for building Cheena Bhavana. In the year 1934, the Sino-Indian Cultural society was set up in Santiniketan with important personalities like Dr. Rajendra Prasad, Dr. Radhakrishnan, Dr. Zakir Hussain and many others from cultural and educational circle as members. The programme of the society was to organize Indian Cultural delegations to go to China and the reciprocal visits of the Chinese delegation to India for conducting research work and delivering lectures on Indian and Chinese culture; recommending Indian students to study in China and Chinese students to study in India; establishing an

Indian institute in China and a Chinese Hall in India; publishing book and journals etc.The work of the Sino-Indian cultural society during this time was focused on the establishment of a China Study Centre and finally Cheena Bhavana came into existence with the following objectives:

i. To conduct research studies in Indian and Chinese Learning.

ii. To promote interchange of Indian and Chinese cultures.

iii. To cultivate friendship and fraternity between the two nations of India and China.

iv. To join and unite the people of India and China.

v. To promote jointly, universal peace and harmony of humanity.

vi. To help in building up "The Great Unity" of the world.

Tagore aspired to see this institution playing a significant role in Sino-Indian relationship, as reflected in the general rules of the university, which is as follows:

> "The objective of this department (Cheena-Bhavana) shall be to establish and promote cultural exchange between China and India for which purpose it will provide facilities for Chinese scholars to study Indian languages, literatures, history, religion, philosophy etc. as well for Indian scholars to study Chinese language, literature, religion, philosophy etc. — Buddhism being regarded as the nucleus for all such studies."[1]

Tagore presided over the function with great joy, because his vision of a cultural renewal between the two nations had been translated into reality, and the Cheena-Bhavana is a living symbol of this reality. Jawaharlal Nehru, India's former Prime Minister send his daughter Indira Nehru to represent him at the opening ceremony of Cheena Bhavana. She read her father's inspiring message which states:

> "It is a very rare opportunity in my life to participate in such a grand ceremony. Therefore, with infinite delight I made a promise to come and take

1 Tan Yunshan, "Twenty Years of The Visva-Bharati Cheena Bhavana-1937-1957" , p.20, Sino Indian Cultural Society of India, Calcutta, 1957

part; I firmly believe that I must come and join in the celebrations. Because the greatness of this ceremony does not confine itself to the ever lasting memories of these two countries in the past, but also points to the great expectation of their friendship in the future. Thus, it will forge a new link which will enable our two countries, India and China to come closer to each other in due time." [1]

Besides, India's Father of the Nation Mahatma Gandhi also sent a message to bless this historical event. In his letter he said:

"I hope this Cheena-Bhavana is a symbol of renewed relations between India and China."[2]

Furthermore, during the inauguration at Cheena Bhavana, Tagore in his speech said:

"This is, indeed, a great day for me, a day long looked for, when I should be able to redeem, on behalf of our people, an ancient pledge implicit in our past, the pledge to maintain the intercourse of culture and friendship between our people and the people of China, an intercourse whose foundations were laid eighteen hundred years back by our ancestors with infinite patience and sacrifice. When I went to China several years ago I felt a touch of that great stream of life that sprang from the heart of India and overflowed across mountain and desert into that distant land, fertilizing the heart of its people. I thought of that great pilgrimage, of those noble heroes, who, for the sake of their faith, their ideal of the liberation of self that leads to the perfect love which unites all beings, risked life and accepted banishment from home and all that was familiar to them. Many perished and left no trace behind. A few were spared to tell their story, a story not of adventurers and trespassers whose heroism has proved a mere romantic excuse for careers of unchecked

---

1 Tan Yunshan, "Twenty Years of The Visva-Bharati Cheena Bhavana-1937-1957" , p.16, Sino Indian Cultural Society of India, Calcutta, 1957

2 Tan Yunshan, "Twenty Years of The Visva-Bharati Cheena Bhavana-1937-1957" , p.16, Sino Indian Cultural Society of India, Calcutta, 1957

brigandage, but a story of pilgrims who came to offer their gifts of love and wisdom, a story indelibly recorded in the cultural memory of their hosts. I read it when I was received there as a representative of a revered race and felt proud as I traced the deep marks our ancestors had left behind on their achievements…"[1]

"The Hall which is to be opened today will serve both as the nucleus and as a symbol of that larger understanding that is to grow with time. Here students and scholars will come from China and live as part of ourselves, sharing our life and letting us share theirs, and by offering their labours in a common cause, help in slowly re-building that great course of fruitful contact between our peoples, that has been interrupted for ten centuries. For this Visva-Bharati is, and will, I hope, remain a meeting place for individuals from all countries, east or west, who believe in the unity of mankind and are prepared to suffer for their faith. I believe in such individuals even though their efforts may appear to be too insignificant to be recorded in history…"[2]

I. Cheena Bhavana in the Initial Phase

Since its inception, Cheena Bhavana has been a unique institution of research, providing facilities for Chinese scholars to study Indian culture, philosophy, religion, language, and for Indian scholars to study Chinese Culture, history, philosophy, language etc. As Buddhism was an important medium for India-China cultural interface, Cheena Bhavana paid special attention to Buddhist studies, study of Buddhist scriptures, and to the re-translation of translated Chinese Buddhist texts back into Sanskrit.

The institution attracted a good number of students and scholars particularly from China and various parts of India, from almost all Asian countries and also from

1 Tan Yunshan, "Twenty Years of The Visva-Bharati Cheena Bhavana-1937-1957" , p.41, Sino Indian Cultural Society of India, Calcutta, 1957

2 Tan Yunshan, "Twenty Years of The Visva-Bharati Cheena Bhavana-1937-1957" , p.42, Sino Indian Cultural Society of India, Calcutta, 1957

Africa, Europe and America. The larger chunk of the foreign students came from Sri Lanka, Japan, Myanmar, Thailand and Nepal. The research outputs of all these scholars were published either in book form or articles in periodicals and other academic journal of India and abroad. Besides, a voluminous amount of translation works was carried out and the department started the publication of the 'Sino-Indian Journal'. The department has also been privileged by the visits of many distinguished personalities and patrons who greatly enriched the institution with their donations for financial support.

From the time of establishment of Cheena Bhavana in 1937 till 1970 was regarded as the golden period for academic activities in Cheena-Bhavana. In the initial period, there were various language courses in Cheena-Bhavana besides Chinese such as Tibetan, Sanskrit etc. During this period, many books were published, various lectures were organized and there were many scholarships for the students studying and pursuing research on China. The research carried out by all these scholars followed the academic ideals of Cheena-Bhavana. Restoration of original Buddhist classics in translation from Chinese to English and modern Indian Languages were also important areas of their research activities. Their main focus was on Buddhism, India-China Relations, History of China, Chinese Art and Comparative Studies. Translation of Rabindranath Tagore's works from Bengali to Chinese was also undertaken by some Chinese scholars.

Later on, these people became the nucleus of China studies research. Moreover there were some others scholars form China's culture and artistic circle like Xu Zhimo（徐志摩）Xu Beihong（徐悲鸿）Tao Xingzhi（陶行知）Zhang Deqian（张德谦）who visited Cheena Bhavana or worked here for a short time. During his stay at Santiniketan Xu Zhimo（徐志摩） forged a profound friendship with Tagore.

II. Contribution of Renowned Scholars in Cheena Bhavana in the India-China Academic and Cultural Interaction in the Last 75 Years

While talking about Cheena-Bhavana we must take into account the association of a galaxy of scholars who contributed immensely in the development of India-China education and cultural exchanges. The fountain-head, the inspiration and the soul was of course Tagore. Next were Professors Tan Yun-shan and P.C. Bagchi. Prof. Tan was a unique personality who combined the Confucian ethic with Buddhist teachings highlighting the values of Ren (benevolence) Yi (righteousness) of the Confucian way of self-cultivation in Synthesis with karuna (compassion,) Prajana (wisdom) and ksanti (forbearance) and other trails of Buddhism, thus uploading the highest value of both the countries. He emphasized the spiritual basis of our culture and ardently hoped that the two peoples set in this strife ridden modern world good examples so that other nations are inspired to emulate them. This was the best way of eliminating conflict and war of ushering in lasting world peace. In this way humankind would bring about Datong (mahasamata) utopia in this globe where greed, insecurity, hatred and conflict would disappear, and the world itself would become a sukhavati dhame (abode of happiness) – a vision that embraces the happiness of all humanity.

Tan Yunshan was responsible for reviving the broken intellectual bonds between India and China after a discontinuation of nearly one thousand years. Unlike Xuan Zang, who came to India to learn and carry her wealth of learning and philosophy back to China for the benefit of his countrymen, Tan Yunshan not only drank deep into the fountain of Indian culture, but imbued with the thoughts of benevolence and charity like a true Confucian, He made India his second home, and settled down at Santiniketan for teaching Indians the cream of Chinese culture and civilization. An ardent Buddhist scholar, deeply religious, unassuming and quiet, he represented all that is best in Chinese civilization. The Poet's true disciple and friend, collaborator and co-worker, Tan was not a visionary but a man of action. He was undoubtedly one of the most fascinating personalities in Visva-Bharati.

P.C.Bagchi was the doyen of Chinese studies in India. He came on the cultural scene at a time when most educated Indians were either ignorant or indifferent to the legacy of the multifaceted Chinese heritage and its importance to Indian history. He was associated with Cheena Bhavana for two years from 1945 to 1947. P.C.Bagchi was a Professor of Cheena Bhavana and also the Director of Research in Visva-Bharati. He was engaged in the study of Buddhism and also went to teach Indology in China. He knew ancient Chinese, Sanskrit, Tibetan, Nepalese and some Central Asian languages. He was engaged in the study of India China Buddhistic cultural exchange. The comprehensive and scientific study of P.C.Bagchi on China's culture as well as the rich results of his research made him heavy weight personality among the Indian scholars engaged in Chinese study in the 20th century. He was also the first author in the world to write a special historical survey of India-China contacts. The book entitled "India and China: A Thousand Years of Cultural Relations" provide information about the ageless affinity between India and China. He gave a very scholarly and comprehensive survey of this phase of India China brotherhood. Dr. Bagchi has also collected and translated several sections of the Ancient Chinese Annals which contain materials for the history and geography of India during the first few centuries of the Christian era. He also translated a Chinese account of India, *She-kia-fang-che* 'the Land of the Sakyas' which was complied by Tao-Xuan in the 7th century A.D. It is a systematic geography of Central Asia and India compiled from the Buddhist point of view and forms an indispensable complement to the famous account of Xuan Zang.In his life and work, P.C.Bagchi exemplifies the perfect Sino-Indologist.

Besides Prof. Bagchi, some other renowned scholars who were associated with Cheena Bhavana were Pandit Vidusekhara Sashtri, P.V. Bapat, V.V. Gokhale, Sujit Kumar Mukhopadhyaya, Santi Bhikksu Sastri, N.Aiyaswami Sastri, Prahlad Pradhan and others. Slightly junior to them were Krishna Kinker Sinha, Amitendranath Tagore, Satiranjan Sen, K. Venkataramanan, V. G. Nair and others.

Prof Krishna Kinkar Sinha, a scholar of Chinese studies, joined Cheena Bhavana, Visva-Bharati in 1942.He learned Chinese Language and Chinese Classical texts under Professor Tan Yunshan. Prof Sinha was appointed as the first Indian Professor of Hindi and Indian Culture in China. He was engaged in the translation work from Chinese into Hindi and some of his works included:

i. Translation of "Modern china" of Prof. Tan Yun Shan, published by "Pandit Hazariprasad Dwivedi", Hindi- Bhavana, Shantiniketan in 1914.

ii.Translation of "San-Min-Chu-I" of Dr. Sun Yat Sen, published by the" Sino-Indian Cultural Society", Santiniketan, in 1948.

iii. Translation of "China's Destiny" of Marshal Chiang, published by "The Sino-Indian cultural society", Santiniketan.

Pandit Aiyaswami Sastri restored into Sanskrit a treatise on Logic named 'Karatalaratna' with critical notes and introduction. It is an important work of the famous Buddhist scholar, Bhavaviveka, who lived in the 6th century A.D. The work long lost is preserved only in a Chinese translation. Mr. Sastri also restored another important text of Buddhist philosophy named *Tattvasiddhi.* The author of the work, Harivarman, lived in the 4th century. The work is preserved in Chinese translation of the 5th century .

Rev. Shanti Bhikshu has restored into Sanskrit another text which was long lost in original. It is the *Bodhicittotpada-sutra-sastra* of Vasubandhu. It is a work on Buddhist philosophy which is preserved in a Chinese translation of the beginning of the 4th century A.D. This underlines the fact that in the initial phase of China Studies programme at Cheena Bhavana, a large portion of the work done by the scholars was related to Buddhism.

Mr. Satiranjan Sen translated into English two medical texts of which the Sanskrit originals were lost. They are only preserved in old translations .

Dr. Amitendranath Tagore translated a number of Jataka stories from Chinese Tripitaka of which the original was lost. He also translated other stories.

Prof. Prahlad Pradhan translated a chapter of the Vinaya of Dharmaguptaka school from its Chinese translation. The original work is now no more. Prof. Pradhan was also engaged in translating the entire Vinaya.

Mr. Sujit Mukherjea translated the Chinese version of a Dhyana text attributed to Kumarajiva and restored a treatise of Vijnanavada translated into Chinese by Paramartha. Mr. Sujit Mukherjea prepared a critical edition of the *Vajrasuci* with the help of available manuscript materials and its ancient Chinese translation.

Dr P.V. Bapat translated from Chinese a lost Sanskrit work called *Arthavargiya-sutra*. It corresponds roughly to the Pali *Atthakavagga*, but there are important differences between the two .Dr. Bapat also analyzed the Chinese Translation of the Pali-text the ‘Samantapasadika’ which is Buddhaghosa’s commentary of the Vinayapitaka.

Rev. Pannasiri carried out a comparative study of the different versions of the Sigalovada *suttanta*, a Buddhist text of great importance. There are four different Chinese translations of the text, besides the Pali version.

Mr. Pa Chow, a Chinese scholar who came from China to study at Cheena Bhavana made a comparative study of the existing Sanskrit version of the Avadanasataka and its ancient Chinese translation and collected important materials which throw light on the original version of the text.

Prof. Venkataramanan has produced a well-documented account of a difficult but important system of thought. His scholarly approach to his materials, his intellectual discrimination, and his command of Chinese sources earned him wide respect in India and abroad. Prof K. Venkataramanan was also well versed in modern Japanese Buddhist studies, and delivered lectures at various Universities in Japan.

A Chinese scholar Dr Wei Kuei Sun who came to Santiniketan under the official exchange programme continued as a faculty in Cheena Bhavana.

It is clear from the contribution made by the above mentioned scholars that, from

1937 till 1971 when Tan Yunshan headed Cheena Bhavana, the works of various scholars of Cheena Bhavana played a significant role in highlighting India-China cultural interaction with Buddhism playing the role of a bridge which is exceptional in the history of cultural connectivity of the world. In the initial stages of the establishment of Cheena Bhavana, a lot of enthusiastic scholars entered the field of Sino-Indian studies. Cheena-Bhavana became the meeting place of Chinese and Indian scholars.

III. India-China Cultural and Educational Exchange with Cheena Bhavana as the Pioneer

Since the establishment of Cheena Bhavana, there had been an increase in the exchange of visit of official and private scholars, some of which were very extraordinary ones. Mahatma Gandhi, Sarojini Naidu, Rajendra Prasad, S.Radhakrishnan, Jawaharlal Nehru, Maulana Abdul Kalam Azad had visited Cheena-Bhavana at least one or more. Jawaharlal Nehru took a special interest in Cheena-Bhavana whenever he visited Santiniketan. The famous Chinese artist Xu Beihong came to Santiniketan in 1939 and stayed in the Cheena Bhavana for about a year as Visiting Professor of Chinese Arts. The most outstanding event was the visit of Generalissimo and Madame Chiang Kai-shek in 1941. They saw the Cheena-Bhavana and made a brief stay in the Uttarayana, the Poet's residence at Santiniketan. The visit of the Prime Minister of China was a great event in the history of India-China relations. Zhou Enlai was accompanied by the Vice-Premier Marshal He Long. The then Premier was conferred the Honorary degree of Desikottama by Visva-Bharati in a special convocation on January 30, 1957. While visiting Cheena Bhavana, he gifted a unique collection of books on modern Chinese literature, history, politics, economics as well as some reprints of classics numbering more than ten thousand. He also donated a sum of rupees sixty thousand for Tagore's memorial. Prior to this, there was the good-will mission of Tai Qitao, President of the Examination Yuan of the Nationalist government in 1940. He wrote an essay in Chinese tracing the historical relations between India and China and praying for its renewal. This document, engraved on a plaque, was installed on a wall of the Cheena-Bhavana hall. The text is his essay on Sino-Indian cultural interface, and his impressions on Buddhist shrines visited by him, as well as his hope for the future improvement of India-China relations. The first Chinese Buddhist Mission to India led by Rev. Tai Xu visited Visva-Bharati and spent a week in Cheena Bhavana.

The Great Buddhist monk Grand Master FaFang, a prominent disciple of Rev. Tai Xu joined Cheena Bhavana, Visva-Bharati as a Research Fellow in Indian Buddhism in 1942.During his stay at Santiniketan, he studied Pali, Sanskrit and English. In 1945 he went to Ceylon to study the Southern School and returned to Santiniketan in 1946 on the invitation of Prof Tan Yunshan and became a Lecturer in Chinese Buddhism. Grand Master FaFang contributed immensely for strengthening Sino-Indian cultural exchange. Some of the books that Master FaFang authored were "Buddhist Outlook on Life", "The Order of a Buddhist, "Culture of India", etc. The keen interest shown by prominent scholars and statesmen towards Cheena Bhavana has been an inspiration for the younger generation in the study of Cultures and civilizations of India and China and Sino-Indian interface and synergy.

Apart from the official exchange of scholars, from the inception of the Cheena Bhavana in 1937 until the late 1960s there were about 40 known researchers or students from India, China, Japan and Ceylon who had, at different times, studied in Cheena-Bhavana. Consequently most of them returned to China for academic pursuits, and three of them were invited to the West to teach Asian studies in American and Canadian universities.

Some of the eminent visiting scholars from China who came to Santiniketan were Wu Xiaolin and Madame Shi Zhen (1941-1945), Wu Baihui(1942-1952), Shi Shulu (1938-1942 and 1948-1956), Zhou Dafu (`1939-1947), Yang Yunyan (1944-1952), Chang Renxia (1944-1945), Xu Hu (1944-1950), Yu Yusan (1948-1950),

Ran Yunhua and his wife (1953-1970), Jin Kemu (1941-1945), etc. Besides these illustrious visitors from China, there were scholars from other countries, namely, Sri Lanka, Germany, United States, Japan, Burma, Thailand, Nepal who visited Cheena Bhavana at different times. Libenthal was a visiting professor from 1954-57. Carrington Goodrich was attached to Cheena-Bhavana from 1953 to 1954. Reverend Sumangala (1937-1941 and 1943-1944) and Reverend Pannasiri (1941-1946), and many others came from Sri Lanka and worked as Research Fellows and teachers in Cheena-Bhavana. Shinya Kasugai from Japan was attached to Cheena Bhavana from 1956-1964.

IV. Recent Development in Cheena Bhavana

The Scholar-Professors who visited Cheena Bhavana in recent years for shorter period and delivered lectures have contributed greatly to fostering academic exchange and friendship between India and China. Among them were Prof. Wei Fengjiang, Prof. Geng Yinzeng, Prof. Du Weiming, Prof. Zhou Fucheng, Prof Lin Chengjie, Prof Charles Willemen Prof.Dong Youchen, Prof Bai Kaiyuan deserve special mention. Two Professors of Ancient Archives Study Centre of Beijing University came to Cheena Bhavana in January, 2009 for a period of two months to help Cheena Bhavana in the cataloguing of the ancient books preserved in the library of Cheena Bhavana. This underscores the fact that the scholars of the universities in China are still very much interested in pursuing research work at Cheena Bhavana.

In view of the increasing India-China exchanges among the scholars of both India and China, it is high time to explore new avenues of academic and cultural cooperation between the Universities of China and India. In order to encourage people to people contact and cooperation between the two countries, Visva-Bharati University, India and Yunnan University, Kunming, People's Republic of China signed an Memorandum of Understanding in July, 2011. Under this programme, about two hundred students from both the Universities had already visited each other's institute. The realization of this programme may be attributed to the lifelong scholarly devotion and contribution of many academic luminaries associated with Cheena Bhavana. In November, 2014 Xi Jinping, President of People's Republic of China has conferred upon Visva-Bharati Cheena Bhavana the "Five Principles of Peaceful Co Existence Award", for Cheena Bhavana's contribution in upholding the five Principles of Peaceful Co existence, strengthening people to people friendship and promoting world peace and development.

Visva-Bharati Cheena Bhavana Library has signed MOA (Memorandum of Agreement) with Shanghai Library, People's Republic of China on November 3rd, 2016 for three years. This MOA between the two libraries possess important significance for India China educational exchanges. Visva-Bharati University signed an MOU with Yunnan Minzu University,Kunming, China on 31st December, 2016 which is intended to further academic objectives of each institution and to promote better understanding between the faculty and students of Visva-Bharati University and the faculty and students of YMU.

Cheena-Bhavana, Visva-Bharati University has been organizing Teacher's Training Course where eminent faculties from Beijing University, China deliver lecture on the new techniques of teaching Chinese Language. Teachers and Research Scholars from various parts of India engaged in teaching and research of Chinese language participate in this programme.

The achievement of Cheena Bhavana can be summarized in three ways:

i) Cheena-Bhavana serves as the venue of India-China cultural dialogue, making ideas flow, resulting in India-China mutual understanding.

ii) Cheena Bhavana functions as the cradle of India-China affection. Starting from Cheena Bhavana, India China affection spread to other parts of India with the tireless efforts of Tagore and Tan Yunshan

iii) Cheena Bhavana acts as the link between India-China cultural and educational interactions.

The establishment of Cheena Bhavana is a significant event in the history of India-China cultural exchange. Since its foundation, Cheena Bhavana provided a stable platform for India-China cultural exchange which helped in the strengthening of India-China relations in various fields. It has already attracted scholars and student from all corners of the earth. As an integral part of Visva-Bharati, Cheena Bhavana is destined to play a very pioneering role in promoting India-China cultural relations.

中非价值观对比：两种和谐理念

塔迪斯·梅茨 【南非】
约翰内斯堡大学特聘教授

一　班图精神和儒家传统思想中“和谐”一词的含义比较

从相似点而言，两种传统都将“和谐”定义为人与人之间的关系，其中也包括人与自然的关系。另外，两种传统都认为和平是和谐关系中的基本要素。然而，他们也否认和平共处会破坏和谐，这两者都需要人与人之间更具整体性的东西。

具体来说，在两种传统中，和谐并非单纯意义上的相同观点或相同生活方式。儒家思想更是重点强调了此点，并经常引用《论语》中的名句“君子和而不同，小人同而不和”。在对中国传统中的和谐进行了多年研究后，李晨阳教授指出：“和谐是通过创造性张力中的不同元素相互作用产生的能量来维系的。”从非洲的价值观来看，和谐关系指的是一种友谊或友爱，要求人与人之间保持友好关系，但并非一定要求同；事实上，成为朋友或相互关爱，就是帮助对方找到其不同于他人之处或独特之处。

此外，对于两种传统而言，和谐关系包括互惠、互助和帮助参与者提高生活品质的行为。虽然和谐是一种关系性的善，而不是对个人固有属性的还原，但它仍然是一种条件，它包含了个人作为其一部分而生活得更好的期待。

最后，儒家与班图精神之间的主要相似点还在于二者均认可“家庭第一”、“仁爱始于家”等相关箴言。虽然两者都认为所有人类都应达到一种道德精神境界，但家庭成员在分配个人财力和其他资源方面原则上具有道德优先权。

除了这些相似性外，儒家世界观中的和谐与班图精神中的有所不同。

首先，虽然“儒家更强调人与人之间的和谐……[儒家] 并未排除内在的和谐”——这点与非洲道德准则不同，后者更在意的是人与人之间的关系。在非洲人看来，与他人分享同一种生活方式、关心他人的生活品质绝对是一种关心他人的做法，至少在哲学意义上确系如此，而儒家的和谐观则强调自我，比如个人的精神状态达到西方人所说的“有机统一”的境界。

其次，非洲人对和谐的理解以友好关系为基点，而“儒家则认为和谐（而不一定是友谊）源自于相反作用力之间的不断相互作用”。举个例子，撒哈拉以南地区希望人们能够创建一种团结一致的生活氛围，也就是说，将彼此称为“我们”，以对方的荣誉为荣。这显然不是中国和谐的必要条件，如果两个有对立态度的政党被适当地组织起来，也可以培养出和谐关系，也就是说，他们之间的紧张关系产生了创造性的东西，对双方都有利。

最后，撒哈拉以南地区对和谐关系的定义偏向于在做决定时的平等主义，而中国则并非如此。事实上，撒哈拉以南的传统社会以酋长和长者为统治阶层，其他人应向他们表示尊重，并且在家庭生活中，父权占统治地位。即便如此，在做决定时，酋长会尊重经大家选举产生的长者或所有牵涉到的成年人的一致决定。此外，在非洲传统中，人类尊严的观念较为显著，在这种传统中，和谐关系包括以寻求合作或咨询的方式尊重他人。相比之下，尊严，至少是将人权纳入政治参与的一种思想，并不是儒家道德思想的核心特征。儒家思想和更普遍的中国思想的特点是，相信“等级体系的自然性、必要性和必然性”。对于中国人来说，所有人都是不平等的，这点不言而喻。这种观点也常常体现在治理和社会地位（而不是财富分配）中。

二 传统非洲与中国和谐观点的当代表现

我认为非洲和中国的和谐价值观可以继续影响当代生活的三个主要方面，特别是政治、经济和社会。

1. 政治

在广泛的层面上，非洲和中国的传统，政治哲学家称之为“完美主义者”，也就是说，他们认为政府的重点应该是改善人们的生活质量，特别是培养他们作为道德存在的自我实现。尽管许多西方人，或至少是西方传统理论家认为，国家应该仅仅强化人们的个人权利，按照他们认为合适的方式生活，而旧时的人们则认为国家应该服务于国王的利益或思想，这两种观点在班图精神和儒家世界观中都没有体现。相反，后者强调了国家的目标应该是帮助其公民过上客观上符合他们需要的生活。这意味着不仅要满足公民的生物需求，使他们成为富裕人士，还要促进他们的良好道德或卓越的人际关系。

完美主义是道德体系的一个明确含义，认为和谐是一种中心价值。对于班图精神而言，请大家回想一下，珍视和谐包括表现出团结一致，即以预期会提高他人生活质量和利益的方式行事。同样，对于儒家来说，抽象的和谐就是通过对所有人都有利的方式缩小差异，往往与等级制度联系在一起。这种观点适用于政治，体现为统治者为提高下属生活而采取的所有行为。

虽然对于和谐的共同关注导致完美主义在非洲和中国的思想和实践中占据主导地位，但对于政府而言，差异性的和谐概念可能会对谁应该控制的观点产生争议。在流行语中，班图精神中的和谐规定双方民主，而儒家的和谐则倾向于“任人唯贤”。

如上所述，许多非洲人普遍认为，对和谐关系的重视是分享生活方式和关心他人生活质量，倾向于支持殖民前撒哈拉以南社会以预先决定为中心、以共识为导向的做法。事实上，非洲大多数著名的政治哲学家常常强调和谐的价值，他们建议应为当代国家提供一种更加丰富的民主政体，而不是多党竞争制度，即议员们就如何造福百姓而寻求一致意见。

虽然当时的非洲国家在独立后的时代没有采取这种共识，但这种趋势显然已经走向了某种民主。撒哈拉以南地区签署了著名的《非洲人权和民族权宪章》或《班珠尔宪章》。该宪章将人的尊严置于非洲价值的核心地位，并承诺政府支持将在日常实践中坚持一系列个人权利，其中许多涉及言论自由和政治结社自由。除了《班珠尔宪章》，包括“直接或通过自由选择的代表自由参与政府的权利”，非洲联盟成员还受其《民主、选举和治理宪章》的约束，许多撒哈拉以南非洲国家在过去30多年来已经开始施行多党选举制度。

与中国形成的对比显而易见。儒家关于和谐作为多样性中互利合一的概念，以及作为等级关系所促进和实现的内容，可能导致中国人民接受这种缺乏民主制度的事实，不仅在过去，也在当下。儒家常常被认为淡化“血统贵族”并坚持“高尚的德行”。

有人认为班图精神和儒家和谐观之间的差异有助于催生不同的政治权力体系，这点看似合理。然而，在这些差异的基础上，我注意到另一种自然归因于对和谐的关注的相似性，这种相似性建立在与现代西方政治力量截然不同的非竞争性和非多数主义决策模式之上。在传统的非洲，要求达到一致同意，而在中国传统意义中，最具资格的人员所制定的规则即为最好的。

2. 经济

社会学家们经常把这些特质放在“儒家动力论”（《中国文化连接》，1987）或“长期定位”的标题下，并强调他们的“前瞻性”维度。也就是说，训练、勤奋、毅力、节俭和节约意味着愿意放缓追求满足的步伐，放弃闲暇时间，并为了未来更大的收益而在传统面前调整。通过“长期定位”，这些理论家们并不是说中国政府或整个社会为了子孙后代果断采取行动，但是建议中国人应对和谐以及家人的福祉，包括他的后代保持基本关心。考虑到迄今为止我所提到的孝道、和谐和宽容的价值观，《中国文化连接》（1987）的研究发现，在构成了儒家集群的中国人价值观中，勤奋排在第二位。

在儒家动力论方面，中国在世界上所有国家中排名第一。相反，据说撒哈拉以南非洲地区坚持“短期定位”，这意味着不仅非洲人没有展现出儒家的活力特征，而且他们更倾向于：展示（民族或族裔）的自豪感，不愿承认他们需要向他人学习；呼吁民间智慧和传统，而不是科学证据；他们将成功或失败归因于命运、运气和环境，而不是努力或缺乏努力。或者说，霍夫斯泰德（Hofstede）和他的团队总结了世界价值观调查的结果，重点是非洲价值观调查也出现了类似结果。本次非洲价值观调查涵盖了撒哈拉以南各个非洲国家，并通过撒哈拉以南地区的本土观点来获取信息。

此外，非洲学者已经注意到，和谐或社群主义与班图精神相关的方式开始倾向于阻碍儒家动力论中的元素。

相比为了长期积累资本而节俭生活，传统非洲人更倾向于将和谐或社群关系解释为希望或至少鼓励他们在短期内消费，特别是用于大家庭和社会。工作和成功的关键不应该是为了自己的利益或财富本身（沃伦·巴菲特），而是要与其他人分享，包括非核心家庭成员。

应该清楚的是，儒家几乎不会把自我利益视为高于一切；相反，对于他们来说，和谐即意味着要调和自己的欲望，调节自己的利益满足，以便能够帮助他人。

然而，儒家和中国人通常更倾向于与自己的家庭保持和睦，并经常考虑到生意，尤其是储蓄和投资，作为为后代提供服务的一种方式。

在中国，研究人员已经注意到生意交易不再严格依据书面协议文字的趋势。西方人倾向于根据对合同的书面解读来解决争端，但中国人并不倾向于这样做。相反，后者经常呼吁和谐关系，双方通过创造性协同确定彼此之间应该发生什么，从而互惠互利。如果发生不可预见的库存短缺，中国的经理人会比美国人更愿意重新谈判合同条款。

这种方法有时总结为“人治”(即贤德之人)，与“法治”相对应。对于那些受儒家思想影响的人来说，负责人因为接受过培训并且具备智慧而处于优越地位，应该对其加以利用，以促进互利关系。书面协议是一种渴望进入或形成和谐关系的象征，以便公司领导人可以根据必要修改其内容以达到期望的目的。

“人治”思想对于中国的经商方式有着额外的影响，即通过知名度的“关系”战略。即中国人寻求建立、维持和丰富的和谐关系或“网络”。虽然关系存在于学校、组织、俱乐部等，但是在经济背景下的讨论最为广泛，因为商人都想发展非正式的互助关系。尽管关系纽带已经超出了家庭范围，但作为儒家思想的反映，它们属于家庭式，因为它们意味着长久可靠，不易被打破。简而言之，关系成员是一个人“组内”的一部分。使用这些连接取得成功是当代中国企业不可或缺的一部分，而西方人通常认为这是腐败现象，因为存在偏袒，缺乏用于分配资源的正式程序。

虽然撒哈拉以南地区与来自相似种族和语言背景的人有业务往来，但是并不存在特殊关系网影响中国业务的情况存在。也就是说，还有其他偏见和关系因素对非洲经济产生显著影响。例如，传统的非洲社会习惯于回报，并在对方给予好处时表示感谢。结果，一些非洲企业领导人向那些帮助过他们生意的人赠礼，有时甚至给政府官员送礼，这种做法被西方人定义为腐败。此外，“家庭第一”的定位并不经常被用来作为裙带关系的理由。

在撒哈拉沙漠以南地区，和谐问题继续影响企业的另一个例子就是时间的考虑方式。任何生活在撒哈拉沙漠以南或熟悉该地区的人都知道“非洲时间”。尽管这有时被认为是一种贬义词，并且不应被用作条条框框，但它代表一种真实的现象，即撒哈拉以南地区认为守时不如参与交易中所涉及的关系重要，和谐即表示给予他人更多的关注。如果一个人正在与某人谈话，并且所需时间超出计划，那么许多非洲人仍然会继续谈话，即使最终导致其他会面迟到。正如一位非洲学者所说的那样，“时间首先与社会义务相关，其次才是专业度”。

此外，传统撒哈拉以南社会的时间流动尚未在任何接近其资本主义的程度上进行管制，在这种情况下，为了公司的产出最大化和投入最小化，个人倾向完全被忽视。例如，期待社会化成为非洲前殖民时期小憩片刻的充足理由。此外，非洲人倾向于基于共识的决策意味着撒哈拉以南的工人希望在进行管理时能够进行实质性的咨询，这点也是非洲商业伦理学家经常推荐的做法，但是需要花费大量时间来寻找适合各方的前进方向。相比之下，中国人的和谐理念认为，下级遵守上级指示，以最适合集体的方式进行指导，更容易与有关守时、效率和工作场所等级制度的资本主义规范保持连贯一致。

3. 社会

与欧美相比，在撒哈拉以南地区和中国社会互动方面，值得注意的是人们思考自身关系的方式。关系不仅告诉我们，在非洲或是中国，一个人应该成为怎样的人，也透露了我们认为一个人应该成为怎样的人。在西方国家，人们习惯于通过自我的内在品质对自身进行定义，比如具体的爱好或价值观以及在特定场合不会因对方是谁而发生改变的品质。相反，在前文论述的两种非西方文化背景下生活的个体更趋向于通过外在品质定义自我。他们认为自己是谁时，经常会考虑存在关系或正在与之建立关系的对方是谁。在这种文化背景下，为了能够回答“我是谁”这个问题，人们需要确定自身的角色，比如某个族系中的成员、教师、教会成员等；而在给定时刻，他们认为自己是谁通常与他们正在担任的角色存在对应关系。在这一点上，曾有一位极具影响力的学者说道，“东方人认为一个人在与不同人打交道时，可以扮演不同的角色。”

现在让我们回到更为严格的评估思考，撒哈拉以南地区和中国社会互动的另一个显著相似点在于二者对于和谐关系的强调的产物为对待家庭的方式。在当代西方国家，鲜有人将结婚生子视为道德义务。婚姻和孩子是打造幸福生活的重要部分，但是对于欧美人或者至少对于西方道德哲学家与职业伦理学家而言，他们很少认为一个人选择单身或丁克属于违背职责，他们应该对自己的做法感到惭愧或羞耻。相反，对和谐的反复关注，特别是家庭生活中，已经表明非洲和中国受本土价值观影响的人群开始认为选择不婚和不生儿育女延续香火属于错误行为，而当代理论学者受其鼓舞，开始认为这种判据有理有据。对于两种传统文化而言，家庭是和谐关系的最重要的表达，凌驾于一个人一生中应追求的所有理想之上。

现在，我们需要做的是思考撒哈拉沙漠以南地区和中国的社会关系差异，以及在不同的和谐观念之下，如何做到纷纷效仿。虽然中非人民都认为在决定如何分配个人金钱、精力、时间和其他资源时，从道德层次出发，家庭应排在第一位，但与他人的社会关系在撒哈拉沙漠以南地区本土价值观的讨论中则更为显著。曾有学者说道，“在非洲社会中，人们热情好客，这点在其价值观中占较大比重”和“热情好客是非洲人民的主要价值观之一，从未曾忘却”。在前殖民时代，陌生人进入村庄后，往往体会到的是热情和慷慨，家庭成员会拿出最好的食物款待来客。并且几乎所有的当代非洲人认为热情好客是班图精神的精髓所在。

相反，这种定位“从传统的儒家观点来看难以证明”。非洲人倾向于认为每个人都有尊严，并坚持共融（同时也倾向于认为共融的实际关系最为重要），但中国人基本上不会抱有这样的思想。对陌生人的欢迎并不是中国社会文献中的一个显要主题，如果有的话，人们会发现，在被纳入他们的关系之前，中国人经常对“外来人群”保持警惕。

最后，非洲和中国社会之间另一个有趣的差异在于沟通的本质以及沟通如何受对和谐的不同理解的影响。为了说明这一点，请参阅一篇由奥古斯丁·萧特（Augustine Shutte）在第一本专门讨论班图精神的伦理书中进行的研究。他注意到一项在修道院里对两组修女进行的调查。这项研究发现，在完成必做的杂务和祷告后，德国的修女们经常通过编织或缝纫继续工作，而非洲的修女则是将时间用在了聊天。研究指出，每个修女群体都认为另一个群体道德缺失；德国人认为非洲人不够勤奋，而非洲人则反对认为德国人更关心实际问题而不是关心人。此外，在史蒂夫·比科（Steve Biko）对撒哈拉以南文化的分析中，他注意到西方人发现奇怪的是，非洲人倾向于为了对话而对话，而非达成任何结论或实现目标。

一般来说，撒哈拉以南地区对培养和谐（理解为身份和团结）关系的注重将人们的注意力引到了关系上，不惜代价，只为完成任务。用社会学的术语来说，则是交际或情感行为在战略或工具行动上占有更大的位置，至少与西方相比，非洲文化为了自身的利益而将前者视为和谐关系的一个实例。尽管学者们对中国人之间的交流持类似的观点，认为目标达成经常因对和谐的注重而被迫缓和，但似乎中国人倾向于少说话，认为沉默是金，西方人和非洲人则恰好相反。粗暴地说，非洲人似乎试图通过谈话来促进和谐，而中国人则是通过不说话来避免冲突。

三　结论

本文的核心目标是分析非洲和中国的本土主要价值观，并提出以下事实：和谐是一种概念，统一了两种传统中对和谐的深刻思考，突出了二者和谐观念之间的相同点和不同点，并以合理的方式提出这些相关概念如何继续影响当代思想和行为。具体地说，笔者关注的是撒哈拉以南地区的班图精神和中国儒学的伦理观，认为和谐关系的某些概念——简言之，前者的身份和团结以及后者的等级差异的互惠——在这两种道德体系中占据核心位置，并且这些传统的和谐理念解释了近期非洲和中国在政治、经济和社会相互作用方面的重要相似性和差异性。

在本文中，笔者发现二者在历史、地理空间和多样性方面都有着举足轻重的位置。笔者通过考察二者如何影响某些当代信仰和实践，对两个社会中存在的不同和谐概念进行了比较。如果本研究旨在发现中国和非洲，甚至与之相关的西方国家的某些事实真相，那么我们可以从和谐的不同表达，与团结或自治相比和谐是否更适合成为基本道德价值观，以及中国或非洲（或其他国家）对和谐的概念定义是否基于系统哲学等角度出发，来进一步扩充方法和途径。

Values in China as Compared to Africa: Two Conceptions of Harmony[1]

Thaddeus Metz / South Africa

Distinguished Professor, University of Johannesburg

I. Comparing Harmony in the African and Confucian Traditions

Let us first consider similarities between the indigenous African and the Confucian traditions when it comes to what is meant by "harmony". Both mainly have in mind certain ways in which people should relate to one another, while also tending to include those ways in which people should relate to nature. In addition, both maintain that peace is an essential element of harmonious relationships. And yet they also deny that peaceful co-existence exhausts harmony, which, for both, requires something much more integrative among people.

More specifically, both traditions reject the notion that harmony is merely a matter of everyone having the same views or living in the same way, about which Confucians are particularly emphatic, often quoting from the Analects: "The gentleman seeks harmony not sameness; the petty person seeks sameness not

1 "Values in China as Compared to Africa: Two Conceptions of Harmony" , cited from *Philosophy East and West*, Vol.67, No.2 (2017): 441-465.

harmony". Chenyang Li, who has most studied harmony in the Chinese tradition, remarks that "harmony is sustained by energy generated through the interaction of different elements in creative tension". On the African side, one need merely remember that a harmonious relationship is roughly a friendly or loving one and that for people to be friendly with one another is not essentially a matter of seeking to become the same; indeed, to befriend or to love another frequently means helping her to realize aspects in which she is different or even unique.

Still more, for both traditions a harmonious relationship is understood to be one that includes reciprocation, mutual aid, and similar behaviors that tend to make its participants better off. Although harmony is a relational good, not reducible to the properties intrinsic to individuals, it nonetheless is a condition that includes the expectation that individuals will live better lives for being a part of it.

For a last major similarity between Confucian and African conceptions of harmony, consider that both accept "Family first", "Charity begins at home", and related maxims. Although both ascribe a moral status to at least all human persons, family members have a principled moral priority when it comes to the allocation of one's financial and other resources, roughly because the harmony there is most intense.

Despite these similarities, the kind of harmony prominent in the Confucian worldview is not identical to what is typically found in the African tradition. First, as Li points out, although "Confucianism puts tremendous weight on interpersonal harmony… [it] does not exclude intrapersonal harmony"—unlike African ethics, which is typically understood to be strictly focused on relationship between persons. The African ideals of sharing a way of life with others and caring for others' quality of life are exclusively other-regarding, at least as a familiar philosophical package, whereas the Confucian notion of harmony can be self-regarding, for example applicable insofar as a single person's mental states form something like what Westerners would call an "organic unity".

Second, while the African understanding of harmony is well understood in terms of friendly relationships, Li further remarks that “Confucians see a harmony (not necessarily friendliness) coming out of this continuous interplay of opposing forces”. So, for example, whereas indigenous sub-Saharans would want people ideally to share a sense of togetherness, say, by thinking of themselves as “we” and taking pride in one another’s accomplishments, this is apparently not essential for Chinese harmony, which could be fostered if two parties with somewhat antagonistic attitudes were organized appropriately, namely so that the tension between them turned out to produce something creative and to be good for both sides.

Third, sub-Saharan notions of harmonious relationships tend toward egalitarianism with respect to decision-making, whereas Chinese ones do not. It is true that traditional societies below the Sahara usually had chiefs and elders, to whom others were expected to express respect, and that power within families tended to be patriarchal. Even so, when making a decision it was common for chiefs to defer to consensus among either elders who had been popularly appointed or all affected adults. In addition, the idea of human dignity has been salient in the African tradition, where a harmonious relationship includes the idea of treating others with respect in the form of seeking their cooperation or consulting with them. In contrast, dignity, at least of a sort thought to ground human rights to political participation, is not a central feature of Confucian moral thought. It has instead been characteristic of Confucian, and more generally Chinese, thought to believe “in the naturalness, necessity and inevitability of hierarchy. It is self-evident to Chinese that all men are born unequal” (according to Michael Bond), where this is understood to apply to governance and status (and not, say, the distribution of wealth).

II. Contemporary Manifestations of Traditional African and Chinese Harmony

I now consider the ways that African and Chinese values of harmony have plausibly continued to influence three major aspects of contemporary life, specifically politics, economics, and society.

1. Politics

At a broad level, both the African and Chinese traditions are what political philosophers call "perfectionist", meaning that they maintain that the point of government should be to improve people's quality of life and, especially, to foster their self-realization as ethical beings. Whereas many Westerners, or at least theorists from the Western tradition, these days maintain that a state should merely enforce people's individual rights to live as they see fit, and others in the past held that it should serve the interests or whims of a king, neither view has been salient in the African and Confucian worldviews. The latter instead highlight the idea that the state's aim should be to help its citizens lead lives that are objectively desirable for them. This means not merely meeting the biological needs of citizens and making them well off as individuals, but also promoting their moral good or relational human excellence.

Perfectionism is a clear implication of ethical systems that deem harmony to be a central value. For the African tradition, prizing harmony includes exhibiting solidarity that is, acting in ways that are expected to improve others' quality of life and for their sake. Similarly, for Confucianism, harmony in the abstract is a matter of bringing differences, often hierarchical, together in ways that are beneficial for all, which, applied to politics, consists of rulers doing what they expect will be best for subordinates.

Although a common focus on harmony has led to perfectionism being dominant in both African and Chinese thought and practice when it comes to the point of a government, differential conceptions of harmony have probably underwritten competing views of who should be in control of it. In catchwords, African harmony prescribes consensual democracy, while Confucian harmony inclines heavily toward meritocracy.

As was mentioned above, a prizing of harmonious relationships, roughly understood as the combination of sharing a way of life and caring for others' quality of life, has tended to support a consensus-oriented approach to decision making among pre-colonial sub-Saharan societies. In fact, often appealing to the value of harmony, several prominent African political philosophers writing in the post-independence era recommend a richer kind of democratic polity than a multi-party competitive system, namely one in which Parliamentarians seek unanimous agreement among themselves about what would be best for the public as a whole.

Although no contemporary African state has taken such a consensual system on board in the post-independence era, the trend has clearly been toward democracy of some kind. The sub-Saharan region is well known for having signed onto the African Charter on Human and Peoples' Rights, or Banjul Charter, which places human dignity at the core of African values and commits governments to upholding a wide array of individual rights, many of which, relating to freedom of expression and political association, are observed in day-to-day practice. And beyond the Banjul Charter, which includes the "right to participate freely in the government of his country, either directly or through freely chosen representatives" (Article 13), members of the African Union are bound by its Charter on Democracy, Elections and Governance, with many sub-Saharan states having introduced multi-party electoral systems over the past thirty years.

The contrast with China is patent. The Confucian conception of harmony as a mutually beneficial unity in diversity, and as something to be promoted by, and realized within, hierarchical relationships, has probably led the Chinese people to accept the lack of a democratic system, not only in the past but also today. Confucianism is often credited with downplaying a "nobility of blood" and upholding a "nobility of virtue".

It is plausible to suggest that the differences between the African and Confucian conceptions of harmony have helped lead to these divergent systems of political power. Yet, underlying these differences I note another similarity that is naturally ascribed to a concern for harmony; it has probably grounded non-competitive and non-majoritarian models of decision-making that are quite distinct from modern Western forms of political power. In the traditional African case, unanimous agreement is thought to be ideal, whereas, in the Chinese case, rule by the most qualified is considered best.

2. Economics

Social scientists have often brought certain traits together under the headings of "Confucian Dynamism" (the Chinese Cultural Connection) or "Long-Term Orientation" (the Hofstedes), and have emphasized their "forward-looking" dimension. Specifically, formal training, hard work, persistence, thriftiness, and saving indicate a willingness to delay gratification, to give up leisure time, and to adjust in the face of tradition for the sake of future, larger gain. By "Long-Term Orientation" these theorists do not mean to suggest that, say, the Chinese government or society as a whole is acting decisively for the sake of future generations, although they would suggest that a given Chinese person is substantially concerned about harmony with, and hence the well-being of, his family, including his descendants. Consider that alongside the values of filial piety, harmony, and tolerance, the Chinese Cultural Connection found industriousness to rank as the second highest value among Chinese people, the thought being that these values all form a Confucian cluster.

This scholarly group has also contended that China ranks first among all nations in the world when it comes to Confucian Dynamism. In contrast, sub-Saharan African is said to have a "Short-Term Orientation", meaning not only that African peoples on average have not exhibited the Confucian Dynamism traits as much, but also that they have been more inclined to the following: they exhibit (national or ethnic) pride, not freely admitting that they need to learn from others; they appeal to folk wisdom and tradition instead of scientific evidence; and they attribute success or failure to destiny, luck, and circumstance, as opposed to effort or its absence. Or so suggest the results of the World Values Survey, summarized by the Hofstedes. Of further interest are the similar results from the African Values Survey, which was developed to cover a wide variety of sub-Saharan countries and to be informed by indigenous sub-Saharan perspectives.

In addition, scholars of Africa have noted the ways in which a characteristically African conception of harmony has tended to militate against elements of Confucian Dynamism. Rather than being thrifty and inclined to save, which would enable them to build up capital in the long term, traditional Africans have tended to interpret a requirement to prize harmonious or communal relationships as expecting, or at least encouraging, them to spend in the short term, particularly on their extended family and society. The point of work and success should not be to amass wealth for its own sake à la Warren Buffett or for one's own sake, but rather to share with others, including people far beyond the nuclear family.

As should be clear, Confucians hardly prize self-interest above all else; instead, harmony for them means that one is to moderate one's desires and temper the satisfaction of one's interests, so as to be able to help others. However, Confucians and the Chinese more generally do prize harmony with their own families above all, and often think of business, and especially savings for and investment in it, as a way to provide for descendants.

For an additional way that the value of harmony influences economics, researchers have noted a tendency for business engagement in China not to be based strictly on the letter of a written agreement. Whereas Westerners tend to want to resolve disputes based on a black-and-white reading of a contract, Chinese are not so much inclined to do this. Instead, the latter often appeal to the expectation of a harmonious relationship, one in which both parties benefit from creative synergy, to determine what should transpire between them. If an unforeseeable shortage of stock was to occur, Chinese managers would be more disposed to renegotiate the terms of the contract than would, say, Americans.

This approach is sometimes summed up by "rule by men" (namely, virtuous people) as opposed to "rule by law". For those influenced by Confucianism, the persons in charge are in a superior position because of their training and wisdom, and they should be using it to foster relationships of mutual benefit. A written agreement is a symbol of a desire to enter into, or a formalization of, a harmonious relationship, so that a firm's leaders may revise its content as judged necessary to obtain that desired end.

The idea of "rule by men" has additional implications for the way business tends to be conducted in China, namely through the well-known strategy of guanxi. This is the term for harmonious relationships or "networks" that the Chinese seek to create, sustain, and enrich. Although they can be found in schools, religious organizations, clubs, and the like, they are most widely discussed in the context of the economy, where businesspeople seek to develop informal bonds of mutual aid. Although guanxi bonds are outside the family, they are, as a reflection of Confucianism, family-like, in that they are meant to be long-lasting and dependable, and not to be broken easily. In short, members of guanxi are part of one's "in-group". The use of these connections to get ahead is integral to contemporary Chinese business, and this is often viewed as corrupt by Westerners because of the partiality involved and lack of formal procedures used to allocate resources.

Although there is certainly some tendency among sub-Saharans to do business with those from a similar ethnic and linguistic background, there is little approaching the extent to which particularistic networks influence Chinese business. That said, there are other partial and relational elements that do notably influence the economy in Africa. For example, it is customary in traditional African societies to reciprocate and to show gratitude to someone when she confers a benefit on you. As a result, some African corporate leaders send gifts to those who have given them business, sometimes even to government officials, a practice that those from a Western background tend to find corrupt. In addition, the "family first" orientation has not infrequently been invoked as a justification for nepotism.

Another example in which a concern for harmony, as construed in sub-Saharan terms, continues to affect business is the manner in which time is regarded. Anyone who has lived below the Sahara, or is otherwise familiar with the region, knows of “African time”. Although this is sometimes meant as a derogatory expression, and should not be used to stereotype people, it denotes a real phenomenon, namely the tendency for sub-Saharans to see punctuality as less important than the need to attend to the relationships involved in a transaction, where an interest in harmony prescribes paying extra attention to the people immediately before oneself. If one is already engaging with someone in conversation, and it requires more time than had been planned, many Africans would stay with that engagement, even at the cost of not showing up on time for the next meeting. As one African scholar has put it, “The time is first related to the social obligations and....professionalism comes later”.

In addition, the flow of time in traditional sub-Saharan societies has not been regimented anywhere near to the degree that it is under capitalism, where personal inclination is utterly disregarded in favor of the firm’s interest in maximizing outputs and minimizing inputs. A desire to socialize, for example, would be a sufficient reason to take a break from work in the pre-colonial era in Africa, quite unlike a 21st century firm in a competitive environment. Moreover, the African inclination toward consensus-based decision-making means that sub-Saharan workers would like there to be substantial consultation on the part of management, a practice frequently recommended by African business ethicists despite the time it would take in order to find a way forward that suits all parties. In contrast, the Chinese idea of harmony, according to which inferiors conform to the dictates of superiors who direct in ways that are best for the group, more easily coheres with capitalist norms regarding punctuality, efficiency, and hierarchy in the workplace.

3. Society

One striking similarity between the sub-Saharan and Chinese social interaction that is a product of their emphasis on harmonious relationships concerns their approach to family. In the contemporary West, it is rare for people to think that there is a moral obligation to wed and to procreate. Marriage and children are typically deemed part of a good life, but it is uncommon for Euro-Americans, or at least Western moral philosophers and professional ethicists, to contend that one would be violating some duty about which one should feel guilt if one elected to remain single or childless. In contrast, the recurrent concern for harmony, particularly as manifested in the family, has meant that those in Africa and China influenced by indigenous values have tended to think that one would be doing wrong not to marry and to continue the family line, with contemporary theorists inspired by them continuing to find such judgment plausible. For both traditions, family is the most important expression of harmonious relationship, and is the one above all to realize during one's life.

Consider, now, some differences in social relationships between sub-Saharans and Chinese, and how they appear to have followed in the wake of their differing conceptions of harmony. Although both Africans and Chinese believe that moral priority goes to one's family when deciding how to allocate one's money, attention, time, and other resources, it is more typical of discussions of indigenous sub-Saharan values to find scholars saying things like "Great value is put on hospitality in African society" and "Hospitality is one of the main African values, which is still alive among Africans". When strangers visited a village in the pre-colonial era, they were typically treated with warmth and generosity, to the point that the best food would often be taken from family members and given to the visitors. And nearly all contemporary African thinkers take hospitality to be a quintessential expression of an ethic of harmony.

In contrast, such an orientation "is difficult to justify from a conventional Confucian standpoint" (according to Bell). Whereas Africans are inclined to think of everyone as having dignity and as being a potential site of communion (while also being inclined to think that actual relationships of communion matter most), the Chinese on average do not. Being welcoming of strangers is not a salient theme in the literature on Chinese society, and, if anything, one finds the suggestion that

Chinese people are wary of those considered part of an "out-group" until they are brought into their guanxi.

Finally, another interesting difference between African and Chinese societies concerns the nature of communication and how it appears to be influenced by different understandings of harmony. To illustrate this point, consider a study recounted by Augustine Shutte in one of the first books devoted to African ethics. He notes a survey that was taken of two groups of nuns at a convent. After the obligatory chores and praying were done, the study found that the German nuns often continued to work by knitting or sewing, while the African nuns did not and instead spent time in conversation. The study noted that each group of sisters deemed the other morally lacking; the Germans judged the Africans insufficiently diligent, while the Africans objectionably considered the Germans to care more about practical matters than about people. In addition, in Steve Biko's analysis of sub-Saharan culture, he notes Westerners finding it odd that Africans tend to engage in conversation for its own sake, and not to reach any conclusion or to achieve a goal.

Generally speaking, the sub-Saharan interest in cultivating harmony, understood as identification with others and solidarity with them, has led to a focus on relationship at some cost to task-fulfillment. To use sociological jargon, communicative or affective action has held a greater place over strategic or instrumental action, at least in comparison to the West, where African culture prizes the former for its own sake as an instance of harmonious relationship. Although scholars have made a similar point about communication among Chinese, to the effect that goal attainment is regularly tempered by an interest in harmony, it appears that Chinese tend to talk less and are comfortable with silence in a way that Westerners and Africans on average probably would not be. Crudely stated, it appears that Africans seek to promote harmony by talking, whereas Chinese seek to avoid conflict by not talking.

III. Conclusion

My central aims have been to analyze salient indigenous values in Africa and

China, to bring out the fact that harmony is a concept that unites much thought about them in both traditions, to highlight similarities and differences between their conceptions of harmony, and to suggest how these respective conceptions continue to influence contemporary thought and behavior. More specifically, I have focused on a widely held sub-Saharan ethic and Chinese Confucianism, argued that certain conceptions of harmonious relationship—roughly, of identity and solidarity for the former, and of mutual benefit from hierarchical difference for the latter—are central to both moral systems, and that these traditional conceptions of harmony explain both important similarities and important differences between recent African and Chinese political, economic, and social interaction.

I naturally have not sought to capture all indigenous values in these contexts, both of which are massive in terms of age, geographical space, and diversity, and I also have not tried to document all the various ways in which these major strands of traditional thought are still influential. Rather, I have sought to compare two different conceptions of harmony that have been salient in both societies by examining how they affect some contemporary beliefs and practices. If the project begun here is revealing with regard to China and Africa—and even the West in relation to them—then it would be worth extending in a variety of ways, say, by considering what additional manifestations of harmony there might be, whether harmony is a better candidate for a basic moral value than, say, utility or autonomy, and whether the Chinese or African (or some other) conception of it is to be preferred on systematic philosophical grounds.

越南语言中的汉文有助于越中关系的相通

阮荣光 【越南】
越中友好协会副主席 / 战略研究与国际发展中心顾问

中越关系可以从三方面来看。一是几千年来的两个民族关系；二是从 20 世纪 20 年代形成的两国执政的共产党之间的关系；三是 1950 年建交以来的两个国家间关系。其中，两个民族的关系是源远流长的，两国文化的交融使之更加紧密。

作为多年从事外交工作的我，深刻认识到任何友好关系都是要在互相了解的基础上建立起来的。没有互相了解就没有互相理解，当然也不会有友好关系。中越两国几千年的文化交流对两个民族互相了解起了骨干作用。

中越两国的文化相通应该包括宗教、哲学、风俗习惯、道德观念等领域。其中语言作为直接交流的桥梁，它的意义超出了文化的范畴。

我虽然不是语言学家，但是因为学过汉语，做过多年翻译，更加了解语言对两国文化相通的重要性，同时越来越看清楚汉语与越南语相同点。

一　汉语在越南语言形成过程中的作用

越南人借鉴和吸收了包括汉语在内的中华文化以便丰富本国文化。越南语受多国语言的影响，但主要的是汉语。

（一）汉文

根据语言学界的研究，在越南汉文出现之前，越南还没有文字。自从公元前 221 年秦朝统治越南起，汉文开始进入越南并成为汉人行政系统的官方文字。汉族文化的传播以及参加宣传汉文的越南贵族知识分子队伍的出现，使汉文字在越南日益流行。

郡县时期之后，虽然越南成为独立自主国家，但是越中两国仍然维持政治、经济、文化等领域的邦交。此时，在行政文件、科举制度、文学艺术创作之中，汉字和汉语始终是官方文字。

10 世纪之前，越南人使用汉字读法正如汉人，然而学汉语总被看成是学外语。10 世纪初，越南进入自主时期，越南人并不将汉语看做外语，继续使用汉字，但为适合越南人语音而改变了读音叫做“汉越音”并从此稳定使用至今。这种读法影响了越南语，使它更加丰富。

（二）喃字

不仅如此，汉字毕竟是外来文字，本来只有官吏、知识分子等上流阶层善于使用，而不可能满足越南广大人民群众的要求。在此环境下，越南人需要拥有自己的一套文字，因此在汉字基础上创造出喃字。喃字大部分借用汉字改变读音来记录普通的越南语。其余部分要借用汉字或汉字部首造成新字。喃字的造字方法有三种：一种是形声法，它是把两个汉字合成一个喃字，其中一个汉字表音，另一个表义。如“南 + 年” = “𢆥”，读音为“南”(năm)，意义为“年”。另一种是假借法，是借用一个汉字来表示与之读音相近的喃字，如借用“别”(biệt) 来表示“知道”(biết) 的含义。还有一种是会意法，也是用两个汉字组合而成，如用“天 + 上” = “𡗶”来表示“天”(trời) 等。喃字就是借用汉字各种要素结合而成的。没有汉字则没有喃字。喃字的普遍推广是越南文化重要成就。当时的越南把喃字看作“国语”“国音”。喃字越来越发展并逐渐能够正确地记录全部越南语词汇，文字也越来越简化。喃字已经成为完全能够记录社会生活中所有活动的真正的一套文字。喃字是保留越南丰富多彩的非物质文化遗产宝库的主要载体。但是喃字的形成以及发展离不开汉字，这是肯定的。

（三）拉丁字母文字

17 世纪初，西方传教士使用拉丁字母拼音越南语，越南文被拉丁化，并逐渐成为越南国语。但是，汉文与越南文的交流互动并未因此而中断。特别是在 19 世纪末 20 世纪初期，越南爱国人士们通过汉语书籍和报纸认识了梁启超、康有为、孙中山等人的进步思想，继而接受了马克思列宁主义。具体说来就是在政治、经济、社会等方面的现行理论术语绝大部分是借用的汉语。

二 汉语对现代越南语的影响

虽然现行越南文字是拉丁字母文字，但是它与汉语关系仍是密不可分。从词汇方面看，汉语的影响最突出。

（一）越南普通话中的汉语

根据越南语言学家的研究，现行的越南语词汇中借用汉语的比例在 60% 以上。这些词语以汉越音为读法，叫做汉越词。这种读法是自 10—11 世纪得到完善并至今稳定使用的。根据研究，汉越音是中国唐代汉语的古音，只是为了适合越南语音，经过稍微调整而成的读音。因此现代汉语和汉越词读音有所差异。如“政治” = “chính trị”，“文化” = “văn hóa”，“国防” = “quốc phòng” 等等。当然也有一些汉越词读音与广东话相近，如“局长”（Cục trưởng）、“五、六、七、八、九、十”（ngũ, lục, thất, bát, cửu, thập）等。还有一些借用汉语含义造成越南语新词，如军队编制名称：小队（班）、中队（排）、大队（连）、小团（营）、中团（团）等；或把汉越词与纯越词合成新词，如“binh lính”（士兵）、“tàu hỏa”（火车）、“thì giờ”（时间）。

越南语借用汉语词有两个目的：一是补充越南语缺少的词汇。越南语形成初期，缺少大量词汇，尤其是在政治、法律、经济、国防、教育、文化、文学、艺术等领域。为了补充所缺词语，越南人一方面根据越南语造词原则创造新词，另一方面借用大量汉语词汇。这主要是科技、政治、社会术语。二是创造出与越南语词语不同色彩的词汇。在郑重、客气环境下，一般不使用通俗词语而借用汉越词。如“夫人”（vợ 老婆）、“贵名”（tên 名字）、“逝世”（chết 死）、“出血”（chảy máu）等。这些是色彩不同的同义词。

（二）越南成语俗语中的汉语

自古以来，成千汉语成语使用在越南语言之中，普遍流行于日常生活中。一方面由于含义丰富而含蓄使这些成语能够广泛应用于日常生活，另一方面是因为越南社会受中国的宗教、道德观念的影响。这些定型的词组或短句是中国古人尤其是孔子、庄子、老子等贤人给后人留下的宝贵遗产，富有深刻的思想内涵。内容反映生活经验、人情世故、为人处世，人人须知。

相当普通、易记易用的成语一般保留原句和汉越音。例如：心投意合、百战百胜、万事起头难、万事如意、无名小卒、贪权固位等等。

其他一种有点改变，译成普通语言使人民群众易懂易用。例如：“Treo đầu dê bán thịt chó”（挂羊头卖狗肉）、“Nghìn cân treo sợi tóc”（千钧一发）、“Ếch ngồi đáy giếng”（井底之蛙）。

（三）越南文学中的汉文诗作

越南汉文诗的创作源远流长，历经丁、黎、李、陈、后黎、西山、阮氏等王朝，都有大量汉文诗作流传至今，它是越南文学艺术宝库中的重要部分，也是越南人精神的一部分。一千年来，从僧侣、王公贵族到广大士庶人等，从都城到各地乡村，万家吟诵汉文诗作，把它看作一种高尚乐趣，一种道德修养、欣赏方式。至今，对现代越南的文艺创作依然具有深远的影响。

从内容来看，越南古代的汉文诗继承和弘扬了儒教和佛教思想，又随着时代的潮流传播了爱国主义、反殖民主义思想，成为激励越南人民革命的犀利武器。

古诗偏爱天然美，
山水烟花雪月风。
现代诗中应有铁，
诗家也要会冲锋。
（胡志明《看〈千家诗〉有感》）

越南汉文诗的一个突出特点是平仄和韵调十分协调。中国的文庄教授是越南通，他认为，用越南语音吟诵汉文古诗比现代汉语语音更协调好听。原因在于，虽经历千年沧桑，越南仍完整地保留着中古汉语的音韵，加上越南语声调丰富（有六声分成平仄两调），并且，越南人作诗非常讲究，严格遵守平仄、韵调格律。例如：

唐代崔护的《题都城南庄》：

去年今日此门中，
人面桃花相映红。
人面不知何处去，
桃花依旧笑春风。

Khứ niên kim nhật thử môn **trung**（仄平平仄仄平平）
Nhân diện đào hoa tương ánh **hồng**（平仄平平平仄平）
Nhân diện bất tri hà xứ khứ（平仄仄平平仄仄）
Đào hoa y cựu tiếu xuân **phong**（平平平仄仄平平）

唐代王翰的《凉州词》:

葡萄美酒夜光杯,
欲饮琵琶马上催。
醉卧沙场君莫笑,
古来征战几人回。

Bồ đào mỹ tửu dạ quang **bôi**（平平仄仄仄平平）
Dục ẩm tỳ bà mã thượng **thôi**（仄仄平平仄仄平）
Túy ngọa sa trường quân mạc tiếu（仄仄平平平仄仄）
Cổ lai chinh chiến kỷ nhân **hồi**（仄平平仄仄平平）

胡志明的《元宵》:

今夜元宵月正圆,
春江春水接春天。
烟波深处谈军事,
夜半归来月满船。

Kim dạ nguyên tiêu nguyệt chính **viên**,（平仄平平仄仄平）
Xuân giang, xuân thuỷ tiếp xuân **thiên**.（平平平仄仄平平）
Yên ba thâm xứ đàm quân sự,（平平平仄平平仄）
Dạ bán quy lai nguyệt mãn **thuyền**.（仄仄平平仄仄平）

（四）贴挂对联，越南人的悠久传统

重视家庭家族是越南民族源远流长的美好传统之一。不少越南人使用对联作为传统建筑的室内装潢，特别是在家族祠堂室内。内容记载祖宗传给后人的为人处世原则、道德伦理或朝向追求的价值，也叫“gia đạo”（家道）。如：“福生富贵家堂盛，禄进荣华子孙兴”。为了表示这些家道源远流长，大部分横批对联使用高质量木材，雕刻汉字（繁体），雕饰讲究。这一文化传统主要在越南北部和中部流传。

此外，在越南一年最重要的节日——春节之际，像中国习惯一样贴挂春联。现在也有一些书法家书写现代越南文字（拉丁字母）做春联，但汉字还是相当普遍。

三 结语

越南语借用汉文或有关汉语词汇在推动双方互相了解起有积极作用，为越中两国人民创造互相理解互相接近的条件与环境。

语言和文化具有非常紧密的关系，各国语言学家都认为语言是文化的构成部分，文化又是语言的构成部分，两者交叉密不可分。它们之间互动互补，共同发展。换种说法，语言是所有知识的载体，也就是说，语言是民族文化的、个人思维的一部分。由此确定，中越两国的文化相通离不开语言相通。

正是文化和语言的相通成为推动越中两国关系的重要优势。在两党、两国、两国人民包括政治、外交、经贸、文化、科技等领域的合作关系都起有积极作用。虽然现今已不在日常生活和行文中使用汉字，但汉越音仍然是现代越南语的重要组成部分，影响着人们的思维与语言习惯，方便两国人民之间的沟通，对对方的思想容易理解。我本人已经翻译过中国的有关改革开放、治党治国、社会主义建设等政治理论书籍，曾多年为两国领导会谈做翻译，2016 年荣获了“中华图书特殊贡献奖”，近年来多次被推荐为越南大学生的《汉语桥》比赛担任评委会组长。我坚信，越中两国语言的相近这一优点，保证了我们两国间的沟通，特别是在民心相通方面将比其他国家间更为顺利。

Chinese Characters in the Vietnamese Language Help Connect the Sino-Vietnamese Relations

Vinh Quang Nguyen / Vietnam

Vice President of Vietnam-China Friendship Association, Consultant at the Center for Strategic Studies and International Development

The relationship between China and Vietnam should be viewed from three perspectives, namely, the relationship between the two ethnic groups over thousands of years; the relationship between the two ruling communists formed in the 1920s; and the relationship between the two countries since the establishment of diplomatic relations in 1950. The relationship between the two countries has a long history, and the intertwining of the cultures of the two countries makes the two countries closer.

I, engaged in diplomatic work for many years, deeply realize that any friendly relationship is built on the basis of mutual understanding. Without mutual understanding, there is no mutual comprehending, not to mention a friendly relationship. The cultural exchanges between China and Vietnam for thousands of years have played a crucial role in helping the two peoples understand each other.

The cultural connection between China and Vietnam covers religion, philosophy, customs, moral concepts, etc. Among them, language serves as a bridge for direct communication, and its meaning is beyond the scope of culture.

Although I am not a linguist, I have learnt Chinese and engaged in translation work for many years, so that I understand more about the importance of language for the cultural connection between the two countries, and the similarities between the Chinese language and the Vietnamese language have become increasingly clearer.

I. The Role of the Chinese language in the process of the formation of the Vietnamese language

Vietnamese people learn from and absorb Chinese culture, including the Chinese language, in order to enrich their home culture. The Vietnamese language is influenced by many languages, but mainly by the Chinese language.

1. Chinese characters

According to the study of linguistics, there was no text in Vietnam before the advent of Vietnamese Chinese characters. Since the Qin Dynasty ruled Vietnam in 221 BC, Chinese characters have begun to enter Vietnam and become the official character of the administrative system of the Han people. The spread of the Han culture and the emergence of the Vietnamese noble knowledge team participating in the promotion of the Chinese language have made Chinese characters increasingly popular in Vietnam.

After the end of the system of prefectures and counties, Vietnam and China have still maintained diplomatic relations in the political, economic, and cultural fields, despite the fact that Vietnam is an independent country. At that time, Chinese characters and the Chinese language were the official language of the administrative documents, the imperial examination system, and literary and artistic creation.

Before the 10th century, the Vietnamese people used and read Chinese characters as did the Chinese people. However, the Chinese language was always regarded as a foreign language. When Vietnam entered the autonomous period in the early 10th century, the Vietnamese people did not regard the Chinese language as a foreign language and continued to use Chinese characters. However, to adapt to the pronunciation of the Vietnamese people, the pronunciation was changed into "Sino-Vietnamese pronunciation", which has been used steadily since then. The Sino-Vietnamese pronunciation affects the Vietnamese language, making it richer.

2. Chu Nom

Chinese characters are foreign characters after all. Originally, only the upper classes, such as bureaucrats and intellectuals, were good at using them, such that the requirements of the vast majority of the Vietnamese people were not fulfilled. In this circumstance, the Vietnamese people needed to have their own characters, so they created Chu Nom on the basis of Chinese characters. Most of the Chu Nom drew on Chinese characters and changed the pronunciation to record the ordinary Vietnamese language. The rest of the Chu Nom draws on Chinese characters or radicals in Chinese characters to create new characters. There are three methods of creating Chu Nom. One is the echoism method. It synthesizes two Chinese characters into one Chu Nom character, one of which is a Chinese phonogram and the other is an ideography. For example, " 南 + 年 "= " 𢆥 ", with the pronunciation of " 南 " (năm) and the meaning of " 年 " (year). The second method is the phonetic loaning method, which uses a Chinese character to represent a Chu Nom character with a similar pronunciation. For example, the Chinese character " 别 " (biệt) is used to express the meaning of "know" (biết). The third method is the ideographic method, which is also a combination of two Chinese characters. For example, " 天 + 上 " = " 𡗶 " to express the " 天 " (trời). Chu Nom is the combination of various elements of Chinese characters. It can be said that if there were no Chinese characters, there would be no Chu Nom. The popularization of Chu Nom is an important achievement of Vietnamese culture. At that time, Vietnam viewed Chu Nom as the "national language" and the "national pronunciation". Chu Nom has developed increasingly and has gradually been able to correctly record all Vietnamese words, also the characters have become more and more simplified. Up to now, Chu Nom has truly become a set of characters that can fully and accurately record all of the activities of the social life. Chu Nom is the main vehicle for retaining the rich treasures of Vietnam's intangible cultural heritage. However, the formation and development of Chu Nom can without doubt not be separated from Chinese characters.

3. Latin alphabetic text

In the early 17th century, Western missionaries used the Latin alphabet to spell Vietnamese characters, and as a result, the Vietnamese language was latinized, and gradually became the Vietnamese national language. However, the interaction between the Chinese language and the Vietnamese language has not been interrupted. Especially in the late 19th century and the early 20th century, Vietnamese patriots came to know the progressive thoughts of Liang Qichao, Kang Youwei and Sun Yat-sen through Chinese books and newspapers, and accepted Marxism-Leninism. Specifically, most of the existing theoretical terms in Vietnamese regarding politics, the economy, and society were borrowed from the Chinese language.

II. The Influence of the Chinese language on the modern Vietnamese language

Although the existing Vietnamese character is the Latin alphabet, its relationship with the Chinese language is inseparable. The influence of the Chinese language is most prominent in terms of vocabulary.

1. Chinese characters in Vietnamese mandarin

According to research carried out by Vietnamese linguists, more than 60% of the current Vietnamese vocabulary has been borrowed from the Chinese language. These characters are written in Sino-Vietnamese pronunciation and are called Sino-Vietnamese characters. The method of pronunciation has been improved since the 10th century and the 11th century and has been used steadily up to now. According to research, the Sino-Vietnamese pronunciation is a pronunciation developed through slight adjustments of the ancient Chinese pronunciation of the Tang Dynasty in order to adapt to the pronunciation of the Vietnamese people. Therefore, there is a difference between the pronunciation of modern Chinese and the Sino-Vietnamese characters, such as, "zhengzhi" = "chính trị", "wenhua" = "văn hóa", "guofang" = "quốc phòng". Certainly, the pronunciation of some Sino-Vietnamese characters is similar to Cantonese, such as, "juzhang" (Cục trưởng), "wu, liu, qi, ba, jiu, shi" (ngũ, lục, thất, bát, cửu, thập). There are also some new Vietnamese characters created by borrowing from the Chinese meanings, such as names of military organizations: squad (class), squadron (platoon), brigade (company), small regiment (battalion), and medium regiment (regiment); or a Sino-Vietnamese character is combined with a Vietnamese character to form a new character, such as "binh lính" (soldier), "tàu hỏa" (train) and "thì giờ" (time).

The borrowing of Chinese characters in the Vietnamese language has two purposes. The first purpose is to supplement the lack of words in the Vietnamese language. The initial stage of the Vietnamese language lacked a large number of words, especially in politics, law, economics, national defense, education, culture, literature, and art. To fill the gap, the Vietnamese people, on the one hand, tried to create new characters based on the rules of the creation of Vietnamese characters, and on the other hand, borrowed a lot of Chinese words, mainly technical, political and social terms. The second purpose is to create the word with different emotional colors from the Vietnamese characters. In a polite environment or in scientific terms, popular characters generally are not used, and Sino-Vietnamese characters are borrowed for use, such as "madam" (vợ wife), "name" (tên name), "die" (chết death), and "bleeding" (chảy máu). These are synonymous with different emotional colors.

2. Chinese characters in Vietnamese idioms and folk adages

Since ancient times, thousands of Chinese idioms have been used in the Vietnamese language and have become very popular in everyday life. On the one hand, these idioms can be widely used in daily life, thanks to rich and implicit meanings. On the other hand, Vietnamese society is influenced by China's religion and moral concepts. These stereotyped phrases or short sentences are a valuable legacy of the Chinese ancients, especially Confucius, Zhuangzi and Laozi, for later generations. They are full of profound ideological connotations and reflect life experience, traditional codes of conduct, and personal behavior. Hence, everyone should know them.

For quite ordinary idioms that are easy to remember and use, the original sentence and Sino-Vietnamese pronunciation are generally retained, such as perfect match, ever-victorious, everything is difficult at the start, everything goes as you wish, nobody, and lust for power.

Other idioms have been slightly changed and translated into common language to make them understandable and easier for use, such as "Treo đầu dê bán thịt chó" (sail under false colors), "Nghìn cân treo sợi tóc" (close call), "Ếch ngồi đáy giếng" (the frog in the well knows nothing of the great ocean).

3. Chinese-style poems in Vietnamese literature

The creation of Vietnamese Chinese-style poetry goes back to ancient times. In all dynasties, such as the Ding, Li, Li, Chen, Later Li, Xishan, Yanshi dynasties, a large number of Chinese-style poems were created and passed down from generation to generation, which constitute an important part of the art treasure of Vietnamese literature, and an integral part of the Vietnamese spirits. Over thousands of years, all walks of life from the monks and nobles to the majority of the common people read Chinese-style poems both in cities and villages around the country. They see it as a kind of noble pleasure, and a method for moral cultivation and appreciation. Chinese-style poems still have a far-reaching influence on the artistic creation of modern Vietnam.

In terms of content, the ancient Vietnamese Chinese-style poems inherited and promoted the thoughts of Confucianism and Buddhism, and later, with the trend of the times, spread thoughts of patriotism and anti-colonialism, becoming a sharp weapon to inspire the revolution of the Vietnamese people.

"Ancient poetry prefers natural beauties,
Such as mountains, rivers, fireworks, snow, moon and wind.
Modern poetry should be imbued with steely strength,
Poets should also charge forward."
(Ho Chi Minh, Feelings during Appreciation of *1000 Poems*)

A prominent feature of Vietnamese Chinese-style poetry is the harmony of level and oblique tones with musical tones. Wen Zhuang, a Chinese professor, is a Vietnamese master, who believes that the reading of ancient Chinese poems with a Vietnamese pronunciation is more harmonious and pleasant compared with the modern Chinese language. It is because that, in spite of the millennia of vicissitudes, Vietnam still fully retains the phonology of medieval Chinese, coupled with a rich tone (with six tones divided into level and oblique tones). In addition, the Vietnamese people are very strict about the creation of poems, and strictly abide by the rules and forms of level tones, oblique tones, and musical tones. Such as:

Nanzhuang, the Capital
Cui Hu
This door, this day, last year,
Her face blushed just like a peach blossom.
But, where is she now?
Peach blossom still laughs at the spring breeze.
Khứ niên kim nhật thử môn **trung**
Nhân diện đào hoa tương ánh **hồng**
Nhân diện bất tri hà xứ khứ
Đào hoa y cựu tiếu xuân **phong**

Liangzhou Words

Wang Han

With wine of grapes, the cups of jade would glow at night,

Drinking to pipa songs, we are summoned to fight.

Don't laugh if we lay drunken on the battleground,

How many warriors ever came back safe and sound?

Bồ đào mỹ tửu dạ quang **bôi**

Dục ẩm tỳ bà mã thượng **thôi**

Túy ngọa sa trường quân mạc tiếu

Cổ lai chinh chiến kỷ nhân **hồi**

Lantern Festival

Ho Chi Minh

What a full moon tonight in the Lantern Festival,

Rivers and waters are full of a sense of spring.

We talk about military affairs in the mist-covered waters,

When we return back, our ship is bathed in the moonlight.

Kim dạ nguyên tiêu nguyệt chính **viên**,

Xuân giang, xuân thuỷ tiếp xuân **thiên**.

Yên ba thâm xứ đàm quân sự,

Dạ bán quy lai nguyệt mãn thuy**ền**.

4. Couplets, a time-honored tradition of Vietnamese people

To attach great importance to family is one of the long-standing and well-established good traditions of the Vietnamese nation. Many Vietnamese people use good couplets as traditional building interior decorations, especially in family ancestral halls. The couplets state ancestors' principles of social behavior, ethics or pursuant values passing down to descendants, known as "gia đạo" (family rules), such as "福生富贵家堂盛，禄进荣华子孙兴" (it's lucky to be born in our wealthy and flourishing family, be sure to study hard and pursue a high position and great wealth to make sure the family thrives)". In order to demonstrate the long history of these family rules, most of the couplets use high-quality wood on which Chinese characters (traditional Chinese characters) are engraved with exquisite carving decorations. This cultural tradition is mainly spread in the northern and central regions of Vietnam.

In addition, just like in China, the Spring Festival couplets are pasted on decorations for the Spring Festival, the most important holiday of the year in Vietnam. Some calligraphers even write modern Vietnamese characters (Latin letters) on Spring Festival couplets. However, Chinese characters are still quite prevalent.

III. Conclusion

The use of Chinese characters or related Chinese vocabulary in the Vietnamese language plays a positive role in promoting mutual understanding between China and Vietnam, and creates a favorable environment for mutual understanding and mutual access for the Vietnamese and Chinese peoples.

There is a very close relationship between language and culture. Linguists from all countries believe that language is a part of culture and culture is also a part of language, so they are inextricably linked to each other. Moreover, due to complementary interaction, they develop together. In other words, language is the vehicle of all knowledge, and language is part of the national culture and personal way of thinking. Hence, it can be said that the cultural exchanges between China and Vietnam are inseparable from each other.

It is the connection of culture and language that has become an important advantage in promoting the relationship between Vietnam and China. It plays an active role in the cooperation between the two parties, the two countries and the two peoples, including politics, diplomacy, economy and trade, culture and technology. Although Chinese characters are no longer used in daily life and writing in Vietnam,

Sino-Vietnamese pronunciation is still an important part of the modern Vietnamese language, which affects the way of thinking and language habits of the Vietnamese people, thereby making it easier for the people of the two countries to communicate with and understand each other. I have personally translated Chinese political theory books on the reform and opening up, the administering of the Party and the country, and the socialist construction, and I have also been a translator for the leaders of the two countries for many years. In previous years, I won the Special Contribution Award of Chinese Books. In recent years, I have been recommended as the leader of the judging panel in the Chinese Language Bridge Competition for Vietnamese university students. I firmly believe that the closeness of the Chinese language to the Vietnamese language is a positive feature, which leads to smoother communication between the two countries, especially the similar popular sentiments. Therefore, the feature should be brought into full play.

书法与诗歌

朱青生 【中国】
北京大学教授 / 国际艺术史学会主席

书法与诗歌有两个方面的问题可以讨论。

第一个问题，作为一种艺术门类的书法和另一种艺术门类的文学（广义的诗歌）之间的关系。这种关系根植于中国文化在某一个阶段时，具体的作家和作者在处理书法和文学的同时所建立的关系，很大程度上是在讨论书法所书写的内容，以及作者的双重身份，即书法家同时也是文学家。关于第一个问题，论述丰富。近年，中国赴欧洲的书法大展《再序兰亭》就约请任平教授发表了专题论文；由方闻教授（Wen Fong）所主编的《书法》一书也有相关章节；诚如龚鹏程教授所言："这种抄录书写，同时兼有文学性与书艺性两方面。也就是同时有两个传统、两个审美原则在起作用。"[1] 而专题研究则甚众。

第二个问题，作为书法的独特性质和文学的独特性质，这两个专业或媒介之间如何发生联系和作用。作为书法艺术的媒介是如何把文学媒介中的成分和内涵平移和纳入其中。本文主要论述第二个问题。

书法的本质是表意，而非造型，这一点我们已经反复论证[2]。如果把书法作为

1　引自龚鹏程《书法与文学》http://book.163.com/15/1008/14/B5DMLQ8B00923P3U.html

2　实际上，书法是一道痕迹，是把一个人的全部的存在放入其中进行表达。这种表达开始时可能仅仅是用一条线，可能出现在旧石器时代的洞窟里，尽管在旧石器时代的洞窟中，很多痕迹曾经被忽视了。例如法国南部的拉斯科洞穴（Lascaux Cave）中，野牛（bison）壁画曾经深受重视，但这实则是受到希腊人"模仿说"（Mimesis）的影响，而洞窟中实际还存在着另一些非象形的点和线。

一种成熟的艺术“样式”，它确实与汉字有关联性；如果把书法视为一种“方法”，其内在的普遍价值就大大超过了汉字的范畴，可以上溯至人类早期旧石器时代的壁画中不画具体物像的那些点和线，这实际上就是书法的根源，用一条线表达了人对于事物的一种态度、观察，人的行为和感觉留下的一道痕迹。甚至可以由此而上溯到前不久发现的旧石器时代中期骨骼上的刻痕。因此，书法实则可被视为一种推进人类的普遍价值和指向广阔的可能性的艺术[1]。

这也可以下沿到绘画的写实功能被机械复制的技术所取代之后，艺术向抽象的方向发展之一，即所谓的“Informal”（所有的线条并不是为了造型的需要，而是本身不造型，而留下来的单纯独立的表达方式）和抽象表现主义。

对于这一本质的归纳，又在第 34 届世界艺术史大会的开幕式和进程中被反复讨论，其主要理论是，书法虽然是中国独特的书写汉字的艺术，翻译 成 calligraphy 却是一个错误的译法，因为 calligraphy 本意为“美术字”[2]。而书法其实是人类艺术表达的一个重要途径，和希腊的模仿与造型构成了不 同的艺术路径。上述这些化石上的刻痕与旧石器洞窟内的点和线，就是“笔 墨”和“心迹”[3]。“笔墨”的意思虽然在书法中获得了充分而长足的发展，但却并不是只有书法中才存在，而是在所有的人为痕迹中都存在，并且也可 以通过对痕迹本身的观察和体悟达到交流和审美的目的。

书法在这道痕迹中贡献了什么？实际就是文学。文学是把人的思维和描述的理性成分灌注到痕迹中去，所以书法和文学的联系实则在这一点。

如果说书法与汉字有关，那么也就是和一种文字有关。而文学是主要通过文字来实现其艺术的功能的，也即书法的媒介共用了文学的媒介——文字。但是，

1 如果顺着这道痕迹走下去，那么重庆奉节云雾土家乡兴隆洞出土的一枚剑齿象门齿化石上，有人工刻画的线条，组成简单而抽象的图案，距今约 12—15 万年，是目前所知最早的人类有意识的刻画作品。而拉斯科洞窟的野牛壁画是距今 3 万到 3 万 5 千年前。所以，如果不以单向的眼光，而是以全面的眼光来看待艺术，人类艺术史的起源就会往前推进 7—10 万年。

2 Calligraphy 在中国叫美术字，calli 是希腊语中“漂亮”的意思，而美术字并不是书法（art of writing），二者的性质完全不同。书法其实就是中间的这一条线，关键不在于写了什么，而在于写的时候线条里面有什么。为什么说写书法就是写中国字不准确？现在我们把中国的书法翻成 calligraphy，是错误的翻译，因为 calligraphy 在中国叫美术字，calli 是希腊语中“漂亮”的意思。我现在给大家看美术字，马上就可以看到美术字 calligraphy 绝对不是书法（art of writing），之间性质完全不同。那书法到底是什么？书法就是中间的这一条线，关键不在于写了什么，而在于写的时候线条里面有什么，这就是书法的含义。

3 英译可译为“trace”，但这和汉斯 · 贝尔廷 Hans Belting 所说的“痕迹”trace 不是一回事，他说的痕迹只是留下来的印记，而我们说的痕迹不是一个印记，而是人为的、对它的表达。

这是一个表面现象，是一句无意义的“命题”。

如果书法是一道寄托和表达“人的意义”的痕迹，它本身就已经可以通过线条和笔墨自身来传达意味，并不需要非得借助文学才能成立。也即，文学和书法可以毫无关系，而各自的意义都可获得各自的表达，它们的借用只不过是一种临时的凑合与遭遇而已，并没有必然性。也就是说，文学的全部作用并不需要书法即可完成，而书法的最高存在不需要文学本自具足。

实际上，书法之所以可以在书法性（即“笔墨”和“心迹”）的层次上达到由这一方向可以达到的极高境界和最高成就，恰恰是因为它和文学有关。关系在于诗歌的状物、表意和抒情使得这条“心迹”随着人的存在价值而获得了扩充。故作赋如下：

笔论

笔者，与墨并称，千古传承。其神也，非道中人不可与语。

笔者，广大无穷，略有涉及，即从会心。笔之广矣，大矣，尽形寿，终精进，如入星天，四顾茫然。念一生有涯，孤闻浅识。但窥笔里疆域，充川瀛海。在无概了之想，遑论习得其功。毕生追随，得一二家衣钵，何望之奢？

破帖万卷，遍搜碑林，盖拾得烽火残叶，风雨遗痕。烟没瑰品，实难以屈数，存世者十之二三耳。即得观上品，离时绝代，难存意味，背俗隔境，胡印心迹？古时人情，且易堪透？但凭猜度，不知就里。先哲用笔妙门得三 四许幸甚！

感笔之大而小我。叹迹之广而恨促。能不怆然？

笔之所能也无穷，若以今日为始，日日加功，代有所归。生在当时，受制于时运，局限于见闻。纵然尽笔力、罄笔形，穷笔意、趣笔势，所可用者，当下为度也。不知器转毫更，墨替色代，帛废纸兴，字变文移，吾何能逆料后世笔墨砚纸之绝异焉？日后天开瑞物，雄视古今。以之诣笔，如何度 之？此笔之材质无穷也。何况后人。自性风发，秉教清纯，云淡气清之常有。老有所养，病无见弃。佑其安定，任其从容。增知广识，虽怅一介之渺，饱 暖荣宠，何喜品类之丰。毕竟远可日游参商，近可出入微尘。心可把换，意 能抄移。今之苦于后愈苦，苦亦无穷，今之乐于后愈乐，乐亦无尽。冲突弥 深，无以相望，皆关笔之前程也。知有明日之笔，不知其所以，能不愁闷？

往日之笔不可追，后日之笔不可晓，固也。然人无我之际遇，尔思我亦曾愁闷。后人无我之心境，尔视我终将怆恨。今当如何？今之为今，今也！ 思虑及此，翻然欣喜，乐我之有我笔也！

我有我笔，我有何笔？

曰笔之用；曰笔之有。

笔之用者，谓笔之状迹之能，构形之所。

状迹者，凡用笔，过处留痕，迹于是能循。一落之际，形状生起。方圆曲折，修短羸盈，如陨石飞花，象朝阳残月。笔之形，何止千化万变矣。至于着落幅中，四边成位。天地生焉，笔厕其间，势动并存。笔势者，比附金戈铁马，非谓其形状类戈与马，其势使之然也。金戈在握、挺向胡虏，铁马飞渡、直下中原，势也。笔因势而可为阵、盖落纸成形，依边布阵，卫夫人图之能留芳千古，既具笔形，又言笔势，此状迹之极能者也。

构形者，一笔为迹，二笔成画，载万物之情形。茹毛饮血之初，已成功用。此处形非笔形，像非迹像。笔随形设，迹为像显。平坦白地，呼出生灵。洞天溪上，可居可游。丽人迁客，背啼侧泣。皆以二画至万画，漾入生机，境界于是浮现。

谓书画同源者，字由画生，聚笔成文。是“一”字，仅一画，其横，笔形不能自绝其字，而独立化形成象。是以亦笔画之笔，非痕迹之笔也。

笔之用，以造幻境、别远近、表金玉、勒妖娆、写愁绪、貌亲疏。但凭手段，无所不可。

笔路皆没入形体，称作无笔，笔无而画有。借形运线，笔路依旧明辨者，称作有笔。无笔之造型，转托影像。有笔之造型，三味依然。而今更须着意，一任信手由心，引几许风流。此笔之用也。

笔之有者，谓笔之个中寄托在人。无论单笔成状之笔迹，亦或复笔成形之笔画。运行必经段落，提按瞬间，百事齐凑。一己之衷情、万世之修养，皆寓其中。君不见人之举手投足、音容笑貌，尚可别贤愚、知忠奸，况乎笔 之用心，又比手足音容更多韫藉。笔必有其有也。

无欲不能生人，有情尚可存活。故原欲本性必在笔中。声色之辨，鼓动好恶；精粗分别，难抑去取。执笔在手，不思度，随心所，笔自行，其情性皆有所以矣。常人不能尽情、尽性者，盖其既非忘怀法度。又无以超脱规矩。牵笔就形，堆划凑字。心牵构形则情散，意注结体则性糜。笔自僵持，唯羁俗格。是故笔中性情之常无也。

人其为人，因有人我。无人则我不得成就，无我则人难具方圆。狼乳为狼，豕处则豕者，因人我绝交而人道无以流行也。人道浸淫笔中，因爱生情，缘仇转亲；人间冷暖，世态炎凉，笔厌之所怨，笔投之所求。笔之于人，或挑或拒，如骂如仇，泣诉淋漓，忿妒交加。寅媚可以在笔，恭谨可以命笔，清高可以走笔，豪放可以使笔。因人成笔，缘缘动毫。书在无声处，笔中自有怀抱耳。常人不能尽行为者，盖其一意不能孤行，笔尚未动，仅知欲左反右，意上先下。居心而不露，敢怒而无言。蓄含富而自在少，城府深则天真无。陈陈相因，驳杂萎顿，是故笔中人道之常无也。

忠良使人向善，天理逼我求全。重义以轻生，怀道常灭欲。自励可恕众，格高则悯天。至理张扬，得失度外。于是心定笔清，量宽笔拙，嫉恶笔凛，超腾笔脱。克己奉公，其笔自正。舍命忘死，其笔方沉。常人不能尽道理者，盖其为人，知其理而不能行其道。知则知也，未曾落到行处。而笔之有者，是其行而非其知也。知行合一，然后精神来聚，存想自张于笔中。总有道貌岸然之徒，中心窃窃，自不便直露内里于笔端。但凭做作，弄清奇、施厚重，欺世盗名，是故笔之精神之常无也。

盖笔中性情常无、人道常无、精神常无，必取外物充之。则转借于造化。飞泉走石，枯藤新篁，湖月江浪，野雨惊风。静若冻原，动有骤雷，壮如啸海，弱似柳蓬。因有所借，则笔势充盈。造化万千，故笔路无穷。所谓笔之有者，一归自然，真似泥牛入海。受尽山水日月之精华。教人不思情欲，洗除哀乐，忘却忧患，疏离神圣。此虽笔中之取借假设，然足以了却人生，游乐无期矣。

至于初浅之功课，非下笔千万遍而不得要领，自不待言。

夫用笔，怀古而得其传，思来而励其志，用形而姿其态，造型而接其交，游心自然而广其意，纵性而从其欲，知人而游其情，尚理而立其德。古人之笔古人也，后人之笔后人也，今人之笔为人也。本性相析，性情润笔，人道练笔，精神使笔。人事汇总，合笔底性情，笔中人道，笔上精神。俯仰天地，思维古今，唯此唯此。

噫唏！笔者，国艺之精髓。脉脉相承，一代有一代之笔！由古至我，由我以至千年。憾笔之奥妙，难以言传。然体古人之心意，念来者之忧思。不得已，作笔论。（1997 年朱青生撰）

这些对人的价值的体悟和表达怎么能够进入“心迹”，中间的过渡就是诗歌

（和文学），由诗歌提取了人的精神并且将之“意识”，然后诉诸文字（歌向诗的转换）。诗歌在史诗和歌谣的口头传唱阶段具有肉身动作形态、语气语调对情绪蕴含和情欲直接表达的部分被忽略（到同步录音和动态影像才得以在更广泛的传播层次上归复），而这种已经成为文字的诗歌，即已经 被意识的诗歌再度被书法来书写时，就在一道运动的线条痕迹中尽量表达人的存在。这道线条非但来自于自我，而且来自于人类有文明以来的全体成就。作为书法的那道痕迹，正是把本来作为个人可以表达的人的价值通过文字，进而连结了诗歌和文学，把整体的人类文明带入了一根线条。此时的线条就不再是旧石器时代洞窟中的点、线，也不是抽象艺术中的个人痕迹所能概括。这种无限的与全体关联的文化使得书法和诗歌之间的关系成为人类艺术中的一根线，连接人性的一切方式。所以，也只有在这种痕迹或“心迹”的艺术的方式与中国的书法传统，亦即写作诗歌与文学的传统关联的时才得以实现。

Calligraphy and Poetry

Zhu Qingsheng / China

Professor of Peking University President of the Comité International d'Histoire de l'Art

There are two issues that could be discussed around calligraphy and poetry.

The first question is about the relationship between calligraphy and poetry (in a broad sense) as two different types of art. This relationship is rooted in the connection between the two built by specific writers or authors in a certain stage of Chinese culture. It is mainly about the content of calligraphy and the dual identity of the author to a great extent, indicating that the calligrapher is also the author in the meantime. There have been abundant discussions on this issue. In recent years, for example, Professor Ren Ping was invited to write a treatise for the exhibition in Europe called "The Orchid Pavilion: The Art of Writing in China in 2009. In *Calligraphy* edited by Wen C. Fong, there are also related discussions. Just as Professor Gong Pengcheng points out, "This action of excerpting and writing possesses both literary and artistic features. That is to say, there are two kinds of traditions as well as two aesthetic principles taking effect at the same time. (Gong, 2015) Not to mention the numerous specific studies.

Either calligraphy or literature has its own unique nature. Thus the second question is about how the two subjects or mediums could relate to and integrate with each other, and how the medium as calligraphy has diverted and absorbed the components and connotation of the medium as literature. This essay will mainly focus on this second question.

Having been repeatedly demonstrated, the essence of calligraphy is ideographic rather than pictographic[1]. If viewing calligraphy as a mature "style of art, it is indeed associated with Chinese characters. However, if we consider calligraphy as a "method of art, then its inner spirit and values would go far beyond the scope of Chinese characters –this could be traced back to the lines and dots in the early Paleolithic cave paintings. They may not present or depict any things, but it is just those lines and dots that are the origin of calligraphy. Calligraphy is to express one's attitude and observation of the world within a single line. It is a *trace* of behaviors and feelings left by human, which can even be traced back to the man- carved trace on a bone during the Middle Paleolithic period. Therefore, calligraphy can be seen as a kind of art that puts forward the universal values of mankind and points to the broader possibilities for the future[2].

The spirit and values of calligraphy can also be followed by the period when the realism function of painting has been replaced by the techniques in the age of mechanical reproduction. It is one of the directions towards abstract art, or "informal art (all the lines are not pictographic, they do not depict or form particular

1 In fact, calligraphy is just a *trace*, it means to express one's entire existence within a line. At the beginning, such expression may refer to any single line – a line in a Paleolithic cave, for instance, though lots of traces have been ignored before. Take the Lascaux Cave for example, people used to focus on the images of the bison, but this actually comes from the Greek's "art as mimesis. In this cave, there are other lines and dots which are non-pictographic and do not depict anything.

2 If we go on following this clue, then on a stegodon fore-tooth fossil unearthed from Xinglong Cave in YunwuTujia Village, Chongqing, there are man-carved lines composing a simple and abstract pattern. This pattern is from 120,000 to 150,000 years ago, and it is currently known as the earliest carving work consciously created by human. The bison cave painting in Lascaux Cave is only from 30,000 to 35,000 years ago. So if we see the history of art not in a single view, but from a comprehensive perspective, then the origin of our art history should have existed 70,000 to 100,000 years earlier.

things, but the lines themselves are pure and independent expressions) or abstract expressionism that we call today.

Such conclusion of the essence of calligraphy was repeatedly discussed in the 34th World Congress of Art History in Beijing. The main idea can be concluded as such: although *Shu Fa* (书法, the art of writing), which is translated into "calligraphy in English, is a unique kind of art about the writing of Chinese characters, this is in fact a false translation, because literally calligraphy refers to "graphic characters (美术字) in Chinese[1]. *Shu Fa*[2] is an important way of the artistic expressions of mankind, which constitutes a different path of art other than the mimesis of the Greek. Actually, the trace on the fossils and the lines and dots in the Paleolithic caves mentioned above are just "the traces of pen and ink (笔墨) and "the traces of the heart (心迹)[3].Though the meaning of "the traces of pen and ink has been fully developed in the filed of *Shu Fa*, it exists not only in this particular art of writing, but in all conscious traces left by human. On the other hand, communication and aesthetic purposes could be achieved through the observation and understanding of such traces per se.

What is the contribution of calligraphy (the art of writing) in these traces? The answer is literature. Literature means to infuse the rational aspect of the thoughts and descriptions of human into the traces. This is the exact relationship between calligraphy (the art of writing) and literature.

If calligraphy (the art of writing) is related to Chinese characters, then it is in

1 Literally, calligraphy refers to "graphic characters (美术字) in Chinese, and "calli means "beauty in Greek. The natures of "graphic characters and "Shu Fa (the art of writing) are totally different. What on earth is "Shu Fa (the art of writing)? It is actually the line in between. The key to the art of writing lies not in the content you write, but just in these lines of your writing.

2 Annotation (译注): Here the English translation for *Shu Fa* is indicated as a false translation, thus *Shu Fa* is used as a replacement for "calligraphy in this paragraph for distinction. In the following paragraphs, when referring to *Shu Fa* or "the art of writing, the expression will be "calligraphy (the art of writing) in order to avoid confusion.

3 The "trace here is not the same as what Hans Belting refers to. Belting's trace is only a trail or a mark left behind, while our trace is not a mark, but a man-made conscious expression.

relation to a certain type of writing. While literature aims to realize its artistic function via writing. That is to say, calligraphy (the art of writing) actually shares the same medium – writing – with literature. However, this is just the superficies, a meaningless "proposition.

If calligraphy (the art of writing) is a trace that holds and expresses "the significance of human, it is able to convey meanings through the brush strokes and lines on its own without any involvement of literature. Thus calligraphy (the art of writing) and literature can be entirely unrelated to each other, while their own meanings can be expressed separately. The mutual borrowing between the two is just a temporary improvise or encounter without any necessity. As a result, the whole purpose of literature could be completed without calligraphy, while there is no need for calligraphy to connect with literature to achieve its utmost existence.

In fact, however, it is just the connection with literature that makes calligraphy (the art of writing)reach the top of this direction and achieve its real essence. The connection or the relationship is that the chanting[1] (状 物), expressive(表 意) and lyrical (抒情) natures of poetry make it possible for "the trace of the heart to expand with the existence values of human.[2]

The path that leads the understanding and expression of the values of human into "the traces of the heart– the transition in between – is poetry (and literature). Poetry extracts the spirit of human and make it "conscious, then resort to words and the process of writing (the transition from "songs to "poems)[3].In the early stage of

---

1 Annotation(译注): A specific word for this kind of poem is called "Dinggedicht (咏物诗), literally meaning "object poems, which is a genre of poetry in which communication of mood or thought is conveyed through the observation of things and symbolic concentration. It was introduced in the early 1900s by the Austrian poet Rainer Maria Rilke.

2 Annotation(译注):In the original Chinese version of this essay, a classical Ode for the Pen, wrote by the author in 1997, is attached after this paragraph. However, it is impossible to translate the verse into English fully with its original meanings to some extent. The meter, metaphor and rhyme are unique and different in every language, and the real charm of poetry can only be sensed in its original language.

3 Annotation (译注): The Chinese word for "poetry is *Shi Ge* (诗歌), literally meaning "poems and songs. In the ancient times, poems were orally created and expressed in the form of songs.

poetry when epics and songs were communicated and sung orally, the tunes and body movements could convey richer expressions of desire and emotion. However, such information was reduced and ignored when it came to the stage of writing (and did not return on a broader sense of dissemination until the emergence of simultaneous recording and moving image). When this kind of poetry began to exist in the term of writing and has been consciously realized by human, and when it is re- written through calligraphy (the art of writing) again, the existence of human is expressed through a line, a moving trace.

This line origins not only from the self, but also from the whole achievements of the civilization of mankind. The values of human could originally be expressed by an individual, but when it is connected with poetry and literature, the overall civilization and spirit of mankind are then brought into a single line, or a *trace*, through writing. It is this trace that is considered as calligraphy– the art of writing. The trace here is no longer the lines and dots in the Paleolithic caves, nor can it be generalized by any personal traces in abstract art. This infinite connection with the whole culture turns the relationship between calligraphy (the art of writing) and poetry into a line among all the arts of human, into a universal way in connection with the human nature. Therefore, only when this trace or “the traces of the heart is linked with the Chinese calligraphy tradition–which is the writing of poetry and literature– can the above connections be fully achieved.